## HE GYMNASIA

the first quarter of the nineteenth century, while British boxing was still at the peak of its
ry, the most popular training hall and hangout for fighters and their followers was the
es Court in London, shown during a sparring session between lightweights Jack Randall
Ned Turner. A century later the center of boxing had shifted to the United States, and,
four decades, there came to Stillman's Gym in New York thousands of fighters from every
tinent but Antarctica, every heavyweight champion from Jack Dempsey through Floyd
terson among them.

# THE FIRESIDE BOOK
## OF
# Boxing

*Edited by*

## W. C. HEINZ

**SIMON AND SCHUSTER**
**NEW YORK    1961**

# ACKNOWLEDGMENTS

THE EDITOR wishes to express his gratitude to the following individuals and publishers for permission to include in this volume the following material:

"Melted Sugar" by Jesse Abramson. Copyright 1952 by the New York Herald Tribune, Inc.., and reprinted by their permission.

"He Swung and He Missed" from *Neon Wilderness* by Nelson Algren. Copyright 1952 by Nelson Algren. Reprinted by permission of Doubleday and Co., Inc.

"Epigrams" by Arthur (Bugs) Baer. Used by permission of the author.

"Billy Miske's Last Christmas" from *My Lifetime in Sports* by George A. Barton. Copyright 1957 by Olympic Press, and reprinted by their permission.

"The Prize Fight" by Arnold Bennett. Reprinted from *The New Statesman* of December 13, 1919, by their permission.

"The Orthodox Champion" by Heywood Broun. Copyright 1941 by Heywood Hale Broun, and used by permission of the author's agents, Marie Rodell and Joan Daves, Inc.

"The Portable A.C." from *Win, Lose, or Draw* by Warren Brown. Copyright 1957 by Warren Brown. Reprinted by permission of G. P. Putnam's Sons.

Selection from *Tale of James Carabine* by Donn Byrne. Copyright 1925, 1953 by The Curtis Publishing Company. Used by permission of the author's widow, Mrs. Dorothea Craig.

"The Joe Louis I Remember" by Jimmy Cannon. Copyright 1955 by *Sport* Magazine, and reprinted by permission of *Sport* Magazine and the author.

"Sullivan–Flood" from *John the Great* by Donald Barr Chidsey. Copyright 1942 by Donald Barr Chidsey, and used by his permission.

"Dempsey–Carpentier" by Irvin S. Cobb. Used by permission of his widow, Mrs. Laura Baker Cobb.

"The Second Louis–Schmeling Fight" by Bob Considine. Copyright 1938 by Hearst Newspapers, and used by permission of the author.

"Sullivan vs. Corbett" from *The Roar of the Crowd* by James J. Corbett. Copyright 1924 by The Curtis Publishing Co.; copyright renewed in 1952 by the author's widow, Mrs. Vera Corbett. Reprinted by permission of G. P. Putnam's Sons.

"Jersey Joe Walcott–Rocky Marciano" by Don Dunphy. Used by permission of the author.

"Twenty-Five Bucks" from *The Short Stories of James T. Farrell*. Copyright 1932 by Pagany; 1934, 1937 by Vanguard Press, Inc. Reprinted by permission of the Vanguard Press.

"Hello, Joe" by William Fay. Copyright 1940 by The Curtis Publishing Company. Used by permission of the author.

"Title Battle in Typhoon" by Nat Fleischer. Copyright 1954 by Nat Fleischer, and used by his permission.

"Pity the Poor Giant" from *Farewell to Sport* by Paul Gallico. Copyright 1937, 1938 by Paul Gallico. Reprinted by permission of Alfred A. Knopf, Inc.

Selection from *The World I Knew* by Louis Golding. Reprinted by permission of Hutchinson and Co.

"All the Way to the Grave" by Frank Graham. Reprinted from the New York *Journal-American* by permission of the author.

"Stillman's Gym" from *Somebody Up There Likes Me* by Rocky Graziano and Rowland Barber. Copyright 1955 by Rocky Graziano and Rowland Barber. Reprinted by permission of Simon and Schuster, Inc.

"Fighter's Wife" by W. C. Heinz. Copyright 1950 by W. C. Heinz.

TO THOSE
WHO DID THE FIGHTING
THIS BOOK
IS DEDICATED

# CONTENTS

## CONTENTS

# LIST OF ILLUSTRATIONS

THE CONTENTS *of this volume might best be described in the terms employed one evening by Harry Balogh when, in the ring at Madison Square Garden, he introduced Gus Lesnevich. Harry was, for some fifteen years, the Garden ring announcer, and Gus was, at that time, the 33-year-old light-heavyweight champion of the world.*

*"And now—" Harry said, making the grand gesture toward Gus, "a man who, like old wine, goes on forever. . . ."*

*That was in 1948 and Lesnevich was enjoying critical notices and popular acclaim he had never known in his prime. At his best Gus had twice finished second to Billy Conn, but now he was finishing first over Billy Fox. Thus the illusion spread that he was better than he had ever been, while the truth was, of course, that it was more of an accomplishment to look reasonably good over thirty rounds with Conn than to appear great popping out Fox in ten and in one.*

*This volume is intended to leave no illusions. Its pieces of writing, painting, drawing and photography are what they always were. They do not, like Tennyson's brook (as I suppose Harry Balogh would say), improve with age, but they do deserve to go on, if not forever, at least for the life of the paper on which they are reprinted and of the covers between which they are bound.*

*That, it has long seemed to me, should be the basic rule of all publishing—to put on good paper and between hard covers only that which deserves to live that long. Over the years I have argued this contention with a number of publishers, but always to no avail. They assure me that that's no way to run a railroad—or a publishing house, either, although lately I detect fewer references to railroads.*

*When I complain that too many four-round writers have been blown up to look like heavyweight contenders they counter me by claiming that if it weren't for these crowd-pleasers they couldn't afford to publish the better, although less popular, boys in the underneath—the eights, sixes and fours. While I recognize the economics of this, I am nevertheless sobered by the thought that some club writer with nothing more going for him than star-bout billing on the best-seller lists is more responsible for this volume than anyone intimately associated with it.*

*This same thing happens, of course, in boxing, for promoters are hardly patrons of the art. If the great Tex Rickard had not exhibited incredibly bad taste but unexcelled promotional acumen in ballyhooing Georges Carpentier into a shot at the heavyweight title and the first million-dollar gate, Gene Tunney would not, that July afternoon of 1921, have had the opportunity of knocking out Soldier Jones in the semifinal.*

*There is a difference, however, and it involves truth. When, in the fourth round, Carpentier lay on his right side, his legs kicking and a small trickle of blood running from his sobbing mouth, as Irvin S. Cobb so well describes in his piece preserved here, that was the truth of him. He was exposed, in his own time and forever, as an adequate light-heavyweight but an impostor among heavyweight contenders. How many preliminary writers go to their graves still celebrated as heavyweight champions I leave to Edmund Wilson and Alfred Kazin. At least anyone who ever boxed Jack Dempsey, Benny Leonard, Joe Louis, Ray Robinson or Willie Pep in their prime knows where he stands.*

*That, I suppose, is why, over almost 3,000 years, so many writers from Homer to Ernest*

*Hemingway, Plato to J. B. Priestley and Virgil to Charles E. Van Loan have been concerned with man in the most fundamental form of competition, in the most completely expressive of the arts. Some may question this definition of boxing, but I submit the painters who have dropped their palettes, the writers who have tossed aside their thesauri, the lawyers who have deserted their briefs to find, in frustration, fulfillment with their bare fists. I do not celebrate this instinct of man, but as long as the six Christian communities cannot agree on the restoration of Jerusalem's Church of the Holy Sepulcher, and the Greek Orthodoxy and the Franciscans tangle on the steps on Christmas, I must hold that boxing, or fighting if you will, at least gives them expression when nothing else does.*

*The pieces in this collection were selected for one or both of two reasons. The best of them stand on their own, and the others are examples of how some of the best boys of their time handled the subject. George Bernard Shaw, for example, made five tries at the novel before he found out that he just didn't have the legs and the wind to go fifteen rounds. His fourth attempt,* Cashel Byron's Profession, *did reveal, however, a keen insight into the meanings of* The Ring, *and so a chapter is included here.*

*Regrettably, the two arts, boxing and literary journalism, did not both reach their peaks at the same time. Thus Joe Gans, perhaps the greatest boxer pound-for-pound and punch-for-punch of all time, is represented only by a photograph of the fine Mahonri Young statue that stands, often obscured by a cardboard cutout of a rodeo performer or ice-show star, in the lobby of Madison Square Garden, and by an Edgren drawing. Happily, John Lardner was able to reconstruct Shelby, Montana, a feat four banks and the Chamber of Commerce never quite acccomplished after*

*Jack Kearns left town; A. J. Liebling and Jimmy Cannon were around for Joe Louis; Frank Graham knew Joe Gould and Jim Braddock; and Red Smith was contemporary with Fritzie Zivic, one of the alltime great genre masters of the digital and cephalic phases of the Sweet Science.*

*This book appears while boxing is at its lowest ebb in the memory of living man, perhaps in 200 years. The decline after the defeat of Jack Broughton in 1750 was due to too many Xs (Pierce Egan's symbol for contests with prearranged outcomes), but the causes this time are economic, sociologic and electronic.*

*The ring has always been the refuge of the underprivileged. The pattern of social persecution in this country is traced in the names and records of the great Irish, then Jewish, Italian and Negro fighters who graced the sport. Now unparalleled prosperity, legislation covering minimum wages, decent working conditions and fair employment practices—in short, the rise of reason and the decline of prejudice—are raising hob with the lists. Added to this, the magic lantern in the living room has killed off the spawning grounds of talent, the small fight clubs. Although the television procurers may, at any moment, cast aside boxing as a jaded female whose faded beauty and tired talents are no longer commercial, it is certain that it will never again enjoy the glory it knew in the first forty free years of this century.*

*Thus I hope that this volume may in some part ease the sorrow and deaden the pain. My appreciation goes to William D. Cox and Harold U. Ribalow for the trail blazing they did in their own research. For help on this book I am indebted to Seymour Adelman, Herbert M. Alexander, Nat Fleischer, A. J. Liebling, Miss Patricia Littlefield, Mitchell Rawson, Peter Schwed and my wife.*

STAMFORD, CONN.                          W. C. HEINZ

# THE FIRESIDE BOOK
## OF
# Boxing

THIS NEWSPAPER STORY describes the most bizarre championship fight of our time, and it is typical of the work of the best all-around, or pound-for-pound, sports reporter of our time. It was written under almost insufferable conditions and in sixty-five minutes for the late editions of the June 26, 1952, New York *Herald Tribune*.

# Melted Sugar

## JESSE ABRAMSON

IN A WEIRD and sensational finish to a duel of champions fought in brutal heat that registered 104 degrees under the Yankee Stadium lights on the hottest June 25 in New York history, Sugar Ray Robinson collapsed on his stool in the corner and could not come out for the fourteenth round when he had an unbeatable lead over Joey Maxim and a third world championship virtually in his grasp.

Sugar Ray could not beat that furnace heat and the fifteen and a half pounds he gave away to the light heavyweight champion. All he had to do was last the limit. But the brilliant middleweight champion, who had made all the fight for thirteen rounds, outpunching and outboxing the plodding, dull defender, exhausted himself by carrying all the fighting load on this roasting, burning night.

Maxim, who did nothing to deserve this Christmas gift in June except to stand up in that furnace, retained his 175-pound crown in his second defense of it and balked Sugar Ray's gallant attempt to become the third triple champion of the Queensberry era.

It was a knockout in the fourteenth round for Maxim—the fourteenth round because the bell rang for that round while all his seconds and Dr. Alexander Schiff were still working over the worn-out lighter man. It was the first knockout, such as it was, ever scored against the great Robinson in 137 professional fights of which he had lost only two previously.

Robinson wasn't the only victim of the stove-box which the Yankee Stadium was last night.

For the first time in the history of championship fights, a referee was knocked out, too. Ruby Goldstein, the referee, began to show distress in the tenth round from his burdensome task of chasing around the ring and repeatedly breaking the fighters out of clinches by force. He took a restorative from the doctor while he pranced around the ring.

But at the end of the tenth round referee Goldstein, on the verge of collapse, was helped from the torture chamber under those 38,500 watts of photo-flood lamps. Ray Miller replaced him in the eleventh round, the first substitute referee that ever was in a title bout.

All Sugar Ray needed was a relief pitcher, too.

It was a heartbreaking blow to the hopes of the thirty-one-year-old New Yorker, so long acclaimed the best and most resourceful fighter of his day. But he had to go fifteen rounds this night, and he failed to pace himself properly, or failed in the end to handle the weight of the bigger man. Maxim did little in this fight except to catch it, but his strength and wrestling and mauling in the interminable clinches and his digs to the body, though they carried little power or authority, helped to weaken the gallant challenger.

Robinson, an authentic middleweight, who, of course, is still the middleweight champion of the world, weighed 157½ pounds to Maxim's 173. Those were the weights for their second weighing yesterday. On Monday when rain forced a two-day postponement, Robinson had weighed 160 to Maxim's 174¾.

A crowd of 47,983, every one of them soaked in his own perspiration, paid more than $400,-000 at the gate. These gate receipts, plus the approximate $100,000 received for theater TV, created a new receipts record for a light heavyweight championship bout. Twenty-six years ago in Ebbets Field, Paul Berlenback and Jack Delaney drew $461,789.

This score card showed Robinson in front, 10 rounds to 3, when the bout ended abruptly. In the confusion and tumult that ensued, it was not possible to get the officials' score cards, except that Artie Aidala, one of the judges, recalled that he scored Robinson in front, 9 rounds to 3, with one even.

So Robinson was home free with his third world championship if he could only stand on his feet.

A sign that he was going to be in trouble standing on his feet came as early as the eleventh round. Though he smote Maxim a tremendous right on the head that shook up the champion just before the bell, Robinson dragged himself to his corner.

But Robinson won that round and he also won the twelfth, staggering Maxim with a smashing hook in an exchange, but taking some hooks to the body in close. Robinson was now more palpably tired going to his corner. He flopped wearily onto his stool. His seconds gave him smelling salts or some restorative.

The signs of approaching disaster became ominously clear in the thirteenth round. Robinson came out of his corner slowly. He tried to move around as he had been moving around. Earlier he had been dancing on springy feet, the lightfooted dazzling Robinson. Now his legs were leaden. He backed away, he clinched. Maxim forced his head through the ropes. Maxim raked his head with a hook. It wasn't any harder than the weak blows he had been landing, but Ray staggered back.

Robinson had been fighting on grit and guts for some rounds, it was now all too evident. Maxim hadn't been able to hit him at all from long range for the first ten rounds. Now Maxim, still plodding, but still strong, was hitting Ray. He hit him with a hook. Robinson turned in desperation and swung a long right that missed.

He missed with another full right-hand swing in mid-ring, missed so completely that he fell flat on his face—the only time either had been on the floor in this fight.

That fall, not from a punch, drained Robinson's last ounce of strength. When he got up they exchanged hard rights, and Maxim followed with a one-two that sent Robinson reeling crazily along the ropes on the northern side of the ring —not so much from the blows, but from his own unutterable weariness. The bell rang.

His seconds, Harry Wiley and Peewee Beal, rushed from the corner and had to lift and carry Robinson to his stool. Dr. Alexander Schiff, commission physician, went to the corner. It was clear that Robinson, completely exhausted from his brilliant fight, had gone as far as a human could in that torture chamber.

When the bell rang for the fourteenth round Maxim rushed to center ring, as he saw that Robinson wasn't coming out. It was the most lively bit of action Maxim had shown all through the fight. He had lasted, Robinson hadn't. He was still the champion.

It was some minutes before Robinson recovered sufficiently to leave the ring, but in the dressing room, where Mayor Impellitteri, his good friend, was the only one admitted besides Robinson's own retinue, there were signs that Robinson was suffering from the exhausting task. He was heard to say, "God willed it," as he went under the shower, the Mayor holding on to him.

One stresses this fact again and again, because Robinson did all the fighting for so many rounds. They say a mule can't beat a race horse, but in this instance a plodding mule did beat the race horse, because the race horse collapsed before the finish.

I scored the first seven rounds for Robinson. Round after round he was the ring master we have known. No one expected he would be so dominant for so long. He was the master of versatility, the virtuoso. He played on Maxim as though he were a violin. He played up and down his body with left leads, he stormed into volleys and barrages and fusillades. He hit and got away clean, or he erupted into two-fisted body attacks in close when he wasn't tying Maxim up in the repeated clinches.

They clinched again and again, and often Ruby Goldstein had to pry them apart as though he were a can-opener. Robinson was tactically the master. He did what he wanted with Maxim, and he wasn't going to let Maxim do anything in close where Maxim, the defensive fighter, is at his best. At long range, Maxim didn't hit Robinson a solid blow until the fight was half over.

If Maxim intended to wear Robinson out by letting him do all the fighting and moving, it was an infernally clever and diabolical plan. In the inferno of last night it worked.

Robinson forced most of the fighting, except when he tactically backed up to lure Maxim in or took a breather for an instant. It was so easy the way he handled Maxim, the Maxim who had fought heavyweights without getting hurt, that Robinson, as it turned out, was lured into his self-destruction.

Round after round Maxim plodded along, hardly threw a punch that counted. He was the negative, defensive fighter he always has been throughout his boxing life. But he did get many chances to clinch, and these clinches were to be Robinson's doom.

Robinson's speed of foot and speed of hand flashed in the night like heat lightning. There's no need to detail all the blows Robinson hit Maxim. Sugar Ray was the more forceful and powerful hitter, though he was hitting a guy who prides himself that he has taken the best punches of heavyweights for years. Maxim was jolted and shaken by the punches, but never in danger of going down. They all added up to an unbeatable lead by the time Maxim won the eighth by a shade with his infighting as Robinson coasted a bit. There were boos from the crowd, chiefly because Maxim was doing so poorly. Robinson came back to win the ninth, landing a couple of direct hits with powerful hooks on the jaw that stung Joey. Maxim showed bruises under both eyes.

By the tenth, Goldstein became the center of attention as he showed signs of distress and had to quit the ring. Maxim won the round, getting a hook and a right to the jaw, though Robbie flared back with a hook that rocked Maxim's head. Then came the mounting tension as Robinson began to tire, and the stunning denouement in his corner at the end of the thirteenth.

ROCCO WAS A PRO. It came out not only in the fight, but in the way he squared his wife.

# He Swung and He Missed

## NELSON ALGREN

IT WAS MISS DONAHUE of Public School 24 who finally urged Rocco, in his fifteenth year, out of eighth grade and into the world. She had watched him fighting, at recess times, from his sixth year on. The kindergarten had had no recesses or it would have been from his fifth year. She had nurtured him personally through four trying semesters and so it was with something like enthusiasm that she wrote in his autograph book, the afternoon of graduation day, "Trusting that Rocco will make good."

Ultimately, Rocco did. In his own way. He stepped from the schoolroom into the ring back of the Happy Hour Bar in a catchweight bout with an eight-dollar purse, winner take all. Rocco took it.

Uncle Mike Adler, local promoter, called the boy Young Rocco after that one and the name stuck. He fought through the middleweights and into the light-heavies, while his purses increased to as much as sixty dollars and expenses. In his nineteenth year he stopped growing, his purses stopped growing, and he married a girl called Lili.

He didn't win every one after that, somehow, and by the time he was twenty-two he was losing as often as he won. He fought on. It was all he could do. He never took a dive; he never had a setup or a soft touch. He stayed away from whisky; he never gambled; he went to bed early before every bout and he loved his wife. He fought in a hundred corners of the city, under a half dozen managers, and he fought every man he was asked to, at any hour. He substituted for better men on as little as two hours' notice. He never ran out on a fight and he was never put down for a ten count. He took beat-

ings from the best in the business. But he never stayed down for ten.

He fought a comer from the Coast one night and took the worst beating of his career. But he was on his feet at the end. With a jaw broken in three places.

After that one he was hospitalized for three months and Lili went to work in a factory. She wasn't a strong girl and he didn't like it that she had to work. He fought again before his jaw was ready, and lost.

Yet even when he lost, the crowds liked him. They heckled him when he was introduced as Young Rocco, because he looked like thirty-four before he was twenty-six. Most of his hair had gone during his layoff, and scar tissue over the eyes made him look less and less like a young anything. Friends came, friends left, money came in, was lost, was saved; he got the break on an occasional decision, and was occasionally robbed of a duke he'd earned. All things changed but his weight, which was 174, and his wife, who was Lili. And his record of never having been put down for ten. That stood, like his name. Which was forever Young Rocco.

That stuck to him like nothing else in the world but Lili.

At the end, which came when he was twenty-nine, all he had left was his record and his girl. Being twenty-nine, one of that pair had to go. He went six weeks without earning a dime before he came to that realization. When he found her wearing a pair of his old tennis shoes about the house, to save the heels of her only decent pair of shoes, he made up his mind.

Maybe Young Rocco wasn't the smartest pug in town, but he wasn't the punchiest either. Just

20

because there was a dent in his face and a bigger one in his wallet, it didn't follow that his brain was dented. It wasn't. He knew what the score was. And he loved his girl.

He came into Uncle Mike's office looking for a fight and Mike was good enough not to ask what kind he wanted. He had a twenty-year-old named Solly Classki that he was bringing along under the billing of Kid Class. There was money back of the boy, no chances were to be taken. If Rocco was ready to dive, he had the fight. Uncle Mike put no pressure on Rocco. There were two light-heavies out in the gym ready to jump at the chance to dive for Solly Classki. All Rocco had to say was okay. His word was good enough for Uncle Mike. Rocco said it. And left the gym with the biggest purse of his career, and the first he'd gotten in advance, in his pocket; four twenties and two tens.

He gave Lili every dime of that money, and when he handed it over, he knew he was only doing the right thing for her. He had earned the right to sell out and he had sold. The ring owed him more than a C-note, he reflected soundly, and added loudly, for Lili's benefit, "I'll stop the bum dead in his tracks."

They were both happy that night. Rocco had never been happier since Graduation Day.

HE HAD A headache all the way to the City Garden that night, but it lessened a little in the shadowed dressing room under the stands. The moment he saw the lights of the ring, as he came down the littered aisle alone, the ache sharpened once more.

Slouched unhappily in his corner for the windup, he watched the lights overhead swaying a little, and closed his eyes. When he opened them, a slow dust was rising toward the lights. He saw it sweep suddenly, swift and sidewise, high over the ropes and out across the dark and watchful rows. Below him someone pushed the warning buzzer.

He looked through Kid Class as they touched gloves, and glared sullenly over the boy's head while Ryan, the ref, hurried through the stuff about a clean break in the clinches. He felt the robe being taken from his shoulders, and suddenly, in that one brief moment before the bell, felt more tired than he ever had in a ring before. He went out in a half-crouch and someone called out, "Cut him down, Solly."

He backed to make the boy lead, and then came in long enough to flick his left twice into the teeth and skitter away. The bleachers whooped, sensing blood. He'd give them their money's worth for a couple of rounds, anyhow. No use making it look too bad.

In the middle of the second round he began sensing that the boy was telegraphing his right by pulling his left shoulder, and stepped in to trap it. The boy's left came back bloody and Rocco knew he'd been hit by the way the bleachers began again. It didn't occur to him that it was time to dive; he didn't even remember. Instead, he saw the boy telegraphing the right once more and the left protecting the heart slipping loosely down toward the navel, the telltale left shoulder hunching—only it wasn't down, it wasn't a right. It wasn't to the heart. The boy's left snapped like a hurled rock between his eyes and he groped blindly for the other's arms, digging his chin sharply into the shoulder, hating the six-bit bunch out there for thinking he could be hurt so soon. He shoved the boy off, flashed his left twice into the teeth, burned him skillfully against the middle rope, and heeled him sharply as they broke. Then he skittered easily away. And the bell.

Down front, Mike Adler's eyes followed Rocco back to his corner.

Rocco came out for the third, fighting straight up, watching Solly's gloves coming languidly out of the other corner, dangling loosely a moment in the glare, and a flatiron smashed in under his heart so that he remembered, with sagging surprise, that he'd already been paid off. He caught his breath while following the indifferent gloves, thinking vaguely of Lili in oversize tennis shoes. The gloves drifted backward and dangled loosely with little to do but catch light idly four feet away. The right broke again beneath his heart and he grunted in spite of himself; the boy's close-cropped head followed in, cockily, no higher than Rocco's chin but coming neckless straight down to the shoulders. And the gloves were gone again. The boy was faster than he looked. And the pain in his head settled down to a steady beating between the eyes.

The great strength of a fighting man is his pride. That was Young Rocco's strength in the rounds that followed. The boy called Kid Class couldn't keep him down. He was down in the fourth, twice in the fifth, and again in the seventh. In that round he stood with his back against the ropes, standing the boy off with his left in the seconds before the bell. He had the trick of looking impassive when he was hurt, and his face at the bell looked as impassive as a catcher's mitt.

Between that round and the eighth Uncle Mike climbed into the ring beside Young Rocco. He said nothing. Just stood there looking down. He thought Rocco might have forgotten. He'd had four chances to stay down and he hadn't taken one. Rocco looked up. "I'm clear as a bell," he told Uncle Mike. He hadn't forgotten a thing.

Uncle Mike climbed back into his seat, resigned to anything that might happen. He understood better than Young Rocco. Rocco couldn't stay down until his knees would fail to bring him up. Uncle Mike sighed. He decided he liked Young Rocco. Somehow, he didn't feel as sorry for him as he had in the gym.

"I hope he makes it," he found himself hoping. The crowd felt differently. They had seen the lean and scarred Italian drop his man here twenty times before, the way he was trying to keep from being dropped himself now. They felt it was his turn. They were standing up in the rows to see it. The dust came briefly between. A tired moth struggled lamely upward toward the lights. And the bell.

Ryan came over between rounds, hooked Rocco's head back with a crooked forefinger on the chin, after Rocco's Negro handler had stopped the bleeding with collodion, and muttered something about the thing going too far. Rocco spat.

"Awright, Solly, drop it on him," someone called across the ropes.

It sounded, somehow, like money to Rocco. It sounded like somebody was being shortchanged out there.

But Solly stayed away, hands low, until the eighth was half gone. Then he was wide with a right, held and butted as they broke; Rocco felt the blood and got rid of some of it on the boy's left breast. He trapped the boy's left, rapping the kidneys fast before grabbing the arms again, and pressed his nose firmly into the hollow of the other's throat to arrest its bleeding. Felt the blood trickling into the hollow there as into a tiny cup. Rocco put his feet together and a glove on both of Kid Class's shoulders, to shove him sullenly away. And must have looked strong doing it, for he heard the crowd murmur a little. He was in Solly's corner at the bell and moved back to his own corner with his head held high, to control the bleeding. When his handler stopped it again, he knew, at last, that his own pride was double-crossing him. And felt glad for that much. Let them worry out there in the rows. He'd been shortchanged since Graduation Day; let them be on the short end tonight. He had the hundred—he'd get a job in a garage and forget every one of them.

It wasn't until the tenth and final round that Rocco realized he wanted to kayo the boy—because it wasn't until then that he realized he could. Why not do the thing up the right way? He felt his tiredness fall from him like an old cloak at the notion. This was his fight, his round. He'd end like he'd started, as a fighting man.

And saw Solly Kid Class shuffling his shoulders forward uneasily. The boy would be a full-sized heavy in another six months. He bulled him into the ropes and felt the boy fade sidewise. Rocco caught him off balance with his left, hook-fashion, into the short ribs. The boy chopped back with his left uncertainly, as though he might have jammed the knuckles, and held. In a half-rolling clinch along the ropes, he saw Solly's mouthpiece projecting, slipping halfway in and halfway out, and then swallowed in again with a single tortured twist of the lips. He got an arm loose and banged the boy back of the ear with an overhand right that must have looked funny because the crowd laughed a little. Solly smeared his glove across his nose, came halfway in and changed his mind, left himself wide and was almost steady until Rocco feinted him into a knot and brought the right looping from the floor with even his toes behind it.

Solly stepped in to let it breeze past, and hooked his right hard to the button. Then the left. Rocco's mouthpiece went spinning in an arc into the lights. Then the right.

Rocco spun halfway around and stood looking sheepishly out at the rows. Kid Class saw only his man's back; Rocco was out on his feet. He walked slowly along the ropes, tapping them idly with his glove and smiling vacantly down at the newspapermen, who smiled back. Solly looked at Ryan. Ryan nodded toward Rocco. Kid Class came up fast behind his man and threw the left under the armpit flush onto the point of the chin, Rocco went forward on the ropes and hung there, his chin catching the second strand, and hung on and on, like a man decapitated.

He came to in the locker room under the stands, watching the steam swimming about the pipes directly overhead. Uncle Mike was somewhere near, telling him he had done fine, and then he was alone. They were all gone then, all the six-bit hecklers and the iron-throated boys in the sixty-cent seats. He rose heavily and dressed slowly, feeling a long relief that he'd come to the end. He'd done it the hard way, but he'd done it. Let them all go.

He was fixing his tie, taking more time with it than it required, when she knocked. He called to her to come in. She had never seen him fight, but he knew she must have listened on the radio or she wouldn't be down now.

She tested the adhesive over his right eye timidly, fearing to hurt him with her touch, but wanting to be sure it wasn't loose.

"I'm okay," he assured her easily. "We'll celebrate a little 'n' forget the whole business." It wasn't until he kissed her that her eyes avoided him; it wasn't till then that he saw she was trying not to cry. He patted her shoulder.

"There's nothin' wrong, Lil'—a couple days' rest 'n' I'll be in the pink again."

Then saw it wasn't that after all.

"You told me you'd win," the girl told him. "I got eight to one and put the whole damn bank roll on you. I wanted to surprise you, 'n' now we ain't got a cryin' dime."

Rocco didn't blow up. He just felt a little sick. Sicker than he had ever felt in his life. He walked away from the girl and sat on the rubbing table, studying the floor. She had sense enough not to bother him until he'd realized what the score was. Then he looked up, studying her from foot to head. His eyes didn't rest on her face: they went back to her feet. To the scarred toes of the only decent shoes; and a shadow passed over his heart. "You got good odds, honey," he told her thoughtfully. "You done just right. We made 'em sweat all night for their money." Then he looked up and grinned. A wide, white grin.

That was all she needed to know it was okay after all. She went to him so he could tell her how okay it really was.

That was like Young Rocco, from Graduation Day. He always did it the hard way; but he did it.

Miss Donahue would have been proud.

THIS WAS a barroom and vaudeville favorite.

# The Kid's Last Fight

## ANONYMOUS

Us two was pals, the Kid and me:
'Twould cut no ice if some gayzee,
As tough as hell jumped either one,
We'd both light in and hand him some.

Both of a size, the Kid and me,
We tipped the scales at thirty-three;
And when we'd spar 'twas give and take,
I wouldn't slug for any stake.

One day we worked out at the gym,
Some swell guy hangin' round called "Slim,"
Watched us and got stuck on the Kid,
Then signed him up, that's what he did.

This guy called "Slim" he owned a string
Of lightweights, welters, everything;
He took the Kid out on the road,
And where they went none of us knowed.

I guessed the Kid had changed his name,
And fightin' the best ones in the game.
I used to dream of him at night,
No letters came—he couldn't write.

In just about two months or three
I signed up with Bucktooth McGee.
He got me matched with Denver Brown,
I finished him in half a round.

Next month I fought with Brooklyn Mike,
As tough a boy who hit the pike;
Then Frisco Jim and Battlin' Ben,
And knocked them all inside of ten.

I took 'em all and won each bout,
None of them birds could put me out;
The sportin' writers watched me slug.
Then all the papers run my mug.

"He'd rather fight than eat," they said,
"He's got the punch, he'll knock 'em dead."
There's only one I hadn't met,
That guy they called "The Yorkshire Pet."

He'd cleaned 'em all around in France,
No one in England stood a chance;
And I was champ in U.S.A.,
And knocked 'em cuckoo every day.

Now all McGee and me could think
Was how we'd like to cross the drink,
And knock this bucko for a row,
And grab a wagonload of dough.

At last Mac got me matched all right,
Five thousand smackers for the fight;
Then me and him packed up our grip,
And went to grab that championship.

I done some trainin' and the night
Set for the battle sure was right;
The crowd was wild, for this here bout
Was set to last till one was out.

The mob went crazy when the Pet
Came in, I'd never seen him yet;
And then I climbed up through the ropes,
All full of fight and full of hopes.

The crowd give me an awful yell
('Twas even money at the bell),
They stamped their feet and shook the place;
The Pet turned 'round, I saw his face!

My guts went sick, that's what they did,
For Holy Gee, it was the Kid–
We just had time for one good shake,
We meant it, too, it wasn't fake.

24

# The Kid's Last Fight ANONYMOUS

Whang! went the bell, the fight was on,
I clinched until the round was gone,
A-beggin' that he'd let me take
The fall for him—he wouldn't fake.

Hell, no, the Kid was on the square,
And said we had to fight it fair,
The crowd had bet their dough on us—
We had to fight (the honest cuss).

The referee was yellin' "break,"
The crowd was sore and howlin' "fake."
They'd paid their dough to see a scrap.
And so far we'd not hit a tap.

The second round we both begin.
I caught a fast one on my chin;
And stood like I was in a doze,
Until I got one on the nose.

I started landin' body blows,
He hooked another on my nose,
That riled my fightin' blood like hell,
And we were sluggin' at the bell.

The next round started, from the go
The millin' we did wasn't slow,
I landed hard on him, and then,
He took the count right up to ten.

He took the limit on one knee,
A chance to get his wind and see;
At ten he jumped up like a flash
And on my jaw he hung a smash.

I'm fightin', too, there, toe to toe,
And hittin' harder, blow for blow,
I damn soon knowed he couldn't stay,
He rolled his eyes—you know the way.

The way he staggered made me sick,
I stalled, McGee yelled, "Cop him quick!"
The crowd was wise and yellin' "fake,"
They'd seen the chance I wouldn't take.

The mob kept tellin' me to land,
And callin' things I couldn't stand;
I stepped in close and smashed his chin,
The Kid fell hard; he was all in.

I carried him into his chair,
And tried to bring him to for fair,
I rubbed his wrists, done everything,
A doctor climbed into the ring.

And I was scared as I could be,
The Kid was starin' and couldn't see;
The doctor turned and shook his head,
I looked again—the Kid was dead!

ARTHUR (BUGS) BAER, into whose hopper of humor vaudeville, radio, night-club and literary comics have dipped for fifty years, was born in Philadelphia in 1886. Starting as a sports cartoonist, he worked on newspapers there and in Washington, where he turned to writing. He joined the New York *Evening World* in 1915 and four years later went to work for Hearst. Present at the Dempsey–Gibbons fight, he described Shelby, Montana, as "so tough that the canaries sing bass."

# Epigrams

## BUGS BAER

[AFTER JACK DEMPSEY knocked out Fred Fulton in 18⅗ seconds on July 27, 1918]—Fulton would do better selling advertising space on the soles of his shoes.

[After Jack Dempsey knocked out Georges Carpentier in the fourth round on July 2, 1921] —The joint was a sellout, and Carpentier had the last seat in the house.

[After Jack Dempsey, knocked out of the ring in the first round, knocked out Luis Firpo in the second round on September 14, 1923]—If the fight had been held on a barge Firpo would be champion because Dempsey would have drowned.

[After Gene Tunney outboxed Jack Dempsey for the second time, on September 22, 1927]— If there had been a gate in the ring, Dempsey would be champion again.

[After Joe Louis knocked out James J. Braddock in the eighth round on June 22, 1937]— The old champion was as game as a butcher's chopping block.

[Before Rocky Marciano knocked out Don Cockell in the ninth round on May 16, 1955]— Cockell's manager is complaining about the size of the ring and demanding one that measures 20 feet. What difference does it make? His man isn't that tall.

GEORGE BARTON wrote sports for Minneapolis newspapers for fifty-three years and covered every heavyweight title fight from Jack Johnson–Jim Jeffries through Floyd Patterson–Ingemar Johansson. He also won a six-round decision over Terry McGovern, sparred exhibitions with Joe Gans, Battling Nelson and Frankie Neil, refereed more than 12,000 bouts and is the source of the Billy Miske story. Since Barton first wrote it for the Minneapolis *Tribune* the story has appeared in hundreds of newspapers and has been rewritten or reprinted in seven magazines. This is from Barton's autobiography, *My Lifetime in Sports*.

# Billy Miske's Last Christmas

## GEORGE A. BARTON

THIS IS THE STORY of Billy Miske, the most courageous fighter I have known in more than half a century of association with professional boxing. Miske came to the end of the fistic trail early in 1923. Although he had not reached his twenty-ninth birthday, Billy was mortally ill with Bright's disease; his days were numbered and he knew it.

Billy Miske's entire ring career, however, marked him as a boxer with a great fighting heart. When he became a victim of Bright's disease in 1916 his family doctor told him he had only five years to live, provided he quit boxing and took care of himself. Miske shrugged off the advice. Knowing that his number was up, he participated in seventy fights in the next six years, meeting the leading light heavyweights and heavyweights. Included were three bouts with Jack Dempsey, three with Tommy Gibbons, three with Jack Dillon, three with Bill Brennan and two with Harry Greb.

At one time Billy was matched with Gibbons for a ten-round fight to be staged at Nicollet Park in Minneapolis on June 19, 1919. A week before the bout, Billy became ill and was ordered to bed by his doctor. An assortment of boils added to his misery in the humid ninety-degree heat.

Four days before the fight Jack Reddy, the St. Paul boxing promoter who was Billy's manager, informed Mike Collins, who was then pro-

moting boxing matches in Minneapolis, that it would be impossible for Miske to go through with the match. Collins, faced with this dilemma, called me and asked if I would go with him to Miske's home in St. Paul.

"Any chance of your fighting on Friday night?" an anxious Collins asked Miske. "We've already got $18,000 in advance sales in the till and the gate is a cinch to hit $30,000. The Minneapolis baseball team is coming home Saturday for a three-week stand and a postponement of that long will kill interest in the fight. It means a big pay day for all of us if you fight Gibbons Friday night. Try to make it, will you, Billy?"

Miske, still in bed and running a temperature, told Collins, "I'll get up tomorrow. If I can walk around the block without falling down, I'll fight Gibbons for you Friday night."

True to his promise, Miske was on hand for the battle. Weak as he was, Billy waged a furious fight for ten rounds and Gibbons was extended to the limit in gaining the decision. As referee of the match, I can vouch for the fury of Miske's fighting.

Due to his health, Billy retired from boxing in the spring of 1920 and entered the automobile business. Within five months he lost $55,000 and needed additional money to carry on. He accepted a guarantee of $25,000 to meet champion Jack Dempsey in a title fight at Benton Harbor, Michigan, on Labor Day.

This match was their third meeting. Miske had lost a ten-round decision to Dempsey after a terrific battle in St. Paul on May 3, 1918. In their second fight, a six-round bout in Philadelphia on November 28 of the same year, Jack had gained a newspaper decision.

Physically ailing, Miske merely went through the motions of training for this third fight with Dempsey and Jack knocked him out in the third round. It was the only knockout suffered by Miske in 150 bouts. After paying Reddy his manager's percentage, Billy had about $18,000 left. Intimate friends, his wife and his manager, all knowing that the automobile business was doomed to failure, begged Billy to go through bankruptcy and save the Dempsey purse for a nest egg.

"Not me," Billy said, proudly. "Nobody is going to point a finger at Billy Miske and say he ever beat them out of even a dime. I'm going to pay off even if I go broke again."

He put $15,000 into the business and eventually was wiped out with a loss of $70,000. Flat broke, Miske returned to the ring in 1921 and participated in twenty-four more fights before his death. He won thirteen by knockouts, ten were no-decision and he was held to one draw.

Miske's illness finally forced him to retire again after he knocked out Harry Foley in one round in Omaha on January 12, 1923. Unable to fight, and too ill to work, Billy stayed home most of the time with his wife, Marie, and their three children. Late November came, with Christmas in the offing. Months of idleness had depleted the Miske bank roll. He needed money badly. That was his predicament as he entered the office of Jack Reddy.

"Jack," Miske said, "get me a fight."

"You must be kidding," replied Reddy. "You're in no condition to fight."

"Get me a fight anyway," Miske said.

"But Billy," answered the manager, "do you want me ruled out of boxing for tossing a sick man into the ring?"

"Look, Jack," pleaded Miske, "here's how it is. I'm flat broke and I haven't done anything for eleven months. I know I haven't long to go, and I want to give Marie and the children one more happy Christmas before I check out. I won't be around for another. Please get me one more pay day. I want to make Christmas this year something Marie and the children will always remember me for."

"This may hurt your feelings, Bill," Reddy said, "but you know as well as I do that if you were to fight in your present condition, you might be killed. You might die right in the ring."

"Sure," answered Miske. "I know better than you do but I'm a fighter and I'd rather die in the ring than sitting home in a rocking chair."

Reddy continued to protest. He offered to do anything he could to help Billy financially. He pleaded with Miske to abandon the idea; he didn't want his pal's death on his conscience.

"Here's what I'll do," Reddy said, finally. "You go to the gym and start working out. If you get into any reasonable kind of shape, we'll talk about getting you a match."

"You know I can't do that," replied Miske. "It's impossible for me to train, but I've got to have one more fight for my family's sake. Please get it for me."

As there was no talking Miske out of his scheme, Reddy reluctantly said he'd look around. After pondering over the matter for several days, Jack engineered a match between Miske and Bill Brennan at Omaha. Billy had decisioned Brennan in three previous fights, all closely contested, and there had been enough excitement created to warrant a fourth meeting.

Bill Brennan was a tough hombre who had fought the best and had been knocked out only once—by Jack Dempsey in the twelfth round of a championship fight at New York in 1920. Brennan led on points in that fight up until the moment the Manassa Mauler flattened him.

I received a tip regarding Miske being matched with Brennan and I immediately called Reddy. I gave him a verbal lashing over the telephone for being willing to risk Miske's life to make a few bucks for himself. I also threatened to expose Billy's condition and promised to blast Reddy for being a party to such an affair.

"Hold everything," said Reddy, when I paused for breath. "Don't write anything until I bring Billy to your office. We'll be there shortly to explain everything."

When they arrived, Miske told me his story and begged me not to reveal it. I was a close friend of both Miske and Reddy; with reluctance I finally agreed to keep Billy's condition secret although, like Reddy, I feared that Miske might die in the ring.

All of these preliminaries took place about a week before Thanksgiving Day with the fight set for December 7. Miske, of course, wasn't able to train. When inquisitive newspapermen and boxing fans asked Reddy why Billy wasn't working out in the Rose Room gym in St. Paul, Jack explained he had a gym rigged up at his Lake Johanna home and Miske intended to do all his training there.

This was all ballyhoo. Billy remained at home, conserving his strength. He didn't go to Omaha until two days before the fight. State athletic commissions weren't as strict with medical examinations as they now are; probably the doctor gave Miske only a cursory examination. I wouldn't know.

What I do know is that Billy knocked out a well-conditioned Brennan in four rounds and picked up a purse of approximately $2,400. Reddy waived his manager's share so Miske kept the entire sum.

Billy spent Christmas Day at home with Marie and their three children—Billy, Jr., aged six, Douglas, four, and Donna, eighteen months—gathered around him. He was just about the happiest man in the world although he knew it would be his last Christmas. Although actually in agony from pain, Billy told Marie he felt fine. He romped with the children and laughed and kidded with relatives.

Early on the morning of December 26, Reddy received a telephone call from Miske. "Come and get me to a hospital, Jack," groaned Billy.

"I can't stand the pain any longer. I know I'm dying."

Reddy and Mrs. Miske rushed the courageous fighter to St. Mary's Hospital in Minneapolis. Billy Miske died there six days later early on New Year's Day, 1924.

Mrs. Miske (now Mrs. Alfred Peterson of St. Paul) remained a widow for seventeen years, working to support the three children. Her eldest son, Billy, Jr., boxed professionally for several years before going to work for a St. Paul meat-packing plant. The second son, Douglas, named after Douglas Fairbanks who was an ardent admirer of Billy, Sr., was an Air Force pilot in the South Pacific in World War II. He returned to service early in the Korean War and was killed in a training-plane crash. The daughter, Donna, received her bachelor's degree in education and a master's degree in recreation from the University of Minnesota. Until her marriage in 1954, she was playgrounds director in St. Louis Park, a suburb of Minneapolis.

Maybe someone can name a gamer boxer than Billy Miske. I can't.

ON DECEMBER 4, 1919, the author of *The Old Wives' Tale* saw Georges Carpentier box Joe Beckett at Holborn Stadium, London, and was deeply interested.

# The Prize Fight

## ARNOLD BENNETT

DURING THE LAST STAGE of the dinner the host came round to you and said, in that politely casual tone of a man who knows more than you do, but who would not like the fact to appear: "Got your ticket safe? Might be as well to keep an eye on it till you're inside." You then divined that you were about to enter another world, a world where the eruptive potentialities of the social organization may show themselves more disconcertingly than in yours. And the inflections of your reply tried to prove that you were an accustomed citizen of that other world. Later, the host said: "I brought a knuckle duster with me." He presented the steely instrument for inspection. "You can do some useful work with that on your fingers," he said, and added fatalistically: "But, of course, it wouldn't be any good if half a dozen of 'em set on you at once." In answer to the naïve query, "How do you get there?" he said: "Oh! That'll be all right. I've got fifteen taxis at the door." Fifteen taxis at the door! It indeed is another world, and one which the taxi driver comprehends and approves. Could anybody get fifteen taxis at any door for an excursion to the Albert Hall for a League of Nations meeting, or to Lowndes Square to hear Robert Nichols recite at Mrs. Kinfoot's? Nobody could.

The crowds began long before the Stadium was reached. The street was narrow and dark, and in an empty space scores of huge policemen were watching the eruptive potentialities. You clutched your ticket, for, after all, it bore the figures £10 10s. Still, there was no difficulty about entering. You noticed the thick solidity of the barriers paneled with barbed wire, but they opened quickly for you, and the strong attendants had none of the geographical indecision which characterizes nonchalant program girls in figleaf white aprons over short black frocks. As you squeezed into the central enclosure of the auditorium, close to the ring (a squared circle), where one of the preliminary bouts was in progress, the final attendant said quickly: "Sit down here until the end of the round, sir." Ferocious homicidal yells from behind reinforced him: "Sit down! Sit down!" You sat down quickly—anywhere. The attendant crouched on his haunches. (This was not *Tristan,* of which ten or twenty bars don't in the least matter. This was pugilism, the most holy and impassioning sacrament of its world.) A few seconds more and you were in your seat, one of four or five thousand. You realized that the affair had been wonderfully organized and rehearsed.

In came Mr. Cochran, the mysterious organizer, escorting the Prince of Wales, the Prince holding a cigar just in the manner of his grandfather, and Mr. Cochran looking rather like one of the Antonines. Mr. Cochran gazed around at the vast advertisements of his own theaters, and at the cinema operators precariously suspended over balconies. Mr. Cochran had thoughtfully provided loops of rope for them to rest their feet in. Mr. Cochran had forgotten nothing. It was his hour. He deserved it. It pains me as a professional observer that I cannot recall whether the Prince and Mr. Cochran wore smoking jackets or swallowtails. Opinion was divided as to the sartorial proprieties. Some star actors and some millionaires wore smoking jackets; some star actors and some millionaires wore swallow-tails. The millionaires were richly represented. There they were, dotted about, the genial wizards who have removed Arlington Street from the map, who are said to have the Government in their pockets, and who assert with calm conviction that "Lloyd George can't put it over *them*." Women were certainly too few; some had sought to atone for the paucity by emulating the attire of the gladiators in the ring. They made futile spots of sex on ten guineas' worth of plush in an environment where Aphrodite had no status whatever.

The raised ring was already well illuminated, but soon many lamps that had been unlit fizzed into activity, and dazzling torrents of bluish light rained down a treble-X radiance on the battleground. The cinema men prepared themselves. The last of the preliminary bouts finished. An M.C. climbed into the ring and besought the audience to stop smoking, so that the champions about to dispute the mastery of a continent might breathe more easily. The celebrated Mr. B. J. Angle, whose word was to be law to the champions, climbed into the ring and delivered a short homily. Mr. B. J. Angle was evidently a man who knew his own mind, and who also knew his world. Some persons were pained because he wore a gray suit and brown boots at ten P.M., in the presence of the Prince, and they did not hesitate to express their narrow-mindedness. A little box, covered with advertisement, was deposited in the center of the ring. It contained the gloves. The sublime moment approached. You had a unique sensation; you admitted to yourself that it was well worth ten guineas, and also that the subject of the reconstruction of Europe lacked actuality.

Beckett and train appeared first, and the train was so numerous as to be bewildering. For a moment you thought that both boxers and both trains must be in the ring. You understood better the immense costliness of a really great fight, and the complexity of the machinery which is necessary to perfect it. You perceived that though eight thousand pounds was to be divided between the combatants, neither would be overpaid when he had reckoned his time and discharged his expenses. When Carpentier and train appeared, the ring was like a market place. One figure, Carpentier, stood out astonishingly from all the rest. All the rest had the faces and the carriage of bruisers. Nobody could have taken Carpentier for a boxer. He might have been a barrister, a poet, a musician, a Foreign Office

attaché, a Fellow of All Souls; but not a boxer. He had an air of intellectual or artistic distinction. And long contact with the very physical world of pugilism had not apparently affected his features in the slightest degree. In the previous six years he had matured, but not coarsened. He seemed excessively out of place in the ring. You could not comprehend what on earth he was doing there. Surely he must have lost his way! Beckett, a magnificent form, but with a countenance from which you would not infer much power of ratiocination, gazed long at Carpentier from under his forehead, whereas Carpentier scarcely glanced at Beckett. At one moment Beckett appeared to you like a dumb victim trying to penetrate the secrets of a higher and inscrutable power; at another moment you were persuaded that grim Beckett was merely contemplating his poor destined intellectual victim with the most admirable British detachment. At one moment you felt that Carpentier must inevitably be crushed; at another moment you were convinced that if Carpentier was not too many for Beckett, then the course of civilization had been very misleading.

I know nothing about boxing; my opinion on boxing would be worth about as much as Beckett's on Scriabin. But I had seen Carpentier, in 1913, when he was a boy, knock out Bombardier Wells at the National Sporting Club in less than two minutes, and the performance was so brilliant, so easy, so natural, that I could not believe that anybody else would ever knock out Carpentier. Now, however, I was overborne by the weight of expert prophecy. All the experts were certain that Beckett must win. Some of them murmured something perfunctory about the million-to-one chance of an early knockout by Carpentier, but none of them had in reality any fear of such a chance. I surrendered, and privily told myself what a simpleton I had been to imagine for a single instant that Carpentier would not be smashed. (I forgot the peculiar accents in which Lord Fisher said to me in 1915, that *his* life then was "nothing but one damned expert after another.") Further, the experts killed Carpentier immediately they saw him. They said he was not in condition; they liked not the color of his skin; they said he had gone right off; they said he was a dead man. And I submissively persuaded myself that this was so.

The ritualistic prologue to the encounter seemed to take a very long time. But it served excellently its purpose of heightening the excitement of expectation. When the bell at length rang, and Beckett and Carpentier approached each other lonely in the ring, beneath a million

candle power of radiance, and the whole bar-
baric Stadium was stilled, and hearts knocked
remindingly under waistcoats—in that moment,
even those who had paid twenty-five guineas
for a ten-guinea seat must have felt that they
had got a bargain.

There had been some grand fighting before
the big event, particularly between Eddie Feathers and Gus Platts, and experts had said: "This
will be the best fighting of the evening. You'll
see. A championship match is never any good."
The devoted experts were wrong again. In five
seconds the championship fighting stood plainly
in a class apart, thanks solely to Carpentier.
Carpentier caught Beckett on the nose at once.
Beckett positively had to rub his nose, an act
which made strong men around me shudder.
Beckett was utterly outclassed. He never had a
chance. . . . The Stadium beheld him lying
stunned on his face. And the sight of Beckett
prone, and Carpentier standing by him listening
to the counting of allotted seconds, was the incredible miraculous consummation of all the
months of training, all the organization, all the
advertising, all the expenditure, all the frenzy.
Aphrodite, breaking loose in the shape of a
pretty girl *bien maquillée*, rushed to the ring.
Men raised her in their arms, she raised her face;
and Carpentier bent over the ropes and kissed
her passionately amid the ecstasies of joy and
disillusion that raged around them. That kiss
seemed to be the bright flower of the affair. It
summed up everything. Two minutes earlier
Beckett in his majestic strength had been the
idol of a kingdom. Now Beckett was a sack of
potatoes, and Carpentier in might and glory was
publicly kissing the chosen girl within a yard of
the Prince of Wales.

We left the Stadium immediately, though the
program of boxing was by no means concluded,
and in Red Lion Square found our taxi driver,
whose claim to distinction was that his grandfather had been a friend of Mr. George R. Sims.

All the streets of the vicinity were full of people
abroad for the event. They were all aware of the
result, for at the very doors of the Stadium, on
our emerging, a newspaper boy had offered us
the news in print. They all stood or moved in
attitudes of amaze, watching with rapt faces the
long lines of departing motors. You perceived
that the English race was profoundly interested
and moved, and that nothing less than winning
the greatest war could have interested and moved
it more profoundly. This emotion was no product
of a press campaign, but the press campaign was
a correct symptom of it. It was as genuine as
British fundamental decency.

Not Beckett alone had been stunned. The experts were stunned. Their prime quality of being
ever cheery had gone from them. They could
scarcely speak; there was naught to say; there
was no ground for any argument. They were
bowed with grief. Fate had heavily smitten them.
One of them murmured: "I consider it's a disgrace to Great Britain." Another: "It's the champion of Great Britain that's been beaten. . . .
This—after Mlle. Lenglen!" Where to go in these
circumstances of woe? Obviously to the Eccen-
tric Club. We went, and were solaced and
steadied with an aged Courvoisier brandy. Sipping the incomparable liquid, and listening to
the exact reconstitution of the battle by the experts, I reflected, all solitary in my own head,
upon what, with such magnificent and quiet
hospitality, I had been taken to see. Was the
show worthy of the talents and the time lavished
on its preparation and accomplishment, worthy
of the tradition, of the prowess, of the fostering
newspapers, of Mr. Cochran? It was. Was it a
moral show? It was—as moral as an Inter-Uni-
versity Rugger match. Was it an aesthetic show?
It was. Did it uplift? It did. Did it degrade? It
did not. Was it offensive? No. Ought the noble
art to continue? It ought. I had been deeply interested.

At 7:30 A.M. on April 17, 1860, at Farnborough, near London, John C. Heenan, the American champion, and Tom Sayers, the English title holder, squared off in the first boxing match to stir public interest on both sides of the Atlantic and intrigue Currier and Ives. In the crowd of 2,500 were the Prince Consort, members of Parliament, William Makepeace Thackeray, Charles Dickens and representatives of the press of both countries. Heenan stood six feet two and weighed 195 pounds; he had six inches and forty-three pounds on Sayers. He was also having the best of it, but choking his opponent when, in the thirty-seventh round, the crowd burst the ropes. The two fought on for five more rounds before the contest was called a draw. (*Bettmann Archive*)

JAMES FIGG,
boxing's first champion
(1719–1730)
painted by William Hogarth

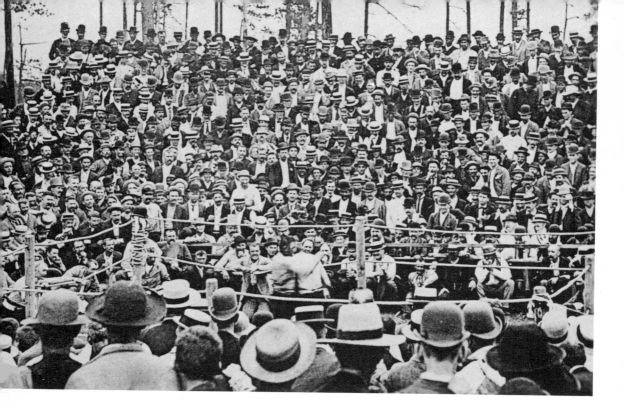

## END OF AN ERA

When John L. Sullivan retained his heavyweight title by knocking out Jake Kilrain in the seventy-fifth round at Richburg, Mississippi, on July 8, 1889, it was the only bare-knuckle fight ever photographed and the last ever fought for a championship. (*Bettmann Archive*)

## TEN SECONDS OF SUNLIGHT

As Luther McCarthy, felled by the blows of Arthur Pelkey, was counted out in the arena in Calgary, Canada on May 24, 1913, the sun broke through the gray overcast for the first time that day. Eight minutes later, as recounted in Barney Nagler's story on page 302, he was pronounced dead. (*The Ring*)

*Ready For The Fr*

IT is a good thing for a girl
to box. Poise, grace and
of movement result from
cise.

The extremely graceful ca
professional boxers is almost p
and to such a science have th
this matter of body balance a
attitude that the man who is q
his feet and quick in his be
ments will often overcome an
of twenty or thirty pounds in
the part of his opponent. Wit
rect body and foot balance
blood circulates more easily
soon comes a buoyancy to
carriage which is most att
look upon.

To take the correct attite
with the feet firmly plante
floor—heelless tennis shoes ar
practice, or the Chinese sl
many girls have for bedroom
ligee use—and place your le
advance of your right anywl
eight to eighteen inches. acc
your height and length
Swing the body back and for
times so that you are perfe
on your feet and find that
swings well with your feet so
Always place the feet so that
swings easily. This is a fur
rule, and must be borne in
ways. It is necessary at all
maintain a perfect balance.
weight of the body divided e
both feet.

The left foot should be p
on the floor pointing straig
front toward your opponent's
the right should be held with
an inch or so off the floor, b
left foot, thus affording imme
portunity to swing quickly i
rection on the ball of the fo
tice this attitude first stand
then moving the body quickly
imaginary blows until perfect
plete balance is established.

In boxing. the left hand. not
is the boxer's main depender
the left hand that delivers
the right hand and arm b
across the body to receive an
body blows, and so protect the
the abdomen and the short ri
your left hand up toward y
nent's chin, just as though.

Although a punch on the nose is hardly intended to improve
the recipient's appearance, boxing's social acceptance was veri-
fied when it made the beauty column of the New York *Evening
World* on February 27, 1905.

# Maid Will Help Her Health by Boxing.

## The Gloves Will Give a Girl Self-Control, Buoyancy and Grace.

Landing on the chin

Ducking a blow.

The Left the ...ing ...nd.

A Solar Plexus Blow

carefully, for each step must be mastered ere you take up the next. ...ing it is the fist, the clinched ...t the flat, open palm, that gives ...wa, and it is quite important to ...ow to double your fist to the ...vantage.

...ising the fist bring the tips of ...gers well over the palm of the ...ith the thumb turned inside and ...e first joint of the first or index

...are a few simple positions and ...vres for girls beginning to box: ...nd in an easy attitude, left foot ...d about eighteen inches in front ...t; left toe pointed straight; ...resting equally on both feet. ...e shoulders back and keep the ...ect. The right forearm should be ...tly across the body, the fist be...r the solar plexus. The left ...ould be slightly advanced, tho ...a position to guard a blow ...g forward the left arm in a ...y straight line, letting the left ...r follow it and at the same ...e slightly on the right so

only with the left arm but with the co-ordination of every muscle of the body.

3. Now, keeping the arm as it was in the first position, bring forward the right fist in similar fashion, again rising on the right heel and bringing the whole body into co-operation. Keep the knees rigid in both these positions.

4. Bending the right knee, lead with the left fist for your opponent's solar plexus, bringing the shoulders forward and raising the right arm high enough to protect your head and face.

5. Bending the right knee again, lead with the right fist for your opponent's heart, raising the left arm to protect the face. Do not lean forward awkwardly nor twist the body to one side, nor in any way disturb the perfection of your balance.

6. Let your opponent lead with the left for your face. As she does so move your head to the right, just far enough to avoid the blow, and at the same time lead with your left for her face, bring-ing your left arm around outside her

on her face. This is called the "left counter."

7. When your opponent makes a left lead for your face move your head to the left, leading with your right for her face. This is the "right counter." Sim-ilarly moving the head to left or right make the two leads for solar plexus and heart.

8. To learn the delicate "boxing bal-ance," practice leaping forward, back-ward and to either side, making sure that your feet and whole body always land in exactly the "first position." This not only teaches balance, but is good exercise.

9. When your opponent leads for the face throw your left shoulder sharply forward to the right, keeping the knee stiff and bringing the head and shoul-ders far enough to the side to avoid the blow. This is the "right duck."

10. When she leads for the face, bend your head to the left, then bring it forward in a semi-circle, low enough to allow her blow to pass over your head. This is the "straight duck."

11. Practice each of the foregoing as follows: First take a step forward, then go through one of these ma-noeuvres and at once step back out of reach. Then taking a step forward make the next lead or counter and again step back. This is not only good

(UPI)

## THE PROMOTERS

The two greatest boxing promoters were George Lewis (Tex) Rickard and Michael Strauss (Mike) Jacobs. Each created, and was himself the creation of, his own great heavyweight champion. Between 1905 and 1929, fights promoted by Rickard, shown at the left with Jack Dempsey, grossed over $21,000,000. Five of these grossed more than $1,000,000 each; one topped $2,000,-000. Between 1933 and 1949, the promotions of Jacobs, shown with Joe Louis in 1938, grossed more than $24,000,000 and included three million-dollar gates.

     (Acme)

## MOST MEMORABLE MOMENT

On September 14, 1923, at the Polo Grounds in New York City, Jack Dempsey and Luis Angel Firpo were participants in what turned out to be, as Frank Menke's account on page 291 makes clear, the most exciting glove fight of all time. When Firpo, down seven times, got up to knock Dempsey out of the ring in the first round, he produced the most dramatic single moment in boxing history, recorded in the best-known of all fight photographs. In return, Dempsey knocked him out in the next round. (*UPI*)

SEATED BOXER
Sculpture from Late Hellenistic period
(*Bettmann Archive*)

JOE GANS
Sculpture by Mahonri V. Young
(*Courtesy of Madison Square Garden Corporation*)

SIX WEEKS BEFORE he knocked out Jake Kilrain in Richburg, Miss., in the seventy-fifth round, John L. Sullivan was interviewed by Nellie Bly (Mrs. Elizabeth Cochrane Seaman). She asked the good questions, and this excellent piece of reporting occupied the first three columns on page 13 of the New York *World* on Sunday, May 26, 1889.

# A Visit with John L. Sullivan

## NELLIE BLY

IF JOHN L. SULLIVAN isn't able to whip any pugilist in the world I would like to see the man who is. I went to Belfast, N. Y., to see him last week and I was surprised. Why? Well, I will tell you.

I have often thought that the sparring instinct is inborn in everything—except women and flowers, of course. I have seen funny little spring roosters, without one feather's sprout to crow about, fight like real men. And then the boys! Isn't it funny how proud they are of their muscle, and how quiet the boy is who hasn't any? Almost as soon as a boy learns to walk he learns to jump into position of defense and double up his fists.

WE REACHED Belfast about 7:30 o'clock in the morning and were the only passengers for that place. Mr. William Muldoon's house, where Mr. Sullivan is training, is in the prettiest part of the town and only a short distance from the hotel. Fearing that Mr. Sullivan would go out for a walk and that I would miss him, I went immediately to the Muldoon cottage.

One would never imagine from the surroundings that a prize fighter was being trained there. The house is a very pretty little two-story building, surrounded by the smoothest and greenest of green lawns, which helps to intensify the spotless whiteness of the cottage. A wide veranda surrounds the three sides of the cottage, and the easy chairs and hammocks give it a most enticing look of comfort. Large maple trees shade the house from the glare of the sun.

I RANG THE BELL, and when a colored man came in answer I sent my letter of introduction to Mr. Muldoon. A handsome young man, whose broad shoulders were neatly fitted with a gray corduroy coat, came into the room, holding a light gray cap in his hand. His face was youthful, his eyes blue, his expression pleasing, his smile brought two dimples to punctuate his rosy cheeks, his bearing was easy and most graceful, and this was the champion wrestler and athlete, William Muldoon.

"We have just returned from our two-mile walk," he said, when I told him I had come to see Mr. Sullivan, "and Mr. Sullivan is just being rubbed down. If you will excuse me one moment I will tell him."

In a few moments Mr. Muldoon returned, followed by a man whom I would never have taken for the great and only Sullivan. He was a tall man, with enormous shoulders, and wore dark trousers, a light cheviot coat and vest and slippers. In his hand he held a light cloth cap. He paused almost as he entered the room in a half-bashful way, and twisted his cap in a very boyish but not ungraceful manner.

"Miss Bly, Mr. Sullivan," said Mr. Muldoon, and I looked into the great fighter's dark, bright eyes as he bent his broad shoulders before me.

"Mr. Sullivan, I would like to shake hands with you," I said, and he took my hand with a firm, hearty grasp, and with a hand that felt small and soft. Mr. Muldoon excused himself, and I was left to interview the great John L.

"I came here to learn all about you, Mr. Sullivan, so will you please begin by telling me at what time you get up in the morning," I said.

"Well, I get up about 6 o'clock and get rubbed down," he began, in a matter-of-fact way. "Then Muldoon and I walk and run a mile or a mile and a half away and then back. Just as soon as we get in I am given a showerbath, and after being thoroughly rubbed down again I put on an entire fresh outfit."

"What kind of clothing do you wear for your walk? Heavy?" I asked.

"Yes, I wear a heavy sweater and a suit of heavy corduroy buttoned tightly. I also wear gloves. After my walk I put on a fresh sweater, so that I won't take cold."

"What's a sweater?" I asked.

"I'll show you," he said, with a smile, and, excusing himself, he went out. In a moment he returned with a garment in his hand. It was a very heavy knit garment, with long sleeves and a standing collar. It was all in one piece and, I imagine, weighed several pounds. "Well, what do you wear a sweater for, and why do you take such violent walks?" I asked, my curiosity being satisfied as to the strange "sweater."

"I wear a sweater to make me warm, and I walk to reduce my fat and to harden my muscles. Last Friday I lost six pounds and last Saturday I lost six and a half pounds. When I came here I weighed 237 pounds, and now I weigh 218. Before I leave here I will weigh only 195 pounds."

"Do you take a cold showerbath when your walk is finished?"

"No, never, I don't believe in cold water. It chills the blood. I always have my showerbath of a medium temperature."

"How are you rubbed down, then, as you term it?"

"I have two men give me a brisk rubbing with their hands. Then they rub me down with a mixture of ammonia, camphor and alcohol."

"What do you eat?"

"I eat nothing fattening. I have oatmeal for breakfast and meat and bread for dinner, and cold meat and stale bread for supper. I eat no sweets nor potatoes. I used to smoke all the day, but since I came here I haven't seen a cigar. Occasionally Mr. Muldoon gives me a glass of ale, but it doesn't average one a day."

"Then training is not very pleasant work?"

"It's the worst thing going. A fellow would rather fight twelve dozen times than train once, but it's got to be done," and he leaned back in the easy chair with an air of weariness. "After breakfast I rest awhile," he continued, "and then putting on our heaviest clothes again we start out at 10:30 for our twelve-mile run and walk, which

we do in two hours. We generally go across the fields to Mr. Muldoon's farm because it is all uphill work and makes us warm. When we get back I am rubbed down again and at one we have dinner. In the afternoon we wrestle, punch a bag, throw football, swing Indian clubs and dumbbells, practice the chest movement and such things until suppertime. It's all right to be here when the sun is out, but after dark it's the dreariest place I ever struck. I wouldn't live here if they gave me the whole country."

The 'Champion Rest,' the name by which Mr. Muldoon's home is known, is surrounded by two graveyards, a church, the priest's home and a little cottage occupied by two old maids.

"I couldn't sleep after 5 o'clock this morning on account of Mr. Muldoon's cow. It kept up a hymn all the morning and the birds joined in the chorus. It's no use to try to sleep here after daybreak. The noise would knock out anything."

"Do you like prize fighting?" I asked Mr. Sullivan, after he had laid his complaint about the "singing cow" before Mrs. Muldoon.

"I don't," he replied. "Of course I did once, or rather I was fond of traveling about and the excitement of the crowds, but this is my last fight."

"Why?"

"Well, I am tired and I want to settle down. I am getting old," and he leaned back wearily.

"What is your age?"

"I was born the 15th of October, 1858. I began prize fighting when I was only nineteen years old. How did I start? Well, I had a match with a prize man who had never been downed, and I was the winner. This got me lots of notice, so I went through the country giving exhibitions. I have made plenty of money in my day, but I have been a fool and today I have nothing. It came easy and went easy. I have provided well for my father and mother, and they are in comfortable circumstances."

"What will you do if you stop fighting?"

"If I win this fight I will travel for a year giving sparring exhibitions, and then I will settle down. I have always wanted to run a hotel in New York, and if I am successful I think I shall spend the rest of my life as a hotel proprietor."

"How much money have you made during your career as a prize fighter?"

"I have made $500,000 or $600,000 in boxing. I made $125,000 from September 26, 1883, to May 26, 1884, when I traveled through the country offering $1,000 to anyone I couldn't knock out in four rounds, which takes twelve minutes."

"How do you dress when you go in a prize ring?"

"I wear knee breeches, stockings and shoes, and no shirt."

"Why no shirt?"

"Because a man perspires so freely that if he wears a shirt he is liable to chill, and a chill is always fatal in a prize ring. I took a chill when I fought with Mitchell, but it didn't last long."

"What kind of shoes do you wear?"

"Regular spike shoes. They have three big spikes to prevent slipping."

"How will you fight Kilrain, with or without gloves?"

"I will fight Kilrain according to the London prize-ring rules. That's without gloves and allows wrestling and throwing a man down. We get a rest every thirty seconds. Under the Marquis of Queensberry rules we wear gloves, anything under eleven ounces. They give us three minutes to a round under the Queensberry, and when the three minutes are up you have to rest whether you could whip your man the next instant or not."

"Your hands look very soft and small for a fighter."

"Do they?" and he held one out to me for inspection. "My friends tell me they look like hams," and he laughed. "I wear number nine gloves."

I examined his hand, he watching me with an amused expression. It looks a small hand to bear the record of so many "knockout" blows. The fingers were straight and shapely. The closely trimmed nails were a lovely oval and pink. The only apparent difference was the great thickness through.

"Feel my arm," he said, with a bright smile, as he doubled it up. I tried to feel the muscle, but it was like a rock. With both my hands I tried to span it, but I couldn't. Meanwhile the great fellow sat there watching me with a most boyish expression of amusement.

"By the time I am ready to fight there won't be any fat on my hands or face. They will be as hard as a bone. Do I harden them? Certainly. If I didn't I would have pieces knocked off of me. I have a mixture of rock salt and white wine and vinegar and several other ingredients which I wash my hands and face with."

"Do you hit a man on the face and neck and anywhere you can?" I asked.

"Certainly, any place above the belt that I get a chance," and he smiled.

"Don't you hate to hit a man so?"

"I don't think about it," still smiling.

"When you see that you have hurt him don't you feel sorry?"

"I never feel sorry until the fight is over."

"How do you feel when you get hit very hard?"

The dark, bright eyes glanced at me lazily and the deep, deep voice said with feeling: "I only want a chance to hit back."

"Did you ever see a man killed in the ring?"

"No, I never did, and I only knew of one fellow who died in the ring, and that was Walker, who died at Philadelphia from neglect after the fight was over."

Although I had my breakfast before reaching Mr. Muldoon's cottage I accepted his proposal to break bread with him and his guests. At a nearer view the dining room did not lose any of its prettiness and the daintiness of everything—the artistic surroundings, the noiseless and efficient colored waiter, the open windows on both sides, giving pretty views of green lawns and shady trees; the canary birds swelling their yellow throats occasionally with sweet little thrills, the green parrot climbing up its brass cage and talking about "crackers," the white table linen and beautiful dishes, down to the large bunch of fragrant lilacs and another of beautifully shaped and colored wild flowers, separated by a slipper filled with velvety pansies—was all entirely foreign to any idea I had ever conceived of prize fighters and their surroundings.

Yes, and they were all perfectly at ease and happy. At one end of the table sat Mrs. Muldoon and facing her was Mr. Muldoon. Next to Mrs. Muldoon sat my companion, then came myself, and next Mr. Sullivan. On the opposite side were the assistant trainers, Mr. Barnitt, a well-bred, scholarly-looking man, and Mr. Cleary, a smooth-faced, mischievous man who doesn't look much past boyhood. Mr. Sullivan's brother, who is anxious to knock out somebody, sat opposite Mr. Sullivan. And the wild flowers which graced the table were gathered by these great, strong men while taking their morning walk through the country.

About a mile from Champion Rest, his town home, is Mr. Muldoon's beautiful farm of seventy acres, which is well stocked with fine cattle. In the rear of Champion Rest are the barn and the training quarters. On the first floor are three stalls, fitted out after the latest improved method, where Mr. Muldoon keeps his favorite horses. Everthing is as clean and pleasant as in a dwelling house.

In the next room, suspended from the ceiling, is a Rugby football, which Mr. Sullivan pounds regularly every day in a manner which foretells hard times for Kilrain's head. The big football with which they play ball daily is also kept here. It is enormous and so heavy that when Mr. Muldoon dropped it into my arms I almost toppled over. Upstairs the floor is covered with a white wrestling pad, where the two champions wrestle every afternoon. In one corner is a collection of dumbbells, from medium weight to the heaviest, and several sizes of Indian clubs. Fastened to one side of the wall is a chest expander, which also comes in for daily use.

Downstairs is Champion Muldoon's den. Everything about it, as about the barn, is of a hardwood finish. There is no plaster nor paper anywhere. In one corner of the den is a glass case, where hang a fur-lined overcoat and several other garments. Along the top of the case is suspended a gold-headed cane. In the center of the room is a writing table, with everything ready for use. Along one side of the hall is a rattan lounge, at the foot of which is spread a yellow fur rug. The floor is neatly carpeted, and several rocking chairs prove that the den is for comfort.

The walls are covered with photographs of well-known people and among them several of Modjeska, with whom Mr. Muldoon at one time traveled. There are also a number of photographs of Mr. Muldoon in positions assumed in posing as Greek statues. On a corner table are albums filled with photographs of prominent athletes, and scrapbooks containing hundreds of notices of Champion Muldoon's athletic conquests. Then there are a number of well-bound standard works and the photographs of Mr. Muldoon's favorite authors—Bryant, Longfellow and, I believe, Shakespeare.

"I DON'T make any money by this," said Mr. Muldoon, in speaking about turning his home into training quarters, "but I was anxious to see Mr. Sullivan do justice to himself in this coming fight. It was a case of a fallen giant, so I thought to get him away from all bad influences and to get him in good trim. This is the healthiest place in the country and one of the most difficult to reach—two desirable things. On the way here we had a special car, but there were more people in our car than in any other. When we go to New Orleans we will keep our car locked and none but Mr. Sullivan's backers and representatives of the press will be admitted. Mr. Sullivan is the most obedient man I ever saw. He hasn't asked for a drink or a smoke since he came here and takes what I allow him without a murmur. It is a pleasure to train him."

"Does Mr. Sullivan never get angry?" I asked.

"If you would hear him and Mr. Barnitt sometimes, you would think they were going to eat one another," said Mrs. Muldoon.

"When he does get angry he runs over the fields until his good humor returns." said Mr. Barnitt, while Mr. Muldoon said that Mr. Sullivan was as docile as a lamb. They all spoke in praise of his strong will power and his childlike obedience.

"You are the first woman who ever interviewed me," said Mr. Sullivan in the afternoon, "and I have given you more than I ever gave any reporter in my life. They generally manufacture things and credit them to me, although some are mighty good fellows."

"When reporters act all right we will give them all they want," said Mr. Muldoon. "The other day a fresh reporter came here, and he thought because he was going to interview prize fighters he would have to be tough, so he said, 'Where's old Sullivan?' That queered him. We wouldn't give him a line."

"Yes, he came up to me first and said, 'Where's old Sullivan?'" said Mr. Sullivan. "And I told him, 'In the barn.' And he soon got put out of there for his toughness."

At suppertime Mr. Cleary had a great story to tell about his Irish bird trap. He had caught one robin, which Mrs. Muldoon released, and another had left his tail behind him. Then Mr. Barnitt and Mr. Sullivan's brother told how they had put some bird feathers in the cage to cheat the bird trapper.

And then the carriage came to take us to the train, and after I bade them all goodby I shook hands with John L. Sullivan and wished him success in the coming fight, and I believe he will have it, too, don't you?

George borrow spent seven years on *Lavengro,* a now classic autobiographical blend of fact and fiction (and prejudice) that first appeared in 1851. His father, Captain Thomas Borrow of the West Norfolk Militia, had once fought Big Ben Bryan (or Brain), and Borrow himself took boxing lessons from John Thurtell, who ran a roadhouse at Ipswich that was a rendezvous of the Fancy.

FROM

# *Lavengro*

## GEORGE BORROW

How for everything there is a time and a season, and then how does the glory of a thing pass from it, even like the flower of the grass. This is a truism, but it is one of those which are continually forcing themselves upon the mind. Many years have not passed over my head, yet, during those which I can call to remembrance, how many things have I seen flourish, pass away, and become forgotten, except by myself, who, in spite of all my endeavors, never can forget anything. I have known the time when a pugilistic encounter between two noted champions was almost considered in the light of a national affair; when tens of thousands of individuals, high and low, meditated and brooded upon it, the first thing in the morning and the last at night, until the great event was decided. But the time is past, and many people will say, thank God that it is; all I have to say is, that the French still live on the other side of the water, and are still casting their eyes hitherward—and that in the days of pugilism it was no vain boast to say that one Englishman was a match for two of t'other race; at present it would be a vain boast to say so, for these are not the days of pugilism.

But those to which the course of my narrative has carried me were the days of pugilism; it was then at its height, and consequently near its decline, for corruption had crept into the ring; and how many things, states and sects among the rest, owe their decline to this cause! But what a bold and vigorous aspect pugilism wore at that time! And the great battle was just then coming off: the day had been decided upon, and the spot —a convenient distance from the old town; and to the town were now flocking the bruisers of England, men of tremendous renown. Let no one sneer at the bruisers of England—what were the gladiators of Rome, or the bullfighters of Spain, in its palmiest days, compared to England's bruisers? Pity that ever corruption should have crept in amongst them—but of that I wish not to talk; let us still hope that a spark of the old religion of which they were priests, still lingers in the breasts of Englishmen. There they come, the bruisers, from far London, or from wherever else they might chance to be at the time, to the great rendezvous in the old city; some came one way, some another; some of tiptop reputation came with peers in their chariots, for glory and fame are such fair things that even peers are proud to have those invested therewith by their side; others came in their own gigs, driving their own bits of blood, and I heard one say: "I have driven through at a heat the whole hundred and eleven miles, and only stopped to bait twice." Oh, the blood-horses of old England! but they too have had their day—for everything beneath the sun there is a season and a time. But the greater number come just as they can contrive; on the tops of coaches, for example; and amongst these there are fellows with dark sallow faces, and sharp shining eyes; and it is these that have planted rottenness in the core of pugilism, for they are Jews, and, true to their kind, have only base lucre in view.

It was fierce old Cobbett, I think, who first said that the Jews first introduced bad faith amongst pugilists. He did not always speak the truth, but at any rate he spoke it when he made that observation. Strange people the Jews—endowed with every gift but one, and that the highest, genius divine—genius which can alone make of men demigods, and elevate them above earth and what is earthly and groveling; without which a clever nation—and who more clever than the Jews?—may have Rambams in plenty, but never a Fielding nor a Shakespeare. A Rothschild and a Mendoza, yes—but never a Kean nor a Belcher.

So the bruisers of England are come to be present at the grand fight speedily coming off; there they are met in the precincts of the old town, near the field of the chapel, planted with tender saplings at the restoration of sporting Charles, which are now become venerable elms, as high as many a steeple; there they are met at a fitting rendezvous, where a retired coachman, with one leg, keeps an hotel and a bowling green. I think I now see them upon the bowling green, the men of renown, amidst hundreds of people with no renown at all, who gaze upon them with timid wonder. Fame, after all, is a glorious thing, though it last only for a day. There's Cribb, the champion of England, and perhaps the best man in England; there he is, with his huge massive figure, and face wonderfully like that of a lion. There is Belcher, the younger, not the mighty one, who is gone to his place, but the Teucer Belcher, the most scientific pugilist that ever entered the ring, only wanting strength to be, I won't say what. He appears to walk before me now, as he did that evening, with his white hat, white greatcoat, thin genteel figure, springy step, and keen, determined eyes. Crosses him, what a contrast! grim, savage Shelton, who has a civil word for nobody, and a hard blow for anybody—hard! one blow, given with the proper play of his athletic arm, will unsense a giant. Yonder individual, who strolls about with his hands behind him, supporting his brown coat lappets, undersized, and who looks anything but what he is, is the king of the lightweights, so called—Randall! the terrible Randall, who has Irish blood in his veins; not the better for that, nor the worse; and not far from him is his last antagonist, Ned Turner, who, though beaten by him, still thinks himself as good a man, in which he is, perhaps, right, for it was a near thing; and

"a better shentleman," in which he is quite right, for he is a Welshman. But how shall I name them all? they were there by the dozens, and all tremendous in their way. There was Bulldog Hudson, and fearless Scroggins, who beat the conqueror of Sam the Jew. There was Black Richmond—no, he was not there, but I knew him well; he was the most dangerous of blacks, even with a broken thigh. There was Purcell, who could never conquer till all seemed over with him. There was—what! shall I name thee last? ay, why not? I believe that thou art the last of all that strong family still above the sod, where mayst thou long continue—true species of English stuff, Tom of Bedford—sharp as winter, kind as spring.

Hail to thee, Tom of Bedford, or by whatever name it may please thee to be called, spring or winter. Hail to thee, six-foot Englishman of brown eye, worthy to have carried a six-foot bow at Flodden, where England's yeomen triumphed over Scotland's king, his clans and chivalry. Hail to thee, last of England's bruisers, after all the many victories which thou hast achieved—true English victories, unbought by yellow gold; need I recount them? nay, nay! they are already well known to fame—sufficient to say that Bristol's Bull and Ireland's Champion were vanquished by thee, and one mightier still, gold itself, thou didst overcome; for gold itself strove in vain to deaden the power of thy arm; and thus thou didst proceed till men left off challenging thee, the unvanquishable, the incorruptible. 'Tis a treat to see thee, Tom of Bedford, in thy "public" in Holborn way, whither thou hast retired with thy well-earned bays. 'Tis Friday night, and nine by Holborn clock. There sits the yeoman at the end of his long room, surrounded by his friends: glasses are filled, and a song is the cry, and a song is sung well suited to the place; it finds an echo in every heart—fists are clenched, arms are waved and the portraits of the mighty fighting men of yore, Broughton, and Slack, and Ben, which adorn the walls, appear to smile grim approbation, whilst many a manly voice joins in the bold chorus:

*Here's a health to old honest John Bull,*
*When he's gone we shan't find such another,*
*And with hearts and with glasses brim full,*
*We will drink to old England, his mother.*

But the fight! with respect to the fight, what shall I say? Little can be said about it—it was soon over. Some said that the brave from town, who was reputed the best of the two, and whose form was a perfect model of athletic beauty, allowed himself, for lucre vile, to be vanquished by the massive champion with the flattened nose. One thing is certain, that the former was suddenly seen to sink to the earth before a blow of by no means extraordinary power. Time, time! was called, but there he lay upon the ground apparently senseless, and from thence he did not lift his head till several seconds after the umpires had declared his adversary victor.

There were shouts—indeed, there's never a lack of shouts to celebrate a victory, however acquired; but there was also much grinding of teeth, especially amongst the fighting men from town. "Tom has sold us," said they, "sold us to the yokels; who would have thought it?" Then there was fresh grinding of teeth, and scowling brows were turned to the heavens. But what is this? is it possible, does the heaven scowl too? Why, only a quarter of an hour ago—but what may not happen in a quarter of an hour? For many weeks the weather has been of the most glorious description; the eventful day, too, had dawned gloriously, and so it had continued till some two hours after noon. The fight was then over and about that time I looked up. What a glorious sky of deep blue, and what a big fierce sun swimming high above in amidst of that blue! Not a cloud—there had not been one for weeks —not a cloud to be seen, only in the far west, just on the horizon, something like the extremity of a black wing. That was only a quarter of an hour ago, and now the whole northern side of the heaven is occupied by a huge black cloud, and the sun is only occasionally seen amidst masses of driving vapor. What a change! But another fight is at hand, and the pugilists are clearing the outer ring. How their huge whips come crashing upon the heads of the yokels! Blood flows—more blood than in the fight. Those blows are given with right good will; those are not sham blows, whether of whip or fist. It is with fist that grim Shelton strikes down the big yokel. He is always dangerous, grim Shelton, but now particularly so, for he has lost ten pounds betted on the brave who sold himself to the yokels. But the outer ring is cleared, and now the second fight commences. It is between two

champions of less renown than the others, but is perhaps not the worse on that account. A tall thin boy is fighting in the ring with a man somewhat under the middle size, with a frame of adamant. That's a gallant boy! He's a yokel, but he comes from Brummagem, he does credit to his extraction; but his adversary has a frame of adamant. In what a strange light they fight, but who can wonder, on looking at that frightful cloud usurping now one half of heaven, and at the sun struggling with sulphurous vapor. The face of the boy, which is turned towards me, looks horrible in that light; but he is a brave boy, he strikes his foe on the forehead, and the report of the blow is like the sound of a hammer against a rock. But there is a rush and a roar overhead, a wild commotion, the tempest is beginning to break loose; there's wind and dust, a crash, rain and hail! Is it possible to fight amidst such a commotion? Yes! the fight goes on; again the boy strikes the man full on the brow; but it is of no use striking that man, his frame is of adamant. "Boy, thy strength is beginning to give way, thou art becoming confused." The man now goes to work amidst rain and hail. "Boy, thou wilt not hold out ten minutes longer against rain, hail, and the blows of such an antagonist."

And now the storm was at its height; the black thundercloud had broken into many, which assumed the wildest shapes and the strangest colors, some of them unspeakably glorious; the rain poured in a deluge, and more than one water spout was seen at no great distance. An immense rabble is hurrying in one direction; a multitude of men of all ranks, peers and yokels, prize fighters and Jews, and the last came to plunder, and are now plundering amidst that wild confusion of hail and rain, men and horses, carts and carriages. But all hurry in one direction, through mud and mire. There's a town only three miles distant, which is soon reached and soon filled; it will not contain one third of that mighty rabble. But there's another town farther on—the good old city is farther on, only twelve miles; what's that!

Who'll stay here? Onward to the old town!

ARTHUR BRISBANE covered the John L. Sullivan–Charley Mitchell fight for the New York *Tribune*. He was twenty-four years old, it was his most important assignment up to that time and, in spite of the fact that Sullivan had befriended him, it marked the start of his disdain for professional pugilism. Like the other thirty-nine spectators, the gladiators and their handlers, Brisbane was rain-soaked and chilled. After eluding the gendarmes he had to rush back to Paris where he wrote this story and filed it by cable. While he was composing, however, the Blizzard of '88 was burying the northeast coast of the United States, and on the day after the fight, March 11, it was impossible to distribute newspapers in New York. It was not, however, until Brisbane had become William Randolph Hearst's strong right hand, or Mary Ann, that he summed up his attitude toward the ring in his classic criticism of two contestants: "A gorilla could lick them both."

# Sullivan–Mitchell

## ARTHUR BRISBANE

PARIS, March 10, 1888—The Sullivan–Mitchell fight at Chantilly today was an even gloomier and more depressing fiasco than the battle between Kilrain and Smith a few months ago on an island in the Seine. It took scarcely twenty minutes of sharp fighting to show that six years of a brutal, dissipated life had sapped the once astonishing power of the American champion. He could not close with his wiry English antagonist, and the effort to force the fighting cost him all the strength which his fatuous admirers counted on for the critical rounds at the finish.

Then the rain came, drenching the pugilists and turning the turf of the prize ring into a mass of slippery mud. Mitchell held out doggedly in the wet, but Sullivan was seized with chills, and after thirty-nine rounds—most of them dragging and ineffectual—the contest ended in a draw. The American pugilist cried with mortification at his ignominious failure to make good the threats he had been hurling so lavishly at Mitchell. Mitchell's friends were equally chagrined at their champion's inability to fight out a decided victory. The credit, at any rate, remained with the London man and it was agreed on all hands—Sullivan's backers not excepted—that the Boston prize fighter had met with a stinging reverse, as crushing to his hopes of international championship as an actual defeat.

The battle was fought on the country place of Baron Alphonse Rothschild, at Apremont, near the Chantilly station. The backers of both men had spent yesterday wrangling at Amiens over the details of the match, unable to agree on a place to pitch the ring. The lookout dispatched from London early in the week had arranged for a battleground nearer at hand, but at the last moment the spot was found unsuitable. The Sullivan party thereupon charged Mitchell was trying to wriggle out of the fight, and much acrimonious discussion followed. Finally, Mitchell's backers agreed to leave the choice of a ring to the American contingent, and "Johnny" Gideon of *The London Sportsman*, who had once hunted up a battleground for Sayers, with two other of *The Sportsman's* representatives, started out late last night at Sullivan's request, to pitch a ring and make all ready for today's contest.

Gideon and his two assistants traveled as far toward Paris as Creil, and early this morning found a quiet spot on the Rothschild grounds, just behind the Baron's stable, the white villa showing through the trees in the distance. Forty people in all were in the secret and saw the fight, the scouting party sending word back at once, and the warring factions at Amiens arriving after a few hours' delay. The French police were on the alert all along the line, short files being drawn up at the different stations which the pugilists and their friends had to pass. Some officers were hanging around even at Creil, but they made no sign as the English and Americans got out of the railway carriages, and shortly afterward straggled by twos and threes over toward the woods at the back of the Baron's country seat.

The last man was on hand, finally, at 11 A.M. The ring was up and the seconds and backers were dividing into two hostile camps. The ropes were drawn about a little plat of turf under the trees. The ground was good and the weather fair enough, except for a threat of rain to the north.

Some well-known English sporting men were in the groups at each end of the ring. "Jake" Kilrain, the Baltimore pugilist, who fought the draw with "Jem" Smith, and Baldock, of the Pelican Club, were Mitchell's seconds. "Jack" Ashton and Macdonald were seconds for Sullivan. A London stockbroker, named Angle, was referee. "Jack" Bennett was Sullivan's umpire, and "Charlie" Rowell, the long-distance pedestrian, did a similar office for Mitchell. "Pony" Moore, Mitchell's father-in-law, and "Chippy" Norton, the well-known London bookmaker, and holder of the stakes in the coming match, stood in a group to one side with Carew Young, Sir Michael Sandys, Lord Wemyss and a few other aristocrats who figure as patrons of the London ring. On the American side were Dominick McCaffrey, "Charley" Dougherty and a few newspaper men.

Mitchell had been talking a good deal all the morning, and his face was flushed with excitement. He had trained hard, and his face was a trifle thin. Still, his spirits were good, and he said he was confident of holding his own. Sullivan had not pushed himself so hard in training, and his face and muscles showed it. He was as arrogant and contemptuous as ever, and boastfully pulled out a £500 note as he entered the ring and, flourishing it aloft, called for Mitchell to cover it. His manager, Phillips, also opened a roll of bills and offered odds of £1,000 to £300 on the Boston pugilist. No takers could be found, however. The English partisans had all their money up at long odds, and as the battle drew near they looked more and more despondently across at the big, self-confident bully who had never yet met his match in the prize ring.

Sullivan, stripped to the waist, stepped out from his corner of the inclosure about half-past twelve. He looked ruddy and burly enough, but as the crucial rounds soon showed, his staying powers had already vanished under the double bombardment of French champagne and American whiskey. Mitchell followed him into the ring four minutes later. The two men were old antagonists and personal enemies, and they glared at each other fiercely. Mitchell made the first movement toward shaking hands, the two men touched palms weakly, the referee called time, and the first round in the fight began. The time taken by the watchers was 12:30 P.M.

The first round opened savagely, Sullivan, as usual, forcing the fighting and making one or two powerful rushes. The American landed his first blow, a heavy left-handed, just to the left of Mitchell's jaw. The Londoner was dazed, but soon got in a light return on Sullivan's chest. Then he sparred cautiously about the ring, warding off successfully two or three of his pursuer's leads. Finally Sullivan got angry and rushed in close. His left hand fell in short, Mitchell dodging, but his big right fist crashed against the unlucky Englishman's head, and the wiry Londoner fell in a heap over toward the ropes in his corner.

The American contingent was jubilant, and odds ran up as high as £1,000 to £100 on the big Bostonian. Sullivan was a trifle winded, but it looked as if the Briton could not stand up before many more rushes like that just ended.

After half a minute or so Mitchell was up again, sponged off and in the ring. Sullivan soon followed. This time Mitchell fought shy, retreating from one part of the ring to the other. Sullivan's fierce rush was too much for him, however, and the two were closed. The first blow caught the Londoner on the chest, and Mitchell staggered as if he had been hit by a pile driver. He made a feeble effort to parry, and then to run away, but another blow on the head from Sullivan's deadly right hand laid him flat on the turf near the middle of the ring. His seconds lifted him over to the corner, where a little sponging brought him to in a minute.

The pace was too fast for the Englishman, but it was also beginning to tell on the greatest of short-distance "sluggers." Sullivan was red in the face, and the cool defensive strategy of his antagonist ruffled the big bully's temper. Still everything looked rose-hued to the little party at his back, which was now frantically waving the Stars

49

and Stripes and the green flag of Ireland in anticipatory triumph. "Pony" Moore had a scowl on his face, and the Union Jack and the Royal ensign over Mitchell's quarters drooped disconsolably in the heavy air that threatened a coming storm.

Mitchell had profited by his experience so far, and from the beginning of the third round fought a waiting battle. He ran all over the ring, Sullivan bounding after him and getting in an occasional ineffective blow. The American champion at last made a desperate rush, broke down the Englishman's defenses and sent him sprawling to the ground with a right-hand blow in the face. Sullivan seemed to have hurt his hand a little in this last rush, and Mitchell, though badly battered, was far from being "knocked out." Sullivan was pushing himself hard, and seemed to feel the strain.

In the fourth round Mitchell squirmed and dodged for several minutes before Sullivan could close with him. When he did reach the Englishman his blows fell lightly, and though Mitchell went down in the last rush, he fell more in the tussle than under any one blow. In the fifth and sixth rounds he took to the tactics that Smith had found so successful in his fight with Kilrain. Sullivan charged again and again, but every time the Londoner got away. Once when he was cornered he dropped to the ground on one hand and one knee—a foul by the London ring rules. Sullivan had come near striking him as he dropped, and the referee cautioned both men about making or causing a foul stroke.

In the next three rounds Sullivan kept up his ineffectual chase after the fleet-footed Englishman. Mitchell got off without any damage to speak of, and even planted his fist two or three times on Sullivan's face.

In the tenth round rain began to fall, and the shower soon turned into a steady pour. Sullivan was chilled to the bone and began to shake with ague. He kept pluckily on, however, pounding through the mud after his opponent, falling shorter and shorter on each rush. His backers kept up their courage, but looked for nothing better than a draw! Mitchell's backers hoped now that their man might outlast the American and win the championship and the £500.

The rounds from the tenth to the thirty-second dragged stupidly. Sullivan, who was beginning to shiver all over, could do nothing. Neither could Mitchell, though he tried with all his might. The terrible punishment of the first four rounds had nearly crippled him. The thirty-second round lasted twenty-seven minutes. The thirty-fifth round was fought through fifteen minutes. Both men were weak and could no longer hit out from the shoulder.

After half an hour's fighting in the last round, Baldock, Mitchell's second, broke into the ring and cried out that the men had had enough. "Make it a draw," he urged. The fight had now lasted three hours and ten minutes. The principals readily agreed to stop, and shook hands, though the champion was soon after looking with rage and chagrin, and his backers folded up their flags, the most heartsore set of sportsmen that has ever traveled 3,000 miles to see a great international fight.

Mitchell was badly trussed. There was a big lump on his jaw, his left eye was bunged up, and his body was a good deal battered. Sullivan was sick and worn out, but not much hurt. Both parties started for this city on the evening train.

The stakes, £500 a side, will be doubled, of course. But it looks as if Sullivan's career was nearly over.

His fight today will be a sad blow, at least, to his "hippodroming" box-office receipts.

JACK BROUGHTON (1704–1789) was the third recognized heavyweight champion of the prize ring and the first great ring scientist. He stood five feet, ten and a half inches, weighed 196 pounds and, a onetime yeoman of the guard of George II, was intelligent and educated. In 1742, while still champion, he erected an amphitheater at Tottenham Court Road in London, and he is called the Father of Boxing because, the following year, he drew up and published the first boxing rules.

# The First Boxing Rules

## JACK BROUGHTON

FOR THE BETTER regulation of the Amphitheater approved of by the gentleman, and agreed to by the Pugilists:

1. That a square of a yard be chalked in the middle of the stage; and every fresh set-to after a fall, or being parted from the rails, each second is to bring his man to the side of the square, and place him opposite to the other, and till they are fairly set to at the lines, it shall not be lawful for one to strike the other.

2. That, in order to prevent any disputes, the time a man lies after a fall, if the second does not bring his man to the side of the square within the space of half a minute, he shall be deemed a beaten man.

3. That in every main battle, no person whatever shall be upon the stage except the principals and their seconds; the same rule to be observed in by-battles, except that in the latter, Mr. Broughton is allowed to be upon the stage to keep decorum, and to assist gentlemen in getting to their places, provided always he does not interfere in the battle; and whoever pretends to infringe these rules to be turned immediately out of the house. Everybody is to quit the stage as soon as the champions are stripped, before set-to.

4. That no champion be deemed beaten unless he fails coming up to the line, in the limited time; or, that his own second declares him beaten. No second is to be allowed to ask his man's adversary any questions, or advise him to give out.

5. That in by-battles, the winning man to have two-thirds of the money given, shall be publicly divided upon the stage notwithstanding any private agreements to the contrary.

6. That to prevent disputes in every main battle, the principals shall, on coming on the stage, choose from among the gentlemen present, two umpires, who shall absolutely decide all disputes that may arise about the battle; and if the two umpires cannot agree, the said umpires to choose a third, who is to determine it.

7. That no person is to hit his adversary when he is down, or seize him by the hair, the breeches, or any part below the waist; a man on his knees to be reckoned down.

THE GUARDIANS of our literature have refused to recognize Heywood Broun as a great essayist because he had one obvious weakness—he wrote for newspapers.   .

In this column Broun presented his interpretation of Benny Leonard's successful defense of his lightweight title against Rocky Kansas on February 10, 1922. The fight went fifteen rounds, but later Patsy Haley, the veteran fighter and referee, announced that never had he seen a short right hand as perfectly executed as that with which Leonard dropped Kansas in the eleventh round.

# The Orthodox Champion

### HEYWOOD BROUN

THE ENTIRE ORTHODOX world owes a debt to Benny Leonard. In all the other arts, philosophies, religions and whatnots conservatism seems to be crumbling before the attacks of the radicals. A stylist may generally be identified today by his bloody nose. Even in Leonard's profession of pugilism the correct method has often been discredited of late.

It may be remembered that George Bernard Shaw announced before "the battle of the century" that Carpentier ought to be a fifty-to-one favorite in the betting. It was the technique of the Frenchman which blinded Shaw to the truth. Every man in the world must be in some respect a standpatter. The scope of heresy in Shaw stops short of the prize ring. His radicalism is not sufficiently far-reaching to crawl through the ropes. When Carpentier knocked out Beckett with one perfectly delivered punch he also jarred Shaw. He knocked him loose from some of his cynical contempt for the conventions. Mr. Shaw might continue to be in revolt against the well-made play, but he surrendered his heart wholly to the properly executed punch.

But Carpentier, the stylist, fell before Dempsey, the mauler, in spite of the support of the intellectuals. It seemed once again that all the rules were wrong. Benny Leonard remains the white hope of the orthodox. In lightweight circles, at any rate, old-fashioned proprieties are still effective.

No performer in any art has ever been more correct than Leonard. He follows closely all the best traditions of the past. His left-hand jab could stand without revision in any textbook. The manner in which he feints, ducks, sidesteps and hooks is unimpeachable. The crouch contributed by some of the modernists is not in the repertoire of Leonard. He stands up straight like a gentleman and a champion and is always ready to hit with either hand.

His fight with Rocky Kansas at Madison Square Garden was advertised as being for the lightweight championship of the world. As a matter of fact much more than that was at stake. Spiritually, Saint-Saëns, Brander Matthews, Henry Arthur Jones, Kenyon Cox, and Henry Cabot Lodge were in Benny Leonard's corner. His defeat would, by implication, have given support to dissonance, dadaism, creative evolution and bolshevism. Rocky Kansas does nothing according to rule. His fighting style is as formless as the prose of Gertrude Stein. One finds a delightfully impromptu quality in Rocky's boxing. Most of the blows which he tries are experimental. There is no particular target. Like the young poet who shot an arrow into the air, Rocky Kansas tosses off a right-hand swing every once and so often and hopes that it will land on somebody's jaw.

But with the opening gong Rocky Kansas tore

into Leonard. He was gauche and inaccurate but terribly persistent. The champion jabbed him repeatedly with a straight left which has always been considered the proper thing to do under the circumstances. Somehow or other it did not work. Leonard might as well have been trying to stand off a rhinoceros with a feather duster. Kansas kept crowding him. In the first clinch Benny's hair was rumpled and a moment later his nose began to bleed. The incident was a shock to us. It gave us pause and inspired a sneaking suspicion that perhaps there was something the matter with Tennyson after all. Here were two young men in the ring and one was quite correct in everything he did and the other was all wrong. And the wrong one was winning. All the enthusiastic Rocky Kansas partisans in the gallery began to split infinitives to show their contempt for Benny Leonard and all other stylists. Macaulay

turned over twice in his grave when Kansas began to lead with his right hand.

But traditions are not to be despised. Form may be just as tough in fiber as rebellion. Not all the steadfastness of the world belongs to heretics. Even though his hair was mussed and his nose bleeding, Benny continued faithful to the established order. At last his chance came. The young child of nature who was challenging for the championship dropped his guard and Leonard hooked a powerful and entirely orthodox blow to the conventional point of the jaw. Down went Rocky Kansas. His past life flashed before him during the nine seconds in which he remained on the floor and he wished that he had been more faithful as a child in heeding the advice of his boxing teacher. After all, the old masters did know something. There is still a kick in style, and tradition carries a nasty wallop.

BEFORE THIS COUNTRY'S leading promoters formed their vicious alliance with the razor-blade tycoons and beer barons, the small fight club was the foundation of boxing. The following tribute by the veteran Chicago sports columnist is from his book *Win, Lose, or Draw* and celebrates a truly talented small-club promoter.

# The Portable A. C.

## WARREN BROWN

WHEN I TOOK up residence in Chicago, late in 1923, the questionable sport of prize fighting was being conducted on a scale peculiar to that area. It was not too hard for me to adjust myself to the surroundings. After all, I had served my time years before, keeping up with the oddities of the four-round game as practiced in California before the game became legalized there.

Chicago's loosely run game would have to move very dizzily to surpass my beloved four-rounders. They were served in San Francisco and Oakland on a regular weekly show basis. Real headliners by any boxing standards would participate occasionally, as was the case when Willie Ritchie, the former lightweight champion, essaying a comeback, was cast as an opponent for Benny Leonard, then the champion of all the world, and so skilled there was a constant argument whether he or Joe Gans had been the greatest of all the lightweights in history.

Benny was not geared for the four-round game. Ritchie, having emerged from it, was able to fit his comeback to its requirements. One night, in the Civic Auditorium, Leonard was somewhat embarrassed when Ritchie hit him a harder punch on the nose than anyone had ever done before. It surprised Benny, but it did not surprise me.

In the four-round game I had learned to expect almost anything. That schooling prepared me for Chicago's boxing, which was of the bootleg variety and presented under something called an injunction, in the days before the solons decided to legalize it.

Nowhere else in the country have I ever witnessed more remarkable exploits of the prize ring than those that Chicagoans patronized when James C. Mullen was promoter and matchmaker, and his club was known to the trade as the Portable A.C.

The reason for that name was valid. Sometimes the shows took place at Aurora. Sometimes they took place at East Chicago. At irregular intervals Mullen would attempt to put over a fast one and come right into a Chicago arena. Usually there were difficulties that only the most resourceful promoter could surmount.

Mullen, for all his promotional eccentricities, was a splendid matchmaker. He might have prospered greatly and found himself ranked with Tex Rickard were it not for one strange turn of his nature. He fancied his ability to find promising fighters and build them into great drawing cards. This he did many times. Then he could hardly wait until he was able to find someone to knock his star crowd-gatherer over. Most promoters other than Mullen have been very careful to protect their drawing cards in and out of all matchmaking clinches.

Mullen was not able to produce any such memorable attractions as Ah Wing, Tanglefoot McGovern, and Cockey O'Brien of my younger days in San Francisco, but with what he had, Mullen did all right. He was a law unto himself. Perhaps that is why he was able to stage some notable events upon which any legalized commission would have frowned quickly.

There were in Chicago's Loop a couple of characters belonging to the set I was pleased to term the Rover Boys of Randolph Street. Each had a leg disability causing him to limp. They became involved in an argument one evening in Henrici's Restaurant, and were about to start swinging when Mullen suggested that they hold their fire. He could use them. He did, too, and after sufficient exploitation the pair appeared in the ring at Aurora as an added attraction to one of Mullen's shows. On that night Randolph Street was as quiet as the main street in Fork-in-the-Road, Utah. Everybody was at Aurora.

Playing baseball (it was alleged) for the White Sox was a character out of Texas, Art Shires, who styled himself "The Great." He thought well of himself as a fighter. First thing he knew he was given a match on one of Mullen's East Chicago cards. When his opponent went out on schedule, Shires became a great attraction.

His major showing in the ring was against George Trafton. Trafton had been a famous Notre Dame center and was later even more famous as a player with the Chicago Bears. The fight between these two created as much excitement among Mullen's clientele as any event he ever staged. It went to East Chicago. It was an awful fight to behold, but it did provoke an incident that indicated the occupational hazards of broadcasting from the ringside.

The broadcaster, Pat Flanagan, a famous figure on Chicago's air lanes, had established his reputation on baseball and football. He was taking this epoch-making fight in stride and showering the air with hysterical words and phrases as Shires and Trafton lumbered about the ring, each wondering what to do next, or whether to skip the whole thing.

Right behind the broadcaster sat one of Trafton's teammates on the Bears. He had come to the show properly fortified with emotional outpourings. In the very thick of the furious battle in the ring, he detected something the broadcaster said that he thought reflected on the fighting character of his pal Trafton. Being a man of action, he reached over and popped the broadcaster right on the nose. This caused a sudden flow of expression that set new heights for airways ring reporting. In the confusion that followed, the fight came to an end, with the sneak-punch victimized broadcaster utterly unable to let his clients know who had won.

Not that this was unusual for radio broadcasting in the twenties. I once sat directly behind Graham McNamee while he was describing the Gene Tunney-Tom Heeney fight. That contest, which marked Tunney's farewell, came to an end under somewhat unusual circumstances.

The champion had steadily cut Heeney down to size, and at the very end of a round deposited the Australian on the floor. Punches were flying from Tunney's fists so fast that McNamee was several wallops behind in his description.

I don't know whether Graham noticed that Heeney was on the floor, or that his seconds had rushed across the ring to carry him to his corner as the bell rang. I know he paid no attention to their frantic efforts to get him up and out for the next round.

For Graham, the instant the bell sounded, plunged into a dramatic reading of the commercial, which was due then in behalf of the tire company that had sponsored the broadcast.

The commercial was timed for a minute's reading. Graham finished just on the dot as the bell for the next round rang. It rang for everybody but Heeney, who couldn't hear it. The fight was over. That much McNamee gathered from a quick survey, but what had caused the sudden ending seemed as dark a mystery to him as it must have been to his listeners.

Under any other circumstances he might have explained, after a quick brushing up on the facts. But it was customary in those days to get at that windup commercial as soon as the fight ended. That's what Graham did, and presently he was on his way out of the arena. He was content to let his clients find out what they wanted to know by reading the papers. Or perhaps he suspected that they had been just as bored with Heeney as he was.

The listening audience of the broadcast of the Shires–Trafton fight was hardly comparable to that of the Tunney–Heeney, but soon after that Mullen came up with another fight project that promised to be national in its scope.

Shires, the White Sox "fighting" first baseman, had been getting so much attention that friends of the Cubs, hated rivals of the White Sox, began to resent it. They looked around for a Cub who might have ring aspirations. In no time at all they found one. At least, Mullen found one for them. One day he announced that "Hack" Wilson, the home-run hitter of the Cubs, would be the next opponent for Shires. That was all the notice this event needed. From then on Mullen had to worry about finding an arena large enough to seat the crowd that wanted in on this battle.

The papers played it up with might and main. There is no telling what might have happened if the event had ever gone through. Even if it did not revolutionize boxing, as it threatened to do, it offered numerous other possibilities. So many, in fact, that Kenesaw M. Landis summoned Wilson and Shires into his presence. He told them how much he appreciated their willingness to prove their athletic versatility, but that he would be sore as hell if he ever heard another word from either of them about fighting each other in a public prize ring as long as they were identified with baseball.

In my private list of the great fights that never took place the Shires–Wilson affair is near the top. It belongs on the same card with the main event of Jack Dempsey in his prime versus Joe Louis in his.

Right behind them is the one that Mullen arranged at East Chicago, outdoors, involving Mickey Walker and Billy Wells, an English warrior who was being handled in this country by Charley Harvey. Harvey was one of the last of the honorable old-line managers and affected a curling, very black mustache.

Walker was a great drawing card, and Wells was a likely enough opponent, so that the arena was sold out many days in advance of the date of the fight. On the day it was scheduled, rain fell, and Mullen ordered a postponement.

Next day he was called by Harvey, who wanted to know if the promoter had any idea where Wells was. Mullen had not. Nor did anyone else. The English fighter simply disappeared. It was several months afterward before he was heard from again. By that time he had crossed the Atlantic. But never a word of why he had walked out on an engagement that figured to return him more money than any in which he participated before or since.

Walker was a performer in several of Mullen's extravaganzas after boxing had become legalized in Illinois. In one of them he was given the decision by referee Benny Yanger over Tiger Flowers, a verdict that made Mickey world's champion. This distinction he held with honor for a long time thereafter.

In its own quiet way, this bout created as much furor as the "long count" episode in Tunney's fight with Dempsey at Soldier Field. There was so much adverse comment over the decision, Yanger was hailed before the Commission to explain.

He told an interesting story. He quoted the rules under which boxing was conducted in Illinois, particularly that part treating of "flicking or hitting with an open glove," a practice at which Flowers was adept. The rule, Yanger went on to say, stated that it was at the discretion of the referee to disqualify the offender *or* award the decision to his opponent.

"With all those people there, I thought there might be trouble if I disqualified Flowers," Yanger explained. So he took the other alternative, and gave the decision to Walker at the end of the fight.

"Oh," said the august Commission, in effect.

Which was all right, except for the fact that the law did *not* offer any alternative. What it said was that the referee at his discretion could disqualify the offender *and* award the decision to his opponent. In other words, the referee, if he were to call into effect that rule, had to do so as soon as he was convinced there was an offense. He was not justified in waiting until the fight was over. But the Commission didn't read the rules too carefully, either.

Well, we had situations like that when Chicago's boxing was very young.

Yet another of Walker's Chicago appearances under Mullen's direction was in a bout with Mike McTigue. The latter was the light-heavyweight whom the incredible Battling Siki, the Singular Senegalese, had the temerity to fight in Dublin on St. Patrick's Day, with the world's championship at stake.

McTigue was something much less than a champion on the night he met Walker. Perhaps Mullen realized that, for in his advertising material he announced that every fight on the card would end in a knockout. It did, too, with Walker draping the unconscious McTigue across the ropes with a punch or two. All of Mullen's clients were back to their normal haunts before ten o'clock from a complete fight show that did not begin until eight-thirty. There should be more of those.

The advent of legalized boxing in Illinois found Mullen putting on the first show, a lightweight contest between Sammy Mandell and Rocky Kansas. Kansas was the lightweight champion going in, but Mandell, a clever sort, outspeeded him and emerged with the title. It was a popular decision.

No other two citizens of Illinois did more to make possible legalized boxing than Ed Hughes, then a member of the Senate, and Michael Igoe, then of the House. They were both regular patrons of the fine arts on display at the Portable A.C.

Once boxing was legalized, it was interesting to observe the demands of the solons for complimentary tickets as their just due for having fostered the sport. But it isn't as interesting as a notation in the memory book of Sol Katz, who was Mullen's head box-office man in the Portable A.C. days and who followed him into the presentation of Illinois' first legalized contest.

His first two purchasers of tickets were Hughes and Igoe, who had put the bill across. Neither had ever acquired the habit of mooching complimentary tickets. Neither cared to start, now that boxing—it was piously hoped—was going on a scale in Illinois that might rival New York.

THERE HAVE BEEN a few trainers like Brian Oswald Donn Byrne's Shadrach Kennedy. In 1925, when Charley Phil Rosenberg signed to fight for the bantamweight title, he weighed 155 pounds. Ray Arcel worked him down to 118.

"He hated me," Arcel has said. "He used to scream at me: 'You copper!' But he made the weight and went fifteen tough rounds with Eddie Cannonball Martin and won the championship of the world."

FROM

# Tale of James Carabine

## DONN BYRNE

IF YOU WERE to meet him on the roads about Destiny Bay, or in Dublin, whither he goes as body servant sometimes to my Aunt Jenepher, with his black clothes, with his erect carriage, with his suspicion of side whiskers, you might take Carabine for a minister of some faith dissenting from the Church of Ireland, by law established. There is something so honest, so clear about his gray eyes. Indeed, you might avoid him, fearing he would pluck you by the sleeve and ask you that most intimate and embarrassing of all questions: Have you found Salvation?

Of course, if you notice his broken nose, his heavy hands, you might say: This man has been a prize fighter in his youth, but there—a Christian missionary might receive these stigmata telling the gentle tale of Bethlehem and Calvary to some emphatic, lusty pagan. We who know the race course and the ring, recognize his craft from the hunched left shoulder, the eye that moves while the head does not. We who know his name recognize him as James Carabine, former champion, the last of the giants of the London prize ring, the conqueror of Simon Kennedy, and Diamond, the Black Man; McCoy, the Glasgow Plasterer, and that most terrible of fighters who was called the Bristol Lamb.

I know the modern glovemongers—they are rather a sordid lot. They are not the thugs and monsters the Society of Friends would have us

believe—indeed, one wishes often they were, watching a fumbling match of men stalling through a ten-round bout. Nor are they the romantics certain journalists would have us think. Good journeymen athletes with a knack of their hands. . . . The prize ring bred better, braver men, the men of the bare knuckles and the finish fights—Tom Cribb, who fought and conquered the Negro Molyneux; Tom Sayers, who drew with Heenan, the Benicia Boy, in a battle thought the most terrific of the ring; that Gully, whom the Game Chicken conquered, whose aspiration it was in early life to be champion of England, owner of the Derby winner, and member of Parliament, and who achieved all three; Sir Daniel Donelly, our great Irish Champion, who was knighted by the Prince Regent after his defeat of the gigantic Captain Cooper at the Curragh of Kildare; Bendigo, who gave his name to a great race horse, and to an Australian city; that Gentleman Jackson, winner over Mendoza, who was friend to Byron, and to our own overrated and greatly loved Tom Moore; the Tipton Slasher, that terrific hitter, who succumbed to great Sayers. Great men these, lion-hearted, proud of their craft—and the last of these was Carabine.

James Carabine is somewhat over sixty years of age. His tale of years he doesn't know exactly, for he can neither read nor write. When he wants to date a matter, he will say it occurred in the spring of the year of So-and-so's Derby, and such a horse's Grand National, or the year that Sullivan beat Paddy Ryan for the championship of America. He has a prodigious memory, and a gift for selecting the outstanding features of comparatives such as we literates, with our science of filing by numbers, can hardly conceive. There is none who knows the mood of the sea better than Carabine, or the approaching changes of the weather. He knows the name of each bird and flower and small animal in our land, and such strength of mind has Nature given him, such innate kindliness, such broad fearless wisdom, that I have come to think very little of the teaching of books. . . .

". . . I came into New York with a cloud in my heart, Mister Kerry," said Carabine, "and what I saw there didn't lift it any. From all I had heard tell of New York, it was a golden city, rich as Jerusalem, and the Irish reigned there. At every corner I expected to see the Irish dancing and fiddling, and jingling the money in their pockets the people had given them just for being Irish, and maybe doing an hour's work now and then, just for the looks of the thing. It is a great city, young and strong, and like everything that is young and strong, cruel, and cruelest of all upon the Irish. The hunger of Famine Days is nothing to the hunger of the unlucky Irish. . . .

"The place where you meet the Irish in America, Mister Kerry," said James Carabine, "is in public drinking houses, but they're not like our public drinking houses at all. At home here, when the sun goes down, you can go into a place that is quiet and orderly, order your pot of beer, smoke your pipe, and talk about the weather and the crops, and play a game of five hundred up. But over there you've got to stand against a bar and drink quick and drink often, or they don't want your custom at all. In the latter end I got very tired of it, Mister Kerry, for I'm not by temperament a drinking man. It was drink, drink, drink, and never a word of getting a fight for me. So that I decided I'd drop the whole thing and get back to Ulster. The old ring had nearly gone in America; the glove men, the tip-and-run fellows were coming along and talking about scientific fighting. People are always for listening to a new thing. So I said: 'I'll go back to the old country where the old things are in honor.' . . .

"All this time I was trying in New York to get a fight according to prize ring rules. The gloves are grand for exercise, but they're not the real measure of a fighting man. Besides, with the gloves there's too much trickery. You can hit harder with the gloves than your bare hands, for

there's protection for the hands in gloves. In the prize ring, you've got to think more of your wrestling than hitting. The hitting is more to prevent a man getting into position for a back heel or a cross-buttock or a flying mare. I don't like these three-minute rounds where a crooked timekeeper can shorten or lengthen the round, Mister Kerry, with his watch in his hand. And these draws, and winning on points—they aren't good. In my day you went into the ring and you came out either beaten or conqueror. And there was no talk about fouling. And the minute's rest between rounds gave an unlucky fellow a chance to come to. A man may be the better man, and have no luck, and that's not a right thing, Mister Kerry.

"I came at a time, Mister Kerry, when the prize ring was setting in glory. The men weren't maybe the equals of Tom Figg, or Sayers, or the Negro Molyneux, though it's hard to say. But they fought like champions. The time when Gentleman Jackson won from Mendoza by holding his hair and hitting him with the other hand, and when a man got his opponent's head in chancery and hammered his face, that time was gone. We fought each other's strength, not infirmities. When I was fighting Simon Kennedy, and slipped on a patch of wet grass, and threw out my hand for the ropes, Simon could have hit me, but he stepped back. And when I twisted my right wrist in a fall against Tom Hill of Bradford, and couldn't use my right hand for hitting, Tom would only use his left, too. And they weren't all just bruisers, Mister Kerry; Simon Kennedy was a schoolmaster, and Deaf Wallace was a maker of fine jewelry, and Dan Lane afterward became a great preacher in Sydney.

"They promised me a fight in New York as soon as they could get a man. They said it would be hard on account of it being against the law, but: 'We'll find a man for you,' they said. . . .

"At last Mills brought this fellow along he was fixing to fight me. 'Meet Blanco Johnson,' he said, 'the champion of Canada.' And there before me was a fellow you would and you wouldn't have taken for a fighter. He was tall and broad in the shoulder, Mister Kerry, but very light below for a prize-ring man. You would think that the very weight of his shoulders would be too heavy for his legs and that he would have little power when it came to wrestling. I'd have great respect for that fellow in a glove fight, but in the London ring I wasn't worried at all. He had beautiful long muscles, and a small head that would be hard to get the range of, and when he walked he had the nice springy step of a fighter. But there's the funny thing, Mister Kerry, he was the handsomest fellow I ever laid my eyes on. He was fair and he had a face that was symmetrical in each degree, but for one. His hair was wavy like a woman's. The only thing wrong about him, Mister Kerry, was that his eyes were too small and a wee bit too close together. But dress that fellow up, and put him on at a smoking concert, and you'd never take him for a fighter. 'Beauty' Johnson was his nickname, and there was never a truer one.

"Well, the match was made, Mister Kerry, for a purse of two thousand five hundred dollars, which was great money, and three hundred pounds a side, London Prize Rules, at a place to be decided later, for this was to put the police off. We signed our names to the articles, I making my mark, and he writing like a schoolmaster. He was a nonpareil.

"Well, Mister Kerry, you'd think I'd done this fellow the honor of the world in fighting him. It was 'Mr. Carabine' here and 'Mr. Carabine' there, and 'What is your opinion of this, Mr. Carabine?' . . .

"The fight was called in New Jersey, across the river from New York, in a clearing in the woods. It was six o'clock of a June morning, and the birds were singing to raise your heart. I never saw a bonnier day. The ring was pitched on fine springy turf and there was a big crowd from New York, Tammany men, gamblers, fellows of society who liked to be known as sportsmen, a big crowd of Irish fellows. . . . The Johnson and I met in the middle of the ring and the referee talked, and Mister Kerry, I've never seen a man in better shape. He shone. He was fit to fight for the world. And his legs that I thought were weak were only light, like a deer's. There was no 'Mr. Carabine' now. He only was curt and ugly. And when I held out my hand he looked at it.

" 'What's that for?' he said.

" 'To shake hands,' I said.

" 'To hell with that!' said he, and walked to his corner.

"I felt hurt at that, Mister Kerry. The men I had fought with before hadn't been like that. It was: May the best man win! I tell you there was a queer feel in the air that morning, for all the birds were singing.

"Time was called and we met, Mister Kerry. And he began sparring like a glove lightweight instead of a prize-ring man. One instant he was in front, in the next breaking ground to the right or left, dancing in and out like a ballet master. I had a trick, as most boxers have tricks, of feinting with the left before leading it, and someone must have told this fellow of it, for as my shoul-

der moved he let fly with his left hand, and Mister Kerry, it was like a slingshot or a golf ball going through the air. He got me fair. And before I could answer he was away dancing. Four times he did it in a row. Once I crowded him in a corner, and began to hit, but he rolled to the punch, and when the crowd began to roar, thinking I was doing for him, I wasn't hurting him at all. And when he got out of the corner he began with the left again. He had great tricks, this fellow. When it looked as if I'd corner him, he'd bend like an acrobat and catch me by the ankles. There was nothing in the rules against or for that. So I'd look down at him and wonder what I'd do. And then he'd straighten up and let go with the right. When I'd set myself, as a heavy man will, to let go with a knockdown punch, he'd drop his hands and walk away laughing, so that I felt like a fool. And then I'd do what a fool will do, rush him furiously to be a mark for his left hand. When I'd get close to throw him, he'd go limp and loose and fall with me of his own accord. Take his minute's rest and come up grinning.

"There's no use telling you about that fight, Mister Kerry; there was only one man in it and that wasn't me. First I could hear the crowd roar for me and then be silent, and then begin to roar for the other man. That is always cruel hearing, Mister Kerry. In the fourth round I couldn't see, so that Nick had to open my eyes with a knife to give me a glimpse of the fellow at all. This man fought a great heady fight. He never let up on my eyes, so that in a little while I didn't know that it was day, only for the singing of the birds. They had to lead me to my corner, and once I hung on by hands to the rope to avoid going down. I had a hope he'd close, so that I could take the strength out of him wrestling, but he was too clever.

"And then in my corner I heard the towel go through the air.

" 'Are you throwing up, Nick?' I asked.

" 'I'm sorry, Shamus,' said he, 'but I can't see a fellow countryman killed.'

"So that was the end of that fight.

"There is no person in the world so friendless as the conquered fighting man. He is like a star that shot across the sky and is lost. The people who were cheering him a month before turn and say: 'Sure, he was no damned good!' The cheering and the handshaking are all for the other fellow, while you are in your corner by yourself, and your trainer and your seconds, even they feel uncomfortable, and wish they were with the other man. The crowd that has been waiting for you before the fight now passes you by as if you were a convict. There is no person in the crowd that doesn't feel he is a better man than you.

"I went across to New York and to a Turkish bath, to steam the sores out of myself, and to get my face patched up, and my eyes painted. . . .

"Well, now, Mister Kerry, I'll tell you a difficult thing. I took to the drink. . . . I was there one night drinking, and a voice came through the place that made me drop the glass from my hands and turn cold. . . . I looked up and it was true. There was your Uncle Valentine before me. . . .

" 'This fellow calling himself champion of Ireland, it's hard,' said he.

" 'It is, Mister Valentine,' I agreed. 'None feels it more than I.'

" 'Did he beat you fair?' asked your Uncle Valentine.

" 'He did,' said I. 'He was too quick for me. His left hand was like a rocket in my face.'

" 'Would you take him on again?' said your Uncle Valentine.

" 'I would,' said I. 'But I don't know if it would be any different. He's too clever for me, and besides, the heart is out of me.'

" 'There was never an attack yet that there wasn't a defense for,' said your Uncle Valentine. 'As to the heart being out of you, you've no right to say that. If it were your own small fight, for a purse of money or a woman, then you could feel any way you liked about it, but this is to keep it from being said that the Irish Belt passed to a cheap bully from overseas.'

" 'Mister Valentine,' I told him, 'get me that match and I'll fight till I die.'

" 'That's better,' said your Uncle Valentine. . . .

"So I said: 'Mister Valentine, when do I start training?'

" 'Come down to Castle Gardens tomorrow,' he said, 'and meet your trainer. He'll tell you.' But who the trainer was I couldn't get out of him.

"I went down with him, and off the Irish boat there comes an old fellow in a beaver hat, and with a gray shawl around his shoulder, and, Living God! Mister Kerry, it would raise the hair on your scalp, for who was it but Shadrach Kennedy, the Irish fighter who had won the championship of Europe at the age of twenty in the camp of Waterloo. I'd often heard of him, and how he was greater than Daniel Donelly himself. He had killed Gaffer Casey at the Curragh of Kildare, and after that had never fought, but the country people said he had sold his soul to the devil for knowledge of boxing. And looking into his eye you might believe that thing. His body was a man's of near ninety, but his eye was a man's of twenty-five. There was no stroke in the game unknown to him.

" 'So you're the young man that lost the championship of Ireland, and have taken me from my deathbed.'

" 'I'm sorry, Mister Kennedy,' said I.

" 'You'll be sorrier before I'm through with you,' he promised, and he looked me over. 'You've got a fighter's frame. Was it cowardice?' he sneered.

" 'He was too quick for me, Mister Kennedy.'

" 'Before I'm through with you, you'll beat a hare in full flight.' . . .

"We had our camp near Stamford in the state of Connecticut which is a seaport town, but not on the sea, on a sort of lake as it were, Mister Kerry, a great healthy place. Your Uncle Valentine chose the boxers and wrestlers. There was a big Pole who couldn't speak English but was a nice fellow, and an American fellow from the Far West, and the boxers were Paddy Moynihan, the Irish-American boxer, and John Rhys, and Cornstalk Bill Ryan, who was looking for a fight. They were the best to be found and if there were better, I'd have had them. They'd all seen men trained in their day, but they themselves had never seen the like of the cruelty of Shadrach Kennedy. Mister Kerry, if I were a poor sinner and he a devil, he couldn't have been worse. He'd sit there with his shawl over his shoulders and his snuffbox in his hand and while I boxed and wrestled, his tongue would cut me like a whip. He would drive out, with me behind the buggy, as they called it, and make me run until I'd nearly drop. It was no trotting. It was swing your legs. And he'd get the Pole to pitch a football at my stomach and ribs, until I could have taken the kick of a mule there. Then he had another trick, which was getting the boys to chuck a bag of sand in the air, and for me to catch it on my jaw and neck. Mister Kerry, at times I could have cried with rage, and killed the old man, and your Uncle Valentine wouldn't stay in the room, he was so sorry for me. But this wasn't the worst, Mister Kerry. One day he had my arms tied to my sides with three twists of rope, and made Paddy Moynihan put on riding gloves with welts.

" 'Now cut the face off him,' he told Paddy.

" 'I'll hit no man that can't put his hands up.'

"Well, Mister Kerry, you'll hardly believe it, but Shadrach Kennedy laid on to Paddy with a driving whip until the big fighting man was nearly crying. In the end he made Paddy go for me. It was cruel. But after a few days of it, I noticed I could sway and duck and draw away my head in a manner I hadn't thought possible. But it was hard.

" 'Mister Kennedy,'' I protested, 'I'm sure you were never trained as hard as this.'

" 'I was not,' he said, 'for two reasons. The one was there was never as good a trainer as myself when I was a boxer. Now, ax me the second,' he said, 'and I'll give you a good answer.'

" 'Well,' said I, 'Mister Kennedy, what is the second?'

" 'I was never,' said he, 'such a traitorous cowardly third-rate tinker's pup as to lose the championship, and to have to go after it again. Is there anything else you'd like to hear?'

" 'No, sir,' said I. For I'd heard enough.

"He was clever, Mister Kerry, He'd have none of the old slip the left and cross-counter. He'd make you catch your man's left on your right wrist and counter with the left straight to the face. A dandy blow. He'd teach you to hit, in a long fight, at the point where a man's left shoulder and arm joins. After a while his left hand is useless. He'd teach you to weave inside a guard instead of breaking it down, and to punish your man with short punches to the body. He taught me to catch my man's left arm, and twisting around pull him over my shoulder in the 'flying mare.' A terrible throw.

"He was good, Mister Kerry. He never pushed me past my strength for all his cruelty. He kept me fresh as new butter. Twice a day he'd work at my hands, fingering the muscles and bones until they were like hard rubber balls with steel inside them. . . .

"He let up on the training one day, and sent me out for a walk. And that evening he called me into his room. 'I've one more thing to tell you,' he went on, 'don't watch your man's eyes, or his feet, or his hands. Watch the point of his jaw, and when he drops that into his shoulder, jump in and punish.'

"Your Uncle Valentine came in and laid his hand on my shoulder. 'We sail over to the Oyster Bay, Jim,' he told me.

"Then I knew I had to fight on the morrow. . . .

"Your Uncle Valentine would not let me out or see anything until the next morning. There was the early note of winter in it, and the trees brown and the black crows in the fields. We left the farmhouse where we were staying after breakfast, and your uncle huddled me up in one of his great frieze coats with a white muffler about my neck.

" 'I have a present here,' he told me, 'for you from the gypsy folk of Destiny Bay.' And out of his pocket he pulls a green scarf of silk so delicate you could pull it through a ring. And on it in gold thread was the Irish harp. 'You'll wear it on your way back, Jim.'

" 'Please God!' said I.

"The ring was pitched on the shore of the bay, fine springy turf, with the sound of the little waves in your ears. And if there were plenty of people at the New Jersey fight there was a multitude here. You wouldn't have thought it was against the law at all. There were folk of quality, acquaintances of your Uncle Valentine, and the scum of the Bowery, horsemen, gamblers, and Irish. There was a sea of faces around the ring, and on the rim of this crowd were carriages of all sorts with people standing on them. I noticed maybe a dozen of our sort, North of Ireland fellows, very quiet men would knock the head off your shoulders for twopence and I saw your Uncle Valentine had taken no chance against the ring being rushed in case of my winning. I was in the ring first and Johnson made me wait a while for him. Your Uncle Valentine was talking to Paddy Moynihan about the trotting horse, and I, I'm not ashamed to admit it, Mister Kerry, I was saying a bit prayer. All around the ring the gamblers were shouting: 'I'll lay fives against the Irishman. Here, I'll lay sixes. Six to one against.' One fellow shouted: 'I'll take tens,' said he. No sooner were the words out of his mouth than a big man with a sealskin waistcoat pulls a roll of bills out of his pocket and passes it up. 'A hundred thousand to win ten thousand dollars on Johnson,' he agreed. The man who offered the bet looked green. There was big money at that ringside.

"Your Uncle Valentine heard the other man coming through the crowd, and had my coat and muffler off, and pulled the sweater over my head. For an instant I stood stripped.

"Then I saw my man was in the ring.

"I went forward to hear the referee go over the rules—his name was Kilrain, a fine fellow and a good fighter in his day!—and there I met Johnson, who had a smile on his face, but it left as I looked at him. He had plaster on his hands.

" 'Do you object to this, Carabine?' the referee asked.

" 'I object to nothing, Mister Kilrain, not even brass knuckles.'

"As we turned to our corners I held out my hand to Johnson, for a prize ring is no place for private spite, and a championship fight is above personal feeling. He looked at my hand without taking it, and turned away. There was a lot of laughing at the ringside, but there was a good deal of hissing. I went back to my corner, and 'Good luck, Jim!' whispered your Uncle Valentine and whipped my coat off, and time was called.

"Mister Kerry, there's nothing in the world as

lonely as a man in the ring when his seconds get out of it, and he's left there with the man he's to fight, and the referee like the blinded woman that's the dispenser of justice on the outside of the law courts. Every one who has fought knows the dropping of the heart. The Southern Irish fellow will cross himself and the Jewish fighter touch a praying shawl. I gave a good pull to the ropes to loosen up and walked out to meet my man.

"I don't know what there was about me, Mister Kerry, but I could see Johnson change his mind as he came forward. He closed up, in a way. We fiddled for a few minutes, breaking ground, moving here and there. Around the ring you could have heard a pin fall, as the saying is, with the silence that was in it. Then Johnson jumped at me with his left hand. I didn't try to stop, but pulled my head away, as Shadrach Kennedy had instructed me, and each time he missed. He looked back and looked puzzled. And when he was thinking I rushed him myself, and letting go with the left caught him with a swash in the ribs that made the wind go through his teeth whistling, and bringing it up caught him on the side of the head and sent him staggering across the ring. I followed him, Mister Kerry, but he covered up on the corner, so I had to clout him a couple of right-handers at the back of the neck to straighten him up. He slipped under my guard and got away. We sparred and I noticed his chin going down and I jumped in and hit. It spread him on his back in the middle of the ring, and the first round was over.

"I never heard such a minute's commotion as there was at the ringside then. The crowd was roaring. It stopped as time was called for the second round. One minute it was shouting and the next it was silent as night. I noticed the marks of my blows on Johnson, the red knuckle marks against the white skin. He had taken it too easy, Mister Kerry. It never does to take a man too easy, even though you've beaten him easily the first shot. He was thinking; he was thinking hard. He feinted at my head and went in for a swing at the ribs, but I got him with right and left as he came in. He was clever, Mister Kerry; he slid behind me to hold and got a full Nelson on. But the Pole had taught me how to beat that. I dropped forward on my knees and threw him over my head. He was quick, so his hands saved him. We were both up on our feet and at it hammer and tongs. He hit hard. He shook me on the neck and jaw. But I got home with an uppercut that finished the round.

"Mister Kerry, in spite of everything, Shadrach Kennedy's instructions nearly did me. He had told me to watch my man's chin and I watched nothing else. In the first fight I had lost to him with my little trick of feinting with my left before leading. The man that beats another to the punch is the man that wins. My feint was a personal trick, but the dropping of the chin to the shoulder is universal. Everyone will protect himself before he attacks. I was doing so well beating him to the punch that I paid no attention to anything else. Once he tried a hard left on me, and dropping my head I caught his knuckles on my skull, and that must have hurt his hand, for he switched with his right hand forward quickly.

" 'For God's sake, look out!' shouted your Uncle Valentine.

"I had only time to set the muscles of my stomach, no time to drop my hands even, before his left with all his body pivoting behind it socked me in the midriff. It was like the blow of a sledge hammer, or a bullet. And the crack of it could be heard all over the ring, so that the people swayed forward, and a big groan came out of them. If I hadn't been in time setting myself for it, it would have been an end of that fight, and maybe of any other fight. And if I hadn't been in condition, I could never have weathered it. Mister Kilrain, the referee, looked at me, and his face was white as a sheet.

"And then some Irish fellow from the ringside shouts: 'Sure, he's laughing at you, Johnson!'

"Well, I wasn't laughing at him, Mister Kerry. My face was just twisted with the grin of pain. Pain does either of two things to you. It makes you senseless or it drives you mad. It drove me crazy and I went for Johnson, hitting him with everything I had, jolt and chop; hooking him, and back-handling him on the return, as we were allowed to do in the prize ring. It must have been like hailstones hitting him, until he went down and lay quiet. The ringside was in a roar, men trying to hedge their bets, taking any money offered on Johnson, where before there wasn't a penny to be taken from his supporters except by the ignorant Irish and your Uncle Valentine. Your Uncle Valentine was the only calm person there. His face was pale and he was whistling 'The Boyne Water,' and he dropped on his knee and began to rub my stomach. Before the minute was up, I was all right. 'I'm fine, Mister Valentine,' I said. 'It's nearly over, Jim,' said he, 'but just keep your eye open.'

"It didn't need any advice from anyone to make me pay attention, for the pivot blow was a master tradesman's punch. I went after Johnson in the next round, giving him the straight left and bringing over the right occasionally. All he did was to try and push me off with the left hand. And then after two minutes of fighting he drew his last trick. He swung his right, high, overhand to my jaw. He brought it from his right heel and as quick as lightning, a punch nobody but a fool or a great boxer uses. If it had caught me on the temple, I'd have been dropped like a felled ox. If it had caught me on the jaw, I'd have been through. I took it on the neck and as it was my knees gave and my hands dropped, and a cloud came before my eyes. And I could hear the roar of the ringside, and the cry: 'Carabine's gone!' But the fog cleared away. I hadn't time to fall, and there was Johnson in front of me, looking more dazed than myself. He couldn't understand I wasn't down. I waded in and began to punch at him. And when I wrestled with him I knew I was strong again. He gave a look over his shoulder at his corner, and threw his shoulders up, and then I knew I was only beating a beaten man.

"He was game, Mister Kerry. There was no black spot on him. He was a better man losing than he ever was winning. I could feel the vitality pouring out of him with every punch I landed. Once he slipped from weakness and fell, and I helped him to his feet. He said: 'Thanks, Jim,' and he put out his right hand and I took it. It was as fine an apology as was ever made.

"The ringside was bawling, Mister Kerry, a mad roar. The men of the North, I noticed, had brass knuckle-dusters on, and worse than that in their pockets, for they weren't going to see the ropes cut and me done out of my fight. I worked Johnson over to his corner, and held him up, he was so weak, and I called to his second: 'Can't you throw in the sponge? Can't you see your man's done? What's the use of punishing any further?' But his seconds were surly and dumb.

"I called to the referee: 'Mister Kilrain,' I said, 'this man's finished. Can't you stop the fight to save him?'

"'It's a championship fight,' said the referee, 'and I've got to give him every chance of keeping his title, if it's only the chance of an earthquake. You've got to knock him out of time,' said Mister Kilrain.

"I appealed to the fellow himself. 'If I land you a light one,' said I, 'will you go down and stay down? There's no disgrace to losing a fight like this. You've given a lot and taken a lot. Will you do that?' said I.

"He shook his head, meaning he wouldn't. . . .

"There was nothing for it, Mister Kerry, but to finish him, so I pushed him off, and bit my heels into the ground for a stance. He knew the end was coming and he tried to get his hands up, but his arms were tired and numb. I let him have it with both hands, and stood back. And he thumped forward on his face. Then I turned and walked to my corner."

In england in the first quarter of the nineteenth century, pugilism and poetry reached their peaks, and although a youthful street fighter and lifelong fistic fan named John Keats had a head start on him, Byron was the foremost contributor to both the arts. He not only frequented the fights but backed fighters and took a lengthy course in sparring from Gentleman John Jackson.

FROM

# Letters and Journal

## GEORGE GORDON, LORD BYRON

September 12, 1830—One of Matthew's passions was "the Fancy"; and he sparred uncommonly well. But he always got beaten in rows, or combats with the bare fist. In swimming, too, he swam well; but with *effort* and *labor,* and *too high* out of the water; so that Scrope Davies and myself, of whom he was therein somewhat emulous, always told him that he would be drowned if ever he came to a difficult pass in the water. He was so; but surely Scrope and myself would have been most heartily glad that

> *"the Dean had lived,*
> *And our prediction proved a lie."*

His head was uncommonly handsome, very like what *Pope's* was in his youth.

His voice, and laugh, and features, are strongly resembled by his brother Henry's, if Henry be *he* of *King's College.* His passion for boxing was so great, that he actually wanted me to match him with Dogherty (whom I had backed and made the match for against Tom Belcher), and I saw them spar together at my own lodgings with gloves on. As he was bent upon it, I would have backed Dogherty to please him, but the match went off. It was of course to have been a private fight, in a private room.

November 24, 1813—Just returned from dinner with Jackson (the Emperor of Pugilism) and an-

other of the select, at Crib's the champion's. I drank more than I like, and have brought away some three bottles of very fair claret—for I have no headache. We had Tom ———— up after dinner; very facetious, though somewhat prolix. He don't like his situation—wants to fight again—pray Pollux (or Castor, if he was the *miller*) he may! Tom has been a sailor—a coal heaver—and some other genteel profession, before he took to the cestus. Tom has been in action at sea, and is now only three-and-thirty. A great man! has a wife and a mistress, and conversations well —bating some sad omissions and misapplications of the aspirate. Tom is an old friend of mine; I have seen some of his best battles in my nonage. He is now a publican, and, I fear, a sinner—for Mrs. ———— is on alimony, and ————'s daughter lives with the champion. This ———— told me; Tom, having an opinion of my morals, passed her off as a legal spouse. Talking of her, he said, "she was the truest of women"—from which I immediately inferred she could *not* be his wife, and so it turned out.

March 20, 1814—Sparred with Jackson again yesterday morning, and shall tomorrow. I feel all the better for it, in spirits, though my arms and shoulders are very stiff from it. Mem. to attend the pugilistic dinner:—Marquess Huntley is in the chair.

APRIL 9, 1814—I am but just returned to town, from which you may infer that I have been out of it; and I have been boxing, for exercise, with Jackson for this last month daily. I have also been drinking, and, on one occasion, with three other friends at the Cocoa Tree, from six till four, yea, unto five in the matin.

APRIL 26, 1814—I can't for the head of me, add a line worth scribbling; my "vein" is quite gone, and my present occupations are of the gymnastic order—boxing and fencing—and my principal conversation is with my macaw and Bayle.

JUNE 19, 1814—My mornings are late, and passed in fencing and boxing, and a variety of most unpoetical exercises, very wholesome, &c., but would be very disagreeable to my friends, whom I am obliged to exclude during their operation.

JOE LOUIS was Jimmy Cannon's favorite fighter. Jimmy Cannon is Joe Louis' favorite writer. The following is as fine a tribute as has ever been paid to any fighter by any writer.

# The Joe Louis I Remember

## JIMMY CANNON

THE TRUTHS OF OUR YOUTH often become falsehoods in our middle years. It is the fee we pay for being alive. We tolerate leniently the rotting of the flesh and the defeat of beauty, but it is harder to accept the decay of ideals. So I am grateful I am still able to admire Joe Louis for what he was. We were young together and he has survived in my estimation. It is because he was a symbol and a force for good, and because he is a decent man.

We have a tendency in this country to praise athletes beyond their worth. It is natural because we are essentially a lighthearted people and this is an age of turbulence. It is a tribute to us that we were able to appreciate Louis. He is a simple man with little education, but the truths he uttered gave him a special radiance. Perhaps his observations were ungrammatical. But often they seemed profoundly witty because they were told with a candor that was unblemished by cleverness. I've never known him to seek the sanctuary of a lie. And I was there from the beginning.

He was an historic heavyweight champion. The others were John L. Sullivan and Jack Dempsey. They were before my time. But I know Joe Louis improved the fight racket with his presence. He ducked no one and he bragged less than any champion I've known. He is a good-humored man who had pride in what he was. The night that Rocky Marciano knocked him out, people who didn't know him wept in Madison Square Garden. Their grief was not restricted by color.

On his fortieth birthday Louis refereed a wrestling match in Decatur, Illinois. Stooging for these comedians of sport demeans a man who was the greatest fighter I've ever covered as a sports writer. I telephoned him long distance to wish him a happy birthday. I expected him to be cranky. Wrestling is a slum, and in this squalid bazaar Louis was selling his tarnished splendor for a night's pay.

"Have you," I asked, "any regrets?"

"No," Louis said. "I had a wonderful time. I still can make as much as I want to make."

I expected him to claim the second fight with Max Schmeling as the finest night of his life or, maybe, the night he beat Jimmy Braddock out of the heavyweight championship. He chose neither. It was, he insisted, the Max Baer fight. "I felt better that night," he explained. "I felt like I could fight for two, three days."

"What was your worst fight?"

"Arturo Godoy," he answered. "I guess I try too hard with him. I was stale. I couldn't do nothing."

So there he is, now nearing forty-one, on the road, performing in the clumsy tableaus of the wrestlers. It is sad, of course, but there is little joy in the fight racket. Maybe Louis is fortunate. At least he doesn't have to bleed for the money he picks up working with the clowns. Maybe I'm being too dramatic about it but I wish he could find another way to exhibit himself. Of course, Dempsey did it and so did a lot of other great fighters. The hours are short and the pay is good. But Louis doesn't belong in a ring to incite laughter. Neither does any other fighter who suffered publicly to make the toughest dollar an athlete earns. We find it hard to forgive the likes of

Louis for submitting to these indignities. We want to remember them as they were, and who was greater than Louis? Let me tell you how I found him to be. He is still my friend and I don't think he really has changed. Of course the years took the skills with them. They made his body a burden. But he never became bitter and nasty, the way some champions do. The history of his fights is in the guides. The matchless record is public knowledge. So this will be a personal recollection of Louis. It is not complete and there will be much that is missing. But none of it is in the files or the books. It is out of my mind and my heart.

THE FIRST TIME I saw Louis fight he humiliated Primo Carnera. The knockout didn't impress me as much as the first left hook that tore Carnera's slack mouth. It was a small punch but it ripped Carnera's high-curved upper lip and his mouth seemed to be crawling up the sides of his face in an agonized grin. The eyes in the big head rolled in terrible wonder, marveling at the force of the blow. Ask me the way Louis punched and I'll tell you about Carnera's mouth breaking into that idiot's smile.

AFTER THE Baer fight, Louis' hands were bruised. Baer was sick with despair. Afterward, Jack Dempsey, who worked his corner, said that Baer had been bragging in the dressing room about what he would do to Louis. But a man shouted it was time for the main event to go on and Baer began to pant.

"I can't go on," said Baer, according to Dempsey.

Dempsey regarded him with loathing and amazement.

"I can't breathe," Baer insisted.

"I conned him into the ring," Dempsey remembers. "After the first round, Max came back to the corner and said he couldn't breathe. I told him I'd kill him with the water bottle if he didn't go back out there and get knocked out."

It wasn't Baer, removing his mouthpiece and waving goodbye to the crowd as he sat on his legs, that I remember. It wasn't Louis' hand-quick ferocity. It was the look on Louis' face when Baer hit him after the bell. Louis' hands were down and he took the punch and a grimace of contempt puckered his face. It degraded Baer, that brief glance. It told what Baer was and what Louis was and never was the difference so clear. The referee didn't have to count.

INSTEAD OF AN OPPONENT, Paolino Uzcudun seemed more of a confederate. No one gave him

a chance. People wondered how long he would last.

Paolino wasn't clever and he couldn't punch much. But he fought with the vanity of the pug who is a fighter in his heart. He stooped over and hunched forward, his face concealed behind the stockade his crossed arms made. The corner had told Louis to be careful. They were afraid he would break his hands on Uzcudun's head. So Louis jabbed, carefully, precisely, lightly. He was patient and cautious. It happened in the fourth round. Paolino looked up and his head came out of the cage of his arms. One punch did it. It was a right hand and Paolino was down. Gold teeth sprinkled on the dirty canvas, the way tiny charms might fall off a woman's broken bracelet.

Paolino began to push himself up. His back was to Louis. But he was in another country, lost and hurt through. The boxing journalists forgot they were reporters. They stood up and shouted to referee Arthur Donovan.

"Stop it!" they yelled. "Stop it!"

And Donovan stopped it.

THE SPORTS EDITOR of the old *American*, the late Eddie Frayne, called me into his office. I had a choice of assignments. Did I want to go West with the Yankees or stay in New York to cover the Schmeling-Louis fight? There was a kid with the Yankees who was making his first road trip. I decided I would rather travel with Joe DiMaggio.

"Schmeling's all washed up," I told Frayne. "It won't be much of a fight."

We were in Detroit. I went to Tony Lazzeri's room. We sat around the radio. Clem McCarthy broadcast the fight. I remember him shouting above the tumult of the crowd.

"He's down!" came McCarthy's hoarse, excited voice.

"I told you," I said.

But it was Louis who was down, and he would be knocked out that night. In the city of Detroit people lit red flares and a parade of automobiles rolled through the downtown streets to celebrate the knockout of a home-town kid. I never understood that.

LET THE OTHERS tell you how stately Jimmy Braddock was in defeat. Go to the library if you would know how Louis won the heavyweight championship of the world. But what belongs to me was what Louis said after it was over. It is not important now but it impressed a sports writer who was still young enough to be moved by a champion.

I had to shove my way into Louis' dressing

room. The special cops on the door barred my way. There was a pushing crowd behind me. They threw me into the room, past the cops who fell and were walked upon. There was a radio announcer clinging to Joe, holding a microphone in his face. I collided with Louis and he grabbed me to hold me up.

"This is Jimmy Cannon," he said, "the assistant heavyweight champion of the world!"

I remember that.

I BELIEVE LOUIS was the greatest fighter who ever lived the night he took Max Schmeling apart. But I'm concerned with the soft evening I spent with him the night before the fight. I had gone to Pompton Lakes after I had written my piece. We had dinner together and sat on the porch of the old farmhouse he lived in.

"You make a pick?" he asked.

"Yes," I said.

"Knockout?" Louis asked.

"Six rounds," I said.

"No," Louis said. "One." He held up a big finger. "It go one," he said.

That's all it went.

I WAS IN the Army when Louis was matched with Lou Nova. I came to New York on a pass and went up to the Polo Grounds early. I was sitting in my seat when John Roxborough, who was one of his managers, came down to the working-press section.

"Joe wants to see you," he said.

I went back to the dressing room. It was a half hour before the fight. But Joe was asleep, burbling little snores. The crowd sounds awakened him and he sat up. We talked about the Army and about people we knew.

"Time to go, Chappie," one of his handlers said, taking up Joe's robe.

"I got to go to work," Louis said.

As long as I've been on the sports beat, I've never seen a cooler guy.

THERE ARE THOSE who are small-hearted and forever afraid, and they shall always fail in every crisis of their lives. But more unfortunate than these are the ones with sufficient courage who betray themselves intentionally by relying solely on caution. When a fighter discards recklessness as though it were a vice he had conquered, it is possible he will survive, but with such a gesture frequently he also abandons his dignity. It was not cowardice that I saw in Jersey Joe Walcott the first time he fought Louis and knocked him down. It is the penalty the mediocre man must pay when he tries to counterfeit greatness. I

made Walcott the winner over Louis, eight rounds to seven. But Louis, although knocked down twice, was still the champion because Walcott refused to reject his concocted meekness and replace it with even an imitation of boldness.

The great champion felt disgraced after that night. He ducked into seclusion and no one could see him. It became a big story because he hadn't told his version of the fight. I made a telephone call to a friend of Louis'. I told him I wanted to see Joe, alone. The champion called me back himself.

"You want me?" asked the thick, soft voice that had awakened me.

"Yeah," I said.

"Come up the apartment then," Louis said.

"Where are you?" I asked.

He gave me the address of an apartment house in upper Manhattan. He told me not to mention his name to the elevator boy but to come directly to the flat which was rented in a friend's name. He had been there a week and hadn't been out. He opened the door himself. He wore pajamas and a black-and-white striped cotton bathrobe. The left eye was still pinched by a discolored mound of flesh. His face was bloated. The knuckles of his right hand were swollen.

"What happened to you?" I asked after we had chatted about inconsequential happenings.

"I made the fight tough for myself," Louis said. "He didn't make it tough for me. He did so many wrong things. I saw every opening. But I couldn't go get him. It was a lousy fight. I saw him when he made the mistakes. It's like a guy running. You can't make a sprint near the end. Your legs feel you can go but you feel bad in the pit of your stomach."

"Sounds like you're getting old," I said.

"Diet and drying out," said Louis, who had weighed 211 pounds for the fight. "I wanted to weigh 12," he continued, omitting the 200 as most fighters do. "I should have weighed 14. I weighed 15, and sometime the day before the fight I killed myself taking off the four pounds. But that ain't no excuse. It was a real lousy fight."

"Why did you dry out?" I asked.

"I don't know," he said. "I guess I figured it was a good weight."

He pointed to a thicket of roses standing in a white vase on the table in the room. "If I water those flowers every day," he said, "and then I don't put no water on them, if I don't keep them alive—the flowers got to die. That's me. The day before the fight I had four lamb chops. No juice. Nothing else. No water all day. I eat no more—not even water—until two o'clock the day I fight.

You got to have strength to go to a guy. I was weak."

"When did you know you weren't right?"

"In the dressing room," Joe said. "I was warming up in there for fifteen minutes. I knew I didn't have the strength in the dressing room."

"The punch that knocked you down in the first was a sucker punch," I told him.

"You can see it coming when you're weak," he said, "but you're late getting up there. I saw every right hand, but it hit me anyway. One thing I'm happy to know . . ."

"What's that?" I asked.

"I made it tough for myself," he said. "He didn't."

Had he been persecuted into panic by the knowledge that he was losing the title? I told him I thought he had lost the fight and didn't deserve the decision.

"On my little daughter—" he said earnestly, "I never thought at any time I lost the fight. I chased his tail all the rest of the night. You knock a man down, you're supposed to go at a man. He knocked me down and then . . . run . . . run . . . run."

"Suppose they had given him the decision?"

"If they had given it to him," he said, "I wouldn't have cared about it. What I mean is it would have been all right with me. What the decision says—you got to go by it. I wouldn't have mentioned it."

"But you were so sore," I reminded him. "You tried to leave the ring before the decision came down."

"I was mad because I was so silly," he said. "Getting hit by them sucker punches. Seeing them coming—and getting hit. This is no excuse —what I told you—it was a lousy fight. Everybody say something. Everyone give a reason why you do this. No one knows what's in your mind, but you do. I can tell you how I feel but you don't *know* how I feel. I know I had no excuse for a lousy fight."

Not once during the three hours I spent with him did Louis call Walcott by his name.

I FOUND OUT afterward that the people who live off Louis had tried to discourage him from giving me an exclusive interview.

"You'll make a lot of enemies if you give this to Cannon," one of them said.

"Cannon's my friend," he said, "if I win or I lose."

THE SECOND TIME he knocked Walcott out and announced he would fight no more. The night after the fight I had dinner with him in the dining room of the Hotel Theresa in Harlem. There were a lot of people standing on the sidewalk when we came out. With us was his wife, Marva, and Leonard Reed, a vaudeville actor, who was his closest friend. The people didn't nag him for autographs but followed him quietly as he walked through the Saturday night crowd to the Alhambra Theater, which is across the street from the Theresa. The usher took us to the loge, off to the side, and from this angle the figures on the screen were thin and very tall. The fight movies started as we sat down. The audience was amused by Walcott's skipping and shoulder-shrugging and they reacted as though they were watching a comedy. They shrieked with laughter as Walcott made his preposterous and solemnly funny gestures. Louis didn't talk to me until the ninth round when he reached Walcott with a solid jab. He nudged me with his elbow. "Got him now," he said.

The audience stood up and shouted when Louis knocked him out, as though the finish was unexpected and had surprised them. We went out through a side door, unnoticed by the majority of the crowd, and strolled back to the hotel.

"It was dreadful," Mrs. Louis said.

"I thought it was terrific," Reed said.

"It might have been the other way," Mrs. Louis said.

"It's all over now," Reed said.

"I hope so," Mrs. Louis said. "But you know how it is . . . like an opera singer with a new role—But I hope not."

"Did you enjoy the picture?" I asked Louis.

"It had a real nice ending," Joe said.

WE WENT UP to the two-room hotel suite after the movies and Louis took off the dark glasses. His left cheek was puffed. The flesh around his eyes was scraped and bruised. He believed he was finished with fighting forever. I asked him about his financial condition.

"I won't ask anybody for nothing," he said.

"Suppose," Reed asked, "you could get a soft fight for, say, half a million clams?"

"If they put half a million in my hand—I got half a million," he replied. "But this way—retired—I can make a hundred thousand a year the rest of my life. The championship is an annuity like."

THERE WAS A night in Philadelphia when he drifted through a four-round exhibition with Arturo Godoy. The dressing room was humid but Louis lay under a woolen blanket on a rubbing table, kidding Ike Williams, who was then the lightweight champion. They were talking about golf.

"If Ike keeps his head down, he's a real good 85 shooter," Louis said.

"That's not me," Williams protested. "My score's 72."

"How about a match for a thousand?" said Blinky Palermo, who managed Williams.

"I don't want to take his money," Louis said. "It would be pitiful. They put people in jail for taking money that way. Seventy-two—he better buy shoes for his caddie. The caddie would wear out his shoes kicking the ball for a 72."

"Do you like these exhibitions?" I asked.

"Sure," Louis said. "There's a lot of difference between fights and exhibitions. Exhibitions. Big gloves. Don't have to fight hard. Expenses ain't much."

That night 7,285 people paid to see him.

THEY PUT LOUIS in with Joe Chesul, a main-event fighter from the obscure clubs of New Jersey, on the exhibition tour. There was a referee to do the counting if there was a knockdown. The seconds acted as though these were genuine contests. But it was show business, not the fight racket.

The cast was the same when I went down into the basement of the Newark Armory. There were cops on the door and inside were the vague hangers-on you know you met before but can't remember where. There was always a guy carried strictly for laughs. This was George Nicholson, who used to be a sparring partner for Louis. There was Manny Seamon, who still trained Joe. There was Marshall Miles, who did the business for him. I had visited Louis in so many bleak rooms like this in so many towns. But the excitement was gone and so was the strain. There was no guessing. Nothing was at stake. It was just another pay night.

Into the place came a guy with a fighter's face. "You remember me, Joe?" the guy asked.

"How are you?" Louis stalled.

"Steve Hamas," the guy said.

This was Steve Hamas, who once licked Max Schmeling, who, until Marciano did it, was the only man ever to knock Louis out. Their conversation was limited to fighters they both knew. After a while, Louis got up and went out to earn his touch.

"Whatever became of Ezzard Charles?" a guy yelled.

This was before Louis fought Charles, and I wonder now what caused the guy to say that. The people there, about 5,000 of them, grumbled when Louis' weight was announced as 228½.

I realized what the years had done to Louis when a kid like Chesul made him miss and lunge. The grace was gone and so was the quickness of hand. I was positive that night that Louis would never try to fight again.

I WAS A WAR correspondent in Korea when Louis was beaten by Ezzard Charles. There had been no mail for us since we made the landing at Inchon. The last radio I had heard had mumbled with static. On the sports page of the last copy of *Stars and Stripes* I had was a photograph of Louis, placid and immense, staring drowsily at Charles. There was no talk about the fight in Korea. But I thought about it one night when I couldn't sleep in a cottage on the road to Seoul. One of the guys was snoring with a whimpering moan. There was the smell of feet and the sound of men turning stiffly in their blankets. I went out onto the porch with a shelter-half wrapped around me to shield my cigarette in the blackout of the command post.

Much of my life had been spent writing about Louis or hanging around his training camps. My youth was gone with his and middle age was upon the both of us. I felt especially old among the very young Marines. That photograph of Louis had aged me. My thigh bones ached from climbing hills. There was a knot on my hip from sleeping on the ground. I was weary with a deep tiredness that never diminished and only seemed to increase. Shaving with cold water had chapped my face. I had worn the same clothes for six days. I was the only sports writer there and I found no companions who cared to argue fights.

I knew Louis couldn't win. But I still had faith in him. At dawn I sat down at a typewriter and filed a sports piece. I wrote that Louis would knock out Charles in six rounds. I was homesick and tired of combat and feeling my age. I wanted to be there when they fought. It seemed to be wrong to be against Louis when I was so far away. So I picked him. It didn't surprise me when I was told that Charles had trimmed him. But it depressed me.

OF COURSE, LOUIS won his fight with Cesar Brion in Chicago. I told him I thought he should quit. But the liars said he still had a couple of more good fights in him. He was thirty-six, but older than Methuselah in the fight racket. One observation he made clarified it all.

"My right hand don't leave me no more," Louis said. "I got to think to throw it now. When you're young, you see an opening and throw punches you can't even remember throwing."

It was said quietly. Louis wasn't being dramatic about it. But here was a guy giving me his own obituary as a fighter.

I WENT TO Pompton Lakes where Louis worked to get ready for Lee Savold. He was obstinate in a courteous way when I asked him about his condition. I told him that he should have taken Brion out because he had a lot of shots at him.

"I ain't lost my punch," he said stubbornly.

"You nailed Brion," I said.

"Not so good," he said sadly, "not so good."

"How's training this time?"

"Very nice," he said. "Very nice. But it's tough to do what you want to do. When you start in boxing, you want to throw a punch but you can't do it. You have to force yourself."

We walked out of the gymnasium and into the glade where the ring was pitched. There was a pigtailed young woman waiting for him with a clump of photographers. She wore boxing gloves, white trunks and a white T shirt. On the T shirt were the figures of two women boxers. Above them, in blocked blue letters, was the legend, "Female Joe Louis."

"I got seventeen knockouts in twenty-two fights," Female Joe Louis said. "I fight boys and everything. I'm a champion, too."

I asked Female Joe Louis where she boxed.

"Mexico City," Female Joe replied. "I'm fighting a girl there for the championship very soon."

"What's her name?" I asked.

"It's in the contract," Female Joe Louis said. "It's an odd name. I don't remember it. I like to fight men. The harder I pop them, the better I like it."

"You scare me," Joe Louis said to Female Joe Louis.

THEY KNEW WHAT he meant even after they had beaten him. It embarrassed Rocky Marciano a little when he knocked out Louis.

"They didn't like me," he said, "because of what I done to Joe."

SMALL REMEMBRANCES return to me as I write this piece. Now it is the dressing room after the first Walcott fight. Louis sat on a rubbing table. He got the decision but he looked like the loser.

"How is your cold?" was the first thing he said to me.

I had been laid up for a couple of days. It impressed me that a guy, bleary and angry, could be that considerate of a friend in such a spot.

I WAS IN Chicago for a football game. Louis telephoned me and said he had a surprise for me. Would I, he asked, come to a night club on the South Side? He wouldn't tell me what would happen. I went and there were people standing in line outside. There was an immense photograph of Louis in the lobby. There was a sticker pasted across the chest. The legend on it read "In Person." He did a comedy act with a straight man. It was very bad and Louis broke up and laughed away the punch lines. The people liked it. Afterward, Louis came to my table and I asked him why he did it.

"Some friends got the joint," he said. "I give them a hand. But don't print that. Just say I'm having some fun."

THERE WERE STORIES in the newspapers that Louis was broke. I met him at Mike Jacobs' offices which were then in the Brill Building on Broadway. I asked him if it were true he had been trimmed.

"No," he said. "I'll let you see my books."

He paused. "I made some investments with friends," he said. "They turned out bad. Look at the books but don't put that in."

THERE WAS A hot day at Yankee Stadium when the Red Sox were playing the Yankees. I came upon Louis, who was sitting behind third base.

"You know Ted Williams?" he asked.

I said I did.

"A good hitter," Louis said.

"Would you like to meet him?"

"Yeah," he said.

I took Louis back to the Boston dressing room. Williams was in his underwear, standing before his locker. They looked at one another and Louis spoke first. He didn't wait to be introduced.

"My," he said, "you skinny."

FRANKIE HARMON, whose father, Paddy, built the Chicago Stadium, promoted an exhibition match between Louis and Billy Conn when both were finished with fighting. Louis dropped by Harmon's office before the fight and asked him:

"What percentage Billy getting?"

Harmon told him.

"Take five per cent of my end," Joe said. "Put it on Billy's."

He never told Conn that.

GEE WALKER, who played the outfield for the Tigers, was the ballplayer Joe admired most. He talked about him continually and explained what a thrill it was to see Walker play. I said the records showed Walker wasn't the best. I told Louis to prove he was.

"You know a man's the best," Louis said, "he's the best. You don't have to prove it."

THERE WAS A season when Louis toured with a softball team and played first base.

"What did you hit?" I asked him.

"Round .200," he said.

We talked awhile about other matters. Louis returned to the topic of softball. "You don't have to put my average in the paper?" he asked.

"I do," I said.

He thought about it a while. "You're a bad hitter," he said, "I guess you're a bad hitter."

THERE WAS A TIME when the late Paul Small, a theatrical agent, arranged a profitable movie deal for Louis. The managers sat at a table and discussed terms. They finally reached an agreement.

"This all right with you?" Small said to Louis.

"Can my softball team be in the picture?" Louis asked.

And that was the only question he asked.

THE REST IS IN the book, but what he was isn't there. There was conceit in him but he controlled it. There was a lot of pride in him, too, but it never took charge of him. He was shy and he hid in silence when there were strangers around, but he was easygoing and good company if you were a friend. I admired him but I tried to see him clearly. At the end, when he needed help, I was sympathetic but I knew he was a goner and I said so. He never complained about it and it never spoiled our relationship. He was a great champion and I'm glad he was a champion in my time. He was mean at his work but he was able to leave it in the ring. The cruelty was there, all right. The poverty of his boyhood formed him as it does all fighters. But he was never resentful and he always did the best he could. His best was wonderful.

The night Marciano knocked him out, a guy said it was pretty sad to see him go that way.

"I've knocked out lots of guys," Louis said.

He was a fighter. Many a guy makes a good living fighting for money and many become champions. They can show you licenses to prove they're fighters, and there isn't any way I can dispute them. But Louis was a boy's dream of a fighter. There was joy and innocence in his skills and this gave him what the others lacked. There have been others but I'm sure of Louis.

Joe Louis was a fighter. It is the finest compliment I can give him.

So I'll stop right here.

## JOE PALOOKA

BY HAM FISHER

In the 6,000 years since the Egyptians introduced boxing, no one dealing with the sport has reached as many people as did Ham Fisher, who started his comic strip on April 19, 1930. Joe Palooka first won the heavyweight crown in 1931 (as shown), and his aseptic adventures in and out of the ring have been followed by hundreds of millions of readers of almost 800 newspapers. Since Fisher's death in 1955 the strip has been drawn by two teams of artists. (Permission of the McNaught Syndicate and the estate of Hammond E. Fisher; courtesy of *Look* Magazine.)

CORBETT'S VICTORY CREATES WILD ENTHUSIASM.
THE CONQUEROR OF MITCHELL GIVEN AN OVATION IN THE CLUB ARENA IN JACKSONVILLE, FLA.
DRAWN BY "POLICE GAZETTE" SPECIAL ARTISTS.

The National Police Gazette, now leading a comparatively subdued existence, was started in a jail cell in 1845, then fell into the talented hands of an Irish immigrant named Richard K. Fox and became the leading sex, crime and sports weekly in the country. For a while Fox had his own American heavyweight champion—Jake Kilrain—but John L. Sullivan settled that when he knocked out Kilrain at Richburg, Miss., on July 8, 1889. Five years later Fox was hailing Sullivan's successor and his third-round kayo of Charley Mitchell with an "Extra!" (*Bettmann Archive*)

THE MOST IMPORTANT single piece of boxing writing ever done was turned out in London in 1865 by John Graham Chambers, a member of the Amateur Athletic Club, who is often confused with Arthur Chambers, who, in 1872, won the lightweight championship of America. Chambers drew up twelve rules to govern the conduct of matches, prescribing gloves, three-minute rounds and the ten-count, and barring wrestling and hugging. When Chambers found a sponsor in John Sholto Douglas, the eighth Marquis of Queensberry, who gained lasting fame merely by lending his name, it was the beginning of the end of bare-knuckle fighting.

The Queensberry Rules supplanted the Revised London Prize Ring Rules, which had grown out of the first boxing rules drawn up by Jack Broughton in 1743. They were applied in full for the first time in a tournament in London in 1872, and in a championship fight when Jim Corbett knocked out John L. Sullivan in twenty-one rounds in New Orleans on September 7, 1892.

# The Marquis of Queensberry Rules

## JOHN GRAHAM CHAMBERS

RULE 1—TO BE a fair stand-up boxing match in a twenty-four-foot ring, or as near that size as practicable.

Rule 2—No wrestling or hugging allowed.

Rule 3—The rounds to be of three minutes' duration, and one minute's time between rounds.

Rule 4—If either man fall through weakness or otherwise, he must get up unassisted, ten seconds to be allowed him to do so, the other man meanwhile to return to his corner, and when the fallen man is on his legs the round is to be resumed, and continued until the three minutes have expired. If one man fails to come to the scratch in the ten seconds allowed, it shall be in the power of the referee to give his award in favor of the other man.

Rule 5—A man hanging on the ropes in a helpless state, with his toes off the ground, shall be considered down.

Rule 6—No seconds or any other persons to be allowed in the ring during the rounds.

Rule 7—Should the contest be stopped by any unavoidable interference, the referee to name the time and place as soon as possible for finishing the contest; so that the match must be won and lost, unless the backers of both men agree to draw the stakes.

Rule 8—The gloves to be fair-sized boxing gloves of the best quality and new.

Rule 9—Should a glove burst, or come off, it must be replaced to the referee's satisfaction.

Rule 10—A man on one knee is considered down, and if struck is entitled to the stakes.

Rule 11—No shoes or boots with springs allowed.

Rule 12—The contest in all other respects to be governed by revised rules of the London Prize Ring.

THIS WAS BARGE fighting. On May 16, 1881, John L. Sullivan fought John Flood at dockside on the Hudson River at Yonkers, New York. Nine months and four fights later he was to knock out Paddy Ryan in nine rounds in front of a hotel in Mississippi City, Mississippi, for the heavyweight title.

# Sullivan–Flood

## DONALD BARR CHIDSEY

NOBODY COULD SAY that John L., his eye on the championship, picked easy ones. John Flood, the Bull's Head Terror, was the biggest and toughest member of the toughest and one of the biggest gangs in New York, that which controlled the neighborhood of the Bull's Head horse market in Twenty-fourth Street. He was redheaded and huge, a good inch taller than John L., at least ten pounds heavier. Called the best rough-and-tumble fighter in the country, conceded at least to be the best in New York, he had no use for fancy things like boxing gloves. Anybody who fought him fought with bare fists. Which was all right with John L. Sullivan. Flood had never failed to knock his man out of time.

The purse was to be one thousand dollars— seven hundred and fifty dollars to the winner, two hundred and fifty dollars to the loser. Somebody else must have made that arrangement, for John L. Sullivan, with his superb confidence, tried as often as possible to have his fights on a winner-take-all basis.

As such things went, the fight was kept tolerably secret. Everybody knew it was going to be held—the night of May 16—but very few knew, up until the last minute, where. Betting was two and three to one in favor of Flood.

The Strong Boy had his picture taken. This is mentionable because the picture is the most familiar one, the one that was used on cigarette cards, among other things, all over the country, the one generations of youngsters gazed at in awe. It's a beauty, too. It shows John L. in profile, fists raised, leaning slightly forward on his

left leg as though ready to attack. Staring at this picture, you can feel a slim shiver of fright; for the young Sullivan, John L. in his prime, must have been a terrible thing to see. He is wearing white tight trunks, black shoes, black stockings, a plain black belt. Above the belt he is naked; and the muscles, not bunched, not protrusive, are bland, sleek, flat. He is clean-shaven, and the hair of his head is shorn close. This was before he developed a taste for evening clothes, diamond studs, candles on the table, wine. Here he is a fighter pure and simple, a lowbrow, a tough, touchy, and a very strong mick from a back street, with an unmatchable talent for using his fists.

At dusk on the sixteenth Boston visitors began drifting into the back room of a certain East Twenty-fourth Street saloon. They were sold tickets for a "chowder party" at ten dollars apiece and told to go to the foot of *East* Forty-Third Street. This was esteemed by the Bull's Head gang a very funny joke, for the barge upon which it had been secretly agreed the fight should be held was moored at the foot of *West* Forty-Third Street. The local crowd wanted to have things its own way.

John L. himself, of course, was directed to the right place. He arrived at eight o'clock, and with him were two followers and nobody else—Billy Madden and Joe Goss. There were about three hundred of the Bull's Head crowd, grinning. There were a few others, members of neither party, among them Al Smith, who was going to referee (not Alfred Emanuel Smith, later governor of New York and a Presidential nominee), and Paddy Ryan, the champion.

John L. had been warned that if he won the Bull's Head crowd, thugs all, and armed, might get nasty. He shrugged. Nervousness was a thing he never knew.

A tug came out of the night and was tied to the barge, and they started up the river. Knowing that the police in both states were looking for them, they showed no light. They stood in little groups, whispering, watching, except that John L. and Madden and Goss remained below.

There was a bar, and it did a lot of business.

They crossed the river, still heading upstream, and somewhere in the hushed shadows of the Palisades they stopped long enough to pitch a ring. It was a very small ring, but large enough. Neither John Flood nor John L. Sullivan was the kind of man to do much running away in a fight.

The tug started up again. After a while the barge bumped softly against a dock in Yonkers. There was nobody around. With very few preliminaries the fight was started.

They did not use bare fists after all but pulled on skintight gloves, which were easier on the hands, though no whit easier on the other fellow's face.

Kerosene lamps were lit at the last moment.

It must have been a great fight. Neither man gave an inch, save when forced backward by the weight of attack. There was nothing scientific about it; it was sheer slugging.

In the middle of it another tug came alongside. The Boston crowd had chartered this and pursued the barge. Now they wanted to come aboard. They were warned to stay away, and knives and pistols were shown. Greatly outnumbered, the Boston crowd backed into midstream, where they waited for the rest of the fight, hearing the shouts that came across the water, "Come on John!" "Kill him, John!" never knowing, agonizingly wondering, which John was meant.

There were eight rounds, all ending in honest falls or knockdowns. There was no stalling. There was a total of sixteen minutes of fight. After that Flood couldn't come to the scratch.

John L. stood panting, fists up, feet spread, the red light of lamps shining on his chest and arms, while wavelets slap-slapped the sides of the barge and every man's breath was held. It was not the first time that he had seen his opponent stretched senseless at his feet, nor was it to be by any means the last; yet I think it was one of the happiest. After a while he lowered his arms, looked around. He caught sight of Paddy Ryan, the champion, and he grinned.

"Ready for yours, Paddy?"

The champion grinned back and shook his head.

It had happened so suddenly, so swiftly, so dramatically too, that if the Bull's Head gang truly had contemplated violence in the event of their leader being beaten, they forgot it. John L. himself helped to pick up the unconscious Flood, and he himself started to pass the hat for the benefit of the loser, contributing a ten-dollar bill. He was always gracious to men he had whipped.

Then the other tug came alongside again, and the Boston men tumbled aboard the barge, nobody trying to stop them. They never got back the money they had paid for "chowder party" tickets, but now they didn't care, having won their bets.

John Flood was taken home and put to bed, where he remained for several days and where John L. visited him. Later he was given a benefit, John L. donating his services free.

John L. and Goss and Madden were carried boisterously down to the St. James Hotel at Broadway and Twenty-sixth Street, where the lobby floor was made up of big black and white marble squares and where there were giddy prism chandeliers and life-sized gilt statues. He ate, it is certain, no less than twelve filets *à la Chateaubriand,* the house specialty, afterward, with the grand manner which was coming naturally to him even in these unaccustomed surroundings, calling in the chef, Mr. Baptiste, to congratulate him. He drank, it is almost equally certain, his first champagne.

WHEN JACK DEMPSEY (188) knocked out Georges Carpentier (172) in four rounds at Boyle's Thirty Acres in Jersey City, New Jersey, on July 2, 1921, it was not much of a fight, but it was a great promotion. The 80,000 persons (see page 108) who paid $1,789,238 to sit in formed the first of the million-dollar gates, and thus the New York *Times* showed journalistic ingenuity in borrowing Irvin S. Cobb from the *Saturday Evening Post* to write its color story.

In his description of the second round Cobb, no boxing expert, hurt Dempsey more than Carpentier ever did. One of the "mute, inglorious, preliminary scrappers" of whom Cobb wrote was Gene Tunney, who knocked out Soldier Jones in the seventh round and five years later beat Dempsey for the heavyweight title.

# Dempsey–Carpentier

## IRVIN S. COBB

THROUGH A HUNDRED ENTRANCES the multitude flows in steadily, smoothly, without jamming or confusion. The trickling streams run down the aisles and are absorbed by capillary attraction in the seats. If it takes all sorts of people to make up the world then all the world must be here already. That modest hero of the cinema, Tom Mix, known among friends as the Shrinking Violet of Death Valley, starts a furore by his appearance at 12:15, just as the first of the preliminary bouts is getting under way. His dress proclaims that he recently has suffered a personal bereavement. He is in mourning. He wears a sea-green sport suit, a purple handkerchief, a pair of solid-gold-filled glasses and a cowboy hat the size of a six-furlong track. Actress ladies in make-up and also some few in citizens' clothes jostle against society leaders and those who follow in their wake.

The arts, the sciences, the drama, commerce, politics, the bench, the bar, the great newly risen bootlegging industry—all these have sent their pink, their pick and their perfection to grace this great occasion. A calling over of the names of the occupants of the more highly priced reservations would sound like reading the first hundred pages of Who's Ballyhooed in America. Far away

and high up behind them, their figures cutting the skyline of the mighty wooden bowl, are perched the pedestrian classes. They are on the outer edge of events if not actually in it.

Conspicuous at the front, where the lumber-made cliffs of the structure shoal off into broad flats, is that type which is commonest of all alongside a fight ring. He is here in numbers amounting to a host. There must be thousands of him present. He is the soft-fleshed, hard-faced person who keeps his own pelt safe from bruises, but whose eyes glisten and whose hackles lift at the prospect of seeing somebody else whipped to a soufflé. He is the one who, when his favorite pug is being hammered to a sanguinary Spanish omelet, calls out: "That's all right, kid, he can't hurt you." I see him countlessly repeated. For the anonymous youths who in the overtures are achieving a still greater namelessness by being put violently to sleep he has a listless eye. But wait until the big doings start. Then will his gills pant up and down as his vicarious lusting for blood and brute violence is satisfied.

Bout after bout is staged, is fought out, is finished. Few know who the fighters are and nobody particularly cares. Who is interested in flea-biting contests when he came to see a combat between young bull elephants? Joe Humphries, the human Cave of the Winds, bulks as a greater figure of interest as he vouches for the proper identities of these mute, inglorious, preliminary scrappers than do the scrappers themselves.

It's one o'clock now. Where an hour ago there were wide vacant stretches of unoccupied seating space, now all is covered with piebald masses—the white of straw hats, the black of men's coats, with here and there bright patches of cola-like peonies blossoming in a hanging garden, to denote the presence of many women in gay summer garb. The inflowing tides of humanity have inundated and swallowed up the desert. Still there has been no congestion, no traffic jams. However the fight may turn out the handling of the crowd has been competent. Tex Rickard is the world's greatest showman.

The hour of one has arrived. Harry Stevens, the official caterer, can't figure within ten thousand of what the full attendance will be and so prepares to slice another ham. One thing is sure —today Boyle's Thirty Acres has given to Tex Rickard a richer harvest than any like area of this world's surface ever yielded.

At this moment—one-sixteen—atmospheric troubles impend. A drizzle has begun to fall. It is a trickle as yet but threatens to develop into an authentic downpour. The air has grown sodden and soggy with moisture, thickened to the saturation point. It is as though one breathed into a wet sponge. I figure this sort of thing, continuing or growing worse, will slow up the two chief clouters when their turn comes.

Governor Edwards of New Jersey comes at one-thirty: the first good solid knockdown in the ring at one-thirty-six. Both are heartily approved with loud thunders of applause. Not everyone can be the anti-dry sport-loving governor of a great commonwealth, but a veritable nobody can win popular approval on a day like this by shoving his jaw in front of a winged fist. There are short cuts to fame though painful.

The shower has suspended, but the atmosphere is still as soppy as a wet shirt. This certainly is a stylish affair. I have just taken note of the fact that the corps of referees all wear white silk blouses and white trousers like tennis players and that the little fat boy who holds up big printed cards with numerals on them to show the number of the next round is done up in spotless white linen like an antiseptically bandaged thumb. The humidity with which the air is freighted is beginning now to be oppressive. Even the exertion of shoving a pencil across paper brings out the perspiration and the two ambitious novices up in the ring are so wet and so slick

with their own sweat that they make you think of a pair of fresh-caught fish flapping about in a new sort of square net.

It's three o'clock. Prompt on the appointed hour, for once in the history of championship goes, the men are brought forth on time. Carpentier comes first, slim, boyish, a trifle pale and drawn-looking, to my way of thinking. He looks more like a college athlete than a professional bruiser. A brass band plays the "Marseillaise," ninety-odd thousand men and women stand to greet him—or maybe the better to see him—and he gets a tremendous heartening ovation. Dempsey follows within two minutes. A mighty roar salutes him, too, as he climbs into the ring and seats himself within the arc of a huge floral horseshoe; but so near as may be judged by the applause for him, an American born, it is not so sincere or spontaneous as the applause which has been visited upon the Frenchman.

He grins—but it is a scowling, forbidding grin —while photographers flock into the ring to focus their boxes first on one and then on the other. Dempsey sitting there makes me think of a smoke-stained Japanese war idol; Carpentier, by contrast, suggests an Olympian runner carved out of fine-grained white ivory. Partisans howl their approval of the champion. He refuses to acknowledge these. One figures that he has suddenly grown sulky because his reception was no greater than it was.

A little crowd of ring officials surrounds Dempsey. There is some dispute seemingly over the tapes in which his knobby brown hands are wrapped. Carpentier, except for one solicitous fellow countryman, is left quite alone in his corner.

Dempsey keeps his eyes fixed on his fists. Carpentier studies him closely across the eighteen feet which separate them. The Gaul is losing his nervous air. He is living proof to give the lie to the old fable that all Frenchmen are excitable.

Overhead airplanes are breezing, and their droning notes come down to be smitten and flung up again on the crest of the vast upheaval of sound rising from the earth. A tiresome detail of utterly useless announcements is ended at last.

As the fighters are introduced, Dempsey makes a begrudged bow, but Carpentier, standing up, is given such an ovation as never before an alien fighter received on American soil. It is more plain by this test who is the sentimental favorite. The bettors may favor Jack; the populace likes Georges.

Without handshaking they spring together; Carpentier lands the first blow. Dempsey, plainly enraged, is fast; Carpentier is faster still. But his blows seem to be wild, misplaced, while Dempsey, in the clinches into which they promptly fall, plans punishing licks with swift, short-armed strokes. The first half minute tells me the story. The Frenchman is going to be licked, I think, and that without loss of time. A tremendous roar goes up as Dempsey brings the first blood with a glancing lick on the side of his opponent's nose; it increases as the Frenchman is shoved half through the ropes. The first round is Dempsey's all the way. He has flung Carpentier aside with thrusts of his shoulders. He has shoved him about almost at will.

But midway of the second round Carpentier shows a flash of the wonderful speed for which he is known. With the speed he couples an unsuspected power. He is not fighting the defensive run-away-and-come-again fight that was expected of him. He stands toe to toe with Dempsey and trades 'em. He shakes Dempsey with a volley of terrific right-handed clouts which fall with such speed you do not see them. You only see that they have landed and that Dempsey is bordering on the state technically known as groggy.

It is a wonderful recovery for the Frenchman. His admirers shriek to him to put Dempsey out. To my mind the second round is his by a good margin. Given more weight I am sure now that he would win. Yet I still feel sure Dempsey's superiority in gross tonnage and his greater aptitude at infighting will wear the lesser man down and make him lose.

The third round is Dempsey's from bell to bell. He makes pulp of one of Carpentier's smooth cheeks. He pounds him on the silken skin over his heart. He makes a xylophone of the challenger's short ribs. The Frenchman circles and swoops, but the drubbing he gets makes him uncertain in his swings. Most of his blows go astray. They fly over Dempsey's hunched shoulders—they spend themselves in the air.

In the fourth round, after one minute and sixteen seconds of hard fighting—fighting which on Carpentier's part is defensive—comes the foreordained and predestined finishment. I see a quick flashing of naked bodies writhing in and out, joining and separating. I hear the flop, flap, flop of leather bruising human flesh. Carpentier is almost spent—that much is plain to everyone. A great spasmodic sound—part gasp of anticipation, part groan of dismay, part outcry of exultation—rises from a hundred thousand throats. Carpentier totters out of a clinch; his face is all spotted with small red clots. He lunges into the air, then slips away, retreating before Dempsey's onslaught, trying to recover by footwork. Dempsey walks into him almost deliberately, like a man aiming to finish a hard job of work in workmanlike shape. His right arm crooks up and is like a scimitar. His right fist falls on the Frenchman's exposed swollen jaw; falls again in the same place even as Carpentier is sliding down alongside the ropes. Now the Frenchman is lying on his side.

Dempsey knows the contract is finished—or as good as finished. Almost nonchalantly he waits with his legs spraddled and his elbows akimbo, hearkening to the referee's counting. At the toll of eight Carpentier is struggling to his knees, beaten, but with the instinct of a gallant fighting man, refusing to acknowledge it. At nine he is up on the legs which almost refuse to support him. On his twisted face is the look of a sleepwalker.

It is the rule of the ring that not even a somnambulist may be spared the finishing stroke. Thumbs down means the killing blow, and the thumbs are all down now for the stranger.

For the hundredth part of a second—one of those flashes of time in which an event is photographed upon the memory to stay there forever, as though printed in indelible colors—I see the Frenchman staggering, slipping, sliding forward to his fate. His face is toward me and I am aware that on his face is no vestige of conscious intent. Then the image of him is blotted out by the intervening bulk of the winner. Dempsey's right arm swings upward with the flailing emphasis of an oak cudgel and the muffled fist at the end of it lands again on its favorite target—the Frenchman's jaw.

The thud of its landing can be heard above the hysterical shrieking of the host. The Frenchman seems to shrink in for a good six inches. It is as though that crushing impact had telescoped him. He folds up into a pitiable meager compass and goes down heavily and again lies on the floor, upon his right side, his face half covered by his arms as though even in the stupor following that deadly collision between his face and Dempsey's fist, he would protect his vulnerable parts. From where I sit writing this I can see one of his eyes and his mouth. The eye is blinking weakly, the mouth is gaping, and the lips work as though he chewed a most bitter mouthful. I do not think he is entirely unconscious; he is only utterly helpless. His legs kick out like the legs of a cramped swimmer. Once he lifts himself halfway to his haunches. But the effort is his last. He has flattened down again and still the referee has only progressed in his fateful sum of simple addition as far as "six."

My gaze shifts to Dempsey. He has moved over into Carpentier's corner and stands there, his arms extended on the ropes in a posture of resting. He has no doubt of the outcome. He scarcely shifts his position while the count goes on. I have never seen a prize fighter in the moment of triumph behave so. But his expression proves that he is merely waiting. His lips lift in a snarl until all his teeth show. Whether this be a token of contempt for the hostile majority in the crowd or merely his way of expressing to himself his satisfaction is not for me to say.

The picture lingers in my mind after the act itself is ended. Behind Dempsey is a dun background of gray clouds, swollen and gross with unspilt rain. The snowy white horizontals of the padded guard ropes cut across him at knee and hip and shoulder line; otherwise his figure stands out clear, a relaxed, knobby figure, with tons of unexpended energy still held in reserve within it. The referee is close at hand, tolling off the inexorable tally of the count—"seven, eight, nine" —but scarcely is one cognizant of the referee's presence, of his arithmetic either. I see only that gnarled form lolling against the ropes and, eight feet away, the slighter, crumpled shape of the beaten Frenchman, with its kicking legs and its sobbing mouth, from which a little stream of blood runs down upon the lolled chin.

In a hush which instantaneously descends and as instantaneously is ended, the referee swings his arm down like a semaphore and chants out "ten."

The rest is a muddle and mass of confusion— Dempsey stooping over Carpentier as though wishful to lift him to his feet; then Dempsey encircled by a dozen policemen who for some rea-son feel called upon to sourround him; two weeping French helpers dragging Carpentier to his corner and propping him upon a stool. Carpentier's long, slim legs dangling as they lift him, and his feet slithering in futile fashion upon the resined canvas; Dempsey swinging his arms aloft in tardy token of appreciation for the whoops and cheers which flow toward him; all sorts of folks crowding into the ring; Dempsey marching out, convoyed by an entourage of his admirers; Carpentier, deadly pale, and most bewildered-looking with a forlorn, mechanical smile plastered on his face, shaking hands with somebody or other; and then the ring is empty of all save Humphries the orator, who announces a concluding bout between Billy Miske and Jack Renault.

As I settle back now to watch with languid interest this anticlimax, three things stand out in my memory as the high points of the big fight, so far as I personally am concerned.

The first is that Carpentier never had a chance. In the one round which properly belonged to him he fought himself out. He trusted to his strength when his refuge should have been in his speed.

The second is that vision of him, doubled up on his side, like a frightened, hurt boy, and yet striving to heave himself up and take added punishment from a foe against whom he had no shadow of hope.

The third—and most outstanding—will be my recollection of that look on Dempsey's towering front when realization came to him that a majority of the tremendous audience were partisans of the foreigner.

# JIMMY HATLO

### THEY'LL DO IT EVERY TIME

ON THE NIGHT of June 22, 1938, when Max Schmeling entered the ring for the second time against Joe Louis, he was, by choice, a representative of the super race and thus an extension of Adolf Hitler. Louis was, by birth, a member of a race Hitler, if successful, would have enslaved or liquidated. Thus this meeting had a political importance never before or since associated with a prize fight, and Louis had his greatest night.

# The Second Louis–Schmeling Fight

## BOB CONSIDINE

LISTEN TO THIS, buddy, for it comes from a guy whose palms are still wet, whose throat is still dry, and whose jaw is still agape from the utter shock of watching Joe Louis knock out Max Schmeling.

It was a shocking thing, that knockout—short, sharp, merciless, complete. Louis was like this:

He was a big lean copper spring, tightened and retightened through weeks of training until he was one pregnant package of coiled venom.

Schmeling hit that spring. He hit it with a whistling right-hand punch in the first minute of the fight—and the spring, tormented with tension, suddenly burst with one brazen spang of activity. Hard brown arms, propelling two unerring fists, blurred beneath the hot white candelabra of the ring lights. And Schmeling was in the path of them, a man caught and mangled in the whirring claws of a mad and feverish machine.

The mob, biggest and most prosperous ever to see a fight in a ball yard, knew that here was the end before the thing had really started. It knew, so it stood up and howled one long shriek. People who had paid as much as one hundred dollars for their chairs didn't use them—except perhaps to stand on, the better to let the sight burn forever in their memories.

There were four steps to Schmeling's knock-out. A few seconds after he landed his only punch of the fight, Louis caught him with a lethal little left hook that drove him into the ropes so that his right arm was hooked over the

top strand, like a drunk hanging to a fence. Louis swarmed over him and hit him with everything he had—until Referee Donovan pushed him away and counted one.

Schmeling staggered away from the ropes, dazed and sick. He looked drunkenly toward his corner, and before he had turned his head back Louis was on him again, first with a left and then that awe-provoking right that made a crunching sound when it hit the German's jaw. Max fell down, hurt and giddy, for a count of three.

He clawed his way up as if the night air were as thick as black water, and Louis—his nostrils like the mouth of a double-barreled shotgun—took a quiet bead and let him have both barrels.

Max fell almost lightly, bereft of his senses, his fingers touching the canvas like a comical stewbum doing his morning exercises, knees bent and tongue lolling in his head.

He got up long enough to be knocked down again, this time with his dark unshaven face pushed in the sharp gravel of the resin.

Louis jumped away lightly, a bright and pleased look in his eyes, and as he did the white towel of surrender which Louis' handlers had refused to use two years ago tonight came sailing into the ring in a soggy mess. It was thrown by Max Machon, oblivious to the fact that fights cannot end this way in New York.

The referee snatched it off the floor and flung it backwards. It hit the ropes and hung there, limp as Schmeling. Donovan counted up to five over Max, sensed the futility of it all, and stopped the fight.

The big crowd began to rustle restlessly toward the exits, many only now accepting Louis as champion of the world. There were no eyes for Schmeling, sprawled on his stool in his corner.

He got up eventually, his dirty-gray-and-black robe over his shoulders, and wormed through the happy little crowd that hovered around Louis. And he put his arm around the Negro and smiled. They both smiled and could afford to— for Louis had made around $200,000 a minute

and Schmeling $100,000 a minute.

But once he crawled down in the belly of the big stadium, Schmeling realized the implications of his defeat. He, who won the title on a partly phony foul, and beat Louis two years ago with the aid of a crushing punch after the bell had sounded, now said Louis had fouled him. That would read better in Germany, whence earlier in the day had come a cable from Hitler, calling on him to win.

It was a low sneaking trick, but a rather typical last word from Schmeling.

THIS WAS THE FIRST heavyweight title fight with gloves (5-ounce) and under the Marquis of Queensberry Rules. Sullivan was 33 and weighed 212. Corbett was 26 and weighed 178. The purse was $25,000, plus a $20,000 stake, and Sullivan got nothing but a beating and the chance to make a speech in which he said he was glad that the title was remaining in America.

The New York *Times* report describes eleven punches landed by Sullivan. Corbett, as he had in the ring, ignores these in this story, but it remains the most lucid account any fighter has left of his crowning experience.

# Sullivan vs. Corbett

## JAMES J. CORBETT

I STARTED IN to do some light training in the Southern Athletic Club and all the time thousands of people were in and out watching me. There were also large audiences at the other club watching Sullivan, and after seeing both of us, the bettors decided that instead of three to one on Sullivan the odds should go up to four to one. This increase was due, I think, to our difference in weights.

If I had ever relied much on others' opinions I wouldn't have had much confidence or strength left for the fight. Even my old friend from California, Tom Williams, who had backed me heavily in the Choinyski fight, and had also seen me fight my sixty-one rounds with Peter Jackson, blew into New Orleans and bet, so someone was kind enough to tell me, five thousand dollars on Sullivan. Not because I was hurt at all, but simply because I liked Williams, I wrote him a letter the day before the fight. In it I said: "Tom, I understand you are betting on Sullivan. I'm not mad, but I wish you would switch your bet and put it on me. I'm in splendid condition. You saw me fight Choinyski and Jackson. You know I can go the distance; and no man who has lived the life that Sullivan has lived can beat me in a finish fight."

A few years later when I was going abroad, I happened to run into Tom Williams on the steamer. We were talking over old times and got down to this fight. "Do you remember the letter you wrote me," he said, "before your fight with Sullivan, telling me to bet on you?"

"Yes," I replied, and somehow managed not to grin.

"Well," continued Williams, "after I received your letter I went out and bet a thousand more on Sullivan!"

I had also written to my father and figured he would receive the letter a day or two before the fight—which he did. I told him in what good condition I was, and prophesied that by taking my time and being careful I would win the fight between the twentieth and the twenty-fifth round; and my dear old dad wore that letter out after the fight, just as he did the telegram after the Kilrain battle.

The excitement in New Orleans was intense from the start, as this was the first heavyweight championship fight ever arranged to be fought under the protection of the police. All other fights up to this time had been under London prize-ring rules and with bare knuckles, and, being against the law, had been pulled off in private.

Just before we left New York for New Orleans, I had told Brady to see how much money he could dig up to bet on me. He took all the money his wife had and what he could skirmish up himself, and it amounted to three thousand dollars. All I had in the world on the day of the fight was nine hundred dollars—we had used up so much for training expenses; but that morning I gave it to Brady and said, "You take this nine hundred and the three thousand you have, and go down and put it on me."

"Jim," he said, "I'll bet my three thousand, but you had better keep your money. If we should lose the fight, that's all we'd have, and we'll have to ride the brakes out of town."

So after thinking it over, I took his advice and kept my nine hundred, Brady going downtown to bet the three thousand—four to one.

In a couple of hours he came back, all excitement, and exclaimed: "They're betting five to one on Sullivan!"

"That's great!" I replied. "Did you put the money up?"

"No," he answered, looking a little sheepish. Then he added, "Don't you think, Jim, we'd better keep it in case you get licked?"

I got angry at this.

"You fool!" I blurted out. "You were willing to take four to one, but now when it's five to one you get cold feet. Sullivan and I are just the same as when it was three to one: we haven't changed any."

Then, pushing him out of the door, I gave him this parting message: "Don't you come back here unless that three thousand is on!"

I had noticed that the strain was beginning to tell on my trainers, and even Delaney. With all his coolness, he was trying to hum little songs to himself to make me feel he was happy and wasn't thinking about the fight at all. And others were whistling too loud and too often. All their actions, I could see, were so unnatural and unlike them. They were all doing it for the effect on me, and, if I do say it myself, I think I was the only one in the whole crowd that really felt normal.

To lead up to the climax, the club had arranged bouts between famous fighters to be fought on successive nights before the heavyweight battle—Monday night, George Dixon fought Jack Skelly for the featherweight championship of the world; on Tuesday, the wonderful lightweight, Jack McAuliffe, defended his lightweight title against Billy Meyers of Streator, Illinois; on Wednesday night, John L. Sullivan was to defend his title.

McAuliffe gave Meyers an awful beating on Tuesday night, and it suddenly occurred to me that it would be a grand idea to have the last meal before I fought Sullivan with poor Billy Meyers. This did not strike me as ominous, for I was never superstitious—in fact, often defied and flew in the face of superstition purposely. This annoyed my companions considerably sometimes, so now when I suggested that I go out with the loser, Billy Meyers, there was a terrible uproar. "Why, he's a 'Jonah'!" they said.

They begged and pleaded with me, but I insisted on going and dragged them all out there with me!

Meyers came down into the dining room and met us. I knew him very well and liked him very much. He had a big black eye and a cracked lip, and I started to "kid" him about these marks of his battle. "You may look worse than I do when Sullivan gets through with you tonight," he retorted.

"No, Billy," I replied. "Sullivan won't have to hit me as many times as McAuliffe did you, to lick me. If it's done, it will be done with one punch!"

So we talked and joked with each other, and finally, about nine o'clock, we started for the Olympic Club.

Now the following incident comes back to me as I write these words, thirty-three years afterwards.

As I was starting to put on a light summer suit, with a straw hat and a little bamboo cane to match, Delaney exclaimed, "You're not going to the fight that way, are you?"

"Certainly, Mr. Delaney," I replied, examining myself in the mirror, as if I thought I looked grand.

It was too much for him. He wanted me to go to the arena like the usual short-haired, big-sweatered type of pug with a scowl that would scare people, and here I looked like a dude that a good man could break in two. For a moment, he couldn't say anything; simply looked his disgust.

"What difference does it make how I'm dressed going up?" I continued, as I gave a little extra twist to my tie. "I don't expect to fight in these clothes."

The streets of the city were black with people, and as our carriage was working through, all I could hear from every side was the murmur: "Sullivan," "Sullivan," "Sullivan!" Not once did I hear the name of "Corbett"; it was all Sullivan in the air.

We reached the club and I stepped out. As I walked in at the door, right ahead of me hurried my old friend, Mose Guntz, from San Francisco, the one who gave Jack Dempsey a thousand dollars to second Choinyski. After that incident we had become great friends, and have been such ever since.

He turned around at my hail and started to speak cheerfully, but when he saw my getup, he looked kind of embarrassed and strange, and, although he didn't *say* anything about my trimmings, I knew what effect they had on him, also that it wouldn't be but a couple of minutes before someone would tell Sullivan that Corbett came to the club with a cane in his hand and a straw hat on, like a dude! I could picture the look on Sullivan's face when he heard this news.

When I reached my dressing room, one of the club managers came in and announced, "Sullivan wants to toss up for the corners."

"Let him take any corner he likes," I answered as I started to get ready. "He's going in the ring first anyway."

Word immediately came back that *I* was to go in the ring first. However, the question was settled by Brady's going down to Sullivan's dressing room and tossing a coin.

Now the only reason for my insisting that Sullivan enter ahead of me was the wonderful ovation I knew Sullivan would receive. Just then I felt quite calm, and I didn't want anything to excite me in any way, and it was possible his great reception might. But Brady had won the toss and finally it was announced that Sullivan was in the ring.

My seconds and I started down the aisle. The seats were banked circus fashion and only a few of the audience could see us, but I could see the ring and Sullivan was not in it. The managers had lied to me. So I stopped.

Now Sullivan thought I was in the ring, because I had started and enough time had elapsed for me to get there. As I stopped and turned back I met Sullivan, for the first time since I had boxed with him in San Francisco at my benefit. I looked him in the eye and said, "You're the champion and I'm the short end. You're going in that ring first, if we stand here all night!"

This enraged Sullivan, who was always aggressive in manner anyway. He gave a roar like a wounded lion, strode down the aisle and bounded into the ring. Never before or since have I heard an ovation equal to that given him as he came through the ropes.

I said a little prayer to myself: "I hope to God I am as cool in the ring as I am now," and then, as the cheers subsided, skipped into the ring, receiving the usual reception that any fellow would get from an audience, which meant about as much as, "Well, anyway he showed up!"

When I entered the ring I noticed that the floor was of turf instead of boards, on which I had always trained and fought. My shoes were of the solid sort used nowadays and I wondered how my feet would hold on turf. As soon as I entered the ring I started dancing around, and found that my feet would hold pretty well—in fact, much better than I had expected—so I was considerably relieved.

There was a reason, you see, for these jumping-jack antics that night, but I wish someone would tell me why present-day fighters do the same thing. They have been training on boards, and are fighting on boards, and using the same shoes and everything, so there is no reason for the practice unless to cover up nervousness. But it has been followed generally by fighters ever since that night. It is funny how customs and habits go down from generation to generation.

Meanwhile, Sullivan sat in his corner trying to catch my eye, his clenched fists on his knees, elbows out, and his head thrust forward in an ugly fashion. He had a wicked eye.

Now, as I had always done before, I was trying to convince him that he was the last person or thing in the world I was thinking about. I was bowing to people I didn't even see, smiling at entire strangers, waving my hand and talking to my seconds, laughing all the time.

Finally the referee, whose name was John Duffy, called us up to the center of the ring for our final instructions. We walked up, Sullivan with his arms still folded, looking right at my eyes—not in them, for I never met his stare—and rising and falling on his toes without a pause. I waited for the referee, my gaze on him, and you could have heard a pin drop in the place. You wouldn't think 10,000 people could be so quiet. At last the referee got down to "hitting in clinches."

"When I tell you to break," he told us, "I want you to drop your arms."

Immediately I grasped the referee by the shoulder—mind you, all for the effect on Sullivan—and sneered, "That's very well for you to say, 'Drop your arms when I say break!' But suppose this fellow"—even then I didn't look at Sullivan, just jerked my thumb at him—"takes a punch at *me* when *I* drop my arms?"

"If he does that, he'll lose the fight; and you'll lose, too, if you try it," Duffy answered.

"Then what about clinching like this?" I asked, and took hold of the referee and put my elbow up under his chin, pushing his head back, and repeated, "What if he does this?"

"That's a foul, of course," he answered. "The one that does it will be cautioned once. If he tries it a second time, he loses the fight."

"All right," I said, as gruffly as I could, "that's all I wanted to know."

Then, for the first time since entering the ring, I looked Sullivan square in the eye and very aggressively, too. He stopped his rising and falling on his toes and stood staring at me as if he were petrified, so surprised was he at this sudden change in my attitude, and I saw at once it had the effect I intended: I had him guessing!

In a very cocksure manner I jerked the towel from my shoulders, turned my back on him and ripped out, "Let her go!"

This piece of business had its effect not only on Sullivan, but also on the audience, for they cheered me louder then than they had when I entered the ring. They must have come to the conclusion, "Why, this fellow thinks he can whip Sullivan. We'll see a fight!"

"Time" was called, and the first round was on.

Now, I knew that the most dangerous thing I could do was to let Sullivan work me into a corner when I was a little tired or dazed, so I made up my mind that I would let him do this while I was still fresh. Then I could find out what he intended doing when he got me there. In a fight, you know, when a man has you where he wants you, he is going to deliver the best goods he has.

From the beginning of the round Sullivan was aggressive—wanted to eat me up right away. He came straight for me and I backed and backed, finally into a corner. While I was there I observed him setting himself for a right-hand swing, first slapping himself on the thigh with his left hand—sort of a trick to balance himself for a terrific swing with his right. But before he let the blow go, just at the right instant, I sidestepped out of the corner and was back in the middle of the ring again, Sullivan hot after me.

I allowed him to back me into all four corners, and he thought he was engineering all this, that it was his own work that he was cornering me. But I had learned what I wanted to know—just where to put my head to escape his blow if he should get me cornered and perhaps dazed. He had shown his hand to me.

In the second round he was still backing me around the ring. I hadn't even struck at him yet, and the audience on my right hissed me for running away and began to call me "Sprinter." Now I could see at a glance that Sullivan was not quite near enough to hit me, so suddenly I turned my side to him, waved both hands to the audience and called out, "Wait a while! You'll see a fight."

That made an awful "sucker" out of Sullivan, as the gallery birds say, and it was quite unex-pected. And since he didn't know that I knew he couldn't reach me when I pulled this stunt, he was the more chagrined. So he dashed right at me, angry as a bull, but immediately I was away again. At the end of the round I went to my corner and said to Brady and Delaney, "Why, I can whip this fellow slugging!"

At this there was a panic in my corner, all of them starting to whine and pleading with me.

"You said you were going to take your time," they said. "What are you going to take any chances for?"

"All right," I replied, to comfort them, "but I'll take one good punch at him this round, anyway."

So far Sullivan hadn't reached me with anything but glancing blows, and it was my intention, when the third round started, to hit him my first punch, and I felt that it *must* be a good one! If my first punch didn't hurt him, he was going to lose all respect for my hitting ability.

So, with my mind thoroughly made up, I allowed him to back me once more into a corner. But although this time I didn't intend to slip out, by my actions I indicated that I was going to, just as I had before. As we stood there, fiddling, he crowding almost on top of me, I glanced, as I had always done before, first to the left, then to the right, as if looking for some way to get out of this corner. He following my eye and thinking I wanted to make a getaway, determined that he wouldn't let me out this time!

For once he failed to slap himself on the thigh with his left hand, but he had his right hand all ready for the swing as he was gradually crawling up on me. Then, just as he finally set himself to let go a vicious right I beat him to it and loosed a left-hand for his face with all the power I had behind it. His head went back and I followed it with a couple of other punches and slugged him back over the ring and into his corner. When the round was over his nose was broken.

At once there was pandemonium in the audience! All over the house, men stood on their chairs, coats off, swinging them in the air. You could have heard the cheers clear to the Mississippi River!

But the uproar only made Sullivan the more determined. He came out of his corner in the fourth like a roaring lion, with an uglier scowl than ever, and bleeding considerably at the nose. I felt sure now that I would beat him, so made up my mind, though it would take a little longer, I would play safe.

From that time on I started doing things the audience were seeing for the first time, judging from the way they talked about the fight afterwards. I would work a left-hand on the nose, then a hook into the stomach, a hook up on the jaw again—a great variety of blows, in fact, using all the time such quick side-stepping and footwork that the audience seemed to be delighted and a little bewildered, as was also Mr. Sullivan. That is, bewildered, for I don't think he was delighted.

In the twelfth round we clinched, and with the referee's order, "Break away," I dropped my arms, when Sullivan let go a terrific right-hand swing from which I just barely got away; as it was it just grazed the top of my head. Some in the audience began to shout "Foul!" but I smiled and shook my head, to tell him, "I don't want it that way."

So the next eight rounds continued much in the fashion of toreador and the bull, Sullivan making his mad rushes and flailing away with his arms, rarely landing on me, but as determined as ever. Meanwhile I was using all the tricks in my boxing repertoire, which was an entirely new one for that day and an assortment that impressed the audience. Then I noticed that he was beginning to puff and was slowing down a little.

When we came up for the twenty-first round it looked as if the fight would last ten or fifteen rounds longer. Right away I went up to him, feinted with my left and hit him with a left-hand hook alongside the jaw pretty hard, and I saw his eyes roll. Quicker than it takes to tell it, I saw that I had then the same chance that I had had in the fight with Peter Jackson, but had failed to take—the same chance that was Firpo's when Dempsey stood helpless before him, and which he also failed to take.

This time I did not let it slip. Summoning all the reserve force I had left I let my guns go, right and left, with all the dynamite Nature had given me, and Sullivan stood dazed and rocking. So I set myself for an instant, put just a little more in a right and hit alongside the jaw. And he fell helpless on the ground, on his stomach, and rolled over on his back! The referee, his seconds, and mine picked him up and put him in his corner; and the audience went wild.

As Sullivan struck the floor, the few people who were for me jumped up and yelled, but the mass of that vast audience were still as death; just clenched their hands, hoping their champion would rise. When the last count ended and it was over beyond doubt, then came an uproar like Niagara tumbling over the cliffs, followed by the greatest shower you ever saw, of hats, coats, canes, belts, flowers from buttonholes, everything, falling on me and my seconds and all over the floor of the ring. I have often thought what a business I could have started down in Baxter Street with such an assorted stock!

So the roar of the crowd went on. I should have felt proud and dazed, but the only thing I could think of, right after the knockout, was Sullivan lying there on the floor. I was actually disgusted with the crowd, and it left a lasting impression on me. It struck me as sad to see all those thousands who had given him such a wonderful ovation when he entered the ring turning it to me now that he was down and out.

In justice to the man who had reigned so long as champion of the world, I think it is only fair to say that I was not fighting the Sullivan I had seen and admired in San Francisco at the Paddy Ryan bout, then twenty-six and in the pink of condition; but a man who had not been careful of his habits and who had enjoyed too much the good fellowship and popularity the championship brings.

I got him when he was slipping; and that goes for all the champions down the line.

"GALLEGHER," OFTEN CITED in bibliographies of boxing, is a newspaper story about a copyboy who masterminded the apprehension of a murderer and "beat the town." Davis used the scene of the fight as the locale of the collar, and left a good description of an illegal prize fight of the late 1890s.

FROM

# "Gallegher"

## RICHARD HARDING DAVIS

As I HAVE SAID, Gallegher lived in the most distant part of the city, not many minutes' walk from the Kensington railroad station, where trains ran into the suburbs and on to New York.

It was in front of this station that a smoothly shaven, well-dressed man brushed past Gallegher and hurried up the steps to the ticket office.

He held a walking-stick in his right hand, and Gallegher, who now patiently scrutinized the hands of everyone who wore gloves, saw that while three fingers of the man's hand were closed around the cane, the fourth stood out in almost a straight line with his palm.

Gallegher stopped with a gasp and with a trembling all over his little body, and his brain asked with a throb if it could be possible. But possibilities and probabilities were to be discovered later. Now was the time for action.

He was after the man in a moment, hanging at his heels and his eyes moist with excitement.

He heard the man ask for a ticket to Torresdale, a little station just outside of Philadelphia, and when he was out of hearing, but not out of sight, purchased one for the same place.

The stranger went into the smoking car, and seated himself at one end toward the door. Gallegher took his place at the opposite end.

He was trembling all over, and suffered from a slight feeling of nausea. He guessed it came from fright, not of any bodily harm that might come to him, but at the probability of failure in his adventure and of its most momentous possibilities.

The stranger pulled his coat collar up around his ears, hiding the lower portion of his face, but not concealing the resemblance in his troubled eyes and close-shut lips to the likenesses of the murderer Hade.

They reached Torresdale in half an hour, and the stranger, alighting quickly, struck off at a rapid pace down the country road leading to the station.

Gallegher gave him a hundred yards' start, and then followed slowly after. The road ran between fields and past a few frame houses set far from the road in kitchen gardens.

Once or twice the man looked back over his shoulder, but he saw only a dreary length of road with a small boy splashing through the slush in the midst of it and stopping every now and again to throw snowballs at belated sparrows.

After ten minutes' walk the stranger turned into a side road which led to only one place, the Eagle Inn, an old roadside hostelry known as the headquarters for pothunters from the Philadelphia game market and the battleground of many a cockfight.

Gallegher knew the place well. He and his young companions had often stopped there when out chestnuting on holidays in the autumn.

The son of the man who kept it had often accompanied them on their excursions, and though the boys of the city streets considered him a dumb lout, they respected him somewhat owing to his inside knowledge of dog and cockfights.

The stranger entered the inn at a side door, and Gallegher, reaching it a few minutes later, let him go for the time being, and set about finding his occasional playmate, young Keppler.

Keppler's offspring was found in the wood-shed.

" 'Tain't hard to guess what brings you out here," said the tavernkeeper's son, with a grin; "it's the fight."

"What fight?" asked Gallegher, unguardedly.

"What fight? Why, *the* fight," returned his companion, with the slow contempt of superior knowledge. "It's to come off here tonight. You knew that as well as me; anyway your sportin' editor knows it. He got the tip last night, but that won't help you any. You needn't think there's any chance of your getting a peep at it. Why, tickets is two hundred and fifty apiece!"

"Whew!" whistled Gallegher. "Where's it to be?"

"In the barn," whispered Keppler. "I helped 'em fix the ropes this morning, I did."

"Gosh, but you're in luck," exclaimed Gallegher, with flattering envy. "Couldn't I jest get a peep at it?"

"Maybe," said the gratified Keppler. "There's a winder with a wooden shutter at the back of the barn. You can get in by it, if you have someone to boost you up to the sill."

"Sa-a-ay," drawled Gallegher, as if something had but just that moment reminded him. "Who's that gent who come down the road just a bit ahead of me—him with the cape-coat! Has he got anything to do with the fight?"

"Him?" repeated Keppler in tones of sincere disgust. "No-oh, he ain't no sport. He's queer, Dad thinks. He come here one day last week about ten in the morning, said his doctor told him to go out in the country for his health. He's stuck-up and citified, and wears gloves, and takes his meals private in his room, and all that sort of ruck. They was saying in the saloon last night that they thought he was hiding from something, and Dad, just to try him, asks him last night if he was coming to see the fight. He looked sort of scared, and said he didn't want to see no fight. And then Dad says, 'I guess you mean you don't want no fighters to see you.' Dad didn't mean no harm by it, just passed it as a joke; but Mr. Carleton, as he calls himself, got white as a ghost an' says, 'I'll go to the fight willing enough,' and begins to laugh and joke. And this morning he went right into the barroom, where all the sports were setting, and said he was going into town to see some friends; and as he starts off he laughs an' says, 'This don't look as if I was afraid of seeing people, does it?' but

Dad says it was just a bluff that made him do it, and Dad thinks that if he hadn't said what he did, this Mr. Carleton wouldn't have left his room at all."

Gallegher had got all he wanted, and much more than he had hoped for—so much more that his walk back to the station was in the nature of a triumphal march. . . .

An hour passed, and the cab was still moving more slowly over the rough surface of partly paved streets, and by single rows of new houses standing at different angles to each other in fields covered with ash-heaps and brick kilns. Here and there the gaudy lights of a drugstore, and the forerunner of suburban civilization, shone from the end of a new block of houses, and the rubber cape of an occasional policeman showed in the light of the lamppost that he hugged for comfort.

Then even the houses disappeared, and the cab dragged its way between truck farms, with desolate-looking glass-covered beds, and pools of water, half-caked with ice, and bare trees, and interminable fences.

Once or twice the cab stopped altogether, and Gallegher could hear the driver swearing to himself, or at the horse, or the roads. At last they drew up before the station at Torresdale. It was quite deserted, and only a single light cut a swath in the darkness and showed a portion of the platform, the ties, and the rails glistening in the rain. They walked twice past the light before a figure stepped out of the shadow and greeted them cautiously.

"I am Mr. Dwyer, of the *Press*," said the sporting editor, briskly. "You've heard of me, perhaps. Well, there shouldn't be any difficulty in our making a deal, should there? This boy here has found Hade, and we have reason to believe he will be among the spectators at the fight tonight. We want you to arrest him quietly, and as secretly as possible. You can do it with your papers and your badge easily enough. We want you to pretend that you believe he is the burglar you came over after. If you will do this, and take him away without anyone so much as suspecting who he really is, and on the train that passes here at 1:20 for New York, we will give you five hundred dollars out of the five-thousand-dollar reward. If, however, one other paper, either in New York or Philadelphia, or anywhere else, knows of the arrest, you won't get a cent. Now, what do you say?"

The detective had a great deal to say. He wasn't at all sure the man Gallegher suspected was Hade; he feared he might get himself in trouble by making a false arrest, and if it should

91

be the man, he was afraid the local police would interfere.

"We've no time to argue or debate this matter," said Dwyer, warmly. "We agree to point Hade out to you in the crowd. After the fight is over you arrest him as we have directed, and you get the money and the credit of the arrest. If you don't like this, I will arrest the man myself, and have him driven to town, with a pistol for a warrant."

Hefflefinger considered in silence and then agreed unconditionally. "As you say, Mr. Dwyer," he returned. "I've heard of you for a thoroughbred sport. I know you'll do what you say you'll do; and as for me I'll do what you say and just as you say, and it's a very pretty piece of work as it stands."

They all stepped back into the cab, and then it was that they were met by a fresh difficulty, how to get the detective into the barn where the fight was to take place, for neither of the two men had $250 to pay for his admittance.

But this was overcome when Gallegher remembered the window of which young Keppler had told him.

In the event of Hade's losing courage and not daring to show himself in the crowd around the ring, it was agreed that Dwyer should come to the bar and warn Hefflefinger; but if he should come, Dwyer was merely to keep near him and to signify by a prearranged gesture which one of the crowd he was.

They drew up before a great black shadow of a house, dark, forbidding, and apparently deserted. But at the sound of the wheels on the gravel the door opened, letting out a stream of warm, cheerful light, and a man's voice said, "Put out those lights. Don't you'se know no better than that?" This was Keppler, and he welcomed Mr. Dwyer with effusive courtesy.

The two men showed in the stream of light, and the door closed on them, leaving the house as it was at first, black and silent, save for the dripping of the rain and snow from the eaves.

The detective and Gallegher put out the cab's lamps and led the horse toward a long, low shed in the rear of the yard, which they now noticed was almost filled with teams of many different makes, from the Hobson's choice of a livery stable to the brougham of the man about town.

"No," said Gallegher, as the cabman stopped to hitch the horse beside the others, "we want it nearest that lower gate. When we newspapermen leave this place we'll leave it in a hurry, and the man who is nearest town is likely to get there first. You won't be a-following of no hearse when you make your return trip."

Gallegher tied the horse to the very gatepost itself, leaving the gate open and allowing a clear road and a flying start for the prospective race to Newspaper Row.

The driver disappeared under the shelter of the porch, and Gallegher and the detective moved off cautiously to the rear of the barn. "This must be the window," said Hefflefinger, pointing to a broad wooden shutter some feet from the ground.

"Just you give me a boost once, and I'll get that open in a jiffy," said Gallegher.

The detective placed his hands on his knees, and Gallegher stood upon his shoulders, and with the blade of his knife lifted the wooden button that fastened the window on the inside, and pulled the shutter open.

Then he put one leg inside over the sill, and leaning down helped to draw his fellow conspirator up to a level with the window. "I feel just like I was burglarizing a house," chuckled Gallegher, as he dropped noiselessly to the floor below and refastened the shutter. The barn was a large one, with a row of stalls on either side in which horses and cows were dozing. There was a haymow over each row of stalls, and at one end of the barn a number of fence rails had been thrown across from one mow to the other. These rails were covered with hay.

In the middle of the floor was the ring. It was not really a ring, but a square, with wooden posts at its four corners through which ran a heavy rope. The space inclosed by the rope was covered with sawdust.

Gallegher could not resist stepping into the ring, and after stamping the sawdust once or twice, as if to assure himself that he was really there, began dancing around it, and indulging in such a remarkable series of fistic maneuvers with an imaginary adversary that the unimaginative detective precipitately backed into a corner of the barn.

"Now, then," said Gallegher, having apparently vanquished his foe, "you come with me." His companion followed quickly as Gallegher climbed to one of the haymows, and crawling carefully out on the fence rail, stretched himself at full length, face downward. In this position, by moving the straw a little, he could look down, without being himself seen, upon the heads of whomsoever stood below. "This is better'n a private box, ain't it?" said Gallegher.

The boy from the newspaper office and the detective lay there in silence, biting at straws and tossing anxiously on their comfortable bed.

It seemed fully two hours before they came. Gallegher had listened without breathing, and with every muscle on a strain, at least a dozen times, when some movement in the yard had led him to believe that they were at the door.

And he had numerous doubts and fears. Sometimes it was that the police had learnt of the fight, and had raided Keppler's in his absence, and again it was that the fight had been postponed, or, worst of all, that it would be put off until so late that Mr. Dwyer could not get back in time for the last edition of the paper. Their coming, when at last they came, was heralded by an advance guard of two sporting men, who stationed themselves at either side of the big door.

"Hurry up, now, gents," one of the men said with a shiver, "don't keep this door open no longer'n is needful."

It was not a very large crowd, but it was wonderfully well selected. It ran, in the majority of its component parts, to heavy white coats with pearl buttons. The white coats were shouldered by long blue coats with astrakhan fur trimmings, the wearers of which preserved a cliqueness not remarkable when one considers that they believed every one else present to be either a crook or a prize fighter.

There were well-fed, well-groomed clubmen and brokers in the crowd, a politician or two, a popular comedian with his manager, amateur boxers from the athletic clubs, and quiet, close-mouthed sporting men from every city in the country. Their names if printed in the papers would have been as familiar as the types of the papers themselves.

And among these men, whose only thought was of the brutal sport to come, was Hade, with Dwyer standing at ease at his shoulder—Hade, white, and visibly in deep anxiety, hiding his pale face beneath a cloth traveling cap, and with his chin muffled in a woolen scarf. He had dared to come because he feared his danger from the already suspicious Keppler was less than if he stayed way. And so he was there, hovering restlessly on the border of the crowd, feeling his danger and sick with fear.

When Hefflefinger first saw him he started up on his hands and elbows and made a movement forward as if he would leap down then and there and carry off his prisoner single-handed.

"Lie down," growled Gallegher; "an officer of any sort woudn't live three minutes in that crowd."

The detective drew back slowly and buried himself again in the straw, but never once through the long fight which followed did his eyes leave the person of the murderer. The newspapermen took their places in the foremost row close around the ring, and kept looking at their watches and begging the master of ceremonies to "shake it up, do."

There was a great deal of betting, and all of the men handled the great roll of bills they wagered with a flippant recklessness which could only be accounted for in Gallegher's mind by temporary mental derangement. Someone pulled a box out into the ring and the master of ceremonies mounted it, and pointed out in forcible language that as they were almost all already under bonds to keep the peace, it behooved all to curb their excitement and to maintain a severe silence, unless they wanted to bring the police upon them and have themselves "sent down" for a year or two.

Then two very disreputable-looking persons tossed their respective principals' high hats into the ring, and the crowd, recognizing in this relic of the days when brave knights threw down their gauntlets in the lists as only a sign that the fight was about to begin, cheered tumultuously.

This was followed by a sudden surging forward, and a mutter of admiration much more flattering than the cheers had been, when the principals followed their hats, and slipping out of their greatcoats, stood forth in all the physical beauty of the perfect brute.

Their pink skin was as soft and healthy-looking as a baby's, and glowed in the lights of the lanterns like tinted ivory, and underneath this silken covering the great biceps and muscles moved in and out and looked like the coils of a snake around the branch of a tree.

Gentleman and blackguard shouldered each other for a nearer view; the coachmen, whose metal buttons were unpleasantly suggestive of police, put their hands, in the excitement of the moment, on the shoulders of their masters; the perspiration stood out in great drops on the foreheads of the backers, and the newspapermen bit somewhat nervously at the ends of their pencils.

And in the stalls the cows munched contentedly at their cuds and gazed with gentle curiosity at their two fellow brutes, who stood waiting the signal to fall upon, and kill each other if need be, for the delectation of their brothers.

"Take your places," commanded the master of ceremonies.

In the moment in which the two men faced each other the crowd became so still that, save for the beating of the rain upon the shingled roof and the stamping of a horse in one of the stalls, the place was as silent as a church.

"Time!" shouted the master of ceremonies.

The two men sprang into a posture of defense, which was lost as quickly as it was taken, one great arm shot out like a piston rod; there was the sound of bare fists beating on naked flesh; there was an exultant indrawn gasp of savage pleasure and relief from the crowd, and the great fight had begun.

How the fortunes of war rose and fell, and changed and rechanged that night, is an old story to those who listen to such stories; and those who do not will be glad to be spared the telling of it. It was, they say, one of the bitterest fights between two men that this country has ever known.

But all that is of interest here is that after an hour of this desperate brutal business the champion ceased to be the favorite; the man whom he had taunted and bullied, and for whom the public had but little sympathy, was proving himself a likely winner, and under his cruel blows, as sharp and clean as those from a cutlass, his opponent was rapidly giving way.

The men about the ropes were past all control now; they drowned Keppler's petitions for silence with oaths and inarticulate shouts of anger, as if the blows had fallen upon them, and in mad rejoicings. They swept from one end of the ring to the other, with every muscle leaping in unison with those of the man they favored, and when a New York correspondent muttered over his shoulder that this would be the biggest sporting surprise since the Heenan–Sayers fight, Mr. Dwyer nodded his head sympathetically in assent.

In the excitement and tumult it is doubtful if any heard the three quickly repeated blows that fell heavily from the outside upon the big doors of the barn. If they did, it was already too late to mend matters, for the door fell, torn from its hinges, and as it fell a captain of police sprang into the light from out of the storm, with his lieutenants and their men crowding close at his shoulder.

In the panic and stampede that followed, several of the men stood as helplessly immovable as though they had seen a ghost; others made a mad rush into the arms of the officers and were beaten back against the ropes of the ring; others dived headlong into the stalls, among the horses and cattle, and still others shoved the rolls of money they held into the hands of the police and begged like children to be allowed to escape.

The instant the door fell and the raid was declared Hefflefinger slipped over the cross rails on which he had been lying, hung for an instant by his hands, and then dropped into the center of the fighting mob on the floor. He was out of it in an instant with the agility of a pickpocket, was across the room and at Hade's throat like a dog. The murderer, for the moment, was the calmer man of the two.

ROBERT PROMETHEUS FITZSIMMONS was born in Cornwall, England, and reared in New Zealand, although he is usually referred to as an Australian. He won the middleweight title from the Nonpareil Jack Dempsey in 1890, the heavyweight championship from Jim Corbett at Carson City, Nevada, in 1897, and in 1903, at the age of forty-one, took the light-heavyweight crown from George Gardner. He finally retired in 1914 at the age of fifty-two, and died three years later of pneumonia.

In the Corbett fight Fitzsimmons introduced the champion to the left hook to the body, and Bob Davis, hearing two San Francisco doctors talking about it, introduced the "solar plexus punch" to the lexicon of boxing.

# Corbett–Fitzsimmons

## ROBERT H. DAVIS

IN PREPARING Fitzsimmons for his fight with Corbett, Dan Hickey, Ernest Roeber, and Jack Stelzner had laid out a careful course of boxing and wrestling with plenty of road running and lots of sleep. Our cuisine was in the hands of a Chinaman, whose idea of high-class cooking was a platter of pork chops with every meal.

About the first of March Bob's wife, with her two sons, Robert and Martin, accompanied by a maid, came to the camp and took entire charge of his diet, much of which she prepared with her own hands. He had an obsession for calf's foot jelly, which he consumed by the pound. Half a chicken, two vegetables, and a rice or custard pudding was an average meal for him. For breakfast he ran to eggs, toast and coffee, ham and eggs, bacon and eggs, and lamb chops. I was a close second at the table.

He was always overweighted with clothing, believing that a continuous mild warmth was preferable to one single chill. He slept under thin blankets and never moved until he rolled out in the morning.

His road work was the most systematic part of his program. Ten, twelve or fifteen miles a day were nothing for him. Roeber, who weighed close to two hundred pounds, did not care much about those jogging exercises, but Hickey and Stelzner followed him valiantly. . . .

The most interesting episode that occurred on the highway was when Corbett and his retinue came over into the bailiwick of Fitzsimmons. The two men met about a mile from the Fitzsimmons camp.

Fitz sighted the Corbett party coming down the penitentiary road, which leads to the state prison and also to the Cook ranch. Billy Delaney, Charley White, Jim Jeffries, and a boxer named McCarthy were with Corbett. The late Bill Naughton, sporting editor of the San Francisco *Examiner,* ambled along in the rear in a two-wheeled cart, waiting to see what he could see. I always thought that Bill negotiated that little meeting by inducing Corbett to go out of his own jurisdiction into the enemy's country.

Fitzsimmons was accompanied by Dan Hickey and the great Dane, Yarum. When the two groups drew together Bob and Hickey walked up and shook hands with Delaney, Charley White, Jeffries, and McCarthy. The next man in the procession was Corbett. Fitz strode forward and offered his palm. Corbett made a gesture as though to accept and then suddenly changed his mind.

"I'll shake hands with you over there," he said, waving his arm in the direction of the nearly completed arena visible across the fields.

Fitz seemed quite embarrassed and flushed.

"I'll shake after I've licked you," continued Corbett, as though to add a period to his statement.

"Then we'll never shake!" replied Fitz.

"You don't think you can lick me?" asked Corbett.

Fitz released a guttural laugh.

"What am I up 'ere training for?"

"I'll see you next Wednesday over there, and you had better bring your dog," retorted Corbett.

"I don't need the dog. You needn't wait until Wednesday," bristled the Australian, preparing to shed a light coat he was wearing. "I can lick you right 'ere and now!"

Bill Delaney took immediate charge of the situation, mumbling something about the absurdity of two gentlemen acting up on the public highway, thus averting what might have been an utterly profitless affair without motion pictures or gate receipts.

I knew nothing about this meeting until Hickey came running into my quarters, breathless and full of glee.

"Fitz just licked Corbett!"

"What do you mean?"

"Exactly what I say! They met on the road above the prison and had some words."

He then described the meeting in full.

"Thought you said he licked him?"

Dan Hickey is a first-class Irish gentleman and believes in banshees, leprechauns and fairies.

"That's the idea," he said hurriedly. "The minute Bob started to take off his coat Corbett knew that Bob wasn't afraid of him. From that moment defeat set on Corbett's shoulders. He will go into the ring a whipped man. He hasn't got a chance! Delaney, Jeffries and Charley White know he is licked, and so far as I'm concerned, the fight's won."

The fire and conviction with which Dan Hickey emitted this observation quite convinced me that there was nothing left except the referee counting "Ten!" over the prostrate Californian. It had quite the opposite effect on Fitz. For several days he brooded over the fact that Corbett had refused what Bob had intended to be a cordial salutation. By nature Fitzsimmons was a more or less sentimental, even-tempered man, slow to anger and swift to forgiveness. Rancor, hatred and enmity had no part in his composition. I have heard him repeatedly say that he never fought a fight in his life but that he always felt sorry when he saw his adversary fall.

In the meeting with the original Jack Dempsey at New Orleans, when the Nonpareil was staggering around that dirt arena helpless and facing defeat, Fitzsimmons begged him to quit.

"The champion never quits," retorted Dempsey, puffing a crimson spray from his bloody lips. "You've got to knock me out."

Fitzsimmons considered it an act of mercy to drop this incomparable man and terminate his agony. Dempsey fell face forward with his shattered mouth in the mud.

"To my dying day," said Fitzsimmons, describing this fight, "I will see Dempsey lying there with the little red bubbles busting as 'e breathed heavily into the red earth. I picked 'im up and helped carry 'im to his corner. I never lifted a braver man to 'is feet." . . .

March 17, 1897—One of those perfect mountain mornings, the atmosphere like crystal, not a cloud in the deep-blue sky. Mrs. Fitzsimmons cooked Bob's breakfast: half a chicken, two slices of toast, one cup of coffee, and a compote of stewed fruit. Bob did a little shadow boxing in the gymnasium and was subjected by Hickey to a thorough rubdown, after which he was wrapped in blankets and remained quiet until eleven o'clock, when we left for the arena in which had gathered about seven thousand customers.

Just before departing we weighed Bob, stripped, on a steelyard, than which there is no more accurate weighing device in the world. He tipped the scale at exactly one hundred and fifty-six and a half pounds.

"I'm still a middleweight. Now let's see wot 'appens," was his only observation.

The dressing room had been built in under the reserved seats and was extremely cold. Fitzsimmons disrobed and was reblanketed so completely that nothing was visible except a lock of his light hair, his eyes, and his nostrils. He remained perfectly quiet and said very little.

Dan Steward, the promoter of the fight, came in and asked one question: "Are you all right?"

"Never better," replied Fitz. . . .

George Siler, the referee, called the principals to the center of the ring and delivered the customary preliminary instructions, after which both men returned to their corners.

The gong sounded. Corbett stepped out of his corner and walked toward Fitzsimmons with his hand extended. Fitz, still smarting under the indignity that had occurred on the highway, declined the hand of his foe. No one at the ringside, not even his wife, had an inkling of Bob's intention. Corbett flushed as Fitzsimmons had flushed a few days before on the open road; but there is a vast difference between embarrassment in the presence of a baker's dozen and before ten thousand fight fans.

For an instant a profound stillness settled over the arena. Both men, in the pink of condition, stood like a pair of stone images, Corbett with his high guard, buoyant in posture, apparently poised on the balls of his feet; Fitzsimmons with his left foot far in advance of his right, apparently standing flat, his massive battering rams swinging from his shoulders.

Action! Lead! Block! Counter! Cross in and out! Blow for blow! Caution! Craft! Each coaxed the other to lead, to come forward, to start a right or a left.

The lithe Californian moved like a shadow. At times the Australian appeared to be like the bronze blacksmith who used to strike the chimes on the New York *Herald* clock, moving only at the hips, waiting to release a sledge hammer at his adversary. A cautious pair.

The gong sounded at the end of the first round. I climbed up behind Fitz and showered him with queries, which he answered by nodding or shaking his head.

Second round. Third round. Fourth round. All pretty much alike. Numerous blows were struck, none of particular consequence. It was plain that Corbett was the better boxer.

At the end of the fourth round, as Fitzsimmons took his seat, he blurted into my right ear: "Ask any questions you want. I'll talk to you. I'm not winded. 'E can't knock me out. I haven't felt a single punch. If 'e will only lead."

Well, from that moment until the end of the fight Fitz and I carried on a running conversation after each round, discussing his condition, his hopes, and his irritation at delay. He chafed at Corbett's activity. He seemed to have one idea, one desire: to get close enough to plant that invincible left.

The morning of the fight S. S. Chamberlain, managing editor of the New York *Journal,* sent me this telegram: PLEASE WIRE YOUR GUESS AS TO RESULT. S. S. CHAMBERLAIN.

Having had no experience with the prize ring, I handed the telegram to Fitz. After a moment of reflection he said, "Tell him I'll win in seven rounds."

"Which hand?"

"Left hand."

"Chin or body?"

"I'll 'it 'im somewhere in the body. It ain't so easy to 'it 'is chin."

I went to my typewriter, thought the matter over for a while, and decided that the seven rounds idea was a bad lay. Being mildly superstitious and believing in the number seven, I decided finally to double Fitzsimmons' guess; to take seven for each of us and let him have his own way with the left hand. I wired: MY GUESS IS FOURTEEN ROUNDS. LEFT-HAND BODY BLOW. FITZSIMMONS WINS. R. H. DAVIS.

The whole transaction was the wild guess of an untutored individual posing as an expert. It was passed around the office and met with wild guffaws. Furthermore, it was chalked on the bulletin board in front of the *Journal* office, where it remained for about half an hour, and was finally erased.

Due to the high, dry atmosphere of the mountains, four thousand feet above sea level, a crack had developed in Fitzsimmons' thick lower lip and widened by Hickey in training bouts. It would not heal. During the fourth and fifth rounds Corbett reached this tender spot with repeated left jabs. At the beginning of the sixth round it began to bleed. A thin stream of blood ran down to Bob's chin, where it began to smear.

Corbett mistook this red badge for something important and stepped in with considerable vigor. He planted a left on Bob's cheekbone. Bob slipped it off with a slight turn to the right. Both men then mixed it and as Bob came out of the clinch he slipped. Corbett was setting himself for a right wallop, but Fitzsimmons, slightly off his balance, seized Corbett around the legs and slid down his body to the floor.

Not a blow was struck during that entire performance. It was merely a question of one man off his balance reaching the floor through a little play of tactical dexterity. The moment his right knee touched he let go of Corbett and Siler began to count. Corbett stepped back with an air of confidence. At the count of nine Fitzsimmons, whose mouth and chin were pretty well covered with blood, got up, backed away, and set himself. Corbett showed no inclination to mix it the rest of that round. He must have known that it was no blow of his that floored his opponent.

There was so little concern in the Fitzsimmons corner between the sixth and seventh rounds that we joked about the prophecy.

"Here comes the seventh, Bob," I said. "What are you going to do?"

"I can't get at 'im. 'E's fast. Wait."

One swipe of a sponge cleared the blood from the lip and chin, upon which there was not the slightest abrasion.

It is a curious commentary upon reportorial accuracy that the eighth, ninth and tenth rounds as described in the American newspapers prove that the human equation plays an important role when even the manly art is under discussion. A review of the files of twenty metropolitan journals will convince the reader that after all the hand is quicker than the eye. There were blows described, shifts analyzed, blocks, feints, etc., carefully pointed out, but somehow or other they seemed to have escaped the cinematograph.

Both men were singularly cautious from the very beginning, and to my unpracticed eye it seemed either man's fight up to the beginning of the thirteenth round, during the latter half of which Fitzsimmons began to land his blows on Corbett's face. During the mix-up Fitzsimmons shot a short right across his own left guard. One of Corbett's gold teeth fell out, smote the canvas and ricocheted among the boxholders.

In this round Bob circled Jim four or five times, seeking a chance to plant his left. On one occasion, when Fitzsimmons stopped with his back to the north, he made a gesture as though to shade his eyes from the blazing sun that was riding a blue sky in the southern quarter.

"Keep out of the sun, Bob," shouted Mrs. Fitzsimmons, waving her hand at her husband. That was the only audible remark uttered by Mrs. Fitzsimmons during the entire fight. She spoke casually to Senator John Ingalls and myself four or five times, generally in monosyllables and always with commendable reserve.

Just before the close of the thirteenth round Fitzsimmons worked close to Corbett and began to plant body blows. The San Franciscan for the first time seemed to be in actual distress, whereas Fitzsimmons was gaining confidence and moving with pantherlike alacrity. When the round ended both men were in the middle of the ring. Fitz took his corner with one bound.

Before I had an opportunity to ask him a question, he placed his left glove against his right cheek, leaned down close to the post where I was standing and said deliberately, "'Ave you got any money on you?"

"Eighty dollars in gold."

"Bet it all on the next round. I am going to knock 'im out."

I jumped down, turned to Fred Bushnell, official photographer for both camps, handed him my own eighty dollars and imparted the thrilling information with instructions to put it all up as fast as he could and in as many directions. There was so much interest centering on the ring at that moment that the little transaction between Bushnell and myself attracted no attention. It was easy for him to place it at odds of two, three, and five to one.

The gong! Fourteenth round. Corbett led and was blocked. He followed with a left at Fitzsimmons' head. Fitzsimmons swung on Corbett's neck and Jim gave ground. Bob stabbed him with a left and a right. Corbett became wild and missed with both hands.

The most accurate description of this fourteenth round came from the lips of Fitzsimmons in the form of dictation. I quote it herewith as follows:

"When the opportunity came in the beginning of the fourteenth round Corbett was fighting a little wild, and made a swing which I sidestepped. In a flash I saw a clean opening on his stomach and came in with the left-hand shift on his wind, and then, without changing position of my feet, shot the same hand against his jaw, thus giving him the identical finish which I administered to Sharkey in San Francisco. I was sure I had done the trick, and although he made a hard struggle to get back on his feet, he was counted out by the referee and lost the championship."

Mr. James W. Coffroth, at that time a young man and a very efficient typist and stenographer, now a boxing and racing promoter of international fame, volunteered to take my dictation after the fight. When I reached the fourteenth round Fitzsimmons insisted upon describing it in his own words, as above.

Threescore and ten correspondents of the ringside have packed that round with the description of the one great punch: *the left shift to the pit of the stomach.* Corbett appeared to be standing still, but such was the speed and violence of the blow that Fitzsimmons' left arm seemed to disappear into Corbett's midst almost to the elbow.

A groan came from Jim's open mouth. He strained as though stricken with lockjaw, the whole upper body retching in apparent effort to reassemble the bodily functions and start to live again.

The late Dr. John W. Girdner, upon reading the dispatches describing the blow, announced that Corbett had been struck in the "solar plexus." This was the birthday of a new blow felt 'round the world.

As soon as Siler counted Corbett out and tapped Fitzsimmons as victor, pandemonium broke loose at the ringside. Instantly the squared circle was filled with seconds, backers, trainers, advisers, officers of the law, and souvenir seekers. Fitzsimmons stepped back to his corner, leaned down over the ropes and kissed his wife thrice full upon the mouth, leaving a little group of red stains upon her trembling lips.

Senator John Ingalls of Kansas, stunned to silence, rose from his seat, inserted his right hand between the folds of his frock coat and surveyed the battleground in the manner of Daniel Webster confronting the Senate just before his reply to Hayne. Above the melee rose the voice of William A. Brady inveighing against something the nature of which nobody could quite understand. Corbett was assisted to his feet, dazed and helpless. All powers of resistance had left him. Presently, however, he recovered with great effort and demanded the privilege of confronting his conqueror.

The confusion was so great that in order to prevent myself from being separated from Fitzsimmons I grabbed a towel hanging on the ropes and tied my right arm to Bob's left, requesting Jack Stelzner to make a double knot as a guarantee of permanency. He made a good job of it and almost stopped the circulation of my blood.

This Siamese twin of press and pugilism was surrounded by twenty people, most of whom had no right in the ring. Suddenly the group separated and Corbett appeared on Fitzsimmons' right.

"You've got to fight me again!" he shouted. "I'm entitled to another chance!"

Fitzsimmons then offered his hand, which Corbett accepted without for one second stemming his clamor for a return match.

"I am through with the ring," said Fitz.

"If you don't fight me," said Jim, "I'll lick you every time I meet you in the street!"

Fitzsimmons replied very earnestly, "If you ever lay a hand on me outside the prize ring, I'll kill you."

PROFESSOR MIKE DONOVAN (1847–1918) was the third of the middle-weight champions, and the first to earn wide acclaim. In thirty-four fights, five of them bare-knuckle, he lost only twice, both times on fouls. He fought at between 145 and 150 pounds, knocked out men who outweighed him by forty-five pounds and twice held his own with John L. Sullivan, who had forty pounds on him.

In 1884 Donovan beat Walter Watson (180 pounds) for a purse and the position of boxing instructor at the New York Athletic Club. Four years later, at the age of forty-one, he came out of retirement to box a six-round draw with Jack Dempsey, "The Nonpareil," then middleweight champion. His son, Arthur Donovan, was for many years instructor at the N.Y.A.C. and refereed more heavyweight title fights—fourteen—than any other man. The Professor's views on training, written in 1893, are included here as those of the most respected teacher and trainer of his time and as a record of the methods of that time.

# How to Train for a Fight

## PROFESSOR MICHAEL J. DONOVAN

METHODS MUST DIFFER according to the habits and constitutions of the men to be trained.

The man who inclines to make flesh must work harder, wear heavier clothes, and undergo a more restricted diet than a man whose habit is the opposite.

Before beginning real work, say about three days, every man should take mild doses of physic to act on the bowels, liver and kidneys, to get the whole system purged from impurities and ready for sustained active work.

The best clothes to work in are fine lamb's wool underclothes; they absorb the perspiration and tend to keep the body free from irritation. The outer garments, sweaters, coats and pants, should fit comfortably, and must be varied according to the season of the year and the amount of flesh to be taken off.

When at work, seven o'clock is a good hour to rise; the trainer should give his man an alcohol bath, followed by vigorous hand-rubbing, to get the blood in good circulation.

Dress leisurely, but before beginning exercise take the yolk of an egg in a glass of sherry, with a cracker or slice of toast. Should you find that the sherry makes you feverish, take, instead, a small glass of cold water with the egg.

Walk, at an easy pace, a mile to a mile and a half, frequently expanding the chest by breathing through the nose to fill your lungs with the pure morning air; this will increase their capacity and give you a good appetite for breakfast. Nothing can equal fresh and pure air as an appetizer.

For breakfast, eat "H-O" oatmeal with milk, broiled lamb chops, one or two poached eggs, with moderately stale bread or toast with a little butter, according to fancy; drink tea, not too strong, with a small amount of sugar. The meat can be varied by eating a broiled steak instead of the chops. After breakfast dress to suit the conditions of the weather; walk briskly, between six and seven miles, genuine heel and toe (this style develops the muscles of the legs more thoroughly than the ordinary easygoing gait). Should this style of walking fail to promote perspiration rapidly enough, vary it by an occasional run of fifty to one hundred yards.

When you return to your quarters strip in a

room free from drafts; let two men rub you gently with soft Turkish towels until dry, then with coarser towels, to quicken the circulation and harden the skin.

Take a sponge bath of half a gallon of water and two gills of alcohol, followed by massage rubbing of the body and limbs; this loosens and rests the muscles, which is especially needed in the legs.

The following incident will show the benefit of massage properly administered: Some two weeks before my fight with Dempsey I injured my left shoulder so that my left arm was almost useless. Of course I was greatly worried. Mr. Edward Rauscher, massage rubber of the New York Athletic Club, undertook to cure me. He massaged my shoulder, vigorously rubbing it with Anti-Stiff liniment. After each treatment I noticed an improvement, and thanks to Mr. Rauscher's efforts, in a week I had entirely recovered.

After your bath make a complete change of clothing from head to foot, and you will be ready for dinner. This meal should consist of roast beef, cooked to your taste, or roast mutton, always well done; but little salt should be used at the table; no pepper; a moderate quantity of mashed or baked potatoes without seasoning; spinach is palatable and aids digestion; eat it as often as you choose for dinner, with very little salt, as salt creates thirst; drink a bottle of Bass's ale, if it does not make you feel heavy and disinclined to work. If you desire to increase your weight, drink Guinness' stout instead of Bass's ale. Should either have a bad effect, drink tea; carbonic and lime water are good to quench thirst and relieve the stomach of surplus gases; rice pudding with currants is a good dessert.

After dinner take one hour's rest.

The afternoon's work can be varied by exercise in the gymnasium or a walk of three to four miles. But the ball should be punched for twenty minutes every afternoon, and you should also spar with your trainer. At the close of the day's exercise let your attendants rub you down, and put on a change of flannels.

For supper, eat cold roast beef, lamb or mutton, or broiled chops or steak, according to fancy, with bread; if you like currant bread and applesauce without sugar and well strained, or baked apples, either can be taken with a cup of tea.

Spend the time between the supper hour and bedtime in strolling gently, reading, or genial conversation.

The man who trains honestly as directed should be ready for bed not later than ten o'clock, as he needs ten hours' sleep and rest. Wholesome rest after a hard day's work makes a man fresh the morrow.

Choose your training quarters in a mountainous or hilly part of the country, where you can be sure of pure air and be free from dust.

It is a good plan to train at a long distance from centers of business and pleasure, where you can be fairly safe from the intrusion and interruption of the curious.

Select for your trainer a man thoroughly informed in his business, one who has been through the mill himself; he should have qualities that will make him a genial companion.

A good boxer is an indispensable qualification. The prize fighter who would select a trainer unable to box is like a gentleman engaging a secretary who cannot write.

The trainer should have two efficient assistants to do the rubbing and principal part of the walking in company with the man in training.

The trainer will have enough to do if he boxes with his man and oversees his daily work.

In sparring with you every day, your trainer should take the place of your expected opponent, imitate his style of fighting, and if he has any peculiar blows practice them constantly, your work being to guard or evade these blows; practice side-stepping and ducking rather than hard hitting, as the latter cannot be done without the risk of injuring your hands. The prize fighter cannot give too much care to his hands. To harden and strengthen them a wash of strong beef brine can be used morning and night, or they can be rubbed with a mixture of fine varnish and one third of alcohol twice a day. Your hands may not look very nice if rubbed with the varnish mixture, but appearances should not count for much in preparing for a fight, for, should your hands give way in the ring, there would not be much chance of your defeating a man inferior to yourself.

Should the skin of your face chap or crack by being exposed to the weather, use a mixture of one third each of glycerine, alcohol and Florida water whenever it becomes sore.

The amount of work and kind of diet must depend upon whether you wish to reduce or retain your weight. In this regard you must depend upon the advice of an experienced trainer, for men in training often become irritable and unreasonable and ask for food that is injurious. Above all things, let common sense rule in your training.

If stale or tired from overwork, rest a day, or even two, to recover your vigor and appetite.

Avoid pastry; it causes indigestion. Many a good man has lost a fight through carelessly eating unwholesome food. The greatest danger is during the week preceding the fight. Tobacco should never be used; smoking parches the throat and weakens the whole nervous system.

In taking walking exercise, take the country "as the crow flies," over hill and dale, and always choose the grass in preference to hard, dusty roads, as it gives better work for your legs. For running, pick out a level stretch of country.

In this way you can get a pleasant change of scene impossible on a beaten road.

Choose your quarters in a place where you can have a small gymnasium fitted up. The most important thing is the punching ball; practicing with it quickens the eyes, develops the hitting muscles, and makes a man a two-handed hitter. The distance from the ceiling to the loop on the ball should be three feet. The center of the ball should swing just below the level of the eyes. Punch it as much as possible alternately with the left and right; this style of hitting is good practice for two-handed infighting, and two hands are always better than one.

By frequently using the bare knuckles on the ball, it will harden the hands, and give you a greater variety of blows.

I regard the punching ball as the most valuable mechanical assistant to a fighter in training. Sixteen years ago I brought it into use; I was then training in Troy to fight William C. McClellan. I began by using an old-fashioned round rubber football with a canvas cover, for arm exercise, in a room, bouncing it alternately with the right and left hand from the floor to the ceiling, when the idea came to me of swinging it from the ceiling. In company with my old friend and, at the time, adviser, Jimmy Killoran,

of Troy, I swung it from the ceiling, and found it gave me invaluable exercise. I used to punch it for hours. It made me a two-handed hitter. My first attempt to make this rig was crude, as I had a ten-and-a-half-foot ceiling to swing it from. I soon found that a lower ceiling was a great improvement as it gave me much quicker work.

I took the ball to California with me, where it created equal surprise and admiration among both pugilists and amateur boxers, foremost among whom I may name dear old Joe Winrow, my trainer, who also trained Tom Hyer for his fight with Yankee Sullivan, Pat Coyle (the assistant trainer), Billy Jordan and Billy Riley, and the two leading amateur boxers of the Pacific Coast, Charley Bennett and J. B. Lewis.

For variety in exercise the skipping rope can be used moderately; in doing so, use the legs as when boxing, stepping forward and backward with the left foot in front, or side-stepping to the left or right. Lawn tennis is an exciting game, and gives splendid exercise for the legs, and improves the wind. It is good training for the eyes, and will make a pleasant change in the afternoon exercises, the movements of the legs being very similar to those required in boxing.

These exercises will give you the sort of practice you want in your actual work. If tired, but not sleepy, just before going to bed take a small glass of Bass's ale, as it tends to produce sound sleep.

If you are unwell, do not trust to the prescriptions of your trainer, but immediately seek the advice of a first-class physician.

Six weeks of honest training should make a thoroughly sound man fit to fight for his life; no other should enter the prize ring.

In 1896 Conan Doyle wrote *Rodney Stone,* a historical romance revolving around the English prize ring at the start of the nineteenth century. Four years later he wrote this story; he may be forgiven the plot, for the rest is good. It has some memorable scenes, and what Rocky Marciano, many years later, was to mean to the shoe workers of Brockton, Massachusetts, is in it, too.

Conan Doyle, himself a gymnasium boxer and a regular at National Sporting Club bouts, was invited to referee the Jack Johnson–Jim Jeffries fight, but turned it down.

# The Croxley Master

## SIR ARTHUR CONAN DOYLE

### I

MR. ROBERT MONTGOMERY was seated at his desk, his head upon his hands, in a state of the blackest despondency. Before him was the open ledger with the long columns of Dr. Oldacre's prescriptions. At his elbow lay the wooden tray with the labels in various partitions, the cork box, the lumps of twisted sealing wax, while in front a rank of empty bottles waited to be filled. But his spirits were too low for work. He sat in silence, with his fine shoulders bowed and his head upon his hands.

Outside, through the grimy surgery window over a foreground of blackened brick and slate, a line of enormous chimneys like Cyclopean pillars upheld the lowering, dun-colored cloudbank. For six days in the week they spouted smoke, but today the furnace fires were banked, for it was Sunday. Sordid and polluting gloom hung over a district blighted and blasted by the greed of man. There was nothing in the surroundings to cheer a desponding soul, but it was more than his dismal environment which weighed upon the medical assistant.

His trouble was deeper and more personal. The winter session was approaching. He should be back again at the University completing the last year which would give him his medical degree; but alas! he had not the money with which to pay his class fees, nor could he imagine how he could procure it. Sixty pounds were wanted to make his career, and it might have been as many thousands for any chance there seemed to be of his obtaining it.

He was roused from his black meditation by the entrance of Dr. Oldacre himself, a large, clean-shaven, respectable man, with a prim manner and an austere face. He had prospered exceedingly by the support of the local Church interest, and the rule of his life was never by word or action to run a risk of offending the sentiment which had made him. His standard of respectability and of dignity was exceedingly high, and he expected the same from his assistants. His appearance and words were always vaguely benevolent. A sudden impulse came over the despondent student. He would test the reality of this philanthropy.

"I beg your pardon, Dr. Oldacre," said he, rising from his chair, "I have a great favor to ask of you."

The doctor's appearance was not encouraging. His mouth suddenly tightened, and his eyes fell.

"Yes, Mr. Montgomery?"

"You are aware, sir, that I need only one more session to complete my course."

"So you have told me."

"It is very important to me, sir."

"Naturally."

"The fees, Dr. Oldacre, would amount to about sixty pounds."

"I am afraid that my duties call me elsewhere, Mr. Montgomery."

"One moment, sir! I had hoped, sir, that perhaps, if I signed a paper promising you interest upon your money, you would advance this sum to me. I will pay you back, sir, I really will. Or, if you like, I will work it off after I am qualified."

The doctor's lips had thinned into a narrow line. His eyes were raised again, and sparkled indignantly.

"Your request is unreasonable, Mr. Montgomery. I am surprised that you should have made it. Consider, sir, how many thousands of medical students there are in this country. No doubt there are many of them who have a difficulty in finding their fees. Am I to provide for them all? Or why should I make an exception in your favor? I am grieved and disappointed, Mr. Montgomery, that you should have put me into the painful position of having to refuse you." He turned upon his heel, and walked with offended dignity out of the surgery.

The student smiled bitterly, and turned to his work of making up the morning prescriptions. It was poor and unworthy work—work which any weakling might have done as well, and this was a man of exceptional nerve and sinew. But, such as it was, it brought him his board and one pound a week, enough to help him during the summer months and let him save a few pounds toward his winter keep. But those class fees! Where were they to come from? He could not save them out of his scanty wage. Dr. Oldacre would not advance them. He saw no way of earning them. His brains were fairly good, but brains of that quality were a drug in the market. He only excelled in his strength; and where was he to find a customer for that? But the ways of Fate are strange, and his customer was at hand.

"Look y'ere!" said a voice at the door.

Montgomery looked up, for the voice was a loud and rasping one. A young man stood at the entrance—a stocky, bull-necked young miner, in tweed Sunday clothes and an aggressive necktie. He was a sinister-looking figure, with dark, insolent eyes, and the jaw and throat of a bulldog.

"Look y'ere!" said he again. "Why hast thou not sent t' medicine oop as thy master ordered?"

Montgomery had become accustomed to the brutal frankness of the Northern worker. At first it had enraged him, but after a time he had grown callous to it, and accepted it as it was meant. But this was something different. It was insolence—brutal, overbearing insolence, with physical menace behind it.

"What name?" he said coldly.

"Barton. Happen I may give thee cause to mind that name, yoong man. Mak' oop t' wife's medicine this very moment, look ye, or it will be the worse for thee."

Montgomery smiled. A pleasant sense of relief thrilled softly through him. What blessed safety valve was this through which his jangled nerves might find some outlet. The provocation was so gross, the insult so unprovoked, that he could have none of those qualms which take the edge off a man's mettle. He finished sealing the bottle upon which he was occupied, and he addressed it and placed it carefully in the rack.

"Look here," said he, turning round to the miner, "your medicine will be made up in its turn and sent down to you. I don't allow folk in the surgery. Wait outside in the waiting room, if you wish to wait at all."

"Yoong man," said the miner, "thou's got to mak' t' wife's medicine here, and now, and quick, while I wait and watch thee, or else happen thou might need some medicine thysel' before all is over."

"I shouldn't advise you to fasten a quarrel upon me." Montgomery was speaking in the hard, staccato voice of a man who is holding himself in with difficulty. "You'll save trouble if you'll go quietly. If you don't you'll be hurt. Ah, you would? Take it, then!"

The blows were almost simultaneous—a savage swing which whistled past Montgomery's ear, and a straight drive which took the workman on the chin. Luck was with the assistant. That single whizzing uppercut, and the way in which it was delivered, warned him that he had a formidable man to deal with. But if he had underrated his antagonist, his antagonist had also underrated him, and had laid himself open to a fatal blow.

The miner's head had come with a crash against the corner of the surgery shelves, and he had dropped heavily onto the ground. There he lay with his bandy legs drawn up and his hands thrown abroad, the blood trickling over the surgery tiles.

"Had enough?" asked the assistant, breathing fiercely through his nose.

But no answer came. The man was insensible. And then the danger of his position came upon Montgomery, and he turned as white as his antagonist. A Sunday, the immaculate Dr. Oldacre with his pious connection, a savage brawl with a patient; he would irretrievably lose his situation if the facts came out. It was not much of a situation, but he could not get another without a reference, and Oldacre might refuse him one. Without money for his classes, and without a situation—what was to become of him? It was absolute ruin.

But perhaps he could escape exposure after all. He seized his insensible adversary, dragged him out into the center of the room, loosened his collar, and squeezed the surgery sponge over his face. He sat up at last with a gasp and a scowl.

"Domn thee, thou's spoilt my necktie," said he, mopping up the water from his breast.

"I'm sorry I hit you so hard," said Montgomery apologetically.

"Thou hit me hard! I could stan' such fly-flappin' all day. 'Twas this here press that cracked my pate for me, and thou art a looky man to be able to boast as thou hast outed me. And now I'd be obliged to thee if thou wilt give me t' wife's medicine."

Montgomery gladly made it up and handed it to the miner.

"You are weak still," said he. "Won't you stay awhile and rest?"

"T' wife wants her medicine," said the man, and lurched out at the door.

The assistant, looking after him, saw him rolling with an uncertain step down the street, until a friend met him, and they walked on arm-in-arm. The man seemed in his rough Northern fashion to bear no grudge, and so Montgomery's fears left him. There was no reason why the doctor should know anything about it. He wiped the blood from the floor, put the surgery in order, and went on with his interrupted task, hoping that he had come scathless out of a very dangerous business.

Yet all day he was aware of a sense of vague uneasiness, which sharpened into dismay when, late in the afternoon, he was informed that three gentlemen had called and were waiting for him in the surgery. A coroner's inquest, a descent of detectives, an invasion of angry relatives—all sorts of possibilities rose to scare him. With tense nerves and a rigid face he went to meet his visitors.

They were a very singular trio. Each was known to him by sight; but what on earth the three could be doing together, and above all, what they could expect from *him*, was a most inexplicable problem.

The first was Sorley Wilson, the son of the owner of the Nonpareil Coalpit. He was a young blood of twenty, heir to a fortune, a keen sportsman, and down for the Easter vacation from Magdalene College. He sat now upon the edge of the surgery table, looking in thoughtful silence at Montgomery, and twisting the ends of his small, black waxed mustache.

The second was Purvis, the publican, owner of the chief beerstop, and well known as the local bookmaker. He was a coarse, clean-shaven man, whose fiery face made a singular contrast with his ivory-white bald head. He had shrewd, light-blue eyes with foxy lashes, and he also leaned forward in silence from his chair, a fat, red hand upon either knee, and stared critically at the young assistant.

So did the third visitor, Fawcett, the horse-breaker, who leaned back, his long, thin legs, with their boxcloth riding gaiters, thrust out in front of him, tapping his protruding teeth with his riding whip, with anxious thought in every line of his rugged, bony face. Publican, exquisite and horsebreaker were all three equally silent, equally earnest and equally critical. Montgomery, seated in the midst of them, looked from one to the other.

"Well, gentlemen?" he observed, but no answer came.

The position was embarrassing.

"No," said the horsebreaker, at last. "No. It's off. It's nowt."

"Stand oop, lad; let's see thee standin'." It was the publican who spoke.

Montgomery obeyed. He would learn all about it, no doubt, if he were patient. He stood up and turned slowly round, as if in front of his tailor.

"It's off! It's off!" cried the horsebreaker. "Why, mon, the Master would break him over his knee."

"Oh, that be hanged for a yarn!" said the young Cantab. "You can drop out if you like, Fawcett, but I'll see this thing through, if I have to do it alone. I don't hedge a penny. I like the cut of him a great deal better than I liked Ted Barton."

"Look at Barton's shoulders, Mr. Wilson."

"Lumpiness isn't always strength. Give me nerve and fire and breed. That's what wins."

"Ay, sir, you have it theer—you have it theer!" said the fat, red-faced publican, in a thick, suety voice. "It's the same wi' poops. Get 'em clean-bred an' fine, and they'll yark the thick 'uns—yark 'em out o' their skins."

"He's ten pund on the light side," growled the horsebreaker.

"He's a welterweight, anyhow."

"A hundred and thirty."

"A hundred and fifty, if he's an ounce."

"Well, the Master doesn't scale much more than that."

"A hundred and seventy-five."

"That was when he was hog fat and living high. Work the grease out of him, and I lay there's no great difference between them. Have you been weighed lately, Mr. Montgomery?"

It was the first direct question which had been asked him. He had stood in the midst of them, like a horse at a fair, and he was just beginning to wonder whether he was more angry or amused.

"I am just eleven stone," said he.

"I said that he was a welterweight."

"But suppose you was trained?" said the publican. "Wot then?"

"I am always in training."

"In a manner of speakin', no doubt, he *is* always in trainin'," remarked the horsebreaker. "But trainin' for everyday work ain't the same as trainin' with a trainer; and I dare bet, with all respec' to your opinion, Mr. Wilson, that there's half a stone of tallow on him at this minute."

The young Cantab put his fingers on the assistant's upper arm. Then with his other hand on his wrist he bent the forearm sharply, and felt the biceps, as round and hard as a cricket ball, spring up under his fingers.

"Feel that!" said he.

The publican and the horsebreaker felt it with an air of reverence.

"Good lad! He'll do yet!" cried Purvis.

"Gentlemen," said Montgomery, "I think that you will acknowledge that I have been very patient with you. I have listened to all that you have to say about my personal appearance, and now I must really beg that you will have the goodness to tell me what is the matter."

They all sat down in their serious, businesslike way.

"That's easy done, Mr. Montgomery," said the fat-voiced publican. "But before sayin' anything, we had to wait and see whether, in a way of speakin', there was any need for us to say anything at all. Mr. Wilson thinks there is. Mr. Fawcett, who has the same right to his opinion, bein' also a backer and one o' the committee, thinks the other way."

"I thought him too light built, and I think so now," said the horsebreaker, still tapping his prominent teeth with the metal head of his riding whip. "But happen he may pull through; and he's a fine-made, buirdly young chap, so if you mean to back him, Mr. Wilson—"

"Which I do."

"And you, Purvis?"

"I ain't one to go back, Fawcett."

"Well, I'll stan' to my share of the purse."

"And well I knew you would," said Purvis, "for it would be somethin' new to find Isaac Fawcett as a spoilsport. Well, then, we make up the hundred for the stake among us, and the fight stands—always supposin' the young man is willin'."

"Excuse all this rot, Mr. Montgomery," said the University man, in a genial voice. "We've begun at the wrong end, I know, but we'll soon straighten it out, and I hope that you will see your way to falling in with our views. In the first place, you remember the man whom you knocked out this morning? He is Barton—the famous Ted Barton."

"I'm sure, sir, you may well be proud to have outed him in one round," said the publican. "Why, it took Morris, the ten-stone-six champion, a deal more trouble than that before he put Barton to sleep. You've done a fine performance, sir, and happen you'll do a finer, if you give yourself the chance."

"I never heard of Ted Barton, beyond seeing the name on a medicine label," said the assistant.

"Well, you may take it from me that he's a slaughterer," said the horsebreaker. "You've taught him a lesson that he needed, for it was always a word and a blow with him, and the word alone was worth five shillin' in a public court. He won't be so ready now to shake his nieve in the face of everyone he meets. However, that's neither here nor there."

Montgomery looked at them in bewilderment.

"For goodness' sake, gentlemen, tell me what it is you want me to do!" he cried.

"We want you to fight Silas Craggs, better known as the Master of Croxley."

"But why?"

"Because Ted Barton was to have fought him next Saturday. He was the champion of the Wilson coalpits, and the other was the Master of the ironfolk down at the Croxley smelters. We'd matched our man for a purse of a hundred against the Master. But you've queered our man, and he can't face such a battle with a two-inch cut at the back of his head. There's only one thing to be done, sir, and that is for you to take his place. If you can lick Ted Barton you may lick the Master of Croxley; but if you don't we're done, for there's no one else who is in the same street with him in this district. It's twenty rounds, two-ounce gloves, Queensberry rules, and a decision on points if you fight to the finish."

For a moment the absurdity of the thing drove every other thought out of Montgomery's head. But then there came a sudden revulsion. A hundred pounds!—all he wanted to complete his education was lying there ready to his hand, if only that hand were strong enough to pick it up. He had thought bitterly that morning that there was no market for his strength, but here was one where his muscle might earn more in an hour than his brains in a year. But a chill of doubt came over him.

"How can I fight for the coalpits?" said he. "I am not connected with them."

"Eh, lad, but thou art!" cried old Purvis. "We've got it down in writin', and it's clear enough. 'Anyone connected with the coalpits.' Doctor Oldacre is the coalpit club doctor; thou art his assistant. What more can they want?"

"Yes, that's right enough," said the Cantab. "It would be a very sporting thing of you, Mr. Montgomery, if you would come to our help when we are in such a hole. Of course, you might not like to take the hundred pounds; but I have no doubt that, in the case of your winning, we could arrange that it should take the form of a watch or piece of plate, or any other shape which might suggest itself to you. You see, you are responsible for our having lost our champion, so we really feel that we have a claim upon you."

"Give me a moment, gentlemen. It is very unexpected. I am afraid the doctor would never consent to my going—in fact, I am sure that he would not."

"But he need never know—not before the fight, at any rate. We are not bound to give the name of our man. So long as he is within the weight limits on the day of the fight, that is all that concerns anyone."

The adventure and the profit would either of them have attracted Montgomery. The two combined were irresistible.

"Gentlemen," said he, "I'll do it!"

The three sprang from their seats. The publican had seized his right hand, the horsedealer his left, and the Cantab slapped him on the back.

"Good lad! Good lad!" croaked the publican. "Eh, mon, but if thou yark him, thou'll rise in one day from being just a common doctor to the best-known mon 'twixt here and Bradford. Thou art a witherin' tyke, thou art, and no mistake; and if thou beat the Master of Croxley, thou'll find all the beer thou want for the rest of thy life waiting for thee at the Four Sacks."

"It is the most sporting thing I ever heard of in my life," said young Wilson. "By George, sir, if you pull it off, you've got the constituency in your pocket, if you care to stand. You know the outhouse in my garden?"

"Next the road?"

"Exactly. I turned it into a gymnasium for Ted Barton. You'll find all you want there; clubs, punching ball, bars, dumbbells, everything. Then you'll want a sparring partner. Ogilvy has been acting for Barton, but we don't think that he is class enough. Barton bears you no grudge. He's a good-hearted fellow, though cross-grained with strangers. He looked upon you as a stranger this morning, but he says he knows you now. He is

quite ready to spar with you for practice, and he will come at any hour you will name."

"Thank you; I will let you know the hour," said Montgomery; and so the committee departed jubilant upon their way.

The medical assistant sat for a little time in the surgery turning it over in his mind. He had been trained originally at the University by the man who had been middleweight champion in his day. It was true that his teacher was long past his prime, slow upon his feet and stiff in his joints, but even so he was still a tough antagonist; but Montgomery had found at last that he could more than hold his own with him. He had won the University medal, and his teacher, who had trained so many students, was emphatic in his opinion that he had never had one who was in the same class with him. He had been exhorted to go in for the Amateur Championships, but he had no particular ambition in that direction. Once he had put on the gloves with Hammer Tunstall in a booth at a fair, and had fought three rattling rounds, in which he had the worst of it, but had made the prize fighter stretch himself to the uttermost. There was his whole record, and was it enough to encourage him to stand up to the Master of Croxley? He had never heard of the Master before, but then he had lost touch of the ring during the last few years of hard work. After all, what did it matter? If he won, there was the money, which meant so much to him. If he lost it would only mean a thrashing. He could take punishment without flinching, of that he was certain. If there were only one chance in a hundred of pulling it off, then it was worth his while to attempt it.

Dr. Oldacre, new come from church, with an ostentatious prayer book in his kid-gloved hand, broke in upon his meditation.

"You don't go to service, I observe, Mr. Montgomery," said he coldly.

"No, sir; I have some business to detain me."

"It is very near to my heart that my household should set a good example. There are so few educated people in this district that a great responsibility devolves upon us. If we do not live up to the highest, how can we expect these poor workers to do so? It is a dreadful thing to reflect that the parish takes a great deal more interest in an approaching glove fight than in their religious duties."

"A glove fight, sir?" said Montgomery guiltily.

"I believe that to be the correct term. One of my patients tells me that it is the talk of the district. A local ruffian, a patient of ours, by the way, is matched against a pugilist over at Croxley. I cannot understand why the law does not step in and stop so degrading an exhibition. It is really a prize fight."

"A glove fight, you said."

"I am informed that a two-ounce glove is an evasion by which they dodge the law, and make it difficult for the police to interfere. They contend for a sum of money. It seems dreadful and almost incredible—does it not?—to think that such scenes can be enacted within a few miles of our peaceful home. But you will realize, Mr. Montgomery, that while there are such influences for us to counteract, it is very necessary that we should live up to our highest."

The doctor's sermon would have had more effect if the assistant had not once or twice had occasion to test his highest and come upon it at unexpectedly humble elevations. It is always so particularly easy to "compound for sins we're most inclined to by damning those we have no mind to." In any case, Montgomery felt that of all the men concerned in such a fight—promoters, backers, spectators—it is the actual fighter who holds the strongest and most honorable position. His conscience gave him no concern upon the subject. Endurance and courage are virtues, not vices, and brutality is, at least, better than effeminacy.

There was a little tobacco shop at the corner of the street where Montgomery got his bird's-eye and also his local information, for the shopman was a garrulous soul, who knew everything about the affairs of the district. The assistant strolled down there after tea and asked, in a casual way, whether the tobacconist had ever heard of the Master of Croxley.

"Heard of him! Heard of him!" The little man could hardly articulate in his astonishment. "Why, sir, he's the first mon o' the district, an' his name's as well known in the West Riding as the winner o' t' Derby. But Lor', sir—" here he stopped and rummaged among a heap of papers —"they are makin' a fuss about him on account o' his fight wi' Ted Barton, and so the Croxley *Herald* has his life an' record, an' here it is, an' thou canst read it for thysel'."

The sheet of paper which he held up was a lake of print around an islet of illustration. The latter was a coarse woodcut of a pugilist's head and neck set in a cross-barred jersey. It was a sinister but powerful face, the face of a debauched hero, clean-shaven, strongly eyebrowed, keen-eyed, with a huge aggressive jaw and an animal dewlap beneath it. The long, obstinate cheeks ran flush up to the narrow, sinister eyes. The mighty neck came down square from the ears and curved outward into shoulders which had lost nothing at the hands of the local artist.

Above was written "Silas Craggs," and beneath, "The Master of Croxley."

"Thou'll find all about him there, sir," said the tobacconist. "He's a witherin' tyke, he is, and we're proud to have him in the country. If he hadn't broke his leg he'd have been champion of England."

"Broke his leg, has he?"

"Yes, and it set badly. They ca' him owd K behind his bock, for thot is how his two legs look. But his arms—well, if they was both stropped to a bench, as the sayin' is, I wonder where the champion of England would be then."

"I'll take this with me," said Montgomery; and putting the paper into his pocket he returned home.

It was not a cheering record which he read there. The whole history of the Croxley Master was given in full, his many victories, his few defeats.

"Born in 1857," said the provincial biographer, "Silas Craggs, better known in sporting circles as The Master of Croxley, is now in his fortieth year."

"Hang it, I'm only twenty-three," said Montgomery to himself, and read on more cheerfully.

"Having in his youth shown a surprising aptitude for the game, he fought his way up among his comrades, until he became the recognized champion of the district and won the proud title which he still holds. Ambitious of a more than local fame, he secured a patron, and fought his first fight against Jack Barton, of Birmingham, in May, 1880, at the old Loiterers' Club. Craggs, who fought at ten stone-two at the time, had the better of fifteen rattling rounds, and gained an award on points against the Midlander. Having disposed of James Dunn, of Rotherhithe, Cameron, of Glasgow, and a youth named Fernie, he was thought so highly of by the fancy that he was matched against Ernest Willox, at that time middleweight champion of the North of England, and defeated him in a hard-fought battle, knocking him out in the tenth round after a punishing contest. At this period it looked as if the very highest honors of the ring were within the reach of the young Yorkshireman, but he was laid upon the shelf by a most unfortunate accident. The kick of a horse broke his thigh, and for a year he was compelled to rest himself. When he returned to his work the fracture had set badly, and his activity was much impaired. It was owing to this that he was defeated in seven rounds by Willox, the man whom he had previously beaten, and afterward by James Shaw, of London, though the latter acknowledged that he had found the toughest customer of his career. Undismayed by his reverses, the Master adapted the style of his fighting to his physical disabilities and resumed his career of victory—defeating Norton (the black), Bobby Wilson, and Levy Cohen, the latter a heavyweight. Conceding two stone, he fought a draw with the famous Billy McQuire, and afterward, for a purse of fifty pounds, he defeated Sam Hare at the Pelican Club, London. In 1891 a decision was given against him upon a foul when fighting a winning fight against Jim Taylor, the Australian middleweight, and so mortified was he by the decision that he withdrew from the ring. Since then he has hardly fought at all save to accommodate any local aspirant who may wish to learn the difference between a barroom scramble and a scientific contest. The latest of these ambitious souls comes from the Wilson coalpits, which have undertaken to put up a stake of £100 and back their local champion. There are various rumors afloat as to who their representative is to be, the name of Ted Barton being freely mentioned; but the betting, which is seven to one on the Master against any untried man, is a fair reflection of the feeling of the community."

Montgomery read it over twice, and it left him with a very serious face. No light matter this which he had undertaken; no battle with a rough-and-tumble fighter who presumed upon a local reputation. This man's record showed that he was first-class—or nearly so. There were a few points in his favor, and he must make the most of them. There was his age—twenty-three against forty. There was an old ring proverb that "Youth will be served," but the annals of the ring offer a great number of exceptions. A hard veteran, full of cool valor and ring craft, could give ten or fifteen years and a beating to most striplings. He could not rely too much upon his advantage in age. But then there was the lameness; that must surely count for a great deal. And, lastly, there was the chance that the Master might underrate his opponent, that he might be remiss in his training, and refuse to abandon his usual way of life, if he thought that he had an easy task before him. In a man of his age and habits this seemed very possible. Montgomery prayed that it might be so. Meanwhile, if his opponent were the best man who ever jumped the ropes into a ring, his own duty was clear. He must prepare himself carefully, throw away no chance, and do the very best that he could. But he knew enough to appreciate the difference which exists in boxing, as in every sport, between the amateur and the professional. The coolness, the power of hitting, above all the capability of taking punishment, count for so much. Those specially developed, gutta-perchalike abdominal muscles of the hardened pugilist will take without flinching a blow which would leave another man writhing on the ground. Such things are not to be acquired in a week, but all that could be done in a week should be done.

The medical assistant had a good basis to start from. He was five feet eleven inches—tall enough for anything on two legs, as the old ring men used to say—lithe and spare, with the activity of a panther, and a strength which had hardly yet ever found its limitations. His muscular development was finely hard, but his power came rather from that higher nerve energy which counts for nothing upon a measuring tape. He had the well-curved nose and the widely opened eye which never yet were seen upon the face of a craven, and behind everything he had the driving force which came from the knowledge that his whole career was at stake upon the contest. The three backers rubbed their hands when they saw him at work punching the ball in the gymnasium next morning; and Fawcett, the horse-breaker, who had written to Leeds to hedge his bets, sent a wire to cancel the letter, and to lay another fifty at the market price of seven to one.

Montgomery's chief difficulty was to find time for his training without any interference from the doctor. His work took him a large part of the day, but as the visiting was done on foot, and considerable distances had to be traversed, it was a training in itself. For the rest, he punched the swinging ball and worked with the dumb-bells for an hour every morning and evening, and boxed twice a day with Ted Barton in the gymnasium, gaining as much profit as could be got from a rushing, two-handed slogger. Barton was full of admiration for his cleverness and quickness, but doubtful about his strength. Hard hitting was the feature of his own style, and he exacted it from others.

"Lord, sir, that's a turble poor poonch for an eleven-stone man!" he would cry. "Thou wilt have to hit harder than that afore t' Master will know that thou art theer. Ah, thot's better, mon, thot's fine!" he would add, as his opponent lifted him across the room on the end of a right counter. "Thot's how I likes to feel 'em. Happen thou'lt pull through yet." He chuckled with joy when Montgomery knocked him into a corner. "Eh, mon, thou art comin' along grand. Thou hast fair yarked me off my legs. Do it again, lad, do it again!"

The only part of Montgomery's training which came within the doctor's observation was his diet, and that puzzled him considerably.

"You will excuse my remarking, Mr. Montgomery, that you are becoming rather particular in your tastes. Such fads are not to be encouraged in one's youth. Why do you eat toast with every meal?"

"I find that it suits me better than bread, sir."

"It entails unnecessary work upon the cook. I observe, also, that you have turned against potatoes."

"Yes, sir; I think that I am better without them."

"And you no longer drink your beer?"

"No, sir."

"These causeless whims and fancies are very much to be deprecated, Mr. Montgomery. Consider how many there are to whom these very potatoes and this very beer would be most acceptable."

"No doubt, sir. But at present I prefer to do without them."

They were sitting alone at lunch, and the assistant thought that it would be a good opportunity of asking leave for the day of the fight.

"I should be glad if you could let me have leave for Saturday, Dr. Oldacre."

"It is very inconvenient upon so busy a day."

"I should do a double day's work on Friday so as to leave everything in order. I should hope to be back in the evening."

"I am afraid I cannot spare you, Mr. Montgomery."

This was a facer. If he could not leave he would go without it.

"You will remember, Dr. Oldacre, that when I came to you it was understood that I should have a clear day every month. I have never claimed one. But now there are reasons why I wish to have a holiday upon Saturday."

Dr. Oldacre gave in with a very bad grace.

"Of course, if you insist upon your formal rights, there is no more to be said, Mr. Montgomery, though I feel that it shows a certain indifference to my comfort and the welfare of the practice. Do you still insist?"

"Yes, sir."

"Very good. Have your way."

The doctor was boiling over with anger, but Montgomery was a valuable assistant—steady, capable, and hard-working—and he could not afford to lose him. Even if he had been prompted to advance those class fees, for which his assistant had appealed, it would have been against his interests to do so, for he did not wish him to qualify, and he desired him to remain in his subordinate position, in which he worked so hard for so small a wage. There was something in the cool insistence of the young man, a quiet resolution in his voice as he claimed his Saturday, which aroused his curiosity.

"I have no desire to interfere unduly with your affairs, Mr. Montgomery, but were you thinking of having a day in Leeds upon Saturday?"

"No, sir."

"In the country?"

"Yes, sir."

"You are very wise. You will find a quiet day among the wild flowers a very valuable restorative. Had you thought of any particular direction?"

"I am going over Croxley way."

"Well, there is no prettier country when once you are past the ironworks. What could be more delightful than to lie upon the Fells, basking in the sunshine, with perhaps some instructive and elevating book as your companion? I should recommend a visit to the ruins of St. Bridget's Church, a very interesting relic of the early Norman era. By the way, there is one objection which I see to your going to Croxley on Saturday. It is upon that date, as I am informed, that that ruffianly glove fight takes place. You may find yourself molested by the blackguards whom it will attract."

"I will take my chance of that, sir," said the assistant.

On the Friday night, which was the last before the fight, Montgomery's three backers assembled in the gymnasium and inspected their man as he went through some light exercise to keep his muscles supple. He was certainly in splendid condition, his skin shining with health, and his eyes with energy and confidence. The three walked round him and exulted.

"He's simply ripping!" said the undergraduate. "By Gad, you've come out of it splendidly. You're as hard as a pebble, and fit to fight for your life."

"Happen he's a trifle on the fine side," said the publican. "Runs a bit light at the loins, to my way of thinkin'."

"What weight today?"

"Ten stone eleven," the assistant answered.

"That's only three pund off in a week's trainin'," said the horsebreaker. "He said right when he said that he was in condition. Well, it's fine stuff all there is of it, but I'm none so sure as there is enough." He kept poking his finger into Montgomery, as if he were one of his horses. "I hear that the Master will scale a hundred and sixty-odd at the ringside."

"But there's some of that which he'd like well to pull off and leave behind wi' his shirt," said Purvis. "I hear they've had a rare job to get him to drop his beer, and if it had not been for that great redheaded wench of his they'd never ha' done it. She fair scratted the face off a potman that had brought him a gallon from t' Chequers.

They say the hussy is his sparrin' partner, as well as his sweetheart, and that his poor wife is just breakin' her heart over it. Hullo, young 'un, what do you want?"

The door of the gymnasium had opened, and a lad about sixteen, grimy and black with soot and iron, stepped into the yellow glare of the oil lamp. Ted Barton seized him by the collar.

"See here, thou yoong whelp, this is private, and we want noan o' thy spyin'!"

"But I maum speak to Mr. Wilson."

The young Cantab stepped forward.

"Well, my lad, what is it?"

"It's aboot t' fight, Mr. Wilson, sir. I wanted to tell your mon somethin' aboot t' Master."

"We've no time to listen to gossip, my boy. We know all about the Master."

"But thou doant, sir. Nobody knows but me and mother, and we thought as we'd like thy mon to know, sir, for we want him to fair bray him."

"Oh, you want the Master fair brayed, do you? So do we. Well, what have you to say?"

"Is this your mon, sir?"

"Well, suppose it is?"

"Then it's him I want to tell aboot it. T' Master is blind o' the left eye."

"Nonsense!"

"It's true, sir. Not stone blind, but rarely fogged. He keeps it secret, but mother knows, and so do I. If thou slip him on the left side he can't cop thee. Thou'll find it right as I tell thee. And mark him when he sinks his right. 'Tis his best blow, his right uppercut. T' Maister's finisher, they ca' it at t' works. It's a turble blow, when it do come home."

"Thank you, my boy. This is information worth having about his sight," said Wilson. "How came you to know so much? Who are you?"

"I'm his son, sir."

Wilson whistled.

"And who sent you to us?"

"My mother. I maun get back to her again."

"Take this half crown."

"No, sir, I don't seek money in comin' here. I do it—"

"For love?" suggested the publican.

"For hate!" said the boy, and darted off into the darkness.

"Seems to me t' redheaded wench may do him more harm than good, after all," remarked the publican. "And now, Mr. Montgomery, sir, you've done enough for this evenin', an' a nine hours' sleep is the best trainin' before a battle. Happen this time tomorrow night you'll be safe back again with your hundred pounds in your pocket."

## II

Work was struck at one o'clock at the coalpits and the ironworks, and the fight was arranged for three. From the Croxley Furnaces, from Wilson's Coalpits, from the Heartsease Mine, from the Dodd Mills, from the Leverworth Smelters the workmen came trooping, each with his fox terrier or his lurcher at his heels. Warped with labor and twisted by toil, bent double by week-long work in the cramped coal galleries, or half-blinded with years spent in front of white-hot fluid metal, these men still gilded their harsh and hopeless lives by their devotion to sport. It was their one relief, the only thing which could distract their minds from sordid surroundings, and give them an interest beyond the blackened circle which inclosed them. Literature, art, science, all these things were beyond the horizon; but the race, the football match, the cricket, the fight, these were things which they could understand, which they could speculate upon in advance and comment upon afterward. Sometimes brutal, sometimes grotesque, the love of sport is still one of the great agencies which make for the happiness of our people. It lies very deeply in the springs of our nature, and when it has been educated out, a higher, more refined nature may be left, but it will not be of that robust British type which has left its mark so deeply on the world. Every one of these ruddled workers, slouching with his dog at his heels to see something of the fight, was a true unit of his race.

It was a squally May day, with bright sunbursts and driving showers. Montgomery worked all morning in the surgery getting his medicine made up.

"The weather seems so very unsettled, Mr. Montgomery," remarked the doctor, "that I am inclined to think that you had better postpone your little country excursion until a later date."

"I am afraid that I must go today, sir."

"I have just had an intimation that Mrs. Potter, at the other side of Angleton, wishes to see me. It is probable that I shall be there all day. It will be extremely inconvenient to leave the house empty so long."

"I am very sorry, sir, but I must go," said the assistant, doggedly.

The doctor saw that it would be useless to argue, and departed in the worst of bad tempers upon his mission. Montgomery felt easier now that he was gone. He went up to his room and packed his running shoes, his fighting drawers, and his cricket sash into a handbag. When he came down Mr. Wilson was waiting for him in the surgery.

"I hear the doctor has gone."

"Yes; he is likely to be away all day."

"I don't see that it matters much. It's bound to come to his ears by tonight."

"Yes; it's serious with me, Mr. Wilson. If I win, it's all right. I don't mind telling you that the hundred pounds will make all the difference to me. But if I lose, I shall lose my situation, for, as you say, I can't keep it secret."

"Never mind. We'll see you through among us. I only wonder the doctor has not heard, for it's all over the country that you are to fight the Croxley champion. We've had Armitage up about it already. He's the Master's backer, you know. He wasn't sure that you were eligible. The Master said he wanted you whether you were eligible or not. Armitage has money on, and would have made trouble if he could. But I showed him that you came within the conditions of the challenge, and he agreed that it was all right. They think they have a soft thing on."

"Well, I can only do my best," said Montgomery.

They lunched together; a silent and rather nervous repast, for Montgomery's mind was full of what was before him, and Wilson had himself more money at stake than he cared to lose.

Wilson's carriage and pair were at the door, the horses with blue-and-white rosettes at their ears, which were the colors of the Wilson Coalpits, well known on many a football field. At the avenue gate a crowd of some hundred pitmen and their wives gave a cheer as the carriage passed. To the assistant it all seemed dreamlike and extraordinary—the strangest experience of his life, but with a thrill of human action and interest in it which made it passionately absorbing. He lay back in the open carriage and saw the fluttering handkerchiefs from the doors and windows of the miners' cottages. Wilson had pinned a blue-and-white rosette upon his coat, and everyone knew him as their champion. "Good luck, sir! Good luck to thee!" they shouted from the roadside. He felt that it was like some unromantic knight riding down to sordid lists, but there was something of chivalry in it all the same. He fought for others as well as for himself. He might fail from want of skill or strength, but deep in his somber soul he vowed that it should never be from want of heart.

Mr. Fawcett was just mounting into his high-wheeled, spidery dogcart, with his little bit of blood between the shafts. He waved his whip and fell in behind the carriage. They overtook Purvis, the tomato-faced publican, upon the road with his wife in her Sunday bonnet. They also dropped into the procession, and then, as they traversed the seven miles of the highroad to Croxley, their two-horsed, rosetted carriage became gradually the nucleus of a comet with a loosely radiating tail. From every side road came the miners' carts, the humble, ramshackle traps, black and bulging, with their loads of noisy, foul-tongued, open-hearted partisans. They trailed for a long quarter of a mile behind them—cracking, whipping, shouting, galloping, swearing. Horsemen and runners were mixed with the vehicles. And then suddenly a squad of the Sheffield Yeomanry, who were having their annual training in those parts, clattered and jingled out of a field, and rose as an escort to the carriage. Through the dust clouds round him Montgomery saw the gleaming brass helmets, the bright coats, and the tossing heads of the chargers, the delighted brown faces of the troopers. It was more dreamlike than ever.

And then, as they approached the monstrous, uncouth line of bottle-shaped buildings which marked the smelting works of Croxley, their long, writhing snake of dust was headed off by another but longer one which wound across their path. The main road into which their own opened was filled by the rushing current of traps. The Wilson contingent halted until the others should get past. The ironmen cheered and groaned, according to their humor, as they whirled past their antagonist. Rough chaff flew back and forwards like iron nuts and splinters of coal. "Brought him up, then!" "Got t' hearse for to fetch him back?" "Where's t' owed K-legs?" "Mon, mon, have thy photograph took—'twill mind thee of what thou used to look!" "He fight?—he's now't but a half-baked doctor!" "Happen he'll doctor thy Croxley Champion afore he's through wi't."

So they flashed at each other as the one side waited and the other passed. Then there came a rolling murmur swelling into a shout, and a great break with four horses came clattering along, all streaming with salmon-pink ribbons. The driver wore a white hat with pink rosette, and beside him, on the high seat, were a man and a woman—she with her arm round his waist. Montgomery had one glimpse of them as they flashed past: he with a furry cap drawn low over brow, a great frieze coat, and a pink comforter round his throat; she brazen, redheaded, bright-colored, laughing excitedly. The Master, for it was he, turned as he passed, gazed hard at Montgomery, and gave him a menacing, gap-toothed grin. It was a hard, wicked face, blue-jowled and craggy, with long, obstinate cheeks and inexorable eyes. The break behind was full of patrons of the sport—flushed iron-foremen, heads of departments, managers. One was drinking from a metal flask, and raised it to Montgomery as he passed; and then the crowd thinned, and the Wilson cortege with their dragoons swept in at the rear of the others.

The road led away from Croxley, between curving green hills, gashed and polluted by the searchers for coal and iron. The whole country had been gutted, and vast piles of refuse and mountains of slag suggested the mighty chambers which the labor of man had burrowed beneath. On the left the road curved up to where a huge building, roofless and dismantled, stood crumbling and forlorn, with the light shining through the windowless squares.

"That's the old Arrowsmith's factory. That's where the fight is to be," said Wilson. "How are you feeling now?"

"Thank you. I was never better in my life," Montgomery answered.

"By Gad, I like your nerve!" said Wilson, who was himself flushed and uneasy. "You'll give us a fight for our money, come what may. That place on the right is the office, and that has been set aside as the dressing and weighing room."

The carriage drove up to it amidst the shouts of the folk upon the hillside. Lines of empty carriages and traps curved down upon the winding road, and a black crowd surged round the door of the ruined factory. The seats, as a huge placard announced, were five shillings, three shillings, and a shilling, with half price for dogs. The takings, deducting expenses, were to go to the winner, and it was already evident that a larger stake than a hundred pounds was in question. A babel of voices rose from the door. The workers wished to bring their dogs in free. The men scuffled. The dogs barked. The crowd was a whirling, eddying pool surging with a roar up to the narrow cleft which was its only outlet.

The break, with its salmon-colored streamers and four reeking horses, stood empty before the door of the office; Wilson, Purvis, Fawcett, and Montgomery passed in.

There was a large, bare room inside with square, clean patches upon the grimy walls, where pictures and almanacs had once hung. Worn linoleum covered the floor, but there was no furniture save some benches and a deal table with a ewer and a basin upon it. Two of the corners were curtained off. In the middle of the room was a weighing chair. A hugely fat man, with a salmon tie and a blue waistcoat with bird's-eye spots, came bustling up to them. It was Armitage, the butcher and grazier, well known for miles round as a warm man, and the most liberal patron of sport in the Riding.

"Well, well," he grunted, in a thick, fussy, wheezy voice, "you have come, then. Got your man? Got your man?"

"Here he is, fit and well. Mr. Montgomery, let me present you to Mr. Armitage."

"Glad to meet you, sir. Happy to make your acquaintance. I make bold to say, sir, that we of Croxley admire your courage, Mr. Montgomery, and that our only hope is a fair fight and no favor and the best man win. That's our sentiment at Croxley."

"And it is my sentiment also," said the assistant.

"Well, you can't say fairer than that, Mr. Montgomery. You've taken a large contrac' in hand, but a large contrac' may be carried through, sir, as anyone that knows my dealings could testify. The Master is ready to weigh in!"

"So am I."

"You must weigh in the buff."

Montgomery looked askance at the tall, red-headed woman who was standing gazing out of the window.

"That's all right," said Wilson. "Get behind the curtain and put on your fighting kit."

He did so, and came out the picture of an athlete, in white, loose drawers, canvas shoes, and the sash of a well-known cricket club round his waist. He was trained to a hair, his skin gleaming like silk, and every muscle rippling down his broad shoulders and along his beautiful arms as he moved them. They bunched into ivory knobs, or slid into long, sinuous curves, as he raised or lowered his hands.

"What thinkest thou o' that?" asked Ted Barton, his second, of the woman in the window.

She glanced contemptuously at the young athlete.

"It's but a poor kindness thou dost him to put a thread-paper yoong gentleman like yon against a mon as is my mon. Why, my Jock would throttle him wi' one hond lashed behind him."

"Happen he may—happen not," said Barton. "I have but twa pund in the world, but it's on him, every penny, and no hedgin'. But here's t' Maister, and rarely fine he do look."

The prize fighter had come out from his curtain, a squat, formidable figure, monstrous in chest and arms, limping slightly on his distorted leg. His skin had none of the freshness and clearness of Montgomery's, but was dusky and mottled, with one huge mole amid the mat of tangled black hair which thatched his mighty breast. His weight bore no relation to his strength, for those huge shoulders and great arms, with brown, sledge-hammer fists, would have fitted the heaviest man that ever threw his cap into a ring. But his loins and legs were slight in proportion.

Montgomery, on the other hand, was as symmetrical as a Greek statue. It would be an encounter between a man who was specially fitted for one sport, and one who was equally capable of any. The two looked curiously at each other: a bulldog, and a high-bred, clean-limbed terrier, each full of spirit.

"How do you do?"

"How do?" The Master grinned again, and his three jagged front teeth gleamed for an instant. The rest had been beaten out of him in twenty years of battle. He spat upon the floor. "We have a rare fine day for't."

"Capital," said Montgomery.

"That's the good feelin' I like," wheezed the fat butcher. "Good lads, both of them!—prime lads!—hard meat an' good bone. There's no ill feelin'."

"If he downs me, Gawd bless him!" said the Master.

"An' if we down him, Gawd help him!" interrupted the woman.

"Haud thy tongue, wench!" said the Master impatiently. "Who art thou to put in thy word? Happen I might draw my hand across thy face."

The woman did not take the threat amiss.

"Wilt have enough for thy hand to do, Jock," said she. "Get quit o' this gradely man afore thou turn on me."

The lovers' quarrel was interrupted by the entrance of a newcomer, a gentleman with a fur-collared overcoat and a very shiny top hat—a top hat of a degree of glossiness which is seldom seen five miles from Hyde Park. This hat he wore at the extreme back of his head, so that the lower surface of the brim made a kind of frame for his high, bald forehead, his keen eyes, his rugged and yet kindly face. He bustled in with the quiet air of possession with which the ring-master enters the circus.

"It's Mr. Stapleton, the referee from London," said Wilson.

"How do you do, Mr. Stapleton? I was introduced to you at the big fight at the Corinthian Club, in Piccadilly."

"Ah, I dare say," said the other, shaking hands. "Fact is, I'm introduced to so many that I can't undertake to carry their names. Wilson, is it? Well, Mr. Wilson, glad to see you. Couldn't get a fly at the station, and that's why I'm late."

"I'm sure, sir," said Armitage, "we should be proud that anyone so well known in the boxing world should come down to our little exhibition."

"Not at all. Not at all. Anything in the interests of boxin'. All ready? Men weighed?"

"Weighing now, sir."

"Ah, just as well I should see it done. Seen you

before, Craggs. Saw you fight your second battle against Willox. You had beaten him once, but he came back on you. What does the indicator say?—one hundred and sixty-three pounds—two off for the kit—one hundred and sixty-one. Now, my lad, you jump. My goodness, what colors are you wearing?"

"The Anonymi Cricket Club."

"What right have you to wear them? I belong to the club myself."

"So do I."

"You an amateur?"

"Yes, sir."

"And you are fighting for a money prize?"

"Yes."

"I suppose you know what you are doing? You realize that you're a professional pug from this onwards, and that if ever you fight again—"

"I'll never fight again."

"Happen you won't," said the woman, and the Master turned a terrible eye upon her.

"Well, I suppose you know your own business best. Up you jump. One hundred and fifty-one, minus two, one hundred and forty-nine—twelve pounds difference, but youth and condition on the other scale. Well, the sooner we get to work the better, for I wish to catch the seven-o'clock express at Hellifield. Twenty three-minute rounds, with one-minute intervals, and Queensberry rules. Those are the conditions, are they not?"

"Yes, sir."

"Very good, then we may go across."

The two combatants had overcoats thrown over their shoulders, and the whole party, backers, fighters, seconds, and the referee, filed out of the room. A police inspector was waiting for them in the road. He had a notebook in his hand—that terrible weapon which awes even the London cabman.

"I must take your names, gentlemen, in case it should be necessary to proceed for breach of peace."

"You don't mean to stop the fight?" cried Armitage, in a passion of indignation. "I'm Mr. Armitage, of Croxley, and this is Mr. Wilson, and we'll be responsible that all is fair and as it should be."

"I'll take the names in case it should be necessary to proceed," said the inspector impassively.

"But you know me well."

"If you was a dook or even a judge it would be all the same," said the inspector. "It's the law, and there's an end. I'll not take upon myself to stop the fight, seeing that gloves are to be used, but I'll take the names of all concerned. Silas Craggs, Robert Montgomery, Edward Barton,

James Stapleton, of London. Who seconds Silas Craggs?"

"I do," said the woman. "Yes, you can stare, but it's my job, and no one else's. Anastasia's the name—four a's."

"Craggs?"

"Johnson. Anastasia Johnson. If you jug him, you can jug me."

"Who talked of juggin', ye fool?" growled the Master. "Coom on, Mr. Armitage, for I'm fair sick o' this loiterin'."

The inspector fell in with the procession, and proceeded, as they walked up the hill, to bargain in his official capacity for a front seat, where he could safeguard the interests of the law, and in his private capacity to lay out thirty shillings at seven to one with Mr. Armitage. Through the door they passed, down a narrow lane walled with a dense bank of humanity, up a wooden ladder to a platform, over a rope which was slung waist-high from four corner stakes, and then Montgomery realized that he was in that ring in which his immediate destiny was to be worked out. On the stake at one corner there hung a blue-and-white streamer. Barton led him across, the overcoat dangling loosely from his shoulders, and he sat down on a wooden stool. Barton and another man, both wearing white sweaters, stood beside him. The so-called ring was a square, twenty feet each way. At the opposite angle was the sinister figure of the Master, with his redheaded woman and a rough-faced friend to look after him. At each corner were metal basins, pitchers of water, and sponges.

During the hubbub and uproar of the entrance Montgomery was too bewildered to take things in. But now there was a few minutes' delay, for the referee had lingered behind, and so he looked quietly about him. It was a sight to haunt him for a lifetime. Wooden seats had been built in, sloping upward to the tops of the walls. Above, instead of a ceiling, a great flight of crows passed slowly across a square of gray cloud. Right up to the topmost benches the folk were banked—broadcloth in front, corduroys and fustian behind; faces turned everywhere upon him. The gray reek of the pipes filled the building, and the air was pungent with the acrid smell of cheap, strong tobacco. Everywhere among the human faces were to be seen the heads of the dogs. They growled and yapped from the back benches. In that dense mass of humanity one could hardly pick out individuals, but Montgomery's eyes caught the brazen gleam of the helmets held upon the knees of the ten yeoman of his escort. At the very edge of the platform sat the reporters, five of them: three locals, and two all the way from London. But where was the all-important referee? There was no sign of him, unless he were in the center of that angry swirl of men near the door.

Mr. Stapleton had stopped to examine the gloves which were to be used, and entered the building after the combatants. He had started to come down that narrow lane with the human walls which led to the ring. But already it had gone abroad that the Wilson champion was a gentleman, and that another gentleman had been appointed as referee. A wave of suspicion passed through the Croxley folk. They would have one of their own people for a referee. They would not have a stranger. His path was stopped as he made for the ring. Excited men flung themselves in front of him; they waved their fists in his face and cursed him. A woman howled vile names in his ear. Somebody struck at him with an umbrella. "Go thou back to Lunnon. We want noan o' thee. Go thou back!" they yelled.

Stapleton, with his shiny hat cocked backwards, and his large, bulging forehead swelling from under it, looked round him from beneath his bushy brows. He was in the center of a savage and dangerous mob. Then he drew his watch from his pocket and held it dial upwards in his palm.

"In three minutes," said he, "I will declare the fight off."

They raged round him. His cool face and that aggressive top hat irritated them. Grimy hands were raised. But it was difficult, somehow, to strike a man who was absolutely indifferent.

"In two minutes I declare the fight off."

They exploded into blasphemy. The breath of angry men smoked into his placid face. A gnarled, grimy fist vibrated at the end of his nose. "We tell thee we want noan o' thee. Get thou back where thou coms't from."

"In one minute I declare the fight off."

Then the calm persistence of the man conquered the swaying, mutable, passionate crowd.

"Let him through, mon. Happen there'll be no fight after a'."

"Let him through."

"Bill, thou loomp, let him pass. Dost want the fight declared off?"

"Make room for the referee!—room for the Lunnon referee!"

And half pushed, half carried, he was swept up to the ring. There were two chairs by the side of it, one for him and one for the timekeeper. He sat down, his hands on his knees, his hat at a more wonderful angle than ever, impassive but solemn, with the aspect of one who appreciates his responsibilities.

Mr. Armitage, the portly butcher, made his way into the ring and held up two fat hands, sparkling with rings, as a signal for silence.

"Gentlemen!" he yelled. And then in a crescendo shriek, "Gentlemen!"

"And ladies!" cried somebody, for indeed there was a fair sprinkling of women among the crowd. "Speak up, owd man!" shouted another. "What price pork chops?" cried somebody at the back. Everybody laughed, and the dogs began to bark. Armitage waved his hands amidst the uproar as if he were conducting an orchestra. At last the babel thinned into silence.

"Gentlemen," he yelled, "the match is between Silas Craggs, whom we call the Master of Croxley, and Robert Montgomery, of the Wilson Coalpits. The match was to be under eleven-eight. When they were weighed just now Craggs weighed eleven-seven, and Montgomery ten-nine. The conditions of the contest are—the best of twenty three-minute rounds with two-ounce gloves. Should the fight run to its full length, it will, of course, be decided upon points. Mr. Stapleton, the well-known London referee, has kindly consented to see fair play. I wish to say that Mr. Wilson and I, the chief backers of the two men, have every confidence in Mr. Stapleton, and that we beg that you will accept his rulings without dispute."

He then turned from one combatant to the other, with a wave of his hand.

### III

"Montgomery—Craggs!" said he.

A great hush fell over the huge assembly. Even the dogs stopped yapping; one might have thought that the monstrous room was empty. The two men had stood up, the small white gloves over their hands. They advanced from their corners and shook hands: Montgomery gravely, Craggs with a smile. Then they fell into position. The crowd gave a long sigh—the intake of a thousand excited breaths. The referee tilted his chair on its back legs, and looked moodily critical from the one to the other.

It was strength against activity—that was evident from the first. The Master stood solidly upon his K-leg. It gave him a tremendous pedestal; one could hardly imagine his being knocked down. And he could pivot round upon it with extraordinary quickness; but his advance or retreat was ungainly. His frame, however, was so much larger and broader than that of the student, and his brown, massive face looked so resolute and menacing, that the hearts of the Wilson party sank within them. There was one

heart, however, which had not done so. It was that of Robert Montgomery.

Any nervousness which he may have had completely passed away now that he had his work before him. Here was something definite —this hard-faced, deformed Hercules to beat, with a career as the price of beating him. He glowed with the joy of action; it thrilled through his nerves. He faced his man with little in-and-out steps, breaking to the left, breaking to the right, feeling his way, while Craggs, with a dull, malignant eye, pivoted slowly upon his weak leg, his left arm half extended, his right sunk low across the mark. Montgomery led with his left, and then led again, getting lightly home each time. He tried again, but the Master had his counter ready, and Montgomery reeled back from a harder blow than he had given. Anastasia, the woman, gave a shrill cry of encouragement, and her man let fly his right. Montgomery ducked under it, and in an instant the two were in each other's arms.

"Break away! Break away!" said the referee.

The Master struck upwards on the break, and shook Montgomery with the blow. Then it was "time." It had been a spirited opening round. The people buzzed into comment and applause. Montgomery was quite fresh, but the hairy chest of the Master was rising and falling. The man passed a sponge over his head, while Anastasia flapped the towel before him. "Good lass! Good lass!" cried the crowd, and cheered her.

The men were up again, the Master grimly watchful, Montgomery as alert as a kitten. The Master tried a sudden rush, squattering along with his awkward gait, but coming faster than one would think. The student slipped aside and avoided him. The Master stopped, grinned, and shook his head. Then he motioned with his hand as an invitation to Montgomery to come to him. The student did so and led with his left, but got a swinging right counter in the ribs in exchange. The heavy blow staggered him, and the Master came scrambling in to complete his advantage; but Montgomery, with his greater activity, kept out of danger until the call of "time." A tame round, and the advantage to the Master.

"T' Maister's too strong for him," said a smelter to his neighbor.

"Ay; but t'other's a likely lad. Happen we'll see some sport yet. He can joomp rarely."

"But t' Maister can stop and hit rarely. Happen he'll mak him joomp when he gets his nieve upon him."

They were up again, the water glistening upon their faces. Montgomery led instantly and got his right home with a sounding smack upon the

Master's forehead. There was a shout from the colliers, and "Silence! Order!" from the referee. Montgomery avoided the counter and scored with his left. Fresh applause, and the referee upon his feet in indignation. "No comments, gentlemen. if *you* please, during the rounds."

"Just bide a bit!" growled the Master.

"Don't talk—fight!" said the referee angrily.

Montgomery rubbed in the point by a flush hit upon the mouth, and the Master shambled back to his corner like an angry bear, having had all the worst of the round.

"Where's thot seven to one?" shouted Purvis, the publican. "I'll take six to one!"

There were no answers.

"Five to one!" There were givers at that. Purvis booked them in a tattered notebook.

Montgomery began to feel happy. He lay back with his legs outstretched, his back against the corner post, and one gloved hand upon each rope. What a delicious minute it was between each round. If he could only keep out of harm's way, he must surely wear this man out before the end of twenty rounds. He was so slow that all his strength went for nothing. "You're fightin' a winnin' fight—a winnin' fight," Ted Barton whispered in his ear. "Go canny; tak' no chances; you have him proper."

But the Master was crafty. He had fought so many battles with his maimed limb that he knew how to make the best of it. Warily and slowly he maneuvered round Montgomery, stepping forward and yet again forward until he had imperceptibly backed him into his corner. The student suddenly saw a flash of triumph upon the grim face, and a gleam in the dull, malignant eyes. The Master was upon him. He sprang aside and was on the ropes. The Master smashed in one of his terrible uppercuts, and Montgomery half broke it with his guard. The student sprang the other way and was against the other converging rope. He was trapped in the angle. The Master sent in another, with a hoggish grunt which spoke of the energy behind it. Montgomery ducked, but got a jab from the left upon the mark. He closed with his man. "Break away! Break away!" cried the referee. Montgomery disengaged, and got a swinging blow on the ear as he did so. It had been a damaging round for him, and the Croxley people were shouting their delight.

"Gentlemen, I will *not* have this noise!" Stapleton roared. "I have been accustomed to preside at a well-conducted club, and not at a bear garden." This little man, with the tilted hat and the bulging forehead, dominated the whole assembly. He was like a headmaster among his boys. He glared round him, and nobody cared to meet his eye.

Anastasia had kissed the Master when he resumed his seat. "Good lass. Do't again!" cried the laughing crowd, and the angry Master shook his glove at her, as she flapped her towel in front of him. Montgomery was weary and a little sore, but not depressed. He had learned something. He would not again be tempted into danger.

For three rounds the honors were fairly equal. The student's hitting was quicker, the Master's harder. Profiting by his lesson, Montgomery kept himself in the open, and refused to be herded into a corner. Sometimes the Master succeeded in rushing him to the side ropes, but the younger man slipped away, or closed and then disengaged. The monotonous "Break away! Break away!" of the referee broke in upon the quick, low patter of rubber-soled shoes, and the dull thud of the blows, and the sharp, hissing breath of two tired men.

The ninth round found both of them in fairly good condition. Montgomery's head was still singing from the blow that he had had in the corner, and one of his thumbs pained him acutely and seemed to be dislocated. The Master showed no sign of a touch, but his breathing was more labored, and a long line of ticks upon the referee's paper showed that the student had a good show of points. But one of this ironman's blows was worth three of his, and he knew that without the gloves he could not have stood for three rounds against him. All the amateur work that he had done was the merest tapping and flapping when compared to those frightful blows, from arms toughened by the shovel and the crowbar.

It was the tenth round, and the fight was half over. The betting now was only three to one, for the Wilson champion had held his own much better than had been expected. But those who knew the ringcraft as well as the staying power of the old prize fighter knew that the odds were still a long way in his favor.

"Have a care of him!" whispered Barton, as he sent his man up to the scratch. "Have a care! He'll play thee a trick, if he can."

But Montgomery saw, or imagined he saw, that his antagonist was tiring. He looked jaded and listless, and his hands drooped a little from their position. His own youth and condition were beginning to tell. He sprang in and brought off a fine left-handed lead. The Master's return lacked his usual fire. Again Montgomery led, and again he got home. Then he tried his right upon the mark, and the Master guarded it downwards.

"Too low! Too low! A foul! A foul!" yelled a thousand voices.

The referee rolled his sardonic eyes slowly round. "Seems to me this buildin' is chock-full of referees," said he.

The people laughed and applauded, but their favor was as immaterial to him as their anger.

"No applause, please! This is not a theater!" he yelled.

Montgomery was very pleased with himself. His adversary was evidently in a bad way. He was piling on his points and establishing a lead. He might as well make hay while the sun shone. The Master was looking all abroad. Montgomery popped one upon his blue jowl and got away without a return. And then the Master suddenly dropped both his hands and began rubbing his thigh. Ah! that was it, was it? He had muscular cramp.

"Go in! Go in!" cried Teddy Barton.

Montgomery sprang wildly forward, and the next instant was lying half senseless, with his neck nearly broken, in the middle of the ring.

The whole round had been a long conspiracy to tempt him within reach of one of those terrible right-hand uppercuts for which the Master was famous. For this the listless, weary bearing, for this the cramp in the thigh. When Montgomery had sprung in so hotly he had exposed himself to such a blow as neither flesh nor blood could stand. Whizzing up from below with a rigid arm, which put the Master's eleven stone into its force, it struck him under the jaw: he whirled half round, and fell a helpless and half-paralyzed mass. A vague groan and murmur, inarticulate, too excited for words, rose from the great audience. With open mouths and staring eyes they gazed at the twitching and quivering figure.

"Stand back! Stand right back!" shrieked the referee, for the Master was standing over his man ready to give him the *coup-de-grâce* as he rose.

"Stand back, Craggs, this instant!" Stapleton repeated.

The Master sank his hands sulkily and walked backwards to the rope with his ferocious eyes fixed upon his fallen antagonist. The timekeeper called the seconds. If ten of them passed before Montgomery rose to his feet, the fight was ended. Ted Barton wrung his hands and danced about in an agony in his corner.

As if in a dream—a terrible nightmare—the student could hear the voice of the timekeeper— three . . . four . . . five—he got up on his hand—six . . . seven—he was on his knee, sick, swimming, faint, but resolute to rise. Eight—he was up, and the Master was on him like a tiger, lashing savagely at him with both hands. Folk held their breath as they watched those terrible blows, and anticipated the pitiful end—so much more pitiful where a game but helpless man refuses to accept defeat.

Strangely automatic is the human brain. Without volition, without effort, there shot into the memory of this bewildered, staggering, half-stupefied man the one thing which could have saved him—that blind eye of which the Master's son had spoken. It was the same as the other to look at, but Montgomery remembered that he had said that it was the left. He reeled to the left side, half felled by a drive which lit upon his shoulder. The Master pivoted round upon his leg and was at him in an instant.

"Yark him, lad! Yark him!" screamed the woman.

"Hold your tongue!" said the referee.

Montgomery slipped to the left again and yet again; but the Master was too quick and clever for him. He struck round and got him full on the face as he tried once more to break away. Montgomery's knees weakened under him, and he fell with a groan on the floor. This time he knew that he was done. With bitter agony he realized, as he groped blindly with his hands, that he could not possibly raise himself. Far away and muffled he heard, amid the murmurs of the multitude, the fateful voice of the time-keeper counting off the seconds.

"One . . . two . . . three . . . four . . . five . . . six . . ."

"Time!" said the referee.

Then the pent-up passion of the great assembly broke loose. Croxley gave a deep groan of disappointment. The Wilsons were on their feet, yelling with delight. There was still a chance for them. In four more seconds their man would have been solemnly counted out. But now he had a minute in which to recover. The referee looked round with relaxed features and laughing eyes. He loved this rough game, this school for humble heroes, and it was pleasant to him to intervene as a *deus ex machina* at so dramatic a moment. His chair and his hat were both tilted at an extreme angle; he and the timekeeper smiled at each other. Ted Barton and the other second had rushed out and thrust an arm each under Montgomery's knee, the other behind his loins, and so carried him back to his stool. His head lolled upon his shoulder, but a douche of cold water sent a shiver through him, and he started and looked round him.

"He's a' right!" cried the people round. "He's a rare brave lad. Good lad! Good lad!" Barton poured some brandy into his mouth. The mists cleared a little, and he realized where he was and what he had to do. But he was still very weak, and he hardly dared to hope that he could survive another round.

"Seconds out of the ring!" cried the referee. "Time!"

The Croxley Master sprang eagerly off his stool.

"Keep clear of him! Go easy for a bit," said Barton, and Montgomery walked out to meet his man once more.

He had had two lessons—the one when the Master got him into his corner, the other when he had been lured into mixing it up with so powerful an antagonist. Now he would be wary. Another blow would finish him; he could afford to run no risks. The Master was determined to follow up his advantage, and rushed at him, slogging furiously right and left. But Montgomery was too young and active to be caught. He was strong upon his legs once more, and his wits had all come back to him. It was a gallant sight —the line-of-battle ship trying to pour its overwhelming broadside into the frigate, and the frigate maneuvering always so as to avoid it. The Master tried all his ringcraft. He coaxed the student up by pretending inactivity; he rushed at him with furious rushes toward the ropes. For three rounds he exhausted every wile in trying to get at him. Montgomery during all this time was conscious that his strength was minute by minute coming back to him. The spinal jar from an uppercut is overwhelming, but evanescent. He was losing all sense of it beyond a great stiffness of the neck. For the first round after his downfall he had been content to be entirely on the defensive, only too happy if he could stall off the furious attacks of the Master. In the second he occasionally ventured upon a light counter. In the third he was smacking back merrily when he saw an opening. His people yelled their approval of him at the end of every round. Even the ironworkers cheered him with that fine unselfishness which true sport engenders. To most of them, unspiritual and unimaginative, the sight of this clean-limbed young Apollo, rising above disaster and holding on while consciousness was in him to his appointed task, was the greatest thing their experience had ever known.

But the Master's naturally morose temper became more and more murderous at this postponement of his hopes. Three rounds ago the battle had been in his hands; now it was all to do over again. Round by round his man was recovering his strength. By the fifteenth he was strong again in wind and limb. But the vigilant Anastasia saw something which encouraged her.

"That bash in t' ribs is telling on him, Jock," she whispered. "Why else should he be gulping t' brandy? Go in, lad, and thou hast him yet."

Montgomery had suddenly taken the flask from Barton's hand, and had a deep pull at the contents. Then, with his face a little flushed, and with a curious look of purpose, which made the referee stare hard at him, in his eyes, he rose for the sixteenth round.

"Game as a pairtridge!" cried the publican, as he looked at the hard-set face.

"Mix it oop, lad; mix it oop!" cried the ironmen to their Master.

And then a hum of exultation ran through their ranks as they realized that their tougher, harder, stronger man held the vantage, after all.

Neither of the men showed much sign of punishment. Small gloves crush and numb, but they do not cut. One of the Master's eyes was even more flush with his cheek than Nature had made it. Montgomery had two or three livid marks upon his body, and his face was haggard, save for that pink spot which the brandy had brought into either cheek. He rocked a little as he stood opposite his man, and his hands drooped as if he felt the gloves to be an unutterable weight. It was evident that he was spent and desperately weary. If he received one other blow it must surely be fatal to him. If he brought one home, what power could there be behind it, and what chance was there of its harming the colossus in front of him? It was the crisis of the fight. This round must decide it. "Mix it oop, lad; mix it oop!" the ironmen whooped. Even the savage eyes of the referee were unable to restrain the excited crowd.

"Mix it oop, lad; mix it oop!" cried the ironmen to their Master.

Now, at last, the chance had come for Montgomery. He had learned a lesson from his more experienced rival. Why should he not play his own game upon him? He was spent, but not nearly so spent as he pretended. That brandy was to call up his reserves, to let him have strength to take full advantage of the opening when it came. It was thrilling and tingling through his veins, at the very moment when he was lurching and rocking like a beaten man. He acted his part admirably. The Master felt that there was an easy task before him, and rushed in with ungainly activity to finish it once for all. He slap-banged away left and right, boring Montgomery up against the ropes, swinging in his ferocious blows with those animal grunts which told of the vicious energy behind them.

But Montgomery was too cool to fall a victim

to any of those murderous uppercuts. He kept out of harm's way with a rigid guard, an active foot, and a head which was swift to duck. And yet he contrived to present the same appearance of a man who is hopelessly done. The Master, weary from his own shower of blows, and fearing nothing from so weak a man, dropped his hand for an instant, and at that instant Montgomery's right came home.

It was a magnificent blow, straight, clean, crisp, with the force of the loins and the back behind it. And it landed where he had meant it to—upon the exact point of that blue-grained chin. Flesh and blood could not stand such a blow in such a place. Neither valor nor hardihood can save the man to whom it comes. The Master fell backwards, flat, prostrate, striking the ground with so simultaneous a clap that it was like a shutter falling from a wall. A yell which no referee could control broke from the crowded benches as the giant went down. He lay upon his back, his knees a little drawn up, his huge chest panting. He twitched and shook, but could not move. His feet pawed convulsively once or twice. It was no use. He was done. "Eight . . . nine . . . ten!" said the timekeeper, and the roar of a thousand voices, with a deafening clap like the broadside of a ship, told that the Master of Croxley was the Master no more.

Montgomery stood half dazed, looking down at the huge prostrate figure. He could hardly realize that it was indeed all over. He saw the referee motion towards him with his hand. He heard his name bellowed in triumph from every side. And then he was aware of someone rushing towards him; he caught a glimpse of a flushed face and an aureole of flying red hair; a gloveless fist struck him between the eyes, and he was on his back in the ring beside his antagonist, while a dozen of his supporters were endeavoring to secure the frantic Anastasia. He heard the angry shouting of the referee, the screaming of the furious woman, and the cries of the mob. Then something seemed to break like an overstretched banjo string, and he sank into the deep, deep, mist-girt abyss of unconsciousness.

The dressing was like a thing in a dream, and so was the vision of the Master with the grin of a bulldog upon his face, and his three teeth amiably protruded. He shook Montgomery heartily by the hand.

"I would have been rare pleased to shake thee by the throttle, lad, a short while syne," said he. "But I bear no ill-feelin' again' thee. It was a rare poonch that brought me down—I have not had a better since my second fight wi' Billy Edwards in '89. Happen thou might think o'

goin' further wi' this business. If thou dost, and want a trainer, there's not much inside t' ropes as I don't know. Or happen thou might like to try it wi' me old style and bare knuckles. Thou has but to write to t' ironworks to find me."

But Montgomery disclaimed any such ambition. A canvas bag with his share—one hundred and ninety sovereigns—was handed to him, of which he gave ten to the Master, who also received some share of the gate money.

Then, with young Wilson escorting him on one side, Purvis on the other, and Fawcett carrying his bag behind, he went in triumph to his carriage, and drove amid a long roar, which lined the highway like a hedge for the seven miles, back to his starting point.

"It's the greatest thing I ever saw in my life. By George, it's ripping!" cried Wilson, who had been left in a kind of ecstasy by the events of the day. "There's a chap over Barnsley way who fancies himself a bit. Let us spring you on him, and let him see what he can make of you. We'll put up a purse—won't we, Purvis? You shall never want a backer."

"At his weight," said the publican, "I'm behind him, I am, for twenty rounds, and no age, country, or color barred."

"So am I!" cried Fawcett. "Middleweight champion of the world, that's what he is—here, in the same carriage with us."

But Montgomery was not to be beguiled.

"No; I have my own work to do now."

"And what may that be?"

"I'll use this money to get my medical degree."

"Well, we've plenty of doctors, but you're the only man in the Riding that could smack the Croxley Master off his legs. However, I suppose you know your own business best. When you're a doctor, you'd best come down into these parts, and you'll always find a job waiting for you at the Wilson Coalpits."

Montgomery had returned by devious ways to the surgery. The horses were smoking at the door, and the doctor was just back from his long journey. Several patients had called in his absence, and he was in the worst of tempers.

"I suppose I should be glad that you have come back at all, Mr. Montgomery!" he snarled. "When next you elect to take a holiday, I trust it will not be at so busy a time."

"I am sorry, sir, that you should have been inconvenienced."

"Yes, sir, I have been exceedingly inconvenienced." Here, for the first time, he looked hard at the assistant. "Good heavens, Mr. Montgomery, what have you been doing with your left eye?"

It was where Anastasia had lodged her protest.

Montgomery laughed. "It is nothing, sir," said he.

"And you have a livid mark under your jaw. It is, indeed, terrible that my representative should be going about in so disreputable a condition. How did you receive these injuries?"

"Well, sir, as you know, there was a little glove fight today over at Croxley."

"And you got mixed up with that brutal crowd?"

"I *was* rather mixed up with them."

"And who assaulted you?"

"One of the fighters."

"Which of them?"

"The Master of Croxley."

"Good heavens! Perhaps you interfered with him?"

"Well, to tell the truth, I did a little."

"Mr. Montgomery, in such a practice as mine, intimately associated as it is with the highest and most progressive elements of our small community, it is impossible—"

But just then the tentative bray of a cornet player searching for his keynote jarred upon their ears, and an instant later the Wilson Colliery brass band was in full cry with "See the Conquering Hero Comes" outside the surgery window. There was a banner waving, and a shouting crowd of miners.

"What is it? What does it mean?" cried the angry doctor.

"It means, sir, that I have, in the only way which was open to me, earned the money which is necessary for my education. It is my duty, Dr. Oldacre, to warn you that I am about to return to the University, and that you should lose no time in appointing my successor."

## CARTOON

### REA

*"He's saving up to buy a piece of a heavyweight."*

© 1955, Time Inc. Permission *Sports Illustrated.*

THE FIRST RADIO broadcast of a fight emanated from Boyle's Thirty Acres in Jersey City, New Jersey, on July 2, 1921, when Jack Dempsey defended his heavyweight title against Georges Carpentier, and the announcer was Major Andrew White. The all-time best of the radio blow-by-blow announcers is Don Dunphy, who reported the weekly Friday-night fights and major championship matches from June 18, 1941, through June 24, 1960. During that period he covered more than 800 fights, and this is a sample of what more than 20,000,000 listeners heard when, on September 23, 1952, Jersey Joe Walcott defended the heavyweight championship against Rocky Marciano in Philadelphia in the best heavyweight title fight since Jack Dempsey vs. Luis Angel Firpo twenty-nine years before.

# Jersey Joe Walcott–Rocky Marciano

## DON DUNPHY

### ROUND ONE

THANK YOU, Harry Curran. Good evening, everyone. They get out there [several words missing due to sound failure] wide with a left hand. They go into a clinch. Marciano tries a left to the body. It's short. And referee Charlie Daggert goes over and gets them apart. Marciano, missing a left hand, goes into a clinch. And the big apple is on the line down here at the Municipal Stadium in Philadelphia. They're still on the inside. Walcott is slow with a right hand to the chin. Now they're at long range. Walcott misses with a right over the head; it grazed the hair. In close, Walcott chops a right to the head, brings it to the body. Marciano tries to tie him up on the inside. Most of the milling is in close. At long range Walcott lands with a jab, puts a right on the face, misses a right, crosses a right, chops away with two more rights to the head, bangs both hands to the body, crosses a right to the jaw. Marciano mainly trying to tie him up for a moment, moves his way into a clinch. And Walcott is throwing heavily here in round one. Marciano rips a long right hand to the body, crosses a right to the jaw. Marciano is hurt, with a left and a right to the head by Walcott as they clinch over in Marciano's corner. Two minutes to go. And Marciano is down by a left hook on the chin. He takes a two-count and he's up. Marciano was down by a left hook. Walcott on top of him again with another left hook, rips a right to the head, misses a left jab. Marciano goes in and holds on for a moment and Walcott was within a few seconds of victory. Walcott misses a left hand over the head, and there they are in a clinch again. Now they're at long range. Walcott takes a light right and a long right hand to the head thrown by Marciano. In close. Half the round is gone. Marciano gets away from a right, smashes a right to the jaw and hurts Walcott. And Walcott may have let him get away. Now they're at long range again. Marciano has recovered from the early battering. He takes a solid left hook on the jaw by Walcott, a right high on the head, and Walcott is in trying for a quick knockout if he possibly can. At long range, Marciano makes Walcott miss, drives a left and a right to the jaw and takes a right chop high on the head by the champion, Jersey Joe Walcott. One minute to go in round one now. Walcott crosses a right hand to the jaw. Marciano, as you know, was down for about a two-count. Now they're at long range again. Walcott, working his way in, takes a solid right hand to the jaw, a light right hand to the body by Marciano. Now they're in close again and the referee is getting them apart. At long range, Walcott comes back with a left to the head, moves in close, and Marciano ties him up on the inside. It's been a rocky round for the challenger so far. He takes a solid left hook to the jaw and throws his own right hand to the head as Walcott comes in on him. They're in close again. Now at long range. Marciano misses a left over the head, takes a right chop a couple of times to the body by Walcott. In a clinch. Out of it again. Parted by referee Charlie Daggert. Walcott misses a right over the head, misses a left, and Marciano has gone into a crouching style and on the inside chops a short right to the jaw. A right to the head and a right and a left to the jaw by Marciano. After Walcott had scored first, Marciano comes back with solid thumps to the head. Marciano digs a left hand to the body. They're in a clinch just above us now. Walcott backs away to the center of the ring and now they tie each other up on the inside and this round is almost over. [Sound of bell] There's the bell.

## ROUND THIRTEEN

ALL RIGHT, Harry. Marciano has been in trouble —in trouble the last couple of rounds—but he gets out there quickly and moves in on Walcott, who paws out with a left hand to the body. It's short. Marciano is short with a left jab aimed at the head. Marciano digs a left hand to the pit of the stomach of Walcott, Walcott backing away now. Here's Marciano moving in on him again, Walcott feinting the left hand, going into a shuffle, Marciano bulling his way in close. Walcott's ageless legs keep taking him back out of trouble whenever he gets into it. Marciano bulling his way in close. Walcott is back to the ropes. Takes a right to the jaw. Walcott is staggered and helpless on the ropes, with a right to the jaw. Walcott is down on his stomach and they're counting over him. It may be a knockout. I don't think Walcott can get up. It's going to be a knockout for Marciano. Rocky Marciano by a knockout. A straight right-hand punch to the jaw. And Walcott rolls over. He is still out cold. It is a knockout, and we have a new heavyweight champion of the world. It is Rocky Marciano, still undefeated, from Brockton, Massachusetts.

PIERCE EGAN (177?–1849) was the first to make a career of sports writing, and boxing's first historian. In 1812 he put out the first paper-bound installment of *Boxiana,* a monthly publication covering boxing, or milling as it was called in Regency England. Between 1813 and 1828 he brought out five bound volumes containing biographical sketches of the fighters, round-by-round descriptions of their key fights and ringside sidelights such as the fluctuations in the price, the weather or the temper of the crowd. He was a stakeholder, a song writer, a novelist and an inspiration to Charles Dickens. Corinthian Tom and Jerry Hawthorne, from his 1821 best seller, *Life in London,* gave their names to the toddy.

# Jem Belcher

### FROM BRISTOL

### *(ONE OF THE MOST HEROIC CHAMPIONS OF ENGLAND)*

## PIERCE EGAN

DESCENDING FROM the mighty *Slack,* of pugilistic celebrity, and grandson of that renowned boxer. The family of the BELCHERS have long been distinguished for their prowess—and the three brothers, JEM, Tom, and Ned, in their various trials of skill, have, in no degree, *sullied* the *milling* fame of their ancestor. In tracing the valorous deeds of BELCHER, candour alone dictates us to observe that, in finding scarcely any thing to condemn, we are almost overwhelmed with circumstances to applaud. To him modern boxing is principally indebted for that extensive patronage and support which it has experienced from the *higher flights* of the Fancy! Upon JEM's first appearance as a pugilist, he was considered a perfect phenomenon in the gymnastic art—*a mere boy,* scarcely twenty years of age, putting all the celebrated heroes of the *Old School* at defiance—their scientific efforts, when placed in competition with his peculiar mode of fighting, were not only completely baffled, but rendered unavailing. BELCHER had a prepossessing appearance, genteel, and remarkably placid in his behavior. There was nothing about his person that indicated superior bodily strength; yet, when stripped,

his form was muscular and elegant. The *science* that he was master of appeared exclusively his own—and his antagonists were not aware of the singular advantages that it gave him over those who studied and fought upon the accustomed principles of pugilism; it was completely intuitive; practice had rendered its effects powerful, and in confusing his antagonists he gained considerable time to improve this native advantage with promptitude and decision. The quickness of his *hits* were unparalleled; they were severely *felt,* but scarcely *seen;* and in springing backwards and forwards, his celerity was truly astonishing—and, in this particular respect, it might be justly said that JEM was without an equal! BELCHER's style was original; the amateur was struck with its excellence; his antagonist terrified from the gaiety and decision it produced; and the fighting men, in general, were confounded with his *sang froid* and intrepidity. It appears that BELCHER made his appearance under the auspices of *Bill Warr;* and it is but justice to observe that the talents of so *finished* a pupil reflected great credit upon that experienced veteran in the gymnastic art.

In his social hours, JEM was good-natured in the extreme, and modest and unassuming to a degree almost bordering upon bashfulness. In the character of a publican, no man entertained a better sense of propriety and decorum than BELCHER did; and the stranger, in casually mixing with the *Fancy* in his house, to behold *Nature* in her *primest* moments of recreation, never felt any danger of being affronted, from the attentive conduct of the landlord. Good order reigned predominant, and frequently very animated criticisms have taken place concerning the merits of the *stage;* and the various talents of most of the first-rate performers, who *sported* their *figures* upon the boards, have given rise to considerable discussion, in which the high and dignified legislator has been heard to *argufy the topic* in the most earnest manner, to convince his *plebeian* opponent (whose situation in life was, perhaps, not more elevated than that of a *coal-porter* or a *costermonger*) of the superior abilities of some particular actor, whose *action* has proved more *convincing* in a few minutes than all the words contained in *Johnson's* folio dictionary could effect; and, in turn, those *composites* of the state have been listening with the most minute attention to the flowing harangue of some *dusty cove, blowing a cloud* over his porter, and lavish with his *slum* on the beauties possessed by some *distinguished* pugilist, whose talents for *serving it out* were elegant and *striking.* And also where *flash* has been *pattered* in all that native purity of style and richness of eloquence that would have startled a *high toby gloque* and put a *jigger screw* upon the alert to find so many *down;* and, even among the heterogeneous crowd have been found admirers of *Hermes,* who have retired well persuaded that all *were not barren!*

*"Yet more; the diff'rence is as great between*
*The optics seeing, as the object seen.*
*All manners take a tincture from our own,*
*Or come discolour'd, through our passions shown,*
*Or Fancy's beam enlarges, multiplies,*
*Contracts, inverts, and gives ten thousand dyes."*

BELCHER's *bottom,* judgment, and activity, have never been surpassed—in his battle with *Paddington Jones,* a pugilist extremely well versed in the *science,* and of good *bottom,* who had also distinguished himself in several fights, and was considered by the amateurs a man that might be depended upon, and one that was not *easily* disposed of, was compelled, in a short conflict, to yield to BELCHER. *Jack Bartholomew* (a thorough-bred and sound pugilist) was defeated by JEM; when the latter performed such prodigies of valour that he astonished the most scientific professors. *Gamble,* who had *milled* all the *primest coves* in the kingdom for some years, *lost,* in a few minutes, all his *consequence,* from the dexterity of BELCHER. In his various fights with *Burke,* either prepared or taken *unawares,* he *hit* away, and gave that most inordinate *glutton* several hearty meals, with all the ease and facility of an experienced caterer. *Fearby* (the *young Ruffian*), who had distinguished himself so manfully in several excellent matches, and who had obtained the appellation of a first-rate pugilist, both for science and bottom, from the best judges among the amateurs, yet, when in competition with BELCHER, his abilities were so reduced as to appear more like that of a third- or fourth-rate boxer, and was *punished* most dreadfully by JEM, while BELCHER scarcely appeared touched: such, most undoubtedly, was the superiority of BELCHER's talents in all the above battles.

It was warmly, if not perhaps ill-naturedly expressed, by one of the most scientific pugilists in the whole circle of boxers, in giving his opinion respecting the battle between the *Game Chicken* and BELCHER, *"That had JEM been in possession of four eyes, he was never able to beat Pearce."* Here it was, for the first time in his life, that his judgment proved defective as a pugilist; and, in acting from the envious impulse of the moment, JEM BELCHER only portrayed the infirmities of human nature, and the want of stability in man. His character was established, and never did any pugilist's fame stand upon a more elevated and stronger basis; he had retired into private life, respected by his friends, and supported and admired by the *Fancy* in general, who were no strangers to his integrity and private worth—there he should have remained, where his days might have glided happily along, without regret, and his life, in all probability, been lengthened from the placid scene—but his rest was unhappily disturbed, and poor JEM, like the greatest part of mankind, had not *fortitude* enough to rise superior to the baleful attacks of

*". . . malicious Envie rode*
*Upon a ravenous wolf, and still did chaw*
*Between his cank'red teeth a venomous toad,*
*that all the poyson run about his jaw*
*But inwardly he chawed his own maw,*
*At neighbour's wealth, that made him ever sad,*
*For death it was, when any good he saw,*
*And wept, that cause of weeping none HE had!"*

In constitution BELCHER had materially declined, independent of the loss of an eye, and the serious effects which his frame sustained upon that afflicting accident had endangered the safety of his life. Upwards of two years had elapsed in retirement, when BELCHER came forward to meet an opponent more formidable than any one he had hitherto met with, and who possessed, in a superior degree, every requisite to constitute a first-rate pugilist, and who, likewise, had improved under his tuition, and might be said *a chicken of his own rearing!* BELCHER, unfortunately, could not be persuaded of the difficulties he would have to encounter from the loss of an eye, and that the *chance* of success was against him, *till it was too late!* and then the error was too glaring to be retrieved. But how did he fight? How he *did fight* will be long remembered by those who witnessed the *grievous,* yet truly honourable combat; a combat in which more unaffected courage was never seen, and where humanity was more conspicuously displayed and gratefully applauded. Animosity appeared to have no resting-place, and it was proud honour, only, struggling for victory. BELCHER fought in his accustomed style, and planted his favourite *hits* with his usual adroitness; but he lost his distance, and became an easy victim to his own incredulity. In the course of the fight, as JEM afterwards acknowledged, his sight became so defective, from the *hits* which he received over his good eye (the peculiar object of his antagonist's aim), that the blows he gave his adversary were merely accidental, his aim was lost in confusion, and certainty was out of the question. BELCHER, with the most undaunted heroism, endeavoured to make up the deficiency of sight by a display of *bottom* and gaiety, astonishing and unequalled. The skill upon both sides claimed universal respect: yet, notwithstanding the spectators perceived a deficiency in BELCHER's fighting in several parts, from his not being able to guard off the attacks as heretofore, and the severe *punishment* which his head and face had sustained in the combat; his afflicting situation made a deep impression, not only upon his friends, but the company in general, and the involuntary tear was seen silently stealing down the iron cheek of many present, for the loss of departing greatness in their favourite hero. JEM's spirits never forsook him; and, in surrendering his laurels, honour consoled him, that he had transferred them *unsullied;* and appeared only affected, by declaring, "that his sorrow was more occasioned from the recollection of the severe loss of a particular friend, who, in fact, had sported everything which he possessed upon his head, and also one of his most staunch backers and supporters through life, than as to any particular consideration respecting himself." Notwithstanding the excellence evinced

by the *Chicken* in science, wind, strength, and bottom, and, by no means, feeling the slightest wish to detract from the merits of so respected and deservedly distinguished a pugilist—yet, if we may be allowed the supposition, that had the above contest taken place when JEM BELCHER possessed his eye-sight in full perfection, we hesitate not in observing, that *its* termination might have been very *doubtful!*

Respecting BELCHER's two battles with *Cribb,* when the circumstances of the case are duly appreciated; when it is recollected that his spirits must have been somewhat damped in descending from his elevated eminence, to rank only with men of minor talents, who, when in the plenitude of his health and strength, dared not to have thus presumed; but JEM was down, and *down with him,* as is too generally the case with the unfortunate, and his powers well known to be on the decay, previous to his *set-to* with the *Chicken,* and which were by no means improved from that circumstance; yet still his heroism and *science* shone resplendent, and he left his opponents at a vast distance.

In the first fight with *Cribb,* as may be traced, JEM's superiority was evidently manifest. The former was severely *punished;* and not until BELCHER had received a most violent *hit* over his good eye, and sprained his right hand did *Cribb* appear to have much *chance.* In the seventeenth round, the odds were two to *one* on BELCHER, and in the eighteenth, five to *one!* when *Cribb* was so much beaten, that considerable doubts were entertained whether he would be able to come again; and even at the conclusion of the battle, *Cribb* was in a very exhausted state. The amateurs were delighted with the uncommon skill BELCHER displayed upon this occasion, and were completely astonished at his gaiety and vigour; and, till he had lost his *distance,* from his confused sight, victory appeared to hover round him.

In the last battle that ever BELCHER fought, his bottom was good in the extreme, and he by no means proved an easy conquest to *Cribb.* Since the loss of his eye, it was the positive wish of his best friends that he would fight no more; but he was not to be deterred, unfortunately neglected good advice, and seemed not aware of the decline of his physical powers. In his last *set-to* the disadvantages he had to contend against were great indeed: his antagonist had made a rapid improvement in the science, was in full vigour, and a glutton that was not to be *satisfied* in a common way; yet still JEM portrayed that the *science* was left in him, but the *strength* had departed; his hands had become enfeebled, and could not execute their accustomed task, and

128

were so dreadfully lacerated for several of the last rounds, that the flesh had separated from the nails. *Death* was almost as agreeable to his feelings as to utter those unwelcome sounds to the courageous mind, as acknowledgment of *defeat.* Never was it given with more reluctance, and his friends positively forced it from him, after a contest of forty minutes!

BELCHER's display with *Tom* (better known by the name of *Paddington*) *Jones*, convinced the amateurs of his peculiar *science, spirit*, and *bottom:* and after a desperate conflict, in which considerable judgment was shown upon both sides, BELCHER was declared the conqueror. He soon rose rapidly into fame, and was matched against the most distinguished pugilists.

The *sporting world* were now all upon the alert, with a match which had long excited considerable attention, between *Jack Bartholomew*, a pugilist of high repute, and JEM BELCHER. The former was a great favourite among the *Fancy*, and had attained the age of thirty-seven; while the latter had not reached his *twentieth year*. The battle was for 300 guineas, and fought upon a stage, on Finchley Common, on Thursday, May 15, 1800.

About half-past one the combatants appeared, and the *set-to* immediately commenced:—sparring was out of the question, and ferocity the leading feature; but BELCHER showed himself off in such good style, and convinced the spectators that the advantage was upon his side, that the odds were now laid upon him. *Bartholomew*, not in the least dismayed, went in boldly, and gave BELCHER a *leveller.* The friends of *Bartholomew* were weak enough, upon this circumstance, to send a pigeon to London with the intelligence, making up their minds that the battle was a *dead thing* in their favour; but they soon had to repent of their temerity, for in the fourth round BELCHER with great agility threw *Bartholomew* upon his head, the shock of which was so violent as nearly to deprive him of his senses, and materially to affect his eye-sight. *Bartholomew*, still *prime*, fought in good style, and contested the battle with great firmness, and dealt out some most tremendous blows, until the close of the seventeenth round, wherein he received a desperate hit in the stomach from BELCHER, that made him vomit great quantities of blood, when he acknowledged he had had *enough.* The battle, for the time it continued, twenty minutes, was very desperate; and considered as obstinate a contest as had been for some years. *Bartholomew* entertained the idea that there was a *chance* left, and ventured a second trial; but he became an easy conquest, and in considerable less time.

*Gamble*, having been successful in eighteen battles, and his knowledge of the *science* being undisputed, it now became the wish of the amateurs that he should enter the lists with JEM BELCHER, who had given such early proofs of excellence, and that it should be decided, whether the honour of the *Championship* was to remain with England or Ireland. Accordingly, a match was agreed upon for one hundred guineas, to be decided in the hollow, near the gibbet of that extraordinary character, *Jerry Abbershaw*, upon Wimbledon-common, on Monday, December 22, 1800. It would be impossible to describe the roads to Wimbledon; the numerous vehicles of all descriptions, and the pedestrians who were flocking to witness this combat. It seemed as if all the inhabitants of London were upon the alert; and the swells of the Fancy were unusually prominent, besides the heroes of the pugilistic art, as *Mr. Jackson, Bill Gibbons, Brown, Back, Paddington Jones*, &c.

BELCHER entered the ring about twelve o'clock, accompanied by his second, *Joe Ward*, and *Bill Gibbons* as his bottle-holder; and *Tom Tring* as an assistant. *Mendoza* was the second to *Gamble;* his bottle-holder *Coady*, and *Crabbe* as deputy. Messrs. *Cullington, Mountain*, and *Lee*, were the umpires. *Cullington*, the publican, held the stakes.

Notwithstanding *Gamble* had beat *James* the Cheshire man, a pugilist that had been successful in seventeen pitched battles, and whose *bottom* was said to be superior to any man in the kingdom; yet still the bets from the first making of the match were *seven* to five in favour of BELCHER; and *Bill Warr*, before the combatants stripped, offered *twenty-five* guineas to twenty. However, on stripping, *Gamble* appeared much the heaviest man, and his friends and countrymen sported *three* to two upon him; but that was by no means the general opinion. A few minutes before one o'clock the fight commenced:—

FIRST ROUND.—The set-to was good, and Gamble put in the first *hit*, which was neatly warded off by BELCHER, and who, with a celerity unequalled, planted in return three severe blows in different parts of Gamble's face: they soon closed, and BELCHER, being well aware of the superiority of his opponent's strength, dropped. The *paddies*, in their eagerness to support their countryman, offered five to four.

Second.—BELCHER, full of spirit, advanced towards Gamble, who retreated. JEM made a feint with his right hand, and with his left struck Gamble so dreadfully over his right eye, as not only to close it immediately, but knocked him down with uncommon violence. Two to one on BELCHER.

Third.—Gamble began to retreat, but put in several severe blows on the body of his antagonist. BELCHER, by a sharp hit, made the *claret* fly copiously from his opponent; but Gamble, notwithstanding, threw BELCHER with considerable violence, and fell upon him cross-ways. The odds rose to four to one upon JEM.

Fourth.—BELCHER, full of coolness and recollection, showed himself possessed of excellent science. His blows were well directed and severely felt, particularly one in the neck, which brought Gamble down. Twenty to one BELCHER was the winner.

Fifth and last round.—Gamble received two such blows that struck him all of a *heap*—one on the stomach, that nearly deprived him of breath; and the other on the kidneys, which instantly swelled as big as a twopenny loaf. Gamble, completely exhausted, *gave in.*

IT IS REPORTED that not less than *twenty thousand pounds* were sported upon this occasion. The Irish were completely *dished,* and full of murmurings at *Gamble's* conduct, who was beaten in five rounds, and in the short space of *nine minutes* and *three quarters! Gamble* fought very badly; and from his former experience much was expected: but he appeared frightened of his opponent's activity. BELCHER laughed at him throughout the fight, and treated his knowledge of the art with the most sovereign contempt. BELCHER was carried upon the shoulders of friends round the ring, in triumph, after the battle was over.

The following conversation immediately afterwards took place between *Mendoza* and BELCHER. A match had been in agitation for some time past between the above celebrated pugilists, for a considerable sum; and, to prevent any injury arising to *Mendoza*, in his capacity as a publican, or the possibility of an interruption to the contest, it was agreed that it should be decided in Scotland; but the match *was off*, and JEM felt rather displeased at the circumstance:—

BELCHER. *Dan Mendoza!*

*Mendoza.* Well, what do you want?

BELCHER. I say, these were the shoes I bought to give you a thrashing in Scotland.

*Mendoza.* Well, the time may come.

BELCHER. I wish you'd do it now.

The parties becoming rather irritated with each other, an immediate *set-to* was nearly the consequence; but their friends stepped in, and prevented it.

BELCHER, witnessing a battle between *Elias, a Jew,* and one *Jones,* which took place upon Wimbledon-common, on Monday, July, 13, 1801, a man of the name of *Burke,* a butcher, who had behaved himself improperly in the outer ring, and who had been *milled* out of it twice by some of the professed pugilists, called out for BELCHER, the Champion. Upon JEM'S mildly asking him what he wanted, the latter received a blow in return for his civility. A dreadful *set-to* instantly commenced—in which *Burke* displayed so much *bottom* and strength, although intoxicated, that the spectators scarcely knew what to think about the termination of the contest. An opinion also prevailed, that had not BELCHER possessed a thorough knowledge of the *science*, there was a great probability of his falling a sacrifice to this outrageous *knight of the cleaver.*

*Burke* having showed so much *game* under such evident disadvantages, *Lord Camelford* was induced to back him, for a second combat in a more *regular* manner, for one hundred pounds. He was accordingly put out to *nurse; a teacher* appointed to initiate him into the mysteries of the *science;* and it was reported of *Burke* that he was a *promising child*—took his food regularly, minded what his master said to him and, for the short time that *he* had taken to *study,* great improvement was visible. *Burke* ultimately turned out one of the most *troublesome* customers, and the hardest to be disposed of, that ever entered the lists with BELCHER.

After some time having elapsed, occasioned by the interruption of magistrates, a stage was erected at Hurley-bottom, a few miles distant from Maidenhead, on November 25, 1801. *Joe Ward* and a *Bristol lad* filled the usual offices for BELCHER—and *Harry Lee* attended as *Burke's* second, and *Rhodes* as his bottle-holder. The odds were nearly two to one, on *setting-to,* upon BELCHER.

FIRST ROUND.—Burke did not give much signs of *improvement* from his tuition—several blows were exchanged, Burke gave BELCHER a terrible blow under his right eye that made him reel. They closed, and fell.

Second, third, and fourth.—Blows were the leading features in these rounds. *Science* was not displayed by either of the combatants.

Fifth.—Burke had his nose laid open, by a severe *hit* from BELCHER, and *floored.*—Ten to one JEM—no takers.

Sixth.—Shyness was prominent; but BELCHER put in a blow upon Burke's forehead; the blood now issued copiously from all parts of his head, that his second found it a difficult task to keep him clean.

Seventh, eighth and ninth.—The former two were of little consequence; but in the latter BELCHER was thrown with considerable violence.

Thirteenth.—*Milling* was the signal, and this round displayed a fine specimen of their talents for *hammering*. The best round in the fight.

Sixteenth.—Burke completely *done up*—yet too much pride to confess he was beat; and his second declared that the fight was over.

SINCE THE DAYS of *Johnson* and *Ben,* it was the opinion of the amateurs, so desperate a battle had not taken place. Twenty-five minutes of hard fighting. *Burke* was heavier than BELCHER, and greatly superior in point of stature; JEM appeared little the worse for the conflict, declaring that he had scarcely felt a blow in the fight: and, in the gaiety of the moment, challenged *Mendoza* to fight in less than a month for three hundred against two hundred guineas: but *Dan* was not to be had, and observed, he had done with pugilism.

Warrants were now issued for the apprehension of BELCHER, *Burke,* and their seconds, *Harry Lee* and *Joe Ward,* "for unlawfully assembling, and publicly fighting, at Hurley, in Berkshire." But this proved to be nothing more than a *reprimand* when brought into Court, on their promising not to break the peace again.

*Burke* was not yet *satisfied;* and another trial of skill was granted, Captain *Fletcher* backing him; and *Fletcher Reid,* Esq., on the part of BELCHER, for fourteen hundred and fifty guineas aside, which were made good. The combatants appeared upon the stage, which was erected in a bye-place, at a village called Grewelthorpe, about nineteen miles from Middleham, in Yorkshire. A dispute taking place about *Burke's* second, BELCHER offered to fight him a few rounds for *love;* but as *Burke* would neither fight for *love* nor *money,* the consequence was, that the *Fancy* were got into a complete *string!* JEM received fifty pounds for his trouble from Mr. *Reid,* who also allowed him five pounds for travelling expenses.

*Burke* now endeavoured to justify himself through the medium of the *Oracle* newspaper, in a long letter to the editor: but it was looked upon as *gammon!*

At Camberwell fair, these heroes met for the first time after the *bubble* in Yorkshire. *Burke* was rather *lushy,* and entertained the *swells* round him, how *he* would *serve it out* to JEM if he was present. BELCHER was nearer than he imagined, and overheard this *bouncing* of *Burke,* and invited him to another *taste;* which the latter readily accepted, and on the bowling-green, at the Golden-Lion, they *set-to.* Burke commenced so furiously, that he attacked BELCHER before he was undressed; but JEM, on being prepared for the fray, put in his blows so hard and fast,

that *Burke* had one of his front teeth knocked out, and a prime *leveller* into the bargain. BELCHER was somewhat indisposed, and *Burke,* now coming a little more to his *recollection*—their friends interfered—and they mutually agreed to postpone the fight till the next day. They met according to appointment (August 20, 1802); and in a field behind St. George's Chapel, near Tyburn turnpike, a most extensive ring was prepared, and though the circumstance was so sudden, and kept very private, yet the spectators were immense. Mr. *Fletcher Reid* and Mr. *Cook* being the only two of the principal amateurs present. A purse of thirty guineas was subscribed for the winner, and five for the loser. *Joe Ward* seconded BELCHER, and *Bill Gibbons* was his bottle-holder; *Burke* had *Owen* for a second, and *Yokel,* a Jew, as bottle-holder. *Burke* expressed a wish that three quarters of a minute might be allowed instead of half, which was resisted.

FIRST ROUND.—Burke was determined to avail himself of his uncommon strength, and ran in upon BELCHER, and endeavoured to throw him, but failed in the attempt. BELCHER, taking advantage of his mistake, soon had him down by his dexterity. Several blows exchanged, but no *corks* were drawn.

Second.—Burke still upon the same suit, but received a *throttler* for his attempt, that made the *claret* fly. They closed, and Burke found himself upon the *ground.*

Third.—Burke, full of spirit, ran in and put home a fierce blow on the right cheek-bone with his left hand; and another between the shoulder and breast, which was of no effect. They closed, and Burke was down.

Fourth.—Burke, still *prime,* rushed upon his opponent, but missing his blow, fell. Some murmurs, and calling out "Burke's at his old tricks"; but he soon showed the charge was false.

Fifth.—Burke, with the most determined resolution, ran in and caught BELCHER by the hams, doubled him up, and gave him a cross-buttock. The spectators were in fear that BELCHER's neck was broken, as JEM pitched upon his head with great violence. "Foul, foul!" was shouted; but BELCHER rose with uncommon gaiety, and said, "No, no—never mind!"

Sixth.—The best round that had been fought. As usual, Burke ran in full of spirit, and severe blows were exchanged. BELCHER put in several severe hits on the head, neck, and throat. They closed, and considerable skill was manifested on both sides in wrestling; but they both fell without any advantage.

Seventh.—Burke on the decline; his strength

was leaving him, but his spirit was good. Closed, and Burke thrown.

Eighth.—Burke wished now to convince the spectators that he was not destitute of *science,* and fought upon the defensive; but BELCHER smiled at the attempt, gave him several severe blows, and ultimately had Burke upon the floor.

Ninth.—Twenty to one on JEM, who was as sprightly as if he had not been fighting—laughing and talking to his antagonist, but not forgetting to put in severe hits. Burke down again.

Tenth.—Burke, full of *pluck,* set-to with great spirit, and close fighting ensued. BELCHER, losing no time, cut Burke under the left eye; under the right; and another blow so dreadful in its effects between the throat and chin, as to hoist Burke off his feet, and he came down head foremost. BELCHER also fell from the force with which he gave it. Both on the floor, when Burke squirted some blood out of his mouth over BELCHER: JEM threatened that in the next round he should have it for such conduct—but Burke declared it was accidental.

Eleventh.—Burke's face was now one mass of blood, and he was completely beaten. But still he stood up; few blows were exchanged—they closed, and Burke was thrown; when JEM, very honourably, fell upon his hands, with an intent not to hurt Burke any more by falling on him, which practice is not unusual, and consistent with fair fighting.

Twelfth.—Burke's weakness was now too evident to be disguised; his second could scarcely get him from the floor.

Thirteenth.—Burke came again, but BELCHER did as he pleased with him; closed and threw Burke. The latter now was convinced there was no *chance,* and wished to give it in; but his seconds persuaded him to proceed.

Fourteenth.—Burke was *game,* but it was useless and only rendered his situation worse; he was knocked about like a feather, and not the least shadow of success remained for him. BELCHER closed, and Burke was thrown upon his chest, he could not come in time, and gave it in.

THUS WAS this *desperate customer* disposed of at last. His face was so disfigured, that scarcely any traces of a human being were left; while, on the contrary, BELCHER was without any visible marks of the contest, excepting a bruise upon his cheek. BELCHER's rapidity of action in this battle claimed universal attention and astonishment—and his judgment was equally sure and good. *Burke* was too strong for him, and he never closed but when necessity compelled him. BELCHER walked round the field several times after the fight, displaying feats of agility.

The *sporting men* were not satisfied of JEM's superiority; and the whole of the immense bets depending upon the Yorkshire contest were decided by the above battle.

Notwithstanding *Burke* suffered so severely from the effects of this battle, his recovery and strength surprised every one—for in three days after, at a pugilistic dinner, given by Mr. *Fletcher Reid,* at the One Tun public-house, St. James's Market, Burke dined there—shook hands with BELCHER, and acknowledged JEM the best man: a match was made for one hundred yards for the best runner, to be decided immediately. *Burke,* to the astonishment of all present, beat *Jack Ward* (son to the veteran) by five yards.

BELCHER, soon after the above battle, was taken into custody for not keeping his promise to keep the peace, and bound over for £200, and two sureties in £100 each.

*Jack Fearby,* better known by the appellation of the Young Ruffian, who had acquired great fame as a pugilist, was now matched with BELCHER for one hundred guineas. The contest was to have been decided at Newmarket; but the magistrates interfering, they travelled out of the country, and halted at a spot of ground about half a mile beyond Linton, and fifteen from Newmarket, and made a ring. The combatants then agreed that the winner should have ninety guineas, and the loser ten. On Tuesday, April 12, 1803, at a quarter past nine, the *set-to* commenced.

FIRST ROUND.—Great anxiety prevailed for the first blow—sparring took place for some seconds, when Fearby put in a blow at BELCHER's head, which JEM parried, and returned two blows right and left; no mischief done: they closed, and BELCHER fell underneath. Offers to take two to one that Fearby would win—Betters shy.

Second.—Fearby received a severe blow on the mouth, the blood from which issued most copiously; and JEM followed it up by a desperate right-handed hit upon the Ruffian's side, that brought him down. Three to one BELCHER was the conqueror.

Third.—Much science displayed on both sides —blows reciprocally given and stopped—when BELCHER fighting half-armed, and following up his adversary close, the Ruffian fell.

Fourth.—A good rally, and several severe blows exchanged. They closed, BELCHER fell upon his knee, and in that situation received a blow from Fearby. "Foul! foul!" was the cry, and

BELCHER wished the point to be decided, but had no desire to take advantage of the circumstance. A constable, followed by a clergyman, now made their appearance; but the clamour was so great that the *exhortations* of the reverend divine could not be heard, and the

Fifth round commenced.—Fearby seemed rather shy of his opponent; his eye now appeared black, and he vomited a great deal of blood—BELCHER smiled and beckoned the *Ruffian* to come forward. Fearby made a blow, but it was too slow, and which BELCHER avoided by bobbing his head aside; and JEM, in aiming to put in a desperate blow on Fearby's ribs, fell. The Ruffian appeared distressed.

Sixth.—The best round in the fight—BELCHER quite gay, but Fearby on the decline. The Ruffian, irritated, made several blows at his antagonist, but they were all thrown away. BELCHER taunted him, and with the most apparent ease put in a severe hit upon the stomach; and, in closing, Fearby received a violent cross-buttock.

Seventh.—*Milling* on both sides. Ten to one on BELCHER.

Eighth.—Fearby rallied with a good spirit, and made a hit at BELCHER, which he parried with great neatness: and, in return, cut the Ruffian's lips severely. Fearby, still *game,* gave JEM a sharp touch, but did not fetch the *claret.* Odds reduced to five to one.

Ninth.—BELCHER, full of gaiety, and without ceremony, put in a desperate hit over his adversary's right eye, and with all the coolness imaginable, put himself in a defensive posture, and sarcastically asked, "How do you like that, Johnny?" This was too much for Fearby, who was not quite so placid as to pass it over without some notice, and immediately endeavoured to answer the question by a severe blow, but overreached himself in so doing, and fell upon the ground. BELCHER smiled, and pointed at him very ironically.

Eleventh.—BELCHER now tried to put an end to the fight, by following Fearby round the ring, and putting in several blows which the Ruffian tried to parry off, but not sufficiently. BELCHER, at length, put in a *leveller,* when Fearby's friends made him decline the contest.

THE AMATEURS were much disappointed in this battle, in not witnessing that excellent display of the science so much expected. *Fearby* had no *chance* whatever, and appeared like a different man—his former excellence seemed *frightened* away. It was over in twenty minutes.

The above extraordinary pugilist was born at his father's house, in *St. James's Church-yard,* Bristol, on the 15th of April, 1781. JEM lived some years with a butcher of that place, but was never apprenticed to the trade; and, when quite a boy, he signalised himself for his pugilistic prowess, and at Lansdown Fair his feats soon rendered him conspicuous. He was about five feet eleven inches and a half in height. On his coming to London, *Bill Ward* invited BELCHER to his house, and a private sparring-match (with the gloves on) took place in *Ward's* dining-room, when the veteran was astonished at JEM's superior knowledge of the art, that he exclaimed, in falling over a table from one of BELCHER's *touches*—"By G—d! JEM, I am perfectly satisfied that you can beat any man in the kingdom." In conversation with *Ward,* after dinner, BELCHER observed, *"I could have done better, Sir, but I was afraid I might hit you too hard, and you should be affronted."*—"Come along, my boy," replied the Veteran, "we'll have no gloves on now, and you shall do your best; I am not, nor ever was afraid of a blow!" The *set-to* instantly commenced, when the guest (out of pure friendship) *levelled* his host several times. Ward wanted no further *convincing* proofs of his talents. They sat down, and spent the remainder of the evening very harmoniously, and *Ward* immediately offered to back JEM against any man in the country.

After the unfortunate circumstance of losing his eye, on July 24, 1803, in playing at Racquets, in company with Mr. *Stuart,* in St. Martin's Street—JEM declined in health; his spirits were not so good as heretofore; and, at times, he felt much depressed from this afflicting loss. Soon after the above accident, he took the *Jolly Brewer,* in Wardour-street, Soho, which house was well attended. In losing the battle with the *Chicken* (which, we are credibly informed, was principally occasioned by a quarrel between *Pearce* and a brother of JEM's since dead), his brave heart was almost bursting with grief. The loss of his eye now preyed upon him so much that his temper became very irritable; and so confident of success was BELCHER, in his last contest with *Cribb,* that, after betting all his money, he sported his gold watch, worth thirty pounds. After this fight he began to droop, and fretted considerably. His confinement in Horsemonger-lane for twenty-eight days, also having to pay a considerable sum for breaking the peace by that battle; added to a cold he caught in the above prison, hastened his death. It was, however, an expressed opinion, that he died more from a family complaint, than from the blows he had received as a pugilist. His circumstances at one time after his defeats were much injured, and he was considerably reduced. The *Fancy* ought not to have let such a man as JEM BELCHER (at any period of his life) suffer loss from his pugilistic efforts;—for more honour, integrity, and affection never resided in the human heart. In his latter moments he displayed much sense, penitence, and resignation, and endeavored to atone for those errors which he had committed, with all the firmness and piety of a good Christian. He suffered a great deal from expectoration, having an ulcer upon his liver. A short period previous to his death, he made his will.

On Tuesday, July 30, 1811, died, at the sign of the Coach and Horses, Frith-street, Soho (of which he was the landlord), the renowned JAMES BELCHER, in the 31st year of his age; and on Sunday, August 4, he was buried in Mary-le-bone ground. The concourse of people eager to witness the last of their once-distinguished Champion was immense. His funeral was of the most respectable kind:

### THE HEARSE

Preceded by a Man carrying a Plume of Feathers.

In the First mourning Coach,

Mrs. Belcher (his Widow), Mrs. Philpot, Tom Belcher, &c.

Second Ditto,

**Mr. Harmer** (his Nephew), Mrs. Harmer, Messrs. Gregson, Richmond, Bitton, &c.

In the Third,

Mr. Summer (an Attorney), Mr. Shabner, Mr. Hawkins, &c.

And in a Glass Coach following,

Bill Wood, Powers, and several Amateur Friends.

As THEY MOVED along in solemn procession, the numbers of people were so great in joining it, that, upon their arrival at the church-yard, which was nearly filled, the mourners could scarcely reach the grave. *Wood* and *Jack Powers* staid to pay the last respects to their departed friend, and dropped a tear to his memory. A more general sympathy was never witnessed among spectators (principally sporting persons), in shedding a profusion of tears; as did most of his pugilistic brethren, at the loss of so great a hero!

In visiting the ground where his remains are deposited, we should think BOXIANA wanting in respect, if not incomplete, were we to omit the words upon his tombstone:—

In Memory of

JAMES BELCHER

Late of St. Anne's Parish, Soho,

who died

The 30th of July, 1811,

Aged 30

Universally regretted by all who knew him.

————

With patience to the last he did submit,
And murmur'd not at what the Lord thought fit,
He with a Christian courage did resign
His soul to God at his appointed time!

THE FIGHT CROWD is the most unreasoning, unjust, vicious, and vindictive of the audiences of sport.

# Twenty-five Bucks

## JAMES T. FARRELL

FIFTEEN YEARS is a hell of a long time to live in grease. Fifteen years is a hell of a long time to keep getting your jaw socked. Fifteen years is a hell of a long time for a broken-down, never-was of a palooka named Kid Tucker. Fifteen years stretched back through a reeking line of stale fight clubs, of jeers and clammy dressing rooms, and lousy gyms, and cheap canhouses, of ratty saloons with sawdust floors—OH, MEET ME TONIGHT IN THE MOONLIGHT—of flophouses whose corridors were fouled with musty lavatory odors, of training camps, gyps, speakeasies—IT'S A LONG, LONG TRAIL A-WINDING INTO THE LAND OF MY DREAMS—of mouldy dumps and joints, of crooks, pikers, louses, lice, and war. . . . Fifteen years stretched back all the way through these things to a boxcar, with *Armour's Meats* printed on its sides in white lettering, moving out of Lima, Ohio, and across sweet Ohio landscapes on a morning when the world was young with spring, and grass, and the hopeful if idiotic dreams of a good-natured adolescent yokel.

It was all over with Kid Tucker and there had never been any shouting—only boos. His face had been punched into hash: cauliflower ears, a flattened nose, a scar above his right eye. His greenish eyes were shifty with the fleeting nervous cowardice of the sacked and broken man. He was flabby. The muscles in his legs were shot. There was a scar on one leg, the medal he had received for carrying a badly wounded farm boy from Iowa through a wheat field near Soissons on a day when the sun was mad over a mad world, the earth nauseous from the stink of corpses, and the wheat fields slashed with ripping machine-gun bullets. Kid Tucker was through.

Toss him aside. Another boloney drowned in grease and defeat.

Sol Levison matched him with K. O. Dane for a six-round preliminary bout at Sol's West Side Arcade Boxing Club. Sol always wore a derby and a race-track vest. He made money out of a mouldy dump of a boxing club. He made money out of a string of ham scrappers. He made money out of everything he touched. Dane was one of Sol's stable, fresh from Minnesota. Sol was nursing him along on pushovers, building up a reputation so that Dane could get a match with a first-rater for a good purse. It did not matter that the big-time boy would slaughter him in a round. He was being prepared for it just as cattle were fed for the Chicago stockyards. Tucker was another setup for Dane. And the Kid needed the twenty-five dollars Sol guaranteed him for the bout. He took the match. He earned his living by taking smashes on the jaw. But Sol told him that this time he would have to fight. No taking a dive in this fight.

"Lissen, now, that ring ain't no swimming pool. See! No divin'! It ain't gonna be nothin' like bed or a park bench. It's a prize ring, and you're in there to fight. So don't act like you ain't never seen a bed for a month. Yuh gotta fight this time . . . or no dough. See!"

Kid Tucker had heard that before.

He reported on time at the West Side Arcade Boxing Club, a rambling building in a shambling district. He dressed for the bout, putting on a pair of faded trunks. With his hands taped, and a dirty bathrobe thrown over his shoulders, he sat on a slivery bench, waiting, watching a cockroach scurry up and down the wall. Two seconds sat on tilted chairs, one sleeping with his mug opened like a fly trap, the other reading a juicy rape story from *The Chicago Questioner*. Tucker sat. He didn't have many thoughts any more. He never became nervous before a fight. He had caught every kind of a punch already. He sat and watched the cockroach on the peeling green wall, with its many spots of broken plaster. It crawled up toward a window, turned back, scrambled sidewise, about-faced, turned downwards, and cut across the floor to lose itself in the shadows of a corner.

Kid Tucker wished that the scrap was over. He might manage to catch this kid off balance, and put him away. But then, he mightn't get any more fights from Levison, because this Dane was one of Sol's comers. Sol wanted him to put up a fight, because he was sure he couldn't take Dane. Anyway, he wished that the fight was over, and he was sitting in a speakeasy with a shot before him. He did not think much any more. Fools think. One day he had been a young ox, puking with excitement in a dressing room, awaiting the gong of his first fight. He watched a second cockroach scurry up and down the wall. Up and down it moved. The seconds lit cigarettes, and opened a discussion of the love-nest suit which had put the abnormal relationships of a rich old sugar daddy and a young gold digger on the front pages of the newspapers. Tucker sat and recalled the mice and cooties in the trenches in France. Up and down the cockroach moved.

When he entered the ring, he received only a small dribble of applause. The crowd knew the bum. Someone yelled at him, asking him if he had gotten his pants pressed for the tea party. Another wanted to know where his patent leather shoes were. Tucker never listened to the comments of the crowd, or its razzberries. He was past the time when he heard or was affected by boos. In France, he had lost all concern and worry when the shells landed. When he had heard one coming, he just casually flopped on the ground. A guy can get used to anything, if he just hangs around long enough. He sat in his corner, waiting, his eyes fastened on the ropes.

The crowd leaped to its feet spontaneously, and roars rose from the murkiness of faces when Dane entered the ring. He was a husky Swede with childish blue eyes, a thick square head, a bull neck, a mountainous pair of shoulders, and legs that resembled tree trunks. Tucker did not look at him.

A slit-mouth of an announcer bellowed out the names of the contending fighters, pointing to their respective corners as he briefly described trumped-up reputations. They shook hands in the center of the ring and returned to their corners. A gong clanged.

The arc lights glared down upon them, revealing a contrast between the fighters that was almost vicious. Dane was strong and full of youth; Tucker worn out and with a paunch of a belly. Both fighters were wary; and the crowd was perfunctory. It wanted Dane to make a corpse of the big fat ham. They faced each other, feinted, tapped, and blocked as they continuously circled around and around. Tucker could see that the kid was nervous; but he had learned to be a bit cautious of shaky young fighters when they looked as powerful as Dane. Dane led with a few light lefts. Tucker caught them easily with his gloves. His confidence perked up, and he retaliated with a straight left. It slid off Dane's jaw. They lumbered, feeling for openings. They clinched and their interlocked bodies made one swaying ugliness in the white glare of the arc lights. The referee danced in and parted them. They clinched again. They broke. Dane hesitantly attacked, and Tucker clumsily skipped backward.

Roars and boos grew out of the sordidness that surrounded the ring.

"Come on, Kayo. He's only a bum!"

"In the bread basket, you Swede! The bread basket!"

"Lam one in the bread basket, you squarehead, and he's through!"

"Come on, fight!"

"This ain't no party!"

"Hey, how about doin' your sleepin' at home? Huh?"

"Siddown in front!"

"Siddown, Tucker, and take a load off your feet!"

"No guts!"

"Murder the sonofabitch!"

"Kill the sonofabitch!"

"Fight, you hams. Fight!"

"Come on, you Swede boy, in the bread basket!"

Dane connected with a few inconsequential left jabs. He was clumsy, and when he led, he stumbled about, losing his balance. A good fighter with a willingness to take a chance, and a heart to mix and trade punches, could have cut him up and polished him off in short order. But Tucker kept backing away out of range, pausing to jab out with a few untimed, ineffective left-handed stabs. Dane danced about him in confusion, and when his opponent retreated, he stood in the center of the ring, hands lowered ungainly, a stupid expression of indecision on his face.

The crowd roared, and suddenly above the disgruntled roaring and booing there rose a throaty-voiced suggestion that sleeping quarters were upstairs. The bell saved them from further exertion.

The razzing increased during the one-minute intermission. Tucker sat heedless of the mob. He rinsed his mouth out from the water bottle, and puffed slightly. The seconds pointed out that Dane was leaving himself so open that a five-ton truck could be driven through his guard; Tucker said he would watch it, and catch the kid in the next round. He waited. He had five more rounds to go. He wondered if he could slip one through when Dane was off balance and stun him, or put him away. If he wanted to last through, he couldn't take many chances, and the kid looked like he had a punch that could kill a mule. He glanced toward the Dane's corner, where the latter's handlers were instructing him with emphatic gestures. He eyed the ropes.

Round two was duller and more slow than the first round. It was a clinching party. A fan called out that they were like Peaches and Daddy. Another suggested a bed. A third asked was it a track meet or a six-day bike race. The crowd grumbled. And repeatedly someone yelled to kill the sonofabitch.

A pimply-faced punk of a kid arose from his chair, yawned, ignored the commands from behind to sit down, and in a moment of quiet, shouted:

"I tank I go home!"

The crowd laughed, and he sat down.

Near the close of the round, Dane connected with a wild but solid right. The accidental wallop had echoed with a thud, and the mob was brought to its feet, yelling for blood and a knockout. Dane hesitated a moment, and stared perplexedly at his opponent. Then he went for Tucker with a look of murderous, if formal and melodramatic, intent stamped on his face.

The bell ended the round. There was a buzz of excitement. Dane was not such a dud after all. That right had been a beaut. Now he was getting warmed up, and he would do his stuff. He'd crush a lemon like Kid Tucker dry; he'd put him away in a hurry. Watch that Swede boy go now; watch him knock that Tucker bastard out now! One to the bread basket, and one on the button, and the lights would go out for that has-been.

Tucker was a trifle groggy as the seconds started working over him. They whispered that he should fake weariness. That would bring Dane in, wide open. Then one solid punch might turn the trick. Tucker nodded his head as if to indicate that he knew the whole story. But when he found himself in there punching and taking them, he found himself unable to put anything behind

his punches. In France, he had gone through two days of a terrific bombardment. Then he had caved in. He had gone on like an automatic man. He could not give himself. It was the same with fighting. He wanted to go in and take a chance trading punches. He told himself that he would. The haze was now cleared from his mind, and he was determined. But things had all happened like this before. Tucker, willing and determined, and then being unable to carry out his will, incapable of giving himself. He couldn't go in and fight. The war and the prize ring had taken all the fight out of him. His nerves and muscles wouldn't respond to his will. There had been too many punches. He awaited the bell, determining in vain. Tucker's state was called being yellow, having no guts. He sat out his final seconds of rest.

Just before the bell, Levison appeared, and told one of the Kid's seconds to warn him that he had to fight if he wanted his dough. Then, the clang of the gong. Some people in the crowd noticed Levison, but their curiosity was drowned by the roar greeting the new round. They were going to watch Dane take the bum for sure in this one.

The tired Tucker backed away. Dane pursued him, determined. His handlers had persuaded him into a state of self-confidence. He unscrewed an awkward left which flushed on Tucker's button. Tucker reeled backwards. The crowd leaped to its feet, yelling for blood. Dane *grew far away from Tucker*. Gloves came at the Kid like *locomotives slowly rising from the distance, coming closer and growing larger until they collided with his face. One ran into his stomach.*

"In the bread basket. Come on, you Swede!"

Tucker experienced a heaving nausea, and *far, far away there was a din of shouting.*

Instinctively, mechanically, Tucker fell into a clinch. He made a weak, hopeless effort to sew Dane up. His head swam in a daze, he was glassy-eyed. Dane, *a billowing mass of flesh grew before his dimmed eyes. Something big closed his eyes.* His feet slid from under him. He was blinded for a few seconds. Then he weakly perceived through his sick daze. He arose feebly. *There was a swinging of gloves, a going around of posts, ropes, and gloves.* He floundered forward to clinch. He was off balance, and Dane came up from the floor with a haymaker that mashed into his jaw; the impact of the punch caused an audible thud. The lights went out for Tucker, and about him, dizzy darkness crashed, like a tumbling nightmarish dream. He fell backward, and his head bounced hard on the canvas. He lay there, quivering slightly, while the referee tolled off the necessary ten seconds. He bled from the mouth; blood trickling out to run in tiny rivulets and mixed with the dust and resin.

The mob rocketed approval.

"That's the ticket, Swede!"

"That's the babee!"

"You put him out for a week. Oh, you beautiful Swede!"

"You got the stuff, kid. Yay!"

"Christ, what a wallop! Dynamite!"

"Out for a week!"

"Oh, you Swede! Wahooooo!"

The punk kid with the pimply face who had yelled about going home in a Swedish accent evidently recalled Levison's visit to the ringside just before the gong. He jumped up on his chair, and shouted:

"Fake!"

As Tucker was lifted back to his corner, and set helplessly on the stool, the cry of fake was suddenly taken up, and it contagiously reverberated through the arena.

Dane left the ring, and the cheers turned to boos as feet stamped and the cry of fake loudened into a booming roar.

The seconds continued working on Kid Tucker. Levison, in the back of the building, nervously spoke with two policemen. Then, after giving hasty instructions to six burly bouncers, he walked to the ringside, climbed through the ropes and stood turning in the center of the ring, his hand raised for quiet.

"Silence, pleez!" he megaphoned.

He finally received relative silence and shouted through megaphoned hands:

"Ladies and gents! Ladies and gents! I wanna say a few words to yuh. I wancha to know I ain't never had nothin' to do with a framed fight, or a faked boxing match of any kind or classification. I wancha to know that any time Sol Levison promotes a bout, then that bout is on the square. A fight that Sol Levison promotes is one hundred per cent on the level. Now to show you all that I'm on the level, I'm gonna offer one hunerd dollars, one hunerd dollars reward to the man that can prove that this last fight was a frameup. Now some one of you spectators here has been so unkind as to insinu-ate that this here last fight has not been on the level. Now, I'm offering one hunerd dollars to the man that proves that this or that any fight that Sol Levison has ever promoted was not on the level, to the very best, I say to the very best, of his knowledge and intentions."

There was a mingling of cheers and boos.

"When one of my fights is not on the level, Sol Levison wants to know about it. This here last fight was not faked to the knowledge of Sol Levi-

son. Kid Tucker here, he asks me for a chanct to go on so's he could make himself a little stake. I gave him his chanct, just as I always do with a boxer. Now, when I came up here just before the last round of this here last bout, it was to instruct Tucker that he had to fight if he wanted to get his purse. It was a square fight. Kid Tucker was yellah. He was just yellah. He was afraid of Kayo Dane, and refused to put up a resistance. He got just what was coming to him becuz he was too yellah to fight like a man, and like he agreed to when I agreed to pay him. He was yellah."

There were cheers. The handlers lifted Tucker down from the ring, and he was carted away to the dressing room amid many boos.

"Now, ladies and gents, to show you how I feel about this here matter, just let me tell you somethin'. When Sol Levison hires fighters, they fight. They fight or Sol Levison knows why. I guarantee that each and every bout I stage will give you your money's worth. If it don't, I guarantee that you kin get your money back at the box office. And when I hire boxers in good faith, they either fight . . . or they get no purse from Sol Levison. Now, to show you how I feel, and to guarantee that you'll get your money's worth after the showing this yellah bum made here, I'm gonna take his purse that was coming to him if he had lived up to his agreement with me and stood up and fought like a man, I'm gonna take his purse because he don't deserve it for breaking the contract he made with me, and I'm gonna give it to the boy who puts up the best fight here this evening, and I'm gonna let you all choose the boy to get it by general acclaim. Now, ladies and gents, I ask you, is that fair? He was yellah and he didn't earn his purse. So I asks you, is it not fair to give it to a boy with a real fighting heart. Now is that fair or isn't it?"

The roars of the crowd approving Levison's speech sounded like far echoes down in the mouldy dressing room where the beaten Kid Tucker lay unconscious. His handlers worked on him in vain, dousing him with water, using smelling salts, working in vain. Two bantams, one a swarthy-skinned Italian boy who had won a Golden Gloves championship before turning professional, and the other a bushy-haired Jewish lad, left to fight the next bout.

"He must have got an awful sock," the Jew said.

"He looks pretty bad," the Italian kid said to his manager.

"We'll bring him around," one of the seconds said.

They worked over Kid Tucker for an hour. Cheers echoed down from the other fights while they worked. A doctor was called in, and he could not bring Kid Tucker to consciousness. An ambulance was called, and Kid Tucker was carted out on a stretcher. As he was being put into the ambulance, the crowd was roaring acclaim, shouting out its decision that the swarthy-skinned Italian bantamweight and former Golden Gloves champion, had merited Tucker's purse.

But Tucker did not need it. He was taken to the hospital and died of a cerebral hemorrhage without ever regaining consciousness.

---

## CARTOON

# HANK KETCHAM

### DENNIS THE MENACE

*"No, No, Dennis! You're supposed to SHAKE HANDS first!"*

THIS IS THE best boy-meets-girl story ever written around boxing. It is also the best job of putting down on paper what it might have been like to be in there with Joe Louis.

# "Hello, Joe"

## WILLIAM FAY

WE STOOD THERE under the lights, and I said, "Hello, Joe." I hadn't met him when we weighed at two o'clock. He said, "Hello, Farmer, boy." He said it soft and touched my gloves, and I could see him just the way he was. You know the way the Bomber is, a sleepyhead, and like a cat, all silk and brown, the champion of the world. The gloves he wears don't mean he don't have claws. Artie Monaghan was referee. "I want a nice clean fight," he said. "You boys have been around. You know the rules."

I know the rules, all right. I ought to know the rules. I got a small lump on my head for every rule they got. Artie knows just who I am and how I am, and talks into the ear that works. The other ear is just a muffin ear. It is a muffin that you wouldn't want to eat.

WE LEFT THE HOTEL at eight o'clock and came to the stadium in a cab. I gave the guy a sawbuck for himself, and Lew said, gagging, to the guy, "You got a high-class load of freight." The cabby only laughed, but you could see he liked to hack a fare like us. We had two motorcycle cops up front, with Lew and me and Marty Manus sitting in the cab.

Lew taped my hands when we got there, and Marty made small strips of tape, like a doctor when he knows you will bleed. Lew put a towel around my head. I didn't want a towel around my head.

"You don't wanna lose your sweat," Lew said.

"How can I lose it? How can anybody lose his sweat? It stinks in here. It's hot!"

Lew smiled. "You're on edge, Farmer, that's

all it is. How you feel?" He smiled some more. He thumped me playful on the arm.

"How the hell you think I feel at a time like this?" I said to him. I was sorry for the way I talked. I never talked like that before. "I'm sorry, Lew," I said. "It's hot, I guess. How'd the Yankees do today?"

Lew said, "How'd the Yankees make out, Marty?"

Marty said he didn't know. "They play two hours later in St. Louie," he said. "I'll ask some guy."

"Never mind," I said. "Forget it. I don't want anybody else in here."

"I can ask the cop outside the door."

"The hell with it," I said.

"He's on edge," Lew said. "That's the way you wanta be, Farmer. It's better that way."

I was on edge, all right, and I am a Yankee fan like Colonel Ruppert was a Yankee fan.

WE WENT TO our corners and Lew took the robe off me. Joe stood in his corner, with the colored boys there. It is hard to take your eyes off Joe, the way he is when the lights are shining down, when his robe is off and there's just the red gloves on his hands.

"The hell with him," said Lew, and then I took my eyes away.

The hell with me, too, was the thought I had, but Lew was being nice. He is always nice. He is a guy to have around. The ball park was black, except for where the ring was, and this is a time, it is always a time, when you're waiting for the bell and the crowd don't say a thing. The crowd just waits and feels the things you feel, except it don't get hit, tonight or any night. Lew shook my glove and said, "Go get 'im, Farmer." I did not say, "With what?" I turned around when I heard the bell, and saw that Joe was gliding easy, the way he always glides, slick and smart, looking at me over his hands.

I KNOW THE THINGS they said about the fight before we climbed in here, the things they wrote in the papers, and all the noise they made. The pictures they made, of Joe and me, and what we ate and what we weighed, and how I nearly beat the guy the last time that we fought. Well, that don't put the teeth back in my head if Joe should knock them out. That don't make me charming when I smile. That don't mean that I can beat one side of Joe. I'm smarter than the boys who write for the papers, though. They don't get hit by Joe, but I get hit, and I know how it feels.

HE'S GOT THAT left hand out. It is a hand that doesn't miss. He feeds it just a little at a time. He's got a spring inside his arm. They tell you he carries the arm too low. They tell the things that Dempsey would have done. Dempsey would take it right on his beard, just the same as me. I took it then. It wasn't hard. Just hard enough to bring the blood into my mouth. I shuffled in and watched the way he moved, his sleepy face. He doesn't have a face. He's got a mask. It doesn't say one thing at all. You don't know when the trouble's coming next.

He's got that left hand on a hinge. He is too smart to take a chance with me. He knows I hit like houses falling down, but not so good as him. He always takes it easy for a round or so, and then he gives you all the guns. Then everyone goes home. I moved in close and tried a short right to his chin. I threw it neat, but Joe just moves his kinky skull away. He chopped me with a right, like only Joe can chop, and then we punched inside a while, got tangled in a clinch. I looked and saw Lew crouching on the steps below the ring. Lew told me, "Easy," with the lips. I smiled a little smile for Lew. It's lonesome in a ring.

YOU'VE SEEN MY picture once or twice, with Joe DiMaggio? With Lefty Gomez? With Selkirk and the boys? You know just how I feel about the Yanks. You know the way I like to see them play. I'm not a slob. I'm in the big leagues too. It's nice when you can walk down through a crowd and people say, "There's Farmer Willy Watson." It's nice to hear them all remembering how I nearly beat the champ, the first time we fought.

I was sitting with Lew in back of third base,

drinking beer and watching the Yankees. The beer was warm in the bottles. This was in May. The sun was bright all over the park and some of the boys wore glasses in the outfield. My vest was open, and it was a wonderful time. It was just three months ago last week.

Lew said, to get a rise from me, "I like Cleveland, Farmer. What'll you lay?"

"Whatta you want?" I said. "I'll lay you ten to five." We always clown around like that.

It was nice, all right, just sitting in the sun, and they'd taken my picture again that day, me with DiMaggio's glove on my hand, and him with his fists held up like he knew how to use them. A gag, it was.

"You'll lay ten to five?" said Lew. "You mean it? Cleveland's got Feller," he said.

"Ten to five," I said, and I hoped I wasn't showing off.

There was a girl on the other side of Lew. "I'll take twenty cents' worth," she said, and she had the nicest voice; her smile was white and nice and clean. She wasn't fresh. She was a friend of Lew's. We'd met her coming down the aisle.

Lew knew the girl from show business, where he used to be a stagehand, and I could see that this was a girl to know.

"Ain't seen you in ten years, Margie," Lew had said. "Ain't seen you since that Ziegfeld show." He sure was glad to see her. So was I.

The girl laughed. "Not so loud," she said.

Ten years are not so much. They didn't hang so heavy on this girl. And you could take a good ten years off me and find I'd still be shaving.

"We don't get any younger," Lew had said. "This is Farmer Watson, Margie."

"Pleased to meet you," I said, but I am strictly a slob when the ladies are around. I can open my eyes, but never my mouth.

"Siddown," said Lew, "and have a beer."

So the girl sat down and had a beer, but she drank her beer from a paper cup. I poured what was left of my beer in a cup, and Lew said, "What's the matter with the bottle, Farmer?" Leave it to Lew to say a thing like that. I kept looking around him at the girl, not so scared as I usually am. She had nice long legs and tidy feet. The clothes she wore were good. I wondered why she kept sitting around with a couple of bums like us.

I'M IN THE second round with Joe and we're moving along. The crowd is screaming the things it feels. They got a right to scream, for the prices they pay, and pretty soon now Joe will get to work. It's watching his face that gets you down, as much as the things he does with his hands. I'm not afraid; don't get me wrong. It's just that Joe is the best in the world. I walked right in and hooked a left. I threw a short right hand inside that must have hurt. It's not that I can't give the man a fight. It's just he's better than I am. It's just there never was a man like Joe, and the dough I get is not enough for getting my brains messed up inside my head. He stabbed me with that long left hand again. He brought it three times to my face. I shuffled in and tossed a right; I know I must have done it wrong, because my back was on the floor. I even bounced a little bit. I've seen Galento go like that, when Louis hit him on the chin, and like Galento, I am tough, and never have been down. I heard the count. I was all right. Of course I would be getting up.

I DON'T KNOW what happened to Lew at the ball game. Somebody came along, some pal, or maybe too many beers. But he was gone, that's all I know, and I was sitting with the girl.

She said, "I saw your fight last summer with the champ." They all say that—then it's not so hard to talk.

"I bet you don't like fights," I said.

"Not much," she said. "But you were really very good. You nearly won."

"Nearly's not enough though," I answered.

"It's closer than anybody else has come." She wanted me to be sure of that. "And you'll probably win the next time. A lot of people think so. I hope so, anyway." I told you she was nice.

"Thanks," I said. "But the man is murder."

"I like ball games," she said. "I really do." And she didn't fool. She always knew the score. She knew why McCarthy used so many left-handers when a guy like Feller was pitching. She was a wonderful girl and it was easy for us to talk.

I said, "Will you have a hot dog?" And she said, "Yes, I love them." Then both of us were laughing about a lot of things, I don't know what; I didn't care, though both of us could see that I owed Lew ten bucks.

THE WAY IT IS, when you are hit by Joe, it hurts more after than it does at first. The count was four, and Artie Monaghan held fingers up in front of me, first four, then five, then six. I rested on one knee. I looked around. I watched the timekeeper, standing up, hitting his club on the floor of the ring. The lights made faces clear around the ring, and some of the faces that I saw were sad. Joe never had me down before, not once in fifteen rounds the other time. I was all right, and Artie rubbed the resin off my gloves. I turned towards Joe and he came fast.

He wore no feeling on his face. No pity, fear or excitement there. No nothing there at all. But he came fast. I moved away. My legs were pretty good. I made him waste a right hand past my ear, and that's a trick that I do good. In fact, that's why the ear is tin. I grabbed Joe's arms and held him tight, and then I punched when we were on the ropes. I shook my head and waited for the bell. It wasn't long.

Lew ran a sponge across my face. He said, "You make 'im come to you." He fixed two cuts that Joe had opened just above my eyes. "You watch 'im, Farmer. Don't get hurt."

*Lew knows I haven't got a chance,* I thought. They know the truth when they start saying, "Don't get hurt."

I SAID IT WAS the springtime. It was May, and it was warm; the trees were pretty when we walked along the street. You can thank the Rockefellers for the trees. We stood in Radio City, by the flowers. She said she liked to watch them. "So do I," I said, and then I felt so good I didn't care the Yankees lost.

That's where she worked—in Rockefeller Center, singing songs. A little beefy now, not much, she didn't dance. She said that she was thirty and I knew she didn't lie. She said Ziegfeld would do a handspring in his grave if she ever tried to dance.

"I bet you could dance like a dream," I said, which was pretty clever stuff for me.

"Willy, you're sweet," she told me then, and I was glad she called me Willy. Why they call me "Farmer" I don't know, because I never farmed so much as one potato. Sometimes they call me "the Ox," sometimes "the Plow," and a lot of silly things that are supposed to describe my style. Farmer or no Farmer, I've done all right. You'd hoe a lot of spinach to make the dough I made. A half million dollars gathering gold dust in the bank.

The place where Margie worked was built up on the roof. The Starlight Club, they call it, where a dinner costs four bucks. She sang and played the piano. The songs she sang were sweet and hot and very good. She's got a soft throb in her voice that sounds like broken hearts. Perhaps she's got a gimmick in her throat, like Crosby's got, that makes her sound so good. She sings so nice. She sings so clean and happily, then sad. The dinner trade don't slam their knives and forks around when Margie sings. I want to say it's all big league. I sat and listened quite a while, and signed some autographs for pretty girls who came along, and then I took a bow. You'd think that I gave flavor to the joint. You'd think that dinner didn't cost four bucks. I can't help wondering all the time what Margie sees in me, when she's a celebrity herself.

That night she drew my picture on a bill of fare. We were sitting in a coffee joint uptown, just off Broadway. She drew my picture, with my cauliflower ear, and I'd been trying all day long to turn my head the other way.

"I got another ear," I said.

She looked surprised. She said, "I'm sorry, Willy. But that's the ear I like. That's you."

"Don't you mind?"

"Mind what?"

"The ear," I said. "The vegetable. That's why I snap my hat down on the side."

She said, "You goose. You big goose. Why, I don't mind at all. I like you as you are."

I nearly cried. I couldn't stand to have her talk like that. I knew I loved her like I never loved my mother. Except I never knew my mother. I never met a pretty girl who didn't have me scared before.

You'll think I'm crazy. I swear you will, but I never knew about those things. The next day I bought her an automobile that cost three thousand bucks, because she'd told me she was fond of driving in the country. They brought it to her house.

I called her on the phone and said, "Hello, Margie." I waited, feeling foolish, for what she'd have to say.

She said, "That fire engine is back where it came from," and then hung up.

I sat there for the longest time. I didn't know what I should do, but I knew that I'd done something wrong. I called her on the telephone again. I said, "I'm sorry, Margie. I'm terrible sorry. You gotta see me. You don't understand."

"I understand," she said.

"Then you'll see me?"

"I don't know."

But she saw me, though. Late that afternoon. She had a package in her hand and she smiled a little bit. She said, "You're nice, Willy. You're really nice." She handed me the package. I opened it up in the street where we met, and I saw it was a necktie.

"A present," she said. "From me to you." And then we walked along the street and she took me into a stocking store. She bought three pairs and held out her hand. "Two dollars, Willy," she told me then. "These are the kind I always wear."

"Three for two bucks?"

"Uh-huh," she said. "This is a present from you to me." We had a perfectly wonderful time, walking down the street.

MARGIE ISN'T HERE tonight. A girl like Margie doesn't like the blood to flow. But Joe is here. He's coming now, and Lew says, "Keep your hands up, Farmer." He shoves me off the stool.

Joe is sweating pretty good. He's oiled like a machine, and Joe is a guy who always takes a proper pride in his work. He doesn't like the last time when I went the full fifteen, and maybe he knows the year just past has slowed me up a bit. A year don't set so easy when you're thirty-two years old. But he'll have to take me the hard way. He knows I won't fold up, not like those other humpty-dumpties, not like those bums who fall right down as soon as he lifts his hands. I got pride in my work, too, except it's not as good as his. He hit me a left hook on the chin, but I held it there with my own right glove, not letting him take the hand away. I belted him clean in his body. I pushed him to the ropes. I brought my two hands up inside, the only way to fight a guy like Joe, who's smart. He got away. He stabbed me with a left. He did it again and cut me again. He cracked me a right hand high, and the way Joe hits, you always got pains for another two weeks, at least. "All right, Joe," I said to myself. "Here we go, just you and me. The way things are, they're not so good." I hooked three times, but he blocked them all. This guy is smooth and hard to find. His hands are hard. They're in my face, and then I'm on the floor again, and Artie holds three fingers up for me to see. I see them, all right, but no so clear as the last time, and I think to myself that a punchy slob is never a prize for a girl. I wonder does it pay me to get up? I hear the crowd that thinks I'm brave. They think I'm a wonderful man. They think I'm great when the going gets tough, and how would they like it in here with Joe?

I NEVER KISSED a pretty girl until I was thirty-two years old. I just kissed her, that was all, and Margie ran her fingers through my hair. She seemed contented in my arms, counting the buttons on my vest.

She said, "I know. I understand. I'm lonely too. Everyone needs a place to rest his head. You're good, Willy, and you're brave. I always loved the people who were brave."

"I'm not so brave," I said, "It's not so smart to be so brave. That's why I got an ear like this."

"Forget the ear," she said.

I told her sometimes I get pains in my head. "That don't do any good," I said.

She understood. "You mean the champ?"

I meant the champ, all right. I told her that. "He's better than I am, Margie," I said. "I'm only second best. I thought that I should tell you that. I wanted you should get it straight."

She was worried, of course. I could see she was worried. "Do you have to fight him, Willy? Is it necessary?"

"I got a contract with Morris Weintraub," I said. "I can't run out on Morris. I never run out on anybody."

"I know, I know," she said. She thought a while. "You're not second best, Willy," she told me then. "It isn't right to think that way. I'll bet it's not the way you used to think. You can beat him, Willy. You nearly beat him the last time." She don't know about the fight game, but it was nice of Margie to talk like that.

"That was the best fight I ever made," I said. "I don't have another one left like that."

"I don't care," she said, and I kissed her again. Her lips were soft and sweet and full of fire. Each man should have a woman for himself. I wondered how I ever got along all by myself before. "I don't care," she said again. "And don't you care. Win, lose or draw," she said. Her eyes were wet when I looked in them, and they were frightened too.

THAT'S WHY I could stay here on the floor. "Win, lose or draw," she said. It's all the same to her. God knows he hit me hard enough to knock me out. He's stopped a dozen other bums with punches only half so good. "You're good and brave," she said. "I like you as you are," she said. There were a lot of things she said, all of them nice, that I'll remember longer than the punches I must take. . . . Okay, Artie, I'll be up. How many fingers, Artie—nine?

I'm up and on my feet. I'm goofy, just a bit. So this is sport? So you can have it, if it's sport. The champ will kill you if you let him do the punching all the time. I put my skull inside my arms. I let him punch a little while. I let my thoughts get clear. I knew my legs were not so good. We clinched, somehow, and Artie stepped between us. I said "Now!" when Joe was walking in. I threw them fast, so fast I don't know where I got the juice inside my arms. Joe slipped away, that easy way. This is the third round. He can wait, can wait forever till I'm gone inside, then bat my head right off into the bleachers—that's a laugh. I heard the bell and I was glad the hands belonged to Lew and not to Joe.

Lew's got collodion and stuff to stop the cuts. The kindest hands, he's got. The water is so good and cold and wonderful to feel, I wish they'd dump the bucket on my head.

"I'm all right," I said to Lew, and to myself I said, *Don't get panicky, you slob. You take it standing up.* Marty combed my hair, just for effect, and I sat straight and steady with my hands set on my knees. Marty said, "The Yankees win both games in St. Louie," and only Marty would think of that at such a time as this. I laughed. I looked around the ringside and I smiled for all my pals. I got so many pals you need a place like this to hold them all. Lew said, "Good luck." Then I was walking back at Joe.

We're in the sixth or seventh—I'm not sure. So far no trouble that a chin like mine can't take. He breaks me down a little at a time, not all at once. They told him how to fight me, not to mess around inside, where maybe he'd be cut. He's a million-dollar piece of chocolate. They don't want to take a chance. He's waiting till my legs give out, and then I'll get it good. He's clean. He got a mark. He's just a shadow with a ball bat in his hands. I keep my hands up and move along. They'll know at least I gave the guy a fight, a helluva fight. He didn't miss the last one that he threw. It caught me right. The best one yet. The lights swam for a minute, like a river made of gold. They come so fast you got no chance to see the punches come. I reach for Joe, but he's not there. His hands are there, but never Joe. I'd like to grab his arms and hold them still. His gloves are just like bullets from a gun.

IN JUNE I trained in Jersey, where I always train, and it was hot. This training isn't fun for me no more. Each morning I did six miles on the road, and in the afternoon, six rounds and sometimes eight, with tough guys who get twenty bucks a round. I can eat these bums I train with, but they got to make a living, too, and I see no sense in punching the heads of guys that I can lick.

Margie came, some days, and every Sunday she would come. We'd sit there on the porch, or walk along the roads when it was night, just holding hands and talking things about the two of us. The lilacs in the fields got smells you can't buy in a store. The night is soft and you can smell the grass; it all is different when you're with a girl. I always liked nice things like that, but now I know it's better with a girl.

One night I said, "It would be nice if I was champ. I wouldn't fight again. We would sit and take our shoes off. We would say, 'We are the champ.' You'd be the champ same as me."

"That would be fun," she said. "But it doesn't matter, Willy. It really doesn't matter."

*The hell it doesn't matter,* I thought then. But I was sorry I had talked like that. The thought just got away, I guess—a foolish thought. But I had never done a thing for her. I couldn't help but think it would be nice if I was champ. What else I got to offer?

ARTIE STEPPED IN between Joe and me, to look at the cuts I had in my eyes. It was the eighth, I guess, or maybe the ninth, and the round had twenty seconds more to go. He must have guessed the eye was not too bad. He clapped his hands, and Joe came banging in again. He wasn't wasting time no more. Joe was teeing off.

Lew washed me up and Marty helped. Marty poured the water down my pants. He rubbed my legs and stuck the salts under my nose. I didn't need the salts. It was a bed I needed most. "Can't even see the guy," I said. I wished that I could see him. It's tough to fight a guy that you can't see. When the eye was fixed, I saw him, though, sitting there across the ring, the black boys talking in his ears, rubbing his lean brown belly, clucking soft and confident to him. Lew shoved me off the stool.

You got to admit I'm tough. I take a punch, all right. Joe hit me clean, right on the chin, and I could hear the crowd blow out its breath. They got a speaker system hanging down from over the ring. It makes the punches sound louder than they are. You hear it loud across the radio. I wondered now did Margie hear the punch, or hear the crowd. I figured that the punches I must take hit Margie too. But what would you do? This guy is hot and getting warmer all the time. I wondered how she liked it when they said, "The Farmer's bleeding bad." That must be nice, indeed.

I ripped a fine right hand at Joe. I felt the punch go home. I tried again. I weaved as best I could from all the jabs he sent my way, those snakes with little razor blades that he's got up his arm. "I like you just the way you are," she said, and just the way I am, I never laid down yet. I hooked a short left hook at Joe when he was coming in. The punch was clean and stopped him for a while. It made him think. But then another made him mad. It made him fight twice as hard, although you couldn't tell it by his face. I knew if I just stood there I'd be killed, so I kept hitting back at Joe the best I could. You hear the crowd like thunder all the time. You know they're getting value for the dough they paid.

SHE TOLD ME, just this afternoon, "Willy, I won't worry. Not a bit. Just give him the evil eye, or something. I know you'll be all right."

"Whatta we got to lose?" I said, then clowned around some stupid way. Lew and Marty tried to clown around and help things out, but they knew, just as well as me, I didn't have a chance. I thought, *What kind of a hero am I? What kind of a fighter will stand around just looking at his corpse?* I could see her disappointment; I knew the way she felt. A woman will love you, win or lose, but a man should have faith when he goes to war. There were other things this afternoon.

I MIGHT GO fifteen rounds, if I am smart. If my legs are good enough for me to run away. If I wrap my arms around my head and don't peek out at Joe. Just let my pride, like the rest of me, be hamburger.

I never thought of that before, when I used to fight alone. I didn't have to save my face for anybody's lips. I only had to worry for myself, and I could say, "You're okay, Willy," or "Willy, you're a bum."

The hell with Joe. She likes me the way I am. I walked on in. I took a tough one in the mouth. I shoved my left hand out and stopped him when he tried again. This is the tenth. He's strong, I see, and here the trouble comes. We stood together and we punched. It seemed forever that we punched, and then we leaned together until Artie came along. He walked between us and we moved into the clear. Joe belted me with all he had. He wondered was I ever going down. A little worry in his eyes. Not very much, but some. It made me proud. I grinned at Joe. "How's it goin', Joe?" I asked him with the grin. But Joe didn't grin. That's not his way when the fight is on. That's why he is the champ, a classy kid. Inside, when we were working in a clinch, I heard him sigh a little sigh. I felt him hold a little bit. He's only human after all. I got it then. I got it good. He brought the fight to me with every gun he had. We stood and fought ourselves to pieces, Joe and me, and then I wasn't standing any more. My gloves were shoving at the floor. . . . Don't show me any fingers, Artie. I don't want to see no fingers. I'll get up. I'll go the whole fifteen. . . . I'm getting up and grinning back at Joe. His chest is going up and down. I never saw him heave like that before.

THIS AFTERNOON, BEFORE we weighed, before I went with Marty and Lew to the Boxing Commission, there was a little church, downtown, and a priest that Margie knew when she was a kid. A long while ago, she said. She said she liked it best this way. She likes it, win or lose. It wasn't in the papers, not today. Nobody knows but Marty, Lew and Marty's wife, and Marty said he'd cut her heart out if she talked, if the thing got in the papers before the fight. She cried and held some flowers in her hand. She said that Margie was so beautiful today. Any day, I said.

WELL, JOE, IT'S you and me. You're getting pretty tired. But not so tired you couldn't kill a horse with that left hook. It's round thirteen.

Joe hit me in the mouth with that left hand, but he was slow, a little bit. Not many guys have ever made Joe travel thirteen rounds. Not any guy will make me travel thirteen rounds again. I don't feel bad. Don't feel so bad I can't stand up.

This Joe is dangerous all the time. His mouthpiece shows. His mouth is open just a little bit. He's breathing through his teeth. He brought one home, downstairs, and that is not so good. Not when I'm getting set to do some tricks myself. He's trying now; he's trying hard; the effort's in his face and eyes. It never was before. He belts me twice and I belt him. When Artie breaks us, I can hear the crowd, the way they yell. It isn't often I can hear the crowd. There's always other things to do.

Joe brings his arms up slow. They must be awful tired. He hits me with another right-hand punch. I bring my own arms up; that's not so hard, because I've traveled more times to the wars than Joe. He's gone; he's tired inside; he isn't any faster than myself.

Well, Joe is young, and he can try again. A guy like me don't get a second chance. There is no other time for me. I'd like to nail him flat against the ropes. But Joe is smart. He's hard to catch. He's smooth and clever in his way. But I'm no dope. I've been around. I'm only starting in to punch. I hit Joe with a left hook on the chin. He wobbled some and didn't like the punch a bit. We've got this round and then two more, and Dempsey stopped Jess Willard in three rounds.

Just let me belt you, Joe. Just once or twice like that again. I've got a chance. A lousy little chance. I wonder what would Margie think, if I should bring the title home—a slob like me.

No OTHER NONCOMBATANT has contributed as much to boxing as Nathaniel Stanley Fleischer. In the past fifty-five years he has written fifty-three books on the subject, donated 190 championship belts and officiated at more than a thousand fights, including two dozen championship contests. Since 1922 he has been editor and publisher of *The Ring,* boxing's foremost magazine, and since 1941 his *Ring Record Book and Encyclopedia* has been the standard reference work. He is also the originator and curator of the Boxing Hall of Fame and the owner of the finest collection of boxiana in the world.

This account of the Jimmy Carruthers—Chamrern Songkitrat bantam-weight championship fight in Bangkok on May 2, 1954, appeared in *The Ring.* Of the fight Fleischer has since said: "This was the most dramatic fight I ever saw—even more dramatic, because of the circumstances, than Dempsey–Firpo."

# Title Battle in Typhoon

## NAT FLEISCHER

IN A SCENE unparalleled in the history of the bantamweight division, a scene that rivaled that in the Dempsey–Tunney fight in Philadelphia, before a gathering of 59,760 persons who paid 5,000,700 ticals, totaling $227,304.90 in U. S. currency, in an arena especially built for the occasion, Jimmy Carruthers of Australia defeated Chamrern Songkitrat by a hairline margin in defense of the Australian's crown. The bout, unlike championship matches staged in our country or in Europe, was scheduled for twelve rounds, the only distance Jimmy would agree upon.

Fortunate for Carruthers that the fight was not a fifteen-rounder, as otherwise, in my opinion, he would have been shorn of his title. Bleeding badly from a deep cut above the right eye and tiring perceptibly, Jimmy used up all his energy in the final session to pull the chestnuts out of the fire, while his opponent, almost as fresh and strong as when he started, could have gone on for several more rounds without tiring. Carruthers was a lucky boy to hold on to his title.

Although referee Bill Henneberry, imported from Down Under, gave the verdict to the champion by a margin of 31½ to 27½, I figured the fight much closer. Scoring the New York system, I had Carruthers ahead by one round and one point, and in the Australian system, used by the only official in the fight, I gave the decision to Jimmy by 31 to 29 points. The fight definitely was that close. In fact the majority of the spectators and many scribes had the local champion ahead at the end of the fight.

Carruthers' jabbing won the fight for him. In hitting, especially body punching, he was outscored by Chamrern.

Those who witnessed the Tunney–Dempsey ten-round title bout in Philadelphia can imagine what was encountered here by picturing a terrific tropical storm that started hours before the fight, increased in intensity as the bout progressed, drenched the spectators and made a lake out of the ring. Bulbs from the overhead lighting system crashed to the canvas every now and then forcing temporary halts while the broom brigade rushed into the ring to sweep it clear, since the fighters, by agreement, were permitted to fight in their bare feet due to the slippery conditions.

Carruthers stepped on glass in the eleventh round and cut his foot.

Carruthers, with the height and reach in his favor, figured to have an advantage, but with equal weights at 117¼ pounds and the conditions more suitable for Chamrern, who is accustomed to barefoot fighting, Jimmy found himself at a disadvantage. Once, in attempting to toss his right for the jaw as Chamrern stepped out of range, Carruthers hit the canvas with a thud and a splash, face down, spun back, and cracked his chin against the floor; his mouth bled from then on. Several times he lost his balance and almost went down, and in the second round, Songkitrat slipped and landed on his back.

But, despite the conditions, the fight was well fought with plenty of action by both lads who put on a splendid performance considering the torrent. Carruthers and his mentor, Dr. McGirr, thought that the champ had won easily and that if the weather had been favorable, he would have scored a knockout, but I didn't agree. He didn't show as much punching power as did his rival. The Australian pair the morning after the fight announced that they were satisfied that had they not imported their own referee, the championship would have changed hands, but that statement carried no weight with me since I found the Siamese most fair in their treatment.

The fight warrants a repeat, especially in view of the throng that packed the new National Stadium, and the thousands who clamored unsuccessfully for admission. Bangkok is definitely the place for the return engagement for which a contract was signed in my presence, with me a witness, but if it takes place, according to Brigadier General Pichai Kullavanijya, who arranged the title match, he will ask the World Championship Committee to appoint a neutral referee to avoid any squawks. It is certain that Dr. McGirr will oppose such a move.

Regarding the next move of the champion, Dr. McGirr stated that he prefers to have Robert Cohen of France get the next shot at the title, but insists that the Frenchman must accept terms offered by the champ. He asked me to present the champion's challenge to the French contender at the European Boxing Union Convention at Monte Carlo. He is willing to have Jack Solomons act as a partner in staging the bout.

Discussing Carruthers' future, Dr. McGirr said: "I know that Solomons has something to say in Cohen's promotions. We offered to have Jimmy fight the Frenchman but he seems to think he, not my Jimmy, is the champion. He wants even more than Jimmy can get out of the fight. If he turns down my offer now, I shall

shunt him to the side lines and give Songkitrat the next championship match."

However, since then Carruthers, who has had difficulty making weight, has officially made known his retirement as undefeated world bantamweight champion.

Despite his hairline defeat by Carruthers, Songkitrat definitely continues to fit into the championship picture. He earned the right to another shot at the crown and remains the number two contender, the post he occupied before the fight here.

Carruthers received 175,000 Australian pounds tax free, round-trip tickets for himself and wife, his trainer and his manager, and all expenses for the entire outfit.

The Bangkok fight in more than one way established a record. It was the first championship bout, or for that matter any other important contest, in which women seconded the title holder. Mrs. Myra Carruthers and Mrs. McConnell, wife of Carruthers' trainer, took their place as aides to Bill during the entire contest.

Dressed in specially made white garments draped with Australian flags, they worked as would our Whitey Bimstein or the Florio brothers when handling the corner of a champion or challenger. Within a few minutes after entering the ring and discarding their huge Siamese umbrellas, the women were drenched by the continuous cloudbursts, but they were game to the core and stuck to their task to the end.

Add to the above the record attendance for a bantam championship match, and that for the first time in ring history champion and challenger fought in their bare feet, and you have something by which to remember the Bangkok affair.

For a city that had never seen a championship bout before, and where Thai or foot-and-hand fighting, of which I shall write in the next issue, is the national pastime, Bangkok's Police Department which staged the bout for the Police Hospital Fund under the direction of General Pichai, as he is commonly known, did itself proud. Except for the storm and the thousands who had to be turned away due to the shortage of accommodations at the vast arena, the gigantic affair was carried out without a flaw.

Since I was the guest of the Thailand government and the official representative of both the National Boxing Association and the European Boxing Union at the fight, the principals in the contest and the Thailand government officials appointed me to supervise the weigh-in to see that the championship regulations were adhered to, and made me the official arbiter in any dispute. There was no need for the latter since at no time did a point arise that required special considerations, so well did General Pichai handle his end of the program.

In every respect, this was a fight crowd such as seldom if ever in my long experience has been seen at the ringside of a world title bout. Dignitaries from Thailand and other nations in this Far Eastern land, most of them in native garb, nobility from many lands, fight fans who traveled by bicycle, train, auto and by foot for many miles—they all headed for the National Stadium hours before the first bout, a hand-and-foot mill, got under way.

Traffic was so congested that it took more than an hour to cover less than a mile from my Government Residence to the arena. But it was little different in that respect from what we ordinarily encounter in any big city when a champion match is being staged, except for the color offered by the mass of humanity of many nations, trudging through the street high in mud, unmindful of the downpour or the ruination of their clothes. As for the latter, all types that give the Far East its picturesqueness, were in evidence, from that of the Hindus, Japs, coolies, Australians and Americans, many of whom were present, to the native garb of the Siamese.

It was a sight to behold—one I shall never forget.

Picture the old Garden Bowl in Long Island, but to a greater depth, with about 20,000 additional seats, and you have a pretty good idea of how the National Stadium of Bangkok looked on this night of all nights. Throughout the day the radio kept announcing that the fight was a sellout but that didn't halt those who had no tickets from flocking to the scene and adding to the congestion. Their national hero, the Jack Dempsey of Thailand, was to fight for a world title, and his admirers were determined to see him.

The lusty cheers that greeted his appearance in the ring, the many gifts that were showered on him after he had bowed in native custom to Buddha, were evidence of the admiration the people of Thailand have for their boy. He is to the Siamese youth what Dempsey is to the American youth, and in his close defeat he became even more of a national figure because he had gone the limit with a fighting champion.

Songkitrat, known as the "Fiery Lizard," is a handsome Thai boy of twenty-four, who took his name from a boxing school he attended. He toughened himself for Siamese-style fighting by plowing behind a water buffalo in the rice paddies as a youth, and so clever was he in the Thai rough-and-tumble style of fighting that he was urged to turn his talents to the European and American style, in which he has met with success.

Though he was defeated on points by the Orient champion, Larry Bataan, in 1952 after he had floored his opponent, he won the Orient lightweight title from Speedy Cabanella that same year in a Bangkok fight. He then whipped Masahi Akiyama, Japanese bantam title holder, Vic Herman of Scotland, Jimmy Pearce of England, Kevin James of Australia and our own Pappy Gault, to gain the title shot at Carruthers.

At the weigh-in, with me in charge, I urged that the bout be postponed for a day. But since we had had three successive days of this Oriental typhoon in which the rain came down like pellets, Brigadier General Pichai, speaking for his government, urged that no postponement be made. "We have arranged half fares on all trains from every part of the country to enable our people to come to see Chamrern fight for the title, and we have no accommodations to handle the throng that is flooding the city," the General said. "The fight I think should be held regardless of the weather. Our people are accustomed to such storms."

Before acting, since the final decision was left to me, I gave each of the fighters an opportunity to express his opinion. They were in favor of going on with the show.

Then came the request of Carruthers to be permitted to fight without shoes. "The ring will be too slippery to fight with regular boxing boots on," he said.

I gave consent after the same request had been made by Chamrern, and thus the stage was set for this historic ring contest. Dr. McGirr, manager of Carruthers, like Brigadier General Pichai, remarked, "Since we have had this heavy downpour for three days, there is no assurance that there will be a clearance by tomorrow and I agree that the fight must go on tonight."

Between weighing-in time and the fight, thousands of visitors went to the various Buddha temples to pray for the rain to halt and the success of their hero. In the national temple, the beautiful Emerald Buddha temple, the scene was most impressive. There hundreds of fight fans from the North and South who had never been to the famous historic building, knelt in prayer with shoes off, the native custom. The National Museum and the King's Palace grounds, all open for the occasion, likewise were jammed with visitors.

It was a picture to behold, to see fight fans, men, women and children, many carrying bags of food, coming to the fight in their gayest festival garments, paying respects to Buddha and their latest national idol, Chamrern Songkitrat.

As for the fight itself, one round followed the other in pattern. Carruthers would flip his right, a stinging sort of jab that knocks his opponent off balance when it lands, while Songkitrat, following instructions, rushed forth to play an attack on Jimmy's body. In the majority of rounds, Chamrern was the aggressor, but Jimmy caught him time and again with effective rights; but he couldn't defend himself against a vicious two-handed body attack that often caused the champ to gasp.

Entering the ninth round, the fight was anyone's. I had Carruthers ahead by only one point. It was in the ninth that Jimmy turned the tide somewhat more in his favor with quickened speed and more effective punching. He was good in that round, which he won.

Then came the tenth in which Songkitrat, urged by his handler to rush his man and attack the head instead of body, opened a deep gash over the champion's right eye, a new cut, which bled profusely. Carruthers, face red with claret, showed signs of weariness as he tried to halt the assault of his opponent, who was widely cheered as his partisan rooters figured he now had the fight in hand and would win. The round belonged to Songkitrat.

The rally by the Thai boy continued in the next round in which he kept piling in blows, giving his opponent no quarter. He pummeled away at the injury above the eye, often forcing Carruthers to jump into a clinch from which he quickly broke and tried desperately to stab his vaunted right, his best punch, to the face of the challenger. Some landed but most failed to reach their objective.

The fight on my card was now even in rounds, with the champion one point ahead in that method of scoring.

The gong sounded for the final round. Chamrern hadn't heard it and stood waiting while Jimmy rushed out of his corner to shake and resume the warfare. Referee Henneberry waved the Thailand boy to the center of the ring, the shake was over and out went Carruthers to clinch the narrow-margin victory. In desperation, apparently realizing his plight, he met the body attack of his rival with equal blows but couldn't avoid punches to the head that kept the blood flowing freely from the wound above the eye.

Carruthers slowed up Songkitrat with punches to the jaw and several good lefts to the body but his best attack in this final session was his effective right, tossed out like one throwing a dart; and though he was hurt several times during the round, he did more damage, landed the more effective blows in that frame and was more effective in the many body exchanges.

That, in my opinion, won the fight for him. It was the round that clinched the victory, but Jimmy knew that he had been in a battle, and from both him and his handlers we learned that it was his toughest fight.

Make no mistake about judging Songkitrat. He's a good fighter who is courageous as all Thai fighters are, has a heavy wallop and is exceedingly fast. All he lacks is some science and this he'll gain as he continues to fight the top men of his divison. He would make a good addition to the bantams and feathers of America, but he can make much more money in the Orient than he could in a country where we are short of men of his weight who possess drawing power.

With the fight over, and many boos penetrating the air when the decision was rendered, Songkitrat grabbed the microphone and standing in the center of the ring, said:

"I am very proud to have been able to bring fame to my country by being the first Thai boxer to contend for the world bantamweight title, and I am personally satisfied that the decision was fair and beyond doubt. If I am not sorry, my friends and my countrymen, why are you?"

Thus in Songkitrat, Thailand has a boxer who lives up to the tradition of fair play and sportsmanship for which his country is noted.

The day following the bout, General Phao Sriyanonda, Director General of National Police and Deputy Minister of the Interior and Minister of Finance, at a banquet tendered in honor of Commissioner of Police Delaney of New South Wales and me, asked me to obtain an American trainer for Thailand boxers. He requested me to sign someone for six months in an effort to boom the sport in Siam and to help organize a Police Athletic League boxing team.

This I shall do upon my return to America.

IN THE CAREER of Primo Carnera the fight game reached its nadir, and Paul Gallico found, in the facts of it, a story surpassing anything that he could invent as a fiction writer. As a footnote, it should be recorded that, in 1946, Carnera returned to the United States, flourished financially as a wrestler and became an American citizen.

# Pity the Poor Giant

## PAUL GALLICO

THERE IS PROBABLY no more scandalous, pitiful, incredible story in all the record of these last mad sports years than the tale of the living giant, a creature out of the legends of antiquity, who was made into a prize fighter. He was taught and trained by a wise, scheming little French boxing manager who had an Oxford University degree, and he was later acquired and developed into a heavyweight champion of the world by a group of American gangsters and mob men; then finally, when his usefulness as a meal ticket was outlived, he was discarded in the most shameful chapter in all boxing.

This unfortunate pituitary case, who might have been Angoulaffre, or Balan, or Fierabras, Gogmagog, or Gargantua himself, was a poor simple-minded peasant by the name of Primo Carnera, the first son of a stonecutter of Sequals, Italy. He stood six feet seven inches in height, and weighed two hundred and sixty-eight pounds. He became the heavyweight champion, yet never in all his life was he ever anything more than a freak and a fourth-rater at prize fighting. He must have grossed more than two million dollars during the years that he was being exhibited, and he hasn't a cent to show for it today.

There is no room here for more than a brief and hasty glance back over the implications of the tragedy of Primo Carnera. And yet I could not seem to take my leave from sports without it. The scene and the story still fascinate me, the sheer impudence of the men who handled the giant, their conscienceless cruelty, their complete depravity toward another human being, the sure,

cool manner in which they hoaxed hundreds of thousands of people. Poor Primo! A giant in stature and strength, a terrible figure of a man, with the might of ten men, he was a helpless lamb among wolves who used him until there was nothing more left to use, until the last possible penny had been squeezed from his big carcass, and then abandoned him. His last days in the United States were spent alone in a hospital. One leg was paralyzed, the result of beatings taken around the head. None of the carrion birds who had picked him clean ever came back to see him or to help him.

No one who was present in Madison Square Garden the night that Primo Carnera was first introduced to American audiences will ever forget him as he came bounding down the aisle from the dressing room and climbed into the ring. It was a masterpiece of stage management.

He wore black fighting trunks on the side of which was embroidered the head of a wild boar in red silk. He disdained the usual fighter's bathrobe and instead wore a sleeveless vest of a particularly hideous shade of green, and on his head a cap of the same shade, several sizes too large for him and with an enormous visor that made him look even larger than he was. Leon See, the Frenchman, then his manager, was a small man. The bucket carriers and sponge wielders were chosen for size, too—diminutive men; everything was done to increase the impression of Primo's size.

Carnera was the only giant I have ever seen who was well proportioned throughout his body for his height. His legs were massive and he was truly thewed like an oak. His waist was comparatively small and clean, but from it rose a torso like a Spanish hogshead from which sprouted two tremendous arms, the biceps of which stood out like grapefruit. His hands were like Virginia hams, and his fingers were ten red sausages.

His head was large, even for the size of his body, and looking at him you were immediately struck with his dreadful gummy mouth and sharp, irregular, snaggle teeth. His lips were inclined to be loose and flabby. He had a good nose and fine, kind brown eyes. But his legs looked even more enormous and treelike than they were, owing to the great blue bulging varicose veins that wandered down them on both sides and stuck out far enough so that you could have knocked them off with a baseball bat. His skin was brown and glistening and he invariably smelled of garlic.

This was the horror that came into the Madison Square Garden ring and sent a sincere shudder through the packed house. That is to say, he was horrible until he commenced to fight, when he became merely pitiful and an object demanding sympathy. Behind what passed for the wild battle blaze in his eyes and the dreadful gummy leer, emphasized by the size of the red rubber mouthpiece (tooth protector) with which they provided him, there was nothing but bewilderment and complete helplessness. The truth was that, handicapped by rules and regulations, a sport he did not understand and was not temperamentally fitted for, and those silly brown leather bags laced to his fingers, never at any time could he fight a lick. His entire record, with a few exceptions, must be thrown out as one gigantic falsehood, staged and engineered, planned and executed by the men who had him in tow and who were building him up for the public as a man-killer and an invincible fighter.

But I think the most dreadful part of the story is that the poor floundering giant was duped along with the spectators. He was permitted, in fact encouraged, to believe that his silly pawings and pushings, when they connected, sent men staggering into unconsciousness and defeat. It was not until late in his career, when in spite of himself he learned something through sheer experience and number of fights, that he ever knocked anyone out on the level. But he never could fight, and never will. In spite of his great size and strength and his well-proportioned body, he remained nothing but a glandular freak who should have remained with the small French traveling circus from which Leon See took him.

This big, good-natured, docile man was exhibiting himself in a small wandering cirque in the south of France as a strong man and Greco-Roman wrestler, engaging all comers and local talent in a nightly show, having found that it paid him more and offered a better life than that of his chosen profession of mosaic-worker. Here he was discovered by a former French boxing champion who signed him up and apprenticed him to one Monsieur Leon See to be taught the rudiments of *la boxe*. It is highly probable that the time spent as a wrestler set his muscles and prevented him from ever becoming a knockout puncher. But Monsieur Leon See was taking no chances. He taught and trained Carnera strictly as a defensive boxer.

Now, it must be understood that Leon See was one of the most intelligent, smart and wily men that ever turned a fighter loose from his corner. He was not much more scrupulous than the bevy of public enemies who eventually took Carnera away from him simply by muscling him, but he was much more far-seeing and he had certain well-thought-out notions and theories about the ridiculous game of boxing. Among them was the excellent and sensible thought that the human head was never intended by nature to be punched, and that secondly, from the manner of its construction out of hundreds of tiny, delicately articulated bones, the closed fist was never meant to be one of man's most effective weapons. In this last idea, Monsieur See was not alone. The coterie of tough guys and mobsters who eventually relieved him of his interest in Carnera rarely used the fist, reckoning it, as did See, an inefficient weapon. The boys always favored the pistol or Roscoe, also known as the Difference, the Equalizer, the Rod, and the Heat.

See was a keen student of the human body— for a prize-fight manager—and he knew something about men. He was aware that abnormalities of size were usually compensated for by weaknesses elsewhere. He found out—exactly how is not known—that Primo Carnera would never be able to absorb a hard punch to the chin. He may have had some secret rehearsal in a gymnasium somewhere in Paris and, having ordered some workaday heavyweight to clout Primo one just to see what would happen, saw that the giant came all undone, wobbled and collapsed. Be that as it may, Monsieur See knew. And never at any time while he was connected with Carnera would he permit anyone to punch Primo in the head—neither his sparring partners nor his opponents. Since both received their pay from practically the same source, this was not so difficult to arrange as might be imagined. But

See also had something else. He was a French-man and so he had a heart. He loved big Carnera.

Years later See proved to be right. When Carnera, through exigent circumstances, was forced to fight without benefit of prearrangement, and the heavyweights began to sight along that big, protruding jaw of his and nail him for direct hits, he was slaughtered. He was brave and game and apparently could take punches to the body all the night long. But one hard, true tap on the chin and he fell down goggle-eyed. For a long time during the early years, however, nobody was permitted to hit him there, and Carnera himself began to think he was invincible.

Primo's first trip to the United States was arranged through an American contact man and importer of foreign fighting talent, a character from Tin Ear Alley named Walter Friedman or, as Damon Runyon nicknamed him, Walter (Good-Time Charley) Friedman. See was smart enough to know that without an American "in," without cutting in an American manager, he would not get very far in America. What he was not quite smart enough to know was how deep his "in" took him, that the ramifications of Friedman's business and other connections were to lead through some very rough and rapacious parties.

Carnera's first fight in New York involved him with a lanky Swede named Big Boy Peterson. In this fight poor Carnera was hardly able to get out of his own way and caused his opponent the most frightful embarrassment through not being able to strike a blow that looked sufficiently hard to enable him to keep his end of the bargain, if there was one. Eventually Peterson succumbed to a push as Carnera lumbered and floundered past him, and to make assurance doubly sure, the Swede hit himself a punch on the jaw as he went down. Someone had to hit him.

Now, this was a shameless swindle from start to finish one way or another. If Peterson was making an honest effort to fight he never should have been permitted to enter the ring. The press unanimously announced beforehand that it would probably be a sell and a fake, and when it was over, suggested strongly that it had been. But it said so in a gay and lighthearted manner as though the whole thing were pretty funny (as indeed it was), and there was no one on the New York State Athletic Commission either sufficiently intelligent or courageous enough to throw Primo and his handlers and fixers right out of the ring and thence out of the country. The Peterson fight in Madison Square Garden, the stronghold of professional boxing, was a sort of test case

by the Carnera crowd to see how much they could get away with. On that score it was a clean-cut success. They found out that they could get away with anything. And so they proceeded to do just that. Primo's first American tour was organized, a tour that grossed something like $700,000, of which handsome piece of money Carnera received practically nothing. He was barnstormed across the country in the most cold-blooded, graceless, shameful series of fixed, bought, coerced, or plain out-and-out tank acts ever. If one of them was contested on its merits it was only because the opponent by no possible stretch of the imagination or his own efforts could harm Carnera or even hit him.

Where the fight could not be bought—that is to say, where the fighter was unwilling to succumb to a tap on the elbow for a price—guns were produced by sinister strangers to threaten him; and where neither threats nor money were sufficient to bag the fight, he was crossed or tricked, as in the case of Bombo Chevalier, a big California Negro who was fascinated by the size of Carnera's chin, and nothing would do but he was going to hit it, just to see what would happen. Between rounds one of Chevalier's own attendants rubbed red pepper or some other inflammatory substance into his eyes so that he lost all interest in tapping anybody's chin.

In Newark, New Jersey, a Negro was visited in his dressing room before the bout by an unknown party not necessarily connected with Carnera's management, and was asked to inspect shooting irons, and in Philadelphia another Negro, Ace Clark, was amusing himself readying up Carnera for a knockout—he had already completely closed one of Primo's eyes—when somebody suggested he look down and see what the stranger beneath his corner was holding under his coat, and what caliber it was.

Every known build-up fighter was lined up for this tour, including faithful old hands like K. O. Christner, Chuck Wiggens, and poor Farmer Lodge. Political and gangster friends in the cities visited volunteered with their private heavyweights for quick splashes that might look well on the record books. It was all for the cause. The more money Carnera made, the more the boys would have to cut up amongst themselves. It was all just one big happy family. It seemed almost as though every scamp in the boxing game contributed his bit somehow to that Carnera build-up.

Friedman, as has been indicated, was the go-between, and although Leon See was quite capable of all the planning necessary to keep Carnera in the victory columns, nevertheless it would have been considered bad form, and down-right dangerous, if See had not cut the local boys in. And, at that, I suspect the said local boys showed the amiable and gifted Frog a few things about building up a potential heavyweight champion that made the two Stribling fights arranged by Monsieur See, one in Paris and the other in London and both ending in fouls, look like Holy Gospel.

An adviser and co-director of the tour, Broadway Bill Duffy was cut in. Bill was then in the night-club and fight-managing business, but in his youth he had been convicted of a little al fresco burgling and had been sent away for a spell. He was still to achieve the highest pinnacle of fame that can come to an American—to be named a Public Enemy. It is a curious commentary upon the conduct of boxing around New York that Duffy was allowed to operate as a manager and a second when there was a rule on the books of the State Athletic Commission, if indeed it was not written directly into the boxing law, that no one ever convicted of a felony was to be eligible for any kind of a license.

Duffy usually split even on things with his dearest friend, Owen Madden, better known as Owney, who had also been away for a time in connection with the demise of a policeman. Owney was out on parole at the time—he was sent back later—making beer (and very good beer it was, too) and acting as silent partner in the operation of a number of prize fighters. Also in this crowd was a charming but tough individual known as Big Frenchy De Mange who made news one evening by getting himself snatched and held for ransom by Mad-Dog Vincent Coll. The Mad Dog was subsequently rubbed out in a West Side drugstore telephone booth. But the subject, after all, is Primo Carnera and not gangsters and racket men, though pretty soon it was all one subject and all one sweet and fragrant mess. The boys had their connections in every town. The Philadelphia underworld collaborated through the medium of the always friendly and helpful Maxmillian Boo-Boo Hoff, and the same courtesies were extended all the way through to the Pacific Coast, where occurred the Bombo Chevalier incident, which was too nauseous even for the local commission there to stomach. There was an investigation resulting in the suspension of a few unimportant people. But Carnera and his swindle went merrily onward.

And it continued until he won the heavyweight championship of the world by ostensibly knocking out Jack Sharkey, then world's champion, in the sixth round, with a right uppercut. I say "ostensibly" because nothing will ever convince me that that was an honest prize fight, contested on its merits.

Sharkey's reputation and the reputation of Fat John Buckley, his manager, were bad. Both had been involved in some curious ring encounters. The reputation of the Carnera entourage by the time the Sharkey fight came along in 1933 was notorious, and the training camps of both gladiators were simply festering with mobsters and tough guys. Duffy, Madden, et Cie., were spread out all over Carnera's training quarters at Dr. Bier's Health Farm at Pompton Lakes, New Jersey. A traveling chapter of Detroit's famous Purple Gang hung out at Gus Wilson's for a while during Sharkey's rehearsals. Part of their business there was to muscle in on the concession of the fight pictures.

If the fight was on the level, it wasn't like either of the companies operating the two pugs. If it was honest, the only explanation was that the boys were going sissy. As far as Primo knew, the right uppercut with which he tagged Sharkey in the sixth round was enough to kill a steer. He had knocked out many men with the same punch. Now he was the heavyweight champion of the world, and even if he didn't have any money to show for it, Italy and Mussolini were going to be very pleased. I have often wondered how long he remained innocent, how long it was before he began to catch on.

For instance, it must have been a terrible surprise and considerable of an eye-opener to Carnera the night he fought Tommy Loughran in Miami as heavyweight champion of the world. It was a no-decision match and a bad one for the gang to make, but they had to do something because they were desperate for money at the time. If the Sharkey fight was crooked, it is probable that the entire end of Primo's purse had to be paid over for the fix.

The Loughran fight had to go on the level because no one had ever managed to tamper with Loughran, and neither he nor his manager was afraid of guns. And Tommy had another curious and valuable protection. He was a good Catholic, and many priests were his friends. The gunmen were a little shy of those padres, who might usually be found in twos and threes at Tommy's home or his training camps. But the mob figured that with a hundred-pound advantage in weight Carnera could take care of Loughran, who was little more than a light heavyweight and never was a hard hitter. During the fight Carnera hit Loughran more than a dozen of the same uppercuts that had stretched Sharkey twitching on the canvas, and never even reddened Tommy's face. Loughran was a cream-puff puncher and yet he staggered Carnera several times with right hands and was himself never in any kind of danger from a punch. He merely got tired from having Carnera leaning on him for half an hour. If nothing else, that fight beneath the Miami moon exposed how incompetent Carnera was as a bruiser, and how utterly false were the stories about his invincibility, besides casting fresh suspicion upon his knockout of Sharkey. We had all seen Loughran put on the floor by a 175-pounder. If a man weighing around 280 pounds, as Primo did for that fight, hit him flush on the jaw and couldn't drop him, and yet had knocked out one of the cleverest heavyweights in the business, it wasn't hard to arrive at a conclusion. It was obvious that he was a phony and the first stiff-punching heavyweight who was leveling would knock him out.

Max Baer did it the very next summer. The following summer Joe Louis did it again, and then an almost unknown Negro heavyweight by the name of Leroy Haynes accomplished the feat for the third time. And that was the beginning of the end of Primo.

His lucrative campaigns and the winning of the heavyweight championship had enriched everyone connected with him except poor Primo, who saw very little of the money he earned. There were too many silent partners and "boys" who had little pieces of him. Monsieur See had long since been dispensed with and shipped back to France for his health; he had served his purpose. But it was an evil day for Carnera when they chased Leon back to Paris, for Leon never would have permitted anyone to belt Carnera on his vulnerable chin. As suggested, the little Frenchman had a love for the big fellow whom he had taught and trained and watched over so carefully. The Duffy crowd had no love for anything. Fighters' chins were made to be smacked and they might just as well get used to taking the punches there.

It seemed as though their power was beginning to lose some of its effectiveness, exhausted perhaps by its own virus and viciousness, shortly after they had made Carnera champion. Primo escaped to Italy with his title and nothing else and later returned here for the disastrous fight with Loughran under the guidance of a little Italian banker by the name of Luigi Soresi, who appeared to be genuinely trying to get and keep for poor Carnera some of the money he was making.

The by-products of the Miami affair were typical and pathetic. Duffy and company were living over a Miami night club in style and spending money like water—Primo's money. Carnera was relegated to a cheap cottage back of the town with a trainer. No one really looked after him. No one cared particularly whether he trained or not. He came into the ring against Loughran twenty pounds overweight. Shortly after that, Duffy was clapped into the jug for a spell for some boyish pranks with his income tax, and from the cooler he wrote pleading letters at the time that Carnera was preparing to defend his title against Baer, maintaining that he was needed to guide, advise, and teach Primo, to prime him for the first serious defense of his title, and that he should be given furlough from quod to attend to this matter. Carnera vigorously denied that he needed him. He was only too delighted to have Duffy held in durance vile. Of course what was really killing Uncle Will was that he was where for the first time he couldn't get his fingers on a nice big slice of the sugar that big, stupid Wop would make for boxing Baer.

It is difficult to bag or fix a heavyweight championship prize fight, though it has been done. But in the postwar sports renaissance there was so much money at stake in a heavyweight championship fight that it took more cash than most could produce to purchase either champion or challenger. It stood to reason that if the champion figured to make a million dollars or more out of his title he wasn't going to sell out for any less. Too, the power of the gangs was weakening. Repeal dealt them a terrible blow and took away their chief source of revenue. Three or four years before, Carnera's title would have been safe because his handlers would not have accepted any challenger for the title unless he agreed to preserve the state of the champion's health throughout the encounter. And there were always ways and means of keeping a challenger from double-crossing.

But Duffy was in the sneezer, as the boys sometimes quaintly called the jailhouse, Carnera was broke and needed money. He could only get it by fighting Baer. And the Baer fight could not be fixed. Baer's reputation was good; at least, he had not been caught out in any shady fights. He was a powerful hitter and it was apparent that now at last the rest of us were going to be made privy to what it was that happened when Carnera was struck forcefully on the chin. We didn't have to wait long. He was knocked down three times in the first round, and lost his championship in the eleventh round on a technical knockout when he was helpless, having been knocked down a total of thirteen times during the ten and a half rounds.

Not, however, until he fought and was knocked out by Joe Louis was it apparent what a dreadful thing had been done to this great hulk of a man.

Strange to feel pity and sympathy excited for one so gross and enormous and strong. But the outsizes of the world are not the happy men, and their bulk is often of little use or help to them. If anything, it is a handicap when up against the speed and timing and balance of a normal man. Carnera's great strength was practically useless to him in the ring. The hardest blow he could strike was little more than a push. True, if he caught you in a corner he could club you insensible, but no smart fighter is caught in corners, and the big man was never fast enough anyway to catch anyone but out-and-out tramps.

When he fought Joe Louis he was defensively but little better than he was the first time I saw him, which, as it happened, was not in Madison Square Garden, but in the smoky, stuffy, subterranean Salle Wagram, a little fight club in Paris where I happened to be one evening when Jeff Dickson was promoting a fight between Primo Carnera, who had then been fighting a little less than a year, and one Moise Bouquillon, a light heavyweight who weighed 174 pounds. Monsieur See was experimenting a little with his giant. It was obvious that Bouquillon was going to be unable to hurt him very much, but what I noted that evening and never forgot was that the giant was likewise unable to hurt the little Frenchman. Curiously, that fight was almost the exact duplicate of the one that Carnera as champion later fought with Loughran. Walter (Good-Time Charley) Friedman was there too. Many years later he told me quite frankly: "Boy, was that a lousy break for us that you come walking into that Salle Wagram that night and see that the big guy can't punch! Just that night you hadda be there. Leon wanted to see if he could go ten rounds without falling down. And you hadda be there. We coulda got away with a lot more if you don't walk in there and write stories about how he can't punch."

Joe Louis slugged Carnera into bleating submission, cruelly and brutally. Handsome Uncle Will Duffy was back in his corner again, jawing angrily at him when he was led trembling and quivering back to his chair after the referee had saved him again, one side of his mouth smashed in, dazed and dripping blood. The very first right-hand punch Louis hit him broke Carnera's mouth and hurt him dreadfully.

Here, then, was the complete sell. He had nothing. His title was gone, his money squandered by the gang. And the one thing he thought he had, an unbeatable skill in defense and an irresistible crushing power in attack that no man living could withstand, never existed. It was a fable as legendary as the great giants of mythology that he resembled. The carrion birds that had fed upon this poor, big, dumb man had picked him clean. They had left him nothing, not even his pride and his self-respect, and that probably was the cruelest thing of all.

In his last fight, the one with Haynes, he was again severely beaten about the head. One of his legs refused to function. The fight was stopped. While he lay in the hospital in New York for treatment, as I have said, he lay alone.

I often wonder what that hulk of a man thinks today as he looks back over the manner in which he was swindled, tricked and cheated at every turn, as he recalls the great sums of money that he earned, all of it gone beyond recall. The world has no place for him, not even as a freak in a circus, from whence he emerged and where he might happily have spent his life and become prosperous. Because as a giant, a terror and a horror, he stands exposed as a poor, unwilling fraud who was no man-killer at all, but a rather helpless, sad creature who, when slugged by a 185-pound mortal, either toppled stricken to the floor or staggered about or bled or had to be saved from annihilation by a third man who obligingly stepped between him and his tormentors.

He was born far, far too late. He belonged to the twelfth or thirteenth century, when he would have been a man-at-arms and a famous fellow with mace and halberd, pike or bill. At least he would have fought nobly and to the limit of his strength, properly armed, because Carnera was a courageous fellow to the limit of his endurance, game and a willing fighter when aroused. In those days he would have won honor afield and would have got himself decently killed, or, surviving, would have been retired by his feudal lord to round out his days and talk over the old brave fights.

Today there is nothing left for this man but reflection upon his humiliations. He was just a big sucker whom the wise guys took and trimmed. What an epitaph for one who came from the ancient and noble race of giants.

All this took place in our country, *Anno Domini* 1930–1935.

# WHITNEY DARROW, JR.

Captain John Godfrey was a patron of Figg's Amphitheater, where he practiced fencing, cudgeling and boxing. In 1747 he published *The Useful Science of Defence,* the two final chapters, reprinted here, being the first treatment of boxing in a book. The work sold out two large printings and was, Pierce Egan noted sixty-five years later, "now extremely scarce." Today there are two copies in the British Museum and one owned by Mitchell Rawson of New York City.

FROM

# The Useful Science of Defence

## CAPTAIN JOHN GODFREY

### BOXING

Boxing is a combat, depending more on Strength than the Sword: But Art will yet bear down the Beam against it. A less Degree of Art will tell for more than a considerably greater Strength. Strength is certainly what the Boxer ought to set out with, but without Art he will succeed but poorly. The Deficiency of Strength may be greatly supplied by Art; but the want of Art will have but heavy and unwieldy Succour from Strength.

Here it may not be amiss to make some little anatomical Enquiry into the advantageous Disposition of the Muscles by the just Posture of the Body, and the acting Arm. I will venture to dabble a little in it; but cry Mercy all the while. If I make a Piece of Botch-Work of it, forgive the poor Anatomist through the Swords-Man.

The Strength of Man chiefly consists on the Power of his Muscles, and that Power is greatly to be increased by Art. The Muscles are as Springs and Levers, which execute the different Motions of our Body; but by Art a Man may give an additional Force to them.

The nearer a Man brings his Body to the Center of Gravity, the truer Line of Direction will his Muscle act in, and consequently with more resisting Force. If a Man designs to strike a hard Blow, let him shut his Fist as firm as possible; the Power of his Arm will then be considerably greater, than if but slightly closed, and the Velocity of his Blow vastly augmented by it. The Muscles which give this additional Force to the Arm, in shutting the Fist, are the Flexors of the Fingers, and the Extensors are the opposite Muscles, as they open or expand the same; yet in striking, or using any violent Efforts with your Hand, these different Orders of the Muscles contribute to the same Action. Thus it will appear, that when you close the Fist of your left Arm, and clap your right Hand upon that Arm, will plainly feel all the Muscles of it to have a reciprocal Swelling. From hence it follows, that Muscles, by Nature designed for different Offices, mutually depend on each other in great Efforts. This Consideration will be of much Advantage in that artificial Force in Fighting, which beats much superior Strength, where Art is wanting.

The Position of the Body is of the greatest Consequence in Fighting. The Center of Gravity ought to be well considered, for by that the Weight of the Body being justly suspended, and the true Equilibrium thereby preserved, the Body stands much the firmer against opposing Force. This depends upon the proper Distance between the Legs, which is the first Regard a *Boxer* ought to have, or all his manly Attempts will prove abortive. In order to form the true Position, the left Leg must be presented some reasonable Distance before the Right, which brings the left Side towards the Adversary; this the right-handed

Man ought to do, that, after having stopped the Blow with his left Arm, which is a Kind of Buckler to him, he may have the more Readiness and greater Power of stepping in with his right Hand's returning Blow. In this Posture he ought to reserve an easy Flexion in the left Knee, that his Advances and Retreats may be the quicker. By this proper Flexion, his Body is brought so far forward, as to have a just Inclination over the left Thigh, insomuch that his Face makes a perpendicular or straight Line with the left Knee; whilst the right Leg and Thigh in a slanting Line, strongly prop up the whole Body, as does a large Beam an old Wall. The Body by this means is supported against all violent Efforts, and the additional Strength acquired by this Equilibrium, is greatly to the Purpose. How much greater Weight must not your Adversary stand in need of, to beat you back from this forward inclining of the Body, than the so much less resisting Reclination of it? By this disposed Attitude you find the whole Body gently inclining forward with a slanting Direction, so that you shall find from the *Outside* of the right Ankle all the way to the Shoulder, a straight Line of Direction, somewhat inclining, or slanting upward, which Inclination is the strongest Position a Man can contrive; and it is such as we generally use in forcing Doors, resisting Strength or pushing forward any Weight with Violence: For the Muscles of the left Side, which bend the Body gently forward, bring over the left Thigh the gravitating Part, which by this Contrivance augments the Force; whereas, if it was held erect or upright, an indifferent Blow on the Head, or Breast, would overset it. The Body by this Position has the Muscles of the right Side partly relaxed, and partly contracted, whilst those of the Left are altogether in a State of Contraction; but the Reserve made in the Muscles of the right Side, is as Springs and Levers to let fall the Body at Discretion.

By delivering up the Power to the Muscles of the left Side, which, in a very strong Contraction, brings the Body forward, the Motion which is communicated, is then so strong, that, if the Hand at that Time be firmly shut, and the Blow at that Instant pushed forward, with the contracting Muscles, in a straight Line with the moving Body, the Shock given from the Stroke will be able to overcome a Force, not thus artfully contrived, twenty times as great.

From this it is evident, how it is in our Power to give an additional Force and Strength to our Bodies, whereby we may make ourselves far superior to Men of more Strength, not seconded by Art.

Let us now examine the most hurtful Blows, and such as contribute most to the Battle. Though very few of those, who fight, know, why a Blow on such a Part has such Effects, yet by Experience they know it has; and by these evident Effects, they are directed to the proper Parts; as for Instance, hitting under the Ear, between the Eye-brows, and about the Stomach. I look upon the Blow under the Ear to be as dangerous as any, that is, if it light between the Angle of the lower Jaw and the Neck; because in this Part there are two Kinds of Blood Vessels considerably large; the one brings the Blood immediately from the Heart to the Head, whilst the other carries it mediately back. If a Man received a Blow on these Vessels, the Blood proceeding from the Heart to the Head, is partly forced back, whilst the other Part is pushed forwards vehemently to the Head: The same happens in the Blood returning from the Head to the Heart, for part of it is precipitately forced into the latter, whilst the other Part tumultuously rushes to the Head; whereby the Blood Vessels are immediately overcharged, and the Sinus's of the Brain so overloaded and compressed, that the Man at once loses all Sensation, and the Blood often runs from his Ears, Mouth and Nose, altogether owing to it's Quantity forced with such Impetuosity into the smaller Vessels, the Coats whereof being too tender to resist so great a Charge, instantly break, and cause the Effusion of Blood through these different Parts.

This is not the only Consequence, but the Heart being overcharged with a Regurgitation of Blood (as I may say with respect to that forced back on the succeeding Blood coming from it's left Ventricle) stops it's Progress, whilst that Part of the Blood coming from the Head, is violently pushed into it's right Auricle; so that as the Heart labours under a violent Surcharge of Blood, there soon follows a Cardiaca or Suffocation, but which goes off as the Parts recover themselves and push the Blood forward. The Blows given between the Eye-brows contribute greatly to the Victory: For this Part being contused between two hard Bodies, *viz* The *Fist,* and *Os frontale,* there ensues a violent Ecchymosis, or Extravasation of Blood, which falls immediately into the Eye-lids; and they being of a lax Texture incapable of resisting this Influx of Blood, swell almost instantaneously; which violent Intumescence soon obstructs the Sight. The Man thus indecently treated, and artfully hoodwinked, is beat about at his Adversary's Discretion.

The Blows on the Stomach are also very hurtful, as the Diaphragm and Lungs share in the Injury. The Vomitions produced by them I might account for, but I should run my anatomical Impertinences too far.

I would recommend to those who Box, that on the Day of Combat they charge not their Stomachs with much Aliment: for by observing this Precaution, they will find great Service. It will help them to avoid that extraordinary Compression on the *Aorta Descendens,* and in a great measure preserve their Stomachs from the Blows, which they must be the more exposed to, when distended with Aliments. The Consequence of which may be attended with a Vomiting of Blood, caused by the Eruption of some Blood Vessels, from the overcharging of the Stomach: Whereas the empty Stomach, yielding to the Blow, is as much less affected by it, as it is more by it's Resistance, when expanded with Food. Therefore I advise a Man to take a little Cordial Water upon an empty Stomach, which, I think, would be of great Service, by its astringing the Fibres, and contracting it into a smaller Compass.

The Injury the Diaphragm is subject to from Blows, which light just under the Breast-bone, is very considerable; because the Diaphragm is brought into a strong convulsive State, which produces great Pain, and lessens the Cavity of the Thorax, whereby the Lungs are a great Measure deprived of their Liberty, and the Quantity of Air retained in them, from the Contraction of the Thorax through the convulsive State of the Diaphragm, is so forcibly pushed from them, that it causes a great Difficulty of Respiration, which cannot be overcome till the convulsive Motion of the Diaphragm ceases.

The artful Boxer may, in some Degree, render the Blows less hurtful on this Part, by drawing in the Belly, holding his Breath and bending his Thorax over his Navel, when the Stroke is coming.

I have mentioned Strength and Art as the two Ingredients of a Boxer. But there is another, which is vastly necessary; that is, what we call a Bottom. We need not explain what it is, as being a Term well understood. There are two Things required to make this Bottom, that is, Wind and Spirit, or Heart, or wherever you can fix the Residence of Courage. Wind may be greatly brought about by Exercise and Diet; but the Spirit is the first Equipment of a Boxer. Without this substantial Thing, both Art and Strength will avail a Man but little. This, with several other Points, will appear more fully in the Characters of the Boxers.

## CHARACTERS OF THE BOXERS

ADVANCE, BRAVE BROUGHTON! Thee I pronounce Captain of the *Boxers.* As far as I can look back, I think, I ought to open the Characters with him: I know none so fit, so able to lead up the Van. This is giving him the living Preference to the rest; but, I hope, I have not given any Cause to say, that there has appeared, in any of my Characters, a partial Tincture. I have throughout consulted nothing, but my unbias'd Mind, and my Heart has known no Call but Merit. Wherever I have praised, I have no Desire of pleasing; wherever decried, no Fear of offending. BROUGHTON, by his manly Merit, has bid the highest, therefore has my Heart. I really think all will poll with me, who poll with the same Principle. Sure there is some standing Reason for this Preference. What can be stronger than to say, that for seventeen or eighteen Years, he has fought every able Boxer that appeared against him, and has never yet been beat? This being the Case, we may venture to conclude from it. But not to build alone on this, let us examine farther into his Merits. What is it that he wants? Has he not all that others want, and all the best can have? Strength equal to what is human, Skill and Judgement equal to what can be acquired, undebauched Wind, and a bottom Spirit, never to pronounce the word ENOUGH. He fights the Stick as well as most men, and understands a good deal of the Small-Sword. This Practice has given him the Distinction of *Time* and *Measure* beyond the rest. He stops as regularly as the Swords-Man, and carries his Blows truly in the Line; he steps not back, distrusting of himself to stop a Blow, and piddle in the Return, with an Arm unaided by his Body, producing but a kind of flyflap Blows; such as the Pastry-Cooks use to beat those Insects from their Tarts and Cheesecakes. No—BROUGHTON steps bold and firmly in, bids a Welcome to the coming Blow; receives it with his guardian Arm; then with a general Summons of his swelling Muscles, and his firm Body, seconding his Arm, and supplying it with all it's Weight, pours the Pile-driving Force upon his Man.

That I may not be thought particular in dwelling too long upon BROUGHTON, I leave him with this Assertion, that as he, I believe, will scarce trust a Battle to a warning Age, I never shall think he is to be beaten, till I see him beat.*

About the Time I first observed this promising Hero upon the Stage, his chief Competitors were PIPES and GRETTING. He beat them both (and I thought with ease) as often as he fought them.

* Three years after Capt. Godfrey's book was published Jack Broughton, on April 11, 1750, lost his title to Jack Slack.—ED.

PIPES was the neatest Boxer I remember. He put in his Blows about the Face (which he fought at most) with surprising Time and Judgement. He maintained his Battles for many Years by his extraordinary Skill, against Men of far superior Strength. PIPES was but weakly made; his Appearance bespoke Activity, but his Hand, Arm, and Body were but small. Though by that acquired Spring of his Arm he hit prodigious Blows; and I really think, that at last, when he was beat out of his Championship, it was more owing to his Debauchery than the Merit of those who beat him.

GRETTING was a strong Antagonist to PIPES. They contended hard together for some Time, and were almost alternate Victors. GRETTING had the nearest way of going to the Stomach (which is what they call the Mark) of any Man I knew. He was a most artful Boxer, stronger made than PIPES, and dealt the straightest Blows: But what made PIPES a Match for him, was his rare Bottom Spirit, which would bear a deal of Beating, but this, in my Mind, GRETTING was not sufficiently furnished with; for after he was beat twice together by PIPES, *Hammersmith* JACK, a meer Sloven of a Boxer, and every Body that fought him afterwards, beat him. I must, notwithstanding, do that Justice to GRETTING'S Memory, as to own that his Debauchery very much contributed to spoil a great *Boxer*; but yet I think he had not the Bottom of the other.

Much about this Time, there was one WHITAKER, who fought the *Venetian* GONDELIER. He was a very strong Fellow, but a clumsy *Boxer*. He had two Qualifications, very much contributing to help him out. He was very extraordinary for his throwing, and contriving to pitch his weighty Body on the fallen Man. The other was, that he was a hardy Fellow, and would bear a deal of Beating. This was the man pitched upon to fight the *Venetian*. I was at *Slaughter's* Coffee-House when the Match was made, by a Gentleman of an advanced Station; he sent for FIG to produce a proper Man for him; he told him to take care of his Man, because it was for a large Sum; and the *Venetian* was a Man of extraordinary Strength, and famous for breaking the Jaw-bone in *Boxing*. FIG replied, in his rough Manner, I do not know, Master, he may break one of his own Countrymen's Jaw-bones with his Fist; but, I will bring him a Man, and he shall not break his Jaw-bone with a Sledge Hammer in his Hand.

The Battle was fought at FIG's Amphitheatre, before a splendid Company, the politest House of that kind I ever saw. While the GONDELIER was stripping, my Heart yearned for my Countryman. His Arm took up all Observation; it was surprisingly large, long, and muscular. He pitched himself forward with his right Leg, and Arm full extended, and, as WHITAKER approached, gave him a Blow on the Side of the Head, that knocked him quite off the Stage, which was remarkable for it's Height. WHITAKER'S Misfortune in his Fall was then the Grandeur of the Company, on which account they suffered no common People in, that usually sit on the Ground and line the Stage round. It was then all clear, and WHITAKER had nothing to stop him but the bottom. There was a general foreign Huzza on the Side of the *Venetian*, pronouncing our Countryman's Downfall; but WHITAKER took no more Time than was required to get up again, when finding his Fault in standing out to the length of the other's Arm, he, with a little Stoop, ran boldly in beyond the heavy Mallet, and with one *English* Peg in the Stomach (quite a new Thing to Foreigners) brought him on his Breech. The Blow carried too much of the *English* Rudeness for him to bear, and finding himself so unmannerly used, he scorned to have any more doings with his slovenly Fist.

So fine a House was too engaging to FIG, not to court another. He therefore stepped up, and told the Gentlemen that they might think he had picked out the best Man in *London* on this Occasion: But to convince them to the contrary, he said, that, if they would come that Day se'nnight, he would bring a Man who should beat this WHITAKER in ten Minutes, by fair hitting. This brought very near as great and fine a Company as the Week before. The man was NATHANIEL PEARTREE, who knowing the other's Bottom, and his deadly way of Flinging, took a most judicious Method to beat him.—Let his Character come in here—He was a most admirable *Boxer*, and I do not know one he was not a Match for, before he lost his Finger. He was famous, like PIPES, for fighting at the Face, but stronger in his Blows. He knew WHITAKER'S Hardiness, and doubting of his being able to give him Beating enough, cunningly determined to fight at his Eyes. His Judgement carried in his Arm so well, that in about six Minutes both WHITAKER'S Eyes were shut up; when groping about a while for his Man, and finding him not, he wisely gave out, with these odd Words—Damme—I am not beat, but what signifies my fighting when I cannot see my Man?

We will now come to Times a little fresher, and of later Date.

GEORGE TAYLOR, known by the Name of GEORGE the BARBER, sprang up surprisingly.

He has beat all the chief Boxers, but BROUGH-TON. He, I think, injudiciously fought him one of the first, and was obliged very soon to give out. Doubtless it was a wrong Step in him to commence a Boxer, by fighting the standing Champion: For GEORGE was not then twenty, and BROUGHTON was in the Zenith of his Age and Art. Since that he has greatly distinguished himself with others; but has never engaged BROUGHTON more. He is a strong able Boxer, who with a Skill extraordinary, aided by his Knowledge of the Small and Back-Sword, and a remarkable Judgement in the Cross-Buttock-Fall, may contest with any. But, please or displease, I am resolved to be ingenuous in my Characters. Therefore I am of the Opinion, that he is not over-stocked with that necessary Ingredient of a Boxer, called a Bottom; and am apt to suspect, that Blows of equal strength with his, too much affect him and disconcert his Conduct.

Before I leave him, let me do him this Justice to say, that if he were unquestionable in his Bottom, he would be a Match for any Man.

It will not be improper, after GEORGE the BARBER, to introduce one BOSWELL, a Man, who wants nothing but Courage to qualify him for a compleat *Boxer*. He has a particular Blow with his left Hand at the Jaw, which comes almost as hard as a little Horse kicks. Praise be to his Power of Fighting, his excellent Choice of *Time* and *Measure,* his superior Judgement, dispatching forth his executing Arm! But fye upon his dastard Heart, that marrs it all! As I knew that Fellow's Abilities, and his worm-dread Soul, I never saw him beat, but I wished him to be beaten. Though I am charmed with the Idea of his Power and Manner of Fighting, I am sick at the Thoughts of his Nurse-wanting Courage. Farewel to him, with this fair Acknowledgement, that, if he had a true *English* Bottom (the best fitting Epithet for a Man of Spirit) he would carry all before him, and be a Match for even BROUGHTON himself.

I will name two Men together, whom I take to be the best Bottom Men of the modern Boxers: And they are SMALLWOOD, and GEORGE STEVENSON, the Coachman. I saw the latter fight BROUGHTON, for forty Minutes. BROUGHTON I knew to be ill at that Time; besides it was a hasty made Match, and he had not that Regard for his Preparation, as he afterwards found he should have had. But here his true Bottom was proved, and his Conduct shone. They fought in one of the Fair-Booths at *Tottenham* Court, railed at the End towards the Pit. After about thirty-five Minutes, being both against the Rails, and scrambling for a Fall,

BROUGHTON got such a Lock upon him as no Mathematician could have devised a better. There he held him by this artificial Lock, depriving him of all Power of rising or falling, till resting his Head for about three or four Minutes on his Back, he found himself recovering. Then loosed the Hold, and on setting to again, he hit the Coachman as hard a Blow as any he had given him in the whole Battle; that he could no longer stand, and his brave contending Heart, though with Reluctance, was forced to yield. The Coachman is a most beautiful Hitter; he put in his Blows faster than BROUGHTON, but then one of the latter's told for three of the former's. Pity —so much Spirit could not inhabit a stronger Body!

SMALLWOOD is thorough game, with Judgement equal to any, and superior to most. I know nothing SMALLWOOD wants but Weight, to stand against any Man; and I never knew him beaten since his fighting DIMMOCK (which was in his Infancy of Boxing, and when he was a perfect Stripling in Years) but by a Force so superior, that to have resisted longer would not have been Courage but Madness. If I were to chuse a Boxer for my Money, and could but purchase him Strength equal to his Resolution, SMALLWOOD should be the Man.

JAMES I proclaim a most charming Boxer. He is delicate in his Blows, and has a Wrist as delightful to those who see him fight, as it is sickly to those who fight against him. I acknowledge him to have the best Spring of the Arm of all the modern Boxers; he is a compleat Master of the Art, and, as I do not know he wants a Bottom, I think it a great Pity he should be beat for want of strength to stand his Man.

I have now gone through the Characters of the most noted Boxers, and finished my whole Work. As I could not praise all in every Article, I must offend some; but if I do not go to Bed till every Body is pleased, my Head will ake as bad as Sir *Roger's.* I declare that I have not had the least Thought of offending throughout the whole Treatise, and therefore this Declaration shall be my quiet Draught.

Let me conclude with a general Call to the true British Spirit, which, like purest Gold, has no Alloy. How readily would I encourage it, through the most threatening Dangers, or severest Pains, or Pledge of Life itself! Let us imitate the glorious Example we enjoy, in the saving Offspring of our King, and blessed Guardian of our Country. Him let us follow with our keen Swords, and warm glowing Hearts, in Defence of our Just Cause, and Preservation of *Britain's* Honour.

In this the English novelist and poet supports boxing as one of the arts, and does it bravely and well.

FROM

# The World I Knew

## LOUIS GOLDING

And there was boxing. Thank the Lord, despite the thousand barriers, there was boxing. For I have been a boxing fan just as much as I have been a ballet fan, and for similar reasons, as I will explain. Whenever I had anything to celebrate, I would go to see boxing. And, as a matter of fact, I would go to see boxing when I had nothing to celebrate too—when I wanted to get away from myself, from my books, from my friends. . . .

I was saying I went boxing on my big nights. I also went boxing on my small nights, quite often two or three nights a week, and an occasional Sunday afternoon, too. It is a seduction to which, of course, infinitely more portentous men of letters than I have been prone, and these have devoted to boxing some of their most inspired writing.

Were they, I among them, mere sadists? That is a reproach I need not waste much time over. I have known gentle insurance clerks who play no more violent game than dominoes who are much more academically sadistic than any bullfight *aficionado*. I have had it said often enough to me: "Oh, yes. We know all about *you*. Boxing, eh? Blood and teeth, eh? Your real heaven would be to horsewhip gangs of naked Negroes with a rhinoceros-hide whip."

Well, it would not. That is enough of that. I found it exciting, I found it beautiful. I found it exciting, not merely when a Big Fight came along and filled countless columns of the newspapers with its vast melodrama. I found it exciting in the most subfusc little hall in the dimmest suburb.

And beautiful, too, not less than painting or dancing or drama. The assertion will sound pretentious only to those who have never seen a boxing match. Or at least only a bad one. And it can be bad, right enough. It can be as slow as waiting in a drizzle for a local train two hours late. It can be as heavy as the sight of two doped seals wallowing about gloomily in a tank. It can be as messy as a butcher's counter. It is not fair to judge boxing, which is at the same time a fine sport, a fine science, and a fine art, from one or two shoddy specimens—any more than one should condemn the cinema and all its works because one once saw a rotten film.

Now about the pure aesthetics of boxing. Clearly there is something magnificent in the spectacle itself. Here are two young fellows in the very pink of physical perfection. Their training has eliminated the last half-ounce of superfluous flesh from every muscle of their body. You can say you prefer tennis or swimming or cycling as a sport, but you cannot get away from the fact that the training that boxing involves makes the male body as perfect as it knows how to be. We know that the job involves more often than not a flattened nose and a thickened ear. But I hardly think that matters unless a boxer has ambitions to be a musical-comedy star, which happens now and again, but not frequently. They have had to forswear delights and live laborious days to attain that condition. You might feel that £50, or £5,000, is a disproportionate payment for a job of work which might last forty-five minutes and might not last two. But it would be like saying that a great violinist is overpaid for his half-hour on the platform, which has only attained that dazzling perfection through heartbreaking application, hour upon hour, year upon year.

The boxers have worked hard, too. They have been as Spartan in their self-denial as monks. There have been strenuous months of work in the gymnasium, topwork, groundwork, skipping, punch-balling, shadowboxing. They have been plugging out on the roads, up hill and down dale, in thick sweaters and flannels. They have attained the taut perfection of a machine.

And then—and then, their great moment comes.

As they stand isolated in the chalky glare from the arc lights, the smoky darkness which frames them makes a picture out of them which has something of the quality of a Michelangelo. But they are something more than canvas. They might stand immobile for one tense moment, each trying to sum up his opponent, to read his mind. In that moment they are superb statuary. You forget—if it is a Big Fight night—you forget the thousands of spectators seething around you, from the journalists just under the canvas, the dinner-jacketed (fancy) in the ringside seats, all the way up, tier beyond tier, to the enraptured errand boys just under the roof. You forget the torrents of newspaper publicity, you forget the purses, the side bets, the commercial angle of it all. It is for that one moment as if you were in a quiet art gallery. They are Greek athletes you are gazing on, molded in bronze to last for all time.

Then the moment snaps. They are not Greek athletes. They are a Cornish miner and a Pimlico greengrocer who have become professional boxers. They are not marble and motionless. They are flesh and blood, and they move. And it is in the nature of their movement that one will often find, in first-rate boxing, at any rate, the quality of ballet, almost as vigorously controlled within the framework of its own patterns.

Then, finally, there is its drama. For boxing is, after all, not merely a contest between two spendidly developed bodies. You will frequently see a boxer of inferior physique make rings round a young Hercules, because he has established a complete intellectual and moral ascendancy over him. The fact is, boxing is also a contest between two minds and two characters—and that is exactly what great drama is. It is an art that both creates character and reveals it. Of course, a fight in the higher levels of the art requires two artists. A Yehudi needs his Stradivarius, a Massine composing his ballet needs his Lichine and his Baronova. But once you have your Jimmy Wilde, your Fidel la Barba, matched against the opponent decreed for him by the stars in their courses, then the rhythm is achieved, that definite musical line, which makes the supreme fights in one's memory abide like the hearing of symphonies.

FOR MORE THAN a quarter of a century Frank Graham has written the cleanest prose to appear in a newspaper and the most accurate dialogue to appear anywhere. No one has ever written more beautifully about boxing. This column, which appeared in the New York *Journal American*, was written on his return home from the funeral of his friend and favorite manager, Joe Gould. His favorite fighter was Jim Braddock.     .

# All the Way to the Grave

## FRANK GRAHAM

ONE OF Joe Gould's favorite stories was about the time Tex Rickard was building up Luis Firpo and wanted Italian Jack Herman as an opponent for him in Havana and Joe, who managed Herman, accepted the match and, on looking for his fighter, found him in a hospital.

"What's the matter with you?" he asked.

"I had a pain in the belly," Herman said, "and the doctor says I'm going to get appendicitis."

"Are you?" Joe asked.

"I don't think so," Herman said. "I feel great."

"Then what are you laying here for," Joe said, "when you are boxing Firpo in Havana on Wednesday?"

"I am?" Herman yelled.

And, the way Joe used to tell it, Herman jumped out of bed and pulled on his pants.

They knew the story well in the fight mob and now some of them were standing in the rain outside the Riverside Memorial Chapel. Funeral services for the little man who guided Jim Braddock to the heavyweight championship were just over and they were standing there, talking about him, and Ernie Braca said:

"He was a very game guy and he gave it a great fight but I knew he was gone when I went into Mt. Sinai to see him a couple of weeks ago. His wife, Lucille, asked me if I couldn't drop in to try and cheer him up and when I walked in, I said to him: 'What are you laying here for when you're boxing Firpo in Havana on Wednesday?'

"I thought it would get a laugh out of him but he couldn't give. He just lay there looking at me and I knew he was a goner."

One of them stood there talking with the others about Joe for a while and then he went away and he was thinking about Joe and the time when Joe and Braddock were broke and the last thing either of them could have figured was that one day Jim would be the heavyweight champion.

But in that time Joe was hustling for him, not knowing where he would be able to take him, but determined that Jim would not stay on the docks and the relief rolls because Jim was too nice a guy for that and he had a wife and children and they rated a better shake than that. Joe's own furniture was in hock and he was sleeping on the bare floor of his apartment and hoping the landlord wouldn't come around looking for the rent too soon, but he never said anything about that to anybody but kept talking Braddock and trying to get a shot for him and finally he got it from Jimmy Johnston.

It was a preliminary bout on the Baer–Carnera card in the Garden Bowl in June of 1934. Braddock was in with a fellow named Corn Griffin, out of Georgia, and knocked him out in the third round. They were on their way back to the dressing room, Joe and Jim, and Jim said to Joe:

"I did that on hash. Get me a couple of steaks and there is no telling what I will do."

A year later they were at Evans Loch Shel-drake, Jim training for the fight with Max Baer in which he was to win the championship. There was a day when Jim, having finished his work, was sitting on the veranda of the main house with Joe and Francis Albertanti. No one could have asked for a more beautiful day. A blue sky . . . a setting sun . . . trees green . . . flowers in bloom . . . birds . . . bees . . . butterflies.

Francis, who hates the country, glared through the haze of his cigar smoke at Jim.

"- - - - - - - you, Braddock," he said. "If it wasn't for you, I wouldn't be here."

Joe laughed.

"If it wasn't for Braddock," he said, "you know where we'd be, don't you?"

"On relief," Francis said.

"Right," Joe said.

Jim laughed with them and he looked at Joe and you could see he was thinking about a lot of things they had gone through together and how it was Joe who was always out there in front of him, showing him the way.

There was the night in the Garden Bowl when Jim took the championship from Max Baer . . . and the night in Chicago when he lost it to Joe Louis.

Louis giving him a frightful beating, and at the end of the sixth round, Joe saying to Jim:

"I'm going to stop it."

Jim, sitting in his corner, looking up at him through the haze of blood in his eyes and saying:

"If you do, I'll never speak to you again as long as I live."

Joe, knowing Jim meant it, let the fight go on and, in the eighth round, Louis hit him on the chin, splitting the flesh on his chin and Jim fell on his face. And, as he lay there, his blood made little pools on the canvas. And when the count was over, Joe helping to lift him and get him back to his corner.

Joe wanting Jim to quit after that but Jim begging for a shot at Tommy Farr and Joe giving in and making the match for him and, in the Garden, Jim coming back to his corner at the end of the eighth round of a ten-round fight and asking Joe:

"How am I doing?"

Joe saying:

"You're losing, Jim."

And Jim saying:

"Watch me do the big apple in the next two rounds."

And going out there and beating Farr in the next two rounds and getting the decision and, in the dressing room, Joe saying:

"That was great, Jim. And that was all. You'll never fight again. But I don't have to tell you we'll still be together, like we have been."

It was raining and the one who had been thinking about this was on his way home and now he was thinking back, just a little while ago, to the funeral services and Rabbi Morris Goldberg intoning in Hebrew. He didn't know what it was then the Rabbi was saying but he knew now, because somebody had told him:

"The Lord is my shepherd: I shall not want. He maketh me to lie down in green pastures; He leadeth me beside the still waters. He restoreth my soul; He leadeth me in the paths of righteousness for His name's sake . . ."

And then he had seen the funeral cars starting for Mount Neboh Cemetery in Brooklyn and Jim getting into one of the cars.

## STEIG

*"I hardly touched him!"*

THE BEST DESCRIPTION of Stillman's, the most famous of all fight gyms, appeared in the best of the boxing autobiographies, *Somebody Up There Likes Me.*

# Stillman's Gym

## ROCKY GRAZIANO

### [WRITTEN WITH ROWLAND BARBER]

MA TOOK my word for it that I was in no kind of trouble. I just got in a simple mix-up with the Army, and someday everything will get straightened out. I am off the hook there, but I still got to pick up some scratch, and how to make any money has got me stumped. I don't want to go on any jobs with Romolo. Benjy is away and so is Sammy. Tommy is waiting trial on a federal rap. I can't locate Big Sal to get back in touch with Eddie Coco.

After all the years Terry Young kept needling me about being a fighter, I didn't want to give him the satisfaction of coming around. But I didn't have no other out. I go to Terry's house. Terry gets all steamed up.

"Jeez, Rocky!" he says. "Howja get outa the Army?"

I just shrugged my shoulders. "I'm out, ain't I?"

"You better get rid of that uniform. Let's see what I got that fits you. I'll take you up to the gym this afternoon and maybe Irving Cohen will give a look at you."

So I get rigged out in an old zoot suit that was too big for Terry, a sweat shirt, and a porcupine hat, and that is how I look when I first walk into Stillman's Gym.

Stillman's Gym don't look no better to me than I do to Stillman's. Up at the end of a long, dark stairway is this barn of a place. In the middle are two regulation-size rings, with big lights over them. It's a good thing there are big lights because the windows look like they haven't been washed in years. Even the pigeons that hang around out there have give up looking in for free at the fighters.

On one side of the rings is a hot-dog stand which don't sell hot dogs, a row of telephone booths which are never empty long enough to clear out the day before's cigar smoke, the door to the locker room, and the stairs up to the balcony where they punch the bags. On the far side of the rings is some exercise space and some training tables. On the left side of the rings is Lou Stillman.

One thing I like about this joint my first day there. I see that everybody spits on the floor at Stillman's, and spitting is an old habit I got.

What I do not like is everything else that is going on. In the ring to the left a couple of guys are slugging each other. They're wearing headgear, but one of the guys is taking a beating in the face and bleeding out of his nose. You can hear his gloves land where he pounds the other guy in the ribs. They're grunting and wheezing with every punch. And nobody is paying much attention to them, except a trainer who leans on the edge of the ring, looking bored and chewing on an old cigar stub.

There must be thirty or forty guys in the room, bundled up in hats and overcoats. They're all talking to each other like they're making big deals, instead of watching the workouts. In ring number two, a half dozen guys are galloping around shadowboxing. Behind the rings, some guys in trunks are shadowboxing, others are doing pushups. From up on the balcony comes the noise of the punching bags—whappity, whappity, whappity. The phones keep ringing and guys keep yelling for guys who ain't there to answer them. Every third and fourth minute the bell rings for the rounds. Guys in overcoats come, make their deals, and go. Or they take their coats off and sit in one of the folding chairs and read the paper or the racing form.

And under the clock, off to the left, is Lou Stillman, who is more bored than anybody else, keeping track of who's in the ring and who's due in next like a checker in a parking lot.

This is the famous Stillman's Gym I heard about all my life. Why, if this joint was down on the East Side, it would be condemned; that was my first thought. And if it was condemned, it wouldn't even be worth our trouble to strip out the lead pipe. What do Lulu and Terry and everybody see in this place?

I go back into the locker room with Terry. This is some cockroach trap, the locker room. There is only one little shower for all the guys with lockers there. It stinks of sweat and old socks and mouthwash and liniment. Guys dressing back there are all mixed, colored and white, but this don't seem to bother Terry. He throws a jock strap and an old pair of trunks at me. "Here, see if these pants fit you."

I threw the things right back at him. "Who you kidding?" I say. "I'm getting out of here."

"What's the matter?" says Terry. "You ain't even met Irving Cohen yet."

"You tell him if he wants to match me in a bout, O.K., I'm ready. But I ain't going to go through none of this shit." I waved towards the training rings outside. "How much they pay you for fighting out there?"

"What you mean, how much they pay you? You crazy? This is only a gymnasium."

"I don't fight no place, gymnasium or no place, unless I get paid," I said. "I come up here with you because I got to make some scratch."

"Just do me a favor. Just stick around until Irving comes. Will ya?"

I sit on the bench there resigning myself to the fact I may have to go back with Romolo to make any money, while Terry puts on his trunks. He throws on this robe that has "Terry Young" on the back of it, and we go outside. Everybody is swarming all around Terry. He is a real important fighter, there's no doubt about it, and probably the next lightweight champion of the world. There's even guys there writing down what Terry is saying. I stand in the corner, under the balcony stairs, thinking that if I beat it out of there, Terry would never know the difference.

Before I can make it, he comes up to me with this short guy with a round face and a big smile, a polite-looking little guy. "This here is Irving Cohen, Rocky," says Terry. "This here is my friend Rocky, Irving."

"Terry told me a lot about you," says the manager in his quiet voice. "He—" Irving stopped like maybe he said the wrong thing and turned to Terry. "This is your friend Rocky, the *fighter*, isn't it?"

"You ain't kidding he's the fighter," says Terry. "You ask anybody was ever in the ring with him in the amateurs." He stepped away, leaving me and Irving alone.

Still smiling, Irving looked me up and down. I must have been some sight for a fight manager —a wise-looking kid with a face still pasty from the can, hair sticking out like a mop under the flattop hat, wearing this sharp green suit that was too long for me with the pants pegged too tight like the year before's style, a ragged sweat shirt under the jacket, and big, stiff GI shoes.

He put his hand on my shoulder. "Kid," he said, "you don't want to be a fighter, do you? A good-looking kid like you?"

"I tell you the truth, Mr. Cohen," I said. "Terry said I could make fifty dollars a fight, that's the only reason."

"Let me tell you straight, Rocky," he says to me, and he talked real soft, like a priest. "You aren't in any shape to fight professional, kid. If you knew what it was like, you wouldn't want to be a fighter. Take my advice. You look like a good kid, a smart fellow. You go find yourself a job that pays fifty a week and you'll be thankful you listened to me." He smiled and shook his head slowly. "Just forget there's any easy dough in fighting. And remember what a favor I'm doing you by telling you this."

"Mr. Cohen," I said. "I give it a chance. Get me a fight and I'll take the chance."

He pointed across the gym. "Rocky," he says, "see the guy in the brown sweater over there, drinking the coffee? See him? He was a nice-looking, clean-cut boy like you once. See his busted nose, smashed all over his face? See the scars over his eyes, where they had to sew him up? You see his right ear? But the worst part you can't see. You just watch the guy the next time the bell rings. You watch him spill his coffee."

Terry comes back then. "You going to take a look at Rocky today, Irving?" he says.

"I'm not sure Rocky wants to go in the ring."

I was confused. I did and I didn't. I had to have that money. Terry saw I was mixed up about what to say. He put his arm around Irving and took him away. Finally Irving stops smiling

169

and holds up his hands, like he was saying, "All right, if that's what you want."

So Terry talked Irving into it, and I went back to put on the trunks. What the hell, I will show them what I can do with some bum there in the training ring—once. I will show them once, and if they don't want to give me no fifty-dollar bout, that's all they will ever see of me.

Irving says do I want to warm up a little first and I say no, let's get this over with. He introduces me to my opponent. I don't get his name, something Spanish. A dark, strong-looking guy, older than me.

Lou Stillman announces to the crowd that Rocky Bob and Antonio what's-his-name will box two rounds in the first ring, and we climb in. Nobody listens to the announcement. Terry and Irving are the only ones who are looking at us. The bell rings.

When we touch gloves, I look down below. A couple guys are sleeping at ringside with newspapers over their faces. There's a bunch of guys talking by the sandwich stand, and another bunch over by the telephone booths. Lou Stillman is clowning around for the newspaper guys.

This is the first time I have been in the ring in over a year since I fought the four-rounder in the Bronx Coliseum under the name of Robert Barber. I felt a little funny up there with my legs bare, the gloves on, the mouthpiece under my lip. Then this guy stung my cheek with a left hook, and I stopped feeling funny. I went after him, swinging for his head. I kept missing and he kept jabbing that left in my face. He ducked my right and I crashed into the ropes. He ducked another right and I almost went down on my knees. Then I caught him in the corner and begun to give it to him.

In the back of my head, I knew that the guys down below were watching me now. Somebody was yelling. Terry was pounding on the canvas, on the apron of the ring.

I finished the guy off with a shot to the temple. He sat there against the post, in a daze. All the characters in the overcoats were crowding in down by the ring. All the phones were ringing and nobody paid no attention. I hopped out through the ropes. Some trainer jumped into the ring to tend to the guy with the Spanish name. The joint was kind of jumping there for a minute. Terry was whacking me on the back.

"That guy you knocked out," he said, "that guy used to be the middleweight champeen of Argentina!"

Irving Cohen had stopped talking softly.

"Whitey! Whitey!" he was yelling. "Whitey! You got to teach this guy!"

He grabs my arms and pumps them. "Where'd you learn to punch like that, Rocky?" he said. Before I could give him an answer, this wiry guy with thin, blond hair come up to us. "Rocky," said Irving, "this is Whitey Bimstein. He's going to train you, Rocky."

"Yah, hi ya, Whitey," I said. I turned to Irving. "You gonna get me a bout for fifty bucks, Mr. Cohen?"

"Don't you worry, Rocky," said Irving. "You start working out with Whitey here, and I'll get you a bout."

I went and had a shower and got dressed in a hurry and almost beat it out of the gym when Irving stopped me at the top of the stairs. "Rocky," he says, "where you going? Whitey's waiting for you."

"You tell Terry when you got a bout for me and Terry will let me know, Mr. Cohen," I said.

"But you got work to do, kid."

"Ya din like that I done to that bum in there today?"

"You landed some good punches, Rocky. But I don't know if your legs will hold up for even four rounds under a pace like that. You got to box a little bit, Rocky. You can't go in swinging like that with every boy you fight."

"That's the way I do it, Mr. Cohen. If you don't like it, I'm sorry. If you do like it, then I'd like to fight somebody." I start down the stairs.

"Will I see you tomorrow, Rocky?" says Irving. He gives me a little smile, like he's hoping and praying I'll say yes.

"I don't know," I tell him. "Depends if I find any better way to pick up a little dough."

It winds up Irving Cohen give me a ten-spot right there on the gymnasium stairs. It looks like he's trying to bribe me to come back the next day to work out with this Whitey guy, the trainer. But a sawbuck looks big when you got an empty pocket, and I took it and told him goodbye and took off down the East Side without even telling Terry so long or thanks.

By the time I reached home and changed back to my uniform, I figured I earned the ten for knocking out this bum. I give all them characters a show, didn't I? I made Lou Stillman's eyes pop out of his head and all the boxers stop shadowboxing and all the customers stop talking and sleeping, and I had Terry pounding the canvas and Irving yelling to blow his top. Sure I earned the ten.

IN THE 140 YEARS since Bill Neat (not Neate) fought Tom Hickman and Hazlitt took his only fling at fight writing, this has been extolled as the all-time, all-around classic. It did get boxing into the English textbooks and the literature courses.

# The Fight

## WILLIAM HAZLITT

"... *The* fight, *the* fight's *the thing*
*Wherein I'll catch the conscience of the King."*

*Where there's a will, there's a way,*—I said to myself, as I walked down Chancery-lane, about half-past six o'clock on Monday, the 10th of December, to inquire at Jack Randall's where the fight the next day was to be; and I found "the proverb" nothing "musty" in the present instance. I was determined to see this fight, come what would, and see it I did, in great style. It was my *first fight,* yet it more than answered my expectations. Ladies! it is to you I dedicate this description; nor let it seem out of character for the fair to notice the exploits of the brave. Courage and modesty are the old English virtues; and may they never look cold and askance on one another! Think, ye fairest of the fair, loveliest of the lovely kind, ye practisers of soft enchantment, how many more ye kill with poisoned baits than ever fell in the ring; and listen with subdued air and without shuddering, to a tale tragic only in appearance, and sacred to the Fancy!

I was going down Chancery-lane, thinking to ask at Jack Randall's where the fight was to be, when looking through the glass-door of the *Hole in the Wall,* I heard a gentleman asking the same question *at* Mrs. Randall, as the author of *Waverly* would express it. Now Mrs. Randall stood answering the gentleman's question, with the authenticity of the lady of the Champion of the Light Weights. Thinks I, I'll wait till this person comes out, and learn from him how it is. For to say a truth, I was not fond of going into this house of call for heroes and philosophers, ever since the owner of it (for Jack is no gentleman) threatened once upon a time to kick me out of doors for wanting a mutton-chop at his hospitable board, when the conqueror in thirteen battles was more full of *blue ruin* than of good manner. I was the more mortified at this repulse, inasmuch as I had heard Mr. James Simpkins, hosier in the Strand, one day when the character of the *Hole in the Wall* was brought in question, observe—"The house is a very good house, and the company quite genteel: I have been there myself!" Remembering this unkind treatment of mine host, to which mine hostess was also a party, and not wishing to put her in unquiet thoughts at a time jubilant like the present, I waited at the door, when, who should issue forth but my friend Joe Toms, and turning suddenly up Chancery-lane with that quick jerk and impatient stride which distinguishes a lover of the Fancy, I said, "I'll be hanged if that fellow is not going to the fight, and is on his way to get me to go with him." So it proved in effect, and we agreed to adjourn to my lodgings to discuss measures with that cordiality which makes old friends like new, and new friends like old, on great occasions. We are cold to others only when we are dull in ourselves, and have neither thoughts nor feelings to impart to them. Give a man a topic in his head, a throb of pleasure in his heart, and he will be glad to share it with the first person he meets. Toms and I, though we seldom meet, were an *alter idem* on this memorable occasion, and had not an idea that we did not candidly impart; and "so carelessly did we fleet the time," that I wish no better, when there is another fight, than to have him for a companion on my journey down, and to return with my friend Jack Pigott, talking of what was to happen or of what did happen, with a noble subject always at hand, and liberty to digress to others whenever they offered. Indeed, on my repeating the lines from Spenser in an involuntary fit of enthusiasm,

*"What more felicity can fall to creature,*
*Than to enjoy delight with liberty?"*

my last-named ingenious friend stopped me by saying that this, translated into the vulgate, meant *"Going to see a fight."*

Joe Toms and I could not settle about the method of going down. He said there was a caravan, he understood, to start from Tom Belcher's at two, which would go there *right out* and back again the next day. Now, I never travel all night, and said I should get a cast to Newbury by one of the mails. Joe swore the thing was impossible, and I could only answer that I had made up my mind to it. In short, he seemed to me to waver, said he only came to see if I was going, had letters to write, a cause coming on the day after, and faintly said at parting (for I was bent on setting out that moment)—"Well, we meet at Philippi!" I made the best of my way to Piccadilly. The mail-coach stand was bare. "They are all gone," said I; "this is always the way with me—in the instant I lose the future—if I had not stayed to pour out that last cup of tea, I should have been just in time"; and cursing my folly and ill-luck together, without inquiring at the coach-office whether the mails were gone or not, I walked on in despite, and to punish my own dilatoriness and want of determination. At any rate, I would not turn back: I might get to Hounslow, or perhaps farther, to be on my road the next morning. I passed Hyde Park corner (my Rubicon), and trusted to fortune. Suddenly I heard the clattering of a Brentford stage, and the fight rushed full upon my fancy. I argued (not unwisely) that even a Brentford coachman was better company than my own thoughts (such as they were just then), and at his invitation mounted the box with him. I immediately stated my case to him—namely, my quarrel with myself for missing the Bath or Bristol mail, and my determination to get on in consequence as well as I could, without any disparagement or insulting comparison between longer or shorter stages. It is a maxim with me that stage-coaches, and consequently stage-coachmen, are respectable in proportion to the distance they have to travel: so I said nothing on that subject to my Brentford friend. Any incipient tendency to an abstract proposition, or (as he might have construed it)

to a personal reflection of this kind, was however nipped in the bud; for I had no sooner declared indignantly that I had missed the mails, than he flatly denied that they were going along, and lo! at the instant three of them drove by in rapid, provoking, orderly succession, as if they would devour the ground before them. Here again I seemed in the contradictory situation of the man in Dryden who exclaims: "I follow fate, which does too hard pursue!" If I had stopped to inquire at the White Horse Cellar, which would not have taken me a minute, I should now have been driving down the road in all the dignified unconcern and *ideal* perfection of mechanical conveyance. The Bath mail I had set my mind upon, and I had missed it, as I miss everything else, by my own absurdity, in putting the will for the deed, and aiming at ends without employing means. "Sir," said he of the Brentford, "the Bath mail will be up presently, my brother-in-law drives it, and I will engage to stop him if there is a place empty." I almost doubted my good genius; but, sure enough, up it drove like lightning, and stopped directly at the call of the Brentford Jehu. I would not have believed this possible, but the brother-in-law of a mail-coach driver is himself no mean man. I was transferred without loss of time from the top of one coach to that of the other, desired the guard to pay my fare to the Brentford coachman for me as I had no change, was accommodated with a great coat, put up my umbrella to keep off a drizzling mist, and we began to cut through the air like an arrow. The mile-stones disappeared one after another, the rain kept off; Tom Turtle, the trainer, sat before me on the coach-box, with whom I exchanged civilities as a gentleman going to the fight; the passion that had transported me an hour before was subdued to pensive regret and conjectural musing on the next day's battle; I was promised a place inside at Reading, and upon the whole, I thought myself a lucky fellow. Such is the force of imagination! On the outside of any other coach on the 10th of December, with a Scotch mist drizzling through the cloudy moonlight air, I should have been cold, comfortless, impatient, and, no doubt, wet through; but seated on the Royal mail, I felt warm and comfortable, the air did me good, the ride did me good, I was pleased with the progress we had made, and confident that all would go well through the journey. When I got inside at Reading, I found Turtle and a stout valetudinarian, whose costume bespoke him one of the Fancy, and who had risen from a three months' sick bed to get into the mail to see the fight. They were intimate, and we fell into a lively discourse. My friend the trainer was confined in his topics to fighting dogs and men, to bears and badgers; beyond this he was "quite chapfallen," had not a word to throw at a dog, or indeed very wisely fell asleep, when any other game was started. The whole art of training (I, however, learnt from him) consists in two things, exercise and abstinence, abstinence and exercise, repeated alternately and without end. A yolk of an egg with a spoonful of rum in it is the first thing in the morning, and then a walk of six miles till breakfast. This meal consists of a plentiful supply of tea and toast and beef-steaks. Then another six or seven miles till dinner-time, and another supply of solid beef or mutton with a pint of porter, and perhaps, at the utmost, a couple of glasses of sherry. Martin trains on water, but this increases his infirmity on another very dangerous side. The Gas-man takes now and then a chirping glass (under the rose) to console him, during a six-weeks' probation, for the absence of Mrs. Hickman—an agreeable woman, with (I understand) a pretty fortune of two hundred pounds. How matter presses on me! What stubborn things are facts! How inexhaustible is nature and art! "It is well," as I once heard Mr. Richmond observe, "to see a variety." He was speaking of cock-fighting as an edifying spectacle. I cannot deny but that one learns more of what *is* (I do not say of what *ought to be*) in this desultory mode of practical study, than from reading the same book twice over, even though it should be a moral treatise. Where was I? I was sitting at dinner with the candidate for the honours of the ring, "where good digestion waits on appetite, and health on both." Then follows an hour of social chat and native glee; and afterwards, to another breathing over healthy hill or dale. Back to supper, and then to bed, and up by six again—Our hero

"*Follows so the ever-running sun,
With profitable* ardour—"

to the day that brings him victory or defeat in the green fairy circle. Is not this life more sweet than mine? I was going to say; but I will not libel any life by comparing it to mine, which is (at the date of these presents) bitter as coloquintida and the dregs of aconitum!

The invalid in the Bath mail soared a pitch above the trainer, and did not sleep so sound, because he had "more figures and more fantasies." We talked the hours away merrily. He had faith in surgery, for he had had three ribs set right, that had been broken in a *turn-up* at Belcher's, but thought physicians old women, for they had no antidote in their catalogue for brandy. An indigestion is an excellent commonplace for two people that never met before. By way of ingratiating myself, I told him the story of my doctor, who, on my earnestly representing to him that I thought his regimen had done me harm, assured me that the whole pharmacopeia contained nothing comparable to the prescription he had given me; and, as a proof of its undoubted efficacy, said, that "he had had one gentleman with my complaint under his hands for the last fifteen years." This anecdote made my companion shake the rough sides of his three great coats with boisterous laughter; and Turtle, starting out of his sleep, swore he knew how the fight would go, for he had had a dream about it. Sure enough the rascal told us how the first three rounds went off, but "his dream," like others, "denoted a foregone conclusion." He knew his men. The moon now rose in silver state, and I ventured, with some hesitation, to point out this object of placid beauty, with the blue serene beyond, to the man of science, to which his ear he "seriously inclined," the more as it gave promise *d'un beau jour* for the morrow, and showed the ring undrenched by envious showers, arrayed in sunny smiles. Just then, all going on well, I thought on my friend Toms, whom I had left behind, and said innocently, "There was a blockhead of a fellow I left in town, who said there was no possibility of getting down by the mail, and talked of going by a caravan from Belcher's at two in the morning, after he had written some letters." "Why," said he of the lapells, "I should not wonder if that was the very person we saw running about like mad from one coach-door to another, and asking if any one had seen a friend of his, a gentleman going to the fight, whom he had missed stupidly enough by staying to write a note." "Pray, Sir," said my fellow-traveler, "had he a plaid-cloak on?" "Why, no," said I, "not at the time I left him, but he very well might afterwards, for he offered to lend me one." The plaid-cloak and the letter decided the thing. Joe, sure enough, was in the Bristol mail, which preceded us by about fifty yards. This was droll enough. We had now but a few miles to our place of destination, and the first thing I did on alighting at Newbury, both coaches stopping at the same time, was to call out, "Pray, is there a gentleman in that mail of the name of Toms?" "No," said Joe, borrowing something of the vein of Gilpin, "for I have just got out." "Well!" says he, "this is lucky, but you don't know how vexed I was to miss you; for," added he, lowering his voice, "do you know when I left you I went to Belcher's to ask about the caravan, and Mrs. Belcher said very obligingly, she couldn't tell about that, but there were two gentlemen who had taken places by the mail and were gone on in a landau, and she could frank us. It's a pity I didn't meet with you; we could then have got down for nothing. But *mum's the word."* It's the devil for any one to tell me a secret, for it's sure to come out in print. I do not care so much to gratify a friend, but the public ear is too great a temptation to me.

Our present business was to get beds and a supper at an inn; but this was no easy task. The public-houses were full, and where you saw a light at a private house, and people poking their heads out of the casement to see what was going on, they instantly put them in and shut the window, the moment you seemed advancing with a suspicious overture for accommodation. Our guard and coachman thundered away at the outer gate of the Crown for some time without effect—such was the greater noise within; and when the doors were unbarred, and we got admittance, we found a party assembled in the kitchen round a good hospitable fire, some sleeping, others drinking, others talking on politics and on the fight. A tall English yeoman (something like Matthews in the face, and quite as great a wag)—

*"A lusty man to ben an abbot able,"*—

was making such a prodigious noise about rent and taxes, and the price of corn now and formerly, that he had prevented us from being heard at the gate. The first thing I heard him say was to a shuffling fellow who wanted to be off a bet for a shilling glass of brandy and water—"Confound it, man, don't be *insipid!"* Thinks I, that is a good phrase. It was a good omen. He kept it up so all night, nor flinched with the approach of morning. He was a fine fellow, with sense, wit, and spirit, a hearty body and a joyous mind, free-spoken, frank, convivial—one of that true English breed that went with Harry the Fifth to the siege of Harfleur—"standing like greyhounds in the slips," &c. We ordered tea and eggs (beds were soon found to be out of the question) and this fellow's conversation was *sauce piquante.* It did one's heart good to see him brandish his oaken towel and to hear him talk. He made mince-meat of a drunken, stupid, red-faced, quarrelsome, frowsy farmer, whose nose "he moralized into a thousand similes," making it out a firebrand like Bardolph's. "I'll tell you what, my friend," says he, "the land-lady has only to keep you here to save fire and candle. If one was to touch your nose, it would go off like a piece of charcoal." At this the other only grinned like an

idiot, the sole variety in his purple face being his little peering grey eyes and yellow teeth; called for another glass, swore he would not stand it; and after many attempts to provoke his humourous antagonist to single combat, which the other turned off (after working him to a ludicrous pitch of choler) with great adroitness, he fell quietly asleep with a glass of liquor in his hand, which he could not lift to his head. His laughing persecutor made a speech over him, and turning to the opposite side of the room, where they were all sleeping in the midst of this "loud and furious fun," said, "There's a scene, by G-d, for Hogarth to paint. I think he and Shakespeare were our two best men at copying life." This confirmed me in my good opinion of him. Hogarth, Shakespeare, and Nature, were just enough for him (indeed for any man) to know. I said, "You read Cobbett, don't you? At least," says I, "you talk just as well as he writes." He seemed to doubt this. But I said, "We have an hour to spare: if you'll get pen, ink and paper, and keep on talking, I'll write down what you say; and if it doesn't make a capital 'Political Register,' I'll forfeit my head. You have kept me alive tonight, however. I don't know what I should have done without you." He did not dislike this view of the thing, nor my asking if he was not about the size of Jem Belcher; and told me soon afterwards, in the confidence of friendship that "the circumstance which had given him nearly the greatest concern in his life, was Cribb's beating Jem after he had lost his eye by racket-playing." —The morning dawns; that dim but yet clear light appears, which weighs like solid bars of metal on sleepless eyelids; the guests drop down from their chambers one by one—but it was too late to think of going to bed now (the clock was on the stroke of seven), we had nothing for it but to find a barber's (the pole that glittered in the morning sun lighted us to his shop), and then a nine miles' march to Hungerford. The day was fine, the sky was blue, the mists were retiring from the marshy ground, the path was tolerably dry, the sitting-up all night had not done us much harm—at least the cause was good; we talked of this and that with amicable difference, roving and sipping of many subjects, but still invariably we returned to the fight. At length, a mile to the left of Hungerford, on a gentle eminence, we saw the ring surrounded by covered carts, gigs and carriages, of which hundreds had passed us on the road; Toms gave a youthful shout, and we hastened down a narrow lane to the scene of action.

Reader, have you ever seen a fight? If not, you have a pleasure to come, at least if it is a fight like that between the Gas-man and Bill Neate. The crowd was very great when we arrived on the spot; open carriages were coming up, with streamers flying and music playing, and the country-people were pouring in over hedge and ditch in all directions, to see their hero beat or beaten. The odds were still on Gas, but only about five to four. Gully had been down to try Neate, and had backed him considerably, which was a damper to the sanguine confidence of the adverse party. About two hundred thousand pounds were pending. The Gas says, he has lost £3,000, which were promised him by different gentlemen if he had won. He had presumed too much on himself, which had made others presume on him. This spirited and formidable young fellow seems to have taken for his motto the old maxim, that "there are three things necessary to success in life—*Impudence! Impudence! Impudence!*" It is so in matters of opinion, but not in the Fancy, which is the most practical of all things, though even here confidence is half the battle, but only half. Our friend had vapoured and swaggered too much, as if he wanted to grin and bully his adversary out of the fight. "Alas! The Bristol man was not so tamed!"—"This is *the grave-digger*," would Tom Hickman exclaim in the moments of intoxication from gin and success, shewing his tremendous right hand, "this will send many of them to their long homes; I haven't done with them yet!" Why should he— though he had licked four of the best men within the hour, yet why should he threaten to inflict dishonourable chastisement on my old master Richmond, a veteran going off the stage and who has borne his sable honours meekly? Magnanimity, my dear Tom, and bravery, should be inseparable. Or why should he go up to his antagonist, the first time he ever saw him at the Fives Court, and measuring him from head to foot with a glance of contempt, as Achilles surveyed Hector, say to him, "What, are you Bill Neate? I'll knock more blood out of that great carcase of thine, this day fortnight, than you ever knocked out of a bullock's!" It was not many, 'twas not fighter-like. If he was sure of the victory (as he was not), the less said about it the better. Modesty should accompany the *Fancy* as its shadow. The best men were always the best behaved. Jem Belcher, the Game Chicken (before whom the Gas-man could not have lived), were civil, silent men. So is Cribb, so is Tom Belcher, the most elegant of sparrers, and not a man for every one to take by the nose. I enlarged on this topic in the mail (while Turtle was asleep), and said very wisely (as I thought) that impertinence was a part of no profession. A boxer was bound to beat his man, but not to thrust his fist, either actually or by implication, in every one's face. Even a highwayman, in the way of trade, may blow out your brains, but if he uses foul language at the same time, I should say he was no gentleman. A boxer, I would infer, need not be a blackguard or a coxcomb, more than another. Perhaps I press this point too much on a fallen man— Mr. Thomas Hickman has by this time learnt that first of all lessons, "That man was made to mourn." He has lost nothing by the late fight but his presumption; and that every man may do as well without! By an over-display of this quality, however, the public had been prejudiced against him, and the *knowing-ones* were taken in. Few but those who had bet on him wished Gas to win. With my own prepossessions on the subject, the result of the 11th of December appeared to me as fine a piece of poetical justice as I had ever witnessed. The difference of weight between the two combatants (14 stone to 12) was nothing to the sporting men. Great, heavy, clumsy, long-armed Bill Neate kicked the beam in the scale of the Gas-man's vanity. The amateurs were frightened at his big words, and thought that they would make up for the difference of six feet and five feet nine. Truly, the *Fancy* are not men of imagination. They judge of what has been, and cannot conceive of any thing that is to be. The Gas-man had won hitherto; therefore he must beat a man half as big again as himself—and that to a certainty. Besides, there are as many feuds, factions, prejudices, pedantic notions in the *Fancy* as in the state or in the schools. Mr. Gully is almost the only cool, sensible man among them, who exercises an unbiassed discretion, and is not a slave to his passions in these matters. But enough of reflections, and to our tale. The day, as I have said, was fine for a December morning. The grass was wet, and the ground miry, and ploughed up with multitudinous feet, except that, within the ring itself, there was a spot of virgin-green closed in and unprofaned by vulgar tread, that shone with dazzling brightness in the mid-day sun. For it was now noon, and we had an hour to wait. This is the trying time. It is then the heart sickens, as you think what the two champions are about, and how short a time will determine their fate. After the first blow is struck, there is no opportunity for nervous apprehensions; you are swallowed up in the immediate interest of the scene—but

*"Between the acting of a dreadful thing*
*And the first motion, all the interim is*
*Like a phantasma, or a hideous dream."*

I found it so as I felt the sun's rays clinging to my back, and saw the white wintry clouds sink below the verge of the horizon. So, I thought, my fairest hopes have faded from my sight!—so will the Gas-man's glory, or that of his adversary, vanish in an hour. The *swells* were parading in their white box-coats, the outer ring was cleared with some bruises on the heads and shins of the rustic assembly (for the *cockneys* had been distanced by the sixty-six miles); the time drew near, I had got a good stand; a bustle, a buzz ran through the crowd, and from the opposite side entered Neate, between his second and bottle-holder. He rolled along swathed in his loose great coat, his knock-knees bending under his huge bulk; and, with a modest cheerful air, threw his hat into the ring. He then just looked round, and began quietly to undress; when from the other side there was a similar rush and an opening made, and the Gas-man came forward with a conscious air of anticipated triumph, too much like the cock-of-the-walk. He strutted about more than became a hero, sucked oranges with a supercilious air, and threw away the skin with a toss of his head, and went up and looked at Neate, which was an act of supererogation. The only sensible thing he did was, as he strode away from the modern Ajax, to fling out his arms, as if he wanted to try whether they would do their work that day. By this time they had stripped, and presented a strong contrast in appearance. If Neate was like Ajax, "with Atlantean shoulders, fit to bear" the pugilistic reputation of all Bristol, Hickman might be compared to Diomed, light, vigorous, elastic, and his back glistened in the sun, as he moved about, like a panther's hide. There was now a dead pause—attention was awe-struck. Who at that moment, big with a great event, did not draw his breath short—did not feel his heart throb? All was ready. They tossed up for the sun, and the Gas-man won. They were led up to the *scratch*—shook hands, and went at it.

In the first round every one thought it was all over. After making play a short time, the Gas-man flew at his adversary like a tiger, struck five blows in as many seconds, three first, and then following him as he staggered back, two more, right and left, and down he fell, a mighty ruin. There was a shout, and I said, "There is no standing this." Neate seemed like a lifeless lump of flesh and bone, round which the Gas-man's blows played with the rapidity of electricity or lightning, and you imagined he would only be lifted up to be knocked down again. It was as if Hickman held a sword or a fire in that right hand of his, and directed it against an unarmed body. They met again, and Neate seemed, not cowed, but particularly cautious. I saw his teeth clenched together and his brows knit close against the sun. He held out both his arms at full length straight before him, like two sledge-hammers, and raised his left an inch or two higher. The Gas-man could not get over this guard—they struck mutually and fell, but without advantage on either side. It was the same in the next round; but the balance of power was thus restored—the fate of the battle was suspended. No one could tell how it would end. This was the only moment in which opinion was divided; for, in the next, the Gas-man aiming a mortal blow at his adversary's neck, with his right hand, and failing from the length he had to reach, the other returned it with his left at full swing, planted a tremendous blow on his cheek-bone and eyebrow, and made a red ruin of that side of his face. The Gas-man went down, and there was another shout—a roar of triumph as the waves of fortune rolled tumultuously from side to side. This was a settler. Hickman got up, and "grinned horrible a ghastly smile," yet he was evidently dashed in his opinion of himself; it was the first time he had ever been so punished; all one side of his face was perfect scarlet, and his right eye was closed in dingy blackness, as he advanced to the fight, less confident, but still determined. After one or two rounds, not receiving another such remembrancer, he rallied and went at it with his former impetuosity. But in vain. His strength had been weakened—his blows could not tell at such a distance—he was obliged to fling himself at his adversary, and could not strike from his feet; and almost as regularly as he flew at him with his right hand, Neate warded the blow, or drew back out of its reach, and felled him with the return of his left. There was little cautious sparring—no half-hits—no tapping and trifling, none of the *petit-maître-ship* of the art—they were almost all knock-down blows: the fight was a good stand-up fight. The wonder was the half-minute time. If there had been a minute or more allowed between each round, it would have been intelligible how they should by degrees recover strength and resolution; but to see two men smashed to the ground, smeared with gore, stunned, senseless, the breath beaten out of their bodies; and then, before you recover from the shock, to see them rise up with new strength and courage, stand ready to inflict or receive mortal offence, and rush upon each other "like two clouds over the Caspian"—this is the most astonishing thing of all: this is the high heroic state of man! From this time forward the event became more certain every round; and about the twelfth it seemed as if it must have been over. Hickman generally stood with his back to me; but in the scuffle, he had changed positions, and Neate just then made a tremendous lunge at him, and hit him full in the face. It was doubtful whether he would fall backwards or forwards; he hung suspended for a second or two, and then fell back, throwing his hands in the air, and with his face lifted up to the sky. I never saw any thing more terrific than his aspect just before he fell. All traces of life, of natural expression, were gone from him. His face was like a human skull, a death's head, spouting blood. The eyes were filled with blood, the nose streamed with blood, the mouth gaped blood. He was not like an actual man, but like a preternatural, spectral appearance, or like one of the figures in Dante's *Inferno*. Yet he fought on after this for several rounds, still striking the first desperate blow, and Neate standing on the defensive, and using the same cautious guard to the last, as if he had still all his work to do; and it was not till the Gas-man was so stunned in the seventeenth or eighteenth round, that his senses forsook him, and he could not come to time, that the battle was declared over. Ye who despise the Fancy, do something to shew as much *pluck,* or as much self-possession as this, before you assume a superiority which you have never given a single proof of by any one action in the whole course of your lives! When the Gas-man came to himself, the first words he uttered were, "Where am I? What is the matter?" "Nothing is the matter, Tom, you have lost the battle, but you are the bravest man alive." And Jackson whispered to him, "I am collecting a purse for you, Tom." Vain sounds, and unheard at that moment! Neate instantly went up and shook him cordially by the hand, and seeing some old acquaintance, began to flourish with his fists, calling out, "Ah, you always said I couldn't fight. What do you think now?" But in all good humour, and without any appearance of arrogance; only it was evident Bill Neate was pleased that he had won the fight. When it was over, I asked Cribb if he did not think it was a good one? He said, *"Pretty well!"* The carrier-pigeons now mounted into the air, and one of them flew with the news of her husband's victory to the bosom of Mrs. Neate. Alas, for Mrs. Hickman!

*Mais au revoir,* as Sir Fopling Flutter says. I went down with Toms; I returned with Jack Pigott, whom I met on the ground. Toms is a rattle-brain; Pigott is a sentimentalist. Now, under favour, I am a sentimentalist too—therefore I say nothing, but that the interest of the excursion did not flag as I came back. Pigott and I marched along the causeway leading from Hungerford to Newbury, now observing the effect of a brilliant sun on the tawny meads or moss-coloured cottages, now exulting in the fight, now digressing to some topic of general and elegant literature. My friend was dressed in character for the occasion, or like one of the *Fancy;* that is, with a double portion of great coats, clogs, and overhauls: and just as we had agreed with a couple of country-lads to carry his superfluous wearing-apparel to the next town, we were overtaken by a return post-chaise, into which I got, Pigott preferring a seat on the bar. There were two strangers already in the chaise, and on their observing they supposed I had been to the fight, I said I had, and concluded they had done the same. They appeared, however, a little shy and sore on the subject; and it was not till after several hints dropped, and questions put, that it turned out they had missed it. One of these friends had undertaken to drive the other there in his gig: they had set out, to make sure work, the day before at three in the afternoon. The owner of the one-horse vehicle scorned to ask his way, and drove right on to Bagshot, instead of turning off at Hounslow: there they stopped all night, and set off the next day across the country to Reading, from whence they took coach, and got down within a mile or two of Hungerford, just half an hour after the fight was over. This might be safely set down as one of the miseries of human life. We parted with these two gentlemen who had been to see the fight, but had returned as they went, at Wolhampton, where we were promised beds (an irresistible temptation, for Pigott had passed the preceding night at Hungerford as we had done at Newbury), and we turned into an old bow-windowed parlour with a carpet and a snug fire; and after devouring a quantity of tea, toast, and eggs, sat down to consider, during an hour of philosophic leisure, what we should have for supper. In the midst of an Epicurean deliberation between a roasted fowl and mutton chops with mashed potatoes, we were interrupted by an inroad of Goths and Vandals—*O procul este profani*—not real flash-men, but interlopers, noisy pretenders, butchers from Tothill-fields, brokers from Whitechapel, who called immediately for pipes and tobacco, hoping it would not be disagreeable to the gentlemen, and began to insist that it was *a cross.* Pigott withdrew from the smoke and noise into another room, and left me to dispute the point with them for a couple of hours *sans intermission* by the dial. The next morning we rose refreshed; and on observing that Jack had a pocket volume in his hand, in which he read in the intervals of our discourse,

I inquired what it was, and learned to my particular satisfaction that it was a volume of the "New Eloise." Ladies, after this, will you contend that a love for the Fancy is incompatible with the cultivation of sentiment? We jogged on as before, my friend setting me up in a genteel drab great coat and green silk handkerchief (which I must say became me exceedingly), and after stretching our legs for a few miles, and seeing Jack Randall, Ned Turner, and Scroggins, pass on the top of one of the Bath coaches, we engaged with the driver of the second to take us to London for the usual fee. I got inside, and found three other passengers. One of them was an old gentleman with an aquiline nose, powdered hair and a pigtail, and who looked as if he had played many a rubber at the Bath rooms. I said to myself, he is very like Mr. Windham; I wish he would enter into conversation, that I might hear what fine observations would come from those finely-turned features. However, nothing passed, till, stopping to dine at Reading, some inquiry was made by the company about the fight, and I gave (as the reader may believe) an eloquent and animated description of it. When we got into the coach again, the old gentleman, with a graceful exordium, said he had, when a boy, been to a fight between the famous Broughton and George Stevenson, who was called the *Fighting Coachman,* in the year 1770, with the late Mr. Windham. This beginning flattered the spirit of prophecy within me, and rivetted my attention. He went on—"George Stevenson was coachman to a friend of my father's. He was an old man when I saw him some years afterwards. He took hold of his own arm and said, 'There was muscle here once, but now it is no more than this young gentleman's.' He added, 'Well, no matter; I have done no more harm than another man.' Once," said my unknown companion, "I

asked him if he had ever beat Broughton? He said Yes; that he had fought with him three times, and the last time he fairly beat him, though the world did not allow it. 'I'll tell you how it was, master. When the seconds lifted us up in the last round, we were so exhausted that neither of us could stand, and we fell upon one another, and as Master Broughton fell uppermost, the mob gave it in his favour, and he was said to have won the battle. But,' says he, 'the fact was, that as his second (John Cuthbert) lifted him up, he said to him, "I'll fight no more, I've had enough," which,' says Stevenson, 'you know gave me the victory. And to prove to you that this was the case, when John Cuthbert was on his death-bed and they asked him if there was any thing on his mind which he wished to confess, he answered, "Yes, that there was one thing he wished to set right, for that certainly Master Stevenson won that last fight with Master Broughton; for he whispered him as he lifted him up in the last round of all, that he had had enough."' This," said the Bath Gentleman, "was a bit of human nature;" and I have written this account of the fight on purpose that it might not be lost to the world. He also stated as a proof of the candour of mind in this class of men, that Stevenson acknowledged that Broughton could have beat him in his best day; but that he (Broughton) was getting old in their last recounter. When we stopped in Piccadilly, I wanted to ask the gentleman some questions about the late Mr. Windham, but had not courage. I got out, resigned my coat and green silk handkerchief to Pigott (loth to part with these ornaments of life), and walked home in high spirits.

P.S. Toms called upon me the next day, to ask me if I did not think the fight was a complete thing? I said I thought it was. I hope he will relish my account of it.

# THOMAS NAST

## HARD ON THE PROFESSIONALS

One slugger to the other—*"We'll have to go to Congress to have our mill out."*

SOME FIGHTERS fall in love and marry. That is why this is included.

# Fighter's Wife

## W. C. HEINZ

IT WAS 9:30 in the evening and they would put the fight on shortly after 10 o'clock. There were about a dozen people in the house, all but two of them women, but it was not noisy. They sat in the carpeted, lush living room on the ground floor of the red-brick, two-family house. For an hour, on and off, she had been a part of their small talk, but now she stood up and walked toward the kitchen and got out the ironing board.

"I hope he should retire," her grandmother said. "I hope he should win and retire healthy. He must be healthy for his family. Allus I hope, he should be healthy with my whole heart."

*One day, when Norma Unger was seventeen years old, she and her friend Alice and Alice's friend Yolanda were sitting at a table in an ice-cream parlor on the corner of Seventh Street and Second Avenue. They were having sodas and talking about boys. Yolanda said her brother was coming out of the Army, and she reached into a pocket and came out with two snapshots of him.*

*"I think you'd like him," she said to Norma while Norma looked at the pictures, "and I think he'd like you. I think it would be fun to arrange a blind date."*

*That was the first time Norma Unger ever heard of Rocky Graziano, the first time in her life.*

"THE LAST TIME he fought Zale," her mother said, "she had her portable radio and was walking up and down the street, turning it on and off."

"Once she sat in the bathtub all through the fight," her grandmother said.

*So they arranged a blind date for the next Saturday night. On Saturday she decided she wanted to do something else, so, still early in the evening, she walked over to Yolanda's house. It was a walkup on First Avenue, and she climbed the steps and rang the bell in the hallway and waited. There was one bulb burning at the ceiling, and after a while Yolanda came downstairs and she explained it to Yolanda. While she was explaining it she heard a noise at the top of the stairs, and there he was, hurrying down the stairs, and she was embarrassed.*

*"Oh," Yolanda said, stopping him when he got to the foot of the stairs, "this is Norma Unger. Norma, this is my brother, Rocky."*

*"Hello," she said, looking at him.*

*"Hello," Rocky said and then he turned. "I'll see you."*

*He left then, but he was wearing a dark-blue suit and he had on a gray hat, porkpie style. He had nice eyes and a nice smile and a nice face, and that was the first time Norma Unger ever saw Rocky Graziano, the first time in her life.*

"THE TIME HE WON the title in Chicago," her mother said. "You remember how he was getting beaten, and she ran crying into the bedroom and locked the door and when she came out he was middleweight champion."

"I don't know," her grandmother said.

"Every time she does something different," her mother said.

*They used to see each other around the neighborhood after that. She saw him in the ice-cream parlor a few times. A couple of times they had* sodas together. *Alice used to go out then with Terry Young, the fighter, and he was Rocky's friend, so the first date they had was a double date with Alice and Terry. That was when she found out he was a fighter, but nobody had ever heard of him then, and she didn't think much about it. After that they went a lot to the movies. He was always in a happy mood, and he wasn't one of those guys who was always trying to kiss a girl good night, and that helped.*

"I DON'T KNOW," her grandmother said. "I wonder what she does tonight."

"I don't know," her mother said, looking around. "Where'd she go?"

It was the first they had missed her. A couple of her friends, the one named Lucille and the other named Innocent, got up and walked out into the kitchen and found her ironing.

"So?" Innocent said.

"Oh," she said, "just a blouse for Audrey for school tomorrow. I thought I could sneak it in. You know, anything to keep busy."

"That's right," Lucille said. "That's why we should do the dresses."

It was 9:35.

*They were married after they had known each other for three months. For a while they had teased one another about getting married. Then one day Rocky met her and said Yolanda was getting married. He said Yolanda was going down for her blood test, and they ought to go along to see what it was like. When they got there with Yolanda they decided to take the blood test themselves. Then, because they had had the blood test, they decided they should get married right away.*

*She was still only seventeen. They went to City Hall, but a man told them she would have to have her mother's consent. She was afraid to ask her mother or her grandmother, so they walked to the Hudson Tubes and rode to Bayonne, New Jersey. They walked along the street and asked some people until they found a place with big windows in the front and it looked sort of like a real-estate office. It said "Justice of the Peace" on the window, but the man said they would have to have the blood test in Jersey and stay there for a while before he could marry them, so they went back to New York.*

*She doesn't remember exactly how they managed it. A few days later they started going around to buildings away downtown. They went around to a hundred buildings, it seemed, and finally a man married them.*

*It was in an office. She had on a beige suit and*

*Rocky had on a dark-blue suit and a white shirt and a dark-blue tie. There were a couple of detectives around the building, and Rocky gave them five dollars each to be witnesses. The ceremony seemed so short. She had never thought anything about a big wedding, because they didn't have the money, but still it seemed so short.*

*The funny thing is, after Rocky became famous he was fighting in the Garden one night. After the fight he was coming out of the ring, and a man stopped him in the aisle.*

*"Hey," the man said. "Remember me? I'm your best man."*

*"Who the hell are you?" Rocky said he said.*

*"Don't you remember?" the man said, and it was one of the detectives. "I stood up with you when you were married, Rock."*

SHE WENT INTO one of the bedrooms then—quietly because Audrey, who is five, and Roxie, who is going on two, were sleeping—and when she came out she had a pile of new girls' dresses in her arms. She dropped them on the table, and she found the sewing basket and she stood there watching, smoking a cigarette, while Lucille and Innocent started to sort through the dresses and, each selecting one, to turn the hems.

It was 9:40.

"I'll take the radio in," Norma said. "I won't listen."

She went to a closet and took out a small radio, the electric cord dangling, and carried it to those sitting in the living room. While she was gone the other two sat sewing, not saying anything.

"She's too nervous," Lucille said finally. "I told her to have some brandy around."

"She doesn't drink," the one named Innocent said.

"She could have some brandy around."

When Norma came back they were silent. She stood, leaning on the sideboard, smoking and just watching them. She is twenty-three now, slim, dark-haired, and she had on a gray-and-green print dress with short sleeves and a flared skirt.

"I called up my husband," Lucille said, sewing, "and he said the whole place is closed down. Everybody went to the fight. Even the bartender went to the fight."

*She used to go to see him fight, but that was at first. One day, while they were still just going together, he asked her to walk over to the gym with him to watch him train. It was the gym on Fourteenth Street, and it was the first time she had ever seen any fighters in a ring. She stood in the gray, dusty-looking gym with all the men, watching Rocky box. Then he always wanted her to go with him when he fought, to Fort Hamilton and the Broadway Arena and the Ridgewood Grove. Less and less she liked it, and the first Frankie Terry fight was the last she saw. It was such a bad thing to watch, because they were cursing and even kicking. It was a real free-for-all, and after that she wouldn't go any more, although for a while she used to stand outside the clubs and wait for him to come out.*

*At first he couldn't understand it. Maybe he thought it meant something else, because he got mad about it once. When she wouldn't go with him for his fight with Leon Anthony he wouldn't fight. They went to a movie together instead that night, and Rocky was suspended by the Boxing Commission because of it. After a while, though, she was able to explain it so he saw it, and now he understands why she doesn't even want to watch him train for a fight.*

"WHAT TIME IS IT?" the one named Babe said.

"It's nine forty-five," Lucille said.

"You people sew so nice," Babe said.

Babe was standing in the doorway, watching the two at the table. Then she walked into the kitchen and sat down on one of the high red-and-white stools.

"The sewing circle," Norma said. "Boys are so much easier."

"Don't say that," Babe said. "You should see my Joseph."

"They make clothes so nice now," Innocent said, sewing.

"Girls' clothes," Babe said.

"Oh, boys', too," Innocent said.

"I'm getting a nervous stomach," Norma said.

She left them, then, and walked back toward the bedrooms and the bath. It was 9:50 by the kitchen clock.

*Their first night they spent in a hotel on Fourteenth Street. Then they went to the flat where Rocky's people lived. They had one bedroom and Rocky's people had the other. There were only four rooms, so Rocky's brother, Lennie, slept in the living room and his sister, Ida, slept in the kitchen. They lived like that for five months, on First Avenue between Eighth and Ninth streets.*

*For two years after that they lived with her mother and stepfather in Brooklyn. There were only three rooms, so they slept in the living room. When Audrey came the crib was in the living room, too.*

"NORMA," ONE OF those from the living room said, "what's the number on that little radio?"

It was the one named Lee and she was standing in the doorway, leaning against the frame. Norma had come back into the kitchen and had just been watching the sewing.

"I don't know," Norma said, and the one named Lee left.

"Listen, Norma," Babe said, "he'll come out all right. You know what my husband said: 'We'll carry him home on our shoulders.' Tony says, 'I shouldn't go to the fight, because I get so nervous, but I'm goin' because Rocky is gonna win.'"

"Like my husband," Lucille said. "Dom was cryin' after the last one. Some fellas from Second Avenue found him and said, 'C'mon, we'll take you home.' So tonight he said he didn't care if he was to go or not."

They could hear them tuning the radio in the living room. In the kitchen they could hear music and then a man's voice coming over the radio very loud and then softer. It was 10 o'clock.

"Say," Norma said, "and what do you think you're doing?"

It was Audrey, standing in the doorway that leads to the bedrooms, a small, dark-haired child in a long white nightgown. She was just standing, blinking in the light, rubbing her eyes with the backs of her hands.

"Aah," Babe said.

"You're makin' too much noise," the child said, still rubbing her eyes, her voice small and whining. "You're makin' too much noise."

"Aah," Babe said. "C'mere."

She reached down and picked the child up and, sitting on the stool, she held her on her lap. Still the child rubbed her eyes.

"How do you like school?" Babe said, turning her head down and talking to the child.

"She won't be able to get up," Norma said. "She has to get some sleep."

"She knows something is happening," Innocent said.

"You're makin' too much noise," the child said.

"What happened?" Norma said, looking up. "You can't get it?"

It was Phil, Lee's husband. He was just standing there, dapper and looking at them and smiling.

"We got it," he said, smiling. "I'm goin' in now."

Now they could hear from the radio the voice of Bill Corum. It was Bill Corum all right, the voice just a little hard and sportslike.

"Bill Corum with Don Dunphy bringing you another major sports event for . . ."

"All right," Norma said softly, getting up and going to the child. She took the child from Babe then, and she carried her out.

"He's got to win," Babe said when Norma was gone.

"That's right," Lucille said, sewing.

"He's gonna win," Innocent said.

"Who feels like sewing?" Lucille said, stopping.

"I don't."

"If you stop I will."

They went on sewing though. They were sewing when Norma came back and Norma, standing and watching, lit another cigarette.

"I don't even think it's ten o'clock yet," Lucille said.

"It's after ten," Norma said, "but they have to get the introductions out of the way."

Now, from the radio far off in the living room they could hear the voice of Johnny Addie, the ring announcer. His voice was very clear, but distant, the only sound in the house.

". . . popular middleweight from Cleveland, Chuck Hunter."

"My husband was like this all day," Babe said, moving her hands. "Back and forth, back and forth. He couldn't eat."

". . . middleweight contender from Brooklyn, Vinnie Cidone."

"If anybody wants to go in—" Norma said.

"No," the two at the table said together, shaking their heads.

"I have to go in," Babe said, sliding off the stool.

"If anybody else wants to go in," Norma said, "because I'm gonna close this door."

"No," her mother, a rather short, trim woman, standing in the doorway now, said, "let's take a walk."

"Wait until it starts," Norma said.

". . . the welterweight king, Sugar Ray Robinson!"

"This is the worst part," Lucille said, "waiting for the introductions."

"No," Norma said. "The worst part is waiting through 'The Star Spangled Banner.'"

"All right," her mother said. "Let's go."

". . . the ring officials are assigned here by the New York State Athletic Commission . . ."

Norma went to get a fresh pack of cigarettes, and then they hurried, the three of them, the one seeming almost to fall over the one ahead, through the dining room and through the living room. In the living room those crowded around

the small radio looked up and shouted something as the three hurried out the front door.

"We're going for a walk," Lucille said, shouting it back.

". . . from Irvington, New Jersey, wearing black trunks . . . Charley Fusari!"

It was the last thing she heard as she hurried out of her own house and into the night.

*She had never, at any time, thought it would be like this. When she was still so young she had listened to the words of Frank Sinatra, but she had always known those were not the truth and that it would never be like that. She had not thought about it much, just that when she did get married it would probably be to some ordinary working guy, and they would live in a little apartment. She could never have known that it would be with a fighter and that they would have two cars and live in their own house, and that she would be driven from it periodically, from her own house, by voices like this.*

"IT'S AN ADVANTAGE I have when he fights in the warm weather," she said. "I can go for nice long walks."

They stood together for a moment under the tree in front of the house. It was a warm, rather humid evening and the street was busy with traffic, the cars shushing by with the lights from their headlights flooding onto the three women in the summer dresses standing under the tree and lighting cigarettes and then starting to walk down the block.

"It's not so warm," her mother said. "I'm cold."

"It isn't really cold," Norma said, "but my teeth are chattering."

"Listen," Lucille said, "you can hear the fight walking along here. Look at them up there."

They could see them sitting on a second-floor sunporch of one of the brick houses, men sitting around, shirt-sleeved, smoking, and through the open windows they could hear, faintly, the voice of Dunphy. They could tell he was calling the fight, but it was impossible to tell what he was saying, and they walked along under the trees, their heels making hard sounds on the pavement.

"Fusari's! . . ."

They heard that much starting by another house, and when Lucille heard it she stopped, dropping back. Then she turned into a driveway, her head forward, and stood motionless.

"Let's walk faster," Norma said.

"All I hear is Graziano, Graziano," her mother said.

"It isn't so much that he wins or loses," Norma

said, "but that he doesn't get hurt. Of course, when you win it leaves a better taste, but it's just that he shouldn't get hurt."

Walking along, their heels clicking faster, they could hear Lucille running up behind them now. Then she was with them again, breathing audibly.

"Your husband must be winning," Lucille said. "Your husband must have knocked Fusari down. I heard him say something about the middle of the ring."

"I don't want to hear it," Norma said, walking.

When they came to the corner they stopped for just a moment. Then they turned left and started walking again.

"Who said being a fighter's wife is easy?" Lucille said.

"It's like being in the ring," Norma said.

"She fights right in the ring with him every fight," her mother said, talking to Lucille.

"That's the trouble," Norma said. "You can't get in the ring with him."

"What could you do?" her mother said.

"Well," she said, "if they put Fusari's wife in the ring."

"He just said Fusari's in trouble," Lucille said quickly.

"You heard it?" Norma said.

"Yes."

"I don't know," Norma said. "It's too much."

"That's the funny thing," Lucille said. "Everybody waits for tonight but you."

"I wait for the night after tonight."

They had reached another corner. They turned left again, but the radio was loud from the house on the corner, the whole first floor lighted beyond the stucco steps. They could hear the hysteria of Dunphy's voice, the crowd noises behind it.

"Shall I ask?" Lucille said. "I could ask here if somebody is knocked out."

"No," Norma said. "Never mind."

She kept walking, but her mother and Lucille stopped. Lucille started up the steps, the radio loud and frantic. When she got to the top of the steps a dog started to bark in the house, and then the door opened and a dog, wild-looking, stood there barking.

"No," Lucille said to the dog, holding up her hands and starting to back down. "Never mind."

A boy showed behind the dog then, a boy of about twelve or thirteen. The boy grabbed the dog and the dog stopped barking, the radio loud again.

"We wanted to know——" Lucille said, halfway down the steps but stopping now—"we wanted to know if one fighter was knocked out."

"No," the boy said, "but Fusari is hurt bad. He's gettin' a beating."

"Norma!" Lucille said, hollering it down the block. "Fusari is hurt!"

"Norma!" her mother said, standing on the sidewalk and hollering it. "Rocky's winning!"

"But when?" Norma said, stopping and turning and shouting it back.

The two were running down the block toward her now. They could make out her dress, the light from a street lamp falling on it through the trees.

"It's the fourth round," Lucille said, running up.

"All I hear," her mother said, "is a left by Graziano, a right by Graziano."

They lighted other cigarettes and started to walk again, Norma between them. A car went by and slowed, approaching the corner, and they could hear the car radio coming through the night.

"It's still going on," Norma said.

"All of a sudden it isn't cold any more," her mother said.

"It got warm," Norma said, trying to laugh it.

"That's a funny thing," Lucille said, "Isn't that funny?"

This is a neighborhood of two-family brick homes. There are small neat lawns in front of the houses and low hedges and cement walks up to the front doors.

"We should have gone to a movie," her mother said.

"That's what I did for the Bummy Davis fight," Norma said. "I saw half a movie. You'd think you'd get over it."

"Every fight it gets worse," her mother said. "At first we used to be able to go to the fights."

They were back in front of the house now. They had slowed down and now they stopped. They could hear, although not distinctly, the radio in the house. They seemed reluctant now to leave the house, to start the walk again, when Babe came running out.

"What?" Norma said. "It's over?"

"No," Babe said, standing in front of them, excited, "but Rocky's ahead. He can't seem to get the left, though. They say something on the radio that he can't seem to get the left."

She was shaking her left fist.

"Was Fusari down?" Lucille said.

"No, but in one round the bell saved him, so we hear. Now it's four rounds for Rocky and three for Fusari or something, but Fusari's bleeding now."

"Is Rocky hurt?" the mother said.

"In the third round he was bleeding over his left eye, but it doesn't bother him now. You should hear it, because . . ."

Norma was rocking a little, back and forth, one foot ahead of the other, smoking and looking at Babe and then down the block.

"You should look on it like any other business," her mother said.

"But you can't do it," Norma said.

"Whatever happens happens," her mother said.

Dunphy's voice came from the house again, excited. When it did Lucille turned and ran up the walk toward the house and Babe followed her. Norma and her mother began to walk.

"Babe said that Rocky slipped, that he crossed his feet and slipped."

"He always does that," Norma said. "Clumsy."

"Once he fell off a ladder."

"Audrey was inside the house watching him through the window and all of a sudden he disappeared. When he's introduced he usually falls into the ring."

"It seems so long," her mother said.

"Well, it takes forty minutes if it goes ten rounds. That's a long time."

"You're telling me."

"I should go to the dentist when he fights. That way I can't worry about him."

"Oh-oh, it's still on."

"I want to hear it, but I don't want to hear it."

"That's it. You want to hear the good part of it."

"It must be the tenth round soon."

". . . Fusari's down! . . ."

It had come loudly and quickly and then was gone, from a car passing swiftly. When they heard it they stopped, their feet poised to go on.

"Fusari's down!" her mother said.

"But did he get up?"

". . . a left hook by Graziano. A right by Graziano . . ."

It was from a house and they stood facing the house, their heads turned to hear it. Even then they could hear only some of it.

"Maybe he'll do what he did in the Cochrane fight," Norma said.

"Norma!"

It was a scream from down the block. When they heard it they turned quickly and they could see figures running through the light and shadow, out of the house.

"Norma! Rocky wins! He wins! He wins!"

They ran, running toward the house. As they ran neighbors came running out of houses, appearing at the low hedges along the sidewalk, shouting to them. The street was all noise now, and when she got to the house she was out of breath, and they were swarming around her, hugging her, kissing her, shouting at her, all of them trying to tell her at once. She ran to the radio where the rest were still gathered and she knelt down in front of it, listening now while Corum told again how it had happened, because now she could not get enough.

"What time will he get home?" somebody said.

*After the last Zale fight she couldn't help it. Even when she heard them bringing him into the house she couldn't stop crying, because that was the first time he had ever really been knocked out like that.*

*The night in Chicago when he beat Zale was the other kind of a night. When he came back to the hotel, the mob around him, they went into the bedroom together to wake Audrey to tell her that her father was the middleweight champion of the world. Audrey was three then, and when they woke her and she stood up in the crib and looked at her father she saw the bandages over one eye and the other eye swollen and closed and the welts on his face.*

*"What happened, Daddy?" Audrey said.*

*"You see what I said?" he said, bending over and pointing his finger at Audrey. "Now stay outa the gutter."*

"I DON'T KNOW," she said. "You never can tell."

It was almost three hours before he came home. In the three hours more people came. The neighbors came in and the men came back from the fight. They congregated in the kitchen, those who had been there and the others, and they fought it all over again for her, swinging their arms, getting more and more excited. They said the same things over and over, and even those who had been in the house all evening, listening to the radio, kept repeating themselves.

"When I was close to the radio," the one named Lee told her twice, "he was losing, and when I walked away he was always winning. So when I walked away Fusari was down so I stayed away and Rocky won the fight."

She stood out on the terrace in the front for a long time, waiting. A couple of reporters—Jim Jennings and Harold Weissman from the *Mirror* —came and Weissman asked her questions about when she had last seen Rocky and if she had been nervous. Behind her, in the house, the phone rang again and again but others answered it.

"You should go to bed," her grandmother said. "The baby will be up early."

At 1:45 a car pulled up and the mob along the curb and on the sidewalk pressed around it. It was Jack Romeo, and he pushed through them and came up the steps, handing her something in a paper bag.

"What is it?" she said, reaching for it. "A bottle?"

"No," he said. "The gloves."

She heard them along the curb then, calling and applauding. In what light there was she could see him. He had on a white cap, and there was a white towel around his neck. Then he had the towel in his hands, and he was pushing through them, acknowledging them in a thick voice until he climbed the steps and saw her.

"Hello, honey," he said, going to her and kissing her quickly.

They walked into the house together, their friends around. They stood for a minute together in the middle of all of them, Rocky answering Weissman's questions.

"No," Rocky said finally, "I'm gonna take a hot bath now, if you'll excuse me. I mean I'm all sweaty. You know? I gotta relax."

"Sure. Sure," they said.

She walked out with him, then, through the dining room and the kitchen and down the hall to the bathroom to run the water into the tub, to be glad again, finally at two o'clock in the morning, that she was this fighter's wife.

*"But don't you want him to retire?" a reporter said to her once. "I mean as soon as you get a little more money?"*

*She was sitting in a chair in the corner of the room and the reporter was sitting across the room from her.*

*"No," she said. "I mean that's not up to me. I think a husband should do whatever work he likes to do. I think if a wife sees her husband happy that's enough."*

THE FIXED FIGHT is the most popular device in boxing fiction, but this surmounts it and is, of course, the best piece of fight fiction ever written. It was first printed in the *Atlantic Monthly,* after having been rejected by *Cosmopolitan* and the *Saturday Evening Post.*

# Fifty Grand

## ERNEST HEMINGWAY

"How ARE YOU going yourself, Jack?" I asked him.

"You seen this Walcott?" he says.

"Just in the gym."

"Well," Jack says, "I'm going to need a lot of luck with that boy."

"He can't hit you, Jack," Soldier said.

"I wish to hell he couldn't."

"He couldn't hit you with a handful of bird-shot."

"Bird-shot'd be all right," Jack says. "I wouldn't mind bird-shot any."

"He looks easy to hit," I said.

"Sure," Jack says, "he ain't going to last long. He ain't going to last like you and me, Jerry. But right now he's got everything."

"You'll left-hand him to death."

"Maybe," Jack says. "Sure. I got a chance to."

"Handle him like you handled Kid Lewis."

"Kid Lewis," Jack said. "That kike!"

The three of us, Jack Brennan, Soldier Bartlett, and I were in Handley's. There were a couple of broads sitting at the next table to us. They had been drinking.

"What do you mean, kike?" one of the broads says. "What do you mean, kike, you big Irish bum?"

"Sure," Jack says. "That's it."

"Kikes," this broad goes on. "They're always talking about kikes, these big Irishmen. What do you mean, kikes?"

"Come on. Let's get out of here."

"Kikes," this broad goes on. "Whoever saw you ever buy a drink? Your wife sews your pockets up every morning. These Irishmen and their kikes! Ted Lewis could lick you too."

"Sure," Jack says. "And you give away a lot of things free too, don't you?"

We went out. That was Jack. He could say what he wanted to when he wanted to say it.

Jack started training out at Danny Hogan's health farm over in Jersey. It was nice out there but Jack didn't like it much. He didn't like being away from his wife and the kids, and he was sore and grouchy most of the time. He liked me and we got along fine together; and he liked Hogan, but after a while Soldier Bartlett commenced to get on his nerves. A kidder gets to be an awful thing around a camp if his stuff goes sort of sour. Soldier was always kidding Jack, just sort of kidding him all the time. It wasn't very funny and it wasn't very good, and it began to get Jack. It was sort of stuff like this. Jack would finish up with the weights and the bag and pull on the gloves.

"You want to work?" he'd say to Soldier.

"Sure. How you want me to work?" Soldier would ask. "Want me to treat you rough like Walcott? Want me to knock you down a few times?"

"That's it," Jack would say. He didn't like it any, though.

One morning we were all out on the road. We'd been out quite a way and now we were coming back. We'd go along fast for three minutes and then walk a minute, and then go fast for three minutes again. Jack wasn't ever what you would call a sprinter. He'd move around fast enough in the ring if he had to, but he wasn't any too fast on the road. All the time we were walking Soldier was kidding him. We came up the hill to the farmhouse.

"Well," says Jack, "you better go back to town, Soldier."

"What do you mean?"

"You better go back to town and stay there."

"What's the matter?"

"I'm sick of hearing you talk."

"Yes?" says Soldier.

"Yes," says Jack.

"You'll be a damn sight sicker when Walcott gets through with you."

"Sure," says Jack, "maybe I will. But I know I'm sick of you."

So Soldier went off on the train to town that same morning. I went down with him to the train. He was good and sore.

"I was just kidding him," he said. We were waiting on the platform. "He can't pull that stuff with me, Jerry."

"He's nervous and crabby," I said. "He's a good fellow, Soldier."

"The hell he is. The hell he's ever been a good fellow."

"Well," I said, "so long, Soldier."

The train had come in. He climbed up with his bag.

"So long, Jerry," he says. "You be in town before the fight?"

"I don't think so."

"See you then."

He went in and the conductor swung up and the train went out. I rode back to the farm in the cart. Jack was on the porch writing a letter to his wife. The mail had come and I got the papers and went over on the other side of the porch and sat down to read. Hogan came out the door and walked over to me.

"Did he have a jam with Soldier?"

"Not a jam," I said. "He just told him to go back to town."

"I could see it coming," Hogan said. "He never liked Soldier much."

"No. He don't like many people."

"He's a pretty cold one," Hogan said.

"Well, he's always been fine to me."

"Me too," Hogan said. "I got no kick on him. He's a cold one, though."

Hogan went in through the screen door and I sat there on the porch and read the papers. It was just starting to get fall weather and it's nice country there in Jersey, up in the hills, and after I read the paper through I sat there and looked out at the country and the road down below against the woods with cars going along it, lifting the dust up. It was fine weather and pretty nice-looking country. Hogan came to the door and I said, "Say, Hogan, haven't you got anything to shoot out here?"

"No," Hogan said. "Only sparrows."

"Seen the paper?" I said to Hogan.

"What's in it?"

"Sande booted three of them in yesterday."

"I got that on the telephone last night."

"You follow them pretty close, Hogan?" I asked.

"Oh, I keep in touch with them," Hogan said.

"How about Jack?" I says. "Does he still play them?"

"Him?" said Hogan. "Can you see him doing it?"

Just then Jack came around the corner with the letter in his hand. He's wearing a sweater and an old pair of pants and boxing shoes.

"Got a stamp, Hogan?" he asks.

"Give me the letter," Hogan said. "I'll mail it for you."

"Say, Jack," I said, "didn't you used to play the ponies?"

"Sure."

"I knew you did. I knew I used to see you out at Sheepshead."

"What did you lay off them for?" Hogan asked.

"Lost money."

Jack sat down on the porch by me. He leaned back against a post. He shut his eyes in the sun.

"Want a chair?" Hogan asked.

"No," said Jack. "This is fine."

"It's a nice day," I said. "It's pretty nice out in the country."

"I'd a damn sight rather be in town with the wife."

"Well, you only got another week."

"Yes," Jack says. "That's so."

We sat there on the porch. Hogan was inside in the office.

"What do you think about the shape I'm in?" Jack asked me.

"Well, you can't tell," I said. "You got a week to get around into form."

"Don't stall me."

"Well," I said, "you're not right."

"I'm not sleeping," Jack said.

"You'll be all right in a couple of days."

"No," says Jack, "I got the insomnia."

"What's on your mind?"

"I miss the wife."

"Have her come out."

"No. I'm too old for that."

"We'll take a long walk before you turn in and get you good and tired."

"Tired!" Jack says. "I'm tired all the time."

He was that way all week. He wouldn't sleep at night and he'd get up in the morning feeling that way, you know, when you can't shut your hands.

"He's stale as a poorhouse cake," Hogan said. "He's nothing."

"I never seen Walcott," I said.

"He'll kill him," said Hogan. "He'll tear him in two."

"Well," I said, "everybody's got to get it some time."

"Not like this, though," Hogan said. "They'll think he never trained. It gives the farm a black eye."

"You hear what the reporters said about him?"

"Didn't I! They said he was awful. They said they oughtn't to let him fight."

"Well," I said, "they're always wrong, ain't they?"

"Yes," said Hogan. "But this time they're right."

"What the hell do they know about whether a man's right or not?"

"Well," said Hogan, "they're not such fools."

"All they did was pick Willard at Toledo. This Lardner, he's so wise now, ask him about when he picked Willard at Toledo."

"Aw, he wasn't out," Hogan said. "He only writes the big fights."

"I don't care who they are," I said. "What the hell do they know? They can write maybe, but what the hell do they know?"

"You don't think Jack's in any shape, do you?" Hogan asked.

"No. He's through. All he needs is to have Corbett pick him to win for it to be all over."

"Well, Corbett'll pick him," Hogan says.

"Sure. He'll pick him."

That night Jack didn't sleep any either. The next morning was the last day before the fight. After breakfast we were all out on the porch again.

"What do you think about, Jack, when you can't sleep?" I said.

"Oh, I worry," Jack says. "I worry about property I got up in the Bronx, I worry about property I got in Florida. I worry about the kids. I worry about the wife. Sometimes I think about fights. I think about that kike Ted Lewis and I get sore. I got some stocks and I worry about them. What the hell don't I think about?"

"Well," I said, "tomorrow night it'll all be over."

"Sure," said Jack. "That always helps a lot, don't it? That just fixes everything all up, I suppose. Sure."

He was sore all day. We didn't do any work. Jack just moved around a little to loosen up. He shadowboxed a few rounds. He didn't even look good doing that. He skipped rope a little while. He couldn't sweat.

"He'd be better not to do any work at all," Hogan said. We were standing watching him skip rope. "Don't he ever sweat at all any more?"

"He can't sweat."

"Do you suppose he's got the con? He never had any trouble making weight, did he?"

"No, he hasn't got any con. He just hasn't got anything inside any more."

"He ought to sweat," said Hogan.

Jack came over, skipping the rope. He was skipping up and down in front of us, forward and back, crossing his arms every third time.

"Well," he says. "What are you buzzards talking about?"

"I don't think you ought to work any more," Hogan says. "You'll be stale."

"Wouldn't that be awful?" Jack says and skips away down the floor, slapping the rope hard.

That afternoon John Collins showed up out at the farm. Jack was up in his room. John came out in a car from town. He had a couple of friends with him. The car stopped and they all got out.

"Where's Jack?" John asked me.

"Up in his room, lying down."

"Lying down?"

"Yes," I said.

"How is he?"

I looked at the two fellows that were with John.

"They're friends of his," John said.

"He's pretty bad," I said.

"What's the matter with him?"

"He don't sleep."

"Hell," said John. "That Irishman could never sleep."

"He isn't right," I said.

"Hell," John said. "He's never right. I've had him for ten years and he's never been right yet."

The fellows who were with him laughed.

"I want you to shake hands with Mr. Morgan and Mr. Steinfelt," John said. "This is Mr. Doyle. He's been training Jack."

"Glad to meet you," I said.

"Let's go up and see the boy," the fellow called Morgan said.

"Let's have a look at him," Steinfelt said.

We all went upstairs.

"Where's Hogan?" John asked.

"He's out in the barn with a couple of his customers," I said.

"He got many people out here now?" John asked.

"Just two."

"Pretty quiet, ain't it?" Morgan said.

"Yes," I said. "It's pretty quiet."

We were outside Jack's room. John knocked on the door. There wasn't any answer.

"Maybe he's asleep," I said.

"What the hell's he sleeping in the daytime for?"

John turned the handle and we all went in. Jack was lying asleep on the bed. He was face down and his face was in the pillow. Both his arms were around the pillow.

"Hey, Jack!" John said to him.

Jack's head moved a little on the pillow. "Jack!" John says, leaning over him. Jack just dug a little deeper in the pillow. John touched him on the shoulder. Jack sat up and looked at us. He hadn't shaved and he was wearing an old sweater.

"Christ! Why can't you let me sleep?" he says to John.

"Don't be sore," John says. "I didn't mean to wake you up."

"Oh no," Jack says. "Of course not."

"You know Morgan and Steinfelt," John said.

"Glad to see you," Jack says.

"How do you feel, Jack?" Morgan asks him.

"Fine," Jack says. "How the hell would I feel?"

"You look fine," Steinfelt says.

"Yes, don't I," says Jack. "Say," he says to John. "You're my manager. You get a big enough cut. Why the hell don't you come out here when the reporters was out! You want Jerry and me to talk to them?"

"I had Lew fighting in Philadelphia," John said.

"What the hell's that to me?" Jack says. "You're my manager. You get a big enough cut, don't you? You aren't making me any money in Philadelphia, are you? Why the hell aren't you out here when I ought to have you?"

"Hogan was here."

"Hogan," Jack says. "Hogan's as dumb as I am."

"Soldier Bartlett was out here wukking with you for a while, wasn't he?" Steinfelt said to change the subject.

"Yes, he was out here," Jack says. "He was out here all right."

"Say, Jerry," John said to me. "Would you go out and find Hogan and tell him we want to see him in about half an hour?"

"Sure," I said.

"Why the hell can't he stick around?" Jack says. "Stick around, Jerry."

Morgan and Steinfelt looked at each other.

"Quiet down, Jack," John said to him.

"I better go find Hogan," I said.

"All right, if you want to go," Jack says. "None of these guys are going to send you away, though."

"I'll go find Hogan," I said.

Hogan was out in the gym in the barn. He had a couple of his health-farm patients with gloves on. They neither one wanted to hit the other, for fear the other would come back and hit him.

"That'll do," Hogan said when he saw me come in. "You can stop the slaughter. You gentlemen take a shower and Bruce will rub you down."

They climbed out through the ropes and Hogan came over to me.

"John Collins is out with a couple of friends to see Jack," I said.

"I saw them come up in the car."

"Who are the two fellows with John?"

"They're what you call wise boys," Hogan said. "Don't you know them two?"

"No," I said.

"That's Happy Steinfelt and Lew Morgan. They got a poolroom."

"I been away a long time," I said.

"Sure," said Hogan. "That Happy Steinfelt's a big operator."

"I've heard his name," I said.

"He's a pretty smooth boy," Hogan said. "They're a couple of sharpshooters."

"Well," I said. "They want to see us in half an hour."

"You mean they don't want to see us until a half an hour."

"That's it."

"Come on in the office," Hogan said. "To hell with those sharpshooters."

After about thirty minutes or so Hogan and I went upstairs. We knocked on Jack's door. They were talking inside the room.

"Wait a minute," somebody said.

"To hell with that stuff," Hogan said. "When you want to see me I'm down in the office."

We heard the door unlock. Steinfelt opened it.

"Come on in, Hogan," he says. "We're all going to have a drink."

"Well," says Hogan. "That's something."

We went in. Jack was sitting on the bed. John and Morgan were sitting on a couple of chairs. Steinfelt was standing up.

"You're a pretty mysterious lot of boys," Hogan said.

"Hello, Danny," John says.

"Hello, Danny," Morgan says and shakes hands.

Jack doesn't say anything. He just sits there on the bed. He ain't with the others. He's all by himself. He was wearing an old blue jersey and pants and had on boxing shoes. He needed a shave. Steinfelt and Morgan were dressers. John was quite a dresser too. Jack sat there looking Irish and tough.

Steinfelt brought out a bottle and Hogan brought in some glasses and everybody had a drink. Jack and I took one and the rest of them went on and had two or three each.

"Better save some for your ride back," Hogan said.

"Don't you worry. We got plenty," Morgan said.

Jack hadn't drunk anything since the one drink. He was standing up and looking at them. Morgan was sitting on the bed where Jack had sat.

"Have a drink, Jack," John said and handed him the glass and the bottle.

"No," Jack said, "I never liked to go to these wakes."

They all laughed. Jack didn't laugh.

They were all feeling pretty good when they left. Jack stood on the porch when they got into the car. They waved to him.

"So long," Jack said.

We had supper. Jack didn't say anything during the meal except, "Will you pass me this?" or "Will you pass me that?" The two health-farm patients ate at the same table with us. They were pretty nice fellows. After we finished eating we went out on the porch. It was dark early.

"Like to take a walk, Jerry?" Jack asked.

"Sure," I said.

We put on our coats and started out. It was quite a way down to the main road and then we walked along the main road about a mile and a half. Cars kept going by and we would pull out to the side until they were past. Jack didn't say anything. After we had stepped out into the bushes to let a big car go by, Jack said, "To hell with this walking. Come on back to Hogan's."

We went along a side road that cut up over the hill and cut across the fields back to Hogan's. We could see the lights of the house up on the hill. We came around to the front of the house and there standing in the doorway was Hogan.

"Have a good walk?" Hogan asked.

"Oh, fine," Jack said. "Listen, Hogan. Have you got any liquor?"

"Sure," says Hogan. "What's the idea?"

"Send it up to the room," Jack says. "I'm going to sleep tonight."

"You're the doctor," Hogan says.

"Come on up to the room, Jerry," Jack says.

Upstairs Jack sat on the bed with his head in his hands.

"Ain't it a life?" Jack says.

Hogan brought in a quart of liquor and two glasses.

"Want some ginger ale?"

"What do you think I want to do, get sick?"

"I just asked you," said Hogan.

"Have a drink?" said Jack.

"No, thanks," said Hogan. He went out.

"How about you, Jerry?"

"I'll have one with you," I said.

Jack poured out a couple of drinks. "Now," he said, "I want to take it slow and easy."

"Put some water in it," I said.

"Yes," Jack said. "I guess that's better."

We had a couple of drinks without saying anything. Jack started to pour me another.

"No," I said, "that's all I want."

"All right," Jack said. He poured himself out another big shot and put water in it. He was lighting up a little.

"That was a fine bunch out here this afternoon," he said. "They don't take any chances, those two."

Then a little later, "Well," he says, "they're right. What the hell's the good in taking chances?"

"Don't you want another, Jerry?" he said. "Come on, drink along with me."

"I don't need it, Jack," I said. "I feel all right."

"Just have one more," Jack said. It was softening him up.

"All right," I said.

Jack poured one for me and another big one for himself.

"You know," he said, "I like liquor pretty well. If I hadn't been boxing I would have drunk quite a lot."

"Sure," I said.

"You know," he said, "I missed a lot, boxing."

"You made plenty of money."

"Sure, that's what I'm after. You know I miss a lot, Jerry."

"How do you mean?"

"Well," he says, "like about the wife. And being away from home so much. It don't do my girls any good. 'Who's your old man?' some of those society kids'll say to them. 'My old man's Jack Brennan.' That don't do them any good."

"Hell," I said, "all that makes a difference is if they got dough."

"Well," says Jack, "I got the dough for them all right."

He poured out another drink. The bottle was about empty.

"Put some water in it," I said. Jack poured in some water.

"You know," he says, "you ain't got any idea how I miss the wife."

"Sure."

"You ain't got any idea. You can't have any idea what it's like."

"It ought to be better out in the country than in town."

"With me now," Jack said, "it don't make any difference where I am. You can't have any idea what it's like."

"Have another drink."

"Am I getting soused? Do I talk funny?"

"You're coming on all right."

"You can't have any idea what it's like. They ain't nobody can have an idea what it's like."

"Except the wife," I said.

"She knows," Jack said. "She knows all right. She knows. You bet she knows."

"Put some water in that," I said.

"Jerry," says Jack, "you can't have an idea what it gets to be like."

He was good and drunk. He was looking at me steady. His eyes were sort of too steady.

"You'll sleep all right," I said.

"Listen, Jerry," Jack says. "You want to make some money? Get some money down on Walcott."

"Yes?"

"Listen, Jerry," Jack put down the glass. "I'm not drunk now, see? You know what I'm betting on him? Fifty grand."

"That's a lot of dough."

"Fifty grand," Jack says, "at two to one. I'll get twenty-five thousand bucks. Get some money on him, Jerry."

"It sounds good," I said.

"How can I beat him?" Jack says. "It ain't crooked. How can I beat him? Why not make money on it?"

"Put some water in that," I said.

"I'm through after this fight," Jack says. "I'm through with it. I got to take a beating. Why shouldn't I make money on it?"

"Sure."

"I ain't slept for a week," Jack says. "All night I lay awake and worry my can off. I can't sleep, Jerry. You ain't got an idea what it's like when you can't sleep."

"Sure."

"I can't sleep. That's all. I just can't sleep. What's the use of taking care of yourself all these years when you can't sleep?"

"It's bad."

"You ain't got an idea what it's like, Jerry, when you can't sleep."

"Put some water in that," I said.

Well, about eleven o'clock Jack passes out and I put him to bed. Finally he's so he can't keep from sleeping. I helped him get his clothes off and got him into bed.

"You'll sleep all right, Jack," I said.

"Sure," Jack says. "I'll sleep now."

"Good night, Jack," I said.

"Good night, Jerry," Jack says. "You're the only friend I got."

"Oh, hell," I said.

"You're the only friend I got," Jack says, "the only friend I got."

"Go to sleep," I said.

"I'll sleep," Jack says.

Downstairs Hogan was sitting at the desk in the office reading the papers. He looked up. "Well, you get your boy friend to sleep?" he asks.

"He's off."

"It's better for him than not sleeping," Hogan said.

"Sure."

"You'd have a hell of a time explaining that to these sports writers, though," Hogan said.

"Well, I'm going to bed myself," I said.

"Good night," said Hogan.

In the morning I came downstairs about eight o'clock and got some breakfast. Hogan had his two customers out in the barn doing exercises. I went out and watched them.

"One! Two! Three! Four!" Hogan was counting for them. "Hello Jerry," he said. "Is Jack up yet?"

"No. He's still sleeping."

I went back to my room and packed up to go into town. About nine-thirty I heard Jack getting up in the next room. When I heard him go downstairs I went down after him. Jack was sitting at the breakfast table. Hogan had come in and was standing beside the table.

"How do you feel, Jack?" I asked him.

"Not so bad."

"Sleep well?" Hogan asked.

"I slept all right," Jack said. "I got a thick tongue but I ain't got a head."

"Good," Hogan said. "That was good liquor."

"Put it on the bill," Jack says.

"What time you want to go into town?" Hogan asked.

"Before lunch," Jack says. "The eleven-o'clock train."

"Sit down, Jerry," Jack said. Hogan went out.

I sat down at the table. Jack was eating a grapefruit. When he'd find a seed he'd spit it out in the spoon and dump it on the plate.

"I guess I was pretty stewed last night," he started.

"You drank some liquor."

"I guess I said a lot of fool things."

"You weren't bad."

"Where's Hogan?" he asked. He was through with the grapefruit.

"He's out in front in the office."

"What did I say about betting on the fight?" Jack asked. He was holding the spoon and sort of poking at the grapefruit with it.

The girl came in with some ham and eggs and took away the grapefruit.

"Bring me another glass of milk," Jack said to her. She went out.

"You said you had fifty grand on Walcott," I said.

"That's right," Jack said.

"That's a lot of money."

"I don't feel too good about it," Jack said.

"Something might happen."

"No," Jack said. "He wants the title bad. They'll be shooting with him all right."

"You can't ever tell."

"No. He wants the title. It's worth a lot of money to him."

"Fifty grand is a lot of money," I said.

"It's business," said Jack. "I can't win. You know I can't win anyway."

"As long as you're in there you got a chance."

"No," Jack says. "I'm all through. It's just business."

"How do you feel?"

"Pretty good," Jack said. "The sleep was what I needed."

"You might go good."

"I'll give them a good show," Jack said.

After breakfast Jack called up his wife on the long-distance. He was inside the booth telephoning.

"That's the first time he's called her up since he's out here," Hogan said.

"He writes her every day."

"Sure," Hogan says, "a letter only costs two cents."

Hogan said goodbye to us and Bruce, the nigger rubber, drove us down to the train in the cart.

"Goodbye, Mr. Brennan," Bruce said at the train, "I sure hope you knock his can off."

"So long," Jack said. He gave Bruce two dollars. Bruce had worked on him a lot. He looked kind of disappointed. Jack saw me looking at Bruce holding the two dollars.

"It's all in the bill," he said. "Hogan charged me for the rubbing."

On the train going into town Jack didn't talk. He sat in the corner of the seat with his ticket in his hatband and looked out of the window. Once he turned and spoke to me.

"I told the wife I'd take a room at the Shelby tonight," he said. "It's just around the corner from the Garden. I can go up to the house tomorrow morning."

"That's a good idea," I said. "Your wife ever see you fight, Jack?"

"No," Jack says. "She never seen me fight."

I thought he must be figuring on taking an awful beating if he doesn't want to go home afterward. In town we took a taxi up to the Shelby. A boy came out and took our bags and we went in to the desk.

"How much are the rooms?" Jack asked.

"We only have double rooms," the clerk says. "I can give you a nice double room for ten dollars."

"That's too steep."

"I can give you a double room for seven dollars."

"With a bath?"

"Certainly."

"You might as well bunk with me, Jerry," Jack says.

"Oh," I said, "I'll sleep down at my brother-in-law's."

"I don't mean for you to pay for it," Jack says. "I just want to get my money's worth."

"Will you register, please?" the clerk says. He looked at the names. "Number two thirty-eight, Mr. Brennan."

We went up in the elevator. It was a nice big room with two beds and a door opening into a bathroom.

"This is pretty good," Jack says.

The boy who brought us up pulled up the curtains and brought in our bags. Jack didn't make any move, so I gave the boy a quarter. We washed up and Jack said we better go out and get something to eat.

We ate lunch at Jimmy Handley's place. Quite a lot of the boys were there. When we were about half through eating, John came in and sat down with us. Jack didn't talk much.

"How are you on the weight, Jack?" John asked him. Jack was putting away a pretty good lunch.

"I could make it with my clothes on," Jack said. He never had to worry about taking off weight. He was a natural welterweight and he'd never gotten fat. He'd lost weight out at Hogan's.

"Well, that's one thing you never had to worry about," John said.

"That's one thing," Jack says.

We went around to the Garden to weigh in after lunch. The match was made at a hundred forty-seven pounds at three o'clock. Jack stepped on the scales with a towel around him. The bar didn't move. Walcott had just weighed and was standing with a lot of people around him.

"Let's see what you weigh, Jack," Freedman, Walcott's manager, said.

"All right, weigh *him* then," Jack jerked his head toward Walcott.

"Drop the towel," Freedman said.

"What do you make it?" Jack asked the fellows who were weighing.

"One hundred and forty-three pounds," the fat man who was weighing said.

"You're down fine, Jack," Freedman says.

"Weigh *him*," Jack says.

Walcott came over. He was a blond with wide shoulders and arms like a heavyweight. He didn't have much legs. Jack stood about half a head taller than he did.

"Hello, Jack," he said. His face was plenty marked up.

"Hello," Jack said. "How you feel?"

"Good," Walcott says. He dropped the towel from around his waist and stood on the scales. He had the widest shoulders and back you ever saw.

"One hundred and forty-six pounds and twelve ounces."

Walcott stepped off and grinned at Jack.

"Well," John says to him, "Jack's spotting you about four pounds."

"More than that when I come in, kid," Walcott says. "I'm going to go and eat now."

We went back and Jack got dressed. "He's a pretty tough-looking boy," Jack says to me.

"He looks as though he'd been hit plenty of times."

"Oh, yes," Jack says. "He ain't hard to hit."

"Where are you going?" John asked when Jack was dressed.

"Back to the hotel," Jack says. "You looked after everything?"

"Yes," John says. "It's all looked after."

"I'm going to lie down awhile," Jack says.

"I'll come around for you about a quarter to seven and we'll go and eat."

"All right."

Up at the hotel Jack took off his shoes and his coat and lay down for a while. I wrote a letter. I looked over a couple of times and Jack wasn't sleeping. He was lying perfectly still but every once in a while his eyes would open. Finally he sits up.

"Want to play some cribbage, Jerry?" he says.

"Sure," I said.

He went over to his suitcase and got out the cards and the cribbage board. We played crib-

bage and he won three dollars off me. John knocked at the door and came in.

"Want to play some cribbage, John?" Jack asked him.

John put his kelly down on the table. It was all wet. His coat was wet too.

"Is it raining?" Jack asks.

"It's pouring," John says. "The taxi I had got tied up in the traffic and I got out and walked."

"Come on, play some cribbage," Jack says.

"You ought to go and eat."

"No," says Jack. "I don't want to eat yet."

So they played cribbage for about half an hour and Jack won a dollar and a half off him.

"Well, I suppose we got to go eat," Jack says. He went to the window and looked out.

"Is it still raining?"

"Yes."

"Let's eat in the hotel," John says.

"All right," Jack says. "I'll play you once more to see who pays for the meal."

After a little while Jack gets up and says, "You buy the meal, John," and we went downstairs and ate in the big dining room.

After we ate we went upstairs and Jack played cribbage with John again and won two dollars and a half off him. Jack was feeling pretty good. John had a bag with him with all his stuff in it. Jack took off his shirt and collar and put on a jersey and a sweater, so he wouldn't catch cold when he came out, and put his ring clothes and his bathrobe in a bag.

"You all ready?" John asks him. "I'll call up and have them get a taxi."

Pretty soon the telephone rang and they said the taxi was waiting.

We rode down in the elevator and went out through the lobby, and got in a taxi and rode around to the Garden. It was raining hard but there was a lot of people outside on the streets. The Garden was sold out. As we came in on our way to the dressing room I saw how full it was. It looked like half a mile down to the ring. It was all dark. Just the lights over the ring.

"It's a good thing, with this rain, they didn't try and pull this fight in the ball park," John said.

"They got a good crowd," Jack says.

"This is a fight that would draw a lot more than the Garden could hold."

"You can't tell about the weather," Jack says.

John came to the door of the dressing room and poked his head in. Jack was sitting there with his bathrobe on, he had his arms folded and was looking at the floor. John had a couple of handlers with him. They looked over his shoulder. Jack looked up.

"Is he in?" he asked.

"He's just gone down," John said.

We started down. Walcott was just getting into the ring. The crowd gave him a big hand. He climbed through between the ropes and put his two fists together and smiled, and shook them at the crowd, first at one side of the ring, then at the other, and then sat down. Jack got a good hand coming down through the crowd. Jack is Irish and the Irish always get a pretty good hand. An Irishman don't draw in New York like a Jew or an Italian but they always get a good hand. Jack climbed up and bent down to go through the ropes and Walcott came over from his corner and pushed the rope down for Jack to go through. The crowd thought that was wonderful. Walcott put his hand on Jack's shoulder and they stood there just for a second.

"So you're going to be one of these popular champions," Jack says to him. "Take your god-dam hand off my shoulder."

"Be yourself," Walcott says.

This is all great for the crowd. How gentlemanly the boys are before the fight! How they wish each other luck!

Solly Freedman came over to our corner while Jack is bandaging his hands and John is over in Walcott's corner. Jack puts his thumb through the slit in the bandage and then wrapped his hand nice and smooth. I taped it around the wrist and twice across the knuckles.

"Hey," Freedman says. "Where do you get all that tape?"

"Feel of it," Jack says. "It's soft, ain't it? Don't be a hick."

Freedman stands there all the time while Jack bandages the other hand, and one of the boys that's going to handle him brings the gloves and I pull them on and work them around.

"Say, Freedman," Jack asks, "what nationality is this Walcott?"

"I don't know," Solly says. "He's some sort of a Dane."

"He's a Bohemian," the lad who brought the gloves said.

The referee called them out to the center of the ring and Jack walks out. Walcott comes out smiling. They met and the referee put his arm on each of their shoulders.

"Hello, popularity," Jack says to Walcott.

"Be yourself."

"What do you call yourself 'Walcott' for?" Jack says. "Didn't you know he was a nigger?"

"Listen—" says the referee, and he gives them the same old line. Once Walcott interrupts him. He grabs Jack's arm and says, "Can I hit when he's got me like this?"

"Keep your hands off me," Jack says. "There ain't no moving pictures of this."

They went back to their corners. I lifted the bathrobe off Jack and he leaned on the ropes and flexed his knees a couple of times and scuffed his shoes in the rosin. The gong rang and Jack turned quick and went out. Walcott came toward him and they touched gloves and as soon as Walcott dropped his hands Jack jumped his left into his face twice. There wasn't anybody ever boxed better than Jack. Walcott was after him, going forward all the time with his chin on his chest. He's a hooker and he carries his hands pretty low. All he knows is to get in there and sock. But every time he gets in there close, Jack has the left hand in his face. It's just as though it's automatic. Jack just raises the left hand up and it's in Walcott's face. Three or four times Jack brings the right over but Walcott gets it on the shoulder or high up on the head. He's just like all these hookers. The only thing he's afraid of is another one of the same kind. He's covered everywhere you can hurt him. He don't care about a left hand in his face.

After about four rounds Jack has him bleeding bad and his face all cut up, but every time Walcott's got in close he's socked so hard he's got two big red patches on both sides just below Jack's ribs. Every time he gets in close, Jack ties him up, then gets one hand loose and uppercuts him, but when Walcott gets his hands loose he socks Jack in the body so they can hear it outside in the street. He's a socker.

It goes along like that for three rounds more. They don't talk any. They're working all the time. We worked over Jack plenty too, in between the rounds. He don't look good at all but he never does much work in the ring. He don't move around much and that left hand is just automatic. It's just like it was connected with Walcott's face and Jack just had to wish it in every time. Jack is always calm in close and he doesn't waste any juice. He knows everything about working in close too and he's getting away with a lot of stuff. While they were in our corner I watched him tie Walcott up, get his right hand loose, turn it and come up with an uppercut that got Walcott's nose with the heel of the glove. Walcott was bleeding bad and leaned his nose on Jack's shoulder so as to give Jack some of it too, and Jack sort of lifted his shoulder sharp and caught him against the nose, and then brought down the right hand and did the same thing again.

Walcott was sore as hell. By the time they'd gone five rounds he hated Jack's guts. Jack wasn't sore; that is, he wasn't any sorer than he always was. He certainly did used to make the fellows he fought hate boxing. That was why he hated Kid Lewis so. He never got the Kid's goat. Kid Lewis always had about three new dirty things Jack couldn't do. Jack was as safe as a church all the time he was in there, as long as he was strong. He certainly was treating Walcott rough. The funny thing was it looked as though Jack was an open classic boxer. That was because he had all that stuff too.

After the seventh round Jack says, "My left's getting heavy."

From then he started to take a beating. It didn't show at first. But instead of him running the fight it was Walcott was running it, instead of being safe all the time now he was in trouble. He couldn't keep him out with the left hand now. It looked as though it was the same as ever, only now instead of Walcott's punches just missing him they were just hitting him. He took an awful beating in the body.

"What's the round?" Jack asked.

"The eleventh."

"I can't stay," Jack says. "My legs are going bad."

Walcott had been just hitting him for a long time. It was like a baseball catcher pulls the ball and takes some of the shock off. From now on Walcott commenced to land solid. He certainly was a socking machine. Jack was just trying to block everything now. It didn't show what an awful beating he was taking. In between the rounds I worked on his legs. The muscles would flutter under my hands all the time I was rubbing them. He was sick as hell.

"How's it go?" he asked John, turning around, his face all swollen.

"It's his fight."

"I think I can last," Jack says. "I don't want this bohunk to stop me."

It was going just the way he thought it would. He knew he couldn't beat Walcott. He wasn't strong any more. He was all right though. His money was all right and now he wanted to finish it off right to please himself. He didn't want to be knocked out.

The gong rang and we pushed him out. He went out slow. Walcott came right out after him. Jack put the left in his face and Walcott took it, came in under it and started working on Jack's body. Jack tried to tie him up and it was just like trying to hold on to a buzz saw. Jack broke away from it and missed with the right. Walcott clipped him with a left hook and Jack went down. He went down on his hands and knees and looked at us. The referee started counting. Jack was watching us and shaking his head. At eight John mo-

tioned to him. You couldn't hear on account of the crowd. Jack got up. The referee had been holding Walcott back with one arm while he counted.

When Jack was on his feet Walcott started toward him.

"Watch yourself, Jimmy," I heard Solly Freedman yell to him.

Walcott came up to Jack looking at him. Jack stuck the left hand at him. Walcott just shook his head. He backed Jack up against the ropes, measured him and then hooked the left very light to the side of Jack's head and socked the right into the body as hard as he could sock, just as low as he could get it. He must have hit him five inches below the belt. I thought the eyes would come out of Jack's head. They stuck way out. His mouth come open.

The referee grabbed Walcott. Jack stepped forward. If he went down there went fifty thousand bucks. He walked as though all his insides were going to fall out.

"It wasn't low," he said. "It was a accident."

The crowd were yelling so you couldn't hear anything.

"I'm all right," Jack says. They were right in front of us. The referee looks at John and then he shakes his head.

"Come on, you polack son-of-a-bitch," Jack says to Walcott.

John was hanging onto the ropes. He had the towel ready to chuck in. Jack was standing just a little way out from the ropes. He took a step forward. I saw the sweat come out on his face like somebody had squeezed it and a big drop went down his nose.

"Come on and fight," Jack says to Walcott.

The referee looked at John and waved Walcott on.

"Go in there, you slob," he says.

Walcott went in. He didn't know what to do either. He never thought Jack could have stood it. Jack put the left in his face. There was such a hell of a lot of yelling going on. They were right in front of us. Walcott hit him twice. Jack's face was the worst thing I ever saw—the look on it! He was holding himself and all his body together and it all showed on his face. All the time he was thinking and holding his body in where it was busted.

Then he started to sock. His face looked awful all the time. He started to sock with his hands low down by his side, swinging at Walcott. Walcott covered up and Jack was swinging wild at Walcott's head. Then he swung the left and it hit

Walcott in the groin and the right hit Walcott right bang where he'd hit Jack. Way low below the belt. Walcott went down and grabbed himself there and rolled and twisted around.

The referee grabbed Jack and pushed him toward his corner. John jumps into the ring. There was all this yelling going on. The referee was talking with the judges and then the announcer got into the ring with the megaphone and says, "Walcott on a foul."

The referee is talking to John and he says, "What could I do? Jack wouldn't take the foul. Then when he's groggy he fouls him."

"He'd lost it anyway," John says.

Jack's sitting on the chair. I've got his gloves off and he's holding himself in down there with both hands. When he's got something supporting it his face doesn't look so bad.

"Go over and say you're sorry," John says into his ear. "It'll look good."

Jack stands up and the sweat comes out all over his face. I put the bathrobe around him and he holds himself in with one hand under the bathrobe and goes across the ring. They've picked Walcott up and they're working on him. There're a lot of people in Walcott's corner. Nobody speaks to Jack. He leans over Walcott.

"I'm sorry," Jack says. "I didn't mean to foul you."

Walcott doesn't say anything. He looks too damned sick.

"Well, you're the champion now," Jack says to him. "I hope you get a hell of a lot of fun out of it."

"Leave the kid alone," Solly Freedman says.

"Hello, Solly," Jack says. "I'm sorry I fouled your boy."

Freedman just looks at him.

Jack went to his corner walking that funny jerky way and we got him down through the ropes and through the reporters' tables and out down the aisle. A lot of people want to slap Jack on the back. He goes out through all that mob in his bathrobe to the dressing room. It's a popular win for Walcott. That's the way the money was bet in the Garden.

Once we got inside the dressing room Jack lay down and shut his eyes.

"We want to get to the hotel and get a doctor," John says.

"I'm all busted inside," Jack says.

"I'm sorry as hell, Jack," John says.

"It's all right," Jack says.

He lies there with his eyes shut.

"They certainly tried a nice double cross," John said.

"Your friends Morgan and Steinfelt," Jack said. "You got nice friends."

He lies there, his eyes are open now. His face has still got that awful drawn look.

"It's funny how fast you can think when it means that much money," Jack says.

"You're some boy, Jack," John says.

"No," Jack says. "It was nothing."

THE O. HENRY ending, like George La Blanche's pivot blow, should have been outlawed in 1889.

# The Higher Pragmatism

## O. HENRY

"SAY," SAID MACK, "tell me one thing—can you hand out the dope to other girls? Can you chin 'em and make matinee eyes at 'em and squeeze 'em? You know what I mean. You're just shy when it comes to this particular dame—the professional beauty—ain't that right?"

"In a way you have outlined the situation with approximate truth," I admitted.

"I thought so," said Mack grimly. "Now, that reminds me of my own case. I'll tell you about it."

I was indignant, but concealed it. What was this loafer's case or anybody's case compared with mine? Besides, I had given him a dollar and ten cents.

"Feel my muscle," said my companion suddenly, flexing his biceps. I did so mechanically. The fellows in gyms are always asking you to do that. His arm was hard as cast iron.

"Four years ago," said Mack, "I could lick any man in New York outside of the professional ring. Your case and mine is just the same. I come from the West Side—between Thirteenth and Fourteenth—I won't give the number on the door. I was a scrapper when I was ten, and when I was twenty no amateur in the city could stand up four rounds with me. 'S a fact. You know Bill McCarty? No? He managed the smokers for some of them swell clubs. Well, I knocked out everything Bill brought up before me. I was a middleweight, but could train down to a welter when necessary. I boxed all over the West Side at bouts and benefits and private entertainments, and was never put out once.

"But say, the first time I put my foot in the ring with a professional I was no more than a canned lobster. I dunno how it was—I seemed to lose heart. I guess I got too much imagination. There was a formality and publicness about it that kind of weakened my nerve. I never won a fight in the ring. Lightweights and all kinds of scrubs used to sign up with my manager and then walk up and tap me on the wrist and see me fall. The minute I seen the crowd and a lot of gents in evening clothes down in front, and seen a professional come inside the ropes, I got as weak as ginger ale.

"Of course, it wasn't long till I couldn't get no backers, and I didn't have any more chances to fight a professional—or many amateurs, either. But lemme tell you—I was as good as most men inside the ring or out. It was just that dumb, dead feeling I had when I was up against a regular that always done me up.

"Well, sir, after I had got out of the business, I got a mighty grouch on. I used to go round town licking private citizens and all kinds of unprofessionals just to please myself. I'd lick cops in dark streets and car conductors and cab drivers and draymen whenever I could start a row with 'em. It didn't make any difference how big they were, or how much science they had, I got away with 'em. If I'd only just have had the confidence in the ring that I had beating up the best men outside of it, I'd be wearing black pearls and heliotrope silk socks today.

"One evening I was walking along near the Bowery, thinking about things, when along comes a slumming party. About six or seven they was, all in swallowtails, and these silk hats that don't shine. One of the gang kind of shoves me off the sidewalk. I hadn't had a scrap in three days, and I just says, 'De-lighted!' and hits him back of the ear."

"Well, we had it. That Johnnie put up as decent a little fight as you'd want to see in the moving pictures. It was on a side street and no cops around. The other guy had a lot of science, but it only took me about six minutes to lay him out.

"Some of the swallowtails dragged him up against some steps and began to fan him. Another one of 'em comes over to me and says:

" 'Young man, do you know what you've done?'

" 'Oh, beat it,' says I. 'I've done nothing but a little punching-bag work. Take Freddy back to Yale and tell him to quit studying sociology on the wrong side of the sidewalk.'

" 'My good fellow,' says he, 'I don't know who you are, but I'd like to. You've knocked out Reddy Burns, the champion middleweight of the world! He came to New York yesterday, to try to get a match on with Jim Jeffries. If you—'

"But when I come out of my faint I was laying on the floor in a drugstore saturated with aromatic spirits of ammonia. If I'd known that was Reddy Burns, I'd have got down in the gutter and crawled past him instead of handing him one like I did. Why, if I'd ever been in a ring and seen him climbing over the ropes, I'd have been all to the sal volatile.

"So that's what imagination does," concluded Mack. "And, as I said, your case and mine is simultaneous. You'll never win out. You can't go up against the professionals. I tell you, it's a park bench for yours in this romance business."

WHEN GEORGE HICKS first spoke into a radio microphone in 1928 he had already been, among other things, a college student, logger, saw-mill hand, factory worker, truck driver and seaman. He became one of the most respected of all radio reporters, covering much of the history of the thirties and forties, including the combat in Europe during World War II. His D-Day broadcast of the Normandy invasion is a classic. He is now finding expression in painting. but because of his sensitivity not only to sights but also to sounds and, above all, to people, he was asked to write for this volume what has remained with him from the adolescent years of the radio coverage of fights.

# A Radio Man Remembers

## GEORGE HICKS

WHEN PRIMO CARNERA defended his heavyweight championship against Max Baer in the Madison Square Garden Bowl on Long Island in June of 1934, the Blue Network of the National Broadcasting Company attempted an experiment. Whether it worked or not was not too important, because they had Graham McNamee doing the blow-by-blow at ringside, but they assigned two of us, an engineer and me, to the champion's dressing room.

I went into the dressing room early with the engineer because I was afraid that I might otherwise be barred. In those days radio had few credentials, and at least the engineer had his equipment to prove what he was.

While the engineer set up in the corner I walked over to Carnera. He was sitting on the rubbing table with one of his handlers standing next to him.

"Excuse me, Champ," I said, "but will it be all right if I interview you over the radio right after the fight?"

Carnera said nothing. He just looked at me with those big, round, brown eyes.

"Maybe," the handler said, shrugging. "We can't say right now."

I watched them prepare the big man then and, finally, when the call came, lead him out. I was afraid to leave the room, afraid that I would not be able to get back in, but after the fight had started and I could hear the roar of the crowd I spoke to the uniformed guard at the door and walked through the tunnel to the beginning of an aisle.

The open arena seemed to me to be the site of an explosion. Under the lights at the bottom of it Carnera was down and the whole pit was filled with a shattering violence of sound. I stood there and watched Carnera get up and, as it went on, get knocked down ten more times, until it ended in the eleventh round.

I was waiting in the dressing room when they brought Carnera back. The big man was breathing heavily but, as they sat him down, he did not seem badly hurt. I stood back, waiting until those who had followed him in had left and only the two handlers still remained with him. Then I walked over to him, the microphone in my hand and the lead line trailing behind me to where the engineer knelt over his portable amplifier in the corner.

"Mr. Carnera," I said, "would you care to speak over the radio now?"

He was sitting on the rubbing table with his head down, still breathing heavily, his robe hanging loose from his shoulders. He lifted that big head and looked at me, and he seemed startled and confused.

"No," one of the handlers said. "He don't want to talk. Beat it."

Then the door behind us opened again, and in walked a short, strutting man followed by several others. I recognized the man, for he was one of this country's best-known sports columnists.

"Hello, Champ," he said, walking up to Carnera.

Carnera's head came up again and he stared out of those brown, hurt eyes. He looked at the man and then he looked away.

"How do you feel about losing it?" the short man said.

Carnera dropped his head and shook it slowly.

"You mean you liked being champion?" the sports writer said.

Carnera lifted his head and looked again at the man. The sweat was still coming out of his forehead and now it was running down and dripping off his nose.

"What do you think the people in Italy will think of you now?" the sports writer said.

"I don't know," Carnera said, and his eyes were starting to fill with tears and he looked away from the man.

"You think Mussolini will like this?" the sports writer said.

Carnera dropped his head, dripping with his sweat.

"Well," the sports writer said, turning, "so long, Champ."

In the silence that followed I put on my earphones and, in them, I could hear McNamee's voice from ringside. I could hear that excited, breathless speech of his slowing down now and beginning to replay the best moments of the fight. In the almost emptiness of that dressing room I walked my microphone back to Carnera.

"Would you care to speak over the radio now?" I said.

Carnera looked up at me and nodded. I signaled the engineer to call Control Room. Now in the earphones I could hear the 11 P.M. correct time and the station break. I got the go-ahead, and I started to speak with the large, suffering man with the injured pride as he sat on the rubbing table, asking him how he felt, if he was physically hurt, about what hopes he might have now.

I no longer remember what Carnera said, but suddenly, answering my questions, he began to cry. No big tears came, but it was the simple, small crying of a boy who has never wished harm to anyone and who has just been terribly mistreated. As it was ending I could hear, in my earphones, McNamee.

"For Christ's sake!" McNamee was shouting. "Get this on the air! It's great! Primo Carnera is crying!"

It never did get on the air. Someone at Radio City had decided not to switch-return to the Bowl. Only those few of us—we in the dressing room, McNamee and his engineer and perhaps those in Control Room—heard Primo Carnera crying. The dressing-room experiment had failed.

JOE LOUIS was not unfriendly but he was an impenetrable man. Perhaps he himself did not know what motivated him. It was a wonderfully warm late summer day, while he was training at Pompton Lakes for the Max Baer fight in 1935, when I was able to stop him as he rounded a corner of the gym. He slouched, bland, quizzical, the sun in his eyes causing him to squint, silently waiting.

I asked how he felt and what his weight was, writing down the answers for a spot I would put on the air later. I was actually afraid to ask him the next question.

"Baer," I said, finally, "says he's going to knock you into the eighth row. What do you think of that?"

Joe changed without moving. Something happened to his eyes.

"Every dog got a right to wag his own tail," Joe said.

He spoke it so fast I could not, at first, understand it, let alone write it down, but it all came back to me years later when I had an appointment with an executive in his hotel room. His wife answered my knock and let me in. She seemed nervous, alone with me, and we were still standing there when her husband came in. When he saw us he moved toward us and, for just that instant, our eyes met and I saw there what I had seen just that once in Joe's. Then it was gone and he apologized for being late.

AL ETTORE was a big, blond Italian-American with pink skin, and that night in 1936 when he fought Joe Louis in Philadelphia he came into the ring healthy and smiling and nodding to those he knew in the press rows. He must have thought he had a chance, but by the fifth round his body was being shocked backward with every punch. The speed and rhythm with which Louis punched at that time made of Joe a brown blur, and there began to settle over Ettore's face a quiet look, a kind of resigned expression. His eyes closed as if he were falling asleep, and Louis made one more blurred move and the flesh on Ettore's left cheek split downward in the same direction as his nose, and he fell forward.

EIGHT years later, in Belgium, I saw another such face. A young man I knew was killed by a bomb. When I looked down at him, lying there on his back on the frozen ground, his face was also split open, and life had so newly left him that a small, steady breath of steam was still rising from the split into the damp, cold air. A long time later, thinking about that, I remembered Ettore.

---

## CARTOON

## O'BRIAN

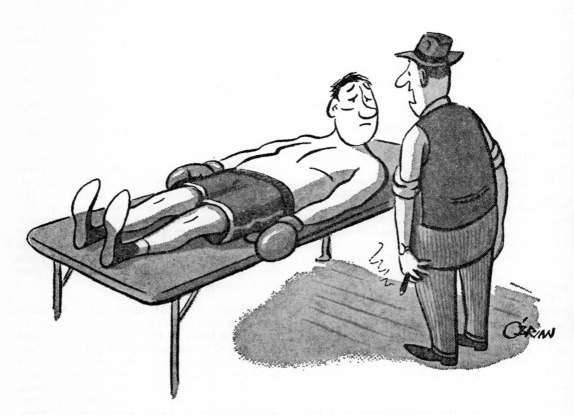

*"What do you mean, 'Who won?' How many people do you think were in it?"*

© 1958, The New Yorker Magazine, Inc. Reproduced by permission.

THIS IS THE first fight story. During the last year of the siege of Troy, and at the funeral games of Patroclus, the fight followed the chariot race and preceded the wrestling and the running. Achilles was the promoter, Epëus the "attraction" and Euryalus the "opponent." Tydides was the well-meaning "amateur" who overmatched his boy.

FROM THE

# Iliad

## HOMER

[TRANSLATED BY ALEXANDER POPE]

The prizes next are order'd to the field,
For the bold champions who the caestus wield.
A stately mule, as yet by toils unbroke,
Of six years' age, unconscious of the yoke,
Is to the circus led, and firmly bound;
Next stands a goblet, massy, large, and round.
Achilles rising, thus: "Let Greece excite
Two heroes equal to this hardy fight;
Who dare the foe with lifted arms provoke,
And rush beneath the long-descending stroke.
On whom Apollo shall the palm bestow,
And whom the Greeks supreme by conquest know,
This mule his dauntless labours shall repay,
The vanquish'd bear the massy bowl away."
   This dreadful combat great Epëus chose;
High o'er the crowd, enormous bulk! he rose,
And seized the beast, and thus began to say:
"Stand forth some man, to bear the bowl away!
(Price of his ruin:) for who dares deny
This mule my right; the undoubted victor I?
Others, 'tis own'd, in fields of battle shine,
But the first honours of this fight are mine;
For who excels in all? Then let my foe
Draw near, but first his certain fortune know;
Secure this hand shall his whole frame confound,
Mash all his bones, and all his body pound:
So let his friends be nigh, a needful train,
To heave the batter'd carcase off the plain."
   The giant spoke; and in a stupid gaze
The host beheld him, silent with amaze!
'Twas thou, Euryalus! who durst aspire

203

To meet his might, and emulate thy sire,
The great Mecistheus; who in days of yore
In Theban games the noblest trophy bore,
(The games ordain'd dead Oedipus to grace,)
And singly vanquish'd the Cadmean race.
Him great Tydides urges to contend,
Warm with the hopes of conquest for his friend;
Officious with the cincture girds him round;
And to his wrist the gloves of death are bound.
Amid the circle now each champion stands,
And poises high in air his iron hands;
With clashing gauntlets now they fiercely close,
Their crackling jaws re-echo to the blows,
And painful sweat from all their members flows.
At length Epëus dealt a weighty blow
Full on the cheek of his unwary foe;
Beneath that ponderous arm's resistless sway
Down dropp'd he, nerveless, and extended lay.
As a large fish, when winds and waters roar,
By some huge billow dash'd against the shore,
Lies panting; not less batter'd with his wound,
The bleeding hero pants upon the ground.
To rear his fallen foe, the victor lends,
Scornful, his hand; and gives him to his friends;
Whose arms support him, reeling through the throng,
And dragging his disabled legs along;
Nodding, his head hangs down his shoulder o'er;
His mouth and nostrils pour the clotted gore;
Wrapp'd round in mists he lies, and lost to thought;
His friends receive the bowl, too dearly bought.

"*Knocked Out*"

*Winston S. Churchill*
*1. 92*

Sir Winston Churchill was 17 when he depicted Peter Jackson's knockout of Frank Slavin at the National Sporting Club, now a fruit warehouse, in London on May 30, 1892. Churchill gave the drawing to the Harrow School tuckshop (candy shop) "in lieu of debts incurred," and forgot it until it turned up again in London in 1959. The bout is recalled by Budd Schulberg's bartender on page 338. (*Pictorial Parade*)

THE JAB THAT MADE JIM CORBETT FAMOUS.

THE PERSISTENT BODY HOOK WITH WHICH BATTLING NELSON WORE JOE GANS DOWN AND KNOCKED HIM OUT.

## THE ILLUSTRATORS

Before the invention of the high-speed camera the boxing fan was dependent upon the eye and hand of the sporting illustrator. Bob Edgren was a University of California hammer thrower and sparring partner of Jim Corbett, had an excellent "eye" for fights and fighters and became a sports writer, illustrator and the sports editor of the New York *Evening World*. (*Courtesy of Arthur "Bugs" Baer*)

GANS, WAITING FOR A LEAD.

CORBETT BEATING DOWN
JOHN L. SULLIVAN.

FITZSIMMONS KNOCKED OUT SCORES OF MEN
WITH THE "SOLAR PLEXUS PUNCH" BEFORE HE
MADE THE BLOW FAMOUS AT CARSON.

R. Edgren.

JOE GANS GREAT PUNCH
WAS A RIGHT, SHOT ACROSS
AFTER BLOCKING A LEAD.

# TAD DOES A BIT ON JACK JOHNSON

This picture was drawn by Tad at Johnson's quarters in San Francisco and forwarded by special delivery mail. The latest news on the fight situation in Reno, also by Tad, is on this page.

T. A. (Tad) Dorgan grew up in the San Francisco neighborhood of Jimmy Britt and Frankie Neil and became a southpaw sports writer and cartoonist following an injury to his right arm. He drew Jack Johnson, in training for Jim Jeffries, for the New York *Evening Journal* of June 22, 1910.

Henry Armstrong won the featherweight, welterweight and lightweight crowns, in that order, was the only man ever to hold three world titles at the same time and introduced "simultaneously" into the lexicon of the fight game. Willard Mullin, who drew this for the New York *World Telegram,* is the best of the sports cartoonists of the middle third of this century and one of the all-time greats.

HENRY ARMSTRONG—
**LITTLE PERPETUAL MOTION—**
GOES THROUGH HIS PACES
IN PREPARATION FOR HIS
WELTERWEIGHT CHAMPIONSHIP
FIGHT WITH BARNEY ROSS—

"All the News That's Fit to Print."

# The New York Times.

VOL. LXXVI....No. 25,080.   * * * *   NEW YORK, FRIDAY, SEPTEMBER 24, 1926.   TWO CENTS In Greater | THREE CENTS | FOUR CENTS
New York | Within 200 Miles | Elsewhere in the U.S.

## THE WEATHER

Showers today and tonight, followed by clearing and cooler tomorrow.
Temperature yesterday—Max. 70, min. 62.
For weather report see Page 46.

# TUNNEY WINS CHAMPIONSHIP, BEATS DEMPSEY IN 10 ROUNDS; OUTFIGHTS RIVAL ALL THE WAY, DECISION NEVER IN DOUBT; 135,000 PAY MORE THAN $2,000,000 TO SEE BOUT IN THE RAIN

## FLORIDA CONSCRIPTS ALL ITS UNEMPLOYED TO CLEAR WRECKAGE

### Police, Militia and Legion Round Up Men in Streets and Set Them to Work.

### CALL ISSUED FOR LABORERS

### Miami Wants 25,000 Men and Hollywood and Fort Lauderdale 2,000 Each.

### LOSS PUT AT $165,000,000

### Known Dead Now 365, With 1,100 Injured, 500 Seriously—Fight on Disease Goes On.

By WARREN IRVIN,
Staff Correspondent of The New York Times.

MIAMI, Fla., Sept. 23.—Conscription of all unemployed persons to aid in the work of clearing away wreckage and to speed the work of rehabilitating the Florida storm-swept area was adopted everywhere in that area today. Militiamen and police, aided by American Legion who have been specially deputized, patrolled all streets and highways, apprehending all persons who could not show that they were employed and putting them immediately to work.

At the same time the city of Miami sent out a call for 25,000 laborers, and officials of Hollywood and Fort Lauderdale announced that they would employ 2,000 laborers in each city.

Mayor E. G. Sewell of Miami predicted that within sixty days every trace of the storm's ravages will have been removed from Miami and the city will be as pros-

## North Carolinians Weave Homespun Suit for Walker

North Carolina mountaineers, reputed by novelists to be a hard-drinking and generally rough lot, are now knitting peacefully in their hillside homes spinning a new suit for Mayor Walker.

The addition to the Mayor's wardrobe will be made of gray homespun and will be presented to him by citizens of Asheville, who arrive on the "Land of the Sky" special train on Oct. 6 on a boosting tour. The color will be gray—chosen by the Mayor himself.

When the delegation reaches the city it will go directly to the City Hall, where, with appropriate ceremony, the suit will be presented.

Copyright, 1926, by The New York Times Company.

## GENEVA CONFERENCE ADOPTS COURT PLAN

### Right of Powers to Withdraw Approval of American Reservations Is Recommended.

### NEW PROTOCOL NEXT STEP

### United States Will Be Invited to Help Draft It—President's Action in Doubt

Special to The New York Times. By Wireless to The New York Times.
GENEVA, Sept. 23.—With a single modification, the conference of signatories of the statute of the Permanent Court of International Justice adopted unanimously the conclusions concerning the American reservations which were presented this morning by the committee.

These conclusions were incorporated in a formal act of the conference, which was submitted for signatures.

## CROWD ARRIVES SMOOTHLY

### Throngs Ushered Into Philadelphia Stadium Without Confusion.

### MANY NOTABLES ATTEND

### Governors of Six States and Mayor Walker Among Long List of Officials.

### OVER 75,000 FROM HERE

### Trains Alone Carry That Number and Others Make the Trip by Automobile.

Special to The New York Times.
PHILADELPHIA, Sept. 23.—One hundred and thirty-five thousand persons, the largest crowd which ever attended a sports event in America, let out a roar when the referee placed the heavyweight crown on the head of Gene Tunney, which must have made the old Liberty Bell at Independence Hall quiver once more.

As the battle began and the heavyweights set to exchanging their jarring blows which rang with a "plop" audible to most of us at the ringside, followed it with a roaring enthusiasm that only the greatest prize-fight crowd in history could produce.

Shortly before the main bout it was announced that the stadium had been completely sold out, breaking both attendance and receipt records. The paid admissions exceeded 130,000 and the gate receipts were over the two-million mark.

In addition to the paid admissions there were unpaid admissions amounting to $30,000 money value. Tex Rickard announced that he had purposely underestimated the crowd in order not to discourage possible last-

## Dempsey's Share $850,000; Tunney to Receive $200,000

Special to The New York Times.
PHILADELPHIA, Sept. 23.—The receipts of the Dempsey-Tunney fight tonight were in excess of $2,000,000. On the basis of $2,000,000, the receipts were divided as follows:

| | |
|---|---|
| Dempsey | $850,000 |
| Tunney | $200,000 |
| Federal Tax | $200,000 |
| State | $100,000 |
| Sesquicentennial | $40,000 |
| Preliminary fights | $40,000 |
| Tex Rickard, promoter | $410,000 |

## TUNNEY ALWAYS MASTER

### Challenger Bewilders His Opponent With His Speed, Accuracy.

### AGGRESSIVE IN ALL ROUNDS

### Sends Rain of Whiplike Lefts Which Champion Cannot Avoid.

### OUTCOME IS A SURPRISE

### Dempsey Lacks All Evidence of His Old Aggressiveness—Victor Is Acclaimed.

By JAMES P. DAWSON.
Special to The New York Times.
RINGSIDE, SESQUICENTENNIAL STADIUM, Philadelphia, Sept. 23.—Gene Tunney is the new world's heavyweight champion. The ex-marine fought like a man-killer tonight in the Sesquicentennial Stadium, when he carried off the decision over Jack Dempsey, once known as the Manassa Mauler and the ring's man-killer, in a ten-round bout which saw the first heavyweight champion lose the championship title on a decision.

Through every round of the ten, Tunney battered and pounded Dempsey. He rained rights on the tottering champion's jaw and he bewildered Dempsey with his speed and the accuracy of a whip-like left hand which Dempsey could not evade. When the decision was announced, the crowd let loose a roar of acclaim for "the man killer," who had conquered the ring's man-killer, and a roar echoing back from the lusty throats of the Pennsylvania State Boxing Commission.

### Confidence Aids Tunney.

The transfer of the title, the ascension of Tunney to the pinnacle last-

## AIRPLANE CARRIES TUNNEY TO SCENE

### Challenger Is First to Make Way to Heavyweight Title Bout Through Air.

### RISK DEPLORED BY MANY

### Tunney, However, Is Calm Throughout—Calls Flying Least Trying on Nerves.

Special to The New York Times.
PHILADELPHIA, Sept. 23.—Not content with the prospect of facing Dempsey and destiny, Gene Tunney had to defy death by flying above the silvery course of the Delaware River, winding through the Pocono Mountains, and landed at the navy yard in plenty of time to weigh in before the scheduled bout.

Gene traveled in a red Curtiss Oriole plan, piloted by the expert hands of

## VICTORY IS POPULAR ONE

### Ex-Marine Gets Ovation as He Enters Ring—Crowd 'Boos' Foe.

### BIGGEST IN SPORT HISTORY

### Rickard's Luck Turns, However, and Distinguished Gathering Is Thoroughly Drenched.

### DEMPSEY'S NOSE SUFFERS

### Rebuilt for Movies, It Is Target of Challenger as He Piles Up Points for Victory.

By ELMER DAVIS.
Special to The New York Times.
RINGSIDE, SESQUICENTENNIAL STADIUM, PHILADELPHIA, Sept. 23.—While the rain poured down on the greatest crowd that ever saw a sporting event, Gene Tunney beat Jack Dempsey, and won the world's heavyweight championship in a ten-round fight here tonight.

The champion, in the phrase of one of the ringside critics, lost his title by a synthetic nose. It was by steady pounding away at the built-in beak which Dempsey acquired a couple of years ago that Tunney piled up a heavy lead on points in the early rounds.

Dempsey rallied toward the middle of the bout, but his effort to come back in a last round finish failed. The ex-marine, against whom the experts were betting three and four to one this afternoon, walked off with the title.

### Crowd is With Tunney.

It was the first time in history that the heavyweight championship of the

## GENE TUNNEY, THE NEW CHAMPION

Times Wide World Photo.

## Champion Tunney Praises the Loser; "I Have No Alibis," Asserts Dempsey

Special to The New York Times.
SESQUICENTENNIAL STADIUM, PHILADELPHIA, Sept. 23.—

## Story of the Fight by Rounds

*Special to* The New York Times.

RINGSIDE, SESQUICENTENNIAL STADIUM, PHILADELPHIA, Sept. 23.—The round by round detail of the Tunney-Dempsey bout fought here tonight follows:

**First Round.**

Dempsey was attired in blue trunks and Tunney in purple. Dempsey looked rather thin as he stepped forward for a consultation.

As the round started Dempsey, with a scowl on his face, rushed out and drove Tunney to his own corner. Dempsey again rushed. Jack sent a terrific left to the jaw. Dempsey kept rushing in and drove Tunney into his own corner. Dempsey went in and Tunney swung a hard right to Dempsey's chin. Tunney weaved in again and sent a heavy right to the chin. Dempsey showered left and right swings to Dempsey's jaw and then Tunney showered lefts and rights to the jaw. They boxed in the centre of the ring for a moment, then Tunney missed a right for the head but ripped two rights to the body. Dempsey jabbed Tunney away, in midring. As they neared the champion's corner Tunney shot a good right to Jack's jaw. Tunney jumped away and sparred cleverly, but Dempsey rushed in again and sent a heavy right to the body and drove Tunney to his corner. Jack drove Gene to a neutral corner and sent two lefts to Jack's head. They wrestled across the ring, Dempsey pounding Gene's ribs, and then sent right and lefts to the

**Second Round.**

Dempsey rushed over to Tunney's corner trying to tie up his man. Dempsey swung his right to the jaw, but Tunney got out of the way. They stepped out in the middle of the ring and Tunney swung right and left, landing a right to the body and drove Tunney to his corner. Jack drove Gene with a right to the body, but still weave in, trying to land a heavy body blow. Dempsey missed a left to the head and then landed a left, but swung a heavy right to Jack's jaw. Dempsey's eye was in bad shape and

**Third Round.**

Dempsey came out slowly for the third and they fought in the middle of the ring. Jack tried a terrific right for the jaw but missed. Gene stood up straight and jabbed lefts and rights to Jack's jaw. Gene put over a heavy right to the head and wrestled Jack back to the ropes with rights and lefts to the jaw. Tunney sent another left to the head but Jack punched him heavily to the body in return. As Jack came in Tunney ripped lefts and rights to the body at the bell.

**Fourth Round.**

Dempsey came out with a terrific rush and with a wild right sent Tunney almost over the ropes. Dempsey was in bad shape, but he continued to jab Jack away with a left. Jack's eye was cut with one of these lefts. Dempsey continued to weave in, trying to land a heavy body

*Continued on Page Two.*

211

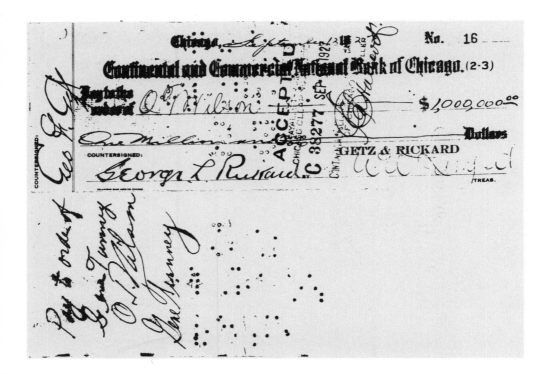

## TOP PAY

The highest fee ever paid for a single performance in any field was received by heavyweight champion Gene Tunney for thirty minutes of strenuous but successful boxing with Jack Dempsey in Chicago on the night of September 22, 1927. Tunney's share of the $2,658,660 gate came to $990,445, so in return for the check for $1,000,000, Tunney gave promoter Tex Rickard a check for $9,555 —not $10,000, as he states in his letter identifying the parties to the payment. (*Courtesy of Gene Tunney.*)

## The McCandless Corporation

52 VANDERBILT AVENUE
NEW YORK 17, NEW YORK

OFFICE OF
CHAIRMAN OF THE BOARD

May 27, 1959

TELEPHONE
MURRAY HILL 9-7820

Mr. W. C. Heinz
Deepwood Road
Stamford, Conn.

Dear Mr. Heinz:

I have your letter of the 19th on my return from Europe.

George F. Getz was a very distinguished Chicago business man. Rickard could not promote the fight since he had no license to promote a fight in Illinois; hence his using Mr. Getz as the official promoter. As a matter of fact a group of six of Chicago's leading businessmen formed a citizens' committee for the promotion of the fight; George F. Getz was chairman of that committee. Actually, Rickard was the promoter.

As to who O. T. Wilson was, the only thing I know about him is that he was with a banking firm in which Madison Square Garden had an account. I gave Tex Rickard a check in the amount of ten thousand dollars and he gave me, through one of the Madison Square trustees, Mr. O. T. Wilson, a check for a million. We just passed checks. I never saw O. T. Wilson after that and have no idea if he is dead or alive though, I presume, the former.

With every good wish,

Sincerely,

Gene

Gene Tunney

S

212

PHELEM-GHE-MADONE was the predecessor of all those large and
lethargic heavyweights. He was, Victor Hugo wrote in 1869, "all
surface more than anything else, and seemed to enter boxing-matches
rather to receive than to give." Had Lady Josiana been French instead
of English she would have been the Madame Defarge of *la boxe*.

FROM

# The Man Who Laughs

## VICTOR HUGO

[TRANSLATED BY ISABEL F. HAPGOOD]

THE FINEST boxing-matches then took place at
Lambeth, a parish where the Lord Archbishop
of Canterbury has a palace—although the air
there is unhealthy—and a rich library which is
open at certain hours to respectable people. Once,
it was in the winter, there took place there, in
a field which was closed with lock and key, a
match between two men, at which Josiana, es-
corted by David, was present. She had inquired:
"Are women admitted?" And David had replied:
*"Sunt feminae magnates."* Free translation: "Not
women of the middle class." Literal translation:
"Great ladies are." A duchess enters everywhere.
That is why Lady Josiana saw the boxing-
match.

Lady Josiana merely made the concession of
dressing like a cavalier, a thing much practiced
then. Women never travelled otherwise. Out of
six persons which the Windsor coach held, it
was rare that there were not one or two women
in male attire. It was a sign of belonging to the
gentry.

Lord David, being in the company of a
woman, could not take part in the match, and
was obliged to remain a simple spectator.

Lady Josiana only betrayed her quality by
looking through an opera glass, which was the
act of a gentleman.

The "noble encounter" was presided over by
Lord Germaine, great grandfather or grand uncle

of that Lord Germaine who, towards the end
of the eighteenth century, was colonel, took to
his heels in battle, was afterwards minister of
war, and escaped the carbines of the enemy only
to fall under the sarcasms of Sheridan, a worse
sort of shot. Many gentlemen laid bets: Harry
Bellew, of Carleton, who had claims on the ex-
tinct peerage of Bella-Aqua, against Henry, Lord
Hyde, member of Parliament for the borough of
Dunhivid, which is also called Launceston; the
Honorable Peregrine Bertie, member for the borough of Truro, against Sir Thomas Colpepper,
member for Maidstone; the Laird of Lamyrbau,
which is on the borders of Lothian, against
Samuel Trefusis, of the borough of Penryn; Sir
Bartholomew Gracedieu, of the borough of Saint-
Ives, against the very Honorable Charles Bod-
ville, who is called Lord Robartes, and who is
Custos Rotulorum of the county of Cornwall;
and others.

The two boxers were an Irishman from Tip-
perary, called from the name of his native mountain, Phelem-ghe-Madone, and a Scotchman
named Helmsgail. This placed two national prides
face to face. Ireland and Scotland were about to
fight; Erin was going to deal blows to Gajothel.
Hence the bets exceeded forty thousand guineas,
without counting the stakes.

The two champions were naked, with very
short breeches, buckled round their hips, and

shoes with hobnailed soles, laced round their ankles.

Helmsgail, the Scotchman, was a little fellow, barely nineteen years of age, but he had his forehead already stitched up; that is why they laid two and a third to one on him. A month previously, he had smashed in a rib and put out the eyes of the boxer Sixmileswater, which explains the enthusiasm.

There had been a gain for those who had bet on him of twelve thousand pounds sterling. In addition to his scarred brow, Helmsgail's jaw was minus some of its teeth. He was alert and quick. He was about the height of a small woman, squat, thickset, of a low and menacing stature, and none of the materials of which he was made had been wasted; not a muscle which did not answer the end—pugilism. There was compactness in his firm torso, as brown and shining as bronze. He smiled, and the three teeth which he lacked added to his smile.

His adversary was large and overgrown, that is to say, weak.

He was a man of forty. He was six feet high, with the chest of a hippopotamus, and a gentle air. The blow of his fist could split the deck of a ship, but he did not know how to deliver it. The Irishman, Phelem-ghe-Madone, was all surface more than anything else, and seemed to enter boxing-matches rather to receive than to give. Only, one felt that he would last a long time. A sort of underdone beef, difficult to chew, and impossible to swallow. He was what is called in local slang "raw flesh." He squinted. He seemed resigned.

These two men had passed the preceding night side by side in the same bed, and had slept together. They had each drunk three fingers of port wine from the same glass.

Each had his group of supporters, people rude of aspect, threatening the umpires at need. In the group for Helmsgail, John Gromane was to be seen, famous for carrying an ox upon his back, and a certain John Bray, who had one day taken upon his shoulders ten bushels of flour, of fifteen gallons to the bushel, plus the miller, and with this burden had walked more than two hundred paces. On the side of Phelem-ghe-Madone, Lord Hyde had brought from Launceston a certain Kilter, who lived at Green Castle, and could throw over his shoulder a stone weighing twenty pounds, higher than the highest tower of the castle. These three men, Kilter, Bray and Gromane, were from Cornwall, which does honor to the county.

The other supporters were brutal fellows, with solid backs, bow legs, big, knotty fists, clumsy faces, in rags, and fearing nothing, being almost all returned convicts. Many of them understood admirably how to render the members of the police force drunk. Each profession must have its talent.

The field chosen was further away than the Bear Garden, where bears, bulls, and dogs had been made to fight in former days, beyond the last buildings in process of construction, beside the edifice of the priory of Saint Mary Overy, ruined by Henry VIII. North wind and hoar frost was the weather; a fine rain was falling, quickly congealed into sleet. Among the gentlemen present some were to be recognized as fathers of families, because they opened their umbrellas.

On the side of Phelem-ghe-Madone, Colonel Moncreif, umpire, and Kilter, to lend him a knee. On the side of Helmsgail, the honorable Pughe Beaumaris, umpire, and Lord Desertum, from Kilcarry, to lend his knee.

The two boxers stood motionless for a few moments in the enclosure while the watches were compared. Then they walked up to each other and shook hands.

Phelem-ghe-Madone said to Helmsgail: "I should like to go home."

Helmsgail replied, honestly, "The gentry must have something, after putting themselves out."

In their naked condition they were cold. Phelem-ghe-Madone shivered. His jaws chattered. Doctor Eleanor Sharpe, nephew to the Archbishop of York, cried to them, "Tap each other, you knaves. That will warm you up."

These kindly words thawed them. They attacked each other.

But neither of them was angry. They had three feeble rounds. The Reverend Doctor Gumdraith, one of the forty Fellows of All Souls' College, shouted, "Pour some gin into them."

But the two referees and the two seconds, all four judges, adhered to the rule. It was very cold, however.

The cry was heard, "First blood!" They were soon replaced face to face with each other.

They looked at each other, approached, stretched out their arms, touched fists, then retreated. All at once Helmsgail, the little man, gave a bound. The real combat began.

Phelem-ghe-Madone was struck full in the forehead between his eyes. His whole face dripped with blood. The crowd shouted, "Helmsgail has tapped his claret!" They applauded. Phelem-ghe-Madone, whirling his arms as a windmill whirls its sails, began to throw his fists about at haphazard.

The honorable Peregrine Bertie said, "Blinded, but not yet blind."

Then Helmsgail heard this encouragement burst forth on all sides—"Bung his peepers!"

In short, the two champions were really well chosen, and although the weather was not very favorable, it was understood that the match would prove a success. The quasi-giant, Phelem-ghe-Madone, had the inconveniences of his advantages, he moved heavily. His arms were clubs, but his body was a mass. The little man ran, struck, leaped, gnashed his teeth, redoubled vigor by swiftness, knew ruses. On one side was the primitive, savage, uncultivated blow with the fist, in a state of ignorance; on the other, the blow of civilization. Helmsgail fought as much with his nerves as with his muscles, and as much with his malice as with his strength; Phelem-ghe-Madone was a sort of inert slaughterer, somewhat slaughtered himself, as a preliminary. It was art against nature. It was the ferocious man against the barbarian.

It was clear that the barbarian would be beaten. But not very soon. Hence the interest. A small man against a large man. The chances in favor of the small man. A cat gets the better of a dog. The Goliaths have always been vanquished by Davids.

A hail of shouts fell upon the combatants—"Bravo, Helmsgail! Good! Well done, highlander! Now, Phelem!"

And Helmsgail's friends kindly repeated to him the exhortation: "Bung his peepers!"

Helmsgail did better. Suddenly ducking and rising again with the undulation of a reptile, he struck Phelem-ghe-Madone on the breast bone. The Colossus tottered.

"Foul blow!" cried Viscount Barnard.

Phelem-ghe-Madone sank back on Kilter's knee saying: "I am beginning to get warmed up."

Lord Desertum consulted the referees, and said: "There will be a suspension of five minutes."

Phelem-ghe-Madone was weakening. Kilter wiped the blood from his eyes, and the sweat from his body with a piece of flannel, and put the neck of the bottle to his mouth. They had reached the eleventh round. Phelem-ghe-Madone, besides the wound on his forehead, had his pectoral muscles disfigured with blows, his abdomen swollen, and his sinciput bruised. Helmsgail had sustained no injury.

A certain tumult arose among the gentlemen. Lord Barnard repeated, "Foul blow."

"Bets off," said the Laird of Lamyrbau.

"I recall my stake," chimed in Sir Thomas Colpepper.

And the honorable member for the borough of Saint Ives, Sir Bartholomew Gracedieu added, "Give me back my five hundred guineas, I'm off."

"Stop the fight," shouted the spectators.

But Phelem-ghe-Madone rose staggering almost like a drunken man, and said, "Let us continue the fight, on one condition—I am also to have the right to deal a foul blow."

On all sides arose the cry: "Agreed!"

Helmsgail shrugged his shoulders.

At five minutes past, the fight was resumed.

The combat, which was agony for Phelem-ghe-Madone, was play for Helmsgail. What a thing is science! the little man found means to put the big one in chancery, that is to say, Helmsgail suddenly took Phelem-ghe-Madone's big head under his left arm, curved like a crescent, and held it there under his armpit, with the neck bent, and the nape of the neck low, while with his right falling again and again, like a hammer upon a nail, but from below and underneath, he smashed the latter's face at his leisure. When Phelem-ghe-Madone, finally released, raised his head, he had no longer any face.

What had been nose, eyes, and mouth, appeared now only like a black sponge soaked in blood. He spat. Four teeth were seen on the ground. Then he fell, Kilter received him on his knee.

Helmsgail was hardly touched. He had a few insignificant bruises, and a scratch on one collarbone.

No one was cold any longer. They were laying sixteen and a quarter to one for Helmsgail against Phelem-ghe-Madone.

Harry Carleton shouted: "There's no longer a Phelem-ghe-Madone. I bet on Helmsgail my peerage of Bella-Aqua, and my title of Lord Bellew against the Archbishop of Canterbury's old wig."

"Give me your muzzle," said Kilter to Phelem-ghe-Madone, and thrusting his flannel into the bottle, he wiped him off with gin. His mouth became visible once more, and Phelem-ghe-Madone opened one eyelid. His temples seemed cracked.

"One round more, my friend," said Kilter. And he added, "For the honor of the low town."

The Welshman and the Irishman understand each other; but Phelem-ghe-Madone gave no sign which could indicate that he had any intelligence left.

Phelem-ghe-Madone rose, Kilter supporting him. It was the twenty-fifth round. By the way in which this Cyclops, for he had now but one eye, placed himself in position, all understood that the end had come, and no one entertained any doubt that he was lost. He placed his guard above his chin, the sign of a failing man. Helmsgail, hardly perspiring, exclaimed: "I bet on myself. A thousand to one."

Helmsgail raised his arm and struck, and, what was strange, both fell. A gay growl of content was heard.

It was Phelem-ghe-Madone who was content.

He had taken advantage of the terrible blow which Helmsgail had given him on the skull, to deal him a foul blow in the navel.

Helmsgail lay and rattled in his throat.

The spectators looked at Helmsgail as he lay on the ground and said: "Paid back."

Every one applauded, even those who had lost.

Phelem-ghe-Madone had returned a foul blow for a foul blow, and acted according to his right.

Helmsgail was carried off on a stretcher. The general opinion was that he would not recover. Lord Robartes exclaimed: "I win twelve hundred guineas." Phelem-ghe-Madone was crippled for life.

As they came out, Josiana took Lord David's arm, which is tolerated between the "engaged." She said to him, "It is very fine. But—"

"But what?"

"I should have thought it would have driven away my ennui. Well, it has not."

THIS IS COMPLETELY believable, and thus one of the best.

# Stop the Fight!

## NORMAN KATKOV

SHE HAD BEEN at him since early morning, and now, during supper, Gino Genovese played with the spaghetti on his plate as he sat at the kitchen table, facing his wife.

"I had enough prize fighters in my family," she said. "My husband was a prize fighter. Not my son. Not while I live; you hear me, Gino?"

"Anna, I told you a thousand times." He spoke quietly and he was very patient. "Young Gino won't fight after tonight. Take my word."

"He's a baby," she said, and Gino realized she hadn't heard him at all.

"He's eighteen, Anna; finished with high school. Young Gino is a man."

"No!" she shouted. She brought her hand down flat on the oilcloth covering the table. "He's not a man." Her voice rose. "He's not a man to me!"

Gino looked at the open window and grimaced. "Anna, please. The neighbors."

"The neighbors," she repeated dully, and pushed her hair back from her forehead. "Is there someone on Water Street who doesn't know my baby is a fighter?"

Some fighter, Gino thought. The kid had won the Golden Gloves and had six pro matches, so that made him a fighter already. He leaned over to close the window, and when he had settled back in his chair, he saw that his wife was staring at nothing, her elbow on the table and her hand to her cheek; her head moving back and forth, back and forth, as though she were in mourning.

"Anna," he said gently, and reached out to touch her. "The spaghetti will get cold, sweetheart," Gino said, but she didn't see him and at last he bent over his plate.

*I should have gone to work today instead of taking off,* he said to himself, thinking of Marin-kov and Stein and Annalora, and the rest of the Park Department crew of which he was foreman. *What good did I do her by staying home?* he thought, as he wound the spaghetti around his fork. *She's like the old women with the kerchiefs over their heads who sit in the sun on Clara Street. She's forty years old and she acts eighty years.*

"Why couldn't he sleep home?" Anna demanded. "Answer me that? My own son. What's the matter with his bed?" she asked, pointing toward Young Gino's room.

Gino sat motionless, the spaghetti trailing from his fork to the plate. "I told you, Anna, his manager wants him to rest. His manager says we would make him excited."

"His manager says," Anna replied. "Who is his manager—chief of police?"

"Anna, what do you want, sweetheart?" He dropped the fork and raised his hands over the plate. "Did I tell Young Gino to fight? Did I go see him fight in the Golden Gloves or since the Golden Gloves? When he came to me and wanted to turn pro, did I tell him yes? When he asked me to be his manager, did I say yes?" Gino reached for a glass of water. "So he went and got Len Farrell for a manager, what should I do then? Should I throw Young Gino out of the house, or turn him over and paddle him because he got my old manager?" He bent forward. "Listen to me, Anna, baby, Young Gino won't fight after tonight. It's the last time tonight."

"He didn't need the boxing gloves," Anna said.

Gino closed his eyes for a moment, and shook his head slowly. "That's five years ago, sweetheart."

"He didn't need them," she said.

Gino sucked in breath and bit his lip. He set the glass down on the table. "Your brother bought him the gloves, Anna."

"My brother, you, Len Farrell, you're all the same." She held the table with both hands, her hair now loose from the pins and falling in disarray about her neck and over her ears and down her cheeks. "You won't be satisfied until they make him a cripple. Then you'll be satisfied. True, Gino?"

And he got up from his chair and walked out of the kitchen. He went through the hall into the living room, and stood with his hands in his pockets, his knees against the cold radiator, looking out onto Water Street.

*I did the right thing,* he thought, as he felt the soft curtain brush against his face. *That Pete Wojick will give Young Gino a good licking, and then finish—the kid won't have a stomach for fighting after tonight, that's all.*

Gino had seen it happen enough times: a lad starting out; being overmatched; getting a beating that took the heart out of him for always. You had to bring a kid along very careful when he started, building up his confidence.

*All right,* Gino thought, and he grimaced again, *it's done with. At least I won't have to listen to her any more after tonight.* He remembered how Len Farrell had protested the match; he remembered pleading with his old manager, agreeing that Wojick was too seasoned for Young Gino, too tricky and wise, with a right hand that could strike like a poleax.

"I've got to stop him fighting, Len," Gino had said. "My wife—she's making me crazy. Let Wojick give him the deep six once and the kid will quit." Gino had gone one afternoon a month ago to the Rose Room Gym downtown to watch his son work out, standing far back among the spectators, so the boy wouldn't see him. "Young Gino's a boxer, a cutie. He won't like getting hurt, Len." He had gone on, talking and talking, until at last Farrell had agreed to make the match —eight rounds in the semifinal at the ball park tonight.

Gino heard Anna moving around in the kitchen, and suddenly, for no reason that he knew, turned away from the window, crossed the living room and went into his son's bedroom.

Gino touched the bed and smoothed the spread, and on the wall above the headboard saw the farm scene Young Gino had painted when he was seven. Anna had taken it to be framed. She had framed the Palmer Method penmanship certificate, and three months ago, in June, she had framed her son's high-school diploma, hanging it there on the wall behind Young Gino's bed.

He turned away and took a step toward the chest of drawers standing at an angle beyond the windows, and knew then why he had come into Young Gino's room. There was the big, double frame that Anna had not bought, which Young Gino had brought home, and in it, the two glossy pictures: the boy on the right and the father on the left.

The boy had dug out Gino's black silk trunks and boxing shoes, and gone to the same photographer across the street from the Rose Room who, twenty years earlier, had taken the father's picture. He had posed the same: right hand high on the bare chest, and left extended; head cocked and shoulders forward.

Standing before the chest of drawers, Gino could see no difference between them, and then noticed the boy's shoulders, sloping more than his father's, and the really enormously big arms for a welterweight.

"I never weighed more than one forty-three," Gino said aloud, and remembered when he had quit. He had finished with fighting one night two blocks from here on the porch of Anna's father's house. She had said she would never see him if he fought again. He'd had thirty fights then, and Len Farrell was ready to take him to Chicago. First to Chicago, and then New York, if he was good enough. That night Gino had asked Anna to marry him.

He remembered, all right, because he had gone into Anna's house and telephoned Len Farrell to tell the manager he was finished.

"No big loss," Gino said aloud. "I wouldn't have been much; I had no punch," and heard Anna behind him; heard her breathing heavy.

"You're proud, Gino, aren't you? Your son is a fighter; you lived to see it," she said, but he would not turn. He didn't turn as he heard her cross the room, but held fast to the chest of drawers.

"You fooled me good, Gino," she said. "Used me for a real dummy, making him a fighter behind my back, lying behind my back," and she reached for the double frame and held it high over her head and flung it to the floor.

He heard the glass smash as he turned. He felt the frame hit his shoe, but didn't look down. He looked at her until her hands went to her cheeks, her lips trembling, the color leaving her face white, and her eyes wide, watching him.

But he said nothing. He went past her, out to the small back porch, taking his jacket off the hook as he pushed open the door and came down the steps. He got into the jacket as he stood beside the car parked in the driveway, and then slid in behind the wheel, turning the key, starting the motor, shifting gears in the old coupé and backing out into the street, his mind blank, not letting himself think as he turned up toward the boulevard leading to the downtown section.

He was driving into the sun, which hung low beyond the green dome of the cathedral on Dayton Avenue, and he squinted as he came into sight of the office buildings. Once he went through a red light, listening to the horns on either side of him. Once he stopped for a semaphore, waiting until long after the light had changed to green and a trailer truck behind him blasted its horn.

Gino came into Kellogg Circle and turned, driving down Washington Street to the bus depot and around it to the alley behind the Rose Room. He parked behind a supermarket and got out of the car, slamming the door behind him and walking out to Exchange Place. He never smoked, but now he went into a drugstore, bought a pack of cigarettes and lit one, inhaling too deeply and coughing as the unfamiliar smoke seared his throat and mouth. He held the cigarette awkwardly and walked toward the newsstand on Seventh Street, but saw Tots Todora, and Bubbling-Over Norris, and Joey Richards, all of them fight fans, and he didn't want to talk with them. He didn't want to see them. He had a feeling to see Young Gino.

He had a feeling to talk to his son or touch him. He remembered, as he walked faster, the years when Young Gino was growing up, sleeping in his own bedroom.

Gino would wake in the night and know—really know—that his son was not sleeping. Gino would get out of bed real slow and careful, not to disturb Anna. Walking in his bare feet, he would turn on the light in the hall, tiptoe into his son's room and stand beside his son's bed and watch him asleep. He would stand there for he never knew how long, looking down at his son, and always, before he left, he would move the covers around his son, and move the hair from his son's forehead, and bend forward to kiss Young Gino.

He never told Anna and he never told his son, and now, turning into the hotel lobby, he had the same feeling he had to see Young Gino. He walked past the room clerk to the house phones and asked for Len Farrell's room.

"Five-o-two, I'm ring . . . ging," the operator said, and in a moment Gino heard Farrell say hello.

"Len?" Gino said. "Gino. I'm downstairs."

"Hello, lieutenant," Farrell said.

"I want to come up, Len."

"Sure, lieutenant; I held out two tickets for you," Farrell said.

"Len, it's Gino. Where's the kid? I want to see the kid."

"I'll bring them down myself, lieutenant. A pleasure. For the police department, any time," Farrell said.

"Len. Len!"

"I'll be down right away," Farrell said, and hung up.

After a moment, Gino dropped the receiver on the cradle. He saw the room clerk watching him, and moved away from the row of telephones, out into the lobby.

He walked to the newsstand near the doors and bought a paper and was looking at the front page when Len Farrell appeared.

"You must be crazy," Len said.

"I'm crazy?" Gino folded the paper and pushed it under his arm. "What's the matter with you? Lieutenant. Police force."

Farrell shook his head. He was a tall thin man with slick black hair, combed straight back. "What if the kid had answered the phone?" he asked. "I've had him quiet all day, and all he'd need would be to talk to you. A good thing I can still think, which is more than you can do."

"How is he, Len?"

"He's fine."

"How does he feel?" Gino asked.

"Like a tiger. How do you expect him to feel? He thinks he can lick the world."

"Yeah."

"I must have been out of my mind to make this match," Farrell said.

"He'll get over it," Gino said.

"Sure," Farrell said. "You just keep telling yourself that."

"What else could I have done?" Gino asked.

Farrell shook his head and carefully buttoned his jacket. "Don't ask me. Don't bring me in this. You're the mastermind," Farrell said. "Wojick. If it was my way, I wouldn't let Young Gino near Wojick for a year."

"You told me that already. Give me a ticket, Len."

"Oh, no," Farrell said, and stepped back, but Gino took the manager's arm. He held the arm, his fingers bunching the coat sleeve, looking at Farrell until the older man reached into his pocket. "Let go of my arm," Farrell said.

"I want a ticket. If I don't get it from you, I buy one," Gino said. "I want to see that fight, Len."

Farrell took a long white envelope from his pocket. "You're not sitting ringside," he said.

"The kid might see you. I'll have enough trouble with him as it is."

"Fifteen rows back," Gino said. "I can't see good any more if I'm any farther away from the ring."

He took the ticket from Farrell and shoved it into his rear pants pocket. "Take care of him, Len," Gino said.

"Yes. Yes, I'll take care of him." Farrell slipped the flap into the envelope. He held the envelope to his lips like a child with a blade of grass, and he whistled softly. "He could have been a real good fighter, Gino. A real classy fighter."

"He'll live without it," Gino said, and didn't want to talk about the kid any more.

He said goodbye to Farrell and left the lobby, walking out into the early evening. The street lights were glowing, the sun was gone from the heavens and the sky was a dull orange, turning black. He went into a diner and ordered a sandwich and a glass of milk and ate it. That took twenty minutes. In the basement of the bus depot he had his shoes shined. That took ten minutes. He watched a Chicago-bound bus load and leave, and afterward found an empty bench and sat down in a corner of it. He squirmed around on the bench, sitting in one position for a moment and then changing to another, and a third, and a fourth, until at last he was bent forward, his legs uncrossed, his elbows on his knees and one hand massaging the other.

Gino heard the dispatcher announce the arrival of a Kansas City bus and got off the bench. "Get it over with," he said aloud, and left the depot, crossing the deserted Federal Building Plaza to the alley where he had left his car.

It was complete night now. Driving out to the ball park, Gino remembered the hours before his own fights. He had been very nervous always, and in the afternoon, when Farrell had put him to bed, Gino had never been able to sleep, but lay motionless, his eyes closed, trying not to think of the fight.

"I wasn't yellow," he said aloud as he came into Lexington Avenue, a mile from the ball park. It was his chief worry always—that the referee, or Farrell, or the sports writers, or those at ringside and those beyond, would think him without courage. Often he would fight with complete abandon, standing toe to toe with an opponent who could hit much harder, in a desperate need to convince everyone of his fearlessness.

He saw the lights of the ball park and drove slowly until a youth standing beside a crudely lettered sign gestured at him. Gino turned into the lad's back yard, converted into a parking lot for the night. He paid the boy and walked along the road until he was across the street from the dark walls of the ball park.

He wasn't going in at the main gate, so that he would have to pass the long refreshment counter behind home plate; he'd made up his mind to that. Gino could see them standing there now: Ernie Fliegel and a few of the Gibbons family; maybe My Sullivan and Billy Light, whom Gino had boxed once in Milwaukee. They would be on him about Young Gino, teasing and baiting him, and he didn't want any of it tonight. He'd had all he could take for one day.

Gino saw the open doors near right field and crossed Lexington Avenue, handing his ticket to the gateman and walking ahead quickly, turning away from the foul line as he neared the stands, crossing out onto the playing field.

The ring was set up on the pitcher's mound. As he crossed second base, Gino could see the permanent stands, spreading in a huge V from home plate. There were twenty rows of chairs around the ring. Gino stood well back from the last row, looking at a couple of inept heavyweights, moving awkwardly through four dull rounds.

Once, during the second four-rounder, an usher asked him if he wanted to sit down, but Gino shook his head. Once, during the six-round bout that followed, Gino saw Frankie Battaglia, who had boxed as a middleweight when he was fighting. Gino turned his back, waiting until he'd heard the bell sound for the end of a round before he looked back at the ring.

It came too soon. One second the ring was clear and Gino could see the cigarette smoke drifting toward the lights, and the next instant Pete Wojick was in the ring, manager and trainers around him.

"He's big. He's too big," Gino said, as Wojick's manager took the robe from the fighter's shoulders and the welterweight began moving about in the corner, punching short lefts and rights, hooks and jabs and uppercuts, into the night air.

The referee stood in a neutral corner, arms resting on the ropes. Across the ring, the announcer looked toward the visiting-team dugout from which the boxers entered the ball field. Gino saw the heads turning, the men standing up in front of their seats, and remembered it was a practice of Farrell's to keep the opponent waiting. He heard the murmurs of the impatient crowd, and saw his son come out of the dugout. Young Gino was wearing his father's old robe, which he had found in the trunk in the front closet. He came down the aisle toward the ring, his gloves pushed against each other and resting on his chest.

Gino lit a cigarette and held it in his hand. He saw Farrell step on the bottom rope and pull up on the middle one for Young Gino. He saw the boy come into the ring and stand absolutely still, arms at his sides, looking across at Wojick. He saw Farrell put his hand in under the robe and massage Young Gino's back, and then he heard the announcer who had come to the center of the ring:

". . . the fighting son of a fighting father, Young Gino Genovese!" as Gino moved to the aisle and bent almost double, hurrying to his seat in the fourteenth row, the cigarette dropping from his hand. He said, "Pardon me," and started moving down the row, holding the backs of the seats in front of him, saying, "Excuse," and "Sorry," until he dropped into the empty folding chair, hearing the bell and raising his head in the darkness to see the two fighters come toward the middle of the ring.

*Just let it be quick,* Gino said to himself, sitting with his hands in his lap, his legs tucked under the chair and his ankles crossed, as he watched the kid jab above Wojick's ear with his left hand.

*He fights like the picture he took,* Gino thought as he watched his son, boxing straight up and down in the classic manner, the left arm out, the right carried high on the chest, the head cocked just a little to one side and the feet far apart.

Wojick took two more lefts and came forward, hooking to the stomach and then to the kidneys as he closed with Young Gino, holding until the referee separated them. Wojick was shorter, carrying absolutely no weight in his legs, with the body of a middleweight.

Young Gino moved around him, jabbing all the time, holding the right on his chest and waiting. They regarded each other carefully for maybe forty-five seconds, circling each other, and then Wojick hooked hard to the stomach.

And again to the stomach, so that Young Gino went back a step and Wojick was on top of him. He came forward all in a rush, his head low, moving in and mauling with both hands, driving Young Gino into the ropes and holding him there. Wojick was in close now, so the kid couldn't punch at all, pushing his head in under Young Gino's chin. He used Young Gino's body as leverage, punching with both hands to the stomach and the kidneys and the stomach again, until at last the kid's arms came down for an instant and Wojick brought the right up and over.

But Young Gino had slipped out, taken a step to his left and moved clear and away from Wojick, out toward the middle of the ring, his stomach pink now from the pounding he'd taken.

Wojick came out to meet him, moving his arms as he shuffled forward, and Young Gino jabbed him. He hit Wojick six times running, long jabs that held the older fighter off balance, moving very carefully, keeping to the center of the ring.

He boxed beautifully, and as Wojick started to hook with his left, Young Gino came in, jabbing short and hard in a perfectly executed counterpunch and bringing the right hand over flush to Wojick's chin.

And Wojick went down as the entire ball park went up on its feet. Young Gino moved to a corner and Wojick took a six count. The referee wiped Wojick's gloves on his shirt, and Young Gino was there swinging. Wojick was in trouble, the legs still wobbly and his eyes glassy, but he had his arms up.

"Wait!" Gino yelled at his son. "Find him!" he yelled, but they were screaming in the ball park, wanting the knockout, and the kid was swinging and punching wildly, as Wojick kept his head down and his forearms covering his face and waited for the bell.

And lasted until the bell, as the crowd settled down slowly, almost one by one, and all around him Gino could hear them shouting at one another and grinning and talking about the kid and how great he was, except they hadn't seen what Gino had seen—that Wojick had not taken another punch, but had caught all the kid's blows on his arms and shoulders and gloves.

Near Gino somebody said, "How do you like that kid, Louie? A champ, isn't he?"

Somebody said, "The best since McLarnin."

And somebody said, "I seen the old man. The kid's better. The kid got the punch the old man never had," and in the darkness Gino rubbed one hand with the other and heard the bell and looked up at the ring.

Young Gino came out very fast, the water from the sponge glistening on his hair and shoulders. He went almost across the ring and jabbed twice and tried the right, missing with the right, as Gino cursed Farrell.

*That Farrell must be nuts,* he thought, *not telling the kid to wait.* He looked over at Young Gino's corner for Farrell, and heard the crowd suck in breath and turned quickly to the ring to see his son against the ropes.

"What happened?" Gino asked. He had the arm of the man next to him. "What happened?" he asked, watching Wojick follow his son around the ring.

"Wojick belted him a right hand," the man

next to him said, and Gino saw his son staggering.

He saw Wojick following Young Gino, fighting cautiously now, out of the crouch, the left arm no more than six inches from his chest and the right pulled back next to the stomach.

Young Gino tried to clinch, but Wojick stepped away and hooked. He hooked twice to the body and then to the head. In the fourteenth row Gino watched Wojick very carefully and saw him push his left foot forward. He saw him weave and he saw Wojick's left glove drop just a couple of inches as the right started down at the stomach and whistled in and caught Young Gino high in the face.

"Down," Gino whispered. "Go down, kid," he said. "Go down!" he said, as he felt the pain in his heart, and saw Wojick jab twice more and get set and drop his left glove again and bring the right hand in along Young Gino's jaw.

"It's over," Gino whispered. "At least, it's finished fast," but his son clinched. Held on and hooked his arms in Wojick's, gaining ten seconds' rest before the referee separated them.

Clinched again immediately, and Gino saw his son straighten up when they were split once more and saw him keep the left out, staying away from Wojick until just before the bell, when he took another right to the chin that spun him clear around so that he fell against the ropes, hanging there until the gong sounded and Farrell was in the ring to lead him to the corner.

The doctor came then. He went into the ring, and Gino whispered, "Stop it. Just stop it."

But the crowd yelled "No!" at the doctor. They yelled, "Let the kid alone!" and "He's okay, doc!" and, "That kid's tough!" until at last the doctor nodded to the referee and left the ring, while Farrell worked over Young Gino.

The kid got up at the ten-second buzzer. He pulled his arm free of Farrell and rose, standing away from the stool in the corner, his arms hanging, looking across at Wojick.

The crowd loved it. They loved it that Young Gino went across the ring to carry the fight to Wojick. They loved it when Young Gino landed a right to Wojick's heart that stopped the older fighter for a few seconds. They loved it that the kid was anxious, and all the time Gino watched Wojick and Wojick's left glove, waiting for it to drop until, after a minute of the round was gone, Young Gino missed with his right and was open.

Gino saw the left glove drop. He saw Wojick get set, the shoulders drooping, and he felt the right when it landed on his son's chin.

Gino waited for the kid to fall. He watched

Young Gino helpless. He saw his son get hit with a second right and a third, and while the boy staggered around the ring, refusing to fall, taking whatever Wojick could deliver, Gino said, "That's enough." He said, "That's all," and got out of his chair.

He heard them yelling "Sit down!" but he started pushing his way toward the aisle, bent forward, feeling the hands against him, as he was shoved from one man to the next until he was in the aisle at last, running toward the ring.

An usher reached for Gino, but missed him. A cop grabbed him, holding his arm, as Gino watched the ring and prayed for the bell, hearing the cop's voice, but not what the cop said, while the kid held on to Wojick, beaten and out on his feet, and nothing holding him up except heart.

"Let me alone," Gino said. "That's my kid," he said to the cop. "Ask Farrell," he said, pointing with his free arm. He turned toward the cop. "My kid," Gino said to the cop. "Let me in my kid's corner," he said, as the bell sounded and the cop released him.

Gino pulled at his jacket as he ran. He got the jacket off and dropped it there at the foot of the three steps leading to the ring, and then he was in the ring, kneeling before his son as Farrell worked on Young Gino.

"Don't talk," Gino warned. "Breathe deep and let it out slow. Wojick's left. It drops when he's going to use the right. The left drops maybe an inch when he shoots the right! You got that? Nod if you got that," and watched his son nod as he rubbed the boy's legs. "Stay away this round. It's only the fourth. Stay away and box him and watch the left. You're a winner, kid; you got that knockdown going for you. Watch the left and bring your right in over it. Remember," as the warning buzzer sounded, and Gino rose, putting his hand flat against his son's chest. "Now you rest, big shot. Rest and watch the left," and Young Gino smiled at him.

Gino felt the smile warming him. He felt the smile all through him, and reached out to brush the kid's hair away from the forehead, and then he had the stool as the bell sounded and Young Gino went out to the center of the ring.

Gino held the stool as he came down the steps. *Let him fight,* Gino decided. *If he wants it that much, let him do what he wants. She'll have to take it, that's all. I'll do what I can, be good and listen to her, but she'll have to get used to it.*

*Me, I'm her husband; she had a right to tell me to quit. Not the kid, she can't tell the kid what to do with his life;* and he turned to look at his son in the ring.

222

# HARPER'S WEEKLY, 1858

## THE PUGILISTIC REVIVAL

GLOVER (who, in consequence of the excitement about the coming prize-fight, can think of nothing but boxing). *"Gloves, Sir?—only pair left, Sir. Rather large, perhaps, but we shall have our assorted stock in next week!"*

MASTER OLIVER. *"Now, Governor, keep your stomach in and chest out and look out for your precious wind when I put in my left."*

Courtesy Culver Pictures, Inc.

THE FIRST OF these poems appeared in the sports column of the New York *Times* on the morning of June 19, 1936, the day of the first Max Schmeling–Joe Louis fight. The second appeared the next day, after Schmeling, an 8–1 underdog, knocked Louis out in the twelfth round. The third ran two years later, on the morning of the return bout, won by Louis in 2:04 of the first round.

# I Still Like Joe

## JOHN KIERAN

### I

They warn me of an ancient day
—I wouldn't know; I wasn't there—
When odds ran wild the other way,
And yet the Tortoise beat the Hare.
So Schmeling may, to my surprise,
Belt out Joe Louis with a blow.
I thank them for their warning wise.
I still like Joe.

They warn me that the Persian host,
In days that long are dead and gone,
Were 1 to 10 in book and boast
To beat the Greeks at Marathon
But sunset saw them on the lope
(Except their dead, who couldn't go).
So Schmeling, too, may cross the dope!
I still like Joe.

They warn me still, in rising wrath,
That little David, brave and bold,
Unplayed at 8 to 1 in Gath,
Came in to knock Goliath cold.
The moral is that Schmeling's fist
May lay the Shuffler very low.
But stubbornly I here insist
I still like Joe.

In final warning, full and fair,
Of what may come when clangs the bell,
They tell of Braddock and of Baer,
On which I do not choose to dwell.
Despite the record of romance
When gallant long shots stole the show
—And giving Schmeling every chance—
I still like Joe.

### II

Lately I wrote in what might be called verse,
Mixing my meter with banter,
Louis would ready Herr Max for the hearse;
Burial service instanter.
That, to be brief, was the theme of my song,
Those of you know who had read it.
Query and Answer: Was I wrong?
You said it!

Lightly I wrote that the Shuffler would bring
Maxie much damage and pain;
Lay him as flat as the floor of the ring;
I said it and said it again;
Stated it broadly and maybe too long,
Thinking I put it astutely.
Was I completely, astoundingly wrong?
Absolutely!

## III

They warned me of an ancient day
—Before the first Joe–Max affair—
When odds ran wild the other way,
And yet the Tortoise beat the Hare.
So Schmeling would—and were they wise!—
Beat Louis down. But even though
It happened right before my eyes,
I still like Joe.

They told me that the Persian host,
Who later ran to hell-an'-gone,
Were 1 to 10 in book and boast
To beat the Greeks at Marathon.
But sunset saw them on the lope,
As moonlight saw Joe Louis low.
Greeklike, Herr Schmeling crossed the dope.
I still like Joe.

They argued eke, in rising wrath,
That little David, brave and bold,
Unplayed at 8 to 1 in Gath,
Rose up to knock Goliath cold.
From this they judged—and were they right!—
But this is yet another night.
I still like Joe.

I've had due warning, loud and long,
Of what must come when clangs the bell,
And how again I will be wrong;
A state in which I often dwell;
Of how, once more, will Joe recline,
And how they'll shout: "We told you so!"
But here I lay it on the line:
I still like Joe.

SAM LANGFORD FOUGHT during that period when the art and science of boxing reached an all-time high, and met the best from lightweights through heavyweights. On January 10, 1944, Al Laney found him as he describes in the first of these two columns from the New York *Herald Tribune*. The second column appeared on Christmas Day, 1944, after Laney had conducted a campaign that resulted in the establishment of a $10,000 trust fund for Langford.

Langford died in Cambridge, Massachusetts, on January 12, 1956.

# Two Visits with Sam Langford

## AL LANEY

ABOUT TWO WEEKS ago we began a search through Harlem for Sam Langford, the old Boston Tar Baby. Inquiries up and down Lenox and Seventh Avenues in bars and grills, cigar stores, newsstands and drugstores failed to turn up a lead. Zoot-suited youths accosted on street corners invariably looked blank and asked, "Who he?" A dozen times we were told positively that Sam was dead.

This is the man competent critics said was the greatest fighter in ring history, the man the champions feared and would not fight, the man who was so good he never was given a chance to show how good he really was. You'd think he'd be a hero to every youth in Harlem.

Sam is not dead. We found him at last in a dingy hall bedroom on 139th Street. He was just sitting there on the edge of his bed listening to the radio. That is all there is for Sam to do now, for he is old and blind and penniless. The Negro woman who admitted us said Mr. Langford's room was the third door down a corridor so dark you had to feel your way. Sam stood up when we entered and fumbled for a string attached to a pale bulb in the ceiling. There was a look of surprise on his flat, broad face.

"You come to see me?" he asked with wonder in his low melodious voice. Sam has been sitting there in the dark for a long time and there have

been no visitors. It took him some time to understand that this was an interview and there would be a story in the paper.

"What you want to write about old Sam for?" he said. "He ain't no good any more. You ever see me fight?"

We lied to Sam, said we had and that he was the greatest we ever saw. That seemed to please him mightily and he laughed loud. Anyone who never saw Sam in the ring is bound to be surprised at his height. He is only 5 feet 6½ inches and yet at 165 pounds he brought down such giants as Jack Johnson, Harry Wills and the towering Fred Fulton. His short legs, long arms, great shoulders and wide girth give him a curiously gnomelike appearance. All of his 210 pounds now seems to be above the hips. But he is a gnome with a prodigiously broad flat nose, a cauliflower ear and an immense amiability.

Sam receives a few dollars a month from a foundation for the blind. It is not enough but he makes it do. His days are all alike. He rises early and two small boys lead him to a restaurant for breakfast. He is back in his room by one o'clock and then he just sits in the dark until late in the afternoon when he goes out to eat again.

This would seem to be a dreary existence, but Sam never was addicted to thinking or to brooding over his fate in the days when they told him he was lucky to get fights at all, and he does not brood now. We had been led to believe by what we had read that this stepchild of fistiana was a stupid man who had been plucked clean by the thieves and then thrown out to starve. A child of the jungle, they used to call him.

It was therefore a surprise to find that Sam is not stupid. He is even intelligent, though ignorant by the world's standards. He never went to school a day in his life and certainly he is a simple creature, almost childlike. His memory is good, he is an excellent mimic, and you would go far to find a more interesting storyteller.

And all the stories Sam tells are amusing ones. He will not be drawn into telling the other kind. He remembers them, but if you ask him about the old days when he was given the business by all and sundry he chuckles and tells another funny story. He laughs all the time he is talking and his laugh is so infectious, his face so expressive, you forget he is blind. When he tells his stories and laughs he seems almost a happy man. There is no drop of hate in his soul for anyone.

Sam said he was born March 4, 1886, in Weymouth, Nova Scotia, but that is just a date he thought up. He admits he doesn't know, and since he was fighting before 1900 he probably is in the middle sixties. He asked about his old friends among the boxing writers and said be sure to get in that he remembered them and sent his greetings. He said he didn't want anybody to feel sorry for him.

In a way Sam is right. His joviality and cheerfulness in adversity envelop you in sadness but he does not inspire pity. He has somehow achieved the feat of rising above it with simple dignity.

"Don't nobody need to feel sorry for old Sam," he said. "I had plenty good times. I been all over the world. I fought maybe three, four hundred fights and every one was a pleasure. If I just had me a little change in my pocket I'd get along fine."

"CHIEF," SAID SAM LANGFORD yesterday, "this gonna be the best Christmas I ever had. Maybe you could put it in the paper."

What Sam wanted was to convey to all his thousands of friends the fact that he is happy and that he understands quite well that it is they who have made it possible. He has a simple faith in the power of the press and he believes that if it is in the paper everyone will see it.

Sam's faith is justified. It is almost a year now since his story was told in this newspaper. At that time Sam was blind and penniless and hungry and he was very lonely indeed. Now he is a man fixed for life so that he never again will be hungry. His friends to the number of several thousand sent money for him, and this money, gathered into a fund, was used to take care of Sam modestly as long as he will live.

Many of these friends never have seen Sam. That is one of his remarkable qualities. You do not have to know him to be his friend and know the kind of man he is. But Sam's friends did not just contribute months ago and then forget that Christmas was coming. Sam wishes this column to acknowledge, besides greetings by mail, the following gifts:

A fine guitar, three boxes of cigars, two of which were purchased by GIs in post exchanges; a pair of gloves, a bottle of gin, several neckties, an anonymous gift of $5 with which he is to buy the best Christmas dinner he can find; a quantity of hard candy, of which someone remembered that he is immensely fond; and various other items good to eat at Christmastime.

All of these things Sam had around him last night. He had friends around him, too, and there will be friends with him today. A year ago Sam's total wealth was twenty cents. With it he bought a meager breakfast and then he sat the day out on the side of his bed, all alone. No one came to see him, for no one knew he was there. He had been a great man in his day, the famous Boston Tar Baby, the greatest fighter of them all, but now he was long since forgotten, believed by many to be dead.

But this is another Christmas Day. He is not alone any more, his dingy room is gay with Christmas decorations, and a candle burned in it last night. His belly will be stuffed with turkey and fixin's today and he will play his guitar and sing and he will laugh. To hear Sam laugh and sing is one of the most profound Christmas experiences a man can have.

He cannot see the decorations or the candle's light, but they make a very great difference to him. Sam is by no means a religious man in the conventional sense, but we were wondering last night how many men there are who understand so well as he the real meaning of Christmas.

Sam wants all of his friends to know that he is happy today and we would like them to know, too, that he is the most completely happy man we have ever seen. Not many are able to be completely happy. For most of us there always are reservations of one kind or another. But not for Sam. He is like a child in the enjoyment of his presents and the remembrance of his friends. He is celebrating Christmas in that spirit.

"You see that bottle, Chief?" he said last night.

"If you come back here on the Fourth of July it'll still be some in it. But tomorrow I'm gonna have myself a couple of good belts. Oil myself up some for a little geetar playin'. Boy! Listen to that thing talk. She shore talk sweet, don't she?

"You tell all my friends I'm the happiest man in New York City. I got a geetar and a bottle of gin and money in my pocket to buy Christmas dinner. No millionaire in the world got more than that, or anyhow they can't use any more. Tell my friends all about it and tell 'em I said God bless 'em."

---

## CARTOON

## AL JOHNS

*"Madison Square Garden—and step on it!"*

© 1954, Time Inc. Permission *Sports Illustrated.*

No one else has ever written as well of the backstage, nonathletic or under-the-table aspect of boxing as did John Lardner. It was his opinion that the art of the fight manager reached its zenith when Jack Kearns took Shelby, Montana, in 1923. As Kearns turned in the classic job, so did Lardner when he reconstructed it a quarter of a century later.

# Shelby, 1923

## JOHN LARDNER

JACK KEARNS, A boxing manager who became almost legendary in the prize-fight business between the two World Wars because of his ability to make money in large, bold scoops without recourse to manual labor, visited New York a while back with his current heavyweight fighter. The fighter, Joey Maxim, will not add luster to Kearns' name in history books. He is just a footnote sort of fighter—pedestrian, the critics say, and practically punchless. There was something like boredom in Kearns' voice as he sat on a desk in the offices of the Twentieth Century Sporting Club, in Madison Square Garden, shortly before Maxim's bout with the Swedish champion, Olle Tandberg, and delivered a routine hallelujah to his latest means of support. "This kid is better than Dempsey in most ways," said Kearns. His soft blue eyes stared vacantly at the floor. "He don't hit quite as hard as Dempsey, but otherwise he's better." Since Kearns managed Jack Dempsey when the latter was heavyweight champion of the world, it may be that he holds a lifetime dispensation from some celestial chamber of commerce to misuse Dempsey's name for advertising purposes. At any rate, no thunderbolt split the ceiling to strike him down for his blasphemous words. His audience, composed of managers, trainers, reporters, and press agents, shifted its feet and withheld comment. There was nothing to be said—nothing polite. Then one of the managers, an old-time boxing man, began to warm to the recollection of the team of Dempsey and Kearns. He turned the talk to happier times. "Remember Shelby, Doc?" he asked. (Kearns is known to his contemporaries as Doc.) "You and Dempsey broke three banks in Montana." Kearns' eyes came to life. "We broke four banks," he said. With rising enthusiasm, he went on to describe his withdrawal after the sack of Shelby, Montana, in 1923, with two bags of silver in a railroad caboose. His listeners drew closer. The career and prospects of Joey Maxim were, for the time being and without regrets, tabled.

To BOXING PEOPLE who have heard of the place, the memory of Shelby is precious for many reasons, one of them being that it brought a man of their own profession—namely, Kearns—into singlehanded combat with a state 146,997 square miles in area, producing copper, gold, silver, zinc, lead, manganese, oil, coal, grain, and livestock. No one who was involved in the Shelby affair, including Kearns and Dempsey, is any longer a perfectly reliable authority on the facts of the story, owing to the blurring influence of the autobiographical instinct on boxing memoirs. However, investigation shows that Kearns' performance compared favorably—for tenacity, at least—with those of the predatory railroad barons Jay Gould, Daniel Drew, Commodore Vanderbilt, and James J. Hill. As it happened, it was on Hill's Great Northern Railway, which opened up the north of Montana, in the eighteen-eighties, that Kearns rode into the state, with a fiery purpose, and out of it again, with great haste, in 1923. The scope of Kearns' raid has been exaggerated somewhat by his admirers, himself among them, but there is no doubt that it had a profound effect on no fewer than two Montana counties, Toole and Cascade. Furthermore, the name, spirit, and wealth of the whole state were invoked by those Montanans who struggled with Kearns first-hand. They stated more than once at the time that "the honor of all Montana" was at stake. Montana today is perhaps in a sounder financial condition than Kearns, but that only goes to show the extent of its natural resources. It took an oil strike to draw Kearns to Shelby, in Toole County, in the first place, and it took another oil strike, years later, to complete Toole County's recovery from Kearns.

The raider, who was born John L. McKernan, is now sixty-five years old. He is still a dapper figure when dressed for pleasure, but his hair is thin and a paunch shows at the conjunction of his pants and sweater when he climbs into the ring on business, as he did at the meeting of his man Maxim with Tandberg, in which Maxim won a close decision and both heavyweights disqualified themselves as white hopes for the championship by their gentle work. The bout netted Kearns and his fighter approximately fifteen hundred dollars. The loser, by the terms of an arrangement based on his drawing power, got fifteen thousand dollars. The bout between Dempsey and Tom Gibbons at Shelby on July 4, 1923, brought Kearns and Dempsey nearly three hundred thousand dollars. The loser got nothing whatever. In those days, though, Kearns was forty years old and at the height of his genius.

A good many people in 1923, including writers of newspaper editorials, likened Shelby after the fight to a Belgian village ravaged by the Huns. They ignored or overlooked the fact that Shelby, like no Belgian village on record, had opened the relationship by begging to be taken. Kearns and Dempsey had never heard of Shelby before its citizens went to the trouble of raising a hundred thousand dollars to entice them there. In the popular view, Dempsey was the archfiend of the episode. His reputation as a draft dodger in the First World War, carefully cultivated by managers of rival fighters like Fightin' Bob Martin, the A.E.F. heavyweight champion, made a strong impression on the public; during the Shelby crisis, people were quite willing to consider him a profiteer as well as a slacker. They lost sight of Kearns in Dempsey's shadow. It was only the men directly concerned with financing the Dempsey-Gibbons match who realized that Kearns was the brains and backbone of the visiting party. In language that will not bear repeating, these men marveled at Kearns' almost religious attachment to the principle of collecting all the cash in Montana that was not nailed down.

It was the booster spirit that got Shelby into trouble—the frontier booster spirit, which seems to have been a particularly red-blooded and chuckleheaded variety. Up to 1922, Shelby had been a village populated by four or five hundred cowhands, sheepherders, and dry-dirt farmers. In 1922, oil was struck in the Kevin-Sunburst field, just north of town. The population rose to over a thousand. It was not much of a jump; the significant difference was that all the new citizens had money. Some of them were oil speculators, some of them were real-estate men from the West Coast buying up land to sell to oil speculators. A few were merchants selling standard boomtown merchandise, much of it liquid, to the oilmen and the real-estate men. Kearns had not yet seen Shelby with his own eyes when he first tried to describe it to skeptics in the East a year later, but his description was not far wrong. "It's one of these wide-open towns," he said spaciously. "Red Dog Saloon, gambling hells—you know, like you see in the movies." It was old Blackfoot country. South of Shelby, the Marias River wound toward the site of a vanished fur-trading post on the Missouri. Not far north was the Canadian border. The Great Northern Railway ran west from Shelby to Glacier Park and the Pacific, east to Duluth and the Twin Cities, south a hundred miles to the nearest real town, Great Falls. In Shelby proper, there were the railroad depot, a few stores, a few houses, a couple of new banks, the Silver Grill Hotel, where fifty extra beds filled the lobby at the height of the boom, and half a dozen saloons.

In one of the saloons, on an evening in January 1923, a bunch of the boys, all of them leading citizens, were whooping it up in a civic-minded way. The party was headed by Mayor James A. Johnson, a large man of fifty-eight who had made a comfortable fortune ranching and had added to it in the boom through oil leases and the ownership of the First State Bank of Shelby. Sitting around him were men named Zimmerman, Sampson, Dwyer, and Schwartz. It was Sam Sampson, a storekeeper and landowner, who first suggested that the best way to make the nation and the world Shelby-conscious —that being the object of everyone in town who owned property—would be to stage a fight there for the heavyweight championship of the world. Dempsey was champion. The two most talked-of contenders for his title at that time were Harry Wills, a Negro, and Tom Gibbons, a white man from St. Paul. The barroom committee skipped lightly over Wills. Gibbons was its choice on two counts: the color of his pelt and the fact that he was a Northwestern man, from a state with which Montana had close commercial connections. The committee toasted Gibbons, Shelby, and itself. Then Sampson began to send telegrams in all directions. He wired Dempsey and Gibbons and their managers, and received no replies, which was not surprising, in view of Shelby's overwhelming anonymity. He also sent a telegram to Mike Collins, a journalist and boxing matchmaker in Minneapolis. Collins, a friend of Gibbons, agreed to come to Shelby at the committee's expense and study the possibilities. His reaction on stepping off the train at the Shelby depot was recorded by himself at a later date. "I was startled," he said. Shelby was small and raw beyond the power of a city man's imagination. Mayor Johnson and Sampson led Collins across a few rods of the Great Plains to a saloon, where the Mayor gave Collins the impression that Mose Zimmerman, another committeeman who owned land, was ready to finance the championship fight out of his own pocket. To substantiate this, the Mayor rounded up Zimmerman, who denied indignantly that he was ready to contribute anything but a small, decent, proportionate piece of the total. The Mayor looked sad. Collins walked back to the depot to catch the 8 P.M. train for Minneapolis. As things turned out, he was the first of a series of people who started to wash their hands of Shelby by catching a train. They were all called back at the last minute. A Fate straight out of Sophocles had matters in her grip.

Before the eight-o'clock train arrived, Mayor Johnson arranged a mass meeting of citizens in a saloon. Collins was persuaded to address it. He said starkly that Shelby had no boxing arena, no population, and, as far as he could see, no money. "You would need a hundred thousand dollars before you even talk to Dempsey and Gibbons," he added. At this point, Shelby startled him for the second time. The Mayor and his friends raised twenty-six thousand dollars on the spot, the contributors receiving vouchers for ringside tickets to the fight in exchange. Collins noted that the vouchers were marked July 4. The Phantom battle already had a date and a ticket sale. This show of *sang-froid* won him over. A short time afterward, he set out, in the company of a gentleman named Loy J. Molumby, state commander of the American Legion, to stump Montana for the balance of the money. Traveling from town to town in Molumby's private airplane, they brought the total of cash on hand to a hundred and ten thousand dollars in a little more than a week's time. The moment had come,

Collins freely admitted, to let Dempsey and Gibbons in on the secret. It was now, he said, just a matter of convincing them that there was such a place as Shelby and showing them the money.

The two things were achieved in reverse order. It was after seeing the money that Dempsey and Gibbons—or, rather, their managers, Kearns and Eddie Kane—brought themselves to believe in Shelby. The rest of the country, having seen no money, did not believe in Shelby for some time to come. At the beginning of May, the boxing critic of the New York *Tribune*, Jack Lawrence, spoke of a meeting that would take place soon at Madison Square Garden between the Dempsey and Gibbons parties. "There," he wrote scornfully, "they will probably hear a counter-proposition from the lips of Tex Rickard that will waft Shelby, Montana, back to the pastoral obscurity from which it emerged so suddenly."

Lawrence was wrong. Kearns and Kane bypassed New York and Rickard and went to Chicago to inspect the cash and negotiate the Shelby deal with Molumby and Collins, who were now the accredited agents of Mayor Johnson's town. It is apparent that both managers were remarkable for the grandeur of their vision. Kane showed it by agreeing to let Dempsey and Kearns have everything the bout drew, up to three hundred thousand dollars, at the box office in Shelby, if there was a Shelby, before taking a percentage for Gibbons. The Gibbons share was to be fifty per cent of the receipts from three hundred thousand to six hundred thousand dollars, and twenty-five per cent of everything above that. Three hundred thousand dollars was exactly what Kearns and Dempsey had made from a spectacular million-dollar-gate fight with Georges Carpentier, which Tex Rickard had promoted two years before on the threshold of New York City. Kearns was now counting on gouging the same sum from an infinitesimal cowtown that had no boxing ring, no grandstand, no professional promoter, and no large city within five hundred miles. At least, he said he was counting on that. Almost no one in New York believed there would be a fight. Kearn's friends suspected, with characteristic misanthropy, that Doc was up to some sort of practice ruse to keep his hand in and his brain lean and sharp for coming campaigns. Rickard, the most famous promoter of the day, who did not think much of either Gibbons or Wills as an opponent for Dempsey, having sped Kearns West with a tolerant wink, went on with plans for his own notion of a Dempsey match with the Argentine Luis Firpo, for autumn delivery.

Kearns, however, was in earnest. It pleased his fancy to undertake this Western adventure on his own. He wanted for once to be free from Eastern entanglements, free from his professional peers. Gibbons and Kane, the parties of the second part, would be amateurs at Shelby in everything but name. At Shelby, every power, privilege, and bargaining weapon would belong to Kearns. If he could carry three hundred thousand dollars out of a town of one thousand population, he would become immortal in his profession. If he couldn't, he had dictated terms that said firmly that all money paid to him and Dempsey in advance was theirs to keep. If they got three hundred thousand dollars, there would be a fight; if they didn't, there would be no fight, and no rebate. Molumby agreed, on behalf of Mayor Johnson, to deliver a second installment of a hundred thousand to Kearns on June 15, and a third, and last, on July 2, two days before the fight. This was Molumby's last major gesture in connection with the Dempsey-Gibbons match. Like half a dozen other Montanans who tried to learn the boxing business in the next few weeks, he flunked the course.

A slight difficulty occurred in the secondary negotiations between Kearns and Kane. The difficulty was that they had not spoken to each other for four years and had no wish to start speaking now. Kearns says today that he does not remember the reason for the breach, which may or may not be true; boxing men are usually shy about revealing the causes of their Grade A feuds—the ones that last anywhere from a year to life. Quartered two floors apart in the Morrison Hotel in Chicago, Kane and Kearns conferred by messenger. The messenger was Collins. One question was who was to referee the fight. It was purely nominal, for Kearns had already decided on his good friend Jim Dougherty, sometimes known as the Baron of Leiperville, Pennsylvania. After four trips by Collins up and down the hotel's emergency stairway, Kane accepted Dougherty. He had no choice. Kearns, as the champion's manager, was in command. Kane, managing the challenger—and a poorly recommended challenger, at that, in the opinion of most critics—could consider himself lucky to have gained a chance at the title for Gibbons. That chance was something, though Gibbons was older and smaller than Dempsey. Beyond it, there was a possibility of making some money if the fight was highly successful, which was the dream that Mayor Johnson had sold to Collins and Collins to Kane. Kane and Gibbons were gambling, like the men of Shelby and the men of the rest of Montana who backed them. That

explains, in part, the deep affection Montana came to feel for Gibbons as the time of the fight drew near.

A few days after the terms were signed, Collins, as "matchmaker," or supervisor of arrangements, announced the ticket price scale: from fifty dollars, ringside, to twenty dollars for the rear seats. There were no seats at the moment, but Mayor Johnson had persuaded Major J. E. Lane, a local lumber merchant, to build an arena at the edge of town to accommodate forty thousand people. There was no money for Major Lane, but the Mayor got him to take a seventy-thousand-dollar chattel mortgage on the arena. Training camps were staked out for both fighters. On May 16, Kearns entrained for Montana with a staff of sparring partners for Dempsey, who made his own way there from his home in Salt Lake City. Kearns was glad to leave the decadent cities of the East, where the newspapers, when they mentioned Shelby at all, still questioned the reality of the fight and half questioned the reality of Shelby. He found Shelby in a holiday mood. The Mayor and his friends had recovered from the strain of getting up the first hundred thousand dollars and had not yet begun to worry about finding the remaining two hundred thousand. The ticket sale would take care of that. Kearns beamed upon these unsophisticated burghers with boots on their feet and guns in their belts. He addressed them at a Chamber of Commerce luncheon at the Silver Grill. With all the sincerity he could muster on short notice, he told them that Gibbons was a great fighter, "the best boxer in the world." "I would not be surprised," Kearns told the meeting lovingly, "if the winner of this contest fought Harry Wills right here in Shelby on Labor Day. You will be the fight capital of the nation. We have come here," he added, "at something of a sacrifice, since we were offered half a million dollars for the same fight in New York. However, Shelby spoke first, and Shelby wins out." Then Kearns took a rapid look at Shelby, whose facilities could all be seen at a glance with the naked eye, and caught the six-o'clock train to Great Falls. All Montana, and Shelby in particular, was well pleased with itself at this point. It is hard to say at just what hour between then and June 15, the first day of open crisis, misgivings began to set in. They must have come soonest to Johnson and Molumby, who were in charge of the ticket sale and the cashbox. Kearns ostensibly had no notion of how things were going. When he was told, Montana was stunned by the change in the manner of the free-and-easy stranger.

Kearns had made his base in Great Falls,

partly because it was a town of thirty thousand, which offered some freedom of movement, and partly because Dempsey was training there, at Great Falls Park, a mile or so outside the city limits. Before June 15, Dempsey trained well and seemed happy. The park, in a hollow in the hills of Cascade County, just east of the Missouri River and in sight of the Little and Big Belt Mountains and the Birdtail Divide, was a pleasant place surrounded by cottonwood trees and had formerly been a scene of revelry. Dempsey lived and sparred in a roadhouse that prohibition and repeated government raids had closed down. Sometimes the champion fished in the Missouri. He had a pet cow, a Hereford bull, a wolf cub, and a bulldog in camp, as well as two of his brothers, Johnny and Bernie; his trainer, Jerry (the Greek) Luvadis; and his stooge, Joe Benjamin, with whom he played pinochle. His sparring partners ranged from giants like Big Ben Wray, seven feet two inches tall, to small, clever middleweights who could simulate Gibbons' style. Gibbons trained in Shelby. He lived with his wife and children in a house on the great, treeless plain, not far from the arena. If anything more was needed to make Gibbons a favorite and Dempsey unpopular in Shelby after June 15, Gibbons' choice of training quarters did it. The town saw him and his family every day. Gibbons at that time was thirty-four, six years older than Dempsey. He had had a long and fairly successful career among middleweights and light heavyweights, though the gifted little Harry Greb had beaten him just the year before. He was a polite and colorless man, with a slim waist, a big chest, and a high shock of pompadoured hair.

On June 15, the day appointed for the payment of the second hundred thousand dollars to Kearns and Dempsey, Kearns went to the Great Falls station to take a train to Shelby. He says now that he was going, in all innocence, to ask Mayor Johnson for the money, that he did not know that the Mayor and Molumby were at that moment wretchedly chewing cigars in a room in the Park Hotel in Great Falls, having just confessed to George H. Stanton, the leading banker of Great Falls, that the day of reckoning found them approximately ninety-eight per cent short. They asked him what to do. Stanton, like all Montanans, had followed the Shelby adventure closely. As the principal capitalist of that part of the state, he had followed it more closely than most, and he probably had a fair notion of the truth before he heard it from the unhappy promoters. However, he told them it was a hell of a note, and he sent someone to get Kearns off the train. Kearns came to the hotel room, looking hopeful. It was his first business contact with Stanton; it would have been better for Stanton if it had been his last. The promoters explained the situation, or what they could understand of it. They admitted frankly that it confused them. It seemed that a great many tickets that had been mailed out, unbonded, to various parts of the state and country were not yet paid for. It seemed that expenses were unexpectedly large. It appeared that there was sixteen hundred dollars in cash on hand for Kearns and Dempsey. Whatever suspicions Kearns may have had before this, the cold facts undoubtedly shocked him. He flew into a rage.

"Why don't *you* take over the promotion and the sale?" suggested Stanton. "From all I can see, you own the fight right now."

"I won't promote!" screamed Kearns. "These guys are the promoters. I'm trying to train a fighter. Let them get our money up or there won't be any fight."

Kearns left the room in a black mood. He went back to the hotel that evening, at Stanton's invitation, and found that most of the money in Great Falls was represented there: Stanton, president of the Stanton Trust & Savings Bank; Dan Tracey, hotel owner; Russell and Arthur Strain, department-store owners; J. W. Speer, lawyer and former judge; and Shirley Ford, vice-president of the Great Falls National Bank. From there on, Kearns was told, the honor of Montana was at stake. The fight would have new promoters. The money would be raised. It *was* raised, within twenty-four hours. At 5:15 P.M. the next day, June 16, the press was summoned to see Stanton present Kearns with a check for a hundred thousand dollars, seventeen hours and a quarter after the deadline of midnight, June 15. Kearns put the check in his pocket and congratulated Montana. "A dead-game state," he said. Stanton accepted his kind words modestly, though it must be said that the newspapermen present got the impression that he himself had put up seventy-three thousand dollars of the money, which was not strictly true. He had supplied cash in that amount, but it was underwritten almost entirely by Mayor Jim Johnson, of Shelby, with land and oil leases from his own estate. The Strain brothers and the O'Neill brothers, Lou and John, who were oilmen, made up the balance. While Molumby and Mayor Johnson sat humbly by—the latter quite silent about his contribution to the salvation of Montana's honor—Dan Tracey delivered a tough speech. The Great Falls committee had appointed Tracey head man of the fight. The old promoters, he said, were through as head men. He would protect the interest of his Great

Falls friends. He would see that they got every nickel back. He would countersign all checks from now on. He paused, and Kearns advanced to shake him by the hand. "This reassures me," said Kearns. "I will stick by Shelby and ignore the countless offers I have got from other states for this fight. I am sure," he added thoughtfully, "that we won't have any trouble with the last hundred thousand dollars—due midnight, July second." Mayor Johnson mopped his brow with a handkerchief. "This is a great relief," he told the press. "I wasn't cut out to be a boxing promoter." Molumby had nothing to say. Earlier that day, he had been denounced by an American Legion post in St. Louis for involving the Legion in Dempsey's affairs.

The reign of Tracey as head man lasted eleven days. It was a time of stress and brooding. The backers of the fight knew that since raising the second hundred thousand dollars had been like pulling teeth, the collection of the third hundred thousand would be on the order of a major amputation. The advance sale of tickets brought in no money to speak of. People could not be expected to buy tickets unless they were sure the fight would take place, and the promoters could not persuade the strong-minded Kearns to guarantee a fight before he was sure of the money. The Great Northern canceled a plan to run special trains from the East and the Pacific Coast. The promoters and their friends snarled at Kearns whenever they saw him, and nervously fondled the butts of their guns. Frank Walker, of Butte, Montana, a lawyer and later Postmaster General under Franklin Roosevelt, came to Great Falls to add weight to the heckling of Kearns. Kearns, however, rode his choppy course serenely and nonchalantly, true to his lofty principle of three hundred thousand dollars or no contest. The strain was much harder on Dempsey than on Dempsey's manager. If Kearns was Public Enemy No. 1 to the financiers of Montana, Dempsey was the people's choice for the part. He was sharply aware of it and of the artillery on the hip of nearly everyone he saw. He said later that he pleaded with Kearns, to no avail, at this time to waive the final payment, to promise a fight, and to take over the box-office management. The champion's state of mind showed in his work. He looked slow and easy to hit in training, and his sparring partners complained of his viciousness when he hit them. On his twenty-eighth birthday, June 24, seemingly angry at his failure to catch Jack Burke, a middleweight, he knocked down another sparring partner seven times in five rounds and broke the jaw of the giant Wray, who subsequently took his meals through a tube.

The crises came fast now. On June 26, Stanton, conferring in Shelby with Tracey and Mayor Johnson, who had been reduced to assistant promoter, was told that the lumber merchant and the contractors were about to foreclose their mortgage on the arena. Stanton stalked angrily to the railroad station, but he was called back into conference, inevitably, at the last minute. Half an hour later, he announced that the creditors had agreed to accept payment on a pro-rata basis from the gate receipts. He said that all was well. Tracey, the tough talker of June 16, could not bring himself to share this view. The mortgage crisis had broken his spirit. On June 27, he resigned his job. "The money my people put up is nowhere in sight that I can see," he said. "I can't be sure they'll get it back, and I'm through." Shelby was excited the next day by a telegram received by Mayor Johnson from Minneapolis signed "Louis W. Till," which it assumed to be from Louis Hill, board chairman of the Great Northern, assuring the Mayor that he was "on way with cash and securities so Tom can have chance to put profiteering Dempsey in hospital." The wire turned out to be a hoax. On June 29, Stanton made a final, desperate move. After consulting with Great Falls leaders on a list of names and sending telegrams to all parts of the state, he proclaimed that "twenty lifelong friends" had pledged five thousand dollars each to meet the final payment to Kearns and "save the honor of Montana." The announcement was given out now, Stanton said, to dispel doubts that the fight would be held, but the payment to Kearns would not be made until the agreed date of July 2, because, he went on sulkily, some of the new sponsors "are disposed to follow the lead taken by the champion's manager and adhere rigidly to the conditions of the contract." It was their opinion, he said, that Kearns "would get out of the fight if he could." Enlarging on the patriotism of his twenty lifelong friends, Stanton said that cancelation of the bout "would have cast reflections on the state that would have been far-reaching in effect." The Northwest, he added, would now save the fight; the Dakotas, Wyoming, Idaho, Washington, Oregon, and western Canada would send at least fifteen thousand people. The members of the committee would take a loss but "are game enough to see this thing through."

Kearns, ignoring the slurs in this manifesto upon his good faith, expressed satisfaction. Dempsey forced a smile and acknowledged the gameness of all Montanans. But on July 2, facing the press, with Kearns present, in Great Falls, Stanton revealed that he had been unable to cash the pledges of his lifelong friends. Eight of them had come through as advertised, he said, but in the circumstances he did not feel like keeping their money. He looked defiantly at Kearns. Kearns shrugged and retired to discuss things with a lieutenant of his from New York, Dan McKetrick. Then he told Stanton that he would make the "gamble" that had been forced on him. He would take over the fight, and the gate receipts with it. From that moment, the concern about paying Kearns was outweighed by a vivid fear that Kearns and Dempsey would slip across the border before July 4 with the money they had already collected, leaving Shelby to whistle for its world-championship fight. There is no evidence that either man contemplated doing this, but practically everyone in Montana was convinced that both of them did contemplate it. Kearns says he remembers Frank Walker, in a state of deep emotion, shaking his fist beneath his nose on July 3, and warning him not to attempt to escape.

SHELBY had built up to the fight, within its limits. There were concession booths and stands all the way from Main Street to the arena. Entertainers had come from every corner of the state. A tent show called the Hyland-Welty Comedians was playing the town; it starred a certain Patricia Salmon, the toast of the out-of-town reporters, who for fifty dollars a week did three song spots a day, yodeled in front of the curtain, and played the lead in *Which One Shall I Marry, Thorns and Orange Blossoms, The Tie That Binds,* and *The Sweetest Girl in Dixie.* An acquaintance of mine from Billings, Montana, drove to Shelby for the fight with his father, an early patriotic ticket buyer. The sign he remembers best on Main Street was "Aunt Kate's Cathouse." All tourists slept in their automobiles the night of July 3. The great Northwestern migration to Shelby had not materialized, but there were enough cars parked on the plain by the arena to show that there was interest in the fight. Part of this interest was speculative; many people had not bought tickets, but they counted on getting in anyway.

Dempsey came from Great Falls in a private railroad car on July 4, arriving in the early afternoon. A switch engine pulled his car to a siding near the arena, where a crowd of men instantly surrounded it. "There were no cheers," recalls Dempsey. His party, which included a Chicago detective named Mike Trant and a celebrated hanger-on of the time, "Senator" Wild Bill Lyons, both strongly and ostentatiously armed, took counsel. Some of the crowd was trying to climb aboard. Lyons told the engineer to keep

the engine hooked on and to run the car up and down the siding till it was time for Dempsey to get off. When that time came, the crowd pressed close around the champion, but there were, according to Dempsey, no gunshots or blows. "Trying to run out, were you?" called some of the men. An emissary from the ringside reported that it was too early for Dempsey's entrance, since the program had been delayed. The crowd, however, got solidly behind Dempsey in a physical sense and pushed him firmly to the arena doors, where he waited with half a dozen retainers by a soft-drink stand, listening to the comments on his character and lineage.

The reason for the delay was the public's reluctance to pay the official prices for tickets. Kearns had opened the gates in the morning, after surrendering five hundred dollars from the advance sale for the privilege to a crew of federal revenue men who were on hand looking closely and hungrily after their country's interests. At noon, however, there were only fifteen hundred people in the grandstand to watch the first preliminary bout. Thousands milled around outside the gates, many of them shouting, "We'll come in for ten dollars!" These were the aristocrats of the mob, and Kearns began to accommodate them at two-thirty, while people inside pushed down from high seats to empty ringside seats, the working press sweltered over typewriters almost too hot to touch, and two bands—the Montana State Elks band on one side of the ring and the Scottish Highlanders of Calgary on the other —alternately administered soothing music. A blind war veteran was singing a ballad in the ring when Kearns finally was overrun by the rest of the crowd outside, which came in free. Dempsey entered at three-thirty-six, thirty-six minutes late. "It was the most hostile crowd a heavyweight champion ever faced," he said a few years later, through a ghost writer, and he was probably right. There was some hissing, he recalls, but mostly "sullen silence." Gibbons made it harder for him by delaying his arrival till three-forty-five and taking ten minutes to have his hands taped in the ring. A few empty bottles descended near Dempsey's corner, tossed by spectators who blamed the champion for the delay. Dodging glassware in the corner with Dempsey were Kearns and Bill Lyons, who wore chaps and a sombrero as well as his arsenal. A number of what Kearns called "my Chicago hard guys" sat watchfully at the ringside just below.

It was a very bad fight. Dempsey, outweighing Gibbons—a hundred and eighty-eight pounds to a hundred and seventy-four—but stale and nervous, could not land his punches squarely. It was widely said later that he would not, out of fear for his safety, but that theory conflicts with the character and testimony of Dempsey and the opinion of expert eyewitnesses. Gibbons won a few of the early rounds. He opened a cut over Dempsey's eye in the second, and Dempsey complained afterward that Kearns, never the most sure-handed of seconds, poured cut medicine into the eye between rounds, making him half blind until the seventh. From the sixth round on, it was Dempsey's fight, easily. The crowd stopped crying "Kill him, Tommy!" and cried "Hang on!" That was all Gibbons tried to do—he had every reason to know he was working for nothing, and Dempsey's strength had soon made him sure he couldn't win. Gibbons scored one moral triumph when he survived the twelfth round, a new record against Dempsey, and another when he survived the fifteenth, and last, and forced the bout to a decision. The last round was one long clinch; Gibbons wrapped his arms around Dempsey, and the onlookers shouted derisively at the champion and threw cushions. Gibbons made no objection to Referee Dougherty's decision for Dempsey. Neither did the crowd.

Dempsey got out with the utmost dispatch when the verdict had been given. The Chicago hard guys, led by Detective Trant, hustled him aboard the private car on the siding. At the Shelby station, his car was hooked to a train for Great Falls. He spent the night at the Park Hotel in Great Falls and caught a regular train the next day for Salt Lake City. Both of Dempsey's eyes were slightly discolored when he boarded the Salt Lake train and exchanged a few last words with residents of Great Falls who came to see him off. "Don't hurry back!" called his well-wishers. "I won't, boys!" said Dempsey sincerely.

Kearns' departure from Montana was a little more complicated. To this day, he holds to the colorful view that he narrowly escaped injury or death from the guns of the West in getting out with the money. The money, the proceeds of the last day's ticket sale, amounted to about eighty thousand dollars in silver and bills. Kearns and McKetrick counted it in the presence of the federal tax men and stuffed it into a couple of canvas sacks. It is altogether possible that if Kearns had then honored an earlier promise to meet with certain fight fans and Shelby citizens in a saloon to talk things over before saying goodbye, he and the cash would not have left the state intact. The temper of Shelby needed only a sprinkling of ninety-proof rye to boil over. But Kearns, holding to his higher purpose, which was to keep all the money, less tax, broke the date. He and McKetrick made straight from the box

office for a caboose attached to a locomotive that stood waiting in the twilight at the station. The getaway transportation had been chartered with the help of the federal men. As Kearns and McKetrick boarded the caboose, they observed in the street nearby the shadowy figure of a small man with a ukelele. This was the late Hype Igoe, a New York sportswriter with a turn for minstrelsy, who, having written his fight piece and lingered in Shelby to take on fuel, was delicately strumming chords for his own entertainment. "This is the New York Special, Hype," called Kearns. Igoe accepted the invitation and got aboard, and the special rolled out of Shelby.

Still playing a cautious game, the Kearns party spent the rest of the night in the cellar of a barbershop in Great Falls. Kearns passed up the Salt Lake City express the next day, and for five hundred dollars, out of one of the canvas bags, hired a locomotive and coach from the Great Northern's Great Falls agent. He and his friends joined Dempsey the next day.

On July 9 began a series of events that canonized Kearns in the boxing business. The Stanton Trust & Savings Bank of Great Falls closed its doors that day. Stanton insisted that the closing had no connection with the Dempsey–Gibbons fight; he blamed it on postwar conditions in general. However, all other reports from Montana then and later agreed that the public knowledge of Stanton's association with the fight caused a run on the bank, which the banker could not meet because of the temporary withdrawal of seventy-three thousand dollars in cash from his own account to pay Kearns on June 16. The state bank examiner, L. Q. Skelton, came to Great Falls to take over the bank. He saved himself an extra trip to the neighborhood by taking over Mayor Johnson' First State Bank of Shelby as well, Johnson having stopped payments to depositors on the morning of July 10. It was now revealed for the first time that much of the cash paid by Stanton to Kearns had been secured by Johnson with his personal property, which he began making over to Stanton after the fight. On July 11, the First State Bank of Joplin, Montana, an affiliate of Stanton's bank, closed down. Newspaper reports from Joplin stated that all closings to date were "generally accredited" to the championship boxing bout in Shelby. Boxing people never doubted this for a moment. Kearns and Dempsey have been pointed out ever since as winners over three Montana banks. The better informed students of the situation, like Kearns, feel that the score should be four, for on August 16 of the same year, almost unnoticed by the press, the First National Bank of

236

Shelby was closed by order of its board of directors, following withdrawals of something like a hundred thousand dollars in the first month after the fight. This left Shelby with, for the time being, no banks at all and practically no assets. The oil boom subsided not long afterward. The arena was torn down and the lumber salvaged by the mortgage holders.

Kearns says that Mayor Johnson wrote to Dempsey and himself that summer asking for a loan of twenty-five thousand dollars, and that it was granted, and repaid within a year. It is certain that the Mayor was comfortably off when he died, in 1938, thanks mainly to another strike in the Kevin-Sunburst oil field a few years after the first one, which reanimated the town. The career of Patricia Salmon, the tent-show actress, took an opposite course. Her New York press reviews from Shelby in 1923 won her a contract with Florenz Ziegfeld and a season in the "Follies." It was thought for a time that she, Dempsey, and Kearns (and the United States government) were the beneficiaries of the Shelby fight. But Miss Salmon was a one-year wonder. Her star declined as Johnson's rose, and in 1928 she was towed off the floor of Madison Square Garden with a set of swollen feet after performing consecutively for a hundred and thirty-five hours and forty minutes in a dance marathon that she had hoped would bring her publicity and another job in the theater.

A WORD should be said about the early unpopularity of Dempsey, for it contributed much to his discomfort at Shelby and to the public's reaction in Montana and elsewhere. Like other entertainers in both World Wars, Dempsey, in 1918, did a certain amount of morale building among war workers. There is evidence that he was popular with sports followers, including some Army and Navy men, in 1919, when he won the championship, and that the change did not set in until after managers of heavyweights with war records, all of them outclassed as prize fighters by Dempsey, began to play up their wartime service in their interviews and advertisements. A photograph was widely circulated of Dempsey striking a pose in a shipyard during the war with a workman's tool in his hands and patent-leather shoes on his feet. He was formally acquitted of draft evasion in 1920. From the time he lost the championship to Gene Tunney, in 1926, he was immensely popular in America and abroad. However, it was plain to anyone who knew him that he never forgot certain aspects of his public life between 1919 and 1926. He was commissioned as a physical director in the Coast Guard in the last war. I saw him during preparations for the Okinawa landing in 1945. He had obtained leave to go to Okinawa on a Coast Guard ship and could hardly control his excitement; in fact, it was almost necessary to gag him to maintain security before the operation began. He went ashore on the Marines' sector of the front shortly after D Day. He did not stay long, since he served no military purpose there, but it probably helped to compensate him for an hour spent with a sharp-tongued crowd outside the wooden arena at Shelby in 1923. Shelby paid as it went for its attitude toward Dempsey, but, like Kearns, he was not an easy man to satisfy.

RING LARDNER, rightly, never thought this one of his better stories. In Midge Kelly he drew a caricature, not a character, and yet, largely because the most successful of all boxing movies was made from it, it became Lardner's best-known work.

# Champion

## RING LARDNER

MIDGE KELLY scored his first knockout when he was seventeen. The knockee was his brother Connie, three years his junior and a cripple. The purse was a half dollar given to the younger Kelly by a lady whose electric had just missed bumping his soul from his frail little body.

Connie did not know Midge was in the house, else he never would have risked laying the prize on the arm of the least comfortable chair in the room, the better to observe its shining beauty. As Midge entered from the kitchen, the crippled boy covered the coin with his hand, but the movement lacked the speed requisite to escape his brother's quick eye.

"Watcha got there?" demanded Midge.

"Nothin'," said Connie.

"You're a one-legged liar!" said Midge.

He strode over to his brother's chair and grasped the hand that concealed the coin.

"Let loose!" he ordered.

Connie began to cry.

"Let loose and shut up your noise," said the elder, and jerked his brother's hand from the chair arm.

The coin fell onto the bare floor. Midge pounced on it. His weak mouth widened in a triumphant smile.

"Nothin', huh?" he said. "All right, if it's nothin' you don't want it."

"Give that back," sobbed the younger.

"I'll give you a red nose, you little sneak! Where'd you steal it?"

"I didn't steal it. It's mine. A lady give it to me after she pretty near hit me with a car."

"It's a crime she missed you," said Midge.

Midge started for the front door. The cripple picked up his crutch, rose from his chair with difficulty, and, still sobbing, came toward Midge. The latter heard him and stopped.

"You better stay where you're at," he said.

"I want my money," cried the boy.

"I know what you want," said Midge.

Doubling up the fist that held the half dollar, he landed with all his strength on his brother's mouth. Connie fell to the floor with a thud, the crutch tumbling on top of him. Midge stood beside the prostrate form.

"Is that enough?" he said. "Or do you want this, too?"

And he kicked him in the crippled leg.

"I guess that'll hold you," he said.

There was no response from the boy on the floor. Midge looked at him a moment, then at the coin in his hand, and then went out into the street, whistling.

An hour later, when Mrs. Kelly came home from her day's work at Faulkner's Steam Laundry, she found Connie on the floor, moaning. Dropping on her knees beside him, she called him by name a score of times. Then she got up and, pale as a ghost, dashed from the house. Dr. Ryan left the Kelly abode about dusk and walked toward Halsted Street. Mrs. Dorgan spied him as he passed her gate.

"Who's sick, Doctor?" she called.

"Poor little Connie," he replied. "He had a bad fall."

"How did it happen?"

"I can't say for sure, Margaret, but I'd almost bet he was knocked down."

"Knocked down!" exclaimed Mrs. Dorgan. "Why, who—?"

"Have you seen the other one lately?"

"Michael? No, not since mornin'. You can't be thinkin'—"

"I wouldn't put it past him, Margaret," said the doctor gravely. "The lad's mouth is swollen and cut, and his poor, skinny little leg is bruised. He surely didn't do it to himself and I think Ellen suspects the other one."

"Lord save us!" said Mrs. Dorgan. "I'll run over and see if I can help."

"That's a good woman," said Dr. Ryan, and went on down the street.

Near midnight, when Midge came home, his mother was sitting at Connie's bedside. She did not look up.

"Well," said Midge, "what's the matter?"

She remained silent. Midge repeated his question.

"Michael, you know what s the matter," she said at length.

"I don't know nothin'," said Midge.

"Don't lie to me, Michael. What did you do to your brother?"

"Nothin'."

"You hit him."

"Well, then, I hit him. What of it? It ain't the first time."

Her lips pressed tightly together, her face like chalk, Ellen Kelly rose from her chair and made straight for him. Midge backed against the door.

"Lay off'n me, Ma. I don't want to fight no woman."

Still she came on, breathing heavily.

"Stop where you're at, Ma," he warned.

There was a brief struggle and Midge's mother lay on the floor before him.

"You ain't hurt, Ma. You're lucky I didn't land good. And I told you to lay off'n me."

"God forgive you, Michael!"

Midge found Hap Collins in the showdown game at the Royal.

"Come on out a minute," he said.

Hap followed him out on the walk.

"I'm leavin' town for a w'ile," said Midge.

"What for?"

"Well, we had a little run-in up to the house. The kid stole a half buck off'n me, and when I went after it he cracked me with his crutch. So I nailed him. And the old lady came at me with a chair and I took it off'n her and she fell down."

"How is Connie hurt?"

"Not bad."

"What are you runnin' away for?"

"Who the hell said I was runnin' away? I'm sick and tired o' gettin' picked on; that's all. So

I'm leavin' for a w'ile and I want a piece o' money."

"I ain't only got six bits," said Happy.

"You're in bad shape, ain't you? Well, come through with it."

Happy came through.

"You oughtn't to hit the kid," he said.

"I ain't astin' you who can I hit," snarled Midge. "You try to put somethin' over on me and you'll get the same dose. I'm goin' now."

"Go as far as you like," said Happy, but not until he was sure that Kelly was out of hearing.

Early the following morning, Midge boarded a train for Milwaukee. He had no ticket, but no one knew the difference. The conductor remained in the caboose.

On a night six months later, Midge hurried out of the "stage door" of the Star Boxing Club and made for Duane's saloon, two blocks away. In his pocket were twelve dollars, his reward for having battered up one Demon Dempsey through the six rounds of the first preliminary.

It was Midge's first professional engagement in the manly art. Also it was the first time in weeks that he had earned twelve dollars.

On the way to Duane's he had to pass Niemann's. He pulled his cap over his eyes and increased his pace until he had gone by. Inside Niemann's stood a trusting bartender, who for ten days had staked Midge to drinks and allowed him to ravage the lunch on a promise to come in and settle the moment he was paid for the "prelim."

Midge strode into Duane's and aroused the napping bartender by slapping a silver dollar on the festive board.

"Gimme a shot," said Midge.

The shooting continued until the wind-up at the Star was over and part of the fight crowd joined Midge in front of Duane's bar. A youth in the early twenties, standing next to young Kelly, finally summoned sufficient courage to address him.

"Wasn't you in the first bout?" he ventured.

"Yeh," Midge replied.

"My name's Hersch," said the other.

Midge received the startling information in silence.

"I don't want to butt in," continued Mr. Hersch, "but I'd like to buy you a drink."

"All right," said Midge, "but don't overstrain yourself."

Mr. Hersch laughed uproariously and beckoned to the bartender.

"You certainly gave that wop a trimmin' tonight," said the buyer of the drink, when they had been served. "I thought you'd kill him."

"I would if I hadn't let up," Midge replied. "I'll kill 'em all."

"You got the wallop all right," the other said admiringly.

"Have I got the wallop?" said Midge. "Say, I can kick like a mule. Did you notice them muscles in my shoulders?"

"Notice 'em? I couldn't help from noticin' 'em," said Hersch. "I says to the fella sittin' alongside o' me, I says: 'Look at them shoulders! No wonder he can hit,' I says to him."

"Just let me land and it's goodbye, baby," said Midge. "I'll kill 'em all."

The oral manslaughter continued until Duane's closed for the night. At parting, Midge and his new friend shook hands and arranged for a meeting the following evening.

For nearly a week the two were together almost constantly. It was Hersch's pleasant role to listen to Midge's modest revelations concerning himself, and to buy every time Midge's glass was empty. But there came an evening when Hersch regretfully announced that he must go home to supper.

"I got a date for eight bells," he confided. "I could stick till then, only I must clean up and put on the Sunday clo'es, 'cause she's the prettiest little thing in Milwaukee."

"Can't you fix it for two?" asked Midge.

"I don't know who to get," Hersch replied. "Wait, though. I got a sister and if she ain't busy, it'll be O.K. She's no bum for looks herself."

So it came about that Midge and Emma Hersch and Emma's brother and the prettiest little thing in Milwaukee foregathered at Wall's and danced half the night away. And Midge and Emma danced every dance together, for though every little onestep seemed to induce a new thirst of its own, Lou Hersch stayed too sober to dance with his own sister.

The next day, penniless at last in spite of his phenomenal ability to make someone else settle, Midge Kelly sought out Doc Hammond, matchmaker for the Star, and asked to be booked for the next show.

"I could put you on with Tracy for the next bout," said Doc.

"What's they in it?" asked Midge.

"Twenty if you cop," Doc told him.

"Have a heart," protested Midge. "Didn't I look good the other night?"

"You looked all right. But you aren't Freddie Welsh yet by a consid'able margin."

"I ain't scared of Freddie Welsh or none of 'em," said Midge.

"Well, we don't pay our boxers by the size of their chests," Doc said. "I'm offerin' you this Tracy bout. Take it or leave it."

"All right: I'm on," said Midge, and he passed a pleasant afternoon at Duane's on the strength of his booking.

Young Tracy's manager came to see Midge the night before the show.

"How do you feel about this go?" he asked.

"Me?" said Midge. "I feel all right. What do you mean, how do I feel?"

"I mean," said Tracy's manager, "that we're mighty anxious to win, 'cause the boy's got a chanct in Philly if he cops this one."

"What's your proposition?" asked Midge.

"Fifty bucks," said Tracy's manager.

"What do you think I am, a crook? Me lay down for fifty bucks. Not me!"

"Seventy-five, then," said Tracy's manager.

The market closed on eighty and the details were agreed on in short order. And the next night Midge was stopped in the second round by a terrific slap on the forearm.

This time Midge passed up both Niemann's and Duane's, having a sizable account at each place, and sought his refreshment at Stein's farther down the street.

When the profits of his deal with Tracy were gone, he learned, by first-hand information from Doc Hammond and the matchmakers at the other "clubs," that he was no longer desired for even the cheapest of preliminaries. There was no danger of his starving or dying of thirst while Emma and Lou Hersch lived. But he made up his mind, four months after his defeat by Young Tracy, that Milwaukee was not the ideal place for him to live.

"I can lick the best of 'em," he reasoned, "but there ain't no more chanct for me here. I can maybe go east and get on somewheres. And besides——"

But just after Midge had purchased a ticket to Chicago with the money he had "borrowed" from Emma Hersch "to buy shoes," a heavy hand was laid on his shoulder and he turned to face two strangers.

"Where are you goin', Kelly?" inquired the owner of the heavy hand.

"Nowheres," said Midge. "What the hell do you care?"

The other stranger spoke:

"Kelly, I'm employed by Emma Hersch's mother to see that you do right by her. And we want you to stay here till you've done it."

"You won't get nothin' but the worst of it, monkeying with me," said Midge.

Nevertheless, he did not depart for Chicago that night. Two days later, Emma Hersch became Mrs. Kelly, and the gift of the bridegroom, when once they were alone, was a crushing blow on the bride's pale cheek.

Next morning, Midge left Milwaukee as he had entered it—by fast freight.

"THEY'S NO USE kiddin' ourself any more," said Tommy Haley. "He might get down to thirty-seven in a pinch, but if he done below that a mouse could stop him. He's a welter; that's what he is and he knows it as well as I do. He's growed like a weed in the last six months. I told him, I says, 'If you don't quit growin' they won't be nobody for you to box, only Willard and them.' He says, 'Well, I wouldn't run away from Willard if I weighed twenty pounds more.'"

"He must hate himself," said Tommy's brother.

"I never seen a good one that didn't," said Tommy. "And Midge is a good one; don't make no mistake about that. I wisht we could of got Welsh before the kid growed so big. But it's too late now. I won't make no holler, though, if we can match him up with the Dutchman."

"Who do you mean?"

"Young Goetz, the welter champ. We mightn't not get so much dough for the bout itself, but it'd roll in afterward. What a drawin' card we'd be, 'cause the people pays their money to see the fella with the wallop, and that's Midge. And we'd keep the title just as long as Midge could make the weight."

"Can't you land no match with Goetz?"

"Sure, 'cause he needs the money. But I've went careful with the kid so far and look at the results I got! So what's the use of takin' a chanct? The kid's comin' every minute and Goetz is goin' back faster'n big Johnson did. I think we could lick him now; I'd bet my life on it. But six mont's from now they won't be no risk. He'll of licked hisself before that time. Then all as we'll have to do is sign up with him and wait for the referee to stop it. But Midge is so crazy to get at him now that I can't hardly hold him back."

The brothers Haley were lunching in a Boston hotel. Dan had come down from Holyoke to visit with Tommy and to watch the latter's protégé go twelve rounds, or less, with Bud Cross. The bout promised little in the way of a contest, for Midge had twice stopped the Baltimore youth and Bud's reputation for gameness was all that had earned him the date. The fans were willing to pay the price to see Midge's haymaking left, but they wanted to see it used on an opponent who would not jump out of the ring the first time he felt its crushing force. Bud Cross was such an opponent, and his willingness to stop boxing gloves with his eyes, ears, nose and throat had enabled him to escape the horrors of honest labor. A game boy was Bud, and he showed it in his battered, swollen, discolored face.

"I should think," said Dan Haley, "that the kid'd do whatever you tell him after all you've done for him."

"Well," said Tommy, "he's took my dope pretty straight so far, but he's so sure of hisself that he can't see no reason for waitin'. He'll do what I say, though; he'd be a sucker not to."

"You got a contrac' with him?"

"No, I don't need no contrac'. He knows it was me that drug him out o' the gutter and he ain't goin' to turn me down now when he's got the dough and bound to get more. Where'd he of been at if I hadn't listened to him when he first came to me? That's pretty near two years ago now, but it seems like last week. I was settin' in the s'loon acrost from the Pleasant Club in Philly, waitin' for McCann to count the dough and come over, when this little bum blowed in and tried to stand the house off for a drink. They told him nothin' doin' and to beat it out o' there, and then he seen me and come over to where I was settin' and ast me wasn't I a boxin' man and I told him who I was. Then he ast me for money to buy a shot and I told him to set down and I'd buy it for him.

"Then we got talkin' things over and he told me his name and told me about fight'n' a couple o' prelims out of Milwaukee. So I says, 'Well, boy, I don't know how good or how rotten you are, but you won't never get nowheres trainin' on that stuff.' So he says he'd cut it out if he could get on in a bout and I says I would give him a chanct if he played square with me and didn't touch no more to drink. So we shook hands and I took him up to the hotel with me and give him a bath and the next day I bought him some clo'es. And I staked him to eats and sleeps for over six weeks. He had a hard time breakin' away from the polish, but finally I thought he was fit and I give him his chanct. He went on with Smiley Sayer and stopped him so quick that Smiley thought sure he was poisoned.

"Well, you know what he's did since. The only beatin' in his record was by Tracy in Milwaukee before I got hold of him, and he's licked Tracy three times in the last year.

"I've gave him all the best of it in a money way and he's got seven thousand bucks in cold storage. How's that for a kid that was in the gutter two years ago? And he'd have still more yet if he wasn't so nuts over clo'es and got to stop at the good hotels and so forth."

"Where's his home at?"

"Well, he ain't really got no home. He came from Chicago and his mother canned him out o' the house for bein' no good. She give him a raw deal, I guess, and he says he won't have nothin' to do with her unlest she comes to him first. She's got a pile o' money, he says, so he ain't worryin' about her."

The gentleman under discussion entered the café and swaggered to Tommy's table, while the whole room turned to look.

Midge was the picture of health despite a slightly colored eye and an ear that seemed to have no opening. But perhaps it was not his healthiness that drew all eyes. His diamond horseshoe tie pin, his purple cross-striped shirt, his orange shoes and his light-blue suit fairly screamed for attention.

"Where you been?" he asked Tommy. "I been lookin' all over for you."

"Set down," said his manager.

"No time," said Midge. "I'm goin' down to the w'arf and see 'em unload the fish."

"Shake hands with my brother Dan," said Tommy.

Midge shook with Holyoke Haley.

"If you're Tommy's brother, you're O.K. with me," said Midge, and the brothers beamed with pleasure.

Dan moistened his lips and murmured an embarrassed reply, but it was lost on the young gladiator.

"Leave me take twenty," Midge was saying. "I prob'ly won't need it, but I don't like to be caught short."

Tommy parted with a twenty-dollar bill and recorded the transaction in a small book the insurance company had given him for Christmas.

"But," he said, "it won't cost you no twenty to look at them fish. Want me to go along?"

"No," said Midge hastily. "You and your brother here prob'ly got a lot to say to each other."

"Well," said Tommy, "don't take no bad money and don't get lost. And you better be back at four o'clock and lay down a w'ile."

"I don't need no rest to beat this guy," said Midge. "He'll do enough layin' down for the both of us."

And laughing even more than the jest called for, he strode out through the fire of admiring and startled glances.

The corner of Boylston and Tremont was the nearest Midge got to the wharf, but the lady awaiting him was doubtless a more dazzling sight than the catch of the luckiest Massachusetts fisherman. She could talk, too—probably better than the fish.

"O you Kid!" she said, flashing a few silver teeth among the gold. "O you fighting man!"

Midge smiled up at her.

"We'll go somewheres and get a drink," he said. "One won't hurt."

IN NEW ORLEANS five months after he had rearranged the map of Bud Cross for the third time, Midge finished training for his championship bout with the Dutchman.

Back in his hotel after the final workout, Midge stopped to chat with some of the boys from up north, who had made the long trip to see a champion dethroned, for the result of the bout was so nearly a foregone conclusion that even the experts had guessed it.

Tommy Haley secured the key and the mail and ascended to the Kelly suite. He was bathing when Midge came in, half an hour later.

"Any mail?" asked Midge.

"There on the bed," replied Tommy from the tub.

Midge picked up the stack of letters and postcards and glanced over them. From the pile he sorted out three letters and laid them on the table. The rest he tossed into the wastebasket. Then he picked up the three and sat for a few moments holding them, while his eyes gazed off into space. At length he looked again at the three unopened letters in his hand; then he put one in his pocket and tossed the other two at the basket. They missed their target and fell on the floor.

"Hell," said Midge, and stooping over picked them up.

He opened one postmarked Milwaukee and read:

DEAR HUSBAND:

*I have wrote to you so many times and got no anser and I dont know if you ever got them, so I am writeing again in the hopes you will get this letter and anser. I dont like to bother you with my trubles and I would not only for the baby and I am not asking you should write to me but only send a little money and I am not asking for myself but the baby has not been well a day since last Aug. and the dr. told me she cant live much longer unless I give her better food and thats impossible the way things are. Lou has not been working for a year and what I make dont hardley pay for the rent. I am not asking for you to give me any money, but only you should send what I loaned when convenient and I think it amts. to about $36.00. Please try and send that amt. and it will help me, but if* *you cant send the whole amt. try and send me something.*

*Your wife,*

EMMA

Midge tore the letter into a hundred pieces and scattered them over the floor.

"Money, money, money!" he said. "They must think I'm made o' money. I s'pose the old woman's after it too."

He opened his mother's letter:

*dear Michael Connie wonted me to rite and say you must beet the dutchman and he is sur you will and wonted me to say we wont you to rite and tell us about it, but I guess you havent no time to rite or we herd from you long beffore this but I wish you would rite jest a line or 2 boy because it wuld be better for Connie then & barl of medisin. It wuld help me to keep things going if you send me money now and then when you can spair it but if you cant send no money try and fine time to rite a letter onley a few lines and it will please Connie. jest think boy he hasent got out of bed in over 3 yrs. Connie says good luck.*

*Your Mother,*

ELLEN F. KELLY

"I thought so," said Midge. "They're all alike." The third letter was from New York. It read:

HON:—*This is the last letter you will get from me before your champ, but I will send you a telegram Saturday, but I can't say as much in a telegram as in a letter and I am writing this to let you know I am thinking of you and praying for good luck.*

*Lick him good hon and don't wait no longer than you have to and don't forget to write me as soon as its over. Give him that little old left of yours on the nose hon and don't be afraid of spoiling his good looks because he couldn't be no homlier than he is. But don't let him spoil my baby's pretty face. You won't will you hon.*

*Well hon I would give anything to be there and see it, but I guess you love Haley better than me or you wouldn't let him keep me away. But when your champ hon we can do as we please and tell Haley to go to the devil.*

*Well hon I will send you a telegram Saturday and I almost forgot to tell you I will need some more money, a couple hundred say and you will have to wire it to me as soon as you get this. You will won't you hon.*

*I will send you a telegram Saturday and remember hon I am pulling for you.*

*Well goodbye sweetheart and good luck.*

GRACE

"They're all alike," said Midge. "Money, money, money."

Tommy Haley, shining from his ablutions, came in from the adjoining room.

"Thought you'd be layin' down," he said.

"I'm goin' to," said Midge, unbuttoning his orange shoes.

"I'll call you at six and you can eat up here without no bugs to pester you. I got to go down and give them birds their tickets."

"Did you hear from Goldberg?" asked Midge.

"Didn't I tell you? Sure; fifteen weeks at five hundred, if we win. And we can get a guarantee o' twelve thousand, with privileges either in New York or Milwaukee."

"Who with?"

"Anybody that'll stand up in front of you. You don't care who it is, do you?"

"Not me. I'll make 'em all look like a monkey."

"Well you better lay down aw'ile."

"Oh, say, wire two hundred to Grace for me, will you? Right away; the New York address."

"Two hundred! You just sent her three hundred last Sunday."

"Well, what the hell do you care?"

"All right, all right. Don't get sore about it. Anything else?"

"That's all," said Midge, and dropped onto the bed.

"AND I WANT the deed done before I come back," said Grace as she rose from the table. "You won't fall down on me, will you, hon?"

"Leave it to me," said Midge. "And don't spend no more than you have to."

Grace smiled a farewell and left the café. Midge continued to sip his coffee and read his paper.

They were in Chicago and they were in the middle of Midge's first week in vaudeville. He had come straight north to reap the rewards of his glorious victory over the broken-down Dutchman. A fortnight had been spent in learning his act, which consisted of a gymnastic exhibition and a ten minutes' monologue on the various excellences of Midge Kelly. And now he was twice daily turning 'em away from the Madison Theater.

His breakfast over and his paper read, Midge sauntered into the lobby and asked for his key.

He then beckoned to a bellboy, who had been hoping for that very honor.

"Find Haley, Tommy Haley," said Midge. "Tell him to come up to my room."

"Yes, sir, Mr. Kelly," said the boy, and proceeded to break all his former records for diligence.

Midge was looking out of his seventh-story window when Tommy answered the summons.

"What'll it be?" inquired the manager.

There was a pause before Midge replied.

"Haley," he said, "twenty-five per cent's a whole lot o' money."

"I guess I got it comin', ain't I?" said Tommy.

"I don't see how you figger it. I don't see where you're worth it to me."

"Well," said Tommy, "I didn't expect nothin' like this. I thought you was satisfied with the bargain. I don't want to beat nobody out o' nothin', but I don't see where you could have got anybody else that would of did all I done for you."

"Sure, that's all right," said the champion. "You done a lot for me in Philly. And you got good money for it, didn't you?"

"I ain't makin' no holler. Still and all, the big money's still ahead of us yet. And if it hadn't of been for me, you wouldn't of never got within grabbin' distance."

"Oh, I guess I could of went along all right," said Midge. "Who was it hung that left on the Dutchman's jaw, me or you?"

"Yes, but you wouldn't been in the ring with the Dutchman if it wasn't for how I handled you."

"Well, this won't get us nowheres. The idear is that you ain't worth no twenty-five per cent now and it don't make no difference what come off a year or two ago."

"Don't it?" said Tommy. "I'd say it made a whole lot of difference."

"Well, I say it don't and I guess that settles it."

"Look here, Midge," Tommy said, "I thought I was fair with you, but if you don't think so, I'm willin' to hear what you think is fair. I don't want nobody callin' me a Sherlock. Let's go down to business and sign up a contrac'. What's your figger?"

"I ain't namin' no figger," Midge replied. "I'm sayin' that twenty-five's too much. Now what are you willin' to take?"

"How about twenty?"

"Twenty's too much," said Kelly.

"What ain't too much?" asked Tommy.

"Well, Haley, I might as well give it to you straight. They ain't nothin' that ain't too much."

"You mean you don't want me at no figger?"

"That's the idear."

There was a minute's silence. Then Tommy Haley walked toward the door.

"Midge," he said, in a choking voice, "you're makin' a big mistake, boy. You can't throw down your best friends and get away with it. That damn woman will ruin you."

Midge sprang from his seat.

"You shut your mouth!" he stormed. "Get out o' here before they have to carry you out. You been spongin' off o' me long enough. Say one more word about the girl or about anything else and you'll get what the Dutchman got. Now get out!"

And Tommy Haley, having a very vivid memory of the Dutchman's face as he fell, got out.

Grace came in later, dropped her numerous bundles on the lounge and perched herself on the arm of Midge's chair.

"Well?" she said.

"Well," said Midge, "I got rid of him."

"Good boy!" said Grace. "And now I think you might give me that twenty-five per cent."

"Besides the seventy-five you're already gettin'?" said Midge.

"Don't be no grouch, hon. You don't look pretty when you're grouchy."

"It ain't my business to look pretty," Midge replied.

"Wait till you see how I look with the stuff I bought this mornin'!"

Midge glanced at the bundles on the lounge.

"There's Haley's twenty-five per cent," he said, "and then some."

The champion did not remain long without a manager. Haley's successor was none other than Jerome Harris, who saw in Midge a better meal ticket than his popular-priced musical show had been.

The contract, giving Mr. Harris twenty-five per cent of Midge's earnings, was signed in Detroit the week after Tommy Haley had heard his dismissal read. It had taken Midge just six days to learn that a popular actor cannot get on without the ministrations of a man who thinks, talks and means business. At first Grace objected to the new member of the firm, but when Mr. Harris had demanded and secured from the vaudeville people a one-hundred dollar increase in Midge's weekly stipend, she was convinced that the champion had acted for the best.

"You and my missus will have some great old times," Harris told Grace. "I'd of wired her to join us here, only I seen the Kid's bookin' takes us to Milwaukee next week, and that's where she is."

But when they were introduced in the Milwaukee hotel, Grace admitted to herself that her feeling for Mrs. Harris could hardly be called love at first sight. Midge, on the contrary, gave his new manager's wife the many times over and seemed loath to end the feast of his eyes.

"Some doll," he said to Grace when they were alone.

"Doll is right," the lady replied, "and sawdust where her brains ought to be."

"I'm liable to steal that baby," said Midge, and he smiled as he noted the effect of his words on his audience's face.

On Tuesday of the Milwaukee week the champion successfully defended his title in a bout that the newspapers never reported. Midge was alone in his room that morning when a visitor entered without knocking. The visitor was Lou Hersch.

Midge turned white at sight of him.

"What do you want?" he demanded.

"I guess you know," said Lou Hersch. "Your wife's starvin' to death and your baby's starvin' to death and I'm starvin' to death. And you're dirty with money."

"Listen," said Midge, "if it wasn't for you, I wouldn't never saw your sister. And, if you ain't man enough to hold a job, what's that to me? The best thing you can do is keep away from me."

"You give me a piece o' money and I'll go."

Midge's reply to the ultimatum was a straight right to his brother-in-law's narrow chest.

"Take that home to your sister."

And after Lou Hersch had picked himself up and slunk away, Midge thought: "It's lucky I didn't give him my left or I'd of croaked him. And if I'd hit him in the stomach, I'd of broke his spine."

There was a party after each evening performance during the Milwaukee engagement. The wine flowed freely and Midge had more of it than Tommy Haley ever would have permitted him. Mr. Harris offered no objection, which was possibly just as well for his own physical comfort.

In the dancing between drinks, Midge had his new manager's wife for a partner as often as Grace. The latter's face as she floundered round in the arms of the portly Harris belied her frequent protestations that she was having the time of her life.

Several times that week, Midge thought Grace was on the point of starting the quarrel he hoped to have. But it was not until Friday night that she accommodated. He and Mrs. Harris had disappeared after the matinee and when Grace saw

him again at the close of the night show, she came to the point at once.

"What are you tryin' to pull off?" she demanded.

"It's none o' your business, is it?" said Midge.

"You bet it's my business; mine and Harris's. You cut it short or you'll find out."

"Listen," said Midge, "have you got a mortgage on me or somethin'? You talk like we was married."

"We're goin' to be, too. And tomorrow's as good a time as any."

"Just about," said Midge. "You got as much chanct o' marryin' me tomorrow as the next day or next year and that ain't no chanct at all."

"We'll find out," said Grace.

"You're the one that's got somethin' to find out."

"What do you mean?"

"I mean I'm married already."

"You lie!"

"You think so, do you? Well, s'pose you go to this here address and get acquainted with my missus."

Midge scrawled a number on a piece of paper and handed it to her. She stared at it unseeingly.

"Well," said Midge, "I ain't kiddin' you. You go there and ask for Mrs. Michael Kelly, and if you don't find her, I'll marry you tomorrow before breakfast."

Still Grace stared at the scrap of paper. To Midge it seemed an age before she spoke again.

"You lied to me all this w'ile."

"You never ast me was I married. What's more, what the hell difference did it make to you? You got a split, didn't you? Better'n fifty-fifty."

He started away.

"Where you goin'?"

"I'm goin' to meet Harris and his wife."

"I'm goin' with you. You're not goin' to shake me now."

"Yes, I am, too," said Midge quietly. "When I leave town tomorrow night, you're going to stay here. And if I see where you're goin' to make a fuss, I'll put you in a hospital where they'll keep you quiet. You can get your stuff tomorrow mornin' and I'll slip you a hundred bucks. And then I don't want to see no more o' you. And don't try and tag along now or I'll have to add another K.O. to the old record."

When Grace returned to the hotel that night, she discovered that Midge and the Harrises had moved to another. And when Midge left town the following night, he was again without a manager, and Mr. Harris was without a wife.

THREE DAYS prior to Midge's Kelly's ten-round bout with Young Milton in New York City, the sporting editor of the *News* assigned Joe Morgan to write two or three thousand words about the champion to run with a picture layout for Sunday.

Joe Morgan dropped in at Midge's training quarters Friday afternoon. Midge, he learned, was doing road work, but Midge's manager, Wallie Adams, stood ready and willing to supply reams of dope about the greatest fighter of the age.

"Let's hear what you've got," said Joe, "and then I'll try to fix up something."

So Wallie stepped on the accelerator of his imagination and shot away.

"Just a kid; that's all he is; a regular boy. Get what I mean? Don't know the meanin' o' bad habits. Never tasted liquor in his life and would prob'bly get sick if he smelled it. Clean livin' put him up where he's at. Get what I mean? And modest and unassumin' as a schoolgirl. He's so quiet you wouldn't never know he was round. And he'd go to jail before he'd talk about himself.

"No job at all to get him in shape, 'cause he's always that way. The only trouble we have with him is gettin' him to light into these poor bums they match him up with. He's scared he'll hurt somebody. Get what I mean? He's tickled to death over this match with Milton, 'cause everybody says Milton can stand the gaff. Midge'll maybe be able to cut loose a little this time. But the last two bouts he had, the guys hadn't no business in the ring with him, and he was holdin' back all the w'ile for the fear he'd kill somebody. Get what I mean?"

"Is he married?" inquired Joe.

"Say, you'd think he was married to hear him rave about them kiddies he's got. His fam'ly's up in Canada to their summer home and Midge is wild to get up there with 'em. He thinks more o' that wife and them kiddies than all the money in the world. Get what I mean?"

"How many children has he?"

"I don't know, four or five, I guess. All boys and every one of 'em a dead ringer for their dad."

"Is his father living?"

"No, the old man died when he was a kid. But he's got a grand old mother and a kid brother out in Chi. They're the first ones he thinks about after a match, them and his wife and kiddies. And he don't forget to send the old woman a thousand bucks after every bout. He's goin' to buy her a new home as soon as they pay him off for this match."

"How about his brother? Is he going to tackle the game?"

"Sure, and Midge says he'll be a champion before he's twenty years old. They're a fightin' fam'ly and all of 'em honest and straight as a die. Get what I mean? A fella that I can't tell you his name come to Midge in Milwaukee onct and wanted him to throw a fight and Midge give him such a trimmin' in the street that he couldn't go on that night. That's the kind he is. Get what I mean?"

Joe Morgan hung around the camp until Midge and his trainers returned.

"One o' the boys from the *News*," said Wallie by way of introduction. "I been givin' him your fam'ly hist'ry."

"Did he give you good dope?" he inquired.

"He's some historian," said Joe.

"Don't call me no names," said Wallie smiling. "Call us up if they's anything more you want. And keep your eyes on us Monday night. Get what I mean?"

The story in Sunday's *News* was read by thousands of lovers of the manly art. It was well written and full of human interest. Its slight inaccuracies went unchallenged, though three readers, besides Wallie Adams and Midge Kelly, saw and recognized them. The three were Grace, Tommy Haley and Jerome Harris, and the comments they made were not for publication.

Neither the Mrs. Kelly in Chicago nor the Mrs. Kelly in Milwaukee knew that there was such a paper as the New York *News*. And even if they had known of it and that it contained two columns of reading matter about Midge, neither mother nor wife could have bought it. For the *News* on Sunday is a nickel a copy.

Joe Morgan could have written more accurately, no doubt, if instead of Wallie Adams, he had interviewed Ellen Kelly and Connie Kelly and Emma Kelly and Lou Hersch and Grace and Jerome Harris and Tommy Haley and Hap Collins and two or three Milwaukee bartenders.

But a story built on their evidence would never have passed the sporting editor.

"Suppose you can prove it," that gentleman would have said. "It wouldn't get us anything but abuse to print it. The people don't want to see him knocked. He's champion."

# B. TOBEY

*"I must say that was a short seven dollars and fifty cents' worth, young man!"*

FOT THE PAST twenty-five years, on and off, Joe Liebling has been writing boxing pieces for *The New Yorker* that have been distinguished examples of scholarship, sagacity, wit and intimate knowledge. Thus one of the most fortunate blows ever struck in behalf of the sport was a left jab landed on Liebling's nose by his Uncle Mike in 1917, when Joe was thirteen years old.

Uncle Mike was a boxing buff and also, to quote Liebling. "a sound teacher and a good storyteller, so I got the rudiments and the legend at the same time." In the pursuit of further knowledge Joe was subsequently struck by Philadelphia Jack O'Brien, who had been hit by Bob Fitzsimmons, who had been hit by Jim Corbett, Corbett by John L. Sullivan, he by Paddy Ryan, Ryan by Joe Goss and Goss by Jem Mace. "I wonder," Liebling wrote, introducing his *The Sweet Science*, "if Professor Toynbee is as intimately attuned to his sources."

# Sparring Partner

## A. J. LIEBLING

JOE LOUIS' knockout of Max Schmeling in their second match was a triumph for the theory that fighters should have tough sparring partners. Each of his bouts since has been a triumph for the same theory. Louis trained for Schmeling with the best colored heavyweights his handlers could hire. They included a man named George Nicholson, who is considered the best sparring partner in the business. Writers covering Louis' camp frequently reported that the partners were outboxing the champion. Schmeling's camp was run on quite a different basis. His sparring partners were four virtually anonymous human punching bags, on whom he practiced his blows with impunity. They seldom hit back except by mistake, and when they did the German punished them. Louis paid twenty-five dollars a day apiece for his sparring partners; Schmeling paid ten. A Schmeling victory, therefore, would have meant economic catastrophe for the sparring-partner industry.

"It goes to show that you got to be in the best of condition no matter who you fighting," George Nicholson says of the German's defeat. And getting in the "best of condition" implies to Nicholson sparring partners at twenty-five dollars a day. "You can hire any kind of cheap help to get theirself hit," says Nicholson. "What you got to pay good money for is somebody that is not going to get hisself hit. By not getting hisself hit, a sparring partner does more good to a fighter, because he sets the fighter to studying why he ain't hitting him." Nicholson's heartfelt interest in the defensive aspect of boxing, critics think, makes him an ideal sparring partner. It is this same interest which prevents him from being a great fighter. He is one of the kindest and least aggressive men who ever pulled on a boxing glove. "My one ambition," George sometimes says, "is to make my parents happy."

One reason he prefers sparring to fighting is that it keeps him out in the country for weeks at a time. George loves nature, usually soaking up its beauties through the pores of his skin, with his eyes closed. He is never more content than when he can sprawl his five-foot-eleven-and-three-quarter-inch body in one of the deep lawn chairs at Dr. Joseph Bier's training camp at

Pompton Lakes, New Jersey, where Louis has trained for eleven Eastern fights and prepared for his match with Tony Galento at the Yankee Stadium. It is pleasant to watch Nicholson in his chair, a straw sombrero cocked over his eyes, which are further protected by smoked glasses with octagonal lenses. His torso slopes backward at an extremely obtuse angle to his thighs. One leg, with a size thirteen shoe at the end of it, is negligently crossed over the other knee. Sometimes he drops off to sleep.

At two o'clock in the afternoon a brisk, pink-cheeked Jewish trainer named Mannie Seamon appears on the lawn and says, "C'mon, George, time to get going." The big man arises and starts for the gymnasium at the back of the house to prepare for the few minutes of acute discomfort whereby he pays for his leisure. Louis in training usually boxes against three sparring partners in an afternoon, two three-minute rounds with each man.

Nicholson is at home at Pompton Lakes. He has been there to help Louis prepare for four fights. In 1936 he spent three weeks in the same camp with Jim Braddock, when Braddock was getting ready to fight Tommy Farr. Now and then, Nicholson gets a fight on his own account, but he doesn't earn much that way. A sparring partner must be a pretty good fighter to give a star a workout, but if he is a financially successful fighter he will not work for training-camp wages. Since there are not many bouts available for a run-of-the-mill Negro heavyweight unless he has a powerful white promoter building him up, the best sparring partners are apt to be Negroes. White boys of commensurate ability are usually in training for their own fights.

A partner's life is not arduous when he has a camp job. He may take some hard punches in a workout with a hitter like Louis, but boxers in training wear headguards and sixteen-ounce gloves, and Nicholson has seldom received a cut. Nor has he ever been knocked down in a sparring match. The trouble with the calling is that stars usually train only four weeks for a bout and fight at most two or three times each year. Sometimes a heavyweight champion skips a year without fighting at all. In the intervals a sparring partner has slim pickings. This sometimes discourages Nicholson, but not for long. His is a sanguine nature.

"When it's no business in the fall," he says, "I go home to my parents' place in Mantua, New Jersey, and hunts rabbits and squirrels with a gun. And when it's no work in the spring I go there and work in the garden. And then, also, I might get a fight in-between-times." He does not say this last with any conviction. He had just fourteen fights in his first four years as a professional, and his net income from them was less than fifteen hundred dollars. George won nine bouts and thinks he got bad decisions in a couple he lost. He was twenty-eight—a ripe middle age for a fighter.

Boxers never start out to be sparring partners, any more than actors start out to be understudies. Fighters take sparring jobs to bridge over gaps between engagements, and even after a boxer has earned his living for years by sparring, he is apt to think of it as a temporary expedient. When Nicholson began boxing he thought he might be a champion.

George was born in Mantua, where his father was a teamster. Later his family moved to Yonkers, and there he played tackle on the high-school football team. His parents have moved back to Mantua since George left school, but he has a brother who still lives in Yonkers, "a govament man," he says, "WPA." One of George's earliest ambitions was to be a prize fighter, because he was always reading about boxing in the newspapers. The beginning of his true career was delayed, though. At Yonkers High he got to thinking he might be a lawyer. He abandoned this project for a peculiar reason. "I got out of the habit of trying to study law," he says, "on account of I saw I couldn't talk fast enough."

For a few years he was bemused. He had got to thinking of himself as a professional man and he couldn't seem to readjust. Even today most of his associates believe he is a college graduate. The misconception, based upon his polished manner, is strengthened by the fact that he played for three seasons on a colored professional football team called the All-Southern Collegians. The Collegians accepted him without a diploma, George explains now. He quit his books after the third year of high school and took a job as porter in a hospital, playing professional football on autumn Sundays. He got the boxing fever again when he was twenty-three, an unusually advanced age for a debut.

George then weighed 243 pounds, which was far too much for his height. "I was so fat that one time I missed and fell right down," he says. "But I always throwed a good right hand anyway." He won two amateur bouts at smokers, both on knockouts, and then lost a decision to a fellow named Moe Levine in a big amateur show in Madison Square Garden. "I bounced him around, but I didn't know enough to finish him," George says now with a hint of cultured regret. A strange accident removed him from the ranks of the amateurs. He entered the 1934 *Daily News*

Golden Gloves Tournament and was rejected because of a heart murmur. Soon after, he went up to Stillman's Gymnasium, where he met a matchmaker and got himself a preliminary bout on a card at a small professional club. The State Athletic Commission doctor found his heart action normal. Once he had fought this professional bout, he was no longer an amateur and after the fight, for which he got twenty-five dollars, he hit a long spell of unemployment. "I was so broke I didn't have *no* money," he says.

It is much easier for an amateur boxer to make a living than it is for a professional. Almost every night of the week several amateur shows are held in the city. Like bingo games and raffles, they are a recognized means of raising money for fraternal organizations. In most shows there are four competitors in each class. They meet in three-round bouts, with the winners competing in a final match later in the evening. There is a standard scale of remuneration. The winner of the final receives a seventeen-jewel watch, which may be sold in the open market for fifteen dollars. The runner-up gets a seven-jewel model, for which he can obtain five or six dollars. The two losers in the first bouts receive cheap timepieces known in amateur boxing circles as "consolations." They have a sale value of two dollars. A preliminary boy "in the professionals" gets forty dollars for a bout, but opportunities for employment are much more limited. Moreover, a State Athletic Commission rule restricts a professional to one bout every five days, whereas an amateur is free to compete every night.

Jim Howell, a Negro who is a frequent colleague of Nicholson as a sparring mate in the Louis camp, had a long career as an amateur. He remembers one week when he won four seventeen-jewel watches. "And it's funny," Howell says, "there's very few even the best amateurs that you can ask him the time and he got a watch. Or if it is, it's just a consolation." Now Howell is a professional and he hasn't had ten fights in the past year. But he still thinks he can break through into the big time.

Unemployment among professional boxers antedates the Hoover depression. There are about a thousand active prize fighters in Greater New York. At the height of the winter season seven boxing clubs operate, with from six to eight bouts on the average weekly card. Only about a hundred fighters out of the available thousand can possibly hope for weekly employment. When they do work most of them get from forty to seventy-five dollars, minus one third for their managers. The average boxer lives from one fight to the next on small loans. When he gets a match, he often owes his entire purse before he enters the ring. Colored boys have even bleaker prospects than their white competitors, but there is a high percentage of Negroes in any training gym. This is because their disadvantage, staggering as it is in the boxing world, is less than in ordinary industry. Even when they cannot get a match, they sometimes have a chance to spar with a white boy in the gymnasium, being paid from three to ten dollars for their trouble.

The plight of the starving boxer is particularly cruel because by his daily exertions he increases his appetite beyond ordinary human bounds. Worse than hunger is the fear of not being able to get up his dues, the dollar a week he must pay for the privilege of using the gymnasium and showers. There are other minuscular expenses which seem huge in the eyes of a boy with no match in sight: he uses ninety cents' worth of gauze and twenty-five cents' worth of tape a week to wrap his fists for sparring matches; he buys rubbing alcohol and Omega Oil, which he applies himself if he cannot afford a dollar for a professional rubdown. In order to avoid cuts he must buy a leather headguard.

Plunged into this athletic slum, Nicholson felt sad and lonely. He was about to go back to his job at the hospital when, in the fall of 1934, his solid form and large white smile attracted the attention of Jim Braddock, at that time making his comeback, who also trained at Stillman's. Braddock had not yet got back to the point where he could pay experienced sparring partners. He noticed that the big colored boy "took a very good punch," a quality which Jim admired, and he offered to teach George some of the inner mysteries of the craft. Braddock got free workouts and Nicholson got free boxing lessons. Within six months Braddock was again in the big money, training for the fight in which he was to win the championship from Max Baer, and Nicholson had learned so fast that he qualified as one of Jim's paid sparring partners. Surprisingly enough, the heavy-set, oldish novice had innate style. He was a natural boxer with a willingness to take punishment when it was necessary. This is not the same as being a natural fighter, which calls for a certain streak of cruelty.

Nicholson still uses Stillman's as a business headquarters when he has no camp job and is running short of money. He loafs for three or four weeks after a training camp breaks up, then makes his appearance at the gymnasium, which is on Eighth Avenue between Fifty-fourth and Fifty-fifth. "More business is transacted there than anyplace in the world," he explains. Trainers and managers are always glad to see him.

"George is a good boy," says Mannie Seamon, who is a sort of personnel director for training camps. "Some sparring partners will throw a head [butt] or throw an elbow and maybe give a man a cut so the fight will have to be postponed, but George don't cross nobody up. He boxes quick so the fighter can't stay lazy, and he keeps throwing punches so the fighter can't make lax. A good boy."

When there is no camp job in sight George will sometimes box with a heavyweight training for a minor bout, receiving five or ten dollars for his afternoon's work, according to the fighter's prosperity. He can usually pick up fifteen or twenty dollars a week, which covers living expenses, until he gets more regular employment. George is a bachelor. "I can't see my ways through to getting married the way things are," he says. When he is in the metropolitan region, he stays with the WPA brother and his family in Yonkers. He doesn't go to Harlem much, because, he says, he doesn't want to change his ways and run wild. George doesn't smoke or drink. At Stillman's he observes the other heavyweights in the training ring. He makes mental note of their styles so that he will be able to imitate them on request. A sparring partner must be versatile. For example, when Louis was training for Nathan Mann his sparring partners were urged to throw left hooks like Mann. But when he was training for Schmeling the script called for George to throw right hands to Louis' jaw. Louis never did learn to block them, but his trainers felt that he would develop a certain immunity through inoculation. In 1939 Nicholson was emphasizing left hooks again, like Tony Galento.

His greatest benefactor, George thinks, was Jim Braddock. "There is no discrimination with Jim," Nicholson says. "When I was training with him in 1936 for that Schmeling fight that never come off he put rocks in my bed just like anybody else." This is a reminiscence of the refined horseplay that always distinguishes Braddock's camps from those of less whimsical prize fighters. A Louis camp is more restful. "All we does is play catch with a baseball and sometimes talk jokes," Nicholson says. He first trained with Louis when the present champion was preparing for his fight with Braddock in Chicago. Having boxed so often with Braddock, Nicholson could illustrate all his moves beautifully. Boxers do not consider such a transfer of allegiance unethical. You hire a sparring partner, and he does his best for you while you pay him. He may be in the enemy's camp for your next fight. Braddock hired Nicholson again before the Tommy Farr fight.

The worst sparring partner in all history was a young giant named James J. Jeffries, who joined Jim Corbett's camp when Corbett was training for his bout with Bob Fitzsimmons in Carson City, Nevada, forty-two years ago. Jeffries knocked Corbett out the first time they put on the gloves, which had an evil effect on Corbett's morale. He lost to Fitzsimmons. Later the ex-sparring partner knocked Fitzsimmons out and became champion of the world. Nicholson has never come near knocking out Braddock or Louis or even Primo Carnera, whom he trained for one of his last fights, but sometimes he is engaged to box with young heavyweights whom he must treat tenderly. A beginner can learn much from a good sparring partner, but if the partner knocks his brains out, as the boys say, the novice loses his nerve. George's most delicate client was a former college football player with the face of a Hollywood star and the shoulders of a Hercules, who was being merchandised by a smart manager. The manager had interested three Wall Street men in his dazzling heavyweight "prospect," assuring them that he was potentially the greatest fighter since Dempsey. The Wall Streeters actually put the boxer and the manager on salary and bought the youngster an automobile. This was before the boy had had even one fight. The manager, in order to prevent his backers from hearing any skeptical reports, arranged to have the football player train in a private gymnasium frequented only by fat businessmen. He then hired Nicholson to spar with him, and each afternoon the Wall Streeters and their friends visited the gymnasium and watched their hopeful knock George about. George got five dollars a workout. They were much astonished subsequently when, after they had supported their coming champion for a year and a half, he was knocked out in a four-round bout they got him with another novice.

George says there was nothing wrong about his conduct. "That manager hired me to box with that boy," he says. "He didn't hire me to hurt him."

There isn't much money in the sparring business, George concedes, but there doesn't seem to be much in anything else, either. The prospect of injury doesn't bother him, because he seldom takes a punch solidly. He "gets on it" before it develops power, or else he takes it on his forearms or shoulders, or at worst "rolls away" from it as it lands. "I like the old word for boxing," he once said. "The manly art of *de*fense. And I don't fear no man. Now, that Joe, he really can punch. He can really punch. What I mean, he can punch, really. Yet he ain't never no more'n shook me. And when I feel myself getting punch-drunk I'm going to quit. I'm going to look me up a profitable business somewhere that's a profit in it."

Nicholson was in his chair at Pompton Lakes when he made this declaration. The chairs at his left and right were occupied by Jim Howell and another large colored man named Elza Thompson. Each of the three had his left leg crossed over his right knee. After a long interval they recrossed their legs in unison, this time with the right on top. There was no spoken word to suggest the shift, just telepathy. Undisturbed by the musical sigh of Nicholson's voice, Howell and Thompson were apparently asleep. Yet the triple movement was perfectly synchronized, like some-thing the Rockettes might do, but in slow time.

At the phrase "punch-drunk" Howell had opened one eye.

"How you going to know you punch-drunk, George?" he inquired. "A man punch-drunk, he don't know he punch-drunk. That the sign he punch-drunk."

Nicholson thought this over in deep gloom for a while.

Then he said, "Sometime when I boxing with a fellow that hit me right on the button, and I know he ain't got no right to hit me on the button, and I boxing with him again and he hit me on the button again, then I going to quit."

After this the three sparring partners all fell asleep.

JOHN L. SULLIVAN and Jake Kilrain fought the last bare knuckle championship fight under a scalding sun and in the oppressive heat and
humidity of Richburg, Mississippi, on July 8, 1889. This is how, many
years later, a celebrated poet-troubadour placed the event within the
frame of its time. Sullivan did not, of course, break "every single rib
of Jake Kilrain" but he knocked him down forty-eight times in a
brutal, bloody fight for which both contestants were arrested and
fined.

# John L. Sullivan,
# the Boston Strong Boy

### VACHEL LINDSAY

[INSCRIBED TO LOUIS UNTERMEYER AND ROBERT FROST]

When I was nine years old, in 1889,
I sent my love a lacy Valentine.
Suffering boys were dressed like Fauntleroys,
While *Judge* and *Puck* in giant humor vied.
The Gibson Girl came shining like a bride
To spoil the cult of Tennyson's Elaine.
Louisa Alcott was my gentle guide . . .
Then . . .
I heard a battle trumpet sound.
Nigh New Orleans
Upon an emerald plain
John L. Sullivan
The strong boy
Of Boston
Fought seventy-five red rounds with Jake Kilrain.

In simple sheltered 1889
Nick Carter I would piously deride.
Over the Elsie Books I moped and sighed.
*St. Nicholas* Magazine was all my pride,
While coarser boys on cellar doors would slide.
The grownups bought refinement by the pound.
Rogers groups had not been told to hide.
E. P. Roe had just begun to wane.

Howells was rising, surely to attain!
The nation for a jamboree was gowned.—
Her hundredth year of roaring freedom crowned.
The British Lion ran and hid from Blaine
The razzle-dazzle hip-hurrah from Maine.
The mockingbird was singing in the lane . . .
Yet . . .
*"East side, west side, all around the town*
*The tots sang: 'Ring a rosie—*
*'London Bridge is falling down.' "*
And . . .
John L. Sullivan
The strong boy
Of Boston
Broke every single rib of Jake Kilrain.

To be sung.
Let the
audience join
in softly on
this tune,
wherever it
appears.

In dear provincial 1889,
Barnum's bears and tigers could astound.
Ingersoll was called a most vile hound,
And named with Satan, Judas, Thomas Paine!
Robert Elsmere riled the pious brain.
Phillips Brooks for heresy was fried.
Boston Brahmins patronized Mark Twain.
The baseball rules were changed. That was a gain.
Pop Anson was our darling, pet and pride.
Native sons in Irish votes were drowned.
Tammany once more escaped its chain.
Once more each raw saloon was raising Cain.
The mockingbird was singing in the lane . . .
Yet . . .
*"East side, west side, all around the town*
*The tots sang: 'Ring a rosie—*
*'London Bridge is falling down.' "*
And . . .
John L. Sullivan
The strong boy
Of Boston
Finished the ring career of Jake Kilrain.

In mystic, ancient 1889,
Wilson with pure learning was allied.
Roosevelt gave forth a chirping sound.
Stanley found old Emin and his train.
Stout explorers sought the pole in vain.
To dream of flying proved a man insane.
The newly rich were bathing in champagne.
Van Bibber Davis, at a single bound
Displayed himself, and simpering glory found.
John J. Ingalls, like a lonely crane
Swore and swore, and stalked the Kansas plain.
The Cronin murder was the ages' stain.
Johnstown was flooded, and the whole world cried.
We heard not of Louvain nor of Lorraine,

## John L. Sullivan, the Boston Strong Boy BY VACHEL LINDSAY

Or a million heroes for their freedom slain.
Of Armageddon and the world's birth-pain—
The League of Nations, and the world one posy.
We *thought* the world would loaf and sprawl and mosey.
The gods of Yap and Swat were sweetly dozy.
We *thought* the far-off gods of Chow had died.
The mockingbird was singing in the lane . . .
Yet . . .
*"East side, west side, all around the town*
*The tots sang: 'Ring a rosie—*
*'London Bridge is falling down.'"*
And . . .
John L. Sullivan knocked out Jake Kilrain.

IN SYDNEY, AUSTRALIA, on the day after Christmas, 1908, Jack London watched Jack Johnson toy with Tommy Burns and win the heavyweight championship of the world. In the last paragraph of his story in the New York *Herald* he started the bigoted ballyhoo that brought Jim Jeffries back, after six years without a fight.

"But one thing remains," London wrote, bravely. "Jeffries must emerge from his alfalfa farm and remove the golden smile from Johnson's face. Jeff, it's up to you!"

In Reno, Nevada, eighteen months later, he watched a fat alfalfa farmer try and, for the first time in a ring, fail.

# Jack Johnson v. Jim Jeffries

## JACK LONDON

RENO, NEVADA, July 5, 1910—Once again has Johnson sent down to defeat the chosen representative of the white race and this time the greatest of them. And as of old, it was play for Johnson. From the opening round to the closing round he never ceased his witty sallies, his exchanges of repartee with his opponent's seconds and with the audience. And, for that matter, Johnson had a funny thing or two to say to Jeffries in every round.

The golden smile was as much in evidence as ever and neither did it freeze on his face nor did it vanish. It came and went throughout the fight, spontaneously, naturally.

It was not a great battle after all, save in its setting and significance. Little Tommy Burns, down in far-off Australia, put up a faster, quicker, livelier battle than did Jeffries. The fight today was great only in its significance. In itself it wasn't great. The issue, after the fiddling of the opening rounds, was never in doubt. In the fiddling of those first rounds the honors lay with Johnson, and for the rounds after the seventh or eighth it was more Johnson, while for the closing rounds it was all Johnson.

Johnson played as usual. With his opponent not strong in attack, Johnson, blocking and defending in masterly fashion, could afford to play. And he played and fought a white man, in the white man's country, before a white man's audience. And the audience was a Jeffries audience.

When Jeffries sent in that awful rip of his the audience would madly applaud, believing it had gone home to Johnson's stomach, and Johnson, defty interposing his elbow, would smile in irony at the audience, play-acting, making believe he thought the applause was for him—and never believing it at all.

The greatest fight of the century was a monologue delivered to twenty thousand spectators by a smiling Negro who was never in doubt and who was never serious for more than a moment at a time.

As a fighter Johnson did not show himself a wonder. He did not have to. Never once was he extended. There was no need. Jeffries could not make him extend. Jeffries never had him in trouble once. No blow Jeffries ever landed hurt his dusky opponent. Johnson came out of the fight practically undamaged. The blood on his lip was from a recent cut received in the course of training and which Jeffries managed to reopen.

Jeffries failed to lead and land. The quickness he brought into the fight quickly evaporated, and while Jeffries was dead game to the end, he was not so badly punished. What he failed to bring into the ring with him was his stamina, which he lost somewhere in the last seven years. Jeffries failed to come back. That's the whole story. His old-time vim and endurance were not there. Something has happened to him. He lost in retirement outside of the ring the stamina that the ring itself never robbed him of. As I have said, Jeffries was not badly damaged. Every day boys take worse lacings in boxing bouts than Jeffries took today.

Jeffries today disposed of one question. He could not come back. Johnson, in turn, answered another question. He has not the yellow streak. But he only answered that question for today. The ferocity of the hairy-chested caveman and grizzly giant did not intimidate the cool-headed Negro. Many thousands in the audience expected the intimidation, and were correspondingly disappointed. Johnson was not scared, let it be said here, and beyond the shadow of any doubt, not for an instant was Johnson scared. Not for a second did he show the flicker of fear that the Goliath against him might eat him up.

But the question of the yellow streak is not answered for all time. Just as Johnson has never been extended, so has he never shown the yellow streak. Just as any man may rise up, heaven alone knows where, who will extend Johnson, just so may that man bring out the yellow streak; and then again he may not. So far the burden of proof all rests on the conclusion that Johnson has no yellow streak.

And now to the battle and how it began! All praise to Tex Rickard, the gamest of sports, who pulled off the fight after countless difficulties and who, cool, calm and quick with nervous aliveness, handled the vast crowd splendidly in his arena and wound up by refereeing the fight.

Twenty thousand filled the great arena and waited patiently under the cloud-flecked, wide Nevada sky. Of the many women present some elected to sit in the screened boxes far back from the ring, for all the world like old-time Spanish ladies at the theater. But more, many more women, sat close to the ringside beside their husbands or brothers. They were the wiser by far.

Merely to enumerate the celebrities at the ringside would be to write a sporting directory of America—at least a directory of the four-hundred sportsmen, and of many more hundreds of near four-hundreds. At four minutes to two Billy Jordan cleared the ring amid cheers and stood alone, the focal point of twenty thousand pairs of eyes, until the great William Muldoon climbed through the ropes to call ringing cheers from the twenty thousand throats for the state of Nevada, the people of Nevada and the governor of Nevada.

Beginning with Tex Rickard, ovation after ovation was given to all the great ones, not forgetting Bob Fitzsimmons, whom Billy Jordan introduced as "The greatest warrior of them all." And so they came, great one after great one, ceaselessly, endlessly. Until they were swept away before the greatest of them all, the two men who were about to do battle.

It was half past two when Johnson entered. He came first, happy and smiling, greeting friends and acquaintances here and there and everywhere in the audience, cool as ice, waving his hand in salute, smiling, smiling, ever smiling with eyes as well as with lips, never missing a name nor a face, placid, plastic, nerveless, with never a signal of hesitancy or timidity. Yet he was keyed up, keenly observant of all that was going on, ever hearing much of the confused babble of the tongues about him—hearing, aye, and understanding, too.

There is nothing beary or primitive about this man Johnson. He is alive and quivering, every nerve fiber in his body, and brain. Withal that it is hidden so artfully or naturally under that poise of facetious calm of his. He is a marvel of sensitiveness, sensibility and perceptiveness. He has the perfect mechanism of mind and body. His mind works like chain lightning and his body obeys with equal swiftness.

But the great madness of applause went up when Jeffries entered the ring two minutes later. A quick, superficial comparison between him and the Negro would have led to a feeling of pity for the latter. For Jeff was all that has been said of him. When he stripped and his mighty body could be seen covered with mats of hair, all the primordial adjectives ever applied to him received their vindication. Nor did his face belie him. No facial emotion played on that face, no whims of the moment, no flutterings of a light-hearted temperament.

Dark and somber and ominous was that face, solid and stolid and expressionless, with eyes that smoldered and looked savage. The man of iron, grim with determination, sat down in his corner. And the carefree Negro smiled and smiled. And that's the story of the fight. The man of iron, the grizzly giant, was grim and serious. The man of summer temperament smiled and smiled. That is the story of the whole fight. It is the story of the fight by rounds.

At the opening of the first round they did not shake hands. Knowing the two men for what they are, it can be safely postulated that this neglect was due to Jeffries or to the prompting from Jeffries' corner. But it is not good that two boxers should not shake hands before a bout. I would suggest to those protagonists of a perishing game, if they wish to preserve the game, that they make the most of these little amenities that by custom grace their sport and give it the veneer of civilization.

Both men went to work in that first round very easily. Johnson smiling, of course; Jeffries grim and determined. Johnson landed the first blow, a light one, and Jeffries in the clinches gave a faint indication of his forthcoming tactics by roughing it, by crowding the Negro around and by slightly bearing his weight upon him. It was a very easy round, with nothing of moment. Each was merely feeling the other out and both were exceedingly careful. At the conclusion of the round, Johnson tapped Jeffries playfully on the shoulder, smiled good-naturedly and went to his corner. Jeffries, in the first, showed flashes of catlike quickness.

Round Two—Jeffries advanced with a momentary assumption of famous crouch, to meet the broadly smiling Johnson. Jeffries is really human and good-natured. He proved it right here. So friendly was that smile of Johnson's, so irresistibly catching, that Jeffries, despite himself, smiled back. But Jeffries' smiles were doomed to be very few in this fight.

And right here began a repetition of what took place down in Australia when Burns fought Johnson. Each time Burns said something harsh to Johnson in the hope of making him lose his temper, Johnson responded by giving the white man a lacing. And so today. Of course, Jeffries did not talk to Johnson to amount to anything, but Corbett, in his corner, did it for Jeffries. And each time Corbett cried something in particular, Johnson promptly administered a lacing to Jeffries.

It began in the second round. Corbett, in line with his plan of irritating the Negro, called out loudly:

"He wants to fight a little, Jim."

"You bet I do," Johnson retorted, and with that he landed Jeffries a stinger with his right uppercut.

Both men were tensely careful, Jeffries trying to crowd and put his weight on in the clinches, Johnson striving more and more than the other to break out of the clinches. And at the end of this round, in his corner Johnson was laughing gleefully. Certainly Jeffries showed no signs of boring in, as had been promised by his enthusiastic supporters.

It was the same story in the third round, at the conclusion of which the irrepressible Negro was guilty of waving his hands to friends in the audience.

In this fourth round Jeffries showed up better, rushing and crowding and striking with more vim than hitherto shown. This seemed to have been caused by a sally of Johnson's, and Jeffries went at him in an angry sort of way. Promptly Jeffries rushed, and even ere they came together Johnson cried out: "Don't rush me, Jim. You hear what I'm telling you?"

No sign there of being intimidated by Jeffries' first dynamic display of ferocity. All he managed to do was to reopen the training cut in Johnson's lip and to make Johnson playful. It was most anybody's round and it was certainly more Jeffries' than any preceding one.

Round five brought Jeffries advancing with his crouch. The blood from Johnson's lip had turned his smile to a gory one, but still he smiled, and to balance things off he opened Jeffries' lip until it bled more profusely than his own. From then until the end of the fight, Jeffries' face was never free from blood, a steady stream, later flowing from his right nostril, added to by an open cut on his left cheek. Corbett's running fire of irritation served but to make Johnson smile the merrier, and to wink at him across Jeffries' shoulder in the clinches.

So far, no problems have been solved, no questions answered. The yellow streak had not appeared. Neither had Jeffries bored in, ripping awfully, nor put it over Johnson in the clinches. Yet one thing had been shown. Jeffries was not as fast as he had been. There was a shade of diminution in his speed.

Johnson signalized the opening of the sixth round by landing stinging blows to the face in one, two, three order. Johnson's quickness was startling. In response to an irritating remark from Corbett, Johnson replied suavely, "Too much on hand right now," and at the same instant he tore into Jeffries. It was Johnson's first real aggressive rush. It lasted but a second or two, but it was fierce and dandy. And at its conclusion it was manifest that Jeff's right eye was closing fast. The round ended with Johnson fighting and smiling strong, and with Jeff's nose, lip and cheek bleeding and his eye closed. Johnson's round by a smile all the way through.

The seventh round was a mild one, opening with Jeff grim and silent and with Johnson leading and forcing. Both were careful and nothing happened, save that once they exchanged blows right niftily. So far Jeff's roughing and crowding and bearing in of weight had amounted to nothing; also he was doing less and less of it.

"It only takes one or two, Jeff," Corbett encouraged his principal in the eighth round. Promptly Johnson landed two stingers. After a pause he landed another. "See that?" he chirruped sweetly to Corbett in the corner. Jeff perceptibly showed signs of slowing down in this round, rushing and crowding less than ever. Jeff's slowing down was not due to the punishment he had received, but to poorness of condition. He was flying the first signals of fatigue. He was advertising, faintly, it is true, that he had not come back.

The ninth round was introduced by a suggestion from Corbett, heroically carrying out the policy that was bringing his principal to destruction. "Make the big stiff fight," was Corbett's suggestion.

"That's right. That's what they all say," was Johnson's answer, delivered with the true Chesterfield grace across his adversary's shoulder. In the previous rounds Johnson had not wreaked much damage with the forecasted cut, the right uppercut.

In this round he demonstrated indubitably that he could drive the left hand in a way that was surprising. Be it remembered that it had long been denied that he had any sort of punch in that left of his. Incidentally, in this round, it led all the others, and he landed a blow near Jeffries' heart that must have been discouraging.

The tenth round showed Johnson with his unexpected left, as quick as ever, and Jeffries going slower and slower. The conclusion of the first ten rounds may be summed up as follows:

The fight was all in favor of Johnson, who had shown no yellow, who had shown condition, who had shown undiminished speed, who had not used his right uppercut much, who had developed a savage left, who had held his own in the clinches, who had gotten the best of the infighting and all the outfighting, who was unhurt, and who was smiling all the way.

Jeff was in bad shape: He was tired, slower than ever, his rushes had been futile, and the sports who had placed their money against him were jubilant.

There were men who proclaimed they saw the end. I refused to see this end, for I had picked Jeff to win, and I was hoping hugely—for what I did not know, but for something to happen, for anything that would turn the tide of battle. And yet I could not hide from myself the truth, that Jeff slowed down.

The eleventh round looked better for Jeff. Stung by a remark of Corbett's, Johnson rushed and provoked one grand rally from Jeff. It was faster fighting and more continuous than at any time in the preceding ten rounds, culminating in a fierce rally in which Jeff landed hard.

Round twelve found Johnson, if anything, quicker and more aggressive than ever. "Thought you were going to have me wild?" Johnson queried sweetly of Corbett. As usual every remark of Corbett's brought more punishment to Jeffries. And by the end of this round the second of the two great questions was definitely answered. Jeff had not come back.

The thirteenth round was the beginning of the end. Beginning slowly enough, but stung by Corbett, Johnson put it all over him in the mouth fighting, and all over Jeff in the outfighting and the infighting. From defense to attack and back again and back and forth Johnson flashed like the amazing fight mechanism he is. Jeff was silent and sick, while as the round progressed Corbett was noticeably silent.

A few entertained the fond hope that Jeff could recuperate, but it was futile; there was no comeback in him. He was a fading, heartsick, heartbroken man.

"Talk to him, Corbett," Jeff's friends appealed in the fourteenth round, but Corbett could not talk. He had long since seen the end. And yet through this round Johnson went in for one of his characteristic loafing spells. He took it easy and played with the big gladiator, cool as a cucumber, smiling broadly as ever, and yet, as careful as ever. "Right on the hip," he grinned out once as Jeff in a desperate dying flurry managed to land a wild punch in that vicinity.

Corbett, likewise desperate, ventured a last sally. "Why don't you do something?" he cried to the loafing, laughing Johnson. "Too clever, too clever, like you," was the reply.

Round fifteen and the end. It was pitiful. There happened to Jeff the bitterness that he had so often made others taste, but which for the first time, perforce, he was made to taste himself.

He who had never been knocked down was knocked down repeatedly. He who had never been knocked out was knocked out. Never mind the technical decision. Jeff was knocked out and through the ropes by the punch he never believed Johnson possessed—by the left and not by the right. As he lay across the lower rope while the seconds were tolled off, a cry that had in it tears and abject broken pride went up from many of the spectators.

"Don't let the Negro knock him out! Don't let the Negro knock him out!" was the oft-repeated cry.

There is little more to be said. Jeff did not come back. Johnson did not show the yellow streak. And it was Johnson's fight all the way through. Jeff was not the old Jeff at all.

Even so, it is to be doubted if this old Jeff could have put away this amazing Negro from

Texas, this black man with the unfailing smile, this king of fighters and monologists.

Corbett and Berger and the others were right. They wanted Jeff to do more boxing and fighting in his training. Nevertheless, lacking the comeback, as he so patently did, this preliminary boxing and fighting would have profited him nothing. On the other hand, it would have saved his camp much of the money with which it backed him.

It was a slow fight. Faster, better fights may be seen every day of the year in any of the small clubs in the land. It is true these men were heavyweights, yet for heavyweights it was a slow fight.

It must be granted that plucky Tommy Burns put up a faster fight with Johnson a year and a half ago. Yet the American fight followers had to see this fight of today in order to appreciate what Burns did against this colored wonder.

Johnson is a wonder. No one understands him, this man who smiles. Well, the story of the fight is the story of a smile. If ever man won by nothing more fatiguing than a smile, Johnson won today.

And where now is the champion who will make Johnson extend himself, who will glaze those bright eyes, remove that smile and silence that golden repartee?

LUCILIUS, the Latin satirical poet of the second century B.C., was the first of the "boxing-is-legalized-brutality" boys.

# Epigrams

## LUCILIUS

### [TRANSLATED BY W. R. PATON]

### I

THIS OLYMPICUS who is now such as you see him, Augustus, once had a nose, a chin, a forehead, ears and eyelids. Then becoming a professional boxer he lost all, not even getting his share of his father's inheritance; for his brother presented a likeness of him he had and he was pronounced to be a stranger, as he bore no resemblance to it.

### II

HAVING SUCH A MUG, Olympicus, go not to a fountain nor look into any transparent water, for you, like Narcissus, seeing your face clearly, will die, hating yourself to death.

### III

WHEN ULYSSES after twenty years came safe to his home, Argos the dog recognized his appearance when he saw him, but you, Stratophon, after boxing for four hours, have become not only unrecognizable to dogs but to the city. If you will trouble to look at your face in the glass, you will say on your oath, "I am not Stratophon."

### IV

YOUR HEAD, Apollophanes, has become a sieve, or the lower edge of a worm-eaten book, all exactly like ant-holes, crooked and straight, or musical notes Lydian and Phrygian. But go on boxing without fear; for even if you are struck on the head you will have the marks you have— you can't have more.

### V

CLEOMBROTUS CEASED to be a pugilist, but afterwards married, and now has at home all the blows of the Isthmian and Nemean games, a pugnacious old woman hitting as hard as in the Olympian fights, and he dreads his own house more than ever he dreaded the ring. Whenever he gets his wind, he is beaten with all the strokes known in every match to make him pay her his debt; and if he pays it, he is beaten again.

### VI

HIS COMPETITORS set up here the statue of Apis the boxer, for he never hurt anyone.

### VII

I, ANDROLEOS, took part in every boxing contest that the Greeks preside over, every single one. At Pisa I saved one ear, and in Platæa one eyelid, but at Delphi I was carried out insensible. Damoteles, my father, and my fellow-townsmen had been summoned by herald to bear me out of the stadium either dead or mutilated.

### VIII

ONESIMUS THE BOXER came to the prophet Olympus wishing to learn if he were going to live to old age. And he said, "Yes, if you give up the ring now, but if you go on boxing, Saturn is your horoscope."

W. O. MC GEEHAN was the founder of the "Aw nuts" school of sports writing. He referred to boxing as "the cauliflower industry" and "the manly art of modified murder" and named the members of the New York State Athletic Commission "The Three Dumb Dukes." He wrote this column about Ad Wolgast in 1927 for the New York *Herald Tribune,* for which he worked from 1914 until he died of a heart attack in 1933 at the age of 54.

Adolph (Ad) Wolgast was lightweight champion of the world from 1910 to 1912. He died, at the age of 67, on April 14, 1955, in a sanitarium in Camarillo, California, still believing that he would someday fight Joe Gans again. Gans had died on August 10, 1910.

# News of a Champion

## W. O. McGEEHAN

AD WOLGAST, once lightweight champion of the world, is in the news again briefly. Friends who have been caring for him in California have made application to have him committed to an asylum as hopelessly insane.

For more than ten years Wolgast has been living in a phantom world populated by old prize-ring ghosts. His mind failed him shortly after he lost his championship, and he labored under the hallucination that he was to meet Joe Gans (long since dead) for the lightweight championship. Jack Doyle, a Los Angeles promoter, with more heart than most of the men who make their money out of the manly art of modified murder, took pity on him and assumed full charge of him.

Through Doyle's generosity Ad Wolgast was provided with a little gymnasium, where he did his training. He seldom used to miss a morning on the road. It was his hallucination that he was to meet Joe Gans, dead even before Wolgast's mind went into the fog, in a championship bout. For years he settled down into this routine with only the idea that he must be in condition for the championship bout.

Sometimes they would take him to boxing matches. He always used to say, "I could whip either of them." But he never insisted on meeting

any of the fighters he saw. He was concentrating on the phantom bout with Gans. Physically Wolgast seemed to be all that he ever had been, but his mind was gone forever.

I saw Wolgast win the lightweight championship from Battling Nelson in a ring pitched in the adobe mud near Port Richmond, California. For concentrated viciousness, prolonged past forty rounds, that was the most savage bout I have ever seen. Both men were badly enough battered, for in giving Nelson a beating, Wolgast was forced to take almost as much as he gave. It was inevitable that the effects would tell.

Somewhere around the thirtieth round I think it was, Wolgast was dropped by a body blow and it looked like the end. But he was up in an instant, snarling and lashing at Nelson. After that it was Nelson, the Durable Dane, who showed signs of weakening and whose face began to look like a raw slab of steak. The features were obliterated and only the slit of one eye remained open.

In the forty-second round Nelson was pressing feebly forward while Wolgast's gloves were hurling crimson splashes around the ring every time they struck the battered face. The Dane would not yield an inch, but it had become so cruel that

262

the most hardened ringsiders were calling upon the referee to stop it.

Finally Eddie Smith stepped between the men and pushed Nelson to his corner. The Dane snarled at him, then tried to protest through the twisted and battered mouth. The only sound that came was one such as might have been made by an exhausted and terribly wounded wild animal. Nelson's seconds caught him and pushed him onto the stool in the corner. The referee raised Wolgast's hand. He had become the lightweight champion of the world.

Not so long after I saw him lose this title to Willie Ritchie of California, then a young graduate from the amateur ranks. It started out as though Wolgast would rush Ritchie off his feet. The "Cadillac Bearcat" was beating the Californian from the start, when Ritchie landed a wild swing that caught Wolgast flush on the jaw. Wolgast dropped to his knees, all but out. As he was about to collapse he drove two foul punches upward at the Californian. He had the rattlesnake's instinct to strike, even when mortally hurt.

It was Wolgast's fate to have won the championship in one of the hardest fights ever staged, only to have lost it through almost a chance blow —if there is such a thing as a chance blow.

Said one of Wolgast's former managers, "He was one of the greatest fighters I ever knew, and it was a pleasure to manage him. He never cared whom he fought or how often. He would fight anybody I signed him up with.

"Once I tried him out for fun. I knew that he was in his hotel room so I rang him up and told him I had signed him as a substitute boxer for some bouts that night. The schedule called for him to appear in three hours. 'All right,' he said. 'Wake me up in a few hours, and I'll get ready to go into the ring.'

" 'But you haven't asked who it is that you are going to fight,' I said. 'No,' said Wolgast, 'and I don't care. Just wake me up so that I won't be late getting into the ring.' He was that way all the time. He would say, 'Get me anybody for any time, and I'll fight him any time you say.'

"You do not meet that kind of fighter these days, the fellow you can have hop into a ring on a few hours' notice. The boys are very careful, particularly the topnotchers, as to the kind of matches you make for them. They never want to take a chance with any of the rough ones. Can you picture any of the later lightweights being careless about whom they are signed up with?"

From the point of view of the manager there is no doubt that Wolgast was the ideal prize fighter. He always was willing to step into the ring at the command of the mastermind, to take a beating, and to listen to the voice of the manager shouting, "Go on in. He can't hurt *us!*"

Nearly all of Wolgast's former managers have their health and are in no danger of the almshouse or the insane asylum. Oh yes. There is no doubt that Ad Wolgast was the ideal prize fighter from the manager's point of view. But poor little Wolgast will be taken to a state insane asylum shortly. The blows that the managers did not feel seem to have had effect upon Wolgast. Perhaps the fighter was just a trifle more sensitive than the manager.

THIS IS BOXING'S most famous poem. Jack Dempsey, "The Non-pareil," was born John Kelly in County Kildare, Ireland, on December 15, 1862. He won the middleweight title in 1884, and was undefeated in sixty-one fights when he was knocked out by George LaBlanche, with an illegal pivot punch, in 1889. Two years later he lost the title to Bob Fitzsimmons, and he died on November 2, 1895, ten months after his last fight, in Portland, Oregon, at the age of 32.

M. J. McMahon, of Portland, Dempsey's lawyer, was so disturbed by the neglect of his idol's grave that he wrote this poem and cir-culated 1,000 copies of it anonymously. One of these reached the *Portland Oregonian*, which printed the poem on December 10, 1899. Dempsey's friends then erected a tombstone, on which the poem is inscribed.

# The Nonpareil's Grave

## M. J. McMAHON

### I

Far out in the wilds of Oregon,
  On a lonely mountain side,
Where Columbia's mighty waters,
  Roll down to the ocean tide;
Where the giant fir and cedar
  Are imaged in the wave,
O'ergrown with firs and lichens,
  I found Jack Dempsey's grave.

### II

I found no marble monolith,
  No broken shaft, or stone,
Recording sixty victories,
  This vanquished victor won;
No rose, no shamrock could I find,
  No mortal here to tell
Where sleeps in this forsaken spot
  Immortal Nonpareil.

### III

A winding wooden canyon road
  That mortals seldom tread,
Leads up this lonely mountain,
  To the desert of the dead.

And the Western sun was sinking
  In Pacific's golden wave,
And those solemn pines kept watching
  Over poor Jack Dempsey's grave.

### IV

Forgotten by ten thousand throats,
  That thundered his acclaim,
Forgotten by his friends and foes,
  Who cheered his very name.
Oblivion wraps his faded form,
  But ages hence shall save
The memory of that Irish lad
  That fills poor Dempsey's grave.

### V

Oh, Fame, why sleeps thy favored son
  In wilds, in woods, in weeds,
And shall he ever thus sleep on,
  Interred his valiant deeds?
'Tis strange New York should thus forget
  Its "bravest of the brave"
And in the fields of Oregon,
  Unmarked, leave Dempsey's grave.

JOSEPH MONCURE MARCH was born and brought up on New York's upper West Side, learned to protect himself in street fights and boxed in the amateurs. In 1928, inspired by his friend James Chapin's painting "Negro Boxer" (page 284), he wrote his long narrative poem "The Setup." Twenty-one years later the poem inspired the movie of the same name. These excerpts describe Pansy Jones, the tragic hero of the piece, and the arena where he fought his last bout.

FROM

# "The Setup"

## JOSEPH MONCURE MARCH

### ONE

Pansy had the stuff, but his skin was brown;
And he never got a chance at the middleweight
Mean as a panther,
Crafty as a fox:
He could hit like a mule,
And he knew how to box.
A jungle jinx
With eyes like a lynx
A head like a bullet
And a face like the Sphinx:
Battered, flat, massive:
Grim:
Always impassive.

He was supple of build
Graceful;
Trim:
Heavy above,
With legs slim.
Compact:
Neat.
Light as a cat on his feet.
His neck was solid.
His arms were long.
His bones were heavy,
And his hands were strong;
And whenever he moved, you could see the lithe
Muscles under his skin writhe.
He was slick:
Quick:
Each movement was like a trick.

In the ring he had the general habits
Of a blacksnake after a couple of rabbits.
He got you nervous:
You never knew
Just what the hell he was going to do—
But he knew all about you.
Lead with your left—
You hit thin air.
Throw in your right—
His shoulder was there.
Always an elbow,
A wrist,
A mitt:
He knew what was coming before you hit.
He slipped what he couldn't block.
His blows were timed like a clock.
He'd warm up slow:
He'd let you go
For maybe a couple of rounds or so.
Then he'd start
One left—
One right—
And you'd wonder who told you
You could fight!
Clinch?
Try and do it!
It was over before you knew it.
He'd carve you up like a leg of mutton
And drop you flat with a sock on the button.
Abrupt,
Emphatic,
His fights were always dramatic.

265

### 2.

He fought all comers,
And he reached his prime:
And he stayed there waiting,
Marking time.
Now was his chance for the title—
Or never:
Each month was vital.
When you get that far, you either click
Or you go to pieces goddamned quick.
His managers sweated.
They did what they could.
They schemed
And they wheedled—
But it did no good.
The months slid by:
The title hung high:
No Pansies need apply.

Some of the sporting pink
Papers raised a stink.
They got sarcastic,
Biting, drastic
On the subject of champs that got the crown
And after they got it, then lay down!
Come on,
Take a sniff at Pansy's glove!
What was the champ so scared of?
No box-office attraction?
Hell!—
They wanted action!

Then,
Sudden disaster:
A final hope-blaster.
The brass-knuckled hand of the law
Hung a hot one on Pansy's jaw.
Dissection of his private life
Revealed he had an extra wife.
And three scrawny brats
Living like sewer rats.

"Not guilty," Pansy pled.
"Guilty," the jury said.

Elections were coming.
The judge was firm.
Pansy went up for a five-year term.

### TWO

Time out.
Ten years pass.
Fighting bodies have gone to grass.
Some lie under grass,
Rotten:
Even their names have been forgotten.

Fresh blood,
New hopes
Inside the old ropes.
Kids that wet their short pants
Ten years back, get their chance;
Giving;
Taking;
Champions in the making.

A fighter's life is short at best.
No time to waste;
No time to rest.
The spotlight shifts:
The clock ticks fast:
All youth becomes old age at last.
All fighters weaken.
All fighters crack.
All fighters go—
And they never come back.

Well—
So it goes:
Time hits the hardest blows.

### FOUR

The Star Arena reeked with age:
It smelled like the bottom of a monkey cage.
Dark,
Stark,
It stood immense
Between small shops and tenements:
Gloomy:
Dim:
Sinister looking:
Grim.

A glittering white
Arc light
Glared against the black night,
Making great shadows sprawl
Over the crumbling brown wall;
And bringing out the rigid shapes
Of long, slanting fire escapes.

Under this lamp, a crowd stirred;
Wading through darkness;
Ghostly:
Blurred.
In high relief, sharp weird
Parts of human forms appeared.
Shoulders jostled, light-splashed:
Hats stuck out,
Dented, gashed.
Wrinkles made black cracks
Across yellow, swaying backs.
Faces nodding,

Turned in talk,
Were masks cut from white chalk.
Mouths were holes:
Eye sockets
Looked like deep, black pockets.

The crowd shivered.
Above their heads
Their breaths rose in white shreds.

They grumbled.
They swore.
They edged towards the main door.
Slowly they stumbled up the wide
Unseen steps, and pushed inside.
Tickets were torn in two.
God!—
They were through!

### 2.

Side entrance
Down the street.
A small group
Clustered there;
Shivered in the cold air:
Swayed;
Stamped their feet.

Gloomy inside:
Dim-lit;
Dusty:
Bare as an old barn:
Echoing:
Musty.
Vestibule stacked with chairs.
A pit of dark rickety stairs;
Deep:
Steep:
Black as a coal heap.

Restless figures
Prowled about:
Shuffled,
Pulled their watches out:
Hung around in twos and threes,
Cold;
Impatient;
Ill at ease.

Down the stairs,
Knots of bent
Cautious-footed figures went.
At the bottom of the long
Creaking flight,
A dirty bulb smeared the wall
Of a long hall
With yellow light.

Under the light,
On a tin sign
Was a pointing hand,
Red on white,
Badly drawn in outline
In heavy raised letters
Of red:
"DRESSING ROOMS"
The sign said.

### 3.

The dressing rooms in the old Star
Had gone out of date with the horse-car.
They were lousy dumps;
Two of a kind.
Enter—
And leave the kiddies behind.

A dirty bulb swung by a cable
Over a battered rubbing table.
The crude glare
Fell on bare
Gleaming flesh, and underwear.
Open trousers bagged,
Sagged.
Shirtails flopped;
Belts dragged.
Backs bent down;
Flushed faces
Scowled over shoelaces.
Shoes thumped.
Knees rose;
Fingers clawed at sweaty hose
With holes in their toes.

Behind,
A row of lockers stood;
Old:
Battered:
Made of wood.
Hinges loose;
Locks rusted.
Doors with half their slats busted.
Yes—
Real Antiques:
Used by them ancient Greeks.

Another Antique—
The toilet.
No modern touch to spoil it.
Pitch black.
You had to go in
With your nose done up in a clothespin.
Wash your hands?
Have a drink?
Observe this handsome

Stopped-up sink.
Here is your shower—
It's on the fritz.
If you don't like it—
Move to the Ritz.
Go in like a little man:
Come out as quick as you can.
Trust to your smell
Instead of your sight—
And be goddamned thankful
There is no light.

There were handlers in the dressing room:
Sweatered,
Capped.
Water splashed.
A bucket banged.
Bath towels flapped.

Some of the handlers lounged at ease;
They sat with their elbows on their knees,
Parked on a bench with stenciled black
Numbers spaced across its back.

It was almost time for the first bout.
They kept pulling their watches out.
They'd give the watch a glance;
Shove it back in their pants:
Then pull it out again, as if in doubt.

No air.
Hot as hell.
The room reeked with the triple smell:
Toilet disinfectant
Blent
With stale sweat and liniment.

# RONALD SEARLE

*"Before I sign I want to know exactly why he's called 'The Bushwick Assassin.'"*

ROCKY MARCIANO had some help, of course, on this one, but it remains his—the feelings, the thoughts and how it was. One year and two fights later, he retired—49 fights, 49 wins, 43 by knockout—the only retired undefeated heavyweight champion in history.

# How It Feels to Be Champ

## ROCKY MARCIANO

AT ABOUT 8:30 on the morning of September 24, 1952, I woke up in a hotel room in Philadelphia. You know how it is when you wake up in a strange place, and at first you don't know where you are.

"Something nice happened to me," I thought to myself, and then I remembered. "That's right. Last night I won the heavyweight championship of the world."

When I tried to turn it seemed like my whole body was sore. I had cuts that had been stitched over both eyes and another on the top of my head, but I was as happy as I think anybody can be. Jersey Joe Walcott had given me the toughest fight I'd ever had, but I'd knocked him out in the thirteenth round, and I was heavyweight champion of the world.

I've had the title now for almost three years. In that time I've found out that, in most ways, it's everything you think it's going to be, and in other ways it's very different.

It's easy for me to remember what I thought it would be like to be champion, because I can remember the first night I ever thought I had a chance. On December 19, 1949, I had Phil Muscato down five times and knocked him out in five rounds in Providence. This was my twenty-fourth win without a loss as a pro and my twenty-second knockout, and after the fight I drove back to Brockton, like I always did after my Providence fights, with my pals Ali Colombo and Nicky Sylvester and Snap Tartarlia.

It was a nice night, clear and cold, but as soon as I got into the car I felt something was different. Usually on the way home after a fight we laughed and kidded a lot, but this night everybody was very serious.

"You know, Rock," one of the guys said while we were driving along, "you haven't got very far to go now."

I said, "To go where?"

"For the title," one of the others said.

"Ah," I said. "Take it easy."

"No," somebody said. "Figure it out. About five good wins and you can be on top of the heap."

Then we started figuring who I'd have to get by—Roland LaStarza, Rex Layne, Joe Louis, if he made a comeback, Jersey Joe Walcott and Ezzard Charles—and when they dropped me off at my house and I went to bed I couldn't sleep. I was a kid who never dreamed he could be heavyweight champion. I wanted to be a major-league catcher, but then I threw my arm out and I started to fight just to help my Pop support the family. Now I got to thinking what it would be like if I could be champion.

I remembered the night Primo Carnera won the title from Jack Sharkey. I was nine years old at the time, and in the Italian section of Brockton they had big bonfires burning and they sang and shouted around them almost all night long. I could remember those fires in the James Edgar playground right across the street from our house and I figured that gee, if I could win the title, I'd come back to Brockton and I'd throw a big party for the whole town and every kid would be invited and get an expensive gift.

Right after he won the title Carnera came to Brockton to referee at the old Arena that was

270

across Pleasant Street from the Brockton Hospital. My uncle, John Piccento, took me that night to see him, and on the way out Carnera walked right by us and I reached out and I touched his arm.

"I saw Carnera and I touched him," I told my Pop when I got home. "I really did."

"How big is he?" my Pop asked me.

"Bigger than this ceiling," I said, "and you should see how big his hands are."

The year before I licked Muscato and was lying there thinking about what it might be like to be the champion of the world I had met Joe Louis for the first time. He was boxing an exhibition with Arturo Godoy in Philadelphia, and I was fighting Gilly Ferron on the card. We were all in the dressing room for the weigh-in when Joe came in.

"Say, Joe," my manager, Al Weill, said, "I want you to shake hands with my heavyweight."

Joe stuck out his hand and we shook. He looked like a mountain, and he had on a big, beautiful overcoat and a mohair hat, light-brown with a nice feather in it. I figured that hat alone must have cost fifty dollars, and now I got to thinking about the money he must have made.

When Louis knocked out Max Schmeling in 2 minutes and 4 seconds in their second fight, Ali Colombo and I were talking about all that dough. We were just kids talking, but it said in the paper that, figuring the purse Louis got for the fight, he made over $150,000 a minute, which is more than the President of the United States gets paid a year.

I got to imagining now what it would mean to have money like that, not just for clothes but the security and what I could do for my family and my friends and others. I thought that boy, when you're the heavyweight champion of the world it means you can lick any man in the world, and wherever you go in the world everything must stop and what an influence you must have.

There were a lot of things I didn't know then that I know now that I'm champion. I didn't know that my life would be threatened a couple of times. I didn't know that, although you do make a lot of money, it isn't what people think it is, expenses and taxes being what they are, and that you can't begin to do the things with it that you dreamed about. I didn't know that being heavyweight champion of the world is almost a full-time job, and that the influence you have on people is sometimes so strong that it worries you and can even bring tears to your eyes.

After I knocked out Joe Louis, for example, my mother got a letter that said that, if I came home to Brockton for the celebration that was planned. I'd be shot. Then, just before my first fight with Charles last June, my folks got another note from a man who said he was a Charles rooter and that if I beat Charles I'd be killed, because Charles is a gentleman and I'm a bully.

The Brockton police found the first letter was written by a thirteen-year-old girl. I don't know, or care, who wrote the second one, but although letters like that don't worry me, they worry my mother.

After that first letter my sisters had to take her to Dr. Rocco Del Colliano, in Brockton, and now every time I fight he picks her up at the house and drives her around all evening until the fight is over. I never imagined I'd put my family through anything like that, because I never realized how many people's lives are tied up in a fight.

I had a friend in Brockton named Miles Dempsey, and he was my first real fan. He used to go to all my amateur fights, and he was the first guy who asked me to arrange for him to buy good seats when I started to fight pro. During the excitement of the sixth round of that June fight with Charles he died at ringside of a heart attack. In my mind this is a part of that fight.

When you're the heavyweight champion the money, of course, is the big thing you're going for, because that's why you became a fighter in the first place. Before I started fighting, the most I ever made was $1.25 an hour as a manual laborer. When I retire, if I'm lucky, I should never have to worry about money again, but it isn't what you think it is, and your security is still a problem.

Last year, for example, I fought Charles twice. At the end of the year, after expenses and taxes, I came out with a lot less than $100,000. When I fight twice in a year I don't figure to net more than about $15,000 out of the second fight, and that's not a lot when you've only got four or five more years of fighting and when, each time you go into the ring, you're risking the heavyweight championship of the world.

I'm not complaining, because I couldn't make that kind of money doing any other thing, and when you come from a poor family you know it's a privilege to pay taxes. It's just that you feel that other people don't understand.

I'll never, you see, be able to afford that big party for all the kids in Brockton. That's not important, just kind of a foolish dream, but the important thing is that you can't do all you want for charities and churches and just good people, and you have a feeling that they go away not liking you because of it. You want to be liked by everybody, not just for yourself, but because when you're heavyweight champion of the world you represent boxing and boxing did everything for you.

There'll be a church that needs $10,000 or a hospital that needs that much to help build a new ward. I'll get a letter from a woman I don't even know but she'll write that if I'd give her $1,500 her little boy could be made well again. How do you think I feel?

They run at you, too, with all kinds of business schemes, but that's only a nuisance, and not like the others. There are people who want me to sign notes for them or loan them money or sponsor them on singing or acting careers. One guy wanted to start a band, and another I had never heard of wanted me to go halves with him in a night club in Buffalo.

They've tried to sell me uranium and copper and oil wells, a dairy and an oil route. Any salesman near Brockton, where I'm home only about two months a year, tries to get me to buy whatever he's handling, and it might be a carving machine or a salad mixer, books, furniture, a car or a horse.

Some of the things you do with your money don't pan out the way you dreamed, either. I always said that, if I became champion, one of the first things I'd do would be to send my Mom and Pop back to their home towns in Italy, and I used to think a lot about what a great time that would be for them.

I did it, right after the first Walcott fight. There were so many things pulling at me at the time, though, that I couldn't even see them off on the plane, and some of the pleasure was lost there. Then, instead of staying three months, they came back after one month, and they never did get to my mother's little town of San Bartholomeo, near Naples. They went only to my Pop's town, Ripiatitina, in Abruzzi, on the Adriatic coast, and it took a couple of months before my mother would tell me why.

"Too much sadness there," she said, and you should understand that my mother is the kind of a woman who can't stand to see suffering and wants to help everybody. "Every place we went they had nothing, and they looked to us and how much could we do? I did not want to go to my own town."

It took my mother that long to tell me about the trip because, when you become heavyweight champion, something comes between you and other people, even your family. Everybody stands back a little, not because of anything you do but because of what you are, even though you try so hard to prevent it. You end up a lonesome guy in a crowd.

"Rocco, there is something I would like to talk with you about," my mother said not long ago while we were at Grossinger's, in the Catskill Mountains of New York, where I always do my training and where I was getting ready for this coming fight with Don Cockell.

"Sure, Mom," I said. "I wish you'd talk to me any time you want."

"You are so important now," she said. "I don't like to bother you."

"Please, Mom," I said. "You can never bother me. I'm your son."

"I have been thinking," she said, and she had probably been carrying this around in her mind for a year or more, "that there is so much pleasure you miss. When your sister has a baby and when somebody gets married it is a beautiful thing. This is a happiness you should enjoy. The most wonderful things in life you cannot enjoy because you are so busy and a big man."

I knew this before she even said it, because it is part of being champion. My sister Concetta's baby is going on two years old now, and I didn't see her until she was almost six months old. When my old friend Nicky Sylvester got married I couldn't even get to the wedding. My own baby, Marianne, is two, and they tell me this is the time when it's the most fun to be with your child, that she's walking around the house now and that every day she's picking up a new word. Instead, I'm with my wife Barbara and the baby about four months a year.

When I get together with my old friends in Brockton it isn't the same, either. They never start a conversation. They answer my questions quickly, and I never do find out how they feel and what they're thinking, and we never have the laughs about the little things we used to have before. They no sooner get out to our house than they're starting for the door, because they're afraid they're bothering me, and I try to tell them they're not.

That's what it's like to be heavyweight champion, when you look at one side. You have to give up something for everything you get, I guess, and when it gets me down and I lie in bed at night and feel a little depressed I think about all the good that there is in it, and it's more than you can imagine.

Take what it has meant to my Pop. He's sixty-one years old now, and came to this country in 1916. He was gassed in World War I fighting with the Second Marines at Chateau Thierry, and he was never really well after that. For over thirty years he worked in the shoe shops in Brockton at the Number 7 bed-laster, which is one of the tough ones. Four years ago I could see to it that he retired.

My Mom was telling me that when I was a kid, day after day would go by when Pop wouldn't say a word. With six kids to support on that little money at that tough job his life was a real drag. Just a few months ago Ali Colombo and I were looking at some old pictures of Pop, and he was skin and bones. Now he's gained about ten pounds, and he has a great time in his quiet way, sitting there and cutting out stories about me and helping around the camp.

Outside of your own family, you can make the title mean so much for other people. One of my greatest pleasures is meeting some nice little guy, like my kind of people, and, when I can make it, going into his town with him. This is a real honest, hard-working quiet little guy that nobody ever paid much attention to, and he takes me around and introduces me to everybody in the town and this makes him somebody important where he works and lives.

Once I made a speech at a dinner in Boston of the big shoe manufacturers. Everybody who spoke was telling jokes and I'm not good at that, so I thought I'd try to make a point in a light way.

I told them that if I was a good fighter, I thought they should take some of the credit for it. I said my Pop worked in the shoe shops for thirty years and I used to carry his lunch to him and I saw how tough it was. I told them that sometimes I saw his pay and I saw how little he got. I said: "He used to tell me, 'I want you to stay out of the shoe shops.' So, to keep away from them, I became a fighter instead, and therefore I think you men had a part in making me a fighter."

I don't know if I got it across. I just thought it was worth a try.

The influence you have and that you can use for good without being a crusader goes so far beyond what you think, that sometimes it frightens you. Right after I won the title from Walcott, Al Weill, Charley Goldman, two sparring partners—Bob Golden and Toxie Hall— and I made a five-week, 30,000-mile exhibition tour of the Pacific, and when they say you're heavyweight champion of the whole world they mean it.

In Manila there were mobs wherever we went. Whenever I'd come out of the hotel for my walk there'd be a hundred people waiting just to look at me. One day I went into a store to buy souvenirs, and there were five hundred people watching for me outside. When I got in a cab, dozens of them ran after it.

Out there they don't look for autographs. All they want is to feel the muscles in your arms. One day I was walking along the street and a little guy stopped his car in the middle of heavy traffic, got out, ran up to me, felt my muscle and got back in his car and drove off.

I tell this to explain something else that happened. I was scheduled to box on a Thursday, but it rained that day and the next two days. Then the promoter suggested I box on Sunday.

"No," I said, "I'm a Roman Catholic, and I go to church on Sunday."

When I'm training for a fight, I have to train on Sundays, too, but I don't have to box exhibitions on Sunday.

I didn't think anything of it, but it was a big front-page story in the newspapers. A little later we went out to visit a leper colony, and a priest spoke to me.

"Rocky," he said, "these people out here are great sports enthusiasts, and we try to get them to be better church people. You've done more for the Catholic religion in that one move than anyone has done here in my time."

That's what I mean when I say that sometimes it frightens you. You might, without realizing it, say a wrong thing. Ali Colombo and I have been taking long walks together since we were kids, and he still goes out on the road with me, and many times when we're walking we work out what I'll say in a speech or how I'll answer if a certain question is asked.

Before we went to the leper colony we were a little nervous, because we didn't know what it would be like. There was a woman who explained that we couldn't contract the disease, and she told us how the poor people in the colony never see anyone important and have so little to look forward to.

There were, maybe, 1,200 people in the place, and when we got there and started to walk through them they just moved back to make a path for us without anyone saying anything to them, and it was one of the saddest things I ever saw. I went up on a stage and they asked if they could see my muscles and how I train, so I took off my shirt and I shadowboxed a couple of rounds.

Then we started out. Again they pulled away to make that path, and they began to call to me.

"God bless you, Rocky," they were calling. "God bless you. May you reign long."

If you think that being heavyweight champion of the world is all happiness you're wrong. In Los Angeles, before we went to the Pacific, we visited the iron-lung patients in a hospital named Rancho Los Amigos, and maybe it was there more than any other place that I realized what being champion of the world means.

We went to the men's polio ward first and there was one kid lying there who knew everything about me, from my earliest fights, and we'd catch each other's eyes in his mirror while we talked. There was another guy who'd been there as long as anybody could remember, and there was one big kid who'd been a basketball player for Loyola, and when I looked in his mirror to talk with him I saw he had my picture pasted on it. They say I had guts in the Walcott fight, but this kid was telling me how he'd lick it and play basketball again.

After that we went to the women's ward, where there were a lot of fourteen and fifteen-year-old kids, and the nurse told us that all that day they'd had all the nurses busy primping them up because I was coming. With us was a friend of mine, Ernie Clivio, who has a dairy in Stoneham, Massachusetts, and when we got out we just looked at one another and I thought we might both cry.

Shortly after I won the title, Al Weill and I received a letter from the White House saying that the President doesn't get to see many sports events and so he was having a sports luncheon to meet some of the sports figures. They wanted to know if we'd be kind enough, if you can imagine, to attend.

I was more nervous than I've ever been going into a fight. Joe DiMaggio, Ty Cobb, Cy Young, Clark Griffith, Ben Hogan, Gene Sarazen, Florence Chadwick and about forty others were there, and to begin with we were all formed in a semicircle in the White House when the President came in.

"So you're the heavyweight champion of the world," he said, when he came to me, and then he stepped back and looked at me and smiled.

"Yes, sir," I said.

"You know," he said, "somehow I thought you'd be bigger."

"No, sir," I said.

After the luncheon we posed on the White House steps, and one of the photographers who's a real fight fan took a picture of the President looking at my right fist. Can you imagine me, Rocco Marchegiano, a shoe worker's son and a PFC in the Army, posing with a five-star general who became the President of the United States?

Everybody, of course, isn't for you when you're champion. There are people who resent you and make remarks, and very often you find that women don't understand.

"What makes you enjoy hurting people?" an elderly woman said to me one night at a dinner party in Milton, Massachusetts.

"I don't enjoy hurting them," I said.

"Then why do you do it?" she said. "Is it some sadistic impulse?"

I dropped it then, but I think it's important for people to understand what you feel about an opponent. I don't want them to think that the heavyweight champion of the world is just a pug.

When I train for a fight I devote eight to twelve weeks getting ready to fight another man. The sports writers say I live a monk's life, because I put all my thoughts and all my efforts into it, and all those around me devote themselves to the same thing.

There are a number of key people who are very important to a fighter getting ready for a fight. They are his wife and family, if he's married, his manager, his trainer and his best friend. In all of these I've been very lucky.

That's the usual thing to say, but I mean it. When a fighter goes into camp for those two or three months his mind should be free and no problems should move in on it. My wife Barbara and I find that even in the four months we have together we don't have the freedom we want, but she has yet to make one complaint. We talk on the phone regularly while I'm in camp, but two weeks before a fight she'll always say that I'm not to call her again until the fight is over, and my family is the same.

I couldn't have made it without Al Weill and Charley Goldman, who trains me. On the way up Al got me opponents who, with only one exception and he got timid after I hit him a good punch, gave me a good fight for as long as it went.

"You see, you're learnin' while you're earnin'," Charley used to tell me.

I'll never forget the first day seven years ago when I met Al and Charley. Ali Colombo and I had bummed down from Brockton with our lunch in a paper bag, and I wanted Al to manage me and I was scared.

"If I manage you," he said, "you got to remember this. With me, I'm the boss. I do the managing and all you do is the fightin'. You don't ask me who you're fighting' or where you're fightin' or how much you're gettin'. When you go to the gym you do what Charley tells you, and after the fight you get your share."

That's the way it should be with a fighter, really. I don't have any of the money worries, and I was a real crude kid as a young fighter and Charley taught me everything I know.

Ali Colombo is a guy who thinks and feels

just like I do. Camp could get pretty grim at the end if you didn't have somebody like that to talk with.

The last month before a fight I don't even write a letter. The last ten days I see no mail and get no telephone calls and meet no new acquaintances. The week before the fight I'm not allowed to shake hands or go for a ride in a car. Nobody can get into the kitchen, and no new foods are introduced. Even the conversation is watched.

By that I mean that the fellas keep it pleasant, with not too much fight talk. My opponent's name is never mentioned, and I don't read the write-ups because, as Charley explained it, somebody might write one idea that might stick in my mind.

"Besides," he said, "think what fun it will be to read the clippings after the fight and see who was right and who was wrong."

For two or three months, then, every minute of my life is planned for one purpose. I don't even think about what I'm going to do the day after the fight, because that's going to be like an adventure and exciting. Everything on my part and on the part of everybody else in camp is directed toward one goal—to lick the other man. I see him in front of me when I'm punching the bag. When I run on the road I've got him in my mind, and always I'm working on certain moves and punches that I hope will lick him.

Take the second Walcott fight. Willie Wilson, one of my sparring partners, had Walcott's moves down very good. He'd feint me and pull away or, after I'd hit him a punch, he'd pull down and try to tie me up. The big problem was to figure out what I was going to hit him with for a second punch, and one night Ali and I were talking about it, walking for about forty-five minutes after dinner, and then we talked it over with Charlie and Al.

We decided to try right-hand uppercuts after a left hook, and I practiced it a lot on the big bag and then against Wilson. As it happened, the fight went less than a round, but the 3-D movies showed why very well. I hit him with a hook, but as he ducked to take it high on the head he moved right into the power of that uppercut, because, with an uppercut, the power is right after you start it.

When he went down I moved to a neutral corner. I listened for the count, and when it got to eight I said to myself: "You know, this fella isn't going to get up."

For the second LaStarza fight—the one with my title on the line—we knew he carried his left high, and always brought it back high. I had to bring that hand down to get to his head, so I practiced throwing right hands to the heart. Finally, along around the tenth round, I got his arm down and I stopped him in the eleventh.

When you work and work like that with only one purpose in mind for weeks on end there's only one thing you want to do—and that's get out there and try it in a fight. Of course, to begin with, you enjoy the fight itself, or you wouldn't be a fighter.

What it comes down to in the ring is that it's the other guy or you. Anybody in there with me is there to get me and I'm in there to get him, but the one thing that people don't seem to understand is that there's nothing personal about it and you don't carry this over outside the ring. You get rid of it in there.

Walcott is an example. I never wanted to lick a man more, because I had to lick him to get his title. Coming up to the second fight his manager was complaining that I'm a dirty fighter and that I hit low and butted Joe in our first fight. One night on television in Chicago he even had a billygoat on with him to represent me, but you know that's only part of the publicity.

When I was training for LaStarza, Walcott came up to see me work in the hangar where I train at the Grossinger airfield. After the photographers had finished posing us, Joe and I got to talking, with nobody listening, over behind the bags.

"Joe," I said, "how's the motel going out there in Jersey?"

"Fine," he said. "Very good."

"I hope you make a lot of money with it," I said. "I really do."

"Rock," he said, "I want to say this. I liked that title. I didn't want to lose it to anybody, but if I had to lose it, I'm glad I lost it to you. You're a good fighter and you're gonna be a great champ."

"I appreciate that, Joe," I said, "and I think you're a great guy."

This was a real warm thing, and why not? Walcott fought his greatest fight against me, and I fought my greatest against him. This is something that people are going to talk about for the rest of our lives, and we can be proud of it. It took two of us to do this together. One can't do it alone.

I have the same kind of fondness for other guys I fought. On the way up I knocked out Johnny Pretzie in five rounds, Gino Buonvino in ten rounds and then in two in a return, and Bernie Reynolds in three. After I became champ I wondered what they were doing and I wrote them post cards.

Reynolds didn't answer me, but I had a nice letter from Buonvino and his wife and one from Pretzie. Buonvino is a carpenter in New York now, and he and his wife sent me their best. Pretzie wrote me that he had a young fighter he was training, and he recalled our fight.

"But don't you think somebody might lick you?" I get asked quite often. "Don't you ever worry about it?"

I don't want to seem like I'm bragging but I don't think anybody in the world can lick me. I've never been defeated in forty-seven fights as a pro, and right now I hope maybe I can hold the title, if I'm lucky, four or five more years and retire undefeated. At the same time, once in a while, maybe seven or eight times when I'm building up to a fight, the thought comes to me on the road or while I'm resting: "Suppose this guy licks me? What will happen to all my plans?"

That's as far as it gets. I never believe it can happen, really. It's just one of the things that come to your mind.

I can remember, though, the night that Joe Louis and Jersey Joe Walcott fought for the first time and Walcott had Louis down twice but didn't get the decision. I had had one pro fight ten months before, and I was working for the Brockton Gas Company and I was sitting on the bed at home listening to the fight.

It never occurred to me that I would be the guy to knock out Louis and retire him and then knock out Walcott and take the heavyweight championship of the world. Now that I'm champion I wonder, once in a while, if there is some other kid nobody ever heard of sitting someplace and listening to one of my fights, or watching it on television, who might, in a few years, do the same thing to me.

Out on the West Coast there's this big, young heavyweight named Charley Powell. He put together a lot of knockouts last year, and they were touting him as a real good prospect. The night last fall when he fought Charley Norkus I watched on television, and when the fight got under way I could see that he was a big guy and boxed nice and could punch.

"You know," I thought to myself, "this might be the guy."

Norkus finally knocked Powell out, but he's still a prospect. I'm heavyweight champion of the world, but is there some young fighter somewhere who wants it as much as I did? The champion never knows.

## THE LONG COUNT

The second Tunney–Dempsey fight at Soldier
Field, Chicago, on the night of September
22, 1927, attracted the largest gate—$2,658,-
660—of any event in history, returned to
Tunney the largest fee—$990,445—ever paid
for a single performance in any field, and

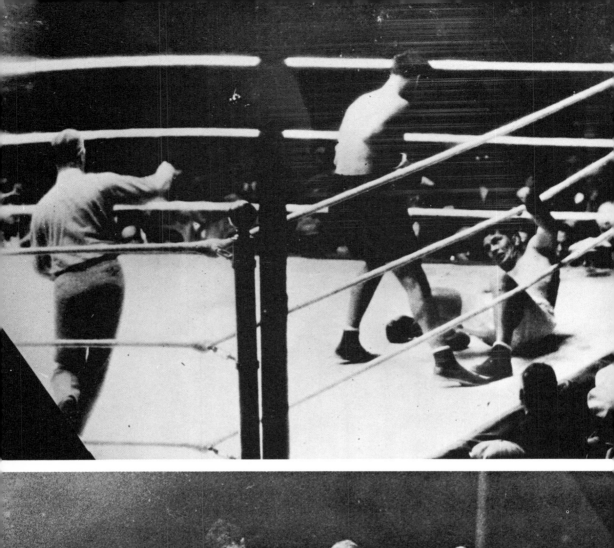

(*continued*)

precipitated the longest-lived controversy in sports. As he had done the year before in Philadelphia, Tunney was outboxing Dempsey again when, in the seventh round, Dempsey floored him with a series of punches near the Dempsey corner. Referee Dave Barry, in accordance with the rules, withheld the start of the count until Dempsey, hovering near Tunney, went to a neutral corner, and at the official count of nine Tunney arose to retreat and box his way out of trouble. Estimates of how long Tunney was down vary from 12 to 17 seconds, but the official timekeeper clocked it at 14. Tunney says he could, if necessary, have arisen after 9 seconds, his mind clear; newspapermen facing him said he was still glassy-eyed at that point. Dempsey partisans claimed their hero was actually the first heavyweight ever to regain the championship; Dempsey says the controversy contributed more than any other single factor to keeping his name and popularity alive.

*(UPI)*

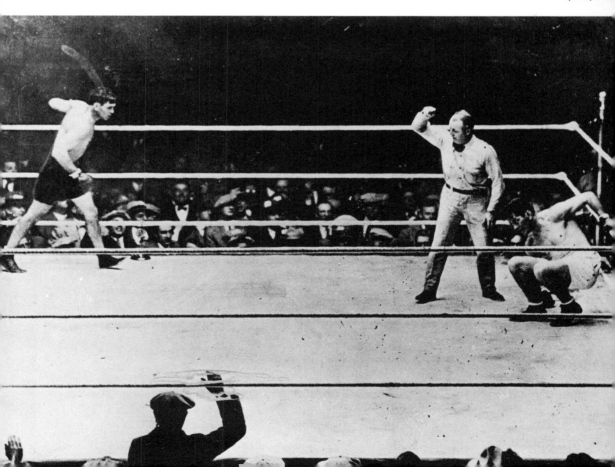

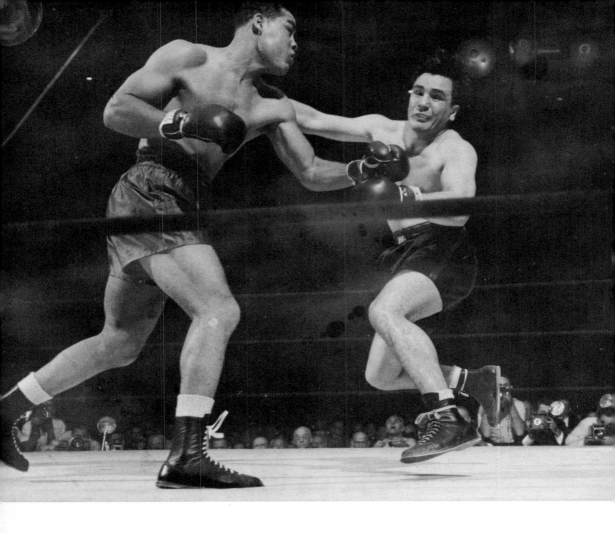

## THE KNOCKOUT

OPPOSITE

Joe Louis was past his prime when he knocked out Tami Mauriello in the first round at Yankee Stadium in New York on September 18, 1946. No other photograph, however, captured as well as this the power of the punch he had in either hand.

BELOW

On January 19, 1945, Johnny Bratton landed a right on the jaw of Robert Earl and literally knocked him stiff. There is no better photograph of the classic coup. (*Carmen Reporto—Chicago* SUN-TIMES)

TAKING THE COUNT
Painting by Thomas Eakins
(*Courtesy Yale University*)

**LITTLE BROWN BROTHER**
Painting by ROBERT RIGGS
(*Courtesy of Philadelphia Museum of Art*)

NEGRO BOXER
Painting by James Chapin
(*Courtesy of the artist and Arthur A. Collins*)

THIS IS THE OPENING of the verse narrative of the redemption of Saul
Kane written in 1911 by the poet laureate and boxing buff. In this
fight Kane behaved like a semipro Floyd Patterson. He had the instincts of a fighter and the compassion of a priest.

FROM

# "The Everlasting Mercy"

## JOHN MASEFIELD

From '41 to '51
I was my folks' contrary son;
I bit my father's hand right through
And broke my mother's heart in two.
I sometimes go without my dinner
Now that I know the times I've gi'n her.

From '51 to '61
I cut my teeth and took to fun.
I learned what not to be afraid of
And what stuff women's lips are made of;
I learned with what a rosy feeling
Good ale makes floors seem like the ceiling,
And how the moon gives shiny light
To lads as roll home singing by't.
My blood did leap, my flesh did revel,
Saul Kane was tokened to the devil.

From '61 to '67
I lived in disbelief of Heaven.
I drunk. I fought, I poached, I whored,
I did despite unto the Lord.
I cursed, 'twould make a man look pale,
And nineteen times I went to gaol.

Now, friends, observe and look upon me,
  Mark how the Lord took pity on me.
By Dead Man's Thorn, while setting wires,
Who should come up but Billy Myers,
A friend of mine, who used to be
As black a sprig of hell as me,
With whom I'd planned, to save encroachin',
Which fields and coverts each should poach in.

Now when he saw me set my snare,
He tells me, "Get to hell from there.
This field is mine," he says, "by right;
If you poach here, there'll be a fight.
Out now," he says, "and leave your wire;
It's mine."
          "It ain't."
                    "You put."
                              "You liar."

"You closhy put."
"You bloody liar."
"This is my field."
"This is my wire."
"I'm ruler here."
"You ain't."
"I am."
"I'll fight you for it."
"Right, by damn.
Not now, though, I've sprained my thumb,
We'll fight after the harvest hum.
And Silas Jones, that bookie wide,
Will make a purse five pounds a side."
Those were the words, that was the place
By which God brought me into grace.

On Wood Top Field the peewits go
Mewing and wheeling ever so;
And like the shaking of a timbrel
Cackles the laughter of the whimbrel.
In the old quarry-pit they say
Head-keeper Pike was made away.
He walks, head-keeper Pike, for harm,
He taps the windows of the farm;

The blood drips from his broken chin,
He taps and begs to be let in.
On Wood Top, nights, I've shaked to hark
The peewits wambling in the dark
Lest in the dark the old man might
Creep up to me to beg a light.

But Wood Top grass is short and sweet
And springy to a boxer's feet;
At harvest hum the moon so bright
Did shine on Wood Top for the fight.

When Bill was stripped down to his bends
I thought how long we two'd been friends,
And in my mind, about that wire,
I thought, "He's right, I am a liar.
As sure as skilly's made in prison
The right to poach that copse is his'n.
I'll have no luck tonight," thinks I.
"I'm fighting to defend a lie.
And this moonshiny evening's fun
Is worse than aught I've ever done."
And thinking that way my heart bled so
I almost stept to Bill and said so.
And now Bill's dead I would be glad
If I could only think I had.
But no. I put the thought away
For fear of what my friends would say.
They'd backed me, see? O Lord, the sin
Done for the things there's money in.

The stakes were drove, the ropes were hitched,
Into the ring my hat I pitched.
My corner faced the Squire's park
Just where the fir trees make it dark;
The place where I begun poor Nell
Upon the woman's road to hell.
I thought of't, sitting in my corner
After the time-keep struck his warner
(Two brandy flasks, for fear of noise,
Clinked out the time to us two boys).
And while my seconds chafed and gloved me
I thought of Nell's eyes when she loved me,
And wondered how my tot would end,
First Nell cast off and now my friend;
And in the moonlight dim and wan
I knew quite well my luck was gone;
And looking round I felt a spite
At all who'd come to see me fight;
The five and forty human faces
Inflamed by drink and going to races,
Faces of men who'd never been
Merry or true or live or clean;
Who'd never felt the boxer's trim
Or brain divinely knit to limb,
Nor felt the whole live body go

One tingling health from top to toe;
Nor took a punch nor given a swing,
But just soaked deady round the ring
Until their brains and bloods were foul
Enough to make their throttles howl,
While we who Jesus died to teach
Fought round on round, three minutes each.

And thinking that, you'll understand
I thought, "I'll go and take Bill's hand.
I'll up and say the fault was mine,
He shan't make play for these here swine."
And then I thought that that was silly,
They'd think I was afraid of Billy;
They'd think (I thought it, God forgive me)
I funked the hiding Bill could give me.
And that thought made me mad and hot.
"Think that, will they? Well, they shall not.
They shan't think that. I will not. I'm
Damned if I will. I will not."
    Time!

From the beginning of the bout
My luck was gone, my hand was out.
Right from the start Bill called the play,
But I was quick and kept away
Till the fourth round, when work got mixed,
And then I knew Bill had me fixed.
My hand was out, why, Heaven knows;
Bill punched me when and where he chose.
Through two more rounds we quartered wide,
And all the time my hands seemed tied;
Bill punched me when and where he pleased.
The cheering from my backers eased,
But every punch I heard a yell
Of "That's the style, Bill, give him hell."
No one for me, but Jimmy's light
"Straight left!! Straight left–!" and "Watch his
    right."

I don't know how a boxer goes
When all his body hums from blows;
I know I seemed to rock and spin,
I don't know how I saved my chin;
I know I thought my only friend
Was that clinked flask at each round's end
When my two seconds, Ed and Jimmy,
Had sixty seconds' help to gimme.
But in the ninth, with pain and knocks
I stopped: I couldn't fight nor box.
But missed his swing, the light was tricky,
But I went down, and stayed down, dicky.
"Get up," cried Jim. I said, "I will."
Then all the gang yelled, "Out him, Bill.
Out him." Bill rushed . . . and Clink, Clink,
    Clink.
Time! and Jim's knee, and rum to drink.

And round the ring there ran a titter:
"Saved by the call, the bloody quitter."

They drove (a dodge that never fails)
A pin beneath my finger nails.
They poured what seemed a running beck
Of cold spring water down my neck;
Jim with a lancet quick as flies
Lowered the swellings round my eyes.
They sluiced my legs and fanned my face
Through all that blessed minute's grace;
They gave my calves a thorough kneading,
They salved my cuts and stopped the bleeding.
A gulp of liquor dulled the pain,
And then the two flasks clinked again.
Time!
      There was Bill as grim as death,
He rushed, I clinched, to get more breath,
And breath I got, though Billy bats
Some stinging short-arms in my slats.
And when we broke, as I foresaw,
He swung his right in for the jaw.
I stopped it on my shoulder bone,
And at the shock I heard Bill groan—
A little groan or moan or grunt
As though I'd hit his wind a bunt.
At that, I clinched, and while we clinched,
His old time right-arm dig was flinched,
And when we broke he hit me light
As though he didn't trust his right,
He flapped me somehow with his wrist
As though he couldn't use his fist,
And when he hit he winced with pain.
I thought, "Your sprained thumb's crocked
      again."
So I got strength and Bill gave ground,
And that round was an easy round.

During the wait my Jimmy said,
"What's making Billy fight so dead?
He's all to pieces. Is he blown?"
"His thumb's out."
"No? Then it's your own.
It's all your own, but don't be rash—
He's got the goods if you've got cash,
And what one hand can do he'll do,
Be careful this next round or two."

Time. There was Bill, and I felt sick
That luck should play so mean a trick
And give me leave to knock him out
After he'd plainly won the bout.
But by the way the man came at me

He made it plain he meant to bat me;
If you'd a seen the way he come
You wouldn't think he'd crocked a thumb.
With all his skill and all his might
He clipped me dizzy left and right;
The Lord knows what the effort cost,
But he was mad to think he'd lost,
And knowing nothing else could save him
He didn't care what pain it gave him
He called the music and the dance
For five rounds more and gave no chance.

Try to imagine if you can
The kind of manhood in the man,
And if you'd like to feel his pain
You sprain your thumb and hit the sprain.
And hit it hard, with all your power
On something hard for half-an-hour,
While someone thumps you black and blue,
And then you'll know what Billy knew.
Bill took that pain without a sound
Till halfway through the eighteenth round,
And then I sent him down and out,
And Silas said, "Kane wins the bout."

When Bill came to, you understand,
I ripped the mitten from my hand
And went across to ask Bill shake.
My limbs were all one pain and ache,
I was so weary and so sore
I don't think I'd a stood much more.
Bill in his corner bathed his thumb,
Buttoned his shirt and glowered glum.
"I'll never shake your hand," he said.
"I'd rather see my children dead.
I've been about and had some fun with you,
But you're a liar and I've done with you.
You've knocked me out, you didn't beat me;
Look out the next time that you meet me,
There'll be no friend to watch the clock for you
And no convenient thumb to crock for you,
And I'll take care, with much delight,
You'll get what you'd a got tonight;
That puts my meaning clear, I guess,
Now get to hell; I want to dress."

I dressed. My backers one and all
Said, "Well done you," or "Good old Saul."
"Saul is a wonder and a fly 'un,"
"What'll you have, Saul, at the Lion?"
With merry oaths they helped me down
The stony wood path to the town.

Daniel mendoza, called "The Light of Israel," was born on July 5, 1764, at Aldgate, London. He stood five feet seven inches, weighed 160 pounds and participated in thirty-seven bouts, the last when he was 56. He was the first Jewish champion of the world, the first proponent of scientific boxing, and his treatise *The Art of Pugilism* was the first technical tract to appear on the subject. He made a fortune, enjoyed it, failed at business, did time in debtor's prison and was constantly on the run from his creditors. He died on September 3, 1836, at the age of 72, leaving a wife, eleven children, no money, but a great name.

The following excerpts are from *The Memoirs of the Life of Daniel Mendoza,* the first such by any champion. published in 1826 and edited anew in 1951 by Paul Magriel. They tell of his penchant, before his two victories over Richard Humphries made him famous, for street fighting, of his visit with King George III, with whom no other Jew had ever spoken, and of an experience not uncommon to fighters whose reputations make them targets.

# From Street Fighting to Fame

## DANIEL MENDOZA

Shortly after my return to town, I was induced to engage in another pugilistic contest, for being present one day in company with a man at a fight at Kentish Town, my friend happened to be grossly insulted by a man whom I challenged in consequence, and we accordingly set to, when after a contest of about half an hour, he was forced to give in, being so severely beaten as to be scarcely able to stand, and indeed, he was obliged to be carried off the field.

Some short time after this I fought three battles in one day, which were occasioned by the following circumstances:

Being at this time out of employment, I was enabled to devote a day or two to amusement and therefore availed myself of the opportunity to go to Barnet to see a battle there between Johnson and Love; and accordingly set out walking, but on reaching Highgate I was overtaken by an old man who was going to the fight in a cart with some friends and being invited to make one of their party, I accompanied them.

On our arrival at Barnet, we were greatly disappointed, for, instead of witnessing a contest of skill between the combatants, Johnson obtained the victory over his opponent in less than five minutes.

On our return, we overtook a young man driving a cart, who boasted greatly of the swiftness of his horse, and invited us to run against him, to which we agreed, and to his great disappointment gained the victory, upon which he was so much out of humor, that he began to vent his spleen upon us. At this moment a gentleman happened to ride up, who, on the circumstance being mentioned to him, declared it would afford him the greatest gratification to see such a fellow well thrashed, and promised to reward anyone who would set about it. Upon which I expressed my determination of having a trial with him myself, for though he appeared to be superior to me in strength, I felt sufficient confidence in my own powers to be but very little dismayed at the circumstance.

Having alighted, therefore, we stripped and set to in an adjoining field, and having fought nearly an hour, the battle ended in my favor.

At the conclusion of the contest, the gentleman by whose persuasion I was induced to fight, being highly pleased, presented me with a guinea and raised a subscription for me among the spectators of between five and six pounds.

The success of this battle and the unexpected pleasure of receiving a few pounds put me in high spirits, and I determined to spend the rest of the day with my companions. We proceeded on the road with great triumph when we were accosted at Finchley by a party of butchers who seemed desirous of provoking a quarrel. A sporting gentleman who was passing by at that time expressed his surprise that I did not get out of the cart and thrash the butchers for their insolence; upon which I acquainted him with the circumstance of my having just fought, but on his promise of a guinea if I again came off victorious I set to with the butcher, who after a battle of half an hour gave in. The gentleman gave me two guineas and also raised a subscription, which with what I had received before amounted to fourteen pounds. I was highly elated and anxious to get to town to spend some of the money which I considered as the honorable reward of my exertions.

I set off to town on horseback but soon found that my day's work was not yet finished, for I had not proceeded far before the disorder of my dress and my awkward manner of riding happened to attract the notice of a fellow who was passing, and who remarked to his companions that I had the appearance of a tailor. They began to shout with a view to frightening the horse and making me the butt of their sport. I immediately dismounted and having singled out the instigator of the disturbance and insisted on his fighting me on the spot, I convinced him in half an hour that he had much better have let me alone.

He found that though I could not ride very well, I could fight quite well enough to give him as severe a thrashing as perhaps he ever received, and from the condition in which I left him, I have no doubt that he was too much in need of ease and rest himself to molest anyone else that evening. I came off this contest as from the two others without receiving a scratched face, or even any blow of material consequence.

I now remounted, and no one offering me any further interruption, proceeded on my journey; on reaching town I determined (notwithstanding the fatiguing exertions of the day) to go to a dance which I knew was to be held in a certain house I was in the habit of frequenting; and accordingly, not choosing to leave my horse in the street, I introduced him into the dancing room, to the surprise and entertainment of the company, chiefly consisting of sailors and their lasses, and having remained here for about two hours, and it drawing near midnight, I thought it high time to quit this place of mirth.

WHEN MY HEALTH was improving, I frequently used to indulge myself with excursions into the country for the purpose of taking the air. On one of these occasions, I went for a few days to Windsor, and, during my stay in that town, had the honor of being introduced to a great personage. This happened one evening on the terrace, where I was walking, and was suddenly surprised at being accosted by a nobleman, who, in a very abrupt manner, mentioned his intention of introducing me to His Majesty. He had scarcely spoken when the King, attended by some lords in waiting, approached the spot, upon which I was introduced, and had a long conversation with His Majesty, who made many ingenious remarks on the pugilistic art, such as might naturally be expected to be made by a person of so comprehensive a mind and such transcendent abilities, as that illustrious personage is generally believed to possess!

Before I quitted the terrace, the Princess Royal (now queen of Württemberg) brought one of the younger branches of the royal family to me, and asked my permission (which I of course readily granted) for this young gentleman to strike me a blow, in order that he might have to boast at a subsequent opportunity of having at an early period of his life, struck a professed pugilist on Windsor terrace.

MY CREDITORS having now discovered that I had arrived in London, seemed resolved to harass and persecute me. A few mornings after my arrival I was arrested for an old debt, which it was not then in my power to discharge, and was consequently obliged to give bail to the action, which I was at length, with considerable difficulty, enabled to settle. In numerous other instances, I was subjected to great expense and inconvenience, but in consequence of a great many gentlemen taking lessons of me, and paying me liberally for my trouble, I contrived to settle many of their demands.

About this time I was introduced to Lord Camelford, whose impetuosity of temper is well known to have led him into many difficulties, and finally to have proved fatal to him. When I attended his lordship, he requested me to spar with him, which I accordingly did, and he professed to feel highly gratified at my exertions, and intimated that he would show me an original attitude of his own, in which he had attained a degree of perfection that would counteract any assault that could be made on him. At his request, therefore, I aimed several blows at him, one of which took place, and in consequence of his lordship's throwing back his head with great violence, he thrust it through the glazed door of a bookcase.

This accident irritated him greatly, and as soon as he was extricated, which was not done without difficulty, he asked, whether I had ever played at the game of single-stick? On my answering I was not entirely unacquainted with the sport, he insisted on my engaging with him; and having procured a pair of weapons from an adjoining room, we set to. At this game I found his lordship a better proficient than myself; he struck with a great force as well as skill, and I speedily received a violent blow over the ear, which caused great pain at the time. However, I was resolved not to yield, and therefore continued till he was tired, when he again proposed to change the amusement to fencing, and though I candidly told him, I knew nothing of this art, he insisted upon my engaging with him, to which I was with reluctance induced to consent. On one of the foils happening to break, he very

coolly observed, we might as well change them for a pair of small swords, with which, he said, if we took proper care, we could not possibly injure each other.

To this proposal I at first strongly objected, and declared my determination not to engage with weapons of such a dangerous nature; upon which my noble antagonist appeared highly irritated, and I began to apprehend the violent effects of his anger; therefore with the view of appeasing his wrath, I pretended to assent to his proposal, merely expressing a wish that he would take care of my family, in case of any accident happening to me. This he promised to do, and left me for the purpose of fetching the swords.

As soon as the coast was clear, I rushed out of the room, and flew down stairs, with all the rapidity in my power: such was my impatience to depart, that I never stopped till I had reached the bottom of the staircase, when I found I had descended too low, and had got to the cellar door; consequently I was obliged to return, and having, at last, reached the street door, departed abruptly from the house, and, as may be imagined, never felt the least inclination to re-enter it.

FRANK MENKE was a good newspaperman, but a more successful ghost writer and encyclopedist. This piece would be an example of gross overwriting, except that it describes the most dramatic of all glove fights and, written more than twenty years after the event, is the best wrap-up of what happened.

# Dempsey–Firpo

## FRANK G. MENKE

NEVER IN THE HISTORY of American pugilism was there staged a battle so sensational as the Jack Dempsey–Luis Firpo affair in New York on the night of September 14, 1923.

From the moment that the first gong banged until the Argentine warrior lay a crumpled heap upon the canvas—total time: 3 minutes, 57 seconds—there was action so rapid, so cyclonic, that the eye could not follow, nor the brain record the exact details.

It was not a boxing match—not a civilized fistic encounter. Two wild men were tossed into the same ring, each with an intent to murder the other—or be murdered in his failure. And 85,000 persons, imbibing the spirit of madness, arose to their feet, and 85,000 voices howled and shrieked in a delirium that made a din which rivaled a thousand Niagaras.

Its like in ring battling had never been seen before—and never will be known again. The story is the epic of ringdom—the fight of all the ages.

With the clang of the first gong, Dempsey fairly catapulted from his corner to meet a huge, hairy giant from the pampas of South America; rushed, crouched, swirled upward and swung a terrific left-hand punch to his foeman's jaw.

It was short—by two inches.

As Dempsey steadied, to try again, Firpo's powerful right hand whistled through the night and struck Dempsey full and solid upon the point of the chin. Every ounce of the South American's gigantic body was concentrated in that blow—one of the hardest ever landed in ring annals.

The knees of the world's champion buckled under him; a world's champion pitched forward. He was toppling, face forward, to dethronement. One punch—the first of the fight—seemed to have sent him to his doom!

If Firpo had been six inches farther away at that very fraction of a second, Dempsey probably would have crumpled into the resin dust, either to rise no more, or, in rising, to be met by a fusillade of blows which probably would have crushed the consciousness from him.

But as Dempsey pitched forward, Firpo was so close that the champion fell against the body of the giant. Instinct made him grab—and hold. Desperately, wildly, Firpo tried to shake off Dempsey. Before he could achieve his purpose, the brief rest saved Dempsey.

Strength and a little power came back to Dempsey's legs; the floodgates of reserve energy opened, revived him, refreshed him—refreshed and revived, however, only the body of him, because Dempsey afterward said he remembered nothing about that first round after he had been hit with that first pile-driver blow.

He had been hit and hurt by the rushing, tearing, lunging form before him. And that form must be destroyed. Such was the prompting of savage instinct. Everything that Dempsey had learned in years of boxing was forgotten; his clear reasoning power, his coolness and calmness were gone. There was nothing left but the fighting fury which made him known as the Tiger Man of the prize ring.

Urged on only by a wild and blazing rage, the champion ripped and tore into the giant and, as he did so, he put into his blows every bit of killing power which he could summon. He was relentless, merciless, forgetful of the ethics of the fighting game; a cruel monster, determined that the man before him must be hammered and pounded into absolute helplessness.

Dempsey, loose from the first clinch, rushed at Firpo, both hands working with the power and speed of a locomotive piston rod. A left hand landed with mighty force upon the chin of Firpo. The Argentinian went down in a heap—perhaps 30 seconds after the round had started.

The official proceeded to drone the count. He had reached "nine" when Firpo started to rise. Then he stopped counting—when he should have gone on, for Firpo was not in a boxing position and should have been counted out then and there. It was at least 13 full seconds before Firpo was back in fighting pose.

Another flurry of blows met Firpo—and again he toppled. He arose, dealt a right-hander to Dempsey's chin and was rewarded with a right to his own, which floored him again. Once more Firpo arose, but Dempsey hurled himself at the huge Argentinian. Even as Dempsey whirled through the air, Firpo steadied on wobbling legs, swung his world-famous right and again caught Dempsey on the rim of the jaw! Dempsey's body quivered, his legs buckled, he stumbled forward, his hands went to the floor.

As the referee raced over, expecting to begin the count, Dempsey pulled himself together, straightened up, lunged at Firpo and caught him on the jaw with a punch that didn't travel more than eight inches. Firpo dropped almost upon the spot where Dempsey, a few seconds before, had been sprawled.

Again Firpo beat the count and rushed at Dempsey. The champion backed to the ropes, more because he was jockeying to get a newer shot at Firpo's jaw than because of fear of the South American's charge.

Then something happened which forms one of the most astonishing chapters in the entire annals of the prize ring. A world's champion, a challenger, a referee were in the ring one second. A second later only two figures were visible. The king of kings of the fistic realms suddenly disappeared as though a trap door had opened and swallowed him.

Over 85,000 persons saw the fight—and perhaps 85,000 different accounts have been given as to how Dempsey went out of the ring—and how he got back. Of the 85,000, perhaps no more than fifty persons in the first row of the ringside press seats actually saw what happened. My seat was in the first row—alongside Jim Corbett. My view was wholly unobstructed.

This is what I saw:

Dempsey was backed to the ropes with Firpo crowding with the left side of his body. Firpo's right arm was free. Six times in succession he hit Dempsey on the chin or head without a return, because Dempsey was in such a position that his arms were practically handcuffed.

Realizing his peril, Dempsey decided to slide out of the trap. Bending his head low toward his own right arm, he attempted to move along the ropes until he was clear of Firpo.

At the exact moment that Dempsey's head was below the upper strand, and at the exact fraction of a second that his right foot was off the floor, Firpo hit the champion on the chin with a right. The middle of Dempsey's body was up against the middle strand of the ropes at that very second.

The result was this:

Dempsey's legs shot off the ground, and his head shot backward. A world champion spun around much as does the piece of wood one uses in playing tiddlywinks. And in a headfirst backward dive, Jack Dempsey, ruler of the fistic world, went into the press row—while 85,000 persons looked on in hushed amazement.

Much has been written about how reporters saved Dempsey in his fall—and how they helped him back into the ring. The real truth is that the reporters handicapped, more than helped, Dempsey in his ring re-entry.

When 194 pounds of humanity came hurtling through the air directly at their heads, those reporters did only the natural thing. They pushed up their hands to protect themselves; they summoned all the power they could to keep Dempsey from falling upon them and breaking their necks. Their thought was to save themselves—not to aid Dempsey, who suddenly had become a 194-pound menace to their existence.

Dempsey landed among the group. Squirming, twisting, lunging with arms, kicking with legs, he strove to get himself steered in the right direction so that he could climb back through the ropes. In one of his wild lurches, his fist hit Kid McPartland, one of the judges, in the eye —and blackened it for ten days.

It is true that reportorial hands shoved Dempsey as he climbed back through the ropes. But they weren't hands of friendship. The men who pushed him did so because they wanted to be sure Dempsey didn't kick them in the face or body. They were passing Dempsey back and forth, because they wanted none of him floundering on their heads and frail necks.

Never did a man look more bewildered, more "all gone," than Dempsey, back in the ring just as the referee counted "nine," flat-footed, legs spread wide for balance, against the ropes. His hands were helpless at his sides. His eyes showed no brain light. His whole body slumped.

This was Firpo's second golden opportunity for world conquest—and for the second and final time it slipped from him.

Had Firpo closed in on Dempsey and thrown every ounce of his titanic power into one punch, Dempsey would have gone down—and his reign would have ended. But Firpo, not sure whether Dempsey was faking, decided to take no chances. He went in cautiously. Precious seconds flew onward into eternity. He finally decided to strike. He swung—and missed—because Dempsey instinctively ducked, as energy came back to him.

The action of Firpo galvanized Dempsey into a new attack. He went forward—revived by some mysterious force. The arms that had been helpless suddenly began whirling through the air. He drove Firpo back—back—and back with his furious charge and, under the avalanche of leather, Firpo crumpled again to the floor. As Dempsey tore at him, Firpo braced and fought back. Toe-to-toe the two men stood, no quarter asked—none given.

The bell banged—the round had passed into official history. But Dempsey never heard it. As Firpo turned to go to his corner the champion's foggy brain construed the act as a new retreat. He went racing after the Wild Bull of the Pampas, showering blows on head, neck and shoulders.

Firpo whirled, a look of surprise on his face—then one of insane rage. He closed in and began slugging viciously, until the referee was able, by locking their arms, to stop the sluggery and tell Dempsey the round was over.

It was a round without dramatic equal in the annals of boxing. Firpo had been down five times; Dempsey had staggered once, was down on his hands later, and out of the ring upon another occasion.

Perhaps a hundred blows had been swung—and about ninety had landed, each with force and power enough to batter any other giant into an hour of unconsciousness. But these were supermen that night.

When the referee finally had stopped the after-bell battling, Dempsey stood in mid-ring. He didn't know the location of his own corner. Jack Kearns, his manager, leaped through the ropes, grabbed Dempsey by the arms, hauled him to his chair, flopped him down, picked up a bucket of ice water and hit Dempsey with its contents. The shock revived Dempsey—brought him back to consciousness for the first time since he was hit with that pile-driver smash in the first round.

There was wild confusion in Dempsey's corner because Kearns couldn't find the smelling salts. They were in the pocket of his shirt. He had forgotten he had placed them there. Kearns was roaring condemnation at Jerry (The Greek) Luvadis, the trainer, and Jerry was trying to grab at Kearns' pocket to get the salts because Kearns was shouting so loudly he couldn't hear Jerry. Kearns hit Jerry in the nose. Jerry grabbed the bottle from Kearns' pocket. Kearns poked the fumes under Dempsey's nose.

The buzzer announced ten seconds before the bell. Kearns leaned over, yelled at Dempsey.

"Quit taking chances—cover—cover! He's a murderer!"

"What round?" asked Dempsey.

"Second," answered Kearns—and the bell rang.

Dempsey came out—cautiously. This time Firpo did the rushing. Dempsey, a keen fighter once again now that his mental faculties were restored, crouched, weaved, feinted, and Firpo lashed out with his right. Dempsey had miscalculated Firpo's nearness, and the blow, a murderous drive, crashed into Dempsey's body, under the heart.

Dempsey sagged back. Firpo "cocked" his right and started to let it go, when, like the flight of a meteor, Dempsey's short left crashed against Firpo's jaw. The South American staggered and fell to the floor with a sickening crash. It seemed that this must be the end. But it wasn't. At "eight" Firpo was up—and Dempsey was upon him.

Scorning a defense, Dempsey pumped lefts into Firpo's face and body with the precision of drum beats. Firpo, in desperation, swung a right, missed, and the momentum carried him close to Dempsey. The champion's short left caught Firpo on the point of the jaw. As he started to fall, Dempsey put all he had into a lifting right hook—and Firpo, in falling, went down as if driven by some terrific explosive force.

For six seconds he lay there inert, seemingly lifeless. Blood streamed from his nose and mouth. His eyes were open—but glazed. At "eight" he made a feeble attempt to rise, lifted himself a few inches—and then toppled back.

"Ten," droned the referee and Dempsey was still the world's champion.

293

AFTER FORTY YEARS of observing and reporting the events of the English ring, Henry Downes Miles authored *Pugilistica,* a three-volume history, published in 1863, covering 144 years of British boxing. He was a conscientious researcher, or heavy borrower, who milked all available sources including Pierce Egan, for whom, he was constantly reminding his reader, he had little respect. This is from his chapter on Mr. John Jackson, that remarkable gentleman who was the first to overcome completely the stigma of being a professional pugilist.

# Mr. John Jackson—1788–1795

## HENRY DOWNES MILES

JOHN JACKSON WAS BORN in London, in 1768, and was the son of an eminent builder, by whom the arch was thrown over the Old Fleet Ditch, near the mouth of the River Fleet, flowing from the Hampstead and Highgate Hills, and crossed by bridges at Holborn and Ludgate. This forms the great sewer of Blackfriars from the north into the new Low Level, over which run Farringdon Street (the site of the old Fleet Market), and Bridge Street, leading to the splendid bridge by Cubitt, with its ugly iron companion carrying the L.C. & D.R. John Jackson's uncles were farmers, and tenants of the Duke of Bedford and the Marquis of Hertford. Nature had bestowed upon him all those athletic requisites which constitute the *beau ideal* of perfect manhood. There was a happy combination of muscular development with proportionate symmetry in his frame (his height was five feet eleven, and his weight fourteen stone), which rendered him a fitting model for the sculptor, and excited the admiration of all those by whom these qualities are appreciated. At the age of nineteen he became a frequenter of the sparring schools, and displayed such talents as proved that he was destined to eclipse the most favoured of his contemporaries; added to which, possessing as he did the *suaviter in modo* as well as the *fortiter in re,* he soon found patrons of the highest grade.

It is stated that a conversation with Colonel Harvey Aston led to his first encounter in the prize ring. Fewterel, a Birmingham boxer, as yet unbeaten, had been the conqueror, says "Pancratia," in eighteen battles. The meeting took place at Smitham Bottam, near Croydon, June 9th, 1788. We copy the report:

"THIS DAY there were decided three boxing matches, which had been long depending, and great bets were depending on. The first was between Jackson, a fine young man of nineteen years only, and Fewterel, of Birmingham. Tom Johnson seconded Jackson, and Bill Warr, Fewterel; Humphries and Dunn were the bottle-holders. Fewterel is a man of extremely great bulk, so much so that, at first setting-to, it was doubted whether Jackson would level such an opponent. Yet this he never failed to do when he could plant his blows at distance. The contest had lasted one hour and seven minutes; its decision being very much procrastinated by Fewterel fighting shifty, getting down to avoid a blow, and then remaining so long on the floor as often to require the interposition of the umpires to remind his seconds of 'time.' Fewterel at last gave up the contest, and Major Hanger, by command of the Prince of Wales, who was present, gave young Jackson a bank note.

JACKSON'S NEXT CONTEST (March 12th, 1789)

was with George Ingleston, the brewer. It closed by an untoward accident, by which Jackson broke the small-bone of his leg, as will be seen under the head of Ingleston, in the Appendix to Period II.

Jackson's next contest was one of the greatest interest to the pugilistic world. The victories of Mendoza had placed him on the pinnacle of fame; and the attempt to defeat the conqueror of Sam Martin, of Humphries (twice), of Bill Warr (twice), to say nothing of minor boxers, was viewed as indeed a bold flight of young ambition. On April 15th, 1795, the men met at Hornchurch, in Essex, for a stake of 200 guineas aside. We copy the contemporary report:—

"A TWENTY-FOUR-FEET STAGE was erected in a most advantageous hollow, which accommodated upwards of three thousand spectators, and so excellently adapted that no one could claim a superiority of situation. All the eminent patrons and amateurs were present: the Duke of Hamilton, Lord Delaval, Sir John Phillipson, Mr. Clark, Mr. Bullock, Mr. Lee, Mr. Fawcett, etc.; and among the pugilists of note were Jackling, Will Warr and Joe Warr, George the Brewer, Tom Tyne, Fearby (the Young Ruffian), etc.

"At one o'clock Mendoza mounted the spot of combat, accompanied by his second, Harry Lea, and Symonds (the Old Ruffian), as his bottle-holder. Jackson immediately followed, with Tom Johnson as his second, and Wood, the coachman, for his bottle-holder. The chosen umpires were Mr. Alexander and Mr. Allen.

"They each politely bowed to the people, and were received with general acclamations. About five minutes after one they, as usual, saluted each other by shaking hands, and immediately set-to. Bets five to four in favour of Mendoza.

## THE FIGHT

"Round 1.—Both having assumed their attitude, displayed the greatest caution; full a minute expired before a blow was struck, when Jackson made a hit, and his antagonist fell.

"2.—Mendoza guarded with great science, avoided the blows of his opponent, and put in several severe ones.

"3.—In this round there was much hard fighting. Odds rose two to one in favour of Mendoza, but the round terminated by Mendoza falling.

"4.—This was the most severely contested round throughout the battle. Jackson seemed to hold his opponent's manoeuvres in contempt, followed him up with great resolution, and put in some dreadfully severe blows, by the last of which Mendoza fell, and his right eye was much cut; Jackson now evidently had the advantage.

"5.—In this round Jackson caught his opponent by the hair, and holding him down, gave him several severe blows, which brought him to the ground; Mendoza's friends called 'foul' but the umpires decided on the contrary. Odds had now changed two to one on Jackson.

"6, 7, 8.—Throughout these three rounds Jackson supported his superiority. Mendoza acted entirely on the defensive.

"9.—This was the last round. Jackson manifestly displayed astonishing advantage; he several times struck his adversary, when he fell quite exhausted, and gave in.

"The battle only lasted ten minutes and a-half, and was acknowledged by every spectator to be the hardest contested that ever was fought in so short a time. Jackson was very little hurt, leaping from the stage with great agility, but Mendoza was quite cut up.

"A subscription purse was made and fought for between a Jew called Black Baruk, who was seconded by Symonds (the Old Ruffian), and Burk a glass-blower, seconded by James the waterman. It was very well contested for half an-hour, when a dispute arose about a foul blow, and it was terminated by sharing the money between them."

NEARLY SEVEN YEARS after his combat with Mendoza, a "gag" paragraph having appeared in the newspaper, announcing a forthcoming fight as in arrangement between Mendoza and Jackson, the latter inserted the following letter to the Editor of the *Oracle and Daily Advertiser* of Wednesday, December 1, 1801:—

"SIR,—*I was somewhat astonished on my return to town on Saturday, to learn that a challenge was inserted in your paper on Thursday last, as if from Mr. Mendoza. Should I be right in my conclusion, by believing that it came from that celebrated pugilist, I beg you will inform the public through the medium of your paper, that for some years I have entirely withdrawn from a public life, and am more and more convinced of the propriety of my conduct by the happiness which I enjoy in private among many friends of great respectability, with whom it is my pride to be received on terms of familiarity and friendship: goaded, however, as I am to a petty conflict. I hope that it will not be considered too much arrogance on my part simply to observe, that, after waiting for more than three years to accept the challenge of any pugilist, however dexterous in the science, and however highly flattered by his friends, I think it rather extraordinary that Mr. Mendoza should add a silence of four years to those three, it being nearly seven years since I had the satisfaction of chastising him; but Mr. Mendoza derived one great good from the issue of that contest—he was taught to be less hasty in forming his resolutions, more slow in carrying them into effect.*

*"This cautious and wise principle of action deserves much commendation; and having served an apprenticeship of seven years to learn a certain portion of artificial courage, he now comes forward with a stock of impudence (the only capital which during that time he seems to have acquired) to force me to appear once more in that situation which I have for years cheerfully avoided.*

*"Reluctant, however, as I am to attract again, even for a moment, the public attention, I shall have no objection to vindicate my character by a meeting with Mr. Mendoza when and where he pleases, PROVIDED he'll promise to fight, and provided he'll also promise not to give previous information to the magistrates at Bow Street, or elsewhere.*

*"I am, Sir, yours and the public's most respectfully,*

"JOHN JACKSON"

*Nov. 20, 1801*

Need we say that this was on the part of Mendoza a mere piece of that absurd system of gagging then so much in vogue, and on which we have elsewhere commented.

Independent of his pugilistic prowess, Mr. Jackson was distinguished for his extraordinary powers as a runner of a short distance, and as a leaper no man of his day was equal to him at a standing jump, of which many extraordinary feats are on record. His muscular strength was equal to his bodily activity, and in the presence of Mr. Harvey Coombe, and other gentlemen, he lifted ten hundred weight and one quarter, and wrote his own name with eighty-four pounds weight suspended from his little finger!

One of the most able and experienced sporting writers, the late Vincent George Dowling, Esq., the founder, and for more than thirty years the editor of *Bell's Life in London,* has left on record a graceful tribute to the memory of his friend of many years, John Jackson, in the form of an obituary notice. From this we shall here make a few extracts.

"JOHN JACKSON was an instance of the glorious truth which this country is constantly evolving—that if a man be true to himself, he may defy the obloquy and malice of millions. No matter in what grade of life a creature be thrown; no matter whether from necessity or choice he mingles with the learned or the illiterate, the high or the low; give him the attribute of genius, or, if that be denied, honesty and perseverance, and he must distinguish himself. The choice of a profession is the puzzle of boyhood—be it so. *A profession never degraded a man, if that man took care not to degrade his profession."* This last axiom deserves to be written in letters of adamant; it contains the philosophy we hope to inculcate by our pages. Mr. Dowling continues: "As there always have been, and always will be, ruffians loose upon society, who can only be met and quelled by the arguments such brutes can appreciate; and as

*Heads, nineteen in twenty, 'tis confest,*
*Can feel a crabstick quicker than a jest,*

it is essential that boxing, as an art, should not fall into desuetude. It empowers the little man to defend himself against the big one; makes the weaker man, to a considerable extent, able to protect himself against the onset of the stronger one, and, in some cases, to punish his want of skill and his presumption. Doubtless much has been done in our great cities by gas and an improved police; but even now things do occasionally occur to call upon every man to know how with his own hands to defend his own head, or, what is doubtless of more consequence, the heads of those near and dear to him, or under his protection. Such a power is a *corps de reserve,* which, though it *may* never be called into action, it is valuable and assuring to possess. So thought our grandfathers' fathers in the days of Fielding. Boxing, to a gentleman, was a more modern and practical application of knight-errantry; it enabled a man to protect himself against aggression, and yet more, to defend an insulted woman. 'Good,' exclaims the anti-pugilist, 'but what say you to the prize-fighter?' The response is plain: He is the exemplar, the professor, the demonstrator of a practice, of an exercise. Could or can the sword or the bow be taught without professors, and can they teach without exemplifying? . . ." After a few facts, which will be found embodied in our *Memoir,* Mr. Dowling concludes: "From 1795, Mr. Jackson ceased to be a public pugilist, having fought but three battles, winning two, and not gaining (for it cannot be called losing) the third by an accident. On what basis, then, rests his fame as a thoroughly tried boxer? On none whatever; the pedestal of his popularity was conduct, the keystone to fortune in every grade of life. There is a singular similarity in the career of John Jackson and John Gully: the latter fought but thrice, was beaten once, won the other two, and then retired to enjoy a better fortune in a higher sphere of society."

Ere quitting the more active sporting career of Mr. Jackson, it may be as well to state that as a runner his speed was extraordinary, but he could not last: he also excelled as a jumper until the celebrated Ireland "tooke the shine out of all England."

The opening of "Jackson's Rooms, 13, Old Bond Street," was literally an era in the gymnastic education of the aristocracy. Not to have had lessons of Jackson was a reproach. To attempt a list of his pupils would be to copy one-third of the then peerage. Byron, who was proud of being thought a pugilist, has in his correspondence spoken highly of his tutor; but the fact is, from lameness, the poet could neither hit nor stop effectively. When Jackson taught the author of "Childe Harold," he was forty-four, Byron about twenty-three; the latter therefore stood a boy before a veteran. In a note to the 11th Canto of "Don Juan," we find this: "My friend and corporeal pastor and master, John Jackson, Esquire, professor of pugilism, who I trust still retains the strength and symmetry of his model of a form, together with his good humour, and athletic as well as mental accomplishments."

And in his diary we read:—"Jackson has been here; the boxing world much as usual, but the club increases (i.e. Pugilistic Club). I shall dine at Cribb's tomorrow."

He records going to this dinner thus: "Just returned from dinner with Jackson (the Emperor of Pugilism), and another of the select, at Cribb's, the Champion's."

The next extract shows the author of "Childe Harold" actually in training: "I have been sparring with Jackson for exercise this morning, and mean to continue and renew my acquaintance with my muffles. My chest, and arms, and wind are in very good plight, and I am not in flesh. I used to be a hard hitter, and my arms are very long for my height (5 feet 8½ inches); at any rate exercise is good, and this the severest of all; fencing and the broad-sword never fatigued me half so much." This latter is dated the 17th of March, 1814.

"Got up, if anything, earlier than usual; sparred with Jackson ad sudorem, and have been much better in health for many days."

Byron kept at his work, for we find him writing thus on the 9th of April, 1814: "I have been boxing for exercise for the last month daily."

In returning to the younger days of the "finest formed man in Europe," we shall take the liberty of borrowing a graphic colloquial sketch from the lips of a veteran: "There were the Lades, the Hangers, the Bullocks, the Vernons, but give me Jack Jackson, as he stood alone amid the throng. I can see him now, as I saw him in '84, walking down Holborn Hill, towards Smithfield. He had on a scarlet coat, worked in gold at the buttonholes, ruffles, and frill of fine lace, a small white stock, no collar (they were not then invented), a looped hat with a broad black band, buff knee-breeches, and long silk strings, striped white silk stockings, pumps, and paste buckles; his waistcoat was pale blue satin, sprigged with white. It was impossible to look on his fine ample chest, his noble shoulders, his waist (if anything too small), his large, but not too large hips (the fulcrum of the human form, whether male or female), his limbs, his balustrade calf and beautifully turned but not over delicate ankle, his firm foot, and peculiarly small hand, without thinking that nature had sent him on earth as a model. On he went at a good five miles and a half an hour, the envy of all men, and the admiration of all women."

As regards his face nature had not been bountiful; his forehead was rather low, and the mode he wore his hair made it peculiarly so. His cheek bones were high, and his nose and mouth coarse. His ears projected too much from his head, but his eyes were eyes to look at rather than look with; they were full and piercing, and formed a great portion of his power as a pugilist—with them he riveted his men.

Anatomists of the first standing examined Jackson, and artists and sculptors without number took sketches and models of his arm; but it was the extraordinary proportion of the man throughout that formed the wonder.

After 1795 Mr. Jackson resolved to teach others the art in which he himself excelled. For an instructor he had that invaluable requisite, temper; he was never too fast with his pupils. This made his initiatory lessons tedious to young gentlemen who go ahead, and it may readily be conceived that amid the aristocracy of England he had plenty of rough assailants to deal with. But he was always on his guard; there was no chance of rushing suddenly in and taking Jackson by surprise—he could not be flurried. Amid the other qualifications he had studied Lavater, and managed to reckon up his customers at first sight, and knew what he had to trust to. It has been said "he defied any man to hit him"; this is the truth, but not the whole truth—he defied any man to hit him whilst he (Jackson) stood merely on the defensive; in a fight, of course, it is impossible to avoid being hit.

"His sparring was elegant and easy. He was peculiarly light upon his feet, a good judge of distance, and when he indulged his friends with a taste of his real quality, the delivery of his blow was only observable in its effect. It literally came like lightning, and was felt before it was seen. Most big men are comparatively slow, but he was as rapid as Owen Swift or Johnny Walker, and this, too, when upwards of fifty years of age.

"Jackson not only told you what to do, but why you should do it; in this essential point many capital instructors are and have been deficient. The want of this power of explaining the purpose of an action made Young Dutch Sam and Richard Curtis bad instructors, though they were finished pugilists, and, which does not always follow, capital sparrers.

"Jackson was not unmindful of the fact that art never ends. If there was anything new in the gymnastic, equestrian, or pedestrian way, there be assured was Jackson; not merely witnessing the exhibition, but examining the means by which the effects were produced. He was consequently often at Astley's and at the Surrey, when Ireland, the jumper, was there, and knew all the famous fencers, funambulists, dancers, and riders of his day, and his day was a long one.

"Of his private character, what can be said more than that all his pupils became his friends. Save with Dan Mendoza, it is not known that he ever had a quarrel. He was a careful man, not a mean man—saving, but not penurious. It is to be remembered, too, from his peculiar situation, continued calls were made upon his purse by the ruffianly and profligate, who claimed a brotherhood that he utterly and properly repudiated."

In 1811, he procured a benefit at the Fives Court, in aid of the subscription for the suffering Portuguese; it realized £114. Next year he did the same for the British prisoners in France; this benefit amounted to £132 6s. He also aided the benefit for the Lancashire weavers (1826).

One old boxer (but who was not of Jackson's day) pestered him incessantly for money. "No," said Jackson, "I'll give you no money; but you may go to the Horse and Groom, and you will find a clean bed, three meals, and a pot of beer a day; stay there until matters mend." The man was thankful in the extreme; but a week had not elapsed ere he was found in the taproom bartering his dinner for gin!

Of course a "lion" like Jackson could not avoid being made a "show" of on particular occasions; accordingly, when the allied sovereigns were in England, his aid was required. On the 15th of June, 1814, at the house of Lord Lowther, in Pall Mall, a pugilistic fete came off in the presence of the Emperor of Russia, Platoff, Blucher, etc. The display so delighted those illustrious fighting men that it was resolved to carry the thing out on a grander scale; accordingly, the King of Prussia, the Prince Royal, Prince of Mecklenburgh, and others assembled. Jackson, Cribb, Belcher, Oliver, Painter, and Richmond, were the principal performers. The foreign nobility now wanted a peep, and at Angelo's rooms some splendid displays took place. It was said that Jackson had inoculated them with a pugilistic fever, but it is believed he never obtained a single pupil from among them. If this be a fact, it is an extraordinary one.

At the coronation of George the Fourth, 1821, Mr. Jackson was applied to to furnish an unarmed force "to preserve order." Cribb, Spring, Belcher, Carter, Richmond, Ben Burn, Harmer, Harry Lee, Tom Owen, Joshua Hudson, Tom Oliver, Harry Holt, Crawley, Curtis, Medley, Purcell, Sampson, and Eales, with Jackson at their head, formed the corps, dressed as Royal Pages.

One gold coronation medal was given to the boxers—they raffled for it at a dinner. Tom Belcher won and wore it.

In 1822, a number of noblemen and gentlemen, admirers of the gymnastic sports of their country, with a Royal Duke (Clarence) at their head, presented John Jackson with a service of plate. The salver, which bears the subjoined inscription, is of magnificent workmanship, weighing one hundred and eighty-seven ounces.

THIS SALVER
(With other Plate)
*Was purchased by Subscriptions from*
A ROYAL DUKE
and Several of the Nobility and Gentry,
And presented to
JOHN JACKSON, ESQ.
*Under the Superintendence of the following Committee:*

| The Most Noble the | Admiral Tollemache, |
|---|---|
| Marquis of Worcester, | Major General Barton, |
| Henry Smith, Bart, M.P., | and John Harrison, Esq. |

MR. JACKSON had for many years been stakeholder, frequently referee, and was always ready to go round personally to solicit a subscription for the beaten man—and who could refuse John Jackson? A match was made in 1822, between Randall and Martin for 500 guineas a side, but Mr. Elliot, Martin's backer, "cried for his toy again," in fact, demanded his money back. Mr. Jackson declared he would never again be a stakeholder, and he kept his word. Thus virtually he retired from the ring, and from that moment the ring declined. Its progress downwards has been checked, now and then, by men of good conduct, and battles of great interest. Spring and Langan (1824) revived the hopes of many. Dutch Sam, from 1827 to 1839, rallied a few of the right sort around him, so did Burn and Owen Swift. A sort of reaction took place when Broome fought Bungaree; another, when Caunt fought Bendigo; again on the occasion of the great resultless battle of Farnborough between Sayers and Heenan in 1861; and lastly, the Benicia Boy's pulley-hauley match with Tom King, awakened attention; but down, down, down, the ring seems doomed to go, unless some thorough reform in the *etiquette* of fights is introduced, or some "Fair Play," or "Pugilistic Club," of respectability, energy, influence, and numbers, can be formed to check its rapid descent. Let us hope to see it revive like "a giant refreshed," to the utter confounding of unmanly, cruel, and bloodthirsty foreign methods of resenting insults by retorting fatal injuries.

John Jackson lived for many years at the house in which he died, No. 4, Lower Grosvenor Street West. The Old "Tattersall's" may be said to have divided his residence from that of another great artist, the late John Liston. "It is with pleasing melancholy we remember," says his old friend Vincent Dowling, "the Yarmouths, the Coombes, the Lades, the Ashtons, wending their way to the house of the one, while the Kembles, with perhaps Charles Mathews and Charles Taylor, Theodore Hook and Young, were standing in converse near, or visiting the low-roofed house of the latter."

There is little more to say. Loved by many, respected by all, enjoying a large circle of excellent society, John Jackson passed his later days. Affluent, but not rich in the vulgar sense, he wanted less than he had, and his income exceeded his expenditure. He was a cheerful companion, sang a good song, told his anecdotes with great tact, and never obtruded them. For the last year or two before his death his health declined, but until then he rarely had a day's illness. Peacefully and trustfully, with his hand in that of his niece (whom he loved, and had assisted as a daughter), John Jackson expired on the 7th of October, 1845, in the seventy-seventh year of his age. His death was as calm and resigned as his life had been exemplary.

The remains of John Jackson rest in Brompton Cemetery, beneath a handsome monument, by Mr. Thomas Butler, of which we give a faithful representation. On the side of the mausoleum nearest to the entrance is inscribed on each side of a medallion portrait of the deceased:—

| HERE LIE THE | Born, Sept. 28, |
|---|---|
| REMAINS OF | 1769, |
| JOHN JACKSON, | Died, Oct. 7, 1845. |

HIC VICTOR CAESTUS
ARTEMQUE REPONO.

On the opposite side to the footpath is a nude gladiator, holding a laurel wreath, and plunged in grief. On the top is a lion couchant, and on the farther end we read the following:—

"Stay, traveller," the Roman records said,
To mark the classic dust beneath it laid;—
"Stay, traveller," this brief memorial cries,
And read the record with attentive eyes.
Hast thou a lion's heart, a giant's strength?
Exult not, for these gifts must yield at length.
Do health and symmetry adorn thy frame?
The mouldering bones below possessed the same.
Does love, does friendship every step attend?
This man ne'er made a foe, ne'er lost a friend.
But death too soon dissolves all human ties,
And, his last combat o'er, here Jackson lies.

This Monument was erected by the subscriptions
of several noblemen and gentlemen,
to record their admiration of one
whose excellence of heart and incorruptible worth
endeared him to all who knew him.

THIS BIT OF political satire was turned out by the Irish bard who wrote, among much else, "Believe Me If All Those Endearing Young Charms," " 'Tis the Last Rose of Summer" and "The Harp That Once Through Tara's Halls." A great friend of Byron's, he never shared the latter's enthusiasm for boxing but he did report in his diary meeting Gentleman John Jackson and attending with him the Jack Randall-Ned Turner fight at Crawley on December 4, 1818. He found it "altogether not so horrid as I expected."

# Epistle from Tom Crib to Big Ben[1]
## CONCERNING SOME FOUL PLAY IN A
## LATE TRANSACTION[2]

### THOMAS MOORE

*"Ahi, mio Ben!"*—METASTASIO [3]
What! Ben, my old hero, is this your renown?
Is *this* the new *go?*—kick a man when he's down!
When the foe has knock'd under, to tread on him then—
By the fist of my father, I blush for thee, Ben!
"Foul! foul!" all the lads of the Fancy exclaim—
CHARLEY SHOCK is electrified—BELCHER spits flame—
And MOLYNEUX—ay, even BLACKY cries "shame!"

Time was, when JOHN BULL little difference spied
'Twixt the foe at his feet, and the friend at his side:
When he found (such his humour in fighting and eating)
His foe, like his beefsteak, the sweeter for beating.
But this comes, Master Ben, of your curst foreign notions,
Your trinkets, wigs, thingumbobs, gold lace and lotions:
Your Noyaus, Curaçaos, and the Devil knows what—
(One swig of Blue Ruin [4] is worth the whole lot!)

[1] A nickname given, at this time, to the Prince Regent.

[2] Written soon after Bonaparte's transportation to St. Helena.

[3] Tom, I suppose, was "assisted" to this motto by Mr. Jackson, who, it is well known, keeps the most learned company going.

[4] Gin.

## Epistle from Tom Crib to Big Ben BY THOMAS MOORE

Your great and small *crosses*—(my eyes, what a brood!
A *cross*-buttock from *me* would do some of them good!)
Which have spoilt you, till hardly a drop, my old porpoise,
Of pure English *claret* is left in your *corpus;*
And (as JIM says) the only one trick, good or bad,
Of the Fancy you're up to, is *fibbing,* my lad.
Hence it comes—*BOXIANA,* disgrace to thy page!—
Having floor'd, by good luck, the first *swell* of the age,
Having conquer'd the *prime one,* that *mill'd* us all round,
You kick'd him, old Ben, as he gasp'd on the ground!
Ay—just at the time to show spunk, if you'd got any—
Kick'd him, and jaw'd him, and *lag'd*[5] him to Botany!
Oh, shade of the *Cheesemonger!*[6] you, who, alas,
*Doubled up,* by the dozen, those Mounseers in brass,
On that great day of *milling,* when blood lay in lakes,
When Kings held the bottle, and Europe the stakes,
Look down upon Ben—see him, *dunghill* all o'er,
Insult the fall'n foe, that can harm him no more!
Out, cowardly *spooney!*—again and again,
By the fist of my father, I flush for thee, Ben.
To *show the white feather* is many men's doom,
But, what of *one* feather?—Ben shows a *whole Plume.*

[5] Transported.

[6] A Life Guardsman, one of the Fancy, who distinguished himself, and was killed in the memorable set-to at Waterloo.

THIS IS THE story of how Luther McCarthy, previously injured in a fall from a horse, was killed in the ring, and the photograph on page 35 substantiates it. When, thirty-five years later, Billy McCarney died from a respiratory ailment contracted at the Cerdan–Zale fight, they found among his effects a rose from Luther McCarthy's grave.

# Ten Seconds of Sunlight

## BARNEY NAGLER

BILLY MC CARNEY is one with the dust now. He slipped away in his seventy-sixth year, quietly, and no church bell tolled his passing. Yet for this old prize-fight manager at least one belfry should have vibrated—the tower of a church in Calgary, Canada. Billy helped purchase the bell for that cupola, and through, of all things, a prize fight.

IT WAS in May 1913, on a sunless day of gloom, that McCarney brought his heavyweight hopeful, Luther McCarthy, into a haphazard arena in Calgary for a bout with Arthur Pelkey, an undistinguished party of the second part. McCarthy, a handsome giant of twenty-one from Wild Horse Canyon in Nebraska, was the favorite to win; and why not? He was a skilled ring fencer and a man who punched with power. Pelkey wasn't accorded the slightest chance against him.

The audience filed into the arena quickly, for outside the sky was a cloudy curtain, unbroken by the merest suggestion of sun. Inside, the fans huddled together in the loneliness of the old barn. The only light came through skylights in the roof.

McCarthy and Pelkey climbed through the ropes and were greeted by the referee, Ed Smith. Then, suddenly, a little man in clerical garb clambered into the ring. "I want to speak to the crowd," the minister told Smith. "There's plenty of time," Smith replied.

The minister began speaking to the quiet audience. "I know you men are going to help us buy a bell for our church," he said. "Your silver tokens will buy a memento for God's house and it will be a credit to you on the Great Ledger."

The audience stirred. They wanted the fight to begin. But the minister went on.

"Everyone must have credit in this Ledger. For who knows whom the Great Referee will call home at any moment?"

A shower of silver covered the ring floor. Referee Smith helped the minister pick up the coins. Billy McCarney assisted, too, and the minister left the ring with his pockets bulging. Then, in the dismal, poorly lighted barn, the fight began.

McCarthy lashed out with left jabs and found his mark on Pelkey's face, leaving reddened skin. But this did not deter Pelkey, a squat, bearish man. He rushed in and scored with a right uppercut. McCarthy's head shook and his neck muscles bulged. From his face went the smile he had carried only moments before. Plainly he was in pain.

Outside the ring, peering through the ropes, McCarney screamed to his fighter: "Keep moving, box—keep moving and stick out your left!"

McCarthy failed to heed the advice. He fumbled his way about the ring, lashed by Pelkey's blows. His face was bloodless, his knees began buckling, and then a left and a right landed on his chin. McCarthy dropped, his body stiffening.

The referee began the count and, as he did, an eerie white glow pierced the skylights. From out of the thick, sunless gloom, a streak of sunlight shone on McCarthy's face.

Smith counted—"two, three, four, five, six, seven, eight, nine, ten and out"—and all the while McCarthy's face was bathed in the halo-like streak. Then, almost at the instant the referee ended the count, the sunlight disappeared. Once again, the arena was wrapped in gloom.

As they dragged the stricken fighter back to his corner and lowered him to the dirt floor where they attempted to revive him, Billy McCarney's ashen face told the story. Luther McCarthy was dead.

BAT NELSON was born in Copenhagen, Denmark, on June 5, 1882, held the lightweight title from July 4, 1908, until February 22, 1910, and died in Chicago, Illinois, on February 7, 1954. His only contribution to the science was a short left hook to the liver, delivered with the thumb and forefinger side of the glove, but his aggressiveness, punching power and ability to absorb punishment made him one of the greats.

The following passage is from his autobiography—*Life, Battles and Career of Battling Nelson, Lightweight Champion of the World,* by Himself—composed with the assistance of Bozeman Bulger and published in 1908. It tells of his return to his home in Hegewisch, Illinois, four years and twenty-nine fights after he had run away, at the age of fifteen, to become a professional fighter.

# The Battler's Old Man

## OSCAR BATTLING MATTHEW NELSON

WHEN I HAD finished my fight with Charley Berry, in December 1901, it was getting close on to Christmas, and it was up to me to hike back to Hegewisch. I am awful strong for Christmas at home and that hanging-up-the-stocking thing still has a hold on me. Every Christmas as regular as a clock I hang up my sock, and my good old mother never fails to see that Santa Claus puts something in it.

With $50 in my pocket I reached Hegewisch two days before Christmas Eve, and I had to get very busy, as all the kids were writing letters to Santa Claus and giving them to me to "mail." The little rascals were wise about Santa Claus, but they tried to make me believe that they were not, and, of course, I "fell." I couldn't buy everything they wanted, because one of them wanted a big balloon with a parachute so that they could go up and make parachute leaps! Can you beat that?

On Christmas Day my father called me into the little parlor and said he wanted to have a talk.

"Now, Bat," he began, and then he told me that he wanted me to stop the fighting business. "Before you leave home," he said, "you must promise."

I wouldn't exactly promise, but told him I would think it over. So we all went downtown. The crowd in Hegewisch usually hangs out at Dad Knight's bar. Just as we went in the door two fellows were having an argument. One of them was from Pullman, where they make the sleeping cars. In Hegewisch we have the largest car works in the world, but we only make working cars, such as flat cars, freight cars, etc.

The Pullman fellows think they have something on us because they make fancy cars, and there is always an argument about which is the better town.

"Maybe you do make the best cars," said the fellow from Hegewisch, "but you can't fight over there."

"Can't fight?" snapped the other fellow. "What's tearing at you? Why we've got the greatest fighter in the world at Pullman, and he can lick anything that ever growed in Hegewisch. I'd like to see you show some guy who could face Frankie Colifer. Why, he's a whirlwind."

"Get out!" cried the Hegewisch man. "Hegewisch can beat anybody in Pullman at anything, and I'll bet you on it." Just then he spied me and the old man as we came in the door.

"Say, kid," he said, "can't you lick anybody your weight in Pullman?"

I said I was willing to try, and would take a chance at it anyway.

"You tink dey got boy over dere vot can beat my boy—vot?" my father flared up in his funny Danish dialect. "Vell, ve'd lack to see him. My boy bane a vonder." And the old man was getting all worked up. He had forgotten all about my promising not to fight any more.

"I bet—I bet—I bet you von tousand dollars," the old man said excitedly, as he kept getting redder in the face. "Leek my boy—vot?"

"Bat," he said, turning to me, "you go an' leek dis Pullman boy, and eef you dake a leekin—vell, I leek some myself, huh? vot—?"

There was nothing to it now. I had to fight for the honor of Hegewisch, and the fellow who was boosting me patted me on the shoulder and said, "Now bring on your fancy Pullman fighter!"

For the next few days the town was wild with talk of the coming fight and they were betting their shoes. The same thing was going on in Pullman, which was just six miles away. We boys had two weeks in which to get ready, and on January 13, 1902, everybody in Hegewisch went over to West Pullman to see the go. The town was closed up. It was a general holiday.

We fought in an empty barn adjoining Pete Kelley's saloon, and the bout was to have gone six rounds.

This fellow Colifer was a pretty good fighter at that, but I remembered that I was battling for the honor of my home town, and I tore at him like a demon. The building was packed so that it bulged out at the sides. On one side the Pullman employees were pulling for their man, and on the other it seemed to me like all the Danes and Swedes in the world were pulling for me. You know I had made peace with the Swedes by this time, and they were working in perfect harmony with us Danes. This time we were all together. Everybody in the town had made a little bet.

The first few rounds went along pretty even, but I was hammering away at Colifer's wind, and it was beginning to tell. In the fifth round, while the Danes and Swedes were talking all sorts of languages and yelling for me to go on, I cracked Colifer in the stomach. He doubled over and as his head came down I hung a beaut squarely on his chin and he flopped over on the mat. By this time the Hegewisch crowd was crazy with joy. Colifer was very limp and took the full count of nine, and then, to everybody's surprise, he got up. He was certainly game to the core. As he got to his feet I set myself and got a clean right-handed swing on his jaw. This put him out for good, and we had a hard time bringing him back to consciousness.

The last word I heard as I started to jump out of the ring was "An' dey dink dey can leek my boy, vot!" followed by a familiar chuckle. The old man was still on the job.

I was handed fifty one-dollar bills for my victory, and I won that much more in bets that I had made with the Pullman employees.

My success in saving the fighting honor of Hegewisch appeared to take all of the talk out of the old man about making me quit the game. From this time on he was a dyed-in-the-wool fight fan. To this day he thinks there is nobody in the world who "can leek his boy, vot!" and, between you and me, his son Battling has got somewhat of the same notion.

*Golden Boy* was the most successful Broadway effort concerned with boxing. It opened at the Belasco Theater on November 4, 1937, and ran for 250 performances. Its excellent cast included Lee J. Cobb, John Garfield (Joe Bonaparte), Morris Carnovsky, Frances Farmer (Lorna Moon), Elia Kazan (Eddie Fuseli) and Luther Adler. Its plot depended upon such tired devices as the gun-bearing gangster (Fuseli) and death in the ring. Its fighters trained on the day of a fight and the day after and put on their robes before they took off their headgear, but it remains the best known theatrical use of the subject.

FROM

# *Golden Boy*

## CLIFFORD ODETS

### ACT III

#### SCENE 2

*The next night.*

*The lights fade in on an empty stage. We are in the same dressing room as seen in Act II, Scene 4. Far in the distance is heard the same roar of* THE CROWD. *The distant bell clangs menacingly. The room is shadows and patches of light. The silence here has its own ugly dead quality.*

LORNA MOON *enters. She looks around nervously, she lights a cigarette, this reminds her to rouge her lips, she puffs the cigarette. The distant bell clangs again.* EDDIE FUSELI *enters, pale and tense. He sees* LORNA *and stops short in his tracks. There is an intense silence as they look at each other.*

LORNA. How's the fight?
EDDIE. I like to talk to you.
LORNA. Is Joe still on his feet?
EDDIE. Take a month in the country, Miss Moon.
LORNA. Why?
EDDIE. (*Repressing a murderous mood.*) Give the boy . . . or move away.
LORNA. I get married tomorrow. . . .
EDDIE. You heard my request—give him or go!

LORNA. Don't Moody count?
EDDIE. If not for Bonaparte they'd find you in a barrel long ago—in the river or a bush!
LORNA. I'm not afraid of you . . . (*The distant bell clangs.*)
EDDIE. (*After turning his head and listening.*) That's the beginning of the eighth. Bonaparte's unsettled—fighting like a drunken sailor. He can't win no more, unless he knocks the Chocolate out. . . .
LORNA. (*At a complete loss.*) Don't look at me . . . what'd you . . . I . . .
EDDIE. Get outa town! (*The roar of* THE CROWD *mounts to a demand for a kill.* EDDIE, *listening intently.*) He's like a bum tonight . . . and a bum done it! You! (*The roar grows fuller.*) I can't watch him get slaughtered. . . .
LORNA. I couldn't watch it myself. (*The bell clangs loudly several times. The roar of* THE CROWD *hangs high in the air.*) What's happening now?
EDDIE. Someone's getting murdered. . . .
LORNA. It's me. . . .
EDDIE. (*Quietly, intensely.*) That's right . . . if he lost . . . the trees are ready for your coffin. (*The roar of* THE CROWD *tones down.*) You can go now. I don't wanna make a scandal around his name. . . . I'll find you when I want you. Don't be here when they carry him in.

LORNA. (*At a complete loss.*) Where do you want me to go?

EDDIE. (*Suddenly releasing his wrath.*) Get outa my sight! You turned down the sweetest boy who ever walked in shoes! You turned him down, the golden boy, that king among the ju-ven-iles! He gave you his hand—you spit in his face! You led him on like Gertie's whoore! You sold him down the river! And now you got the nerve to stand here, to wait and see him bleeding from the mouth! ——

LORNA. Fuseli, for God's sake ——

EDDIE. Get outa my sight!

LORNA. Fuseli, please ——

EDDIE. Outa my sight, you nickel whoore! (*Completely enraged and out of control,* EDDIE *half brings his gun out from under his left armpit.* JOE *appears in doorway. Behind him are* ROXY, MOODY *and a* SECOND.)

JOE. Eddie! (EDDIE *whirls around. The others enter the room. In the ensuing silence,* MOODY, *sensing what has happened, crosses to* LORNA.)

LORNA. (*Quietly.*) What happened?

ROXY. What happened? (*He darts forward and picks up* JOE'S *arm in the sign of victory. The arm drops back limply.*) The monarch of the masses!

EDDIE. (*To the* SECOND.) Keep everybody out. Only the newspaper boys. (*The* SECOND *exits and closes the door.* JOE *sits on a table. Physically he is a very tired boy. There is a high puff under one eye, the other is completely closed. His body is stained with angry splotches.*)

TOKIO. (*Gently.*) I have to hand it to you, Joe. . . .

ROXY. (*Explaining to the frigid* EDDIE, *elaborately.*) the beginning of the eighth: first the bell! Next the Chocolate Drop comes out like a waltz clog, confident. Oh, he was so confident! Haha! The next thing I know the Chocolate's on the floor, the referee lifts our arm, we got on our bathrobe and we're here in the dressing room! How do you like it?

EDDIE. (*Narrowly.*) I like it.

TOKIO. (*Taking off* JOE'S *gloves.*) I'll have you feelin' better in a minute. (*After which he cuts the tapes.*)

JOE. I feel all right.

EDDIE. (*To* TOKIO.) Gimme his gloves.

MOODY. (*Wary of* JOE.) That's a bad lump under your eye.

JOE. Not as bad as the Chocolate Drop got when he hit the floor!

ROXY. Darling, how you gave it to him! Not to my enemies!

JOE. 'Twas a straight right—with no trimmings

or apologies! Aside from fouling me in the second and fifth ——

MOODY. I called them on it ——

ROXY. I seen the bastard ——

JOE. That second time I nearly went through the floor. I gave him the fury of a lifetime in that final punch! (EDDIE *has taken the soggy boxing gloves for his own property.* TOKIO *is daubing the bruise under* JOE'S *eye.*) And did you hear them cheer! (*Bitterly, as if reading a news report.*) Flash! As thousands cheer, that veritable whirlwind Bonaparte—that veritable cock-eye wonder, Bonaparte—he comes from behind in the eighth stanza to slaughter the Chocolate Drop and clinch a bout with the champ! Well, how do you like me, boys? Am I good or am I good?

ROXY. Believe *me!*

TOKIO. (*Attempting to settle* JOE.) You won the right for a crack at the title. You won it fair and clean. Now lay down. . . .

JOE. (*In a vehement outburst.*) I'd like to go outside my weight and beat up the whole damn world!

MOODY. (*Coldly.*) Well, the world's your oyster now!

TOKIO. (*Insistently.*) Take it easy. Lemme fix that eye, Joe —— (*Now a bustling little Irishman,* DRISCOLL, *hustles into the room.*)

DRISCOLL. Who's got the happy boy's gloves?

EDDIE. Here . . . why? (DRISCOLL *rapidly takes gloves, "breaks" and examines them.*)

TOKIO. What's the matter, "Drisc"?

JOE. What's wrong?

DRISCOLL. (*Handing the gloves back to* EDDIE.) Chocolate's a sick boy. Your hands are clean. (DRISCOLL *hustles for the door.* JOE *is up and to him.*)

JOE. What happened?

DRISCOLL. (*Bustling.*) It looks like the Pride of Baltimore is out for good. Change your clothes.

JOE. How do you mean?

DRISCOLL. Just like I said—out! (DRISCOLL *pats* JOE'S *shoulder, hustles out, closing door in* JOE'S *face.* JOE *slowly sits on the nearest bench. Immediately* TOKIO *comes to him, as tender as a mother.*)

TOKIO. You didn't foul him—you're a clean fighter. You're so honest in the ring it's stupid. If something's happened, it's an accident. (*The others stand around stunned, not knowing what to do or say.*)

MOODY. (*Very worried.*) That's right, there's nothing to worry about.

ROXY. (*Ditto.*) That's right. . . .

JOE. Gee. . . . (JOE *stands up, slowly crosses the room and sits on the table, head in his hands, his back to the others. No one knows what to say.*)

EDDIE. (*To* MOODY.) Go out there and size up the situation.

(MOODY, *glad of the opportunity to leave the room, turns to the door which is suddenly violently thrust open.* BARKER, *the* CHOCOLATE DROP'S *manager, pushes* MOODY *into the room with him, leaving door open. From outside a small group of curious people look in.* BARKER, *bereft of his senses, grabs* MOODY *by the coat lapel.*)

BARKER. Do you know it? Do you know it?

MOODY. Now wait a minute, Barker —— (BARKER *runs over to* JOE *and screams:*)

BARKER. You murdered my boy! He's dead! You killed him!

TOKIO. (*Getting between* JOE *and* BARKER.) Just a minute!

BARKER. (*Literally wringing his hands.*) He's dead! Chocolate's dead!

TOKIO. We're very sorry about it. Now pull yourself together.

(EDDIE *crosses room and slams door shut as* BARKER *points an accusing finger at* JOE *and screams:*)

BARKER. This dirty little wop killed my boy!

EDDIE. (*Coming to* BARKER.) Go back in your room.

BARKER. Yes, he did!! (EDDIE'S *answer is to shove* BARKER *roughly toward door, weeping.*) Yes, he did!!

EDDIE. Get out before I slug your teeth apart!

JOE. (*Jumping to his feet.*) Eddie, for God sakes, don't hit him! Let him alone! (EDDIE *immediately desists.* BARKER *stands there, a weeping idiot.*)

MOODY. Accidents can happen.

BARKER. I know . . . . know. . . .

MOODY. Chocolate fouled us twice.

BARKER. I know, I know. . . . (BARKER *stammers, gulps and tries to say something more. Suddenly he dashes out of the room. There is a long silent pause during which* JOE *sits down again.*)

EDDIE. We'll have to wait for an investigation.

TOKIO. (*To* JOE.) Don't blame yourself for nothing. . . .

JOE. That poor guy . . . with those sleepy little eyes. . . .

ROXY. (*Solemnly.*) It's in the hands of God, a thing like that.

(LEWIS, *the sports writer, tries to enter the room.*)

EDDIE. (*Herding him out.*) Stay outside. (*To*

MOODY.) See what's happening? (MOODY *immediately leaves.*) Everybody out—leave Bonaparte to calm hisself. I'll watch the door.

TOKIO. Don't worry, Joe. (*He exits, followed by* ROXY. EDDIE *turns and looks at* LORNA.)

EDDIE. You too, Miss Moon—this ain't no cocktail lounge.

LORNA. I'll stay here. (EDDIE *looks at her sharply, shifts his glance from her to* JOE *and back again, he exits.*) Joe. . . .

JOE. Gee, that poor boy . . .

LORNA. (*Holding herself off.*) But it wasn't your fault.

JOE. That's right—it wasn't my fault!

LORNA. You didn't mean it!

JOE. That's right—I didn't mean it! I wouldn't want to do that, would I? Everybody knows I wouldn't want to kill a man. Lorna, you know it!

LORNA. Of course!

JOE. But I *did* it! That's the thing—I *did* it! What will my father say when he hears I murdered a man? Lorna, I see what I did. I murdered myself, too! I've been running around in circles. Now I'm smashed! That's the truth. Yes, I was a real sparrow, and I wanted to be a fake eagle! But now I'm hung up by my finger tips—I'm no good —my feet are off the earth!

LORNA. (*In a sudden burst, going to* JOE.) Joe, I love you! We love each other. Need each other!

JOE. Lorna darling, I see what's happened!

LORNA. You wanted to conquer the world ——

JOE. Yes ——

LORNA. But it's not the kings and dictators who do it—it's that kid in the park ——

JOE. Yes, that boy who might have said, "I have myself; I am what I want to be!"

LORNA. And now, tonight, here, this minute—finding yourself again—that's what makes you a champ. Don't you see that?

JOE. Yes, Lorna—yes!

LORNA. It isn't too late to tell the world good evening again!

JOE. With what? These fists?

LORNA. Give up the fighting business!

JOE. Tonight!

LORNA. Yes, and go back to your music ——

JOE. But my hands are ruined. I'll never play again! What's left, Lorna? Half a man, nothing, useless. . . .

LORNA. No, *we're* left! Two together! We have each other! Somewhere there must be happy boys and girls who can teach us the way of life! We'll find some city where poverty's no shame— where music is no crime!—where there's no war in the streets—where a man is glad to be himself, to live and make his woman herself!

JOE. No more fighting, but where do we go?

LORNA. Tonight? Joe, we ride in your car. We speed through the night, across the park, over the Triboro Bridge ——

JOE. (*Taking* LORNA'S *arms in his trembling hands.*) Ride! That's it, we ride—clear my head. We'll drive through the night. When you mow down the night with headlights, nobody gets you!

You're on top of the world then—nobody laughs! That's it—speed! We're off the earth—unconnected! We don't have to think!! That's what speed's for, an easy way to live! Lorna darling, we'll burn up the night! (*He turns and begins to throw his street clothes out of his locker.*)

MEDIUM FADEOUT

## CARTOON

## LYONS

"*Keep away from him.*"                    "*Keep away from him.*"

THIS IS HERE for the shop talk and the beginnings of a sparring partner—all in the first half. The second half is about Nathan Hale and Patrick Henry.

# Brooklyn Mick

## EDDIE ORCUTT

THE MICK WAS supposed to be resting, getting ready to fight the Argentine at the Coliseum that night. He had stripped to his shorts and he was sitting up on his bed in this dollar-a-day hotel room, with a blanket over his legs. He had hung his sweat clothes in the window to get a little sun before he packed them, and the air in the room had a bitter smell. This Brooklyn Mick was a black Irishman, sailor-tattooed on his arms and big chest, and he had grown a one-day stubble of beard to protect his face against glove cuts. His face had two deep lines down the cheeks, and they curved along his jaw and made an inverted U over the deep cleft in his chin. These lines wreathed his wide mouth when he laughed, but when he looked serious, the lines hardened and his chin had the character that a bulldog's jowls have.

"Hype Igoe put a piece in the newspapers about me, and he called me the Dean of Sparring Partners. I been sparring partners to five world champions. Six, because Tommy Loughran was the light-heavy champ. You can put in your story that I probably boxed more rounds with Mr. Joe Louis than any other white man in the world."

"You don't have to go yet," the Mick said.

They had picked the Mick up in Los Angeles, working out with Maxie Rosenbloom, earning a couple dollars a round and trying to get back in some kind of shape. The Mick was tough and he knew his way around, but he was twelve pounds overweight and he had not had a ring fight in six months, and so he was exactly what they wanted for the Argentine. They were pointing the Argentine for big money, so, naturally, they would not give him anybody who was in shape to make trouble for him. The Mick would go in and take a beating. He was broke and a long way from home, and he needed the money.

"You don't have to go yet." This thing was on his mind, this jam that he was in back East, and finally he wanted to give me the story. If it had not been for this trouble, he would have been in New York right then, working for Joe Louis or Tommy Farr. He saw where the Garden had signed Max Baer and Jim Braddock, too, and either of them would have been glad to have him, he said. He had boxed each of them. The year before, when Schmeling began training at Napanoch for Joe Louis, the Mick had been the second man to arrive in Schmeling's camp, and the last to leave. Schmeling had paid him thirty-five dollars a day, all expenses and a bonus. The Mick had been tops at his trade.

"Schmeling told me: 'Make yourself at home. If there is anything you don't see, ask for it. You'll get it.' He was tanned and brown. He had a solid grip and his eyes were clear. He looked like a real clean-living man, which he was. . . . But I hadda take it on the duffy outa New York," the Mick said. "Wit' a wife an' two kids, I couldn't stay back there, see, because you can't tell what these guys will do. Like I told you," he said, "they got something wrong wit' their mind."

This trouble was bad.

"Wit' a wife an' two kids, I couldn't stay back there—"

On this last afternoon, resting up for his hundred-dollar pasting, the Mick wanted to spill his trouble to somebody. To understand it, though, you would have to get some of this talk that he gave me about his trade. Because if the Mick had never taken up a good trade, if he had not worked hard at it and then been good at it, he never would have been in this jam.

The Mick was a good Irish talker with a tang of Brooklyn in his brogue, and I ribbed him to talk shop because I liked to hear it.

"Sparrin' wit' a guy," the Mick said, "you learn him like a book. Carnera couldn't let go his right, bein' muscle-bound, see, but if you run into his left, it would knock your teeth out. He was always holdin' it out, stickin' wit' it, an' stickin' an' stickin'. He could stick good wit' it."

You had to watch out for that left, and you had to ride him in the clutches, not try to rassle with him. If you watched those things, the Mick said, you could give Primo a good workout without getting hurted.

"Workin' wit' these champeens," he explained, "you got to be kind of a cutie. You got to give 'em what they're payin' you for, but you don't wanta just let 'em punch you up. You got to learn 'em." If they wanted to punch somebody around, they could hire some has-been or some punk that didn't know any better, but a real sparring partner was not just a punching dummy.

The Mick had gone with Carnera back in '31, when Da Preem was prepping for his first Sharkey fight. The Mick had been down on his luck then, because it was right after they killed Kid Ritchie, the Mick's first manager. He had been glad to go with Carnera for fifteen dollars a day. Carnera had hired him again for the second Sharkey fight, then taken him on a stage tour, and then brought him back to camp again when Carnera began readying up for Max Baer.

"I will never forget the first time I seen this Carnera. He was out on the lawn at Doc Bier's place, playin' wit' a little brown dog. He sure was very big. He looked like a sea sperrint playin' wit' a goldfish."

Max Baer had hired him next. "But I only worked wit' him a week, on account they said I was not the type." The Mick laughed. He had a sort of hell-may-care, chuckling laugh. "He was a good guy, though. He was all right. He would be always trying to knock your brains out, but if he hurt you, he would clown around an' give you time to stall out of it."

Carnera's left hand had been made to order for Baer, the Mick said, but Braddock's was not. "Baer was a sucker for a left—but he was a smart sucker, see? Carnera goes in stickin' wit' his left, but he moves back after a jab, like most guys do. Well, if you jab Max Baer and pull back, you are going to pull back into his right

hand, see, an' he'll hit you so hard wit' it that you bust an ankle. 'At's what this Carnera did. But Braddock was always movin' in behind his left, an' if you swing the right you just wrapped it around his neck. Braddock was awful tough, too, in them days," the Mick said. "Awful tough. But a nice guy, though. A prince."

Most of the guys that get up around the top are nice guys, the Mick said, no matter how they were raised. "They been places, see, an' they met high-class people," he explained. "It all adds up. It's education," the Mick said. "Even watchin' 'em an' workin' wit' 'em, it's kind of an education.

"This Carnera was like a kid. Always happy, an' we even hadda save the funny papers for 'im. But when you was introduced to him, he would make a good impression on you."

The Mick was glad to talk shop, I think. When he was telling about rowboat riding with Max Schmeling at Napanoch, or explaining what Tommy Loughran used the thumb of his glove for, or trying to tell me how it felt to be in with Joe Louis that first time, it was easier to forget all this about being broke and in a jam and a long way from home. Schmeling and Mr. Joe Louis interest him most.

"After bein' wit' Mr. Joe Louis so much, when he was first sensational, see," the Mick explained, "I sure was interested in workin' wit' Schmeling. I knew right away that Schmeling was no bum, because he had plenty of brains. A big heart too. The last day Schmeling worked, it began rainin' an' we hadda box indoors. I boxed 'im third. In the second round he was really fightin', an' I hit 'im square under the eye wit' the hardest punch I ever throwed. I didn' go to do it. It raised a bump under his eye. 'Are you hurted?' I asked him. 'Nah! Nah! Come on in! I feel good!' he said. Gee, I liked that guy. An' I knew he was right for Mr. Joe Louis too.

"The night before Schmeling–Louis," the Mick said, "I went on the radio, which Francis Albertanti got me into, for two hundred and fifty dollars. When I said Schmeling would win, everybody laughed. 'Schmeling by a knockout,' I said, 'on account of his big heart an' a good right hand!' Everybody in the studio laughed."

It was funny, but the Mick had not seen the fight itself. He and his wife had had another young couple in, and they had sat around the Mick's living room with a pitcher of beer, listening to the radio.

"In the second, remember how the Dutchman's eye began swelling? Oh-oh, did I feel bad," the Mick said, "because it was me that started that eye!" But pretty soon the radio gave off a *Boff* and they said the German was reaching Joe Louis with his right.

"I jumped outa me chair! I leapt in the air! An' you shoulda seen the way me wife got laughing at me!" the Mick said.

The Mick's black eyes twinkled with his grin, because that had been one of the big nights of his life, and it was funny to think of him sitting there in his home with his wife and friends and getting this big bang over the radio.

"Certain'y, I had tickets to the fight. I had two tickets, but I hadda give 'em away," he said. "I didn't wanta see the fight—I was too excited!" The Mick laughed at himself. "I had been sparring partners wit' both these guys, see?

"Mr. Joe Louis hired me for one week when he was training for Carnera. He hired me for three weeks when he was training for Max Baer. I and three other fighters then accompanied him on an exhibition tour of Canada and New England, staying at the best hotels everywhere, and nothing was too good for us, and we boxed Mr. Joe Louis in twelve different cities. He stopped me once. This was in Bangor, Maine, on account of a cut over me eye which Mr. Mushkey Jackson feared might result in a permanent injury, him being the referee."

Talking about Louis, the Mick made sentences carefully, the way he believed they would look good in a newspaper story. He referred to the colored boy as "Mister."

"They was four sparrin' partners. Stanley Ketchell, two-twenty pounds, which Mr. Joe Louis knocked out nine times. Andy Wallace, two-ten, which Mr. Joe Louis knocked out seven times. Me, which Mr. Joe Louis did not knock out, but he stopped me in Bangor, Maine, on account of this eye. And Paul Cavalier, which Mr. Joe Louis did not knock out at all."

They had opened in Montreal; then going to a place called Ottawa, the Mick said. He told me how the four sparring partners had spent a day loafing around Montreal, and it seems that the town was full of Frenchies, talking French. Talking back to them, the fighters gave them the double-talk. "Look, will you or me get me that two-three on the outside, inside, over here, see, so the inside over the outside—" The Mick said that the Frenchies went nuts.

Talking about Mr. Joe Louis as a fighter or as a boxer, the Mick was very earnest and respectful, but he was full of chuckles about the tour. The crowds had mobbed in everywhere to see Joe Louis, because he was supposed to be dynamite and murder, but the sparring partners had made a picnic out of it. In Bangor, after the show, a friend had thrown a party for Louis, and the Mick gave me a long story about the doings. Afterwards, in the hotel room, he and Cavalier had short-sheeted Andy Wallace's bed, and the four two-hundred-pounders had wound up with a big towel fight. "Wit' wet towels too!"

"We returned to Boston, and here Mr. Joe Louis swang over to go back to Detroit, and we came on home. Before leaving, Mr. Joe Louis bought us presents. Mine was a swell wrist watch, and you can say it is a sacred piece, which I will never part with. I did not question the other boys the extent to which Mr. Louis gave them presents, but you can put it in that he sure done so."

Well, this was the shop talk of the Mick's trade, and he had added it all up in his mind. "It's a good business," he told me. "It's a good business for a guy that was raised tough." At another time he said: "If I hadda do it all over again, I would do the same. I think I done right."

On this last afternoon, even when he got to thinking about this trouble that he was in, the Mick said the same thing.

"I was raised tough. I been knocked around all me life," he said. "I don't go out easy." You had to be tough, he explained, if you were going to earn your thirty-five a day off Max Schmeling, or Mr. Joe Louis, or any of the good ones. When you got him to talking about this angle of it, though, you began to understand about the choice this Brooklyn Mick had made.

The Mick had been born down on Sands Street, in the Williamsburg district of Brooklyn, near the Navy Yard, and his first playground had been the city dump. "In them days, I t'ought it was the biggest place in the world." Al Capone and Johnny Torrio had started in that district. Vincent Coll, the baby killer, nicknamed Mad Dog Coll, had been the Mick's friend when they were going to grammar school. "Him and me was raised kids together," the Mick said. He had gone to school there, too, with Barney Souza, the boy who talked too much. Telling me this, giving me these names, the Mick would go somber, deadpan, and his voice held a tone that I tried, in my mind, to label. It was not terror, because it was blank and quiet, but it had some recollection of terror in it. Kids grew up on fighting in this neighborhood.

"You hadda fight. You hadda learn to fight good," the Mick said. Even these tough kids knew, though, that there were things there that you could not fight. The Mick said: "There was big guys, see?" And he watched me to see if I got it. That meant Coll, or Capone, or such names, and their shadow was on the rats and the hoodlums and the lesser tough guys of the district.

"But even when I was a kid, sometimes I would get away from the neighborhood and live different for a day. That does a guy good. I would play like I was explorin' around in the country, wit' tree forests an' hills an' lakes, an' stuff like that.

"The city dump was a good place," the Mick told me, "an' when I was maybe nine or ten I would play hooky there. I would get up before daylight, an' I would find bread an' maybe half a bottle of port wine on the table from me folks havin' a party the night before. So I would cop it an' beat it over to the city dump, see, an' I would stay there all day. Not go to school, not go home or nuttin'. There was places like hills or caves, because there was all kinds of junk on this dump, see? I would go explorin' around all day.

"An' they was always dumpin' cans there by the millions, but some of these cans from the restaurants would not be opened yet. If I would find a full can, I would open it an' eat whatever was in it. Maybe beans, maybe salmon—whatever was in it, I would eat it, see?

"You know how I would open them cans? I wouldn' swipe a can opener from home, because that would be, like you say, civilized. I would get me a big rusty nail an' a brick, an' I would hammer holes all around under the edge of the can till I could bust the top off!" The Mick had a laugh at these things he did when he was little. "That's a kid for you!" he said.

In the neighborhood, though, the Mick said, there were some very tough guys, and the smaller kids would imitate them. They would gang up and fight, or they would prowl around on the clip, like these older guys, and the best fighters would very likely grow up to be hoodlums.

"I had a good reputation in street fightin', but I never would be a hoodlum, because what kind of a heart do them guys have? How could I stand a guy up against the wall and punch him around and tell him he has to do business with my boss or I will hurt him? Maybe he might be an old fella—old enough to be my father. Guys that do that, what do they have for a heart?"

Fighting was natural, but this other business was not. The Mick told me about this Barney Souza, and how the cops finally fished him out from the foot of Bridge Street, swollen from a couple of days in the East River and with his lips mottled green from copper wire. "They sewed his mouth wit' wire, see, so's to show he shouldn'a talked so much. If you can do things like that, your mind is not right."

The Mick went on a beer truck when he was seventeen, working nights and making good money, because it was prohibition times. After that he did a two-year hitch in the Navy. He went on a coal truck when he got out. It was not much money, but jobs were scarce, and this job kept him from getting mixed up in anything.

"In me spare time, I would go over to New York, an' would hang around the fight gyms—the Pioneer, see, or Stillman's. This prevented me hangin' around wit' any neighborhood guys." The Mick twinkled his wide grin at me, and added a word.

"Ambition," he said. "See what I mean?"

And then it seems that the Mick really got a break, because old Kid Ritchie picked him up at the Pioneer and liked the look of him. Kid Ritchie took him off the coal truck and made a fighter of him. Kid Ritchie was high-class, the Mick said. In the old days he had been a fighter, and a good one, and he had saved his money. He had bought property, raised a family and settled down to running a good saloon, and when the Mick knew him, he was well-to-do and a respected man.

"Me, I could fight," the Mick said, "but I didn't know nuttin'. This Kid Ritchie knew everything. He showed me how to live right an' take care of meself, see, an' goin' in the ring he wouldn' leave me bust in sluggin' an' take a lot of punches. He would make me be smart. He never got me no fights until I was ready, an' then he got me main events in these neighborhood clubs. I was wit' him a year an' a half," the Mick said. "I win twelve straight knockouts. You know," the Mick told me, "I begun feelin' like a real prize fighter, see?"

This ended when Kid Ritchie got killed. The old man had eased a drunk out of the saloon one night, talking nice to him, in the way that old-timers have, but the drunk had come back with a gun. Kid Ritchie never had a chance.

"He used to take me home to dinners in his own house, like he was me own father," the Mick said. And then, mourning Kid Ritchie, he added it up in words that he had made careful and formal, out of respect to the Kid's memory. "He survived all me workouts," the Mick said. "I was continuously in his company all the time wit' 'm."

All this about Kid Ritchie had a bearing on what the Mick wanted to tell me about, on this last afternoon, so he went over it again. It was five years after Kid Ritchie died, he said, before he began really getting ambition again.

"Sure, I boxed on me own," he said. "I would take this fight, or that fight; sometimes win an' sometimes lose. If the other guy would be nice. I've took the handcuffs, also, when I had to. I done all right," he said, "but I was not like I was when Kid Ritchie had me, see?" The Mick watched me carefully, to make sure I would get all this. "After I finished wit' Schmeling, though," he said, "I got ambition again. Bein' wit' high-class people, see, it makes you want to be high-class yourself."

So it was this ambition, the Mick said, that got him into the trouble. He made a couple of good fights. He got himself a manager who had strong connections. And then—

"Last December—the sixt' of last December," the Mick said, "I got pinched by the Feds in Baltimore for transportin' twenty-five ounces of heroin." He said it in a flat voice. He looked square at me. The reckless Irish grin swaggered into his face for a second, but his eyes were dead black, intent, watching me. I waited.

"Ever hear of George Kubel?" the Mick asked. I said, "No."

"When I made a couple good fights, George Kubel come around to me," the Mick said, "an' asked me how about him handling me business. He tol' me what he could do for me. I knew he had good connections, see, an' I hadda have somebody with the ins, so I said okay. George Kubel was kind of big, but he was a racket guy," the Mick told me. "I knew that, but I never knew what his racket was, see?" The Mick was still watching me. "It was none of my business. I said okay, an' he started han'ling me. Look," the Mick said, "I would of had a lotta nerve to go askin' 'm if maybe he was peddling coke. He's never been pinched, see, and I don't go askin' 'm what his racket is." The Mick's eyes were dead black, somber. "There was big guys mixed up wit' 'm, see?"

But the Mick said it looked like a good break, because Kubel started getting him work right away. He got him a bout in Boston. He got him one in Detroit. He sent the Mick over to Paterson for a couple of fights. They were not big fights —$600 was the best, the Mick said—but the Mick had this ambition in him again, and he began to go good. George Kubel had all kinds of dough and he rolled around New York in a limousine with a Filipino chauffeur, and the Mick knew that Kubel was not interested in just taking his cut out of $600 purses. Kubel had something bigger in mind.

"I figured he really went for me," the Mick explained. "The way this Kid Ritchie had. I figured he was takin' me up into money. Maybe I never got over Kid Ritchie tellin' me I would be champion of the world. Sometimes it would make me laugh. But workin' wit' Mr. Joe Louis or Schmeling or them, sometimes I would re-member it. Bein' wit' high-class people, see, it makes you want to be high-class yourself.

"George got me these fights, but he never went wit' me, see? He got me this one in Detroit," the Mick said. "He sent me—he didn't go wit' me. In Boston, he sent me—he didn' go wit' me. He got me a fight in Chicago. A good fight. But he sent me—he didn't go wit' me." The Mick watched to see if I was getting it. He said, "In New York, I went around wit' him a lot, ridin' in this big limousine, see? Like I was a bodyguard. I always dressed good an' I would stick around an' keep my mouth shut, an' so George would take me along when he was goin' around, meeting guys. Some of them was plenty big. But when he set me for a fight, he wouldn't go out of town wit' me. He just sent me."

The payoff came early last December, when George Kubel got the Mick a fight in Richmond, Virginia. This time he told the Mick that they would take the big car and go down together. Naturally, the Mick thought that Kubel figured he was about ready for big money. "So I was gonna show'm a hell of a fight," the Mick said.

He finished a light workout on a Sunday noon, and Kubel drove around to the gym and picked him up. "Put your bag in the car," Kubel told him, "and go out and grab some lunch. I got an errand to do; I'll pick you up in half an hour."

The Mick did it, of course. He left his training bag in Kubel's car and packed away a meal while Kubel was doing his errand. Then Kubel called for him again, and they got away on schedule. They stopped somewhere in Jersey for a cup of coffee several hours later, and got into Baltimore at about ten o'clock that night. George Kubel had another errand in Baltimore. He had to see a guy at a certain hotel, he said. "But I guess you're good and hungry," he told the Mick. "You hop out at this restaurant and get some grub. I'll meet you here inside an hour." This time, though, he had the Mick take his bag with him.

The training bag was just a big black leather satchel with the Mick's boxing things in it, and the Mick lugged it with him into the restaurant. He set the bag down beside the counter where he could watch it, and ordered up a square meal. He ate fast, expecting Kubel to be back soon.

Kubel didn't come.

"An' so I guess now you know what the racket was," the Mick told me. "Dope, see? George went to talk to a guy about a deal, but the guy he talked to was a stool pigeon," the Mick explained. "When George came down out of the hotel, the cops closed in an' made the pinch. Me, I was waitin' for 'm an' waitin' for 'm, an' he never showed up," the Mick said. "So finally I asked the boss if I could leave this bag in the restaurant while I went up to this hotel to look for me manager."

Two blocks down the street, a couple of tough Government cops walked up to the Mick, shoved a gun at him.

George Kubel and the Filipino chauffeur were already in this room in the Baltimore post-office building when the cops threw the door open and shoved the Mick in. Right behind them there was another guy with the Mick's bag. When George Kubel looked at the bag, the Mick said, he turned the same color as the chauffeur, which was kind of a yellowish tan.

"They set this bag on the desk, an' the head man of the office was there. These cops give me plenty of rough talk, but the head guy was quiet. He was high-class. College, an' like that. 'What's in your bag, buddy?' he asked me. I told 'm. 'Is that all?' 'Yes, sir,' I says. So the boss asked these cops if I had give 'em my name when they asked me. They told him I had. He asked if I told 'em where me bag was when they asked me. They said, 'Yes.' Then he pushed a button an' a stenographer come in. It must of been midnight, see, but she was there, waitin'. So this guy says to me: 'Set down an' talk to this stenographer. Tell her everything that you got in that bag.' I set down. I thought of everything I put in that bag. I give her the list—"

The Mick told it to me earnestly. He named the things he carried in this bag, and he told me how the stenographer took them down, *chck-chck-chck-chck,* on the typewriter. When he had finished, the head man asked him again if that was all. The Mick said it was. Then the cops opened this bag. The Mick's things were there. "Me mout'piece, me boxin' helmet, bandages, bag-punchin' gloves, protector, shoes, trunks— everything I told 'em about was there. Only down at the bottom there was this package like a cigar box wrapped in paper." The Mick watched me.

"Remember," he asked, "how George had me put this bag in his car while I got me lunch that noon?"

The head man said: "There's twenty-five ounces of heroin in that package. You transported it from New York to Baltimore. What's your story?"

The Mick gave it to him.

"An' this guy believed me. He said so," the Mick told me.

But they kept the Mick eleven days in the Baltimore city jail, because a narcotics charge is dynamite, and the Government will check all the angles on any guy that gets mixed up in it. The Mick had been on edge for this fight, and the

jail food—what with worry and all, he said— poisoned him. He bought three sandwiches and a can of coffee every day from a place across the street, but he got good and sick. He was in bad shape when he got out. And he had to stick around Baltimore an extra day, trying to get his bag and his boxing gear back.

They kept his bag. He finally got them to give him his ring equipment, seeing that he needed it to earn a living with, but they kept the bag for an exhibit. So then the Mick borrowed eight dollars off George Kubel to get back to New York with. Kubel had $18,000 cash on him when he was pinched, and the Mick tried to borrow ten dollars, but eight dollars was all Kubel let him have.

"So it was a fine way to get home, see?" the Mick said. "Me sick, me wife sick wit' worryin', an' me wit' the change out of eight dollars in me pockets. I felt like crawlin' in a hole. The funny thing is that if I had been a hoodlum or a racket guy, this George Kubel would never of picked me up. I wouldn' of been no use to him. If I hadn' of got me a good reputation, I never would of been in this jam. That's funny, ain't it?"

Two months later, the Government sent him a letter. It said that if he would go to the Federal building in New York City, he could get his bag. The Mick went.

"It was a good bag," the Mick said, "an' it was mine."

Everything was all right by that time, of course, and the Government had nothing on the Mick; but when he got inside the Federal building, and went to the property office to claim his bag, they told him that the Major wanted to see him. "Major? What Major?" the Mick asked. They told him who the Major was. They steered him to the Major's office, and the next thing the Mick knew, he was talking to the head of the Government's narcotics division for the whole New York district.

"He was a swell guy. High-class. When he talked to you, you could believe in him," the Mick said.

But the Major asked this Brooklyn Mick a hard question—a question that might be tough on any of us, but a very strange one to put up to a boy raised where the Mick was. They were alone in the Major's office, and after they had talked for a while, the Major asked his question.

"How good a citizen are you?" the Major asked.

Telling me about it, the Mick's grin was twisted. "That makes you stop an' think, don't it? That's a hell of a question!" he said. But in the Major's office he had finally figured an answer. "I guess I am as good as I want to be," he told the Major. "I try to be good."

Well, you will understand what the Major wanted. Down in the Baltimore jail, George Kubel had cracked. The Government had him dead to rights, of course, and Kubel had asked for a deal. He had talked. He had named names and he had signed affidavits. He had been big, but there were others that were bigger, and Kubel had even named the biggest guy of all. The Government had pinched this big guy.

"All right," the Major said, "you can help us."

"How can I help you?" the Mick asked. The Major's office was part of the United States Government, and the Major and the Federal cops and agents were a part of it. The Mick felt funny, having the United States Government ask him for help.

"You went around a lot with Kubel. He used you for kind of a bodyguard."

"That's right," the Mick said.

Doing business in New York, a big dealer had to buy direct from the higher-ups. The Major named them. "You saw Kubel meet these men, one time and another?" "I might of," the Mick admitted. Then the Major named the big guy himself. He named a time and a place that Kubel had put in an affidavit.

"You saw him hand Kubel these packages?"

"I might of. I didn' know what was in them, though." Since he was a kid, the Mick had known enough not to see what he was not supposed to see. "George never told me," the Mick said. "I never asked."

The Major nodded. He was no country boy. "But you see what I want," he said.

The Major could have put George Kubel on the stand, perhaps, and Kubel might have spilled everything he had. But the big guy's lawyers would have made him look bad. They would have called him a rat and a squealer, and they would have claimed that he would say anything to cut time off his own rap.

If the Government could get the Mick on the witness stand, though, it would be different. The Mick was no rat. He was no peddler, no racket guy, and he had a good record. The Government could prove what he did for a living, and they could show that he was high up in his trade— sparring partner to six world champions. When the Mick told what he had seen, a jury would believe him.

"Will you do that?" the Major asked.

The Mick said: "Oh-oh!"

So, IN THIS cheap hotel room where he was resting for his fight, the Mick held his answer and waited, and there was a kind of suspense in the room. This prize fighter from the Navy Yard district, born on Sands Street, raised kids with Vincent Coll, had made his choice long before the Major ever got him into the Federal building and asked him how good a citizen he was. He had made his choice when he got that job on the coal truck. He had made his choice when he began hanging around the fight gyms in New York, getting away from the neighborhood guys. Watching him in this hotel room, I knew what answer he had had to give the Major, but suspense tightened while I waited for him to name it. The Mick leaned forward, resting his arms on his knees and staring at the window where his sweat clothes were catching the last of the afternoon sun.

"Ever see a cokie?" the Mick asked.

I said I had, and the Mick nodded. "They showed me one," he said.

Then he shrugged. He spoke flatly, almost indifferently, the suspense ended and the story finished. "What the hell else could I do?" he said. "I told the Major: 'All right, I will do it.' " He kept on staring at the window. "A thing like that," he said, "is your duty. You hafta do it."

So, at the big guy's trial, the Mick took the stand for the United States Government, in a courtroom where the big guy's torpedoes watched him, and where some of the Mick's own friends gave him the eye and pretended that they had never seen him before. He faced men who had done murder for hire, and men who had paid hire for murder. He gave his name and his record and described his trade. The judge on the bench questioned him, asking him what money he earned at this trade, about the family he supported and his home, and about the champions he had worked for. "I believe this man's word," the judge said. When the Government asked questions, the Mick answered them and the judge and jury believed him. They did not have to depend on any frightened squealer, any stoolie or spy, because this Brooklyn Mick was an American citizen testifying under oath. You could say that he was a special kind of citizen that day. A citizen by choice.

The dope racket's big guy went to the Federal prison at Leavenworth.

"So I come out here for me health," the Mick said. He gave me his grin again suddenly. "After it was over, I was not a Gover'ment witness any more, an' I didn' know how soon somebody might start ringin' me doorbell. So I took it on the duffy outa New York. I come out here, bummin' around."

It was not very funny. I told him so.

"Gee, it's late all of a sudden," the Mick said. "I better lay back an' take me a nap." He still sat there, though, while I stood up. "You've got plenty of heart, kid," I told him, but he was not listening. He sat with his knees hunched up, his arms resting on them, and he stared thoughtfully at this window where he had hung up his sweat clothes. The sun was almost gone. The Mick still wanted to tell me something, and he was thinking it out.

"You know," he said finally, "it's all right. Stuff like that is your duty." He gave it to me soberly and confidentially, the way he had told me about Carnera's invisible uppercut and how Max Baer had acted at the weigh-in for Braddock. "You got to do it." Then he broke out this wide Irish grin of his, but he looked at me almost bashfully, because he was telling me something

I should have known from a long time ago, when I was a kid in school.

"That's how our country got like it is," the Brooklyn Mick said. "People doing something for their gover'ment. Nat'an Hale. Patrick Henry. Guys like them."

He gave me those names.

Nat'an Hale. Patrick Henry. Guys like them. . . . People doing something for their gover'ment. . . . That's how our country got like it is.

After I had shaken hands with the Mick and wished him good luck, and left him to rest up for his beating, I went down into the streets and saw an unaccustomed thing. This Mick, and the Brooklyn city dump where he played when he was a kid, were a part of what I saw. I went out and walked through ordinary streets, and I looked at the ordinary people in them, and what I saw was the United States of America.

## CARTOON

## BILL YATES

"Tryin' to win the Nobel Peace Prize?"

IN JULY OF 1940, fourteen years after he lost the heavyweight title to Gene Tunney, Jack Dempsey fought his last three fights, such as they were. This account of the first part of this trilogy, in which no opponent survived the second round, appeared in the Chicago *Tribune*.

# Dempsey Knocks Out Wrestler

## STEWART OWEN

ATLANTA, GA., July 1, 1940—Jack Dempsey proved several things here tonight in his return to the ring, by knocking out one Clarence (Cowboy) Luttrell in one minute and fifty-eight seconds of the second round of a heavyweight boxing match that was scheduled to go ten rounds.

The principal thing he proved was that despite the years that have passed since the former heavyweight champion was in his prime, he still carries a punch as powerful as that of almost any other man in the ring today. Whether the bout proved, as Dempsey said it would, that a boxer can whip a wrestler any day in the week is not certain, but at least it proved that this particular boxer can whip this particular wrestler any time he wants to.

It also proved that this fight was not what a great many people suspected it might be: just another of those fantastic spectacles which are common to the wrestling game. No man, not even a wrestler, would take the beating Luttrell took tonight just to make it look good. Luttrell, in the brief space of a round and a half, was pounded into a bloody mass, floored three times, and then knocked from the ring and under the front row of the press section. Helpless, semiconscious, he was carried to his dressing room.

The fight had been billed as a grudge fight growing out of a brief flurry of fists in an Atlanta ring two months ago. Luttrell had protested referee Dempsey's action in disqualifying him by punching Dempsey's jaw. That is merely routine histrionics in the wrestling game and only the extremely gullible regarded the Texas cowboy's subsequent glares and taunts as anything more

until after tonight's match had been arranged. Even then it couldn't be regarded very seriously.

The aroma of the phony wrestling match still clung to it when Luttrell, a bald-headed, paunchy man of thirty-four years, entered the ring. Dempsey had preceded him amid an uproar that attested his right to the introduction as the most popular sports figure America has ever known. Then Luttrell climbed into the ring to the tune of a magnificent jeer that he had earned as the villain of many an Atlanta wrestling piece. He cast the customary malign leer that a wrestler always bestows upon his opponent.

There was something pitiful about finding Dempsey here in this ring. There was no stool in his corner. His seat was an inverted, empty beer case. He was a little fat around the middle and the elastic of his trunks, biting into the excess flesh, gave him a modified hourglass figure. The fighting face was still there and his legs and shoulders looked as trim as ever. But still it was a 45-year-old Dempsey, a middle-aged man, who was sitting there ready to try his hand at the sport of youth.

It was like finding Sarah Bernhardt tap dancing in a burlesque show, a Michelangelo drawing smutty pictures on a washroom wall, a Man o' War hitched to a garbage wagon. Nay, the contrast was worse than that. It was the Manassa Mauler, the scourge of the ring of two decades ago, sitting on a beer box in a bush-league ball park about to fight a small-time wrestler.

Dempsey's weight was announced as being 205 pounds. Perhaps it was; it looked a little more. Luttrell's weight was given as 224 pounds.

There was an appeal made from the ring for the American Red Cross and humanity.

Then the bell rang and there was no thought of humanity. Dempsey came out fast, faster than one would have thought his aged legs could carry him. He pounded Luttrell with both rights and lefts to the head and to the body. The wrestler covered up and crouched in a neutral corner, seldom attempting to counter, more seldom connecting with his wild swings when he did try. Long before the end of the first round it was obvious Dempsey was going to win before the end of the second, as he had said he would. But there was no inkling of the fury of the attack he was to launch in that final minute.

The second round started as the first had. Luttrell essayed a few wild rights, and three in a row landed well below Dempsey's midsection. Nat Fleischer, the referee, stepped between the two men. He warned Luttrell against punching low. Perhaps it was those low punches; perhaps Jack knew he couldn't go on for many rounds himself. At any rate there was for a few brief moments a flash of speed and a flash of power that was reminiscent of the Dempsey of old.

Jack sent a left hook to the jaw, a left hook to the jaw, a left hook to the jaw, and Luttrell crumpled up for a count of eight. Again a left to the jaw, a right to the jaw, a left to the jaw, and the Texan was down for nine. Gamely he came up and as quickly went down again, this time in Dempsey's corner. One terrific left hook caught him full on the chin, and the wrestler went bowling through the ropes, across the press table and to the ground, where he lay unconscious.

When efforts to revive Luttrell in his dressing room failed, he was taken to a hospital. There he regained consciousness an hour later. Attendants say he is suffering from a broken nose and is being kept under observation for possible concussion of the brain.

The match had been ballyhooed as drawing 20,000. The promoter, Jim Dowling, said the actual attendance was 15,000 and that gate receipts were around $20,000. An estimate of 10,000 or 12,000 would be fair.

No OTHER WRITER has ever been as avidly read by the members of the fight mob as Dan Parker. This column, which appeared in 1938, or fourteen years after Parker joined the New York *Mirror*, is typical of him in his dual roles as judge and jester.

# I Went to See Tony Galento

## DAN PARKER

*Oh, Tony Galento, he trains on pimento*
  *And gargles the ale when it's cool.*
*My pronunciamento concerning Galento*
  *Is: "Switch to that pasta fazoole!"*
*—From Oscar O'Ginsburg's "Odes of Orange"*

ORANGE, NEW JERSEY, which likes to consider itself a suburban community, became a tank town Wednesday night when Charley Massera played the role of a barrel of beer to Bartender Tony Galento's bung starter. Ordinarily, under the same circumstances, the whole town would be asking: "Did he fall or was he pushed?" but these little technical points bother residents of Orange not at all. The end always justifies the means with them where the sainted Galento is concerned.

*They say a left hook*
*To the chops closed the book*
*Of the prize fighter, Charley Massera.*
*Though it may not have landed*
*It left Charley stranded.*
*(And how is your dear old Aunt Sarah?)*
*—From Moses McGillicuddy's "Musings of*
  *Massera"*

THE WHOLE THING was a fifteen-minute interlude in Tony's career as a boniface. One minute he was slicing layers of foam off scuttles of suds with the bone cleaver in his tonsil-irrigating studio down the block. The next thing you knew, he was in the ring, covered all over from head to foot, covered all over with Vaseline, like the greased pig at the annual field day of the Iron Puddlers' Local No. 365. There was majesty in

his manner as he clasped his gloved hands and held them aloft in acknowledgment of the applause with which his public greeted him.

And may I be vouchsafed permission to say that no sovereign, replying to expressions of fealty from his subjects, ever acknowledged them with more regal dignity?

*They seen their duty and they done it*
*They cheered for Tony and he won it.*
*He put Massera on the shelf*
*And proved it's "everyone for THEIR self!"*
*—From Gabriel Googarty's "Gurgles of Galento"*

NOR DID HE STOP at this all-embracing acknowledgment, as your fly-by-night celebrities of the prize ring might have done. Some of the beer he has drunk in his day may have gone to Tony's head, but success hasn't. He's still the same Democratic Tony who has always voted for Mayor Hague's candidate. Didn't he prove it by acknowledging every greeting from a galleryite or ringsider, individually, after having taken care of his public as a unit?

*He bowed to the left and he bowed to the right*
*And came close to bowing right out of the fight.*
*Next he dropped 'em a curtsy, a regular wow,*
*And he would have salaamed had he only known*
  *how.*
*—From Murgatroyd the Mope's "Murdering the*
  *Muse"*

FINALLY, THE FIGHT was on—the epic clash that had caused the biggest turnout of Orangemen since the Battle of the Boyne. The armory was packed to the last available inch and the halitosis quotient was dreadful. Tony's admirers and customers were everywhere. They hung by their toes from above, literally, as the girders across the drillshed were infested with them. Outside thousands lingered, hoping to hear the thud. Everyone knew Massera was going out like an empty beer barrel, the only element of doubt being "when?"

*Tony's belly rolled like jelly*
*And Massera's fist*
*Bounced into it—almost through it—*
*Right up to the wrist.*
*—From "Mendel's Mutterings"*

As a boxer, Tony uses the Ely Culbertson, or approach system. He approaches an opponent wide open, as if inviting a liver massage. After getting what he wants, he switches to the Irish attack, better known as "The back of me fisht to you!" Next, he tries "The Shoemaker's Revenge," or "Giving It the Heel." Two rounds of this and Tony decided the customers had had enough. Did I say Tony? I meant Charley. One of Tony's left hooks landed somewhere—no one is quite sure—and Charley landed on his haunches. He's up. He's down. He's out. It all happened in 45 seconds. Yussel Jacobs, in Tony's corner, summed it up succinctly when he warbled: "He certainly stood down the second time when you left him have that left."

Some of the boys said Charley almost choked on his mouthpiece after he had been counted out. If he did, it was from laughing.

Tony was back behind the bar in his white apron, with most of the grease wiped off him, in about ten minutes, and from then until dawn his cash register burned out six bearings handling the biggest night's trade in the history of the jernt.

Louis Phal, called Battling Siki, was born in 1897 in Senegal, French West Africa. On September 24, 1922, he knocked out Georges Carpentier in six rounds in Paris to become the light-heavyweight champion of the world. Six months later he made the classic error of boxing Mike McTigue on St. Patrick's Day in Dublin, Ireland, and lost the title on a twenty-round decision. He was killed in a street brawl in New York City on December 15, 1925.

James Westbrook Pegler was born in 1894 in Minneapolis, Minnesota. He was a war correspondent for the United Press from 1916 through 1918, and a great sports commentator for the UP from 1919 to 1925 and for the Chicago *Tribune* from 1925 to 1933. Then he gave up his title and deserted the division to campaign among the heavies.

# Siki and Civilization

## WESTBROOK PEGLER

New york, December 17, 1925—Battling Siki, who tried hard to understand civilization but never quite got the idea, will be trundled out over the roads of Long Island tomorrow and buried in the civilized way without a single thump of the tom-tom. A Negro minister will commend him to the mercy of the Christian God, and Negroes will shoulder the casket, but there will be nobody there who really understood the Mohammedan-born Siki because the difference was no mere matter of complexion.

The one person who knew Battling Siki best and loved him as a man loves a friendly but mischievous pet was a white man, Bob Levy, his manager. Siki called him Papa Bob and often assaulted him with moist kisses in the same conciliatory way a chicken-killing Airedale with feathers in his whiskers might slap his master on the cheek with a sopping tongue.

Siki had heard a lot about the virtues of civilization in a dozen years of exposure to its decorous influence, but in the last minute of his life, when he fell in a dirty gutter in Hell's Kitchen, where the lights of Broadway throw deep shadows and churches face speakeasies across the street, civilization must have been a puzzle and a

josh to him. As Siki stumbled over the curb and his dented plug hat bounced away, he may have laughed at the irony of it all, for he had come all the way from the jungle to the haunts of civilization and chivalry to be shot in the back.

Siki was one who could giggle with his last gasp, too. He laughed in Paul Berlenbach's face throughout their fight in the old Garden, and the harder Paul slugged him the more he seemed to enjoy the joke.

As Siki got the idea, civilization was something supposed to make men do things they didn't want to do and to curtail their natural enjoyment of life. Civilization was a good thing in theory, but it didn't work, and Siki saw proof it didn't work.

For one thing, under civilization, if a man stole your woman or your ox you were not allowed to go over to that man's house and razor his head off in person. It was against the rules to kill people. And then civilization fell out with itself and Siki was given a gun with a knife on the end of it and invited to kill everyone he saw wearing a certain uniform.

Under civilization a man was allowed just one wife at a time. But Siki rattled around Paris enough to learn civilization was, in civilized language, the bunk in this respect.

Siki came to the United States, and they told him civilization had made a law whereby it was wrong to drink liquor. And then Siki toured half of the country and found civilized men everywhere, white and black, who would sell him liquor and get him stewed contrary to the statutes.

Siki went to night clubs and, to the weird squealing of the wood winds and the muffled thump of tom-toms, the music of civilization, he saw half-naked black-and-tans wiggling and squirming in the dances of an enlightened tribe.

He fought in the ring, and when blood showed, the civilized crowds came up from their chairs, roaring approbation.

So, from what he saw of it, Siki frankly didn't get the plot of this business called civilization. The whole thing was too much for this simple mind of a primitive African who got a late start at the racket.

SINCE SOCRATES and Gorgias (and Plato) found in boxing a universal reference, no other form of athletic endeavor has supplied such a stockpile of simile and metaphor.

FROM THE

# Dialogues

## PLATO

[TRANSLATED BY BENJAMIN JOWETT]

**GORGIAS**                    *Socrates and Gorgias*
AND IN A CONTEST with a man of any other profession the rhetorician more than any one would have the power of getting himself chosen, for he can speak more persuasively to the multitude than any of them, and on any subject. Such is the nature and power of the art of rhetoric! And yet, Socrates, rhetoric should be used like any other competitive art, not against everybody; the rhetorician ought not to abuse his strength any more than a pugilist or pancratiast or other master of fence; because he has powers which are more than a match either for friend or enemy, he ought not therefore to strike, stab, or slay his friends. Suppose a man to have been trained in the palestra and to be a skillful boxer—he in the fullness of his strength goes and strikes his father or mother or one of his familiars or friends; but that is no reason why the trainers or fencing-masters should be held in detestation or banished from the city; surely not. For they taught their art for a good purpose, to be used against enemies and evildoers, in self-defense not in aggression, and others have perverted their instructions, and turned to a bad use their own strength and skill. But not on this account are the teachers bad, neither is the art in fault, or bad itself; I should rather say that those who make a bad use of the art are to blame. And the same argument holds good of rhetoric; for the rhetorician can speak against all men and upon any subject.

**REPUBLIC**                   *Socrates and Adeimantus*
HERE, THEN, IS a discovery of new evils, I said, which the guardians will have to watch, or they will creep into the city unobserved.

What evils?

Wealth, I said, and poverty; for the one is the parent of luxury and indolence, and the other of meanness and viciousness, and both of discontent.

That is very true, he replied; but still I should like to know, Socrates, how our city will be able to go to war, especially against an enemy who is rich and powerful, if deprived of the sinews of war.

There may possibly be a difficulty, I replied. in going to war with one such enemy; but there is no difficulty where there are two of them?

How so? he asked.

In the first place, I said, our side will be trained warriors fighting against an army of rich men.

That is true, he said.

And do you not suppose, Adeimantus, that a single boxer who was perfect in his art would easily be a match for two stout and well-to-do gentlemen who were not boxers?

Hardly, if they came upon him at once.

What, not, I said, if he were able to run away and then turn and strike at the one who first came up? And supposing he were to do this several times under the heat of a scorching sun,

323

might he not, being an expert, overturn more than one stout personage?

Certainly, he said, there would be nothing wonderful in that.

And yet rich men are probably not so inferior to others in boxing as they are in military qualities.

Likely enough.

Then probably our athletes will be able to fight with three or four times their own number?

I agree with you, for I think you right.

## LAWS

*Athenian Stranger:* . . . The regulations about war, and about liberty of speech in poetry, ought to apply equally to men and women. The legislator may be supposed to argue the question in his own mind:—Who are my citizens for whom I have set in order the city? Are they not competitors in the greatest of all contests, and have they not innumerable rivals? To be sure, is the natural reply. Well, but if we were training boxers, or pancratiasts, or any other sort of athletes, would they never meet until the hour of contest arrived; and should we do nothing to prepare ourselves previously? Surely, if we were boxers, we should have been learning to fight for many days before, and exercising ourselves in imitating all those blows and wards which we were intending to execute in the hour of conflict; and in order that we might come as near to reality as possible, instead of cestuses we should put on boxing gloves, that the blows and the wards might be practiced by us to the utmost of our power. And if there were a lack of competitors, the fear of ridicule would not deter us from hanging up a lifeless image and practicing at that. Or if we had no adversary at all, animate or inanimate, should we not venture in the dearth of antagonists to spar by ourselves? In what other manner could we ever study the art of self-defense?

*Cleinias:* The way which you mention, Stranger, would be the only way.

*Athenian Stranger:* And shall the warriors of our city, who are destined when occasion calls to enter the greatest of all contests, and to fight for their lives, and their children, and their property, and the whole city, be worse prepared than boxers? And will the legislator, because he is afraid that their practicing with one another may appear ridiculous, abstain from commanding them to go out and fight; will he not ordain that soldiers shall perform lesser exercises without arms every day, making dancing and all gymnastic tend to this end; and also will he not require that they shall practice some gymnastic exercises, greater as well as less, as often as every month; and that they shall have contests one with another in every part of the country, seizing upon posts and lying in ambush, and imitating in every respect the reality of war; fighting with boxing gloves and hurling javelins, and using weapons somewhat dangerous, and as nearly as possible like the true ones, in order that the sport may not be altogether without fear, but may have terrors and to a certain degree show the man who has and who has not courage; and that the honor and dishonor which are assigned to them respectively, may prepare the whole city for the true conflict of life? If any one dies in these mimic contests, the homicide is involuntary, and we will make the slayer, when he has been purified according to law, to be pure of blood, considering that if a few men should die, others as they will be born; but that if fear is dead, then the citizens will never find a test of superior and inferior in desert, which is a far greater evil to the state than the loss of a few.

*Cleinias:* We are quite agreed, Stranger, that we should legislate about such things, and that the whole state should practice them.

THIS IS A picture by the English novelist, critic and playwright of a typical London fight club of the 1920s.

# The Ring

## J. B. PRIESTLEY

NOT WAGNER'S but the boxing hall in the Blackfriars Road. It was once the Old Surrey Chapel, and it still suggests a chapel. I remember that when I first saw it, all that remains of my Nonconformist boyhood was wickedly thrilled at the thought of seeing some boxing matches in such a setting. Dick Burge, who was responsible for the transformation, must have been the sort of man I dreamed about when I was a boy, compelled to sit, hot and glowering, under a Children's Address. Its deaconly appearance gave me no thrill last night, however, though it was my first visit for several years. It was not a night for easy thrills. The Blackfriars Road, black and dripping, was being swept by sleet, and I trust that Mrs. Burge, now the director of The Ring, will forgive me if I say that, even after the miserable Blackfriars Road, her hall did not seem very snug and lively. The big lights above the ring itself had not been turned up, for it still wanted some minutes to eight; the place was still dim, chill, cheerless; the cries of the youths who offered us apples and bars of chocolate went echoing hollowly, forlornly; and there was nothing to see, to do. I was alone—with a whole row of ringside seats to myself—and I began to wish I had stayed at home. The program looked dull. Even the "Important 15 (3–min.) Rounds Contest" did not suggest anything very exciting.

Then the officials made their appearance. The referee climbed into his high chair, and the timekeeper sat down beside his stop watch and bell. The fat men in white sweaters brought out their pails of water, bottles, and towels, and stumped round to their corners. The announcer climbed into the ring, which was immediately flooded with hard, bright light. I like the announcer at The Ring. He looks as if he were taken over from the original chapel. He has an air of mellowed Nonconformity. His trim white hair and white mustache, his black tie, black morning coat, and dark, striped trousers—these things give him dignity; and even when he bellows "Ler-hay-dees an' Ger-hentle-men, Ser-hix Rer-hound Contest," you still feel that he is probably the last of the Old Surrey Deacons.

Two thin but muscular youths, whose street-corner faces seemed almost an insult to their excellent bodies, climbed into the ring, grinned, touched gloves, and then instantly began pummeling one another. They were poor boxers but good stouthearted fighters, and they pleased the rapidly growing audience. One of them got a cut early in the contest, with the result that both their faces were quickly crimsoned and there were marks of blood on their bodies. Somebody who knew nothing about the sport might have imagined that they were trying to kill one another and that the roaring crowd in the cheap seats was filled with a blood lust, but of course actually they were both good-humoredly slogging away, doing little or no harm to one another, and the crowd was merely applauding their lively spirit. It ended in a draw, a great round of applause, and an astonishing shower of coppers in the ring, so many indeed that it took the announcer and an assistant several minutes to pick them up. These two novices had pleased the crowd, and so it had rained pennies on them. The man sitting in front of me—a fellow with huge shoulders, a battered face, and a professional air —had registered the general verdict when he cried: "A bloody good fight!"

The next two were not so satisfactory. They

325

were dapper, dark lads, better boxers than the others but far less pugnacious. One of them was a trifle affected in his footwork and had a funny little trick of his own, a sort of back-kick not unlike that of a stage dancer. This amused the crowd at the back of me. They decided that these antics were effeminate, and immediately, unanimously, christened the author of them "Cissie." They indulged in waggish irony. "Oh, Cissie!" they screamed, as if in girlish terror. "Don't 'urt Cissie," they implored. In the last of their six rounds, however, these two improved and hammered one another to such a tune that the crowd was won over, dropped all talk of "Cissie," and gave them a round of applause as a benediction.

The contest that followed, though it rose to the dignity of twelve rounds, pleased nobody. The two boys appeared to be engaged in a kind of double-shadow boxing. They seemed determined to get their twelve rounds without giving one another any real trouble at all. "Oh! 'ave a fight, 'ave a fight!" cried a disgusted sportsman at the back. The referee stopped them at one point and apparently uttered words of reproof. But they did not have a fight. The crowd at the back, tired of giving them ironical congratulations, now began to stamp in unison and to whistle "All by Yourself in the Moonlight." The announcer appealed for order, but not very passionately. The timekeeper chatted with his neighbor, smoked cigarettes, and mechanically shouted "Seconds out" and sounded his bell. The referee yawned harder than ever. The two boys danced round and round the ring, went back to their corners, were slapped and toweled and massaged, returned to the center each time looking very ferocious, but did not fight. We were all glad to see the last of them. Now came the event of the evening. The fat men with cigars and the little hard-bitten men with cigarettes stopped roaming up and down the corridor that led to the dressing rooms. They all came out, looking knowing and important. The lights above the ring looked harder and brighter than ever. You could not see the other side of the building; everything there was a mysterious blue haze, in which a match occasionally twinkled. "Cher-hoc-lait," cried the white-coated youth, more hopefully. "Fine Aipple," retorted the opposition caterer, sticking his tray of green fruit under our noses. The announcer entered the ring, and there waited, grave, important. There was a cheer. Tom had come out, an old favorite and a Bermondsey lad. A grin lights up his broad flat face; he puts his two gloves together, holds them up to salute friends and patrons. He is attended by several

enormous fellows with cauliflower ears, old hands. Another round of applause. The Frenchman is out, with Messieurs Dubois and Dupont in close attendance. "Ler-hay-dees an' Ger-hentle-men." Tom has cast aside his beautiful dressing gown, to reveal himself as a brown, stocky little fellow in blue shorts. The Frenchman is performing those mysterious exercises with the elastic ropes that girdle the ring. He is taller and longer in the reach than Tom, but does not look so strong or so fit—a queerly made ugly fellow, this "Froggy," as they quickly decide to call him. He does not look as if he will last more than a round or two.

At first Tom seems to have it all his own way. You hear the thump-pad-thud of his glove on Froggy's lean body. But Froggy does not seem to mind. Now and then that long left of his flashes out and sends Tom staggering. "Don't take it too easy, Tom," the crowd tells him. The other Bermondsey lads at the back are full of advice. "Poke it out, Tom," they cry; and then "Turn 'im round, Tom." And Tom's only too anxious to do all these things, but somehow the ungainly Frenchman never allows himself to be hurt. Now and then it is true, he blinks and gives a queer little grin, all of which suggests that Tom's blows to the body have made some impression, but he comes back from his corner as fresh as ever. Indeed, somewhere about the tenth round, it stops being Tom's fight, and there is now no talk of his taking it too easy. Froggy is not only very quick with that long left of his, but he is also a crafty fellow. Every time Tom rushes in, he is stopped, and you hear the dull thump of the wet glove. And there are moments when Froggy drives Tom round the ring or bounces him against the ropes. If Tom were softer, he might easily find himself on his back, with the timekeeper's voice measuring out his doom; but Tom is very tough, an old taker of punishment. The last round sees him almost as lively as ever, but now it is Froggy's glove you hear thump-pad-thudding. The final clang—and the referee jerks a thumb toward Froggy's corner. The announcer cannot be heard above the cheers. We do not know Froggy and—to speak candidly—do not like the look of him; but he has proved himself the better man; and so we give him the best cheer of the evening. (Perhaps Froggy's friends in Paris would do the same for Tom—perhaps; it is just possible.) Tom puts his gloves together, shakes them at us, still grinning, and we give him a cheer too. Everybody is good-humored.

There was more to come, but a great many people were drifting out, now that the great event was over, and I followed them. The Black-friars Road looked exactly as it had done when I hurried out of it earlier in the evening, a black misery, but the thought of the good humor I had left behind me kept me warm. When the old Ring is transformed into a gigantic boxing arena, where really big purses are won and lost in a few minutes under glaring film-studio lights, I hope it will keep its good humor. I hope it will, but I have my doubts.

JOHN HAMILTON REYNOLDS was the Tony Janiro or Coley Wallace of English poetry. At the age of 19 he was a protégé of Byron, at 22 he was bracketed with Shelley and Keats and now he is remembered, if at all, as a friend of Keats, with whom he shared a great affection for boxing, and as an associate of Lamb, DeQuincey, Hazlitt and Hood.

In 1820, Reynolds' most celebrated book, *The Fancy*, was issued by the publishers of Keats' "Lamia." Jack Randall, eulogized in it, fought from 1815 to 1821, was the original "Nonpareil" and the most accomplished middleweight ever developed in England. Philip Samson, advised in *The Fancy* to give up the quest, four years later twice fought Jem Ward and took two beatings.

FROM

# The Fancy

## JOHN HAMILTON REYNOLDS

SONNET

### On the Nonpareil

'None but himself can be his parallel!'

With marble-colored shoulders,—and keen eyes,
    Protected by a forehead broad and white,—
    And hair cut close lest it impede the sight,
    And clenched hands, firm, and of punishing size,—
Steadily held, or motion'd wary-wise,
    To hit or stop,—and kerchief too drawn tight
    O'er the unyielding loins, to keep from flight
    The inconstant wind, that all too often flies,—
The Nonpareil stands!—Fame, whose bright eyes run o'er
    With joy to see a Chicken of her own,
    Dips her rich pen in *claret*, and writes down
Under the letter R, first on the score,
    "Randall,—John,—Irish parents,—age not known,—
    "Good with both hands, and only ten stone four!"

From *The Fancy* BY JOHN HAMILTON REYNOLDS

LINES TO PHILIP SAMSON,

## The Brummagem Youth

Go back to Brummagem! go back to Brummagem!
 Youth of that ancient and halfpenny town!
Maul manufacturers; rattle, and rummage 'em;—
 Country swell'd heads may afford you renown:
Here in Town-rings, we find Fame very fast go,
 The exquisite *light weights* are heavy to bruise;
For the graceful and punishing hand of Belasco
 Foils,—and *will* foil all attempts on the Jews.

Go back to Brummagem, while you've a head on!
 For bread from the *Fancy* is light weight enough;
Moulsey, whose turf is the sweetest to tread on,
 Candidly owns you're a good *bit of stuff:*
But hot heads and slow hands are utterly useless,
 When Israelite science and caution awake;
So pr'ythee go home, Youth! and pester the Jews less,
 And work for a *cutlet,* and not for a *stake.*

Turn up the *raws* at a fair or a holiday,
 Make your fists free with each Brummagem rib;
But never again, Lad, commit such a folly, pray!
 As sigh to be one of the messmates of Crib.
Leave the P. C. purse, for others to handle,—
 Throw up no hat in a Moulsey Hurst sun;—
Bid adieu, by the two-penny post, to Jack Randall,
 And take the outside of the coach,—one pound one!

Samson! forget there are such men as Scroggins,
 And Shelton and Carter, and Bob Burns and Spring:
Forget *toss for sides,* and forget all the floggings,—
 While shirts are pull'd off,—to make perfect the ring.
Your heart is a real one, but skill, Phil, is wanted;
 Without it, all uselessly bravery begs:—
Be content that you've beat Dolly Smith, and been chaunted,—
 And train'd,—stripp'd,—and pitted,—and hit off your legs!

GRANTLAND RICE was the most beloved and famous of all sports writers. From the end of World War I until he died, working at his typewriter at the age of 73 on July 13, 1954, he was also the friend and confidant of more of the sporting great than any other writer who ever lived. What follows was excerpted from his autobiography, completed twelve days before his death.

# On Dempsey and Tunney

## GRANTLAND RICE

IN SPORT, you'll find there are great defensive stars and brilliant offensive competitors. Among the great offensive athletes I've studied I must include Ty Cobb, Bill Tilden, Babe Ruth, Harry Greb and Jesse Owens. But I found the greatest attacking, or pure offensive, star one June day in 1919 in Toledo, off the hot and steamy shores of Maumee Bay.

His name was Jack Dempsey. I had been in France during 1917 and 1918, so had seen no prize fights in that period. When I first met Dempsey, he was burnt purple. He had trained down to 180 pounds in getting ready for Jess Willard, the 250-pound giant. Dempsey was then twenty-four years old. He was keen and lithe, almost as fast as Cobb. It was his speed, speed of hand as well as foot, that made him such a dangerous opponent.

Dempsey was the oddest mixture of humanity I've known. In the ring he was a killer—a superhuman wild man. His teeth were frequently bared and his complete intent was an opponent's destruction. He was a fighter—one who used every trick to wreck the other fighter.

Yet, outside the ring, Jack is one of the gentlest men I know. I've seen him in his restaurant at times when some customer, with more enthusiasm than good sense, would grab his vest or part of his shirt—strictly for a souvenir—with no kickback from Jack. I've known the man closely for more than thirty years and I've never seen him in a rough argument or as anything except courteous and considerate.

Looking at Dempsey and Willard in 1919, it was hard to give Dempsey a chance. Dempsey, slightly over 6 feet, weighed 180. Willard, at 6 feet 6, weighed 250 at least.

Willard looked on Dempsey as a little boy. The night before the fight Bob Edgren and I called on Jess. He thought the fight was a joke.

". . . . outweigh him seventy pounds," Willard said. "He'll come tearing into me . . . I'll have my left out . . . and then I'll hit him with a right uppercut. That'll be the end."

Next day when the first round opened, Dempsey circled Willard some twenty-five or thirty seconds. He was a tiger circling an ox. Finally Willard couldn't wait any longer. He jabbed at Dempsey with his left, and the roof fell in. Jack ducked under Willard's left, threw a right to the body. At the same time he nailed Willard on the right side of the head with a smashing left.

"I knew it was over then," Jack said later. "I saw his cheekbone cave in."

LINING UP GEORGES CARPENTIER for the Dempsey vs. Carpentier fight, at Boyle's Thirty Acres, Jersey City, for July 1921, was a shrewd piece of work by Tex Rickard. Tex "sensed" more and better gate-building tricks in one minute than today's promoters can dream up in a year. I realize that television has taken a lot of the steam off the need for a "live" gate—what with TV rights selling for great chunks of cash. But the fact remains that Rickard, yes, and Mike Jacobs, had the kind of promotional touch that would have them storming the gates today instead of taking in the fight through a camera.

Carpentier, with a gaudy if superficial war record, had returned to Paris in one piece—and hungry. He was a pretty fair light-heavyweight, but they couldn't have ballooned the Frenchman into a bona fide heavyweight, except in the papers, with two sandbags for added ballast. At any rate, Rickard—knowing the public's love of a hero-and-villain tangle—cast Dempsey, the scowling, wire-bearded "draft dodger," as the villain, with apple-cheeked Carpentier, the amiable, personable soldier boy, as the hero. Pictures of Dempsey, riveting battleships in patent leather shoes—all at [Jack] Kearns' behest—flooded the sports pages, along with those of Carpentier, practically winning the war singlehanded.

The fight was the first to be broadcast—with Graham McNamee describing the action—and it had the whole nation taking sides for or against Dempsey. . . .

It was all over in four rounds, but had Dempsey wanted to put the slug on Carpentier, I think he could have nailed him in the first round. From ringside, all French ships at sea received this cabled flash: "Your Frog flattened in fourth"—for a new high in international diplomacy.

I WAS HAVING BREAKFAST with Jack and Max Baer one February morning back in 1931 at the Warwick Hotel. The day before, Jack had refereed the Baer–Tommy Loughran fight at Madison Square Garden. Max had been decisioned in ten rounds.

"I've been looking at left jabs all night," Max said. "Lefts . . . lefts . . . lefts . . . that's all I've seen!"

"The funny part," said Dempsey, "is that you could have stopped that 'Lefty' in the first round."

"How?" said Baer.

"Take off your coat," replied Jack to big Maxie, 6 feet 3 and 220 pounds. Max shucked off his coat and faced Dempsey.

"Now lead with a left, just as Loughran did," said Jack. Max led . . . and there was an immediate yelp. "You broke my arm," Max howled as he backed away, holding it.

As Baer led with his left, Dempsey had dropped his huge right fist across the left biceps with paralyzing force. The left arm became useless for thirty minutes.

"I'll show you another punch," Jack said. He spun Baer and then socked him.

"You can't do that," Max said. "It's illegal."

"They'll only warn you the first time," Dempsey said.

I ONCE ASKED DEMPSEY why college athletes never made good fighters. "Football is just as rough," I said. "They star in those games. But seldom in boxing where the big money is."

"They're too smart," Dempsey said. "The fight game is the toughest game on earth. When I was a young fellow I was knocked down plenty. I wanted to stay down. I couldn't. I had to collect that two dollars for winning—or go hungry. I had to get up. I was one of those hungry fighters. You could hit me on the chin with a sledge hammer for five dollars. When you haven't eaten for two days you'll understand.

"Few college fellers ever get that low. I had one early fight when I was knocked down eleven times before I got up to win. You think I'd have taken that beating if I had had as much as twenty-five bucks with me? No chance."

He would have.

THE GIANTS WERE PLAYING AT HOME and Heywood Broun, covering for the *World,* and I were in the press box at the Polo Grounds when Walter Trumbull, sports editor of the old New York *Post,* appeared in our midst with a young fellow in tow. Trumbull introduced his guest, Gene Tunney, all around, and I recall that Broun made quite a fuss over the handsome youngster.

I had glimpsed Tunney several days earlier when he fought "Soldier" Jones, a tough trial horse in a supporting bout to the Dempsey–Carpentier fight at Jersey City. Tunney scored a knockout in seven rounds. He was known only as a soldier-boxer who had won the light-heavyweight title of the AEF in France. However, he had not fought as a bona fide heavyweight and certainly looked no part of one.

"What are your plans?" I asked.

"My plans are all Dempsey," he replied.

"Very interesting," I said. "But why not sharpen your artillery on Harry Greb, Carpentier or Tom Gibbons before you start hollering for Dempsey?"

"I suppose I'll have to beat them on the way up," Tunney said. "But Dempsey is the one I want."

I said no more and turned my attention back to McGraw's Giants, who with George (High Pockets) Kelly at first base, were headed for their first pennant since 1917. I recall Tunney later volunteered that he was twenty-three years old. I couldn't help thinking that this forthright young fellow would make a fine insurance salesman but certainly had no business having his features and brains scrambled by Dempsey's steel fists.

In January of 1922, Tunney defeated Battling

Levinsky for the [American] light-heavyweight crown, but lost it the following May to Harry Greb in perhaps the bloodiest fight I ever covered. A great fighter—or brawler—Greb handled Tunney like a butcher hammering a Swiss steak. How the Greenwich Village Irishman with the crew haircut survived fifteen rounds I'll never know—except that Tunney always enjoyed more and better physical conditioning than anybody he ever fought. By the third round, Gene was literally wading in his own blood.

I saw Gene a few days later. His face looked as though he'd taken the wrong end of a razor fight. "You know," he said, "I must have lost nearly two quarts of blood in there."

Abe Attell, the former fighter-gambler and longtime "character" in the fight game, probably saved Tunney from bleeding to death.

"Abe was sitting near my corner—a spectator," continued Tunney. "When he saw the shape I was in after the second round, he ducked out to the nearest druggist and bought his entire supply of adrenalin chloride. Hustling back, Attell slipped the bottle to Doc Bagley. Between rounds Doc's long fingers flew. A superb 'cut' man, he'd managed to stop the bleeding only to watch Greb bust my face apart in the following round. It was discouraging."

To me, the fight was proof that Tunney meant to stick with prize fighting. I tried to tell Gene that Greb was too fast for him . . . to go after a softer touch. But less than a year later they fought again and Tunney won the decision in fifteen rounds. I scored that fight for Greb, but then Tunney met Greb four times more without defeat.

IN 1925 Tunney fought another fight that has never been recorded. I was the matchmaker and promoter.

Jim Corbett, the old champion and the world's greatest boxer, had written a book called *The Roar of the Crowd.* I was in the business of making sports pictures for the *Sportlight,* and I finally sold Corbett the idea of boxing three rounds, for pictures, with Gene Tunney.

My "assistant" promoter was Frank Craven, the actor. At that time Tunney had heard of Will Shakespeare and, having met Craven, he was quite keen about it all. He also knew of Corbett's reputation as a boxer and what Jim had meant from the viewpoint of science and skill. We arranged a spot in midtown Manhattan, atop the Putnam Building.

Anxious to pick up any possible tip from the old stylist, Tunney arrived at the appointed hour, ready to go and attired in trunks. Corbett took one look at them and said, "I'd like to wear long white trousers. I had a pair of good-looking legs in the old days, but they don't look so good now. I'm nearly sixty and they are kinda shriveled."

They boxed three two-minute rounds. Tunney was on the defensive. Corbett was brilliant. He feinted with his left—then punched with his left. A left feint . . . a left hook; a right feint . . . a left jab; a right feint; a right cross. He still had bewildering speed! He mixed up his punches better than practically any fighter I've seen since —with the possible exception of Ray Robinson.

After the exhibition, Tunney turned to me. "I honestly think he is better than Benny Leonard. It was the greatest thing I've ever seen in the ring. I learned plenty," he said.

At fifty-nine Corbett was still the master.

That winter in Florida I played golf with Tommy Armour and Tunney. Gene would hit his drive, toss aside his club and run down the fairway throwing phantom punches—left and right hooks—and muttering, "Dempsey . . . Dempsey . . . Dempsey."

"He's obsessed," observed Armour. "His brain knows nothing but Dempsey. I believe Jack could hit him with an ax and Gene wouldn't feel it. I don't know if Dempsey has slipped, but I'll have a good chunk down on Tunney when that fight arrives."

DAMON RUNYON was closer to boxing than to any other sport. He not only covered most of the major fights from the end of World War I until he died in 1946, but he owned pieces of a number of fighters and was one of a triumvirate that assisted Mike Jacobs in the formation of the Twentieth Century Sporting Club, the most powerful promotional organization in the history of the sport.

# Bred for Battle

## DAMON RUNYON

ONE NIGHT a guy by the name of Bill Corum, who is one of these sport scribes, gives me a Chinee for a fight at Madison Square Garden, a Chinee being a ducket with holes punched in it like old-fashioned Chink money, to show that it is a free ducket, and the reason I am explaining to you how I get this ducket is because I do not wish anybody to think I am ever simple enough to pay out my own potatoes for a ducket to a fight, even if I have any potatoes. Personally, I will not give you a bad two-bit piece to see a fight anywhere, because the way I look at it, half the time the guys who are supposed to do the fighting go in there and put on the old do-se-do, and I consider this a great fraud upon the public, and I do not believe in encouraging dishonesty.

But of course I never refuse a Chinee to such events, because the way I figure it, what can I lose except my time, and my time is not worth more than a bob a week the way things are. So on the night in question I am standing in the lobby of the Garden with many other citizens, and I am trying to find out if there is any skullduggery doing in connection with the fight, because any time there is any skullduggery doing I love to know it, as it is something worth knowing in case a guy wishes to get a small wager down. Well, while I am standing there, somebody comes up behind me and hits me an awful belt on the back, knocking my wind plumb out of me, and making me very indignant indeed. As soon as I get a little of my wind back again, I turn around figuring to put a large blast on the guy who slaps

me, but who is it but a guy by the name of Spider McCoy, who is known far and wide as a manager of fighters.

Well, of course I do not put the blast on Spider McCoy, because he is an old friend of mine, and furthermore, Spider McCoy is such a guy as is apt to let a left hook go at anybody who puts the blast on him, and I do not believe in getting in trouble, especially with good left-hookers.

So I say hello to Spider, and am willing to let it go at that, but Spider seems glad to see me, and says to me like this: "Well, well, well, well, well!" Spider says.

"Well," I say to Spider McCoy, "how many wells does it take to make a river?"

"One, if it is big enough," Spider says, so I can see he knows the answer all right. "Listen," he says, "I just think up the greatest proposition I ever think of in my whole life, and who knows but what I can interest you in same."

"Well, Spider," I say, "I do not care to hear any propositions at this time, because it may be a long story, and I wish to step inside and see the impending battle. Anyway," I say, "if it is a proposition involving financial support, I wish to state that I do not have any resources whatever at this time."

"Never mind the battle inside," Spider says. "It is nothing but a tank job, anyway. And as for financial support," Spider says, "this does not require more than a pound note, tops, and I know you have a pound note because I know you put the bite on Overcoat Obie for this amount not an hour ago. Listen," Spider McCoy says, "I know where I can place my hands on the greatest heavyweight prospect in the world today, and all I need is the price of carfare to where he is."

Well, off and on, I know Spider McCoy twenty years, and in all this time I never know him when he is not looking for the greatest heavyweight prospect in the world. And as long as Spider knows I have the pound note, I know there is no use trying to play the duck for him, so I stand there wondering who the stool pigeon can be who informs him of my financial status.

"Listen," Spider says, "I just discover that I am all out of line in the way I am looking for heavyweight prospects in the past. I am always looking for nothing but plenty of size," he says. "Where I make my mistake is not looking for blood lines. Professor D just smartens me up," Spider says. Well, when he mentions the name of Professor D, I commence taking a little interest, because it is well known to one and all that Professor D is one of the smartest old guys in the world. He is once a professor in a college out in Ohio, but quits this dodge to handicap the horses, and he is a first-rate handicapper, at that. But besides knowing how to handicap the horses, Professor D knows many other things, and is highly respected in all walks of life, especially on Broadway.

"Now then," Spider says, "Professor D calls my attention this afternoon to the fact that when a guy is looking for a race horse, he does not take just any horse that comes along, but he finds out if the horse's papa is able to run in his day, and if the horse's mamma can get out of her own way when she is young. Professor D shows me how a guy looks for speed in a horse's breeding away back to its great-great-great-great-grandpa and grandmamma," Spider McCoy says.

"Well," I say, "anybody knows this without asking Professor D. In fact," I say, "you can look up a horse's parents to see if they can mud before betting on a plug to win in heavy going."

"All right," Spider says, "I know all this myself, but I never think much about it before Professor D mentions it. Professor D says if a guy is looking for a hunting dog he does not pick a Pekingese pooch, but he gets a dog that is bred to hunt from away back yonder, and if he is after a game chicken he does not take a Plymouth Rock out of the back yard. So then," Spider says, "Professor D wishes to know why, when I am looking for a fighter, I do not look for one who comes of fighting stock. Professor D wishes to know," Spider says, "why I do not look for some guy who is bred to fight, and when I think this over, I can see the professor is right.

"And then all of a sudden," Spider says, "I get the largest idea I ever have in all my life. Do you remember a guy I have about twenty years back by the name of Shamus Mulrooney, the Fighting Harp?" Spider says. "A big, rough, tough heavyweight out of Newark?"

"Yes," I say, "I remember Shamus very well indeed. The last time I see him is the night Pounder Pat O'Shea almost murders him in the old Garden," I say. "I never see a guy with more ticker than Shamus, unless maybe it is Pat."

"Yes," Spider says, "Shamus has plenty of ticker. He is about through the night of the fight you speak of, otherwise Pat will never lay a glove on him. It is not long after this fight that Shamus packs in and goes back to bricklaying in Newark, and it is also about this same time," Spider says, "that he marries Pat O'Shea's sister, Bridget.

"Well, now," Spider says, "I remember they have a boy who must be around nineteen years old now, and if ever a guy is bred to fight it is a boy by Shamus Mulrooney out of Bridget O'Shea, because," Spider says, "Bridget herself can lick half the heavyweights I see around nowadays if she is half as good as she is the last time I see her. So now you have my wonderful idea. We will go to Newark and get this boy and make him heavyweight champion of the world."

"What you state is very interesting indeed, Spider," I say. "But," I say, "how do you know this boy is a heavyweight?"

"Why," Spider says, "how can he be anything else but a heavyweight, what with his papa as big as a house, and his mamma weighing maybe a hundred and seventy pounds in her step-ins? Although of course," Spider says, "I never see Bridget weigh in in such manner.

"But," Spider says, "even if she does carry more weight than I will personally care to spot a doll, Bridget is by no means a pelican when she marries Shamus. In fact," he says, "she is pretty good-looking. I remember their wedding well, because it comes out that Bridget is in love with some other guy at the time, and this guy comes to see the nuptials, and Shamus runs him all the way from Newark to Elizabeth, figuring to break a couple of legs for the guy if he catches him. But," Spider says, "the guy is too speedy for Shamus, who never has much foot anyway."

Well, all that Spider says appeals to me as a very sound business proposition, so the upshot of it is, I give him my pound note to finance his trip to Newark.

Then I do not see Spider McCoy again for a

week, but one day he calls me up and tells me to hurry over to the Pioneer gymnasium to see the next heavyweight champion of the world, Thunderbolt Mulrooney.

I am personally somewhat disappointed when I see Thunderbolt Mulrooney, and especially when I find out his first name is Raymond and not Thunderbolt at all, because I am expecting to see a big, fierce guy with red hair and a chest like a barrel, such as Shamus Mulrooney has when he is in his prime. But who do I see but a tall, pale-looking young guy with blond hair and thin legs.

Furthermore, he has pale-blue eyes, and a faraway look in them, and he speaks in a low voice, which is nothing like the voice of Shamus Mulrooney. But Spider seems satisfied with Thunderbolt, and when I tell him Thunderbolt does not look to me like the next heavyweight champion of the world, Spider says like this: "Why," he says, "the guy is nothing but a baby, and you must give him time to fill out. He may grow to be bigger than his papa. But you know," Spider says, getting indignant as he thinks about it, "Bridget Mulrooney does not wish to let this guy be the next heavyweight champion of the world. In fact," Spider says, "she kicks up an awful row when I go to get him, and Shamus finally has to speak to her severely. Shamus says he does not know if I can ever make a fighter of this guy because Bridget coddles him until he is nothing but a mush-head, and Shamus says he is sick and tired of seeing the guy sitting around the house doing nothing but reading and playing the zither."

"Does he play the zither yet?" I asked Spider McCoy.

"No," Spider says, "I do not allow my fighters to play zithers. I figure it softens them up. This guy does not play anything at present. He seems to be in a daze most of the time, but of course everything is new to him. He is bound to come out okay, because," Spider says, "he is certainly bred right. I find out from Shamus that all the Mulrooneys are great fighters back in the old country," Spider says, "and furthermore he tells me Bridget's mother once licks four Newark cops who try to stop her from pasting her old man, so," Spider says, "this lad is just naturally steaming with fighting blood."

Well, I drop around to the Pioneer once or twice a week after this, and Spider McCoy is certainly working hard with Thunderbolt Mulrooney. Furthermore, the guy seems to be improving right along and gets so he can box fairly well and punch the bag and all this and that, but he always has that faraway look in his eyes, and personally I do not care for fighters with faraway looks.

Finally one day Spider calls me up and tells me he has Thunderbolt Mulrooney matched in a four-round preliminary bout at the St. Nick with a guy by the name of Bubbles Browning, who is fighting almost as far back as the first battle of Bull Run, so I can see Spider is being very careful in matching Thunderbolt. In fact, I congratulate Spider on his carefulness. "Well," Spider says, "I am taking this match just to give Thunderbolt the feel of the ring. I am taking Bubbles because he is an old friend of mine, and very deserving, and furthermore," Spider says, "he gives me his word he will not hit Thunderbolt very hard and will become unconscious the instant Thunderbolt hits him. You know," Spider says, "you must encourage a young heavyweight, and there is nothing that encourages one so much as knocking somebody unconscious."

Now of course it is nothing for Bubbles to promise not to hit anybody very hard because even when he is a young guy, Bubbles cannot punch his way out of a paper bag, but I am glad to learn that he also promises to become unconscious very soon, as naturally I am greatly interested in Thunderbolt's career, what with owning a piece of him, and having an investment of one pound in him already.

So the night of the fight, I am at the St. Nick very early, and many other citizens are there ahead of me, because by this time Spider McCoy gets plenty of publicity for Thunderbolt by telling the boxing scribes about his wonderful fighting blood lines, and everybody wishes to see a guy who is bred for battle, like Thunderbolt.

I take a guest with me to the fight by the name of Harry the Horse, who comes from Brooklyn, and as I am anxious to help Spider McCoy all I can, as well as to protect my investment in Thunderbolt, I request Harry to call on Bubbles Browning in his dressing room and remind him of his promise about hitting Thunderbolt. Harry the Horse does this for me, and furthermore he shows Bubbles a large revolver and tells Bubbles that he will be compelled to shoot his ears off if Bubbles forgets his promise, but Bubbles says all this is most unnecessary, as his eyesight is so bad he cannot see to hit anybody, anyway.

Well, I know a party who is a friend of the guy who is going to referee the preliminary bouts, and I am looking for this party to get him to tell the referee to disqualify Bubbles in case it looks as if he is forgetting his promise and is liable to hit Thunderbolt, but before I can locate the party, they are announcing the opening bout, and there is Thunderbolt in the ring looking very far away indeed, with Spider McCoy behind him.

It seems to me I never see a guy who is so pale all over as Thunderbolt Mulrooney, but Spider looks down at me and tips me a large wink, so I can see that everything is as right as rain, especially when Harry the Horse makes motions at Bubbles Browning like a guy firing a large revolver at somebody, and Bubbles smiles, and also winks.

Well, when the bell rings, Spider gives Thunderbolt a shove toward the center, and Thunderbolt comes out with his hands up, but looking more far away than somewhat, and something tells me that Thunderbolt by no means feels the killer instinct such as I love to see in fighters. In fact, something tells me that Thunderbolt is not feeling enthusiastic about this proposition in any way, shape, manner, or form. Old Bubbles almost falls over his own feet coming out of his corner, and he starts bouncing around making passes at Thunderbolt, and waiting for Thunderbolt to hit him so he can become unconscious. Naturally, Bubbles does not wish to become unconscious without getting hit, as this may look suspicious to the public.

Well, instead of hitting Bubbles, what does Thunderbolt Mulrooney do but turn around and walk over to a neutral corner, and lean over the ropes with his face in his gloves, and bust out crying. Naturally, this is a most surprising incident to one and all, especially to Bubbles Browning.

The referee walks over to Thunderbolt Mulrooney and tries to turn him around, but Thunderbolt keeps his face in his gloves and sobs so loud that the referee is deeply touched and starts sobbing with him. Between sobs he asks Thunderbolt if he wishes to continue the fight, and Thunderbolt shakes his head, although as a matter of fact no fight whatever starts so far, so the referee declares Bubbles Browning the winner, which is a terrible surprise to Bubbles. Then the referee puts his arm around Thunderbolt and leads him over to Spider McCoy, who is standing in his corner with a very strange expression on his face. Personally, I consider the entire spectacle so revolting that I go out into the air, and stand around awhile expecting to hear any minute that Spider McCoy is in the hands of the gendarmes on a charge of mayhem.

But it seems that nothing happens, and when Spider finally comes out of the St. Nick, he is only looking sorrowful because he just hears that the promoter declines to pay him the fifty bobs he is supposed to receive for Thunderbolt's services, the promoter claiming that Thunderbolt renders no service.

"Well," Spider says, "I fear this is not the next heavyweight champion of the world after all. There is nothing in Professor D's idea about blood lines as far as fighters are concerned, although," he says, "it may work out all right with horses and dogs, and one thing and another. I am greatly disappointed," Spider says, "but then I am always being disappointed in heavyweights. There is nothing we can do but take this guy back home, because," Spider says, "the last thing I promised Bridget Mulrooney is that I will personally return him to her in case I am not able to make him heavyweight champion, as she is afraid he will get lost if he tries to find his way home alone."

So the next day, Spider McCoy and I take Thunderbolt Mulrooney over to Newark and to his home, which turns out to be a nice little house in a side street with a yard all around and about, and Spider and I are just as well pleased that old Shamus Mulrooney is absent when we arrive, because Spider says that Shamus is just such a guy as will be asking a lot of questions about the fifty bobbos that Thunderbolt does not get.

Well, when we reach the front door of the house, out comes a big fine-looking doll with red cheeks, all excited, and she takes Thunderbolt in her arms and kisses him, so I know this is Bridget Mulrooney, and I can see she knows what happens, and in fact I afterwards learn that Thunderbolt telephones her the night before.

After a while she pushes Thunderbolt into the house and stands at the door as if she is guarding it against us entering to get him again, which of course is very unnecessary. And all this time Thunderbolt is sobbing no little, although by and by the sobs die away, and from somewhere in the house comes the sound of music I seem to recognize as the music of a zither.

Well, Bridget Mulrooney never says a word to us as she stands in the door, and Spider McCoy keeps staring at her in a way that I consider very rude indeed. I am wondering if he is waiting for a receipt for Thunderbolt, but finally he speaks as follows: "Bridget," Spider says, "I hope and trust that you will not consider me too fresh, but I wish to learn the name of the guy you are going around with just before you marry Shamus. I remember him well," Spider says, "but I cannot think of his name, and it bothers me not being able to think of names. He is a tall, skinny, stoop-shouldered guy," Spider says, "with a hollow chest and a soft voice, and he loves music."

Well, Bridget Mulrooney stands there in the

doorway, staring back at Spider, and it seems to me that the red suddenly fades out of her cheeks, and just then we hear a lot of yelling, and around the corner of the house comes a bunch of five or six kids, who seem to be running from another kid. This kid is not very big, and is maybe fifteen or sixteen years old, and he has red hair and many freckles, and he seems very mad at the other kids. In fact, when he catches up with them, he starts belting away at them with his fists, and before anybody can as much as say boo, he has three of them on the ground as flat as pancakes, while the others are yelling bloody murder.

Personally, I never see such wonderful punching by a kid, especially with his left hand, and Spider McCoy is also much impressed, and is watching the kid with great interest. Then Bridget Mulrooney runs out and grabs the frecklefaced kid with one hand and smacks him with the other hand and hauls him, squirming and kicking, over to Spider McCoy and says to Spider like this:

"Mr. McCoy," Bridget says, "this is my youngest son Terrence, and though he is not a heavyweight, and will never be a heavyweight, perhaps he will answer your purpose. Suppose you see his father about him sometime," she says, "and hoping you will learn to mind your own business, I wish you a very good day."

Then she takes the kid into the house under her arms and slams the door in our kissers, and there is nothing for us to do but walk away. And as we are walking away, all of a sudden Spider McCoy snaps his fingers as guys will do when they get an unexpected thought, and says like this: "I remember the guy's name," he says. "It is Cedric Tilbury, and he is a floorwalker in Hamburgher's department store, and," Spider says, "how he can play the zither!"

I see in the papers the other day where Jimmy Johnston, the matchmaker at the Garden, matches Tearing Terry Mulrooney, the new sensation in the lightweight division, to fight for the championship, but it seems from what Spider McCoy tells me that my investment with him does not cover any fighters in his stable except maybe heavyweights. And it also seems that Spider McCoy is not monkeying with heavyweights since he gets Tearing Terry.

THIS IS THE opening chapter of *The Harder They Fall,* a paraphrase
of the career of Primo Carnera and the most popular of boxing novels.
It was published in 1947, and eight years later was translated into a
vividly photographed, ill-conceived motion picture. The first sentence
misses by a city block. Mickey Walker's is at Forty-ninth Street and
Eighth Avenue.

FROM

# The Harder They Fall

## BUDD SCHULBERG

WHEN I CAME into the story I was having a
quiet conversation over a bottle of Old Taylor
with my friend Charles the bartender at Mickey
Walker's, the place Mickey hasn't got any more
at 50th and Eighth Avenue, right across the
street from the Garden. I like Charles because
he always serves up a respectable two-ounce
whisky and because of the talks we have about
old-time fighters. Charles must know as much
about the old days as Granny Rice. He must be
sixty or seventy years of age, with baby-pink
skin and hardly a wrinkle in his face. The only
giveaway to his age is his spare white hair that
he insists, for some reason, on dyeing a corny yellow. He's seen a lot of the fighters who are just
names to me—legendary names like Ketchell and
Gans and Mexican Joe Rivers. One of the last
things he did before he left London (a faint
cockney echo lingers in his speech) was to see
the famous Peter Jackson–Frank Slavin fight at
the National Sporting Club. This afternoon, as
on so many other afternoons, we were back in
the crucial twentieth round, and Charles, with
his hands raised in the classical nineteenth-cen-
tury boxing stance, was impersonating the dark-
skinned, quiet-spoken, wonderfully poised Jackson.

"Fix the picture in your mind, sir," Charles
was always saying. "Here's Jackson, a fine figure
of a man, the first of the heavies to get up on his
toes, faster than Louis and every bit the puncher.

And here in front of him is solid Frank, a great
rock of a man who's taken everything the black
man had to offer and had him on the verge of
a kayo in the early rounds. They're locked for a
moment in a furious clinch. Jackson, who's made
a remarkable recovery, a miraculous recovery,
sir, breaks away and nails old Frank with a right
that travels just this far—" Charles demonstrated,
reaching over the bar and rapping me sharply
on the side of the jaw—"just that far."

At this point in the battle Charles switched
sides. He had been in vaudeville once, and during the early days of the depression he had picked
up a couple of bucks playing butlers on Broadway. He should be paying regular dues to Actors
Equity because he's acting all the time. Now he
was the staggering, glassy-eyed Slavin, reeling
back from Jackson's short punishing blow. "Fix
the picture in your mind, sir," he repeated. His
chin was resting on his chest and his body had
gone limp. "His hands are at his side, he can't
raise his head or lift his feet, but he won't go
down. Peter Jackson hits him again, and Frank
is helpless to defend himself, but he won't go
down. He just stands there with his arms at his
side, waiting to be hit again. He's made quite a
boast of it before the fight, you see, sir, that
there's no nigger in the world good enough to
make Frank Slavin quit to him. I never use the
word 'nigger' myself, you understand, sir, I'm
just trying to give you the picture as it was. In

my business, you see, sir, I judge a man by the color of his deeds, not the color of his skin. This Peter Jackson, for instance. A finer sportsman never climbed through the ropes than this dark gentleman from Australia."

Now Charles was Jackson again, magnificently proud and erect as the crowd waited for him to finish off his battered opponent. "But at this moment, a memorable thing happened, sir. Instead of rushing in and clubbing the helpless Slavin to the canvas, Jackson stood back, risking the chance that Slavin with his bull-strength might recover, and turned to the referee. You could hear his calm, deep voice all the way back to where I was sitting, sir. Sounded more like a preacher than a fighter, he did. 'Must I finish him off, Mr. Angle?' he said. 'Box on,' said Mr. Angle. Black Peter turned back to his man again. In spite of all those taunts about the color of his skin, you could see he had no stomach for the job. He tapped Frank on the chin once, twice, three times—little stiff punches that would put him away without breaking his jaw—and finally on the fourth, down went old Frank, cold as the proverbial mackerel, for all his boasts. And all the gentlemen who had come to the Sporting Club to see the white man get the better of the black couldn't help rising to their feet and giving Jackson one of the longest rounds of applause that had ever been heard in the Sporting Club."

"Give me another shot," I said. "Charles, you're wonderful. Did you really see the Jackson–Slavin fight?"

"Would I lie to you, Mr. Lewis?"

"Yes," I said. "You told me you were one of Joe Choynski's handlers the time he fought Corbett on that barge off San Francisco. Well, over on Third Avenue I found an old picture of Choynski and Corbett with their handlers just before the fight. You don't seem to be in it."

Charles uncorked the Old Taylor again and poured me another one. "You see, a man of my word," he said. "Every time you catch me in an inaccuracy, Mr. Lewis, I buy you a drink."

"An inaccuracy is an accidental mistake," I said. "What I caught you in, Charles, was a good old-fashioned lie."

"Please, Mr. Lewis," said Charles, deeply offended. "Don't use that word. I may on occasion, for dramatic emphasis, fib. But I never lie. A lie is a thief, sir, and will steal from anybody. A fib just borrows a little from people who can afford it and forgets to pay them back."

"But you actually saw this Jackson–Slavin fight?"

"Say 'bout,' sir, the Jackson–Slavin bout. You'd never hear a gentleman calling a boxing contest a fight."

"Here on Eighth Avenue," I said, "a gentleman is a fellow who calls a woman a broad instead of something else."

"It is unfortunately true," Charles agreed. "The gentlemen in the pugilism business are conspicuous by their abstinence."

"That includes me in," I said. "What do I owe you for this week, Charles?"

"I'll tell you before you leave," Charles said. He never liked to talk about money. He would always scribble the amount on the back of a tab and then slip it under my glass like a secret message.

A sharply dressed, nervous-looking little man stuck his head in the door. "Hey, Charley—you seen the Mumbler?"

"Not today, Mr. Miniff."

"Jeez, I gotta find him," the little man said.

"If he shows up I'll tell him you're looking for him," Charles told him.

"T'anks," said Miniff, "You're m' boy." He disappeared.

Charles shook his head. "It's a sad day, Mr. Lewis, a sad day."

I looked at the big oval clock over the door. A little after three. Time for Charles's over-the-bar address on the decline and fall of the manly art. "The people who come into this place," Charles began. "Grifters, chiselers, two-bit gamblers, big-time operators with small-time minds, managers who'd rather see their boys get killed than make an honest living and boxers who've taken so many dives they've got hinges on their knees. In the old days, sir, it was a rough game but it had some . . . some character to it, some dignity. Take Choynski and Corbett fighting on that barge. Skin gloves on Choynski, two-ouncers on Corbett, to a finish. No fancy percentages, no non-title business, just winner take all, may the best man win. A man squared off for his own pride in those days. He was an athlete. If he made a little money at it, fine and dandy. But what have we got today? Champions with mobsters for managers who stall for years fighting overweight bouts because they know the first time they climb into the ring with a good man it's goodbye, championship."

Charles turned around to see if the boss was watching and had one himself. The only time I ever saw him take one was when we were alone and he got going on this decline-and-fall thing.

He washed his glass and wiped it clean, to destroy the evidence, and looked at me steadily. "Mr. Lewis, what is it that turned a fine sport into a dirty business?"

"Money," I said.

"It's money," he went on, as if he hadn't heard me. "Money. Too much money for the promoters, too much money for the managers, too much money for the fighters."

"Too much money for everybody except the press agents," I said. I was feeling sorrier for myself at the moment than I was for the game. That's what the bottle always did to me.

"I tell you, Mr. Lewis, it's money," Charles was saying. "An athletic sport in an atmosphere of money is like a girl from a good family in a house of ill fame."

I pulled out the gold-banded fountain pen Beth had given me for my birthday, and made a couple of notes on what Charles was saying. He was made to order for that play I was going to write, the play on the fight game I had been talking about so long, the one Beth seemed to be so sure I was never going to finish. "Don't spill it all out in talk," she was always saying. Damn Beth and her bright sayings. If I had had any sense I would have found myself a nice dumb broad. But if I could only set the play down the way I felt it sometimes, in all its sweaty violence—not a nine-dollar bill like *Golden Boy*—no violinists with brittle hands, no undigested poetry subtle as a train wreck, but the kids from the streets as they really were, mean and money-hungry, and the greed of the mobsters who had the game rigged; that was the guts of it and I was the boy to write it.

One solid job could justify all the lousy years I had frittered away as a press agent for champions, deserved and otherwise, contenders and bums, plenty of the latter. You see, that play would tell Beth, I haven't really fallen so low as you thought. All the time it seemed as if I were prostituting myself by making with the adjectives for Honest Jimmy Quinn and Nick (The Eye) Latka, the well-known fistic entrepreneurs, I was actually soaking up material for my masterpiece. Just as O'Neill spent all those years as a common sailor and Jack London was on the bum.

Like O'Neill and London. It always made me feel better to make those notes. My pockets were full of notes. There were notes in every drawer of my desk at the hotel. The notes were kind of an escape valve for all the time I wasted getting loaded, cutting up touches with Charles, sitting around with the boys, going up to Shirley's, and ladling out the old craperoo about how old Joe Roundheels, who couldn't lick my grandfather and who had just been put away in two over at the Trenton Arena, was primed (I would be starving to death without that word *primed*)

to give Jack Contender the fight of his life.

"What are you doing there, Mr. Lewis?" Charles said. "Not writing down something I say."

A good bartender, Charles never pried into his customers' affairs. But he was beginning to break down with me because he liked the idea of getting into my play. I wish Beth had as much faith in me as Charles. "You know what you ought to do, you ought to quit leaning on your elbows and get to work," she was always saying. But Charles was different. He'd tell me something and then he'd say, "You ought to put *that* in your play." We talked about it so long that my work of art came to have a real identity. "If you're going to put me in your show," Charles would say, "please call me Charles. I like to be called Charles. My mother always called me Charles. Charley sounds like—a puppet, or a fat man."

The door swung open and Miniff popped his head in again. "Hey, Charley, still no signa the Mumbler?"

Charles shook his head gravely. "No signa the Mumbler whatsoever, Mr. Miniff." Charles was a snob. It gave him pleasure to exercise his talent for mimicry at the expense of his ungrammatical clientele. Miniff came in and climbed up on the stool next to mine. His small feet didn't reach the footrest at the base of the stool. He pushed his brown felt hat back on his head desperately. He ran his hands over his face and shook his head a few times, his fingers covering his eyes. He was tired. New York is hot when you run around all day.

"Have one with me, Miniff," I said. He waved me off with a small, hairy hand.

"Just the juice of the cow," he said. "Gotta keep my ulcer quiet." From his breast pocket he took a couple of short, stubby cigars, shoved one into his mouth and offered the other one around.

"No, thanks," I said. "If I smoked those six-for-a-quarters I'd have ulcers too. If I'm going to have them, I want expensive ulcers, bottled in bond."

"Listen," Miniff said, "it ain't the hemp. It's the headaches I got. Nervous digestion." He drank his milk carefully, letting it trickle slowly down his throat for maximum therapeutic effect.

"Jeez, I gotta find the Mumbler," he said. The Mumbler was Solly Hyman, the matchmaker for St. Nick's. "I looked everywhere already, Lindy's, both of them, Sam's. Up at Stillman's I hear Furrone can't go Tuesday. Gotta bad toot'. Jeez, I gotta guy to take his place. My bum'll look good in there."

"Who you got, Mr. Miniff?" Charles said, still mimicking.

"Cowboy Coombs."

"Oh, my God," I said.

"He can still go," said Miniff. "I tell ya he c'n stay three-four rounds with the shine, maybe go the limit."

"Cowboy Coombs," I said. "The grandfather of all the bums."

"So he ain't no Tooney," Miniff said.

"Fifteen years ago, he wasn't Tunney," I said.

Miniff pushed his hat back an inch or two on his forehead. His forehead was shiny with perspiration. This Cowboy Coombs thing was no joke. It was a chance to hustle a fast fifty. The way Miniff works he picks up some down-and-outer or some new kid from the amateurs and he angles a spot or two for him, if he can. It's strictly quick turnover. If the bum goes down, Miniff can't do anything more for him anyway. If the kid is good, smarter managers with better "ins" always steal him away. So for Miniff it's mostly a substitution business, running in a bum or a novice at the last minute, so the box office doesn't have to buy the tickets back, or picking up a quiet C by arranging for one of his dive artists to do an el foldo.

"Listen, Eddie," Miniff said to me, working all the time, "Coombs has got a wife and five kids and they gotta eat. All he's been doin' is spar work the last year or two. The bum needs a break. You could maybe write up something in one of the rags about him. How he got canned for settin' the Champ down in a workout . . ."

"That's not the way I heard he got canned," I said.

"All right, all right, so it happened a little different, maybe the Champ slipped. I suppose you never write stuff it ain't a hunnert per cent kosher!"

"Mr. Miniff, you impugn my integrity," I said. The stuff a guy will write to pay his rent and keep himself in whisky! The things a guy will do for a hundred bucks a week in America! Eddie Lewis, who spent almost two years at Princeton, got A's in English, had a by-line in the *Trib* and has twenty-three pages of a play that is being systematically devoured by a little book club of hungry moths who can't tell a piece of literature from a square meal.

"Go on, Eddie, for a pal," Miniff pleaded. "Just one little lineroo about how the Cowboy is back in great shape. You could work it into almost any colyum. They go for your crap."

"Don't give me that Cowboy Coombs," I said. "Coombs was ready for the laughing academy when you had to talk through a little hole in the door to get a drink. The best thing that could happen to Mrs. Coombs and those five kids is for you to climb down off Mr. Coombs's back and let him go to work for a change."

"Aaaah," said Miniff, and the sound was so bitter it could have been his ulcer talking. "Don't sell that Coombs short. He c'n still lick half the heavyweights in the business right now. Whadcha thinka that?"

"I think half the heavyweights in the business should also climb back on their trucks," I said.

"Aaaaaah," Miniff said. He finished the milk, wiped his lips with his sleeve, pulled some of the wet, loose leaves from the end of his cigar-butt, stuck it back between his teeth again, pulled down the brim of his old brown hat, said, "Take it easy, Eddie, see ya, Charley," and got out in a hurry.

I drank slowly, letting the good warm feeling fan out gradually from my belly. The Harry Miniffs of the world! No, that was taking in too much territory. America. Harry Miniff was American. He had an Italian name or an Irish name or a Jewish name or an English name, but you would never find an Italian in Italy, a Jew in Palestine, an Irishman in Ireland or an Englishman in England with the nervous system and social behavior of the American Harry Miniff. You could find Miniffs everywhere, not just the fight game but show business, radio, movies, the rackets, wholesale houses, building trades, blackjack unions, advertising, politics, real estate, insurance—a disease of the American heart—successful Harry Miniffs, pushing their way to the top of steel institutes, oil companies, film studios, fight monopolies; unsuccessful Harry Miniffs, born with the will but not the knack to catch up with the high dollar that keeps tempting them on like a mechanical rabbit which the whippet can't catch unless the machine breaks down, and can't eat if it does.

"The last one in the bottle, Mr. Lewis," Charles said. "On the house."

"Thanks," I said. "You're an oasis, Charles. An Eighth Avenue oasis."

Someone in a booth had dropped a nickel in the juke slot. It was the only good record in the box, the Bechet version of "Summertime." The haunting tone of Sidney's clarinet took over the place. I looked around to see if it was Shirley. She was always playing it. She was sitting in a booth by herself, listening to the music.

"Hi, Shirley, didn't hear you come in."

"I saw you was talking with Miniff," she said. "Didn't want to interrupt a big important conversation like that."

She had been around for ten or twelve years,

but there was still a little Oklahoma left in her speech. She came to town with her husband, Sailor Beaumont—remember Billy Beaumont?— when he was on the upswing, after he had licked everything in the West and was coming to New York for a shot at the big time. He was the boy who crossed the wise money by going in on the short end of 10–1 to win the welterweight title. He and Shirley rode pretty high for a while. The Sailor was an unreconstructed reform-school graduate from West Liberty who threw most of his dough into such routine channels as the flesh-pots, the ponies and the night spots. All the rest went for motorcycles. He had a white streamlined motorcycle with a sidecar on which, if you were good at reading print cutting through downtown traffic at sixty miles an hour, you could make out the words "Sailor Beaumont, the Pride of West Liberty." That's the kind of a fellow he was. Lots of times, especially in the beginning when they were still getting along together, I remember Shirley riding in that sidecar, with her dark-red hair flying out behind her. She was something to look at in those days, before the beers and the troubles caught up with her. You could still see some of it left, even with the crow's-feet around the eyes and the telltale washed-out look that comes from doing too many things too many times. She still had something from the neck down too, even if her pinup days were ten years behind. She was beginning to spread, just this much, in the rump, the belly and the bust, but there was something about the way she held herself—sometimes I thought it was more in her attitude toward men than anything physical—that made us still turn around.

"Have one with me, Shirley?" I called over.

"Save it, Eddie," she said.

"Not even two fingers, to be sociable?"

"Oh, I don't know, maybe a beer," Shirley said.

I gave Charles the order and went over to the booth. "Waiting for anyone?"

"For you, darling," she said, sarcastic. She didn't bother to look at me.

"What's the matter? Hung?"

"Aah, not really, just, oh, the hell with it . . ."

Shirley was in a mood. She got that way every now and then. Most of the time she was feeling good, a lot of laughs—"What the hell, I'm not getting any richer and I'm not getting any younger, but I'm having fun." But once in a while, especially when you caught her alone in the daytime, she was this way. After it got dark and she had had a few, it would be better. But I've seen her sit there in a booth for hours, having solitary beers and dropping nickels in the slot, playing "Summertime" or "Melancholy Baby" or another of her favorites. "Embraceable You." I suppose those songs had something to do with the Sailor, though it always struck me as profane to associate the tender sentiments of those excellent lyrics with a screwball slugger like Beaumont. He'd lay anything that stood still for thirty seconds. If Shirley ever asked for an explanation she got it—on the jaw. He was one of the few professionals I ever knew who indulged in spontaneous extracurricular bouts in various joints, a practice which did not endear him to Jacobs' Beach and brought him frequently and forcibly to the attention of the local gendarmerie. When he finally had a blowout on that hotcha motorcycle of his and left in a bloody mess on the curb at Sixth Avenue near 52nd Street what few brains he had salvaged from ninety-three wide-open fights, the people who took it hard could be counted on one finger of one hand, and that was Shirley.

She reached into her large red-leather purse, took out a little white bag of fine-cut tobacco, carefully tapped it out onto a small rectangle of thin brown paper with a practiced hand. She was the only woman I had ever seen roll her own cigarettes. It was one of the habits she brought with her from the hungry years in West Liberty. While she twirled the flat wrapper into an amazingly symmetrical cylinder, she stared absently through the glass that looked out on Eighth Avenue. The street was full of people moving restlessly back and forth in two streams like ants, but with less purpose. "Summertime," she sang under her breath lackadaisically, a snatch here and a snatch there.

The beer seemed to do something for her. "You can draw me another one, Charles," she said, coming up out of her mood a little, "with a rye chaser."

After all these years, that was still one of the pub's favorite jokes. Shirley looked at me and smiled as if she were seeing me for the first time.

"Where you been keeping yourself, Eddie? Over in Bleeck's with my rival again?"

This had been going on for years. It had been going on so long there probably was something in it. Shirley was all right. I liked the way she was about men. She never really let you forget that there were anatomical differences between you, and yet she didn't make a conflict of it. I liked the way she had been about Sailor Beaumont, even if he was a wrongo. There were so many American wives who gave most of their energy to trying to make their husbands vice-presidents or head buyers or something. Twice a week they did him a big favor. That was called being a good wife. Shirley, if she hadn't fallen in love with an irresponsible, physically precocious kid who came in wide-open but had a knockout punch in his right hand, would have made somebody in West Liberty an exceptional wife instead of making Eighth Avenue an exceptional madam.

"Favor us with your presence this week, Eddie," she said. "Come in early and I'll have Lucille fry us some chicken and we'll play a little gin."

"Maybe Friday night, before the Glenn–Lesnevich fight," I said.

"That kid Glenn! A jerk thing Nick did, bringing him along so fast," Shirley said. "Those overgrown boys who get up in the heavy dough because they can sock and can take it—thinking they're King of the May because they got their names in lights outside the Garden, when all they got is a one-way ticket to Queer Street. Glenn draws four good gates to the Garden because the customers know he's going to try, gets himself slapped around by men he's got no business in the same ring with, goes back to L.A. to be a lousy runner for a bookie or something, and the manager gets himself another boy. That's what he did with Billy. Nick Latka, that crumb!"

"Nick isn't so bad," I said. "Pays me every Friday, doesn't look over my shoulder too much, kind of an interesting fella, too."

"So is a cockroach interesting if it's got Nick's money in the bank," Shirley said. "Nick is marked lousy in my book because he don't look out for his boys. When he has a good one, he's got the dough and the connections to get him to the top, but down under that left breast pocket, he got nothing there for the boys. Not like George Blake, Pop Foster. Their old boys were always coming back for a touch, a little advice. Nick, when you're winning nothing's too good for you. You're out to that estate over in Jersey every weekend. But when you're out of gas, that's all, brother. You got about as much chance of getting into that office as into a pay toilet without a nickel. I know. I was all through that already, with Billy. And how many has he had since Billy? And now Glenn. And next week maybe some skinny-legged speedball from the Golden

Gloves. They're so pretty when they start, Eddie. I hate to see 'em run down."

Now that Billy was gone, I think Shirley was in love with all fighters. She loved them when they were full of bounce and beans, with their hard trim bodies moving gracefully in their first tailor-made full-cut double-breasteds with pegtop trousers narrowing at the ankles in a modified zoot. And she loved them when the shape of their noses was gone, their ears cauliflowered, scar tissue drawing back their eyes, when they laughed too easily and their speech faltered and they talked about the comeback that Harry Miniff or one of his thousand-and-one cousins was lining up for them. Lots of ladies have loved winning fighters, the Grebs, the Baers, the Golden Boys, but it was the battered ones, the humiliated, the washed-ups, the TKO victims with the stitches in their lips and through their eyelids that Shirley took to her bosom. Maybe it was her way of getting Billy back, the Sailor Beaumont of his last year, when the younger, stronger, faster boys who did their training on Eighth Avenue instead of on 52nd Street were making him look slow and foolish and sad.

"Well, first one today," Shirley said, and tossed it off, exaggerating the shudder for a laugh.

She reached into her purse again and took out a very small Brownie snapshot, slightly overexposed, of a well-set-up kid grinning under a ten-gallon hat.

"New picture of my kid the folks just sent me."

While I took a dutiful hinge at it she said, "He's the image of Billy. Isn't he a doll?"

He did look like Beaumont—the same overdevelopment from the waist up, with the legs tapering down nicely. On his face was a look of cheerful viciousness.

"He'll be nine next month," Shirley said. "He's with his grandparents on a ranch near home. He wants to be a veterinary. I don't care what he does, as long as he stays out of the ring. He can be a card player or a drummer or a pimp if he wants to. But, by God, if I ever hear that he's turning out to be a fighter like his old man, I'll go home and kick his little annyfay for him."

THIS IS CHAPTER IX of *Cashel Byron's Profession,* the fourth of Shaw's five unsuccessful novels, and written when he was twenty-six years old. He acquired what knowledge he had of the prize ring by attending a few fights and, as he put it, "wading through *Boxiana* and the files of *Bell's Life* at the British Museum." As is evident in the words of his hero, here pleading his case before his beloved, Shaw was less intrigued by boxing than by the hypocrisy of a society that looked down upon it.

FROM

# Cashel Byron's Profession

## GEORGE BERNARD SHAW

CASHEL'S PUPILS sometimes requested him to hit them hard—not to play with them—to accustom them to regular, right-down severe hitting, and no nonsense. He only pretended to comply; for he knew that a black eye or loosened tooth would be immoderately boasted of if received in combat with a famous pugilist, and that the sufferer's friends would make private notes to avoid so rough a professor. But when Miss Carew's note reached him, he made an exception to his practice in this respect. A young guardsman, whose lesson began shortly after the post arrived, remarked that Cashel was unusually distrait, and exhorted him to wake up and pitch in in earnest. Instantly a blow in the epigastrium stretched him almost insensible on the floor. His complexion was considerably whitened when he was set on his legs again; and he presently alleged an urgent appointment and withdrew, declaring in a shaky voice that that was the sort of bout he really enjoyed.

When he was gone, Cashel walked distractedly to and fro, cursing, and occasionally stopping to read the letter. His restlessness only increased his agitation. The arrival of a Frenchman whom he employed to give lessons in fencing made the place unendurable to him. He changed his attire, went out, called a cab, and bade the driver, with an oath, drive to Lydia's house as fast as the horse could go. The man made all the haste he could, and was presently told impatiently that there was no hurry. Accustomed to this sort of inconsistency, he was not surprised when, as they approached the house, he was told not to stop, but to drive slowly past. Then, in obedience to further instructions, he turned and repassed the door. As he did so, a lady appeared for an instant at a window. Immediately his fare, with a groan of mingled rage and fear, sprang from the moving vehicle, rushed up the steps of the mansion, and rang the bell violently. Bashville, faultlessly dressed and impassibly mannered, opened the door. In reply to Cashel's half-inarticulate inquiry, he said, "Miss Carew is not at home."

"You lie," said Cashel, his eyes suddenly dilating. "I saw her."

Bashville reddened, but replied coolly, "Miss Carew cannot see you today."

"Go and ask her," returned Cashel sternly, advancing.

Bashville, with compressed lips, seized the door to shut him out; but Cashel forced it back against him and went in, shutting the door behind him. He turned from Bashville for a moment to do this; and before he could face him again he was tripped and flung down upon the tessellated pavement of the hall. When Bashville was given the lie, and pushed back behind the door, the excitement he had been suppressing since his visit to Lucian exploded. He had thrown Cashel in Cornish fashion, and now desperately awaited the upshot.

Cashel got up so rapidly that he seemed to rebound from the flags. Bashville, involuntarily cowering before his onslaught, just escaped his right fist, and felt as though his heart had been drawn with it as it whizzed past his ear. He turned and fled frantically upstairs.

Lydia was in her boudoir with Alice when Bashville darted in and locked the door. Alice rose and screamed. Lydia, though startled, and that less by the unusual action than by the change in a familiar face which she had never seen influenced by emotion before, sat still, and quietly asked what was the matter. Bashville checked himself for a moment. Then he spoke unintelligibly, and went to the window, which he opened. Lydia divined that he was about to call for help to the street.

"Bashville," she said authoritatively, "be silent; and close the window. I will go downstairs myself."

Bashville then ran to prevent her from unlocking the door; but she paid no attention to him. He did not dare to oppose her forcibly. He was beginning to recover from his panic, and to feel the first stings of shame for having yielded to it.

"Madam," he said, "Byron is below; and he insists on seeing you. He's dangerous; and he's too strong for me. I have done my best; on my honor I have. Let me call the police. Stop," he added, as she opened the door. "If either of us goes, it must be me."

"I will see him in the library," said Lydia composedly. "Tell him so; and let him wait there for me—if you can speak to him without running any risk."

"Oh pray let him call the police," urged Alice. "Don't attempt to go to that man."

"Nonsense!" said Lydia good-humoredly. "I am not in the least afraid. We must not fail in courage when we have a prize fighter to deal with."

Bashville, white, and with difficulty preventing his knees from knocking together, but not faltering for a second, went devotedly downstairs and found Cashel leaning upon the balustrade, panting, and looking perplexedly about him as he wiped his dabbled brow. Bashville halted on the third stair, and said, "Miss Carew will see you in the library. Come this way, please."

Cashel's lips moved but no sound came from them: he followed Bashville in silence. When they entered the library, Lydia was already there.

Bashville withdrew without a word. Then Cashel sat down and, to her consternation, bent his head on his hand and yielded to a hysterical convulsion. Before she could resolve how to act, he looked up at her with his face distorted and discolored, and tried to speak.

"Please don't cry," said Lydia. "I am told that you wish to speak to me."

"I don't wish to speak to you ever again," said Cashel hoarsely. "You told your servant to throw me down the steps. That's enough for me."

Lydia caught from him the tendency to sob which he was struggling with; but she repressed it, and answered firmly, "If my servant has been guilty of the least incivility to you, Mr. Cashel Byron, he has exceeded his orders."

"It doesn't matter," said Cashel. "He may thank his luck that he has his head on. But *he* doesn't matter. Hold on a bit—I can't talk—I shall get—second wind—and then—" Cashel raised his head with a curiously businesslike expression; threw himself supinely against the back of his chair; and in that position deliberately rested until he could trust himself to speak. At last he pulled himself together, and said, "Why are you going to give me up?"

Lydia ranged her wits in battle array, and replied, "Do you remember our talk at Mrs. Hoskyn's?"

"Yes."

"You admitted then that if the nature of your occupation became known to me, our acquaintance should cease."

"That was all very fine to excuse my not telling you. But I find, like many another man when put to the proof, that I didn't mean it. Who told you I was a fighting man?"

"I had rather not tell you that."

"Aha!" said Cashel, with a triumph that was half choked by the remnant of his hysteria. "Who is trying to make a secret now, I should like to know?"

"I do so in this instance because I am afraid to expose a friend to your resentment."

"And why? He's a man, of course: else you wouldn't be afraid. You think that I'd go straight off and murder him. Perhaps he told you that it would come quite natural to a man like me— a ruffian like me—to smash him up. That comes of being a coward. People run my profession down, not because there is a bad one or two in it—there's plenty of bad bishops, if you come to that—but because they're afraid of us. You may make yourself easy about your friend. I am accustomed to get well paid for the beatings I give; and your own common sense ought to tell you that any one who is used to being paid for a job is just the last person in the world to do it for nothing."

"I find the contrary to be the case with first-rate artists," said Lydia.

"Thank you," retorted Cashel sarcastically. "I ought to make you a bow for that."

"But," said Lydia seriously, "it seems to me that your art is wholly antisocial and retrograde. And I fear that you have forced this interview on me to no purpose."

"I don't know whether it's antisocial or not. But I think it hard that I should be put out of decent society when fellows that do far worse than I are let in. Who did I see here last Friday, the most honored of your guests? Why, that Frenchman with the gold spectacles. What do you think I was told when I asked what *his* little game was? Baking dogs in ovens to see how long a dog could live red hot! I'd like to catch him doing it to a dog of mine. Aye; and sticking a rat full of nails to see whether pain makes a rat sweat. Why, it's just sickening. Do you think I'd have shaken hands with that chap? If he hadn't been a friend of yours, I'd have taught him how to make a Frenchman sweat without sticking any nails into him. And *he's* to be received and made much of, while I am kicked out! Look at your relation the general, too! What is he but a fighting man, I should like to know? Isn't it his pride and boast that as long as he is paid so much a day, he'll ask no questions whether a war is fair or unfair, but just walk out and put thousands of men in the best way to kill and be killed—keeping well behind them himself all the time, mind you. Last year he was up to his chin in the blood of a lot of poor blacks that were no more a match for his armed men than a featherweight would be for me. Bad as I am, I wouldn't attack a featherweight, or stand by and see another heavy man do it. Plenty of your friends go pigeon shooting to Hurlingham. *There's* a humane and manly way of spending a Saturday afternoon! Lord Worthington, that comes to see you when he likes, though he's too much of a man or too little of a shot to kill pigeons, thinks nothing of fox hunting. Do you think foxes like to be hunted, or that the people that hunt them have such fine feelings that they can afford to call prize fighters names? Look at the men that get killed or lamed every year at steeplechasing, fox hunting, cricket, and football! Dozens of them! Look at the thousands killed in battle! Did you ever hear of any one being killed in the ring? Why, from first to last, during the whole century that my sort of fighting has been going on, there's not been six fatal accidents at really respectable fights. It's safer than dancing:

many a woman has danced her skirt into the fire and been burnt. I once fought a man who had spoiled his constitution with bad living; and he exhausted himself so by going on and on long after he was beaten that he died of it, and nearly finished me, too. If you'd heard the fuss that even the old hands made over it, you'd have thought a blessed baby had died from falling out of its cradle. A good milling does a man more good than harm. And if all these damned dog bakers, and soldiers, and pigeon shooters, fox hunters, and the rest of them, are made welcome here, why am I shut out like a brute beast?"

"Truly I do not know," said Lydia, puzzled, "unless it be that your profession is not usually recruited from our ranks."

"I grant you that boxers aren't gentlemen, as a rule. No more were painters or poets, once upon a time. But what I want to know is this. Supposing a boxer has as good manners as your friends, and is as well born, why shouldn't he mix with them and be considered their equal?"

"The distinction seems arbitrary, I confess. But perhaps the true remedy would be to exclude the vivisectors and soldiers, instead of admitting the prize fighters. Mr. Cashel Byron," added Lydia, changing her manner, "I cannot discuss this with you. Society has a prejudice against you. I share it; and I cannot overcome it. Can you find no nobler occupation than these fierce and horrible encounters by which you condescend to gain a living?"

"No," said Cashel flatly. "I can't. That's just where it is."

Lydia looked grave, and said nothing.

"You don't see it?" said Cashel. "Well, I'll just tell you all about myself, and then leave you to judge. May I sit down while I talk?" He had risen in the course of his remarks on Lydia's scientific and military acquaintances.

She pointed to a chair near her. Something in the action brought color to his cheeks.

"I believe I was the most unfortunate devil of a boy that ever walked," he began. "My mother was—and is—an actress, and a tiptop crack in her profession. One of the first things I remember is sitting on the floor in the corner of a room where there was a big glass, and she flaring away before it, attitudinizing and spouting Shakespeare like mad. I was afraid of her, because she was very particular about my manners and appearance, and would never let me go near a theater. I know nothing about my people or hers; for she boxed my ears one day for asking who my father was, and I took good care not to ask her again. She was quite young when I was a child: at first I thought her a sort of angel. I should have been fond of her, I think, if she had let me. But she didn't, somehow; and I had to keep my affection for the servants. I had plenty of variety in that way; for she gave her whole establishment the sack about once every two months, except a maid that used to bully her and give me nearly all the nursing I ever got. I believe it was my crying about some housemaid or other who went away that first set her abusing me for having low tastes—a sort of thing that used to cut me to the heart, and which she kept up till the very day I left her for good. We were a precious pair: I sulky and obstinate; she changeable and hot-tempered. She used to begin breakfast sometimes by knocking me to the other side of the room with a slap, and finish it by calling me her darling boy and promising me all manner of toys and things. I soon gave up trying to please her or like her, and became as disagreeable a young imp as you'd ask to see. My only thought was to get all I could out of her when she was in a good humor, and to be sullen and stubborn when she was in a tantrum. One day a boy in the street threw some mud at me, and I ran in crying, and complained to her. She told me I was a little coward. I haven't forgiven her for that yet—perhaps because it was one of the few true things she ever said to me. I was in a state of perpetual aggravation; and I often wonder I wasn't soured for life at that time. At last I got to be such a little fiend that when she hit me I used to guard off her blows, and look so wicked that I think she got afraid of me. Then she put me to school, telling me I had no heart, and telling the master I was an ungovernable young brute. So I, like a little fool, cried at leaving her; and she, like a big one, cried back again over me—just after telling the master what a bad one I was, mind you—and off she went, leaving her darling boy and blessed child howling at his good luck in getting rid of her.

"I was a nice boy to let loose in a school. I could speak as well as an actor, as far as pronunciation goes; but I could hardly read words of one syllable; and as to writing, I couldn't make pothooks and hangers respectably. To this day, I can no more spell than old Ned Skene can. What was a worse sort of ignorance was that I had no idea of fair play. I thought that all servants would be afraid of me; and that all grown-up people would tyrannize over me. I was afraid of everybody; afraid that my cowardice would be found out; and as angry and cruel in my ill-tempers as cowards always are. Now you'll hardly believe this; but what saved me from going to the bad altogether was my finding out that I was a good one to fight. The bigger boys were like grown-up people in respect of liking to see other people fight; and they used to set us young ones at it, whether we liked it or not, regularly every Saturday afternoon, with seconds, bottle-holders, and everything complete, except the ropes. At first, when they made me fight, I shut my eyes and cried; but for all that I managed to catch the other fellow tight round the waist and throw him. After that, it became a regular joke to make me fight; for I always cried. But the end of it was that I learned to keep my eyes open and hit straight. I had no trouble about fighting then. Somehow, I could tell by instinct when the other fellow was going to hit me; and I always hit him first. It's the same with me now in the ring: I know what a man is going to do before he rightly knows himself. The power this gave me, civilized me. In the end it made me cock of the school; and, as cock, I couldn't be mean or childish. There would be nothing like fighting for licking boys into shape if every one could be cock; but every one can't; so I suppose it does more harm than good.

"I should have enjoyed school well enough if I had worked at my books. But I wouldn't study; and the masters were all down on me as an idler, though I shouldn't have been like that if they had known how to teach: I have learned since what teaching is. As to the holidays, they were the worst part of the year to me. When I was left at the school I was savage at not being let go home; and when I went home, my mother did nothing but find fault with my schoolboy manners. I was getting too big to be cuddled as her darling boy, you understand. Her treatment of me was just the old game with the affectionate part left out. It wasn't pleasant, after being cock of the school, to be made to feel like a good-for-nothing little brat tied to her apron strings. When she saw that I was learning nothing, she sent me to another school at a place in the north called Panley. I stayed there until I was seventeen; and then she came one day, and we had a row, as usual. She said she wouldn't let me leave school until I was nineteen; and so I settled that question by running away the same night. I got to Liverpool where I hid in a ship bound for Australia. When I was starved out, they treated me better than I expected; and I worked hard enough to earn my passage and my victuals. But when I was left ashore in Melbourne, I was in a pretty pickle. I knew nobody, and I had no money. Everything that a man could live by was owned by someone or other. I walked through the town looking for a place where they might want a boy to run errands or to clean the windows. But I hadn't the cheek to go into the shops and ask.

Two or three times, when I was on the point of trying, I caught sight of some cad of a shopman, and made up my mind that I wouldn't be ordered about by *him,* and that since I had the whole town to choose from I might as well go on to the next place. At last, quite late in the afternoon, I saw an advertisement stuck up on a gymnasium; and while I was reading it I got talking to old Ned Skene, the owner, who was smoking at the door. He took a fancy to me, and offered to have me there as a sort of lad-of-all-work. I was only too glad to get the chance; and I closed with him at once. As time went on, I became so clever with the gloves that Ned matched me against a lightweight named Ducket, and bet a lot of money that I would win. Well, I couldn't disappoint him after his being so kind to me—Mrs. Skene had made as much of me as if I were her own son. What could I do but take my bread as it came to me? I was fit for nothing else. Even if I had been able to write a good hand and keep accounts, I couldn't have brought myself to think that quill-driving and counting other people's money was fit employment for a man. It's not what a man would like to do that he must do in this world: it's what he *can* do; and the only mortal thing I could do properly was to fight. There was plenty of money and plenty of honor and glory to be got among my acquaintance by fighting. So I challenged Ducket, and knocked him all to pieces in ten minutes. I half killed him, because I didn't know my own strength and was afraid of him. I have been at the same work ever since; for I never was offered any other sort of job. I was training for a fight when I was down at Wiltstoken with that old fool Mellish. It came off the day you saw me at Clapham when I had such a bad eye. Wiltstoken did for me. With all my fighting, I'm no better than a baby at heart; and ever since I found out that my mother wasn't an angel, I have always had the notion that a real angel would turn up some day. You see, I never cared much about women. Bad as my mother was as far as being what you might call a parent went, she had something in her looks and manners that gave me a better idea of what a nice woman was like than I had of most things; and the girls I met in Australia and America seemed very small potatoes to me in comparison with her. Besides, of course, they were not ladies. I was fond of Mrs. Skene because she was good to me; and I made myself agreeable, for her sake, to the girls that came to see her; but in reality I couldn't stand them. Mrs. Skene said they were all setting their caps at me—women are death on a crack fighter—but the more they tried it on the less I liked them. It was no go: I could get

on with the men well enough, no matter how common they were; but the snobbishness of my breed came out with regard to the women. When I saw you that day at Wiltstoken walk out of the trees and stand looking so quietly at me and Mellish, and then go back out of sight without a word, I'm blessed if I didn't think you were the angel come at last. Then I met you at the railway station and walked with you. You put the angel out of my head quick enough; for an angel, after all, is only a shadowy, childish notion—I believe it's all gammon about there being any in heaven—but you gave me a better idea than Mamma of what a woman should be, and you came up to that idea and went beyond it. I have been in love with you ever since; and if I can't have you, I don't care what becomes of me. I know I am a bad lot, and have always been one; but when I saw you taking pleasure in the society of fellows just as bad as myself, I didn't see why I should keep away when I was dying to come. I am no worse than the dog baker, anyhow. And hang it, Miss Lydia, I don't want to brag; but there are clean ways and dirty ways in prize fighting the same as in anything else; and I have tried my best to keep in the clean ways. I never fought a cross or struck a foul blow in my life; and I have never been beaten, though I'm only a middleweight, and have stood up with the best fourteen-stone men in the Colonies, the States, or in England."

Cashel ceased. As he sat eyeing her wistfully, Lydia, who had been perfectly still, said bemusedly, "I was more prejudiced than I knew. What will you think of me when I tell you that your profession does not seem half so shocking now that I know you to be the son of an artist, and not a journeyman butcher or a laborer, as my cousin told me."

"What!" exclaimed Cashel. "That lantern-jawed fellow told you I was a butcher!"

"I did not mean to betray him; but, as I have already said, I am bad at keeping secrets. Mr. Lucian Webber is my cousin and friend, and has done me many services. May I rest assured that he has nothing to fear from you?"

"He has no right to tell lies about me. He is sweet on you too: I twigged that at Wiltstoken. I have a good mind to let him know whether I am a butcher or not."

"He did not say so. What he told me of you, as far as it went, is exactly confirmed by what you have said yourself. I happened to ask him to what class men of your calling usually belonged and he said that they were laborers, butchers and so forth. Do you resent that?"

"I see plainly enough that you won't let me

348

resent it. I should like to know what else he said of me. But he was right enough. There are all sorts of blackguards in the ring: there's no use denying it. Since it's been made illegal, decent men won't go into it. All the same, it's not the fighting men, but the betting men, that bring discredit on it. I wish your cousin had held his confounded tongue."

"I wish you had forestalled him by telling me the truth."

"I wish I had, now. But what's the use of wishing? I didn't dare run the chance of losing you. See how soon you forbade me the house when you did find out."

"It made little difference," said Lydia gravely.

"You were always friendly to me," said Cashel plaintively.

"More so than you were to me. You should not have deceived me. And now I think we had better part. I am glad to know your history; and I admit that you made perhaps the best choice that society offered you. I do not blame you."

"But you give me the sack. Is that it?"

"What do you propose, Mr. Cashel Byron? Is it to visit my house in the intervals of battering and maiming butchers and laborers?"

"No, it's not," retorted Cashel. "You're very aggravating. I won't stay much longer in the ring now: my luck is too good to last. Anyhow, I shall have to retire soon, luck or no luck, because no one can match me. Even now there's nobody except Bill Paradise that pretends to be able for me; and I'll settle him in September if he really means business. After that, I'll retire. I expect to be worth ten thousand pounds then. Ten thousand pounds, I'm told, is the same as five hundred a year. Well, I suppose, judging from the style you keep here, that you're worth as much more, besides your place in the country; so if you will marry me we shall have a thousand a year between us. I don't know much of money matters; but at any rate we can live like fighting cocks on that much. That's a straight and businesslike proposal, isn't it?"

"And if I refuse?" said Lydia, with some sternness.

"Then you may have the ten thousand pounds to do what you like with," said Cashel despairingly. "It won't matter what becomes of me. I won't go to the devil for you or any woman if I can help it; and I—but where's the good of saying *if* you refuse? I know I don't express myself properly: I'm a bad hand at sentimentality; but if I had as much gab as any of those long-haired fellows on Friday, I couldn't be any fonder of you, or think more highly of you."

"But you are mistaken as to the amount of my income."

"That doesn't matter a bit. If you have more, why, the more the merrier. If you have less, or if you have to give up all your property when you're married, I will soon make another ten thousand to supply the loss. Only give me one good word, and, by George, I'll fight the seven champions of Christendom, one down and t'other come on, for five thousand a side each. Hang the money!"

"I am richer than you suppose," said Lydia, unmoved. "I cannot tell you exactly how much I possess; but my income is about forty thousand pounds."

"Forty thousand pounds!" ejaculated Cashel. "Holy Moses! I didn't think the Queen had as much as that."

For a moment he felt nothing but mere astonishment. Then, comprehending the situation, he became very red. In a voice broken by mortification, he said, "I see I have been making a fool of myself," and took his hat and turned to go.

"It does not follow that you should go at once without a word," said Lydia, betraying nervousness for the first time during the interview.

"Oh, that's all rot," said Cashel. "I may be a fool while my eyes are shut; but I'm sensible enough when they're open. I have no business here. I wish to the Lord I had stayed in Australia."

"Perhaps it would have been better," said Lydia, troubled. "But since we have met, it is useless to deplore it; and— Let me remind you of one thing. You have pointed out to me that I have made friends of men whose pursuits are no better than yours. I do not wholly admit this; but there is one respect in which they are on the same footing with you. They are all, as far as worldly gear is concerned, much poorer than I. Most of them, I fear, are poorer—much, *much* poorer than you are."

Cashel looked up quickly with returning hope; but it lasted only a moment. He shook his head dejectedly.

"I am at least grateful to you," she continued, "because you have sought me for my own sake, knowing nothing of my wealth."

"I should think not," groaned Cashel. "Your wealth may be a very fine thing for the other fellows; and I'm glad you have it, for your own sake. But it's a settler for me. So goodbye."

"Goodbye," said Lydia, almost as pale as he had now become, "since you will have it so."

"Since the devil will have it so," said Cashel ruefully. "It's no use wishing to have it any other way. The luck is against me. I hope, Miss Carew, that you'll excuse me for making such an ass of myself. It's all my blessed innocence: I never was taught any better."

"I have no quarrel with you except on the old score of hiding the truth from me; and I forgive you that—as far as the the evil of it affects *me*. As for your declaration of attachment to me personally, I have received many similar ones that have flattered me less. But there are certain scruples between us. You will not court a woman a hundredfold richer than yourself; and I will not entertain a prize fighter. My wealth frightens every man who is not a knave; and your profession frightens every woman who is not a fury."

"Then you— Just tell me this," said Cashel eagerly. "Suppose I were a rich swell, and were not a—"

"No," said Lydia, peremptorily interrupting him. "I will suppose nothing but what is."

Cashel relapsed into melancholy. "If you only hadn't been kind to me!" he said. "I think the reason I love you so much is that you're the only person that is not afraid of me. Other people are civil because they daren't be otherwise to the cock of the ring. It's a lonely thing to be a champion. You knew nothing about that; and you knew I was afraid of you; and yet you were as good as gold."

"It is also a lonely thing to be a very rich woman. People are afraid of my wealth, and of what they call my learning. We two have at least one experience in common. Now do me a great favor by going. We have nothing further to say."

"I'll go in two seconds. But I don't believe much in you being lonely. That's only fancy."

"Perhaps so. Most feelings of this kind are only fancies."

There was another pause. Then Cashel said, "I don't feel half so downhearted as I did a minute ago. Are you sure that you're not angry with me?"

"Quite sure. Pray let me say goodbye."

"And may I never see you again? Never at all?—world without end, amen?"

"Never as the famous prize fighter. But if a day should come when Mr. Cashel Byron will be something better worthy of his birth and nature, I will not forget an old friend. Are you satisfied now?"

Cashel's face began to glow, and the roots of his hair to tingle. "One thing more," he said. "If you meet me by chance in the street before that, will you give me a look? I don't ask for a regular bow, but just a look to keep me going?"

"I have no intention of cutting you," said Lydia gravely. "But do not place yourself purposedly in my way."

"Honor bright, I won't. I'll content myself with walking through that street in Soho occasionally. Now I'm off: I know you're in a hurry to be rid of me. So goodb— Stop a bit, though. Perhaps when that time you spoke of comes, you'll be married."

"It is possible; but I am not likely to marry. How many more things have you to say, that you have no right to say?"

"Not one," said Cashel, with a laugh that rang through the house. "I never was happier in my life, though I'm crying inside all the time. I'll have a try for you yet. Goodbye. No," he added, turning from her proffered hand, "I daren't touch it: I should eat you afterwards." He made for the door, but turned on the threshold to say in a loud whisper: "Mind, I'm engaged to you. I don't say you're engaged to me; but it's an engagement on my side." And he ran out of the room.

In the hall was Bashville, pale and determined, waiting there to rush to the assistance of his mistress at her first summons. He had a poker concealed at hand. Having just heard a great laugh, and seeing Cashel come downstairs in high spirits, he stood stock still, not knowing what to think.

"Well, old chap," said Cashel boisterously, slapping him on the shoulder, "so you're alive yet. Is there anyone in the dining room?"

"No," said Bashville.

"There's a thick carpet there to fall soft on," said Cashel, pulling Bashville into the room. "Come along. Now shew me that little trick of yours again. Come! Don't be afraid: I won't hit you. Down with me. Take care you don't knock my head against the fire irons."

"But—"

"But be hanged. You were spry enough at it before. Come!"

Bashville, after a moment's hesitation, seized Cashel, who immediately became grave and attentive, and remained imperturbably so whilst Bashville expertly threw him. He sat thinking for a moment on the hearthrug before he arose. "*I* see," he said then, getting up. "Now do it again."

"But it makes such a row," remonstrated Bashville.

"Only once more. There'll be no row this time."

"Well, every man to his taste," said Bashville, complying. But instead of throwing his man, he found himself wedged into a collar formed by Cashel's arms, the least constriction of which would have strangled him. Cashel again roared with laughter as he released him.

"That's the way, ain't it?" he said. "You can't catch an old fox twice in the same trap. Do you know any more falls?"

"I do," said Bashville, "but I really can't show them to you here. I shall get into trouble on account of the noise."

"You come down to me whenever you have an evening out," said Cashel, handing him a card, "to that address, and show me what you know; and I'll see what I can do with you. There's the making of a man in you."

"You're very kind," said Bashville, pocketing the card with a grin.

"And now let me give you a word of advice that will be of use to you as long as you live," said Cashel impressively. "You did a damned silly thing today. You threw a man down—a fighting man—and then stood looking at him like a fool, waiting for him to get up and kill you. If ever you do that again, fall on him as heavily as you can the instant he's off his legs. Double your elbow well under you, and see that it gets into a soft place. If he grabs it and turns you, make play with the back of your hand. If he's altogether too big for you, put your knee on his throat as if by accident. But on no account stand and do nothing. It's flying in the face of Providence."

Cashel emphasized each of these counsels by an impressive tap of his forefinger on one of Bashville's buttons. In conclusion, he nodded, opened the house door, and walked away in buoyant spirits.

Lydia, standing near the library window, saw him go down the long front garden, and observed how his light, alert step, and a certain gamesome assurance of manner, marked him off from a genteelly promenading middle-aged gentleman, a trudging workman, and a vigorously striding youth passing without. The railings that separated him from them reminded her of the admirable and dangerous creatures passing and repassing behind iron bars in the park yonder. But she exulted, in her quiet manner, in the thought that, dangerous as he was, she had no fear of him. When his cabman had found him and taken him off, she went to a private drawer in her desk and took out her father's last letter. She sat for some time looking at it without unfolding it.

"It would be a strange thing, Father," she said, as if he were actually there to hear her, "if

your paragon should end as the wife of an illiterate prize fighter. I felt a pang of despair when he replied to my forty thousand pounds a year with an unanswerable goodbye. And now he is engaged to me."

She locked up her father, as it were, in the drawer again, and rang the bell. Bashville appeared, somewhat perturbed.

"If Mr. Byron calls again, admit him if I am at home."

"Yes, madam."

"Thank you."

"Begging your pardon, madam, but may I ask has any complaint been made of me?"

"None." Bashville was reluctantly withdrawing when she added, "Mr. Byron gave me to understand that you tried to prevent his entrance by force. You exposed yourself to needless risk by doing so; and you may make a rule in future that when people are importunate, and will not go away when asked, they had better come in until you get special instructions from me. I am not finding fault: on the contrary, I approve of your determination to carry out your orders; but under exceptional circumstances you may use your own discretion."

"He shoved the door in my face; and I acted on the impulse of the moment, madam. I hope you will forgive the liberty I took in locking the door of the boudoir. He is older and heavier than I am, madam; and he has the advantage of being a professional. Else I should have stood my ground."

"I am quite satisfied," said Lydia a little coldly, as she left the room.

"How long you have been!" cried Alice, almost in hysterics, as Lydia entered. "Is he gone? What were those dreadful noises? *Is* anything the matter?"

"Dancing and late hours are the matter," said Lydia. "The season is proving too much for you, Alice."

"It is not the season; it is the man," said Alice, with a sob.

"Indeed? I have been in conversation with the man for more than half an hour; and Bashville has been in actual combat with him; yet we are not in hysterics. You have been sitting here at your ease, have you not?"

"I am not in hysterics," said Alice indignantly.

"So much the better," said Lydia gravely, placing her hand on the forehead of Alice, who subsided with a sniff.

# CHON DAY

*"They ought to give <u>him</u> a glass of their tangy, healthful, invigorating beer."*

WHEN A FIGHTER comes out of his corner, his chin on his chest, and looking at the other man out of the tops of his eyes, that seems to be the whole truth of him right there. The whole truth of any fighter is that he probably has a woman and she may be his wife and, although he will not do his gym work mornings, it may be as bad as this.

# Return to Kansas City

## IRWIN SHAW

ARLINE OPENED the bedroom door and softly went over between the twin beds, the silk of her dress making a slight rustle in the quiet room. The dark shades were down and the late afternoon sun came in only in one or two places along the sides of the window frames, in sharp, thin rays.

Arline looked down at her husband, sleeping under the blankets. His fighter's face with the mashed nose was very peaceful on the pillow and his hair was curled like a baby's and he snored gently because he breathed through his mouth. A light sweat stood out on his face. Eddie always sweated, any season, any place. But now, when she saw Eddie begin to sweat, it made Arline a little angry.

She stood there, watching the serene, glove-marked face. She sat down on the other bed, still watching her husband. She took a lace-bordered handkerchief out of a pocket and dabbed at her eyes. They were dry. She sniffed a little and the tears started. For a moment she cried silently, then she sobbed aloud. In a minute the tears and the sobs were regular, loud in the still room.

Eddie stirred in his bed. He closed his mouth, turned over on his side.

"Oh, my," Arline sobbed, "oh, my God."

She saw, despite the fact that Eddie's back was toward her, that he had awakened.

"Oh," Arline wept, "sweet Mother of God."

She knew that Eddie was wide awake listening to her and he knew that she knew it, but he hopefully pretended he hadn't been roused. He even snored experimentally once or twice. Arline's sobs shook her and the mascara ran down her cheeks in straight black lines.

Eddie sighed and turned around and sat up, rubbing his hair with his hands.

"What's the matter?" he asked. "What's bothering you, Arline?"

"Nothing," Arline sobbed.

"If nothing's the matter," Eddie said mildly, "what're you crying for?"

Arline didn't say anything. She stopped sobbing aloud and turned the grief inward upon herself and wept all the more bitterly, in silence. Eddie wiped his eye with the heel of his hand, looked wearily at the dark shades that shut out the slanting rays of the sun.

"There are six rooms in this house, Arline darling," he said. "If you have to cry why is it necessary to pick the exact room where I am sleeping?"

Arline's head sank low on her breast, her beautiful beauty-shop straw-colored hair falling tragically over her face. "You don't care," she murmured, "you don't care one dime's worth if I break my heart."

She squeezed the handkerchief and the tears ran down her wrist.

"I care," Eddie said, throwing back the covers neatly and putting his stockinged feet onto the floor. He had been sleeping in his pants and shirt, which were very wrinkled now. He shook his head two or three times as he sat on the edge of the bed and hit himself smartly on the cheek with the back of his hand to awaken himself. He looked unhappily across at his wife, sitting on the other bed, her hands wrung in her lap, her face covered by her careless hair, sorrow and despair in every line of her. "Honest, Arline, I care." He went over and sat next to her on the bed and put his arm around her. "Baby," he said. "Now, baby."

She just sat there crying silently, her round, soft shoulders shaking now and then under his arm. Eddie began to feel more and more uncomfortable. He squeezed her shoulder two or three times, exhausting his methods of consolation. "Well," he said finally, "I think maybe I'll put the kid in the carriage and take him for a walk. A little air. Maybe when I come back you'll feel better."

"I won't feel better," Arline promised him, without moving, "I won't feel one ounce better."

"Arline," Eddie said.

"The kid." She sat up erect now and looked at him. "If you paid as much attention to me as to the kid."

"I pay equal attention. My wife and my kid." Eddie stood up and padded around the room uneasily in his socks.

Arline watched him intently, the creased flannel trousers and the wrinkled shirt not concealing the bulky muscles.

"The male sleeping beauty," she said. "The long-distance sleeping champion. My husband."

"I don't sleep so awful much," Eddie protested.

"Fifteen hours a day," Arline said. "Is it natural?"

"I had a hard workout this morning," Eddie said, standing at the window. "I went six fast rounds. I got to get rest. I got to store up my energy. I am not so young as some people any more. I got to take care of myself. Don't I have to store up energy?"

"Store up energy!" Arline said loudly. "All day long you store up energy. What is your wife supposed to do when you are storing up energy?"

Eddie let the window shade fly up. The light shot into the room, making it harder for Arline to cry.

"You ought to have friends," Eddie suggested without hope.

"I have friends."

"Why don't you go out with them?"

"They're in Kansas City," Arline said.

There was silence in the room. Eddie sat down and began putting on his shoes.

"My mother's in Kansas City," Arline said. "My two sisters are in Kansas City. My two brothers. I went to high school in Kansas City. Here I am, in Brooklyn, New York."

"You were in Kansas City two and a half months ago," Eddie said, buttoning his collar and knotting his tie. "A mere two and a half months ago."

"Two and a half months are a long time," Arline said, clearing away the mascara lines from her cheeks, but still weeping. "A person can die in two and a half months."

"What person?" Eddie asked.

Arline ignored him. "Mamma writes she wants to see the baby again. After all, that is not unnatural, a grandmother wants to see her grandchild. Tell me, is it unnatural?"

"No," said Eddie, "it is not unnatural." He combed his hair swiftly. "If Mamma wants to see the baby," he said, "explain to me why she can't come here. Kindly explain to me."

"My husband is of the opinion that they are handing out gold pieces with movie tickets in Kansas City," Arline said with cold sarcasm.

"Huh?" Eddie asked, honestly puzzled. "What did you say?"

"How can Mamma afford to come here?" Arline asked. "After all, you know, there are no great prize fighters in *our* family. I had to *marry* to bring one into the family. Oh, my God!" Once more she wept.

"Lissen, Arline," Eddie ran over to her and spoke pleadingly, his tough, battered face very gentle and sad, "I can't afford to have you go to Kansas City every time I take a nap in the afternoon. We have been married a year and a half and you have gone to Kansas City five times. I feel like I am fighting for the New York Central Railroad, Arline!"

Arline shook her head obstinately. "There is nothing to do in New York," she said.

"There is nothing to do in New York!" Eddie's mouth opened in surprise. "My God! There's something to do in Kansas City?" he cried. "What the hell is there to do in Kansas City? Remember, I have been in that town myself. I married you in that town."

"I didn't know how it was going to be," Arline said flatly. "It was nice in Kansas City. I was an innocent young girl."

"Please," said Eddie. "Let us not rake up the past."

"I was surrounded by my family," Arline went on shakily. "I went to high school there."

She bent over and grief took possession once more. Eddie licked his lips uncomfortably. They were dry from the morning's workout and the lower lip was split a little and smarted when he ran his tongue over it. He searched his brain for a helpful phrase.

"The kid," he ventured timidly, "why don't you play more with the kid?"

"The kid!" Arline cried defiantly. "I take very good care of the kid. I have to stay in every night minding the kid while you are busy storing up your energy." The phrase enraged her and she stood up, waving her arms. "What a business! You fight thirty minutes a month, you got to sleep three hundred and fifty hours. Why, it's laughable. It is very laughable! You are some fighter!" She shook her fist at him in derision. "With all the energy you store up you ought to be able to beat the German army!"

"That is the business I am in," Eddie tried to explain gently. "That is the nature of my profession."

"Don't tell me that!" Arline said. "I have gone out with other fighters. They don't sleep all the time."

"I am not interested," Eddie said. "I do not want to hear anything about your life before our marriage."

"They go to night clubs," Arline went on irresistibly, "and they dance and they take a drink once in a while and they take a girl to see a musical show!"

Eddie nodded. "They are after something," he said. "That is the whole story."

"I wish to God you were after something!"

"I meet the type of fighter you mention, too," Eddie said. "The night-club boys. They knock my head off for three rounds and then they start breathing through the mouth. By the time they reach the eighth round they wish they never saw a naked lady on a dance floor. And by the time I get through with them they are storing up energy flat on their backs. With five thousand people watching them. You want me to be that kind of a fighter?"

"You're wonderful," Arline said, wrinkling her nose, sneering. "My Joe Louis. Big-Purse Eddie Megaffin. I don't notice you bringing back the million-dollar gate."

"I am progressing slowly," Eddie said, looking at the picture of Mary and Jesus over his bed. "I am planning for the future."

"I am linked for life to a goddam health-enthusiast," Arline said despairingly.

"Why do you talk like that, Arline?"

"Because I want to be in Kansas City," she wailed.

"Explain to me," Eddie said, "why in the name of God you are so crazy for Kansas City?"

"I'm lonesome," Arline wept with true bitterness. "I'm awful lonesome. I'm only twenty-one years old, Eddie."

Eddie patted her gently on the shoulder. "Look, Arline." He tried to make his voice very warm and at the same time logical. "If you would only go easy. If you would go by coach and not buy presents for everybody, maybe I can borrow a coupla bucks and swing it."

"I would rather die," Arline said. "I would rather never see Kansas City again for the rest of my life than let them know my husband has to watch pennies like a streetcar conductor. A man with his name in the papers every week. It would be shameful!"

"But, Arline, darling—" Eddie's face was tortured—"you go four times a year, you spread presents like the WPA and you always buy new clothes . . ."

"I can't appear in Kansas City in rags!" Arline pulled at a stocking, righting it on her well-curved leg. "I would rather . . ."

"Some day, darling," Eddie interrupted. "We're working up. Right now I can't."

"You can!" Arline said. "You're lying to me, Eddie Megaffin. Jake Blucher called up this morning and he told me he offered you a thousand dollars to fight Joe Principe."

Eddie sat down in a chair. He looked down at the floor, understanding why Arline had picked this particular afternoon.

"You would come out of that fight with seven hundred and fifty dollars." Arline's voice was soft and inviting. "I could go to Kansas . . ."

"Joe Principe will knock my ears off."

Arline sighed. "I am so anxious to see my mother. She is an old woman and soon she will die."

"At this stage," Eddie said slowly, "I am not ready for Joe Principe. He is too strong and too smart for me."

"Jake Blucher told me he thought you had a wonderful chance."

"I have a wonderful chance to land in the hospital," Eddie said. "That Joe Principe is made out of springs and cement. If you gave him a pair of horns it would be legal to kill him with a sword."

"He is only a man with two fists just like you," Arline said.

"Yeah."

"You're always telling me how good you are."

"In two years," Eddie said, "taking it very easy and careful, making sure I don't get knocked apart . . ."

"You could make the money easy!" Arline pointed her finger dramatically at him. "You just don't want to. You don't want me to be happy. I see through you, Eddie Megaffin!"

"I just don't want to get beaten up," Eddie said, shaking his head.

"A fine fighter!" Arline laughed. "What kind of fighter are you, anyhow? A fighter is supposed to get beaten up, isn't he? That's his business, isn't it? You don't care for me. All you wanted was somebody to give you a kid and cook your goddam steaks and lamb chops. In Brooklyn! I got to stay in a lousy little house day in and . . ."

"I'll take you to the movies tonight," Eddie promised.

"I don't want to go to the movies. I want to go to Kansas City." Arline threw herself face down on the bed and sobbed. "I'm caught. I'm caught! You don't love me! You won't let me go to people who love me! Mama! Mama!"

Eddie closed his eyes in pain. "I love you," he said, meaning it. "I swear to God."

"You say it."

Her voice was smothered in the pillow. "But you don't prove it! Prove it! I never knew a young man could be so stingy. Prove it . . ." The words trailed off in sorrow.

Eddie went over and bent down to kiss her. She shook her shoulders to send him away and cried like a heartbroken child. From the next room, where the baby had been sleeping, came the sound of his wailing.

Eddie walked over to the window and looked out at the peaceful Brooklyn street, at the trees and the little boys and girls skating.

"O.K.," he said, "I'll call Blucher."

Arline stopped crying. The baby still wailed in the next room.

"I'll try to raise him to twelve hundred," Eddie said. "You can go to Kansas City. You happy?"

Arline sat up and nodded. "I'll write Mama right away," she said.

"Take the kid out for a walk, will you?" Eddie said, as Arline started repairing her face before the mirror. "I want to take a little nap."

"Sure," Arline said, "sure, Eddie."

Eddie took off his shoes and lay down on the bed to start storing up his energy.

RED SMITH is the most widely read and quoted sports writer of all time. He is the Willie Pep of his profession—all solid skill and inventiveness and the master of the unexpected—and, when it has to be done, he can take his man out as cleanly as anyone writing today. After all, Pep, not celebrated primarily as a puncher, had sixty-two KOs, and broke Sal Bartolo's jaw in three places.

Fritzie Zivic, handled here, had 232 fights, held the welterweight title and was the master of the unorthodox. Ray Robinson, who beat him twice, once said, "Fritzie Zivic taught me more than anybody. Why, he even taught me how you can make a man butt open his own eye."

# The Nose

## RED SMITH

PITTSBURGH, February 18, 1947—The most un-retired man in North America went all retired again today, this time for beauty's sweet sake. Fritzie (the Nose) Zivic, fresh back from a fist fight in Mexico City—"I run second"—unbuttoned a plaid sports jacket, hooked a thumb into the pocket of a chamois waistcoat as casually as he ever thrust it into an adversary's eye, stretched suede-shod feet out beneath the luncheon table and pensively caressed the beak that looks like a mine cave-in.

"That's all," he said. "I'm through. That last fight was my last."

"How many retirements is this, Fritzie, not counting those suggested by boxing commissions?"

"Two. Yeah, that's right, only two of my own. Of course, the newspapers probably retired me about ten times."

He introduced Justo Fontaine, a stake performer in his expanding fight stable. He handed over a folder of matches labeled: "Send your boy to Fritzie Zivic's new boxing school."

He mentioned the surburban arena where he is proprietor, promoter, manager, second, ticket-taker, and janitor and where he once pleaded vainly for permission to substitute for one of his main-eventers. He displayed the photograph of a lovely child in a boxing pose inscribed: "Janis Zivic, paperweight, aged five, twenty-seven fights, twenty-seven KOs." He brought out a letter from Lew Burston advising that he could "pick up a couple grand" boxing "some local boy" in Puerto Rico.

Then he came through with the convincer. It was a letter from a Philadelphia plastic surgeon, who wrote: "I have often admired your skill at reshaping the noses of your unhappy opponents. You and I have directed our talents along parallel lines." The doctor offered to rebuild Fritzie's sway-backed prow for free, "just for the satisfaction it would give me."

"I talked to him on the phone," the Nose said. " 'Doc,' I ast him, 'can you fix up a scar under my left eye?' A cinch, he says. 'One more question, Doc,' I ast him. 'Can you grow hair on my head?' He says, hell, I can be handsome without it. So I'm takin' no more punches on this schnoz. Fella named Perfecto Lopez give it to me in L.A. in 1933. He butt me and busted all the cartilages and I got a doctor out there—a doctor? A horse-doctor—and he took out too much cartilage, so in my next fight it caved in like this. I want a big one, big enough to wear a mustache under it."

"You'll be beautiful with a mustache behind the wheel of that Cadillac of yours."

"You remember that Cadillac? Ever since I was a kid, that's what I always wanted. Figured then I'd be a success. So the day I'm fighting Henry Armstrong for the title in New York, I go and look at the biggest Cadillac I can find.

"That night Henry's givin' it to me pretty good and I can see that Cadillac rollin' farther and farther away from me. Henry's givin' me the elbows and the shoulders and the top of the head, and I can give that stuff back pretty good, but I don't dare to or maybe they'll throw me out of the ring.

"Well, in the seventh round I give him the head a couple times and choke him a couple times and use the elbow some, and the referee says: 'If you guys want to fight that way, it's okay with me.' 'Hot damn!' I told Luke Carney in my corner. 'Watch me go now.' And from there out I saw that Cadillac turn around and come rollin' back.

"But I sold it when I was in the Army. I'm down in Texas and get a chance to fight in Houston. I ast the lieutenant if I could get a pass and he says: 'We'll ast the Old Man.' I'm in the Army three months and don't know who the Old Man is. Well, he's the colonel and I'm scared. But the lieutenant takes me in and the Old Man puts his arm around my shoulders and says: 'Sit down and have a cigar, son. What'll it be?' He gives me a lousy cigar. The lieutenant explains and I sit there kind of groggy because I never smoked a cigar, but I got to make out I enjoy it. The Old Man says sure I can have a pass and I said I'd give part of the purse to the camp athletic fund. Forget it, he says, in the Army I can keep what I get. So I take a couple of guys with me to Houston and I flatten the guy in about four and get a thousand dollars and we have a hell of a party.

"Next time, though, the Old Man says I can have another pass, but he figures I should donate something to the athletic fund. It was me smartened him up, see, and now it's his idea. Well, I promise $500, but my end for the second fight comes to only $850 and with expenses and all I got to write my personal check for about $150.

"Next time it's the same thing but my end is only $300. I can't admit to anybody that I fight that cheap, so I got to write a bigger check. I win about seven or eight fights and it costs me more money all the time. Altogether I give the camp about $7,200 out of $11,000.

"Finally Mike Jacobs calls me up and offers me twenty-five per cent in the Garden with Billy Arnold, that I never heard of. I had a furlough coming to me, so I had Mike wire me a thousand dollars and a bunch of us drove to Pittsburgh; I had the Cadillac then. At home here, we tore into the champagne something terrific before we went to New York. There they tell me this Arnold that I never heard of is four to one to beat me and has twenty-seven knockouts in thirty-three fights. Well, I says, nobody's four to one against Fritzie, and we started betting, the whole crowd of us. I win, all right, and when we collect the bets we got $16,000 wrapped up in a newspaper. I win $4,200 in bets and my end is $11,000. So, I give the Old Man another $500 because he don't know I'm getting $11,000, which if he ever found it out he'd of thrown me in the brig.

"I also send him two boxes of Corona Coronas so the next time I go in his office I'll have a decent cigar to smoke."

PUBLIUS PAPINIUS STATIUS delivered, in his epic the *Thebaid,* this description of the classic combat—the slugger versus the boxer. In the first century his Alcidamas knew more about pace, footwork, blocking, slipping, hand-feinting and counterpunching than 95 per cent of his twentieth-century counterparts.

FROM THE

# *Thebaid*

## STATIUS

[TRANSLATED BY J. H. MOZLEY]

"AND NOW IS courage needed; wield ye the terrible cestus in close conflict; valor here comes nighest to that of battle and the sword."

Argive Capaneus took his stand—awful his aspect, awful the terror he inspires—and, binding on his arms the raw ox-hide black with lumps of lead, himself no softer, "Send me one," says he, "from all those thousands of warriors; and would rather that my rival were of Aonian stock, whom it were right to slay, and that my valor were not stained with kindred blood." They stood aghast and terror made them silent. At last Alcidamas, unexpected, leaped forth from the naked crowd of Laconians, while the Dorian princes marvel but his comrades knew he relied on his master Pollux, and had grown up in the wrestling school of a god. Pollux himself guided his hands and molded his arms—love of the sport constrained him—and oft he set him against himself, and admiring him as he stood up in like mood caught him up, exultant, and pressed his naked body to his breast. Capaneus thinks scorn of him and mocks at his challenge, as though in pity, and demands another foe; at last perforce he faces him, and now his languid neck swells at anger's prompting. With bodies poised at their full height, they lift their hands, deadly as thunderbolts, safe withdrawn are their faces on their shoulders, ever watching and closed is the approach to wounds. The one is as great in broad expanse of every limb and terrible

in size of bone as though Tityos should rise up from the Stygian fields, did the fierce birds allow him; the other was lately but a boy, yet his strength is riper than his years, and his youthful vigor gives promise of a mighty manhood; him would none wish to see defeated nor stained with cruel gore, but each man fears the spectacle with eager prayers.

Scanning each other with their gaze and each awaiting the first opening, they fell not at once to angry blows, but stayed awhile in mutual fear, and mingled caution with their rage; they but incline their arms against each other as they spar, and make trial of their gloves, dulling them by mere rubs. The one, more skillfully trained, puts by his fury, and taking thought for the future delays and husbands up his strength; but the other, prodigal of harm and reckless of his powers, rushes with all his might and in wild blows exhausts both arms, and attacks with fruitless gnashing of teeth, and injures his own cause. But the Laconian, prudent and crafty, and with all his country's vigilance, now parries, now avoids the blow; sometimes by throwing back or rapid bending of his head he shuns all hurt, now with his hands he beats off the aimed assault, and advances with his feet while keeping his head drawn back. Often again, as his foe engages him with superior power—such strength is in his cunning, such skill in his right hand—with bold initiative, he enters his guard and overshadows him, and towering high assails him. Just as a mass of water hurls itself headlong on a threatening rock, and falls back broken, so does he wheel round his angry foe, breaking his defense; look! he lifts his hand and threatens a long time his face or side, and thus by fear of his hard weapons diverts his guard and cunningly plants a sudden blow, and marks the middle of his forehead with a wound; blood flows, and the warm stream stains his temples. Capaneus, yet ignorant, wonders at the sudden murmur of the crowd, but when, as he chanced to draw his weary hand across his face, he saw the stains upon the cowhide, no lion nor tiger feeling the javelin's smart was e'er so mad; hotly he drives the youth before him in headlong retreat over the whole field, and is forcing him on to his back; terribly he grinds his teeth and whirls his fists in countless repeated blows. The strokes are wasted on the winds, some fall on the gloves of his foe; with active movement and aid of nimble feet the Spartan eludes the thousand deaths that shower about his temples, yet not unmindful of his art he flees still fighting, and though fleeing meets blows with blows.

And now both wearied with the toil and their exhausted panting; slower the one pursues, nor is the other so swift to escape; the knees of both fail them and alike they rest. Thus when long wandering o'er the sea has wearied the mariners, the signal is given from the stern and they rest their arms awhile; but scarce have they taken repose, when another cry summons them to the oars again. Lo! a second time he makes a furious dash, but the other tricks him and goes at him with a rush of his own and sinking into his shoulders; forward he pitches his head, and as he rises the merciless boy smote him another blow and himself grew pale at his success. The Inachidae raise a shout louder than the noise of shore or forest. But when Adrastus saw him struggling from the ground, and lifting his hands, intent on hideous deeds, "Haste, friends, I pray you, he is mad! hasten, prevent him! he is out of his mind—quick! bring the palm and prizes! He will not cease, I see well, till he pounds the brain within the shattered skull. Rescue the doomed Laconian!" At once Tydeus darts forth, and Hippomedon, obedient to command; then scarce do the two with all their might master his two arms and bind them fast, and forcefully urge him: "Leave the field, thou art victorious; 'tis noble to spare the vanquished. He too is one of us, and a comrade in war." But no whit is the hero's fury lessened; he thrusts away the proffered branch and cuirass, and shouts: "Let me free! Shall I not smash in gore and clotted dust those cheeks whereby that eunuch-boy gained favor, and send his unsightly corpse to the tomb, and give cause for mourning to his Oebalian masters?"

So says he, but his friends force him away, swelling with wrath and protesting that he has not conquered, while the Laconians praise the nursling of famed Taygetus, and laugh loud at the other's threats.

ON SEPTEMBER 9, 1905, during the reign of Joe Gans, Battling Nelson and Jimmie Britt fought for "the white lightweight championship of the world" at Colma, California. A celebrated, and overwrought, drama critic reviewed the contest for the San Francisco *Examiner*.

# Old Man Britt

## ASHTON STEVENS

MELODRAMA WOULD BE a hollow word—poor old cut-and-dried melodrama! For this duel between Jimmie Britt and Battling Nelson had a nerve-wrecking shudder for every moment of the fifty-two minutes of actual fighting. It was a sight such as I hope never to see again; and yet it was the greatest matinee I have ever witnessed. The most colossal audience—and the most expensive, too, that I have ever known—played the horrible mob.

When the right fist of Nelson emerged from a tangle of blows in the eighteenth round and came invincibly against the jaw of Britt, and the champion of his lightweight kind fell numb against the ropes and sank to the canvas floor, his lips geysers of blood, his tongue a protruding, sickening blade of red, the mob went mad.

Referee Graney had declared "all bets off," and it was more merely a matter of passion.

So the crowd opened its throat in unmercenary rapture. The King was dead—curse him!—and long live the Battling One!

A thousand cushions from the hard seats of the Colma arena were thrown into the afternoon air, and picked up and thrown, and thrown again.

Nelson the Great!

Britt the Beaten!

For ten minutes after the determining blow, hell was lidless.

Jubilant arms tossed Nelson again and again in the air as college kids are tossed in blankets. He was the gloat of fifteen thousand throats. The prize ring filled for him, and the policemen detailed to clear it fought to retain their clubs.

In the corner of the vanquished mourned the seconds, and if the truth must be told—for I sat at the ringside in Britt's corner where Britt fell—mourned also the referee, who that afternoon at the last moment had accepted the post in the face of what had appeared to be an implacable grudge 'twixt himself and the Britts.

But more touching still in that near corner was Old Man Britt, pillowing the gore-flecked head of his heretofore undefeated first-born. He bent his body over his broken son and made of his back a shield against the flying cushions.

As well as fake the prize ring has its tragedy, and one sees it with ghastly vividness at the ringside.

Quickly permit me to admit that my small change and my large sympathies had been with Jimmie. I had interviewed him for the Sunday *Examiner* as fistrion and plumber boy. His mind had won me. His neck had appeared to be a bit too long and thin "for the game," yet he had more brains than all of the ringsters I had ever chanced to fall in with. Also he had quickness, muscle and a left arm like a foil. His mentality and fleetness I would have pitted against the brawn of any man of equal weight. And I had seen him defeat Nelson in twenty rounds—where yesterday in a contest of the practically unlimited number of forty-five, he went down in the eighteenth.

So I motored out to Colma with the rest of the experts and impostors (like myself), wondering just what sort of a foolish dramatic critic's point of view I should be able to bring to bear on Jimmie Britt's victory.

On everything save paper I had my story written before the gong rang. Presently, when I turned and looked two rows behind into the troubled features of Old Man Britt, I felt like a living obituary.

During the fiercest rounds, Mr. Britt was the only man that stood in the great open-air auditorium. Others that attempted to keep their feet were hissed and cussed down.

But the Old Man stood, and even those directly behind him made no murmur. He stood with his black hat in his hand, close against his black coat, like a mourner at a funeral. When big Dean Naughton turned and said, "Nothing but a miracle can save Britt," the foreboding was echoed in the face of the father. When he said, "It's all over now for Jimmie; we have only to wait for the rounds," the Old Man's mouth was working with every blow and his breathing was hopelessness against hopelessness.

Before the finale came, the senior Britt had surrendered. To have taken his game youngster out of that padded square he looked as though he would have given one plumbing shop and some flats.

But Jimmie knew that he was beaten only after he had been lifted to his corner. It's a pity that such grit has to be sold in the market place for purses and percent. It's a crime against what we are pleased to call civilization. If the bloody wage of war must come, and come in response to national pride and protection, then Jimmie Britt should be foremost with the fighters. They deserve a dearer heroism than this cheap one of the glove.

Almost throughout the battle was a fury. Britt seemed bent on throwing fancy boxing to the winds and piercing his opponent by main strength. Vainly the picturesque "Spider" Kelly and the other Britt seconds cautioned him to caution—just as vainly as they urged him to wildness in the fatal eighteenth. He fought his own fight, and the cheers that greeted his defeat were for a stronger but not for a braver man.

I am not depreciating the courage of Battling Nelson. No one can but admire the sand and strength and skill of him. There were times when his expressionless face was a crimson jelly under the thud of Britt's sodden gloves; there were times when his Greek body seemed to be stung through and through by the merciless flogging from Britt's left. But invariably Nelson returned for more, and gradually, cumulatively, he gave rather than took that more. He had rounds to spare, yet, like Britt, he wanted no boxing. The man that called this a "boxing match" was a merry jester. I will leave it to the experience of Otto Floto, Naughton and Hamilton if a harder, bloodier battle has ever been fought in the vision of paying spectators.

Some of these spectators should have been excluded. They were women. A few of them looked like decent women, but the most gave token of being jaded jades in search of some new torment for their sagging nerves. Hoots of mock applause properly met the entrance of each.

Man at a prize fight is not a polite animal. In fact, he has no politeness at all and is much more animal than man.

I saw yesterday professional men, doctors and lawyers high in practice and clubs, writhing rapturously with every blow. Each was "fighting the fight" by himself.

And I saw the eyes of Jack London, who in his novel *The Game* has translated to the stage a prize fight better than Bernard Shaw in either novel or play—I saw the eyes of this great primitive fictionist turn from sympathy with Britt to contempt for the mob that thundered at Britt's fall.

Even London has not written the whole "Game"; and no melodramatist has approached it. Oh, these miserable sublimations of fights that you see in the casual melodrama! They have nothing of the spirit, nothing of the ring; and after all, the ring and those immediately about it are about all you could hope to show within the confines of an ordinary stage.

If we must have the fighter in drama let him be dramatized accurately. Let him have a "Spider" Kelly in his corner screaming:

"That's the candy, Jimmy! Once more where he bleeds! Draw more of the claret; I like to see it run! Go in, you tiger, you, and finish him before he faints on your shoulder!"

I admit, ladies, that this sounds brutal, but it is only a scented version of what actually is shouted at the ringside.

Then again, if we must have the ring on the stage, give us the real surroundings; the telegraph instruments clicking against shout; the hooded telephone operators; the worried correspondents from all ends of the earth. And if we must have prize fights on the stage, give us an actor to play the part of a Naughton, so that in one of those deadly climaxes where the tension of the crowd is too great for clamor, when what London calls the "blood-cry" is choked in the throats —then I say give us a Naughton on the stage, talking like a phonograph to his telegrapher, the news to be carried from ocean to ocean, from newspaper to newspaper.

"A — couple — of — lefts — to — the — — body — brought — Britt's head — forward.

As — Britt's — head — came — in — Nelson — showered — rights — and — lefts — on — the — jaw. Nelson — tore — loose — with — a — hard — left — on — the — body. Britt — began — to crumble. Then — Nelson — unloaded — a — right — on — the — head — and — a — left — on — the stomach. It — was — hard — to — say — which — blow — ended — the — fight — but — Britt — sank — to — the — floor — and — rolled — over — his — tongue — protruding. It — was — blood — red — and — he — was — gasping — for — breath. He — grasped — the — ropes — and — tried — to — arise — but —"

If women and children and sedentary gents must see prize fights on the stage, give them to them as they are. This will show the ring for its true worth. Give us everything, I say—save one. Not Old Man Britt erect in the mob and holding his hat like a mourner at his son's funeral. To show "the game" as it is you don't have to go quite that far. I saw a fighter kill a man in the ring; the picture was not half so sad as that of Old Man Britt.

THE VENAL, callous manager of fighters is the most overworked of characters in sports literature, but Robert Switzer has written him better than anyone else.

# Death of a Prize Fighter

## ROBERT SWITZER

IT WAS TWO A.M. Billy Murdoch was at the airport, his small, sharp-chinned face pale with strain. He was catching a plane for Detroit. It was the wise thing to do because a kid named Tony Casino had died here tonight and the way people were acting you would think Billy Murdoch had killed him.

Tony Casino had been a prize fighter. Billy Murdoch had been his manager. And the kid had been hit too hard and had died of cerebral hemorrhage—and it was all Billy Murdoch's fault, of course.

*Yes,* Billy Murdoch thought sourly. *Oh, hell, yes.*

He slouched low on the bench in the waiting room, the collar of his camel's-hair topcoat turned up and his hat pulled down. He heard somebody say, "Hello, Billy."

He looked up and saw a fair-haired young man. *Another reporter,* he thought. *I haven't seen enough reporters tonight.*

"Hello," Billy Murdoch said.

The young man sat down. "I guess you've had a pretty tough night," he said sympathetically.

Billy Murdoch knew better than to answer that one. Nice traps these sports experts set. If he said yes, he had had a tough night, the paper would say Billy Murdoch felt sorrier for himself than he did for the dead boy. If he said he was all right, the paper would talk about the unfeeling manager. If he said something like, "It was worse for Tony," then he would be making jokes while the boy lay dead. It did not matter what you said; these guys could make you into the worst slob that ever walked.

So he said nothing. He wished he could get aboard the plane.

"Going to New York?" the reporter asked.

"Yes," Billy Murdoch said, and got up and walked across the waiting room to get away from the reporter, hoping the reporter would leave. But as he walked across the room the loud-speaker blared, "Flight 34 for Detroit," and Billy Murdoch knew that the press would be waiting for him in Detroit.

He sat to the rear of the plane. After what seemed a long time, the plane started to roll and then they were in the air. Billy Murdoch closed his eyes and thought of how it had been.

In the last second of the first round, Tony Casino had taken a terrific punch on his left temple, and, as the other boy was about to tear his head off, the bell rang. Tony just stood there, crouching a little, arms hanging straight down from his shoulders. Billy Murdoch and the handler brought him back to his corner. His eyes were glazed. Billy Murdoch and the handler worked on him frantically, with Billy Murdoch thinking: *He was knocked out last week, and now if he quits after one punch I'll have one sweet time matching him again.* Some expression came back into Tony's eyes.

"How you feel?" Billy Murdoch said.

"I'm all right," Tony said blurrily.

"Good. Good. Now listen. Stay away from him. Keep away from him this round."

"Yeah," Tony said.

So the bell rang and Tony went back in and took one more punch. They tried to revive him in the ring, but could not. They carried him to the dressing room and tried to revive him, but could not. Then there was a doctor and a flock of reporters and the other fighters standing around in the dressing room they all shared and the very white body lying completely still on the rubbing table under the light bulb that dangled from the ceiling on the end of a long cord and threw a clear, brittle light on the blue-black smear of Tony's left temple. The doctor bent over the barely breathing body and without looking up said, "Call an ambulance. Quick." There was a scuffling sound on the cement floor as somebody went to telephone, but it was wasted effort because Tony died almost immediately. The doctor looked across the dry, white body at Billy Murdoch and said, "He's dead. Cerebral hemorrhage, probably."

Billy Murdoch kept his eyes on Tony Casino and felt everybody looking at him. There were a lot of men in the room and they were all watching him and waiting for him to say something.

"He was a nice boy," Billy Murdoch said. "It's a lousy thing."

For a moment nobody said anything. It was very hot in the room. Billy Murdoch could feel the sweat running down his sides.

"He was too tall for a welter," one of the fighters said.

"He should have been a middle with that height," a reporter said. "Only his bones weren't big enough."

"You got to have that bone," another fighter said. "Bone soaks it up."

Billy Murdoch wanted to leave, but there were too many people around. Somebody might get mad if he tried to leave too quickly.

"He was knocked out last week," a reporter said. "Just like tonight. He went down like he'd been shot."

The doctor said sharply, "Was he unconscious long? Last week, I mean?"

"No," Billy Murdoch said. "I've seen them out a lot longer. He was all right."

For the first time, Billy Murdoch noticed the man standing next to the doctor. A cop. Not in uniform but one hundred per cent cop. You can tell. The cop was staring at him. Billy Murdoch felt a flash of terror, and then he thought: *They can't do anything to me. I didn't kill the kid. The cop must have been at the fights and heard about this. Cops can't stay away from corpses.*

"How long was he out?" the cop said in a low voice.

"I don't know," Billy Murdoch said. "Not very long."

"About how long?"

"A few minutes, that's all."

The cop's heavy face suddenly looked heavier. "How long is a few minutes?"

"What are you trying to do?" Billy Murdoch said shrilly. "Blame me for this?"

It was very quiet in the room. Billy Murdoch felt his fingers trembling.

"I was here last week," a colored lightweight said. "Tony was out ten minutes anyway. Maybe fifteen."

"So what?" Billy Murdoch said. "I'd like to have a nickel for every boy that's been out ten minutes."

"He looked real bad when he came out of it," the lightweight said. "He was awful pale. I sat here with him for a while after Mr. Murdoch left. He was dizzy. He was sick, too, but he couldn't throw up anything. Just some of that green stuff that burns."

"Dizzy," the cop said. He looked at Billy Murdoch. "Did you ever see him dizzy?"

"No," Billy Murdoch said, thinking of the dizzy spells Tony Casino had had for the past six months. Ever since that night in Cleveland.

"I saw him fight in Cleveland," a reporter said. "About six months ago. He took one of the worst beatings I've ever seen. It was enough to finish any fighter."

"Did he lose all his fights?" the doctor asked in a puzzled voice.

"No," the reporter said. "He had a whole lot of guts. He won his share of fights. Nobody lost money on him."

Billy Murdoch heard grunts from the fighters and saw the angry eyes of the reporters and the flat eyes of the cop, and he thought: *Sure, that's what they're all thinking. I killed the kid for a few crummy bucks.*

He began to edge his way toward the foot of the rubbing table. The door was that way.

"How was he between rounds tonight?" a reporter asked. "When he came out for the second he didn't seem to know where he was going."

"I asked him how he was," Billy Murdoch said. "He said he was all right."

"They're always all right. How did he look?"

"He was hit hard. Maybe he didn't look perfect, but you can't stop a fight every time your boy gets hit."

"Where's the handler?" the cop said.

"Here," the handler said.

"How did he look?"

"He looked bad. I don't think he could see."

"Yeah," the cop said.

"Now, look," Billy Murdoch said, shrilly again. "You're all talking as if I was trying to kill the kid. That's enough of that. I don't have to take that." He started straight for the door and was faintly surprised when nobody tried to stop him.

The cop said viciously, "Murdoch!"

Billy Murdoch stopped.

"I'd like to get you bastards," the cop said in the same vicious voice. "I wish I could figure a way to get you bastards."

Billy Murdoch got out of there. A fat man followed him and caught up with him in the tunnel. He was the man who promoted the fights in this arena.

"Billy," the promoter said, "you better get out of town."

"I was leaving tomorrow, anyway. I got a couple of boys going in Detroit tomorrow night."

"Get out tonight. Don't hang around. Everybody's mad as hell. The papers will have a field day with this. I'm going to have enough trouble. It'll be better if you're not around. You know."

"Sure," Billy Murdoch said. "Tonight."

"About the kid," the promoter said. "Where'll I send him?"

"Somewhere in Brooklyn. I don't know where. The sports writers will find out for you. They'll be looking up his mother."

"I'll take care of it," the promoter said. "So long, Billy."

"So long," Billy Murdoch said, and left the arena, thinking: *Yes, you'll take care of it, you bighearted rat. You'll take care of it out of the purse you didn't pay me. You'd ship the kid C.O.D. if you could get away with it. Keep the money. I'm not stupid enough to argue about that.*

Billy Murdoch went to his hotel, threw his stuff in his bag and went out to the airport, and had to wait two hours for the fog to blow away so the plane could take off.

And now he was in the air for Detroit. The press would be waiting for him. He would have to say something to them. You can't just say, "No comment," when somebody's been killed. He would have to tell them something and it would have to be better than what he had done in the dressing room. He had handled that all wrong. Well, he had been scared. It was foolish, but he had been scared. God, he would hate to have that cop get at him. But what would he say to the reporters? He thought back again and remembered what he had said about you can't stop a fight every time somebody gets hit. He could work on that. He would have to say it right, though.

The plane came down at Detroit and four reporters jumped him. There was light in the sky now, but the sun was not up and it was chilly.

"We heard about Casino," a reporter said. "What happened?"

Nice and innocent, Billy Murdoch thought. When these guys go innocent, hang on.

"Tony was hit very hard," Billy Murdoch said. "I thought he was all right. But he was hit harder than I thought."

"Did you think of stopping the fight?"

"I thought he was all right," Billy Murdoch said again. "He was hit hard, but you can't stop a fight every time your boy gets hit. What would happen to the fight game if you stopped a fight every time somebody got hit?"

"I know what should happen to it," another reporter said. "They should take it out and bury it."

"Sure," Billy Murdoch said. "Nobody likes the fights. That's why they all go to them."

"What are you doing in Detroit?"

"Just passing through."

"To where?"

"Toronto," Billy Murdoch said. "I'm working on a main go for Danny O'Brien up there."

"How do you feel about this Casino kid?"

"How do you think I feel?"

"He was like a son to you."

"Don't be like that," Billy Murdoch said. "That's not funny."

"Forgive me," the reporter said.

Billy Murdoch got away from them, caught a cab, and checked in under a phony name at a small hotel. He slept until two in the afternoon. Then he got up, bathed, shaved, had something to eat, and felt better. He read what the papers had done about Tony Casino. It was just plain murder, the way they told it. Tony Casino had been having head trouble for months, but his manager, Billy Murdoch, had kept right on making him fight. Tony Casino should never have been a fighter, anyway. He had not been rugged enough to take the punishment. But the fight business was savage and could use kids like Tony Casino, and men like Billy Murdoch were licensed to break these kids, physically or mentally or both. The fight business was rotten from top to bottom and it was high time something was done about it.

Billy Murdoch was glad to read that last sentence. They were spreading their fire. They were shooting at the whole fight game and the target was too big and nobody would get hurt.

Billy Murdoch went to see Max Green. Green was putting on the card tonight that included Billy Murdoch's two boys. Green did not look happy at seeing him.

"I heard you were in town," Green said. "They got the finger on you good."

"I got two boys going for you tonight. Don't you remember?"

"They'll go on all right, but I don't want you out there, Billy. There might be trouble. I don't want to get mixed up in this thing. It's one of those messes and I don't want any part of it."

"All right," Billy Murdoch said. "I'll go to a movie. I'll have a time."

"I wouldn't do that, either. You should go on to New York. Dig in there for a while. A man's better off at home at a time like this."

"I'm getting tired of being run out of towns."

"So stay," Green said. "Stay and get your ears beat in. This is a small town. They'll find you and that'll just keep them all excited. I never saw so much excitement as over this one. But New York is big. You won't stir up anything there. Is that right?"

"Sure," Billy Murdoch said. "I'll see you around."

"Goodbye," Max Green said.

Billy Murdoch caught a plane for New York without being seen, and so there were no reporters waiting for him at LaGuardia Field.

He bought a paper. The Tony Casino death was splashed on page one. Billy Murdoch was surprised. He had not thought it would be played up here like this. They were really going to work on this one. Billy Murdoch could not understand it. Fighters were being killed all the time. Why did they have to knock themselves out over this one?

It was ten P.M. when Billy Murdoch stood on the corner of 58th and Sixth Avenue. There was a hotel down the street. Billy Murdoch and nine other managers kept a room in it. Most nights you could get a poker game there. Billy Murdoch went to the hotel and up to the fourteenth floor.

There were five men in the room, sitting around a table littered with chips and ash trays and glasses. They looked up casually when Billy Murdoch came in and then they all jumped to their feet and gave him a royal welcome.

"Hell," Billy Murdoch said. "I thought you might throw me out. Everybody else has."

"Yeah," Jack Latimer said. "What are you trying to do? Give us a bad name?"

"You got a tough break, Billy," Pete Torelli said. "It was too bad."

"All this hollering," Manny Gold said. "Don't let it get you, Billy. It means nothing. Every so often they got to yell. They'll yell for maybe two more days and then they'll forget it."

From across the room another man called, "What do you take in Scotch, Billy?"

"Water," Billy Murdoch said. "Just plain water."

They all went back to the table and sat down. Billy Murdoch relaxed. It was nice to be back among friends again.

A FIGHTER HAS fifteen years in which to make it, so he ages three times as fast as an insurance salesman or an account executive. He knows this is so, but he does not accept it until, one night, he thinks it is the last round and there are two more to go.

# A Boxer: Old

## HARRY SYLVESTER

### I

COBURN WAS VERY WEARY. His neck hurt from the constant, bent, stilted position he held it in to protect his chin with his shoulder. One eye was half closed but did not hurt. Where his jaw hinged was a dull ache, and blood was caked in his nostrils. His arms, too, had begun to pain, partly from blows received, partly from the constant, guarding position. His breath would have been sobbing had he let it. His thighs were no longer springy, moving only with a dull flexibility.

Only his courage was unwearied. It moved in him like an animal, inexorable, insistent, for all that Coburn was unconscious of it.

But Coburn was very weary and he knew that Machter knew it. He could tell this from the crooked smile on Machter's face. It was a strange face, the nose shapeless, the lips leaden and hard, the cheekbones raised. Only the eyes differed from those of the other boxers of Machter's type; feral, yes, but with a depth, an understanding, transcending mere animal cleverness.

This head was on a lower level than Coburn's; it seemed to sway alone, outthrust as it was from the bent, moving body. It wove as wove the lithe, powerful torso. It came in again. And of its own volition Coburn's wet left glove found it once more, and Coburn's weary legs took him away in stiff, dancing motion.

Still the dark head followed, what might have been a smile on its crooked lips; still the damp, dark gloves swayed beneath it, weaving, weaving as wove the head and body. They came on, head and hard gloves and feline body, in a rhythm of their own, savage in its beat. They came in, and Coburn's balled left glove found the blunted features in a flurry of quick little jabs which seemed intentional, but whose rapidity and number were due to a small frenzy born of near panic. This time, Coburn knew, he had danced back into a corner; knew it instinctively, neither by touch nor sight; Coburn had been a boxer a long time. Automatically his legs moved left to take him sidewise from the angle of rope, but Machter slid to his own right, took the jabs on his creased forehead, and was in. . . . Pain of body, extreme, dull, came to Coburn in two brief, sudden waves; and the gasp wrung from him was half a sob. He slid away, holding Machter's left glove under his arm. Machter's right was poised, the face more grimly smiling than before. He seemed to sense he could hit Coburn . . . and was waiting; perhaps to make sure, perhaps because he liked to wait.

The bell rang. What was probably a laugh came from the crooked lips in two guttural sounds, and Machter turned, walked all the way across the ring to his own corner. Even in this time of pain and weariness, Coburn's feet and body had taken him near his own corner, as instincts a decade old and perfect told him the round was nearly over. By the ringside they said he was still clever.

Coburn sank, without looking, onto the small seat he knew Trant had swung into place in the corner. He closed his eyes, relaxing as his buttocks met the support. He relaxed completely. This he could do very well. He felt Trant ministering to him, felt him hold the elastic of the trunks away from the heaving belly muscles; felt the wet sponge move over face and neck and base of head.

The wind of the towel Vanny swung was good. Trant was talking, jerkily, through the cotton-tipped swabs between his teeth: ". . . las' roun' . . . stay away; stay away from the punk . . ."

Coburn knew what Trant was saying, but did not know that this was a remarkable thing. For few boxers hear what their seconds say.

Coburn knew he was weary. This time he knew it more than he ever had before. In the past he had known weariness, but it had usually been a thing fleeting, bitter, perhaps, but quickly gone. Now, permeating everything as dampness the air on a day heavy with rain, weariness was in his body. The terrible weariness of the flesh, but, too, the less combatable, the more insidious, weariness of the mind. Coburn was nearly thirty-three.

Three times he had fought Machter, winning each time, but each time with more difficulty. This time, in the early rounds when his body was strong and swift, he had gained a lead on points which still existed, paper thin.

A whistle sounded, the seconds-out-of-the-ring signal. Coburn could hear Trant climbing backward through the ropes as it seemed Trant had been doing always. Then Trant's hands slid, each between an arm of Coburn's and Coburn's body, and Trant's bony wrists rose until they were hard in Coburn's armpits. The bell rang and Coburn stayed relaxed. Trant's stiffened arms raised Coburn to a standing position, and Coburn finally allowed life and what vigor remained to become active in thews and body.

The gray-shirted referee, Deady, stood in the center, Machter already by him, smiling his crooked smile, waiting to touch gloves for the last round. Otherwise, Coburn knew, Machter would have been three quarters of the way across the ring.

Deady said: "Last round." They touched gloves, pushing. Coburn could feel the terrific power that still flowed in Machter; even in this brief contact Coburn could feel it. They broke away, but Machter dropped into his swaying crouch.

He wove in, was short with hooked left and right to the body, short as Coburn's rigid left arm sent wet leather into his face. Machter licked his crooked lips, and came on, insistent. Again and again Coburn jabbed, once whipping a long right over, but Machter inclined his head, took most of its force on his forehead, hesitated only a little, then came on, steady and unsmiling.

Instinctively Coburn knew he was in a corner;

his feet moved, automatically, in the square, sidling movements necessary to get him out . . . but unaccountably, Machter was in front of him, his right swinging up and home to send pain again through Coburn.

At the ringside they said, he's slowing down.

Coburn hung to the other wet body, his lips tight against the rubber mouthpiece, his head bowed over Machter's shoulder, as if in a gesture to hide, only half-knowingly, his pain from some vague, critical body. . . . A strange pair of lovers, they seemed, to one minded at the moment to note the grotesque.

Light, quick hands were slapping Coburn's gloves down from behind Machter's body. Deady's voice came, impersonal, harsh: ". . . when I tell yuh! Come up!"

Coburn let Deady push him away, then allowed himself to breathe through the mouth a little. The air whistled strangely as it passed the mouthpiece. Things seemed blank, even his pain dull and apart . . . only his left arm leaped into quick, short, pumping action without his willing it. . . . Then he was against the ropes, wrestling, wrestling as futilely as must Jacob have wrestled with the angel; wrestling with quick, blocking, holding movements to stem, to pad, the terrific, bitter power of those short, thick arms. . . .

And again Deady was pulling them apart, and Coburn was skipping with halting, almost spastic, grimly humorous movements, circling behind Deady, away from the ropes. Machter pawed at his own nose where the lacing of Coburn's glove had roughed it . . . then followed, followed.

The weary, incredible left arm and fist straightened Machter up for another innumerable time, and the right, a little bent now, crashed full and clean against the beard-dark jaw. Machter stood, shook it off, smiled a little. Time was when it would have jarred and shaken, perhaps dropped him briefly . . . but the time was long gone. . . .

He came on, head weaving on his body like that of some dull beast. But only seemingly. Machter was not dull. Twice more he took the flurries of lefts, felt a wild, slightly desperate, right glance off the top of his head . . . was in, swinging, jolting.

Coburn's breath was rasping in his ear, Coburn's body arching, arching backward, to get away from the punishment flying with the moving leather. Machter could feel the other body turn, move, fairly writhe to escape the ripping fists, and Machter laughed a little, although he didn't know it.

He brought his left to the jaw, not hard, just priming the clever, dodging head for his right; but when he slung the right, the pain-racked face and wet hair went under it, sliding away. Machter turned, saw Coburn in the middle of the ring. Machter leaned against the angle of rope, an arrogant play, then started to sway in. But the pale figure did not wait; it came to meet him, jolted his head back with lefts, again threw the long right. Machter did not grow angry. He grinned again. A lot of moxie this guy Coburn had, a lot of moxie, but not much stuff left. . . .

Now he had him against the ropes, and as he threw an overhand right, landing high on the once handsome head, the gong sounded. He laughed and dropped his right glove heavily on Coburn's right shoulder.

"Lot of moxie, keed," he said. Machter couldn't hear what the puffed lips replied. He turned away.

Coburn walked to his corner, head hanging despite his knowledge that he should hold it up. The crowd—his crowd, the only one in years to follow a boxer in a day of fighters—liked him to hold it up. Trant met him with a cool, wet sponge.

Coburn said: "What do you think?"

Trant said, "Close," as he spat the swabs from his lips. "You got 'im, though—again." He started to wipe Coburn's body with a dirty towel. He took the dead arms and thrust them through the holes of the robe, pulling the garment tight around Coburn's body. Coburn moved as though without interior volition, on legs held locked and stiff. More than anything else in the world right now, more than desire to hear himself proclaimed winner, he wanted to sit down. But he couldn't. The crowd would have thought it looked funny. . . . You had to stand. . . . Coburn closed his eyes.

"Here it comes," Trant said.

Coburn opened his eyes, turning to the ring. The announcer had two slips of paper in his hand, and was stooping to get a third from a judge reaching up from his little coop by the ring. The announcer looked at the slips a little longer than usual. It must have been close as hell, Coburn thought. Now he knew, but very dimly, the old, repeated tension of the moment before the decision was announced; the kick that always came even when you knew you'd won. The announcer looked up from the slips in his hand, took a single long step toward Coburn, and even as the harsh, full-throated chorus of praise started to rise like some gigantic and invisible flock of birds whirring upward, seized Coburn's right wrist and raised the limp arm high and straight overhead.

The chorus was crescendo now; but interspersed with definite sounds of booing. Through it, as through muffling cloth, came Trant's voice, harsh: "Well, we got 'im again. How many times we got to lick the punk? . . ."

Coburn did not think of this, although he did not know why; rather, it seemed that he knew why, but kept it away from his active consciousness. He turned a little to walk to Machter's corner for the customary amenities. But Machter met him halfway across the ring, grinning, the skirt of his robe billowing a little from the briskness with which he moved.

Machter, too, laid arms on Coburn in the cold, boxer's embrace. He said: "Close one, huh, keed? Every one is a close one. Every one is closer, huh, keed?"

Coburn had murmured the customary, "Good fight, lotta guts, kid." If almost any other fighter but Machter had made Machter's remark, Coburn would have known it to be said for the possible effect. It wasn't that Machter was dumb. It was—well, Coburn didn't know exactly what it was. . . .

He walked back to his corner. The sweat was becoming slightly cold and sticky, and the weight of his weariness eased a very little. Trant and Vanny held the middle rope down, and Coburn climbed through onto the sort of plinth that ran around the outside of the ring. The crowd was still yelling, sporadically now; but as he started down the short, wooden steps, the noise became continuous again, though duller than before. The booing, too, rose, dimly echoing. Coburn forced, half consciously, a smile to his lips, feeling the new, dried cracks in them open again as his mouth curved. The faces before him and at angles as he walked up the aisle had open mouths; some of them bright, admiring eyes. They moved and turned. He should dislike them, but didn't. He'd had the feeling often.

His smile faded as he walked through the entrance under the stands and away from the gaze of the eyes. He could feel the lines of the smile smooth out of his face. He was colder and the weariness, the outer weariness, seemed gone for the moment. Inside him it was different. And not just imagination, he thought. Hell, he knew himself. It was weariness of the inside of his body.

Someone threw open a door and bright yellow light fell upon the concrete runway in a weird oblong. He went into the light, bowing his head against it, closing his eyes. It was warmer here. He lay onto a slanted rubbing table and let them undress him.

## II

Once more the lights blared as would the music of a brassy band, beating down with an intensity that seemed to have the tangibility of a weight. Coburn stood in his corner smiling, smiling brightly, but only with his mouth. The resin rose in invisible waves, making him inhale more deeply.

A hoarse, yelling chorus rose, growing stronger. Coburn knew it was Machter coming down the aisle. He swung into the ring through the ropes, the skirt of his silk robe rising briefly, stiffly, like the short costume of a ballerina. He half trotted across the ring, grinning. "Howdy, keed," he said, and his handclasp through the bandaging was strong and firm; but how much from sincerity and how much from his natural and spilling exuberance, Coburn did not know. He said: "Good; how's yourself?"

"Swell, keed, swell." Machter turned away, laughing a little, half trotting. The lights did not seem quite so oppressive. The old imagination, Coburn thought. He turned to Trant, muttering to himself. Trant tried to be light. He said: "What's the matter, mug? A guy like you shouldn't put money in the bank. He should spend it. If you put it in the bank, someone'll take it away from you with a first mortgage on the Empire State Building."

Presently all the lights were dim except the big, bright ones directly over the ring; these threw their white, even illumination on the soiled canvas, shutting the three within their rays from the outside world as surely as though the line of demarcation between light and dusk was a transparent casing of steel.

The loneliest place in the world. Coburn looked across at the swart figure in the purple-and-blue trunks. Five months had passed since their last meeting. Again Machter had come up, fighting two, three times a month, knocking his men out, technically usually, sometimes clean. Twice Coburn had fought, beating inferior men easily, taking the first five or six rounds, coasting the rest, finishing tired. Tired, but not weary. Only Machter could make him weary. Coburn was thirty-three.

For the first time in his life he hadn't wanted to fight an opponent. This he knew while unadmitting it. . . . Why couldn't he get a crack at the champ, anyhow? He'd beaten everyone else. They had said he must fight Machter again. Machter had beaten others more decisively than Coburn had. Machter had given him a tough go last time. Two judges had voted draw, one for Coburn. They must fight again, winner to meet the champ.

"But I made the punks pay," Trant had squealed. "Thoity-seven an' a half per cent. I made them give it to us." It had annoyed Coburn

at the moment, Trant's exulting over the money. . . .

Coburn looked at the swart figure in the dark trunks. The features, the outline of the head, seemed vague against the tenebrous background, their shapelessness making for an unnatural and sinister air of invincibility. Coburn shook his head as though to clear it. Too damn much imagination. He drew a deep breath, expelled it hard, through the nose.

The gong rasped and he slid out, circling to the right of the crouching, weaving figure. It swung vicious left and right for the body, missing by almost a foot with each. The crowd was raucous. Coburn jabbed the flattened nose twice without a return, moved easily away from the looping left swing. He was a little conscious of the yells. "Give him a boxin' lesson, Billy!" For a moment Coburn forgot himself, went in, snapped lefts easily to the face, whipping his long, swift right over, straight. They yelled. They still went for him, he thought. Then he remembered about saving himself.

At the ringside they said: "Boy, oh boy-howdy, for five roun's they ain't none can hit him with a handful of birdshot. For five roun's they . . ."

Coburn worked in real close, brought his left up in that rarest of punches, a left uppercut, moved under Machter's vicious hook, and standing a little to the side, visibly shook Machter with a right cross.

"Oh, lovely, lovely," someone said in the uproar. . . .

Machter was angry and bleeding. He came in, lips in a snarl. Coburn's left moved more rapidly than the eye could count, not an inch of Machter's face escaping the flickering leather. . . . Coburn moved beautifully, skillfully, cleanly, feet in precise but swift movement, in perfect concatenation with hand and arms as they, too, sped in sure, certain, controlled, if unthought, gesture. Coburn moved as must have moved the Negro, Peter Jackson; as must have moved the Nonpareil.

Machter rushed him clumsily to the ropes, Coburn giving ground easily before the harmless rush. Coburn held Machter's left glove under his right armpit, held Machter's right arm at the crook of the elbow with the notch formed of left thumb and forefinger. They froze still. Like a snake's head, Coburn's left glove went away from Machter's right arm, smacked clean against the dark jaw, then was back, holding. The yelling was of sheer delight.

Machter surged, raging a little; in close, inside his punches, Coburn ran the rough lacing of his right glove across Machter's mouth and nose.

Machter cursed. A left landed low on Coburn's thigh. He danced away, laughing, made Machter look foolish with jabs. . . . Near the end of the round, unconsciously he started to sidle a little toward his corner. He turned, still facing Machter, let the other rush, drew blood from Machter's mouth with stinging jabs. Coburn laughed.

COBURN WAS VERY weary. One eye half-closed but did not hurt. His arms, where they met his body and flowed into the pectorals and trapezii, were so weary as to be near numbness. His neck hurt dully and seemed to have a little crick in it from the crooked, inclined position he held it in to guard his jaw with shoulder and upper arm. One corner of his mouth was slit a little, and he held it unconsciously sucked in. Where the fine muscles of the thigh met, lapping over each other just above the knee, was pain, dull and sheer; and Coburn's legs moved woodenly, almost like those of marionettes, locked. . . . The salt of the blood in his mouth mingled with the taste of the rubber of his mouthpiece. Breathing seared his lungs, and the arches of his feet hurt. He was very weary.

Only his courage was unwearied. It was within him, filling him with that swift and perfect permeability with which light fills a room. It stood in his torn flesh, holding it up. It surged at times with the plangency of surf, sending him against the insistent, pain-giving form before him. Only Coburn's courage was unwearied.

But his body was very weary. And he knew that Machter knew of this. He could tell it from the crooked smile on Machter's face, could tell it from a thing unnamed in Machter, but which in almost anyone else would have been a nonchalance.

The flat-featured, dark face, darker because of the smeared blood, moved on a lower level than Coburn's own face. It seemed to sway alone, projecting a little above and beyond the swaying, weaving body. Under the face, Coburn knew, the dark, wet gloves, pain-laden, moved in small motions.

Now the face came in again as it seemed it had been coming for an interminable time. And again Coburn's left glove, the padding pushed away from the knuckles by Trant's kneading fingers, flickered into motion, spontaneous, automatic, briefly effective. And Coburn's weary legs took him away, still in dancing, sidling motion, grotesque to one who had seen only the first round or two, and then had come back for this one. . . . But there were none who had, and so the change, in the eyes of those who watched, was gradual, not sharply defined . . . and Coburn's leg movements did not look grotesque . . . only a little pathetic; if any of the watchers knew the meaning of the term.

Still the dark, smeared face followed. Now it took the lefts glancingly on its creased forehead . . . and was in, its beard rough against Coburn's shoulder, the fists finding Coburn's twisting, arching body in hard blows, partly blocked.

Coburn panted, his breath rasping past the rubber of the mouthpiece; he would have sobbed had he let himself. Once Machter's right came free, came high, but the wet, clever head on the aching shoulders went inside the bent arm, and the blow shot harmlessly around the neck. Machter relaxed, dropping his arms, and Coburn knew he had done this to show it was not he who was holding. Coburn felt Deady's light, quick slaps knocking his own curled gloves away from Machter's body.

"Break. Come on now, break."

They were apart near the center. A voice was suddenly clear: "Give it to him, baby! He's all through! . . ." And Coburn knew that for a long time he had not heard the voices.

The head and gloves and weaving body came on with a wavelike insistence; and again Coburn's wet, balled glove met the face, flickering over the features. But the flurry was born in part of an unconscious fear; and the long right followed only automatically. Coburn danced away with the spastic puppet motions, danced toward a corner, for it was near the end of the round. Machter came fast, his swinging right driving Coburn against the angle of rope. Coburn gasped, doubling over, yet raising his left arm high for protection rather than dropping it to his body in the more instinctive gesture. He straightened a little. Machter's right was poised for the opening, the face more grimly smiling than ever. He seemed to sense he could put Coburn away whenever he chose, and was waiting, easily; perhaps to make sure, perhaps because he liked to wait. The gong sounded.

The crooked lips opened about a certain laugh; Machter turned and walked all the way across the ring to his own corner. The seat Trant shoved out barely got under Coburn's settling body. Coburn lay against the rope corners, relaxing completely. Water was cool on his head, flowing down his face and dribbling off mouth and nose and chin onto his chest. Trant held the elastic of the trunks away from Coburn's belly and rubbed the heaving muscles. Vanny did not swing the towel. He took Coburn's mouthpiece out, washed it rapidly, put it aside. Then he massaged Coburn's thigh muscles.

Coburn opened his eyes. A boy was walking

slowly around the inside of the ring, holding high a placard with a number on it. Only one number. There was something wrong. There should be two numbers on the card. It was the last round, the tenth. Sure it was. Something partly panic and partly annoyance came to Coburn. He said: "Last round?" His voice sounded husky to himself.

"Nah, Billy." Trant was trying to give his voice an assuring quality. "Nah, Billy. The nint'. You gotta stay away from him, Billy; stay away, an' when he gets in close . . ."

The voice faded. Surely there had been a mistake. He'd never felt so gone at the start of the ninth. At the start of the tenth, yes; but never the ninth. Surely a mistake. The ten-second whistle. Vanny holding the mouthpiece against his lips, waiting for them to open. Trant's bony wrists going under his arms, lifting just after the bell rang.

Still Coburn walked out slowly, more than half expecting Deady to make them touch gloves for the final round. But Deady was near a corner . . . and Machter half way across the dirty canvas. He swung a right from the hip and Coburn only partly blocked it. Coburn moved away, back, left extended. For a time he was swift, but a little startled at his lack of accuracy. Then, gradual but sure, came weariness, creeping through his muscles, seeping into joints. There was the taste of blood.

He saw his own long right flash whitely out, saw the smear on Machter's face darken, grow, fed from a hidden source; perhaps the nose, or the small cut over the eye that he had opened twice tonight. But still, as inevitable as a wind, the figure came on. It made no pretense to defend itself. It took three, five, if necessary, to get one in. But it was rarely necessary.

Things seemed misty. All things but the thing you couldn't see called pain. This and weariness that was like death must be.

He saw the right coming, knew his own left should rise, block—if he were fresher, counter with the same movement. He saw the right coming, raised the left . . . but it seemed something was the matter with his legs . . . and the left didn't get up because something was the matter

with his legs. But it must have gotten up in time because it always had. But it mustn't have this time because—well, because something had happened and he was half lying on the floor, and there was a great, dull noise and pain and dryness of throat. And there was a pounding, definite, regular. And something waving by his face . . . and suddenly Coburn knew it was Deady's arm, counting, keeping time . . . and Coburn knew he had been dropped.

Knocked down. Strange. He had been knocked down before. Ten, twelve or was it fifteen years ago. A long time. He had been knocked down then and had gotten up. He would get up now. He would wait for the nine and get up. He would be smart then and stay away for the rest of the fight, and win. He would be very smart. At nine he would get up and be smart. He wasn't hurt. No pain now. Just kind of tired. The smallest, nearest noise he made out to be—"six—"

He turned over a little, prone, legs sprawled on the floor. His head was bowed, but his bent arms supported his body. He drew up a leg. It was terribly slow. How did your legs get that way? Like wood. Heavy wood. Now he had it up though, foot on the floor. Now the other . . . the other . . . God! Something had happened. He had moved the other foot . . . and then both legs had fallen, straightening out along the floor, and he had fallen and it had all been a little blank . . . and he would have to get up again because he was lying on the canvas full length. . . .

He licked his lips and they were bitter with resin. Now how the hell had that happened? But he'd get up all right. He hadn't been knocked down much in his life; just two or three times in ten or twelve or fifteen years. But he'd always gotten up . . . and he would now . . . and he'd stay away and be smart and win. Now he'd just gather himself and get up . . . but hell he didn't need any help. Why the hell didn't they keep their hands away? He'd get up. He'd always gotten up. He didn't need any help. Why the hell didn't they stay away, keep their hands away? He could have gotten up without them. Hell, he'd . . .

GEORGE BERNARD SHAW once said of Thackeray that he "loved a prize fight as he loved a fool." Thackeray, being dead by then, never denied this, but he did deny, although recognized by friends and journalists at ringside, that he attended the Heenan–Sayers fight, eulogized here in a paraphrase of Macaulay.

Although the Crimean War, which involved England, France, Turkey and Russia, attracted only two special correspondents from the United States, four years later four American newspapers sent reporters across the Atlantic to cover the fight between Tom Sayers, champion of England, and John C. Heenan, champion of America. They met at Farnborough, England, on April 17, 1860, in the first truly international boxing contest, and in the thirty-seventh round, when the 195-pound Heenan seemed about to annihilate his 149-pound opponent, the ropes were cut. The two fought five more rounds until the contest was declared a draw, a decision that ignited the first international post-fight controversy.

# A Lay of Ancient London

## WILLIAM MAKEPEACE THACKERAY

*(Supposed to be recounted to his great-grandchildren, April 17, 1920 A.D., by an Ancient Gladiator.)*

Close round my chair, my children,
    And gather at my knee,
The while your mother poureth
    The Old Tom in my tea:
The while your father quaffeth
    His rotgut Bordeaux wine,—
'Twas not on such potations
    Were reared these thews o' mine.
Such drinks come in the very year
    —Methinks I mind it well—
That that great fight of HEENANUS
    With SAYERIUS befell.
These knuckles then were iron;
    This biceps like a cord;
This fist shot from the shoulder
    A bullock would have floored.
Crawleius his Novice,
    They used to call me then,
In the Domus Savilliana,

Among the sporting men.
There, on benefit occasions,
    The gloves I oft put on,
Walking round to show my muscles
    When the set-to was done;
While ringing in the arena
    The showered denarii fell.
That told Crawleius, Novice
    Had used his mauleys well.
'Tis but some sixty years since
    The times whereof I speak,
And yet the words I'm using
    Will sound to you like Greek.
What know ye, race of milksops,
    Untaught of the P. R.,
What stopping, lunging, countering,
    Fibbing, or rallying are?
What boots to use the *lingo*,
    When you have not the *thing*?
How paint to *you* the glories
    Of BELCHER, CRIBB, or SPRING,—
To *you*, whose sire turns up his eyes
    At mention of the Ring?

Yet, in despite of all the jaw
  And gammon of the time,
That brands the art of self-defense
  —Old England's art—as crime,
From off mine ancient memories
  The rust of time I'll shake,
Your youthful bloods to quicken
  And your British pluck to wake.
I know it only slumbers;
  Let cant do what it will,
The British bulldog *will* be
  The British bulldog still.
Then gather to your grandsire's knee,
  The while his tale is told,
How SAYERIUS and HEENANUS
  Milled in the days of old.

The Beaks and Blues were watching,
  Agog to stop the Mill,
As we gathered to the station
  In the April morning chill.
By twos and threes, by fours and tens,
  To London Bridge we drew;
For we had had the office,
  That were good men and true;
And, saving such, the place of fight
  Was ne'er a man that knew.
From east and west, from north and south,
  The London Fancy poured,
Down to the sporting Cabman,
  Up to the sporting Lord.
From the Horse-Shoe in Titchfield Street,
  Sharp OWEN SWIFT was there;
Old PETER left the Rising Sun,
  All in the street of Air;
LANGHAM forsook his beer-taps,
  With nobby ALEC REED;
And towering high above the crowd
  Shone BEN CAUNT'S fragrant weed.
Nor only fighting covies,
  But sporting swells besides,—
Dukes, Lords, M.P.s, and Guardsmen,
  With county beaks for guides;
And tongues that sway our Senators,
  And hands the pen that wield,
Were cheering on the champions
  Upon that morning's field.

At last the bell is ringing,
  The engine puffs amain,
And through the dark towards Brighton
  On shrieks the tearing train;
But turning off when Reigate
  Unites her clustering lines,
By poultry-haunted Dorking
  A devious course it twines;
By Wotton, Shier, and Guilford,

Across the winding Wey,
  Till by heath-girded Farnborough
Our doubling course we stay,
  Where Aldershort lay snoring
All in the morning gray,
  Nor dreamed the Camp what combat
Should be fought here today!

The stakes are pitched, the ropes are tied,
  The men have ta'en their stand;
HEENANUS wins the toss for place,
  And takes the eastward hand.
CUSICCIUS and MACDONALDUS
  Upon the Boy attend;
SAYERIUS owns BRUNTONUS,
  And JIM WELSHIUS for friend.
And each upon the other now
  A curious eye may throw,
As from the seconds' final rub
  In buff at length they show,
And from their corners to the scratch
  Move stalwartly and slow.
Then each his hand stretched forth to grasp,
His foemen's fives in friendly clasp;
Each felt his balance trim and true,—
Each up to square his mauleys threw;
Each tried his best to draw his man—
The feint, the dodge, the opening plan,
Till left and right SAYERIUS tried;
HEENANUS' grin proclaimed him wide;
He shook his nut, a lead essayed,
Nor reached SAYERIUS' watchful head.
At length each left is sudden flung,
  We heard the ponderous thud,
And from each tongue the news was rung,
  SAYERIUS hath "First blood!"
Adown HEENANUS' Roman nose
Freely the telltale claret flows,
While stern SAYERIUS' forehead shows
That in the interchange of blows
  HEENANUS' aim was good!
Again each iron mauley swung,
And loud the counter-hitting rung,
Till breathless all, and wild with blows,
Fiercely they grappled for a close;
A moment in close hug they swing
Hither and thither, round the ring,
Then from HEENANUS' clinch of brass
SAYERIUS, smiling, slips to grass!

I trow mine ancient breath would fail
  To follow through the fight,
Each gallant round's still changing tale,
  Each feat of left and right.
How through two well-spent hours and more,
  Through bruise, and blow, and blood,
Like sturdy bulldogs, as they were,

Those well-matched heroes stood.
How nine times in that desperate Mill
    HEENANUS, in his strength,
Knocked stout SAYERIUS off his pins,
    And laid him all at length;
But how in each succeeding round
    SAYERIUS smiling came,
With head as cool, and wind as sound,
As his first moment on the ground,
    Still confident, and game.
How from HEENANUS' sledgelike fist
Striving a smasher to resist,
SAYERIUS' stout right arm gave way,
Yet the maim'd hero still made play,
And when infighting threatened ill,
Was nimble in outfighting still,
    Did still his own maintain—
In mourning put HEENANUS' glims;
Till blinded eyes and helpless limbs,
    The chances squared again.
How blind HEENANUS in despite
Of bleeding mug and waning sight
So gallantly kept up the fight,
    That not a man could say
Which of the two 'twere wise to back,
Or on which side some random crack
    Might not decide the day:
And leave us—whoso won the prize,—
Victor and vanquished, in all eyes,
    An equal meed to pay.

Two hours and more the fight had sped,
    Near unto ten it drew,
But still opposed—one-armed to blind,—
    They stood, the dauntless two.
Ah, me, that I have lived to hear
    Such men as ruffians scorned,
Such deeds of valor brutal called,
    Canted, preached down, and mourned!
Ah, that these old eyes ne'er again

A gallant Mill shall see!
No more behold the ropes and stakes,
    With colors flying free!
But I forget the combat—
    How shall I tell the close,
That left the Champion's Belt in doubt
    Between those well-matched foes?
Fain would I shroud the tale in night,—
The meddling Blues that thrust in sight,—
    The ringkeepers o'erthrown;—
The broken ring,—the cumbered fight,—
HEENANUS' sudden, blinded flight,—
SAYERIUS pausing, as he might,
Just when ten minutes used aright
    Had made the fight his own!

Alas! e'en in those brighter days
    We still had Beaks and Blues,—
Still, canting rogues, their mud to fling
On self-defense and on the Ring,
    And fistic arts abuse!
And 'twas such varmint had the power
    The Champion's fight to stay,
And leave unsettled to this hour
    The honors of the day!
But had those honors rested
    Divided as was due,
SAYERIUS and HEENANUS
    Had cut the Belt in two.

And now my fists are feeble,
    And my blood is thin and cold,
But 'tis better than Old Tom to me
    To recall those days of old.
And may you, my great-grandchildren,
    That gather round my knee.
Ne'er see worse men or iller times
    Than I and mine might be,
Though England then had prize fighters—
    Even reprobates like me.

CASTOR AND POLLUX (Polydeuces) were the twin sons of Zeus and fought their way to seats on Olympus. Theocritus, regarded as the creator of pastoral poetry, lived in the third century B.C., and his is one of several versions of the go between the undefeated Pollux and the muscle-bound Amycus.

FROM

# The Dioscuri

## THEOCRITUS

[TRANSLATED BY ANDREW LANG]

WE HYMN THE children twain of Leda, and of aegis-bearing Zeus—Castor and Pollux, the boxer dread, when he hath harnessed his knuckles in thongs of ox-hide. Twice hymn we, and thrice the stalwart sons of the daughter of Thestias, the two brethren of Lacedaemon. . . .

Even already had Argo fled forth from the Clashing Rocks, and the dread jaws of snowy Pontus, and was come to the land of the Bebryces, with her crew, dear children of the gods. There all the heroes disembarked, down one ladder, from both sides of the ship of Iason. When they had landed on the deep seashore and a sea bank sheltered from the wind, they strewed their beds, and their hands were busy with firewood.

Then Castor of the swift steeds, and swart Polydeuces, these twain went wandering alone, apart from their fellows, and marveling at all the various wildwood on the mountain. Beneath a smooth cliff they found an ever-flowing spring filled with the purest water, and the pebbles below shone like crystal or silver from the deep. Tall fir trees grew thereby, and white poplars, and planes, and cypresses with their lofty tufts of leaves, and there bloomed all fragrant flowers that fill the meadows when early summer is waning—dear worksteads of the hairy bees. But there a monstrous man was sitting in the sun, terrible of aspect; the bruisers' hard fists had crushed his ears, and his mighty breast and his broad back were domed with iron flesh, like some statue of hammered iron. The muscles on his brawny arms, close by the shoulder, stood out like rounded rocks that the winter torrent has rolled and worn smooth in the great swirling stream, but about his back and neck was draped a lion's skin, hung by the claws. Him first accosted the champion, Polydeuces.

P. Good luck to thee, stranger, whosoe'er thou art! What men are they that possess this land?

A. What sort of luck, when I see men that I never saw before?

P. Fear not! Be sure that those thou look'st on are neither evil, nor the children of evil men.

A. No fear have I, and it is not for thee to teach me that lesson.

P. Art thou a savage, resenting all address, or some vainglorious man?

A. I am that thou see'st, and on thy land, at least, I trespass not.

P. Come, and with kindly gifts return homeward again!

A. Give me no gifts, none such have I ready for thee.

P. Nay, wilt thou not even grant us leave to taste this spring?

A. That shalt thou learn when thirst has parched thy shriveled lips.

P. Will silver buy the boon, or with what price, prithee, may we gain thy leave?

A. Put up thy hands and stand in single combat, man to man.

P. A boxing match, or is kicking fair, when we meet eye to eye?

A. Do thy best with thy fists and spare not thy skill!

P. And who is the man on whom I am to lay my hands and gloves?

A. Thou see'st him close enough, the boxer will not prove a maiden!

P. And is the prize ready, for which we two must fight?

A. Thy man shall I be called (should'st thou win), or thou mine, if I be victor.

P. On such terms fight the red-crested birds of the game.

A. Well, be we like birds or lions, we shall fight for no other stake.

So AMYCUS SPOKE, and seized and blew his hollow shell, and speedily the long-haired Bebryces gathered beneath the shadowy planes, at the blowing of the shell. And in like wise did Castor, eminent in war, go forth and summon all the heroes from the Magnesian ship. And the champions when they had strengthened their fists with the stout ox-skin gloves, and bound long leathern thongs about their arms, stepped into the ring, breathing slaughter against each other. Then had they much ado, in that assault—which should have the sun's light at his back. But by thy skill, Polydeuces, thou didst outwit the giant, and the sun's rays fell full on the face of Amycus. Then came he eagerly on in great wrath and heat, making play with his fists, but the son of Tyndarus smote him on the chin as he charged, maddening him even more, and the giant confused the fighting, laying on with all his weight, and going in with his head down. The Bebryces cheered their man, and on the other side the heroes still encouraged stout Polydeuces, for they feared lest the giant's weight, a match for Tityus, might crush their champion, in the narrow lists. But the son of Zeus stood to him, shifting his ground again and again, and kept smiting him, right and left, and somewhat checked the rush of the son of Poseidon, for all his monstrous strength. Then he stood reeling like a drunken man under the blows, and spat out the red blood, while all the heroes together raised a cheer, as they marked the woeful bruises about his mouth and jaws, and how, as his face swelled up, his eyes were half closed. Next the prince teased him, feinting on every side, but seeing now that the giant was all abroad, he planted his fist just above the middle of the nose, beneath the eyebrows, and skinned all the brow to the bone. Thus smitten, Amycus lay stretched on his back, among the flowers and grasses. There was fierce fighting when he arose again, and they bruised each other well, laying on with hard weighted gloves; but the champion of the Bebryces was always playing on the chest, and outside the neck, while unconquered Polydeuces was smashing his foeman's face with ugly blows. The giant's flesh was melting away in his sweat, till from a huge mass he soon became small enough, but the limbs of the other waxed always stronger, and his color better, as he warmed to his work.

How then, at last, did the son of Zeus lay low the glutton? Say goddess, for thou knowest, but I, who am but the interpreter of others, will speak all that thou wilt, and in such wise as pleases thee.

Now behold the giant was keen to do some great feat, so with his left hand he grasped the left of Polydeuces, stooping slantwise from his onset, while with his other hand he made his effort, and drove a huge fist up from his right haunch. Had his blow come home, he would have harmed the King of Amyclae, but he slipped his head out of the way, and then with his strong hand struck Amycus on the left temple, putting his shoulder into the blow. Quick gushed the black blood from the gaping temple, while Polydeuces smote the giant's mouth with his left, and the close-set teeth rattled. And still he punished his face with quick-repeated blows, till the cheeks were fairly pounded. Then Amycus lay stretched all on the ground, fainting, and held out both his hands, to show that he declined the fight, for he was near to death.

There then, despite thy victory, didst thou work him no insensate wrong, O boxer Polydeuces, but to thee he swore a mighty oath, calling his sire Poseidon from the deep, that assuredly never again would he be violent to strangers.

378

FEW WRITERS of fiction have understood and enjoyed the realm of the fighter as did Charles Emmet Van Loan, who wrote this in 1913 for the *Saturday Evening Post*. He was discovered, ten years earlier, in San Francisco by T. A. Dorgan, who recommended him to the New York *Journal* and started a chain reaction. In Denver, Van Loan discovered Damon Runyon and recommended him to the New York *American*. He also, in Chicago, persuaded Ring Lardner to send some baseball fiction to the *Saturday Evening Post*.

# One-Thirty-Three—Ringside

## CHARLES E. VAN LOAN

CHARLES FRANCIS HEALY, known to all the world as "Young Sullivan," sat on the edge of his bed and stared incredulously at Billy Avery, his manager, press agent and bosom friend.

"Naw," said Healy, shaking his head, "you don't mean that, Billy. You're only kidding."

"It ain't what *I* mean, Charles," said Avery, discouragement showing in the dispirited droop of his shoulders and the flat tones of his voice. "It's what Badger means that cuts the ice. I talked to him for four hours—the obstinate mule!—and that's the very best we get—one-thirty-three at the ringside."

"But, man alive," wailed the little fighter, "that's murder in the first degree! He'd be getting me in the ring so weak that a featherweight could lick me!"

"Yes," said Avery, "and he knows that as well as you do. That's what he's playing for—a cinch."

"The public won't stand for it!" stormed Healy.

"The public be damned!" said Billy Avery, unconsciously quoting another and greater public character. "It stands for anything—everything. We're on the wrong side of this weight question, Charles. Badger has got the champion, and it's just our confounded luck that Cline can do one-thirty-three and be strong. Cline won it from Fisher at one-thirty-three ringside, and Badger says that every man who fights Cline for the title must make the same weight—the lightweight limit."

"Huh!" snarled Healy. "There ain't any such thing as a limit! I notice that they called Young Corbett a champion after he licked McGovern, and Corbett couldn't get within a city block of the featherweight limit! They make me sick! It's the champion that makes the weight limit—not the rules!"

"All true," said Avery; "and that's exactly why we're up against it. Cline can do the weight. Badger opened up and talked straight off his chest, Charlie. He says he isn't anxious to fight us because he's got softer matches in sight where Cline won't have to take a chance. He thinks that this weight restriction will stop us bothering him with challenges and chasing him around the country with certified checks and things. I hollered like a wolf for one-thirty-five at three in the afternoon, and he only laughed at me. 'We're not fighting welters, this season,' he says. 'One-thirty-three ringside, or nothing. Take it or leave it.' The Shylock!"

"Well, leave it, then!" said Healy angrily. "If Mike Badger thinks I'm sucker enough to cut off an arm and a leg, just to get a fight with that hunk of cheese that he's managing, he's got another guess coming. I'll go into the welterweight class first!"

"Y-e-e-s," said Avery slowly, "and there isn't a welter in the country today that would draw a two-thousand-dollar house. I suppose we'll have to go back to the six- and ten-round no-decision things, splitting the money even, and agreeing to box easy! Yah! A fine game, that is."

"I suppose you think I ought to grab this fight with Cline?" It was more than a question; it was an accusation.

"Well," said the business manager, looking at the ceiling, for he had no wish to meet Young Sullivan's eyes just then, "the bank roll ain't very fat, Charlie. We could use a few thousand, you know, and there's more money in losing to Cline—don't get excited, kid; let me talk—than we could get by winning from a flock of pork-and-bean welters. That fight would draw forty thousand if it draws a cent. If you *win*—and it's no cinch that Cline will be as good as he was two years ago—we can clean up a fortune the first year, like shooting fish!"

"If I win!" said Healy bitterly. "I tell you, it'll *murder* me to get down to one-thirty-three! I'd have to cut the meat right off to the bone to do it. You know I made one-thirty-five for Kelly, and it was all I could do to outpoint him in twenty rounds when I should have stopped him with a punch!"

"The loser's end ought to be eight thousand, at least," said Avery, still looking at the ceiling. "And in case you don't get him, you've got a fine alibi—the weight stopped you. It was your stomach that bothered you in the Kelly fight, remember that."

"See here, Billy," said Charles Francis, "you want me to fight Cline, don't you? Even at one-thirty-three?"

"We need the money," said the manager simply.

"I'll gamble you!" said Healy, producing a silver half-dollar. "Heads, I fight him; tails, I don't. Will you stick by it, Billy, if it comes tails?"

"Sure!" said the manager. "Will you go through with it if she comes heads?"

"It's a promise!" said Healy.

The coin spun, flickering, in the air, struck the carpet, and rolled to the fighter's feet.

"Heads!" he groaned. "I lose, Billy!"

WHENEVER A SPORTING writer had reason to rake over his vocabulary for the sort of an adjective which should best fit Mike Badger, manager of "Biddy" Cline, the choice usually lay between two words. The scribes who liked Mike selected "astute." The others said he was "obstinate." Both were right.

To be absolutely fair in the matter, Mike was neither better nor worse than any other manager. Only wiser. When he made a business contract, he was prudent enough to demand at least seventy-five per cent the best of the bargain, and tenacious enough to hold out until he got it. Mike simply did what the other fellows would have done if they had been given the opportunity, and everyone knows what an unprincipled course that is to pursue. One fight promoter, hoping to secure certain concessions and smarting under Mike's steady refusal to recede from the original proposition, burst out thus:

"Ain't you got any sportsmanship in you at all?"

"Not a stitch," answered Mike. "Sportsmanship and business are two different things. I'm a businessman, and you know my terms. I've got something to sell—buy it or let it slide."

In the "good old days," which some of the scarred bare-knuckle veterans still mourn with sorrowful pride, a fighter needed no business manager for the excellent reason that fighting was not then a business. It was a habit. With the era of large purses and profitable theatrical engagements came the shrewd businessman, and Mike Badger was the shrewdest of them all. He could smell a five-dollar note farther than a bird dog can smell a glue factory.

A champion is the greatest asset a wise manager can have—and vice versa. The very word "champion" is a valuable trade-mark. It means easy money, free advertising, and last and most important, the right to dictate terms. Every ambitious fighter dreams of winning a title some day; the man who has one dreams only of keeping it until the last dollar has been squeezed out and then retiring undefeated.

It is because of the financial value of this trade-mark that championships are so carefully guarded. It is easier to hale a multimillionaire before an investigating committee than it is to get a champion of the world into the ring with a fighter who has an even chance to defeat him. All sorts of tactics are used in order to sidestep dangerous matches. Managers of heavyweights, lacking poundage restrictions, often bid the ambitious challenger goodbye until such time as he has secured a reputation, fondly hoping that in the process he will be soundly licked and eliminated. Managers of bantams, feathers, and lightweights insist that husky aspirants shall "do the weight, ringside." Many a man has saved his title by starving an opponent for a week before a match. The old-time bare-knuckle warriors sneer at this sort of thing. They were used to making matches, "give or take ten pounds," but, as has been pointed out, they were not businessmen. The slogan "May the best man win" has been changed to "May the best-managed man win."

Biddy Cline was a great little fighter—probably the greatest at his weight that the ring had seen during his generation. He was no boxer, but a sturdy, willing, courageous chap, who began fighting when the bell rang and continued to fight as long as the other man could stand in front of him. His record was black with knockouts, though Biddy was not the typical one-punch fighter. His victims succumbed to the cumulative effect of a thousand blows as well as the terrific pace they were compelled to travel. It was a very strong lightweight indeed who could play Cline's game with the champion and hear the gong at the end of the fifteenth round. Biddy's best fighting weight was slightly below one-thirty-three, he had held the championship for three years and, under Mike Badger's careful guidance, expected to hold it for three years more.

Charles Francis Healy had been a large, sharp thorn in the champion's side for some time. He was a dashing, sensational performer, a clever boxer, a hard, clean hitter, and a tremendous finisher—the very ideal of the average fight follower. He had beaten nearly all the men whom Cline had defeated—most of them in shorter fights—but this was only natural, as Healy's best fighting weight was close to one hundred and forty pounds. When he trained below one hundred and thirty-eight he was sacrificing strength and stamina, and one hundred and thirty-five pounds at three in the afternoon was the lowest notch he had been able to make with any degree of safety. In spite of this, Billy Avery challenged the champion once a month with clocklike regularity, and was as frequently informed that the holder of the title had other pressing matters on his hands. The end of Avery's campaign had been the private conference with Badger and the latter's ultimatum:

"One-thirty-three ringside, or no fight."

Then, with the hardihood of a man who gambles when he knows he cannot afford to lose, Healy had risked certain defeat on the flip of a coin.

The match was made with a tremendous thrumming of journalistic tom-toms, and sporting America sat up cheerfully, for this was the one great fight it really wished to see. When the articles of agreement were drawn up—a queer document, half legal, half sporting in its phraseology—Mike Badger dropped a large fly in Billy Avery's ointment. It came with the dictation of the forfeiture clause—Mr. Badger speaking:

"For weight, five thousand dollars; for appearance,—"

"Hold on, there!" yelled Avery. "Who ever heard of a weight forfeit of five thousand dollars?"

"You did—just now," said the imperturbable Mike, with a grin. "I'm going to make it an object for your man to do one-thirty-three. I've had fighters forfeit their weight money on me before this."

Avery argued and Healy glared across the table at Biddy Cline, who glared back, such conduct being customary in the presence of newspapermen; but Mike was firm as Gibraltar.

"Here's the point, gentlemen," said he, ignoring the sputtering Avery. "I don't want this man to come into the ring weighing a ton. This fight is to be for the lightweight championship of the world, at the lightweight limit. If we are overweight, we shall expect to forfeit five thousand dollars. If Avery's man can't do one-thirty-three, I want to know it now. If he *can* make it, why should he object to a large forfeit? Come on, Avery. Now's your chance to spring some of those certified checks you've been flashing around the country so recklessly!"

In the end Mike Badger won out, as was his habit. Billy Avery had the added worry of knowing that his entire fortune, as well as the sweepings and scrapings of Healy's bank roll, was forfeit unless the challenger reached the lightweight limit.

"We're hooked," said Avery gloomily, when he was alone with his warrior. "If the weight forfeit had been a thousand bucks or so, we could have let it slide and still made money; but now it's one-thirty-three or bust!"

"Bust is good!" said Healy. "We bust if we don't and we bust if we do. You might have known that Badger would slip one over on you somehow. A fine mess you've got us in, Billy!"

"Me?" exclaimed the manager, virtuously indignant. "Say, what's the matter with you? Who offered to toss the coin? Whose idea was that?"

"Shucks!" growled Healy. "I only did that because I knew you intended to make the match anyway."

"You took a chance—"

"Yes; and so did Steve Brodie," interrupted the fighter. "He ought to have had his head examined for doing it, and I'm worse, because Steve had a chance to win and I haven't. I was kind of figuring on forfeiting my weight money if I saw I couldn't get that low without trouble; but now I've got to hang up my hat in a Turkish bath joint for a week before that fight, and I'll be as weak as a kitten! You're one swell manager, you are!"

"And you're a grand squealer," said Avery. "Your own proposition and now you blame me."

Thus, with mutual reproaches and a general disarticulation of family skeletons, the challenger and his manager set out to secure training quarters for the coming event, the shadow of which loomed dark about them.

## II

"Can Healy do the weight and be strong?"

This momentous question agitated every sporting center in the country. It was discussed as far away as London, Paris and Melbourne. Men wrote about it, talked about it, argued about it; and all agreed that the outcome of the match hinged upon the correct answer, and nowhere was there such uncertainty as in Healy's training camp. There were only two men who really knew, and they were not committing themselves. Even the trainer was excluded from the daily weighing process.

The newspapermen argued that the public had a "right to know", spies from the other camp nosed about daily; betting men begged the lowdown and on-the-level; curious ones sought to satisfy their curiosity; close personal friends went away disappointed. Billy Avery would talk about everything but the weight, and when that subject was mentioned, he became an oyster, gripping tight the pearl of information. Healy had but one answer: "See Billy about it."

The best judges had no chance to form an opinion, for they never saw Healy stripped. Whenever he appeared in the gymnasium he was loaded down with sweaters and woolens.

Public opinion was divided. Half the fight followers inclined to the belief that Healy could not make the weight and was therefore secretive; the other half pointed out that Avery might be preparing an unpleasant surprise for the opposition.

"He's keeping Cline guessing," said the optimistic ones. "If he couldn't make the weight, he'd have been a fool to post five thousand bucks."

At the end of three weeks Mike Badger received a telephone message from Billy Avery. He hung up the receiver with a hard little edge of a smile, for he had been expecting something of the sort.

"They're on the run, Biddy," he remarked to his champion. "Avery wants to see me tonight— on the strict QT. I knew that big sucker couldn't do the weight, or anywhere near it!"

"Did he say so?" asked the literal Cline.

"Bonehead!" retorted Mike. "He didn't have to *say* it. What else could he want to see me about? I'll call the turn now—he wants to rat out on their forfeit. A swell chance he's got!"

"Serves 'em right for going around the country trying to make a bum out of me!" said Cline feelingly. "Hand it to 'em good, Mike!"

"That's the best thing to do," remarked Mr. Badger.

The real heart-to-heart business of the fight game is transacted without witnesses, and it shrinks from publicity. The newspapermen were not invited to attend the moonlight conference of the managers, and the meeting was as secret as if they had been preparing to dynamite a national bank.

"Hello, Mike!" said Avery. "Have a cigar?"

"Thanks! Well, out with it! What's on your mind?"

"I wanted to have a chat with you about this weight proposition," said Avery.

"Haven't you got a copy of the articles of agreement?"

"Yes," said Billy.

"Well, if I remember," said Badger calmly, "it says there that the men are to do one-thirty-three, ringside. Is that correct?"

"Yes."

"That's all there is to it," said Badger. "Have you just found out that Healy can't get down that low?"

"He can get down there, all right," said Avery, "but it'll weaken him pretty bad. Chances are it won't be a very good fight. Can't we get together somehow—and give the people a run for their money? Suppose we should come in a pound or so overweight. You wouldn't grab that forfeit, would you?"

"Why wouldn't I?" asked Badger grimly. "That's business, ain't it? A contract is a contract, and it ain't my fault that you went into this thing without knowing whether your man could do the weight or not. You came to me and asked me for this match. I wasn't anxious to make it, but I turned down some good theatrical offers and signed up. You mustn't expect me to lose money on your mistakes. My dough is posted, and I'm going to carry out my part of the contract. You must do the same thing. I wouldn't let you come in a pound over, or an ounce over. One-thirty-three, ringside, and you'll do it, or I'll claim your five thousand."

"Looking for a cinch, ain't you?" sneered Avery.

"You bet I am; and if you had a champion you'd be looking for cinches, too! Now, I'm going to tell you something else: Don't pull any of that moth-eaten stuff about breaking a hand or an arm or a leg, and having to call off the match. I won't stand for it. I'll claim your appearance money, and I'll show you up from one end of the country to the other."

"Won't you listen to *reason?*" begged Avery.

"I haven't heard any, yet," said Badger, "and, what's more, I've said all I'm going to. Better have your man down to weight if you want to save that forfeit. I never make any agreements on the side, and when I sign my name to a thing I go through. Good night."

Avery went home, talking to himself. Healy was waiting for him.

"What luck?" asked the fighter anxiously. "Would he do business?"

"Of course, he wouldn't! He's got us, and he knows it. Shylock was a piker beside this guy!"

"I can break my leg," suggested Healy hopefully.

"Yes, and he'll send out a flock of doctors to examine you, and they'll all be from Missouri. It'll take something more than a lot of bandages and a crutch to get by this bird. He'll snatch our appearance money and put us in Dutch all over the country."

"But we've got to do something!" There was a note of desperation in Healy's voice. "Typhoid fever might bring me down to weight; but it's a cinch sweating won't do it. One-thirty-nine tonight, and I've done enough work already to sweat an elephant to a shadow. I simply *can't* make it, and that's all there is to it. You know what the doctor said—that this excess baggage is due to natural growth. It's in the bone and muscle, and it won't come off! Why the devil didn't we think of that before we got hooked in so strong?"

"Give me a chance to think," said Avery. "I may dig up a way to wriggle out of this match and save the appearance money, anyway. You tear into the hay and leave it to me."

"I wish you'd done your thinking before we made this match!" sighed Healy.

"There you go again!" mumbled Avery. "Always putting it up to me! Didn't you toss a coin, and—"

"I've heard all that before," said Healy. "By the way, there was a man here to see you about eight o'clock. Says he'll be back about ten."

"Another nut!" growled the manager.

"Not this fellow," said Healy. "He looks like class, and he's got a letter for you—from Jim Quinn.'"

"Quinn!" said Avery. "Holy cat! I wish Jim was here. He might think of some way to get us out of this jam."

Promptly at ten o'clock the stranger returned. He was small, neatly dressed, of middle age, and wore a close-trimmed beard and nose glasses. He presented Quinn's letter without comment:

*DEAR BILLY: I don't know how you're fixed on the weight proposition, but the last time I saw Healy he was falling away to a mere cartload, and I don't think he can do one hundred and thirty-three ringside without the aid of a saw. On the chance that you've got a bad match on your hands, I am sending Mr. George Harden to see you. George is an expert in his line, knows how to keep his mouth shut, and you can bank on anything he tells you being right.*

*Of course, if Healy can do one hundred and thirty-three without weakening himself, you won't need Harden. If he can't, put Harden on the job. I can't explain here, for obvious reasons, but Harden can make your man a winner, and save you the weight forfeit. Wire me three days before the fight whether I can bet on Healy or not. Yours in haste,*

*JAS. QUINN*

Billy folded the letter and placed it in his pocket.

"This listens well," said he slowly. "What's the idea?"

"The idea is that I can put your man in the ring as strong as he is now and save you the weight forfeit. It'll cost you five hundred dollars."

"It would be worth it," said Avery. "My boy is having trouble getting down to weight. We didn't figure that he has put on several pounds by growth and development, and it's coming off hard."

"I'll take him the way he is," said Harden, "and make him weigh one-thirty-three—on any scales they pick out."

"A fake?" demanded Avery suddenly.

"Yes, and a darned good one," said Harden.

Avery shook his head.

"Mike Badger is a pretty wise bird," said he. "He's seen the chewing-gum trick and the little chunk of lead, and all that. I'd hate to try and get by him with a weight-stealing device."

"Has he seen this, do you think?" asked Harden, drawing something from his pocket.

"What is it?" demanded Avery, staring at what appeared to be a stiff black thread in the palm of Harden's hand.

"Nothing but an innocent little piece of horsehair," said the visitor quietly. "Do you think he's seen that?"

"Horsehair is a new one to me," said Avery. "How does it work?"

"That's *my* business," said Harden. "Leave me alone with your weighing machine for a few minutes and I'll give you a demonstration."

"Fair enough!" said Avery, leading the way.

THREE DAYS BEFORE the fight Billy Avery presented himself at the office of the promoter of pugilistic events—a wise young man of Hebraic extraction.

"Moe," said Billy, "have you made any arrangements about the scales the men are to weigh in on?"

"Not yet," said Goldstein. "Why?"

"Well, this is a special occasion," said Avery, "and I want a pair of scales that there can't be any question about. I've got a lot of money up and I can't afford to take chances."

"You don't want to use your own, do you?" asked Moe slyly.

"No, and I don't want to use Mike Badger's, either!" snapped Billy angrily. "We're going to be at weight, right enough, but we'll just barely make it and that's all. It'll be so close that there won't be any fun in it, and that darned Shylock says that if we're an ounce over he'll grab the five thousand. Now, I wish you'd write a letter to some reputable hardware concern and ask 'em to send you a brand-new weighing machine to be used at the ringside. They probably have an expert, too, and they might be willing to send him along. I want the scales tested by a government official and balanced by a man who hasn't the slightest interest in the fight either way. I'm not going to monkey with 'em myself, and I want Badger to keep *his* hands off. There ain't much that fellow wouldn't do for five thousand bucks! Is that a fair proposition?"

"As fair as a June day!" replied Goldstein. "I'll write a letter to Messmore & Jones immediately."

Avery smoked a cigar while the letter was written, and after that he chatted about the coming fight, the advance sale, the probable "cut," and kindred topics. When he rose to go, he picked up the envelope containing the letter.

"I'll drop this in the mail chute when I go out," he said.

The next day the office boy brought Mr. Goldstein a neatly engraved business card, bearing the name of a firm of national reputation as manufacturers of scales. In the lower left-hand corner appeared these words:

"Presented by Mr. Henry C. Darling, Western Representative."

Goldstein tossed the card over to Mike Badger, who happened to be present.

"Let's see what he wants," said Goldstein.

Mr. Henry C. Darling proved to be a dapper little person, with a close-cropped beard and nose glasses. He spoke with the crisp, incisive tones of a businessman, and Mike Badger, surreptitiously running his thumbnail over the pasteboard which he held, was impressed. An engraved card, to ninety-nine men out of one hundred, is a convincing argument; an embossed trade-mark in three colors in the upper corner clinches matters.

"Mr. Darling—Mr. Badger," said Goldstein.

"I beg pardon—I didn't quite catch the name," said the visitor. It had to be repeated, and even then it was evident that it meant nothing to the Western representative, who turned immediately to Goldstein.

"I happened to be calling on Mr. Messmore when your letter arrived," said Darling. He produced Goldstein's letter and laid it upon the desk. "Mr. Messmore suggested that as you needed an expert, it was more in my line than his. I will be very glad to accommodate you. If you will tell me where you wish the scales delivered and when, the details will be attended to."

"I wouldn't want to take up your time—" began Goldstein.

"Oh, that's all right!" chirped Mr. Darling. "It will be a pleasure to do it, I assure you. As a matter of fact, I am—ah—rather interested in the manly art myself. My son is an amateur boxer—you may have heard of him? Peter C. Darling, Chicago Athletic Club? No? Only sixteen years old, but clever as they make 'em! I like to see a good bout when I can."

"Of course!" said Moe. "Why not?" He reached into his desk and brought forth a ticket. "Here's a box seat for the show Friday night."

Mr. Darling fairly gushed thanks as he put the ticket carefully away in his pocketbook.

"Very, very kind of you, I'm sure!" he said. "Now, it is understood that I am to furnish a new weighing machine which shall be tested and certified correct by the Board of Weights and Measures on Friday afternoon. I will then take charge of it myself and deliver it at the fight pavilion that night. Is that satisfactory?"

"Suits *me!*" said Badger, thumbing the card.

Mr. Darling paused at the door, and there were traces of nervous hesitation in his voice when he spoke.

"May I suggest—ah—that the name of my firm—or my own name—does not appear in the newspapers?" he asked. "This is—ah—rather an unusual service, and—"

"I understand!" said Moe heartily. "You'll be kept under cover, all right. Only three people need to know who you are—the other one is Avery."

Mr. Darling seemed immensely relieved.

"If you are interested in seeing the scales tested," said he, "come to the Bureau of Weights and Measures at four o'clock on Friday afternoon."

"I'll be there," said Mr. Badger. "Moe, you notify Avery."

Mr. Goldstein looked after his visitor with a grin.

"Ain't it funny what some people will do for a free fight ticket?" he remarked. "There's a traveling man whose time is worth money, yet he's willing to go to fifty dollars' worth of trouble to get a twenty-dollar seat! Can you beat it?"

"It saves paying him a fee," said the frugal Badger. "And did you get that about not wanting his name in the paper? I'll bet he's a deacon in a church or something, when he's home!"

### III

THE OFFICIAL TESTING of the scales took place on schedule time. The shiny, new weighing machine—of the portable platform variety— balanced to a hair. Mr. Badger almost precipitated a fight by remarking over and over again that an ounce might mean five thousand dollars, and every time he said it Avery snarled.

"Now, gentlemen, if you are satisfied," said Mr. Darling, "we will ask that the scales be placed under lock and key here until I shall call for them this evening. I guarantee that they will not be out of my sight from that time until you are ready to use them. Is that satisfactory?"

"Perfectly!" said Mike Badger, and Billy Avery mumbled something under his breath.

"Well, old top," chuckled Badger to Avery, as they left the room, "my man is under weight. How's yours?"

"We may have to sweat him a bit," answered Avery shortly, "but I'd cut off one of his legs before I'd let you have that five thousand!"

"Cut off his head, instead," suggested Badger pleasantly. "He never uses that when he fights!"

"You make me sick!" growled Avery.

The weight of the contender was still a mystery, but there was an unconfirmed rumor that Moe Goldstein—sworn to secrecy—had been present at the Healy camp on Thursday afternoon and had seen the challenger raise the beam at one hundred and thirty-four pounds. This may have had something to do with the flood of Healy money which appeared as if by magic.

Shortly after the doors of the fight pavilion were opened an express wagon drove up to the main entrance and the weighing machine was carefully unloaded, under the personal supervision of Mr. Henry C. Darling. Moe Goldstein, who was standing in the door, cheerfully contemplating the long line of humanity stretching away from the general-admission window, waved his cigar at Darling and grinned.

"You're here early enough, I see!" remarked the promoter.

"Better early than late!" said Mr. Darling. "Is there a room where we can lock this thing up until it's wanted? I have made myself personally responsible for it."

"Put it in the first dressing room," said Moe. "You can't lock the door, though, except from the inside."

A few minutes later the "Western representative" was alone with the weighing machine, behind a locked door. In two seconds he had the wooden platform unshipped and set aside, exposing the levers underneath. These levers, sensitive to the touch as human ingenuity can make them, are V-shaped and meet in the center, forming an X, the short lever passing underneath the long one.

Mr. Darling whipped a black horsehair from his pocket, tested it carefully for strength, and then bound it about both arms of the short lever, some three inches above the point of contact in the center. Instead of tying the hair in a knot, he fastened it with a dab of beeswax, replaced the floor of the platform, weighed himself carefully, nodded approvingly, and left the room. The entire operation had consumed less than a minute. The next time that Moe Goldstein looked in that direction Mr. Darling was standing in front of the closed door, like a sentinel on guard.

Two tremendous roars announced the entry of the gladiators, naked, save their socks and bathrobes. Behind them came four strong young men carrying the weighing machine, Mr. Darling trotting behind and urging them to handle it as they would a crate of eggs.

Biddy Cline, grinning in his corner, looked up at his manager.

"Here's where we get that five thousand!" he said.

In silence and breathless curiosity the house waited the weighing-in ceremony.

Mr. Henry C. Darling, fussy and important, fluttered about like an old hen, commanding everyone to stand back while he demonstrated that the scales balanced to a hair. At a signal, the fighters rose from their corners and climbed through the ropes, their handlers trooping after them.

"Stand back, everybody!" chirped Mr. Darling. "We must have room here! Stand back! You observe that the scales balance perfectly. I will set the bush poise exactly at one hundred and thirty-three pounds—no more and no less. On the dot. So! Now, then, gentlemen, who goes first?"

Charlie Healy, who had been removing his socks, slipped his bathrobe from his shoulders and stood forth, naked.

"Might as well get it over with!" he said.

Mike Badger, his thin arms folded over his flat chest, flashed a keen, appraising glance at the challenger, as if anticipating the verdict of the scales. Healy's face was lean and leathery, and his cheekbones stood out prominently, but he had not the haggard, drawn appearance of a man who had sapped his vitality by making an unnatural weight, and his muscular armament bulked large under his smooth, pink skin.

"In great shape!" thought Badger. "But he's heavy, good Lord, he's heavy! He ain't anywhere near one-thirty-three!"

Healy stepped gently upon the scales and dropped his hands at his sides. Mike Badger bent forward, his gimlet eyes fixed upon the notched beam. He expected it to rise with a bump, instead of which it trembled slightly, rose half an inch, and remained there, quivering.

"Just exactly!" chirped Mr. Darling. "Next!"

Charlie Healy threw his hands over his head with a wild yell of triumph.

"By golly, I made it! I made it!" he shouted; and then, as if carried away by an excess of feeling, he jumped six inches in the air and alighted upon his heels with a jar that made the weighing beam leap and rattle, and brought a sudden, sharp strain upon the concealed levers—enough of a strain, let us say, to snap a strand of horse-hair and allow it to fall to the floor. Healy's action was natural enough, but it was his jump which roused Mike Badger to action and crystallized his suspicion. He had seen that sort of thing before.

"No, you don't!" howled Mike. "You ain't going to put anything like that across on me! I want to look at those scales!"

The "Western representative" bristled with sudden anger, strutting about like an enraged bantam rooster.

"Preposterous!" he said. "Examine them yourself!"

He pushed the weighing machine over toward Badger. Mike removed the wooden platform in a twinkling and bent over the levers. That was the reason he did not see Mr. Darling place the sole of his foot upon a dab of beeswax and the horse-hair which clung to it, removing the only bit of evidence.

Sweating and swearing, Mike Badger sought earnestly for wads of chewing gum or other extraneous matter, after which fruitless quest he demanded that Healy weigh again. By this time the challenger was in his corner, calmly partaking of a bowl of beef tea.

"Well, I should say we won't weigh him again!" said Avery. "You've examined the scales, and they're all right. My man has got a pound of beef tea in him by now. He made the weight at the time set, and we won't weigh again. Ain't that right, Goldstein?"

The promoter nodded.

"Go on and weigh your man, Badger," he said. "The crowd is getting restless."

"But I tell you we've been jobbed!" wailed Mike. "Why, *look* at that fellow! He's as big as a house."

"Forget it!" growled Avery. "My boy has been at weight for the last three days! You saw him weigh yesterday, didn't you, Moe?"

"That's right, Mike," said Goldstein.

"I dare you to put him on the scales again!" raved Badger. "I'll give you a thousand dollars if you'll weigh him *now!*"

"And him full of beef tea? I should say you would! G'wan and get your champion on there!"

Mr. Henry C. Darling, still bristling in a quiet, gentlemanly manner, stepped forward to adjust the plummet on the notched bar, but Mike swept him aside.

"That'll be about all for you!" he said brusquely. "I'll attend to this myself!"

And Billy Avery was so well pleased with the turn of events that he allowed Mike to weigh his own man. The bar did not rise for Cline. He was safe by a full pound and a half.

He was far from safe after the fight started, however. Biddy Cline, tough little battler that he was, found himself as helpless as a toy in the hands of the challenger. In the clinches, which were Biddy's specialty, Healy worried him and tossed him about like a rag doll.

"This guy is strong as a middleweight!" panted the champion, after the third round. "See the way he hauls me around? It's a job, Mike, as sure as you live!"

"We can't help it now," said Badger. "You've got to lick him if it kills you!"

Let it be placed to Biddy's credit that he did his honest best to follow out instructions. He set a slashing, whirlwind pace, fighting with the desperation of one who feels his laurels slipping away from him; but Healy met him considerably more than halfway, and after the tenth round the most rabid Cline sympathizer in the house was forced to admit that the end was only a matter of time.

The championship of the world passed in a spectacular manner toward the end of the fifteenth round. Cline, knowing that he had been badly beaten thus far, summoned every ounce of his reserve strength and hurled himself upon the challenger in a hurricane rally, hoping to turn the tide with one lucky blow. Healy, cautious, cool, and steady as a boxing master, waited until the opening came, and then shot his right fist to the point of the chin. The little champion reeled, his hands dropped at his sides, and a vicious short left hook to the sagging jaw ended the uneven battle.

Biddy Cline took the long count for the first time in his life, and a dapper gentleman in a box seat smiled through his nose glasses and played with a bit of horsehair in his pocket. Such a trivial thing had changed the pugilistic map.

According to custom, the conqueror offered his hand to the conquered before he left the ring. Biddy would have taken it, but Mike Badger restrained him.

"Don't shake with him!" said Mike. "You've been licked, but by a welterweight."

"You think anybody will believe that?" cackled Healy.

"I'll make 'em before I'm through," said Mike grimly.

## IV

The new champion ceased in the midst of the pleasant duty of inscribing his name and title upon photographs.

"Badger!" he said. "What does he want, Billy?"

"Don't know. He's coming right up."

Mike Badger entered and helped himself to a chair. "You're a nice pair of burglars, ain't you?" he demanded.

"You're a sorehead," said the new champion cheerfully. "Are you still harping on that weight business? Everybody in the country is giving you the laugh!"

"Oh, you think so, do you?" said Mike. "I've been doing a little detective work lately. That fellow—that Darling—I've been on his trail, and I know all—"

"I didn't have a thing to do with him," protested Avery quickly. "Goldstein wrote a letter to a hardware firm and—"

"And *you* posted it," said Mike. "Remember that? I happened to keep his business card, so yesterday I wired his firm asking for information. Here's the answer." He tossed a telegram across to Avery.

"It says there," remarked Mr. Badger, "that no such man is known to the concern. It was a smooth trick, Billy, but it won't do. I'm going to show you fellows up from one end of the country to the other, and I'll never quit hounding you until you give us another match—at the proper weight. And what's more, we still claim the championship." He picked up one of the new photographs and read the inscription scornfully. "Lightweight champion of the world!" he said. "You ain't a lightweight any more'n I am!"

"Well," said Charlie Healy softly, "they're still pointing me out on the street as the man that licked Biddy Cline– That's good enough for me."

GOADED BY THE fight mob, an old champion comes back.


FROM THE

# Aeneid


## VIRGIL

[TRANSLATED BY H. H. BALLARD]


After the races were run, and all the prizes awarded,
"Now," Aeneas exclaimed, "if any be bold and courageous,
Let him stand forth with his hands and arms enveloped in gauntlets."
Having said this he announced a twofold reward for the contest;
Unto the victor a bull bedecked with gold and with fillets,
And to console the vanquished, a sword and a marvelous helmet.
Instantly, waiting for naught, gigantic and powerful Dares
Lifted his head, and stood mid the loud acclaim of the heroes;
Dares, the only man who used to stand out against Paris:
He, too, it was, by the tomb where Hector the mighty lies buried,
Butes, the giant, smote, the victor who haughtily boasted
Kinship with Amycus' line by descent from Bebrycian princes,
Stretching him hurt to the death on the yellow sand. Such is Dares,
Who is now tossing his head on high for the opening combat,
Vaunting his shoulders' breadth, and his arms, one after the other,
Stretching defiantly forth, and beating the air with a flourish.
Where is his mate to be found? Not one in the whole great assembly
Ventures to meet this man, or to put on the gauntlets against him.
Eagerly, therefore, believing that all have withdrawn from the contest,
Facing Aeneas he stands, and short is his limit of patience,
Then by the left horn seizing the bull; "O son of a goddess,
Since there is none," he cries, "dares trust himself to the battle,
What is the term of delay? How long is it meet to detain me?
Bid me lead off my prize!" The Trojans, all shouting together,
Roar their assent, and demand the promised reward for the hero.
Frowning Acestes, then, with irony lashes Entellus,
Next unto whom he reclines on the verdant couch of the hillside,
"Ah, Entellus! in vain the bravest of heroes aforetime,
Dost thou so meekly allow such prizes, without any contest,
Thus to be won? Where now is that Eryx we worshiped, whom vainly
Thou for thy trainer hast claimed? Where now is thy fame which o'ershadowed
All the Trinacrian isle; and those trophies that hung in thy palace?"
Quickly he answered, "Not quenched by fear is my passion for glory,
Or my desire for praise; but age is retarding the icy
Flow of my blood, and the languishing forces congeal in my body.

Had I what once I had, and in which yon braggart confiding,
Vaunteth himself; were mine that youth which has long since departed,
Lured by no thought of a prize, nor hope of a beautiful bullock,
Would I have come! nor now do I tarry for gifts!" and so speaking,
Into the midst he hurled a pair of ponderous gauntlets.
Eyrx the dauntless with these had once been wont to do battle,
Binding on hand and arm these thongs of well-seasoned bull's hide.
Hearts were appalled; seven folds of the hides of bulls so enormous
Stiffened in rigid coils, insewn with lead and with iron.
Dares, himself, was the first to draw back from the sight in confusion;
E'en the brave son of Anchises was moved by the terrible weapons,
While, now this way, now that, he turned the huge links of the cestus.
　　Then the old hero flung forth from his heart these words of defiance:—
"What, then, if one could have seen the arms, and looked on the gauntlets
Hercules owned; and have viewed upon this very shore the grim battle!
Eryx once wore these arms, yes, Eryx, the son of thy mother;
Still canst see how with blood and with brains they are stained and bespattered,
'Gainst the great son of Alcaeus with these did he stand; and I used them
Long as more vigorous blood gave strength; while Age, my dread rival,
Had not yet whitened my locks, not scattered his frost on my temples
But, if your Dares of Troy object to these arms of our choosing,
If good Aeneas approve, and Acestes, my sponsor, be willing,
Make me the fight more fair; I spare you the bull's hide of Eyrx;
Banish thy fear; yet thou must relinquish those Ilian gauntlets."
Having thus spoken, he flung from his shoulders the folds of his mantle;
Then the huge joints of his limbs, his powerful frame, and great muscles
Baring, gigantic he stood in the midst of the yellow arena.
Father Aeneas, then, with gauntlets more fairly proportioned
Bound with equal arms the palms of both the contestants.
　　Instantly both stand forth, with body erect, and on tiptoe;
High aloft in the air his arms each fearlessly raises;
Back, far away from the stroke, their high-flung heads they are tossing;
Hands intermingle with hands; they challenge each other to combat;
That one, the better of foot, on the quickness of youth is reliant,
This one excels in the bulk of his limbs, but his knees' tardy hinges
Fail, and his giant frame is racked by laborious breathing.
Many blows in vain do the champions thrust at each other;
Many on echoing ribs they rain; and loudly they thunder
Full on the chest, while hands about ears and temples are playing
Heavy and fast, and jaws 'neath terrible buffets are cracking.
Firmly Entellus stands, and, fixed in the same alert posture,
Only with body and vigilant eye is avoiding the gauntlets;
Dares, like one who assails a fortified city with engines,
Or with tented array besieges a hill-crowning fortress,
Craftily tries now these and now the other approaches,
Circling the ring, and attacking in vain with varied maneuvers.
Rising against him, Entellus outstretches his right and uplifts it
High overhead; but his foe, as the blow comes down from above him,
Quickly foresees, and escapes by a sudden swerve of his body.
Wasting his strength on the air, Entellus, untouched by his rival,
By his own ponderous bulk overborne, lurching heavily forward,
Falls to the earth; as oft upon Mount Erymanthus or Ida,
Pine trees, hollow and huge, have suddenly fallen uprooted.
Teucrian men and Trinacrian youth spring up in confusion;
Rises a shout to the sky, and Acestes is first to run forward,
And in compassion uplift from the earth the old friend of his boyhood.
But, unhurt by his fall, and wholly undaunted, the hero

Keener returns to the fight, and rouses his strength by his fury;
Shame and conscious worth are also rekindling his vigor;
Fiercely o'er all the plain he drives the fugitive Dares;
Now and again his blows with right and left hand are redoubled.
Neither delay nor rest; with strokes as incessant as hailstones
Rattling from cloud to roof, with blow after blow is the hero
Ceaselessly buffeting Dares and driving him o'er the arena.
    Father Aeneas, now, not brooking so violent passion,
Also restraining Entellus from growing too bitter in temper,
Instantly ends the fight, and rescues discomfited Dares,
Comforts his heart with words, and thus addresses him kindly:
"Ill-fated man! What madness so great hath o'ermastered thy spirit!
Dost thou not recognize here the might and displeasure of Heaven?
Yield to the god." He speaks, and speaking closes the contest.
Faithful young comrades, however, lead Dares away to the galleys,
Dragging his faltering knees, his head all listlessly swaying,
Spitting thick gore from his mouth, and teeth with blood intermingled.
Then they are summoned back and awarded the sword and the helmet,
While they resign to Entellus the bull and the glory of conquest.
Then cries the victor, elated in mind, and proud of his bullock,
"Child of a goddess, and Teucrians all, be taught by this token
Both what strength was mine ere age had enfeebled my body,
And from what death redeemed ye have rescued the life of this Dares."
When he has uttered these words he turns and faces the bullock
Which, as the gift of the fight, is standing beside him; then, backward
Raising his hand on high, he dashes the terrible gauntlet
Midway the horns, through skull, and bursting brain, to the brain pan.
Staggers the bull, and falls, head foremost, trembling and lifeless.
Standing above it, such words as these he pours from his bosom:
"Better than Dares' death, this life do I pay thee, O Eryx!
Here, as a victor, henceforth resigning my art and my gauntlets."

THIS COLUMN APPEARED, on February 12, 1953, in the Seattle *Post-Intelligencer*. It tells, with great beauty, not only of the end of a fine prospect but of one of the great teacher-trainer-managers.

# End of the Line for Leo

## EMMETT WATSON

IT WAS LATE afternoon and there were a few people hanging around the gym watching Harry Mathews skip rope. Jack Hurley motioned toward the back room, which was bare of furniture and looked out on First Avenue. Leo Lokovsek propped himself on the window ledge and looked down at the people hurrying about their business.

The side of his face away from the window was shadowed, and you could hardly see the jagged scars around his cheek, ear and temple. It had been three weeks now since the automobile crash outside Everett; three weeks since they had called the priest to the hospital where Leo lay unconscious for twelve hours.

"I got you down here," Hurley said, "to tell you that Leo is through. He isn't going to fight no more."

Lokovsek had come into the gym, feeling well, ready to work out. The Deacon called him into the office, where he told him: "You're all through." Lokovsek argued and pleaded. The X rays had shown no fracture; the doctor had assured him his head was sound.

Hurley tried to explain how it was with Ernie Schaaf, when Primo Carnera killed him with a light left jab. He told him about Lem Franklin, who had a previous head injury that nobody knew about, and how Franklin collapsed and died in the ring without being hit a solid punch.

"Not if all the doctors in the Mayo Clinic told me this boy could fight," Hurley said. "Not even then. He's finished."

"Would you fight for somebody else, Leo?"

Hurley answered the question. "I can't control his life," the Deacon said. "What he does is his own business now. But I think I've convinced him he shouldn't."

Lokovsek nodded.

It was easy then to remember the months of patient training in the gym, the long lean strong body, with the sharp reflexes, the smooth blend of balance and leverage. Experts conceded Lokovsek was a real possibility. It was easy to remember the night in Hoquiam, his first fight, his first knockout, how he drew the deep breath of satisfaction and there was nothing ahead but fight and build-up and fight again—with perhaps a fortune waiting.

Nothing had changed except, possibly, a minute broken blood vessel in his head; something Hurley was afraid of.

"You're young," Hurley said. "You've got a wife and baby to look out for. You got your whole life ahead of you, and if you've got the guts to fight, you should have the guts to start over."

Hurley walked to the door, paused and turned. The steel-rimmed glasses and the tight mouth gave his face a prissy expression.

"They'll come at you," he was saying, in a soft voice. "They'll come at you with money. Parasites. They'll give you money to fight again, because they know you're good and they know they can get it back out of you. Don't go.

"Just remember, I could let you fight. I chase a buck as hard as any man. I could use you for a year in easy fights and then I could back off. I like money real well, but I won't make my money that way."

Hurley went through the door and on out into the gym. Lokovsek was staring hard at his fists, clenched in his lap, and it was easy to think how things might have been.

The build-up already was well on its way. Even now, in the East, they are waiting the word on Hurley's heavyweight. Lokovsek was a natural for the build-up, with his easy, friendly ways, handsome, photogenic face, and a deep, warm sense of humor.

"When he first told me," the fighter said, "I got all sorts of crazy notions. I went away from him mad and disappointed, and I thought about getting somebody else to manage me. I was going to show him.

"Then I remembered something that happened in that fight in Vancouver. The guy was mussing me up a little. I got a flash of Jack in my corner and I remember thinking: 'Nobody can beat me. I'm Hurley's fighter.' Then I knew that Jack was right, and I would have to quit."

Outside the lights were coming on and traffic thickened in the streets. The faint sound of a bag being punched came through the walls, and Leo again looked down at his hands.

"I was going to do so much," he said. "I was going to be champion of the world. All through my life I'll wonder if I could have made it. Now I'll never know."

TOO FEW WRITERS have availed themselves of the knowledge of Abe Attell. After all, he survived 166 fights, eleven years as featherweight champion, eleven managers and the charge that he did the leg work for Arnold Rothstein in the X (as Pierce Egan would have put it) that was the 1919 World Series. Here he is, in 1950, on the lost science of carrying.

# Abe Attell Takes the Stand

## JOE WILLIAMS

IT IS TO BE doubted that Abe Attell will ever be canonized in the Cooperstown Monastery due to certain vague peccadilloes dating back to 1919, but in the fight racket the old featherweight champion commands respect.

I do not claim to have been the first white child born on the banks of the Mississippi but I did see Attell fight twice. Down through the years I've seen all the other featherweight champions. Only three or four stand out. Johnny Kilbane, Johnny Dundee, Tony Canzoneri and Willie Pep. But Attell still leads 'em all in my book.

"You gotta put Pep up near the top," Attell said as we sat in Shor's discussing tonight's title fight with Saddler in Yankee Stadium. "He learned his trade good. And he's got it up here, too." Attell tapped his head. Nothing rattled either. . . . "Still I can't go for him in this one. I'm afraid the old guy's caught up with him." The old guy being, I was amazingly quick to sense, Father Time.

Attell, fighting twenty-rounders at sixteen, had held the featherweight championship eleven years when Kilbane took it from him.

"I think Kilbane had the best one-two punch of all us little fellows," Attell said. "Yet he seldom made a sensational fight. That was because he wouldn't take no chances. Nobody ever hit him when he was good, you know—and he never started a punch until he was sure it was going to land first."

A long time ago Benny Leonard, on the subject of Kilbane, had said to me: "The Mick was just yellow enough to be a great fighter."

Attell blinked. You could see he found it hard to associate the opprobrious adjective with a champion. "Overcautious," he finally compromised.

Attell was twenty-nine when he lost his title. Pep, at twenty-eight, is spotting Saddler four years tonight. Attell got $15,000 against Kilbane. Pep figures to pull down close to $75,000.

"Naturally, we didn't get the dough fighters get today," Attell admitted. "But I used to do all right. Better 'n some of the big guys. If it was a betting fight I always bet on myself, usually my whole end. Like the night I fought Freddie Weeks in 'Frisco. I win $10,000."

Attell had been at the ringside the night Ray Robinson took particular pains not to overbruise little Charley Fusari in a fight which interested the insiders very keenly. The betting was 2½ to 1 Fusari would be on his feet at the finish. He was. Everybody seemed to agree the welterweight champion had carried Fusari, and not for reasons of mercy. Attell frowned. "It was not a pro job. You could see the rough edges from the back rows."

An old pro was talking. Attell grew humpbacked carrying fighters in his day. But he was a consummate artist. It takes superlative skill to make a bad fighter look good. Attell made 'em look great. And there'd always be a demand for a return bout—which was the main idea from the start. Then if the return was a betting fight

Attell would send it in and go to work on the startled young man in front of him.

"The trick was to let the yokel hold you even," Attell said. "In those days the newspapers gave the decisions. I always felt I'd turned in a bad job when they gave me a shade. The line I liked to read was: 'The champion was entitled to no more than a draw.'"

Old-timers still jabber about the fight Attell had with England's Jem Driscoll. Versions differ. I didn't see it. Driscoll was the best boxer John Bull ever developed, fast and smart with it. Some say Attell had a bad night. Others insist the Britisher stabbed him silly.

"I was saving him for 'Frisco," Attell explained. "Jim Coffroth (the promoter out there) and I had it all arranged in advance. Another thing, Charley Harvey had Driscoll, and Harvey was just like this with Little and Big Tim Sullivan, Tammany big shots. They were at ringside that night. I decided it would be wise to make everybody happy."

Years back I had discussed this particular fight with Harvey and what he said supports Attell's disclosure—"For his inches and pounds Attell was the greatest fighter I ever saw."

Incidentally, while Attell may have made the Sullivan boys and others happy that night he wasn't to get another crack at Driscoll. Coffroth had the fight booked but it never took place. Driscoll cabled from London. "I can't make it. I'm sick."

"So was I," Attell grimaced. "I had $20,000 bet on myself."

---

## CARTOON

## W. F. BROWN

TO THE ARENA

*"You seldom see a much harder left to the midsection."*

THE TENDER-HEARTED heavyweight has always been a mark for humorists. Wilberforce Billson, a sort of Bermondsey Saint Bernard, turns up three times in *He Rather Enjoyed It,* the saga of Stanley Featherstonehaugh Ukridge, first published in 1924.

# The Debut of Battling Billson

## P. G. WODEHOUSE

IT BECOMES INCREASINGLY difficult, I have found, as time goes by, to recall the exact circumstances in which one first became acquainted with this man or that; for as a general thing I lay no claim to the possession of one of those hair-trigger memories which come from subscribing to the correspondence courses advertised in the magazines. And yet I can state without doubt or hesitation that the individual afterward known as Battling Billson entered my life at half-past four on the afternoon of Saturday, September the tenth, two days after my twenty-seventh birthday. For there was that about my first sight of him which has caused the event to remain photographically limned on the tablets of my mind when a yesterday has faded from its page. Not only was our meeting dramatic and even startling, but it had in it something of the quality of the last straw, the final sling or arrow of outrageous Fortune. It seemed to put the lid on the sadness of life.

Everything had been going steadily wrong with me for more than a week. I had been away, paying a duty visit to uncongenial relatives in the country, and it had rained and rained. There had been family prayers before breakfast and bezique after dinner. On the journey back to London my carriage had been full of babies, the train had stopped everywhere, and I had had nothing to eat but a bag of buns. And when finally I let myself into my lodgings in Ebury Street and sought the soothing haven of my sitting room, the first thing I saw on opening the door was this enormous redheaded man lying on the sofa.

He made no move as I came in, for he was asleep; and I can best convey the instantaneous impression I got of his formidable physique by saying that I had no desire to wake him. The sofa was a small one, and he overflowed it in every direction. He had a broken nose, and his jaw was the jaw of a Wild West motion-picture star registering Determination. One hand was under his head; the other, hanging down to the floor, looked like a strayed ham congealed into stone. What he was doing in my sitting room I did not know; but, passionately as I wished to know, I preferred not to seek firsthand information. There was something about him that seemed to suggest that he might be one of those men who are rather cross when they first wake up. I crept out and stole softly downstairs to make inquiries of Bowles, my landlord.

"Sir?" said Bowles, in his fruity ex-butler way, popping up from the depths accompanied by a rich smell of finnan haddie.

"There's someone in my room," I whispered.

"That would be Mr. Ukridge, sir."

"It wouldn't be anything of the kind," I replied, with asperity. I seldom had the courage to contradict Bowles, but this statement was so wildly inaccurate that I could not let it pass. "It's a huge redheaded man."

"Mr. Ukridge's friend, sir. He joined Mr. Ukridge here yesterday."

"How do you mean, joined Mr. Ukridge here yesterday?"

"Mr. Ukridge came to occupy your rooms in your absence, sir, on the night after your departure. I assumed that he had your approval.

He said, if I remember correctly, that 'it would be all right.' "

For some reason or other which I had never been able to explain, Bowles's attitude toward Ukridge from their first meeting had been that of an indulgent father toward a favorite son. He gave the impression now of congratulating me on having such a friend to rally round and sneak into my rooms when I went away.

"Would there be anything further, sir?" inquired Bowles, with a wistful half-glance over his shoulder. He seemed reluctant to tear himself away for long from the finnan haddie.

"No," I said. "Er—no. When do you expect Mr. Ukridge back?"

"Mr. Ukridge informed me that he would return for dinner, sir. Unless he has altered his plans, he is now at a matinee performance at the Gaiety Theater."

The audience was just beginning to leave when I reached the Gaiety. I waited in the Strand, and presently was rewarded by the sight of a yellow mackintosh working its way through the crowd.

"Hallo, laddie!" said Stanley Featherstonehaugh Ukridge, genially. "When did you get back? I say, I want you to remember this tune, so that you can remind me of it tomorrow, when I'll be sure to have forgotten it. This is how it goes." He poised himself flat-footedly in the surging tide of pedestrians and, shutting his eyes and raising his chin, began to yodel in a loud and dismal tenor. "Tumty-tumty-tumty-tum, tum tum tum," he concluded. "And now, old horse, you may lead me across the street to the Coal Hole for a short snifter. What sort of a time have you had?"

"Never mind what sort of a time I've had. Who's the fellow you've dumped down in my rooms?"

"Redhaired man?"

"Good Lord! Surely even you wouldn't inflict more than one on me?"

Ukridge looked at me a little pained.

"I don't like this tone," he said, leading me down the steps of the Coal Hole. "Upon my Sam, your manner wounds me, old horse. I little thought that you would object to your best friend laying his head on your pillow."

"I don't mind your head. At least I do, but I suppose I've got to put up with it. But when it comes to your taking in lodgers—"

"Order two tawny ports, laddie," said Ukridge, "and I'll explain all about that. I had an idea all along that you would want to know. It's like this," he proceeded, when the tawny ports had arrived. "That bloke's going to make my everlasting fortune."

"Well, can't he do it somewhere else except in my sitting room?"

"You know me, old horse," said Ukridge, sipping luxuriously. "Keen, alert, farsighted. Brain never still. Always getting ideas—bing—like a flash. The other day I was in a pub down Chelsea way having a bit of bread and cheese, and a fellow came in smothered with jewels. Smothered, I give you my word. Rings on his fingers and a tie pin you could have lit your cigar at. I made inquiries and found that he was Tod Bingham's manager."

"Who's Tod Bingham?"

"My dear old son, you must have heard of Tod Bingham. The new middleweight champion. Beat Alf Palmer for the belt a couple of weeks ago. And this bloke, as opulent-looking a bloke as ever I saw, was his manager. I suppose he gets about fifty per cent of everything Tod makes, and you know the sort of purses they give for big fights nowadays. And then there's music-hall tours and the movies and all that. Well, I see no reason why, putting the thing at the lowest figures, I shouldn't scoop in thousands. I got the idea two seconds after they told me who this fellow was. And what made the thing seem almost as if it was meant to be was the coincidence that I should have heard only that morning that the Hyacinth was in."

The man seemed to me to be rambling. In my reduced and afflicted state his cryptic method of narrative irritated me.

"I don't know what you're talking about," I said. "What's the Hyacinth? In where?"

"Pull yourself together, old horse," said Ukridge, with the air of one endeavoring to be patient with a half-witted child. "You remember the Hyacinth, the tramp steamer I took that trip on a couple of years ago. Many's the time I told you all about the Hyacinth. She docked in the Port of London the night before I met this opulent bloke, and I had been meaning to go down next day and have a chat with the lads. The fellow you found in your rooms is one of the trimmers. As decent a bird as ever you met. Not much conversation, but a heart of gold. And it came across me like a thunderbolt, the moment they told me who the jeweled cove was, that if I could only induce this man Billson to take up scrapping seriously, with me as his manager, my fortune was made. Billson is the man who invented fighting."

"He looks it."

"Splendid chap—you'll like him."

"I bet I shall. I made up my mind to like him the moment I saw him."

"Never picks a quarrel, you understand—in

fact, used to need the deuce of a lot of provocation before he would give of his best; but once he started—golly! I've seen that man clean out a bar at Marseilles in a way that fascinated you. A bar filled to overflowing with A.B.s and firemen, mind you, and all capable of felling oxen with a blow. Six of them there were, and they kept swatting Billson with all the vim and heartiness at their disposal, but he just let them bounce off, and went on with the business in hand. The man's a champion, laddie, nothing less. You couldn't hurt him with a hatchet, and every time he hits anyone all the undertakers in the place jump up and make bids for the body. And the amazing bit of luck is that he was looking for a job ashore. It appears he's fallen in love with one of the barmaids at the Crown in Kennington. Not," said Ukridge, so that all misapprehension should be avoided, "the one with the squint. The other one. Flossie. The girl with the yellow hair."

"I don't know the barmaids at the Crown in Kennington," I said.

"Nice girls," said Ukridge, paternally. "So it was all right, you see. Our interests were identical. Good old Billson isn't what you'd call a very intelligent chap, but I managed to make him understand after an hour or so, and we drew up the contract. I'm to get fifty per cent of everything in consideration of managing him, fixing up fights, and looking after him generally."

"And looking after him includes tucking him up on my sofa and singing him to sleep?"

Again that pained look came into Ukridge's face. He gazed at me as if I had disappointed him.

"You keep harping on that, laddie, and it isn't the right spirit. Anyone would think that we had polluted your damned room."

"Well, you must admit that having this coming champion of yours in the home is going to make things a bit crowded."

"Don't worry about that, my dear old man," said Ukridge, reassuringly. "We move to the White Hart at Barnes tomorrow, to start training. I've got Billson an engagement in one of the preliminaries down at Wonderland two weeks from tonight."

"No; really?" I said, impressed by this enterprise. "How did you manage it?"

"I just took him along and showed him to the management. They jumped at him. You see, the old boy's appearance rather speaks for itself. Thank goodness, all this happened just when I had a few quid tucked away. By the greatest good luck I ran into George Tupper at the very moment when he had had word that they were

going to make him an under-secretary or something—I can't remember the details, but it's something they give these Foreign Office blokes when they show a bit of class—and Tuppy parted with a tenner without a murmur. Seemed sort of dazed. I believe now I could have had twenty if I'd had the presence of mind to ask for it. Still," said Ukridge, with a manly resignation which did him credit, "it can't be helped now, and ten will see me through. The only thing that's worrying me at the moment is what to call Billson."

"Yes, I should be careful what I called a man like that."

"I mean, what name is he to fight under?"

"Why not his own?"

"His parents, confound them," said Ukridge, moodily, "christened him Wilberforce. I ask you, can you see the crowd at Wonderland having Wilberforce Billson introduced to them?"

"Willie Billson," I suggested. "Rather snappy."

Ukridge considered the proposal seriously, with knit brows, as becomes a manager.

"Too frivolous," he decided at length. "Might be all right for a bantam, but—no, I don't like it. I was thinking of something like Hurricane Hicks or Rock-Crusher Riggs."

"Don't do it," I urged, "or you'll kill his career right from the start. You never find a real champion with one of these fancy names. Bob Fitzsimmons, Jack Johnson, James J. Corbett, James J. Jeffries—"

"James J. Billson?"

"Rotten."

"You don't think," said Ukridge, almost with timidity, "that Wildcat Wix might do?"

"No fighter with an adjective in front of his name ever boxed in anything except a three-round preliminary."

"How about Battling Billson?"

I patted him on the shoulder.

"Go no farther," I said. "The thing is settled. Battling Billson is the name."

"Laddie," said Ukridge in a hushed voice, reaching across the table and grasping my hand, "this is genius. Sheer genius. Order another couple of tawny ports, old man."

I did so, and we drank deep to the Battler's success.

My formal introduction to my godchild took place on our return to Ebury Street, and—great as had been my respect for the man before—it left me with a heightened appreciation of the potentialities for triumph awaiting him in his selected profession. He was awake by this time and moving ponderously about the sitting room, and he looked even more impressive standing than he had appeared when lying down. At our first meeting, moreover, his eyes had been closed in sleep; they were now open, green in color, and of a peculiarly metallic glint which caused them, as we shook hands, to seem to be exploring my person for good spots to hit. What was probably intended to be the smile that wins appeared to me a grim and sardonic twist of the lip. Take him for all in all, I had never met a man so calculated to convert the most truculent swashbuckler to pacifism at a glance; and when I recalled Ukridge's story of the little unpleasantness at Marseilles and realized that a mere handful of half a dozen able-bodied seamen had had the temerity to engage this fellow in personal conflict, it gave me a thrill of patriotic pride. There must be good stuff in the British Merchant Marine, I felt. Hearts of oak.

Dinner, which followed the introduction, revealed the Battler rather as a capable trencherman than as a sparkling conversationalist. His long reach enabled him to grab salt, potatoes, pepper, and other necessaries without the necessity of asking for them; and on other topics he seemed to possess no views which he deemed worthy of exploitation. A strong, silent man.

That there was a softer side to his character was, however, made clear to me when, after smoking one of my cigars and talking for a while of this and that, Ukridge went out on one of those mysterious errands of his which were always summoning him at all hours, and left my guest and myself alone together. After a bare half-hour's silence, broken only by the soothing gurgle of his pipe, the coming champion cocked an intimidating eye at me and spoke.

"You ever been in love, mister?"

I was thrilled and flattered. Something in my appearance, I told myself, some nebulous something that showed me a man of sentiment and sympathy, had appealed to this man, and he was about to pour out his heart in intimate confession. I said yes, I had been in love many times. I went on to speak of love as a noble emotion of which no man need be ashamed. I spoke at length and with fervor.

"R!" said Battling Billson.

Then as if aware that he had been chattering in an undignified manner to a comparative stranger, he withdrew into the silence again and did not emerge till it was time to go to bed, when he said "Good night, mister," and disappeared. It was disappointing. Significant, perhaps, the conversation had been, but I had been rather hoping for something which could have been built up into a human document, entitled "The Soul of the Abysmal Brute," and sold to some editor for

that real money which was always so badly needed in the home.

Ukridge and his *protégé* left next morning for Barnes and, as that riverside resort was somewhat off my beat, I saw no more of the Battler until the fateful night at Wonderland. From time to time Ukridge would drop in at my rooms to purloin cigars and socks, and on these occasions he always spoke with the greatest confidence of his man's prospects. At first, it seemed there had been a little difficulty owing to the other's rooted idea that plug tobacco was an indispensable adjunct to training: but toward the end of the first week the arguments of wisdom had prevailed and he had consented to abandon smoking until after his debut. By this concession the issue seemed to Ukridge to have been sealed as a certainty, and he was in sunny mood as he borrowed the money from me to pay our fares to the Underground station at which the pilgrim alights who wishes to visit that Mecca of East End boxing, Wonderland.

The Battler had preceded us and, when we arrived, was in the dressing room, stripped to a breath-taking semi-nudity. I had not supposed that it was possible for a man to be larger than was Mr. Billson when arrayed for the street, but in trunks and boxing shoes he looked like his big brother. Muscles resembling the hawsers of an Atlantic liner coiled down his arms and rippled along his massive shoulders. He seemed to dwarf altogether the by no means flimsy athlete who passed out of the room as we came in.

"That's the bloke," announced Mr. Billson, jerking his red head after this person.

We understood him to imply that the other was his opponent, and the spirit of confidence which had animated us waxed considerably. Where six of the pick of the Merchant Marine had failed, this stripling could scarcely hope to succeed.

"I been talkin' to 'im," said Battling Billson.

I took this unwonted garrulity to be due to a slight nervousness natural at such a moment.

" 'E's 'ad a lot of trouble, that bloke," said the Battler.

The obvious reply was that he was now going to have a lot more, but before either of us could make it a hoarse voice announced that Squiffy and the Toff had completed their three-round bout and that the stage now waited for our nominee. We hurried to our seats. The necessity of taking a look at our man in his dressing room had deprived us of the pleasure of witnessing the passage of arms between Squiffy and the Toff, but I gathered that it must have been lively and full of entertainment, for the audience seemed in excellent humor. All those who were not too busy eating jellied eels were babbling happily or whistling between their fingers to friends in distant parts of the hall. As Mr. Billson climbed into the ring in all the glory of his red hair and jumping muscles, the babble rose to a roar. It was plain that Wonderland had stamped our Battler with its approval on sight.

The audiences which support Wonderland are not disdainful of science. Neat footwork wins their commendation, and a skillful ducking of the head is greeted with knowing applause. But what they esteem most highly is the punch. And one sight of Battling Billson seemed to tell them that here was the Punch personified. They sent the fighters off to a howl of ecstasy, and settled back in their seats to enjoy the pure pleasure of seeing two of their fellow men hitting each other very hard and often.

The howl died away.

I looked at Ukridge with concern. Was this the hero of Marseilles, the man who cleaned out barrooms and on whom undertakers fawned? Diffident was the only word to describe our Battler's behavior in that opening round. He pawed lightly at his antagonist. He embraced him like a brother. He shuffled about the ring, innocuous.

"What's the matter with him?" I asked.

"He always starts slow," said Ukridge, but his concern was manifest. He fumbled nervously at the buttons of his mackintosh. The referee was warning Battling Billson. He was speaking to him like a disappointed father. In the cheaper and baser parts of the house enraged citizens were whistling "Comrades." Everywhere a chill had fallen on the house. That first fine fresh enthusiasm had died away, and the sounding of the gong for the end of the round was greeted with censorious catcalls. As Mr. Billson lurched back to his corner, frank unfriendliness was displayed on all sides.

With the opening of the second round considerably more spirit was introduced into the affair. The same strange torpidity still held our Battler in its grip, but his opponent was another man. During round one he had seemed a little nervous and apprehensive. He had behaved as if he considered it prudent not to stir Mr. Billson. But now this distaste for direct action had left him. There was jauntiness in his demeanor as he moved to the center of the ring; and, having reached it, he uncoiled a long left and smote Mr. Billson forcefully on the nose. Twice he smote him, and twice Mr. Billson blinked like one who has had bad news from home. The man who had

had a lot of trouble leaned sideways and brought his right fist squarely against the Battler's ear.

All was forgotten and forgiven. A moment before the audience had been solidly anti-Billson. Now they were as unanimously pro. For these blows, while they appeared to have affected him not at all physically, seemed to have awakened Mr. Billson's better feelings as if somebody had turned on a tap. They had aroused in Mr. Billson's soul that zest for combat which had been so sadly to seek in round one. For an instant after the receipt of that buffet on the ear the Battler stood motionless on his flat feet, apparently in deep thought. Then, with the air of one who has suddenly remembered an important appointment, he plunged forward. Like an animated windmill he cast himself upon the bloke of troubles. He knocked him here, he bounced him there. He committed mayhem upon his person. He did everything to him that a man can do who is hampered with boxing gloves, until presently the troubled one was leaning heavily against the ropes, his head hanging dazedly, his whole attitude that of a man who would just as soon let the whole matter drop. It only remained for the Battler to drive home the final punch, and a hundred enthusiasts, rising to their feet, were pointing out to him desirable locations for it.

But once more that strange diffidence had descended upon our representative. While every other man in the building seemed to know the correct procedure and was sketching it out in nervous English, Mr. Billson appeared the victim of doubt. He looked uncertainly at his opponent and inquiringly at the referee.

The referee, obviously a man of blunted sensibilities, was unresponsive. Do It Now was plainly his slogan. He was a businessman, and he wanted his patrons to get good value for their money. He was urging Mr. Billson to make a thorough job of it. And finally Mr. Billson approached his man and drew back his right arm. Having done this, he looked over his shoulder once more at the referee.

It was a fatal blunder. The man who had had a lot of trouble may have been in poor shape, but, like most of his profession, he retained, despite his recent misadventures, a reserve store of energy. Even as Mr. Billson turned his head, he reached down to the floor with his gloved right hand, then, with a final effort, brought it up in a majestic sweep against the angle of the other's jaw. And then, as the fickle audience, with swift change of sympathy, cheered him on, he buried his left in Mr. Billson's stomach on the exact spot where the well-dressed man wears the third button of his waistcoat.

Of all human experiences this of being smitten in this precise locality is the least agreeable. Battling Billson drooped like a stricken flower, settled slowly down, and spread himself out. He lay peacefully on his back with outstretched arms like a man floating in smooth water. His day's work was done.

A wailing cry rose above the din of the excited patrons of sport endeavoring to explain to their neighbors how it had all happened. It was the voice of Ukridge mourning over his dead.

At half-past eleven that night, as I was preparing for bed, a drooping figure entered my room. I mixed a silent, sympathetic Scotch and soda, and for a while no word was spoken.

"How is the poor fellow?" I asked at length.

"He's all right," said Ukridge, listlessly. "I left him eating fish and chips at a coffee stall."

"Bad luck his getting pipped on the post like that."

"Bad luck!" boomed Ukridge, throwing off his lethargy with a vigor that spoke of mental anguish. "What do you mean, bad luck? It was just dam' boneheadedness. Upon my Sam, it's a little hard. I invest vast sums in this man, I support him in luxury for two weeks, asking nothing of him in return except to sail in and knock somebody's head off, which he could have done in two minutes if he had liked, and he lets me down purely and simply because the other fellow told him that he had been up all night looking after his wife who had burned her hand at the jam factory. Infernal sentimentalism!"

"Does him credit," I argued.

"Bah!"

"Kind hearts," I urged, "are more than coronets."

"Who the devil wants a pugilist to have a kind heart? What's the use of this man Billson being able to knock out an elephant if he's afflicted with this damned maudlin mushiness? Who ever heard of a mushy pugilist? It's the wrong spirit. It doesn't make for success."

"It's a handicap, of course," I admitted.

"What guarantee have I," demanded Ukridge, "that if I go to enormous trouble and expense getting him another match, he won't turn aside and brush away a silent tear in the first round because he's heard that the blighter's wife has got an ingrowing toenail?"

"You could match him against bachelors."

"Yes, and the first bachelor he met would draw him into a corner and tell him his aunt was down with whooping cough, and the chump would heave a sigh and stick his chin out to be walloped. A fellow's got no business to have red hair if he isn't going to live up to it. And yet," said Ukridge, wistfully, "I've seen that man—it was in a dance hall at Naples—I've seen him take on at least eleven Italians simultaneously. But then, one of them had stuck a knife about three inches into his leg. He seems to need something like that to give him ambition."

"I don't see how you are going to arrange to have him knifed just before each fight."

"No," said Ukridge, mournfully.

"What are you going to do about his future? Have you any plans?"

"Nothing definite. My aunt was looking for a companion to attend to her correspondence and take care of the canary last time I saw her. I might try to get the job for him."

And with a horrid, mirthless laugh Stanley Featherstonehaugh Ukridge borrowed five shillings and passed out into the night.

I did not see Ukridge for the next few days, but I had news of him from our mutual friend George Tupper, whom I met prancing in uplifted mood down Whitehall.

"I say," said George Tupper without preamble, and with a sort of dazed fervor, "they've given me an under-secretaryship."

I pressed his hand. I would have slapped him on the back, but one does not slap the backs of eminent Foreign Office officials in Whitehall in broad daylight, even if one has been at school with them.

"Congratulations," I said. "There is no one whom I would more gladly see under-secretary-ing. I heard rumors of this from Ukridge."

"Oh, yes, I remember I told him it might be coming off. Good old Ukridge! I met him just now and told him the news, and he was delighted."

"How much did he touch you for?"

"Eh? Oh, only five pounds. Till Saturday. He expects to have a lot of money by then."

"Did you ever know the time when Ukridge didn't expect to have a lot of money?"

"I want you and Ukridge to come and have a bit of dinner with me to celebrate. How would Wednesday suit you?"

"Splendidly."

"Seven-thirty at the Regent Grill, then. Will you tell Ukridge?"

"I don't know where he's got to. I haven't seen him for nearly a week. Did he tell you where he was?"

"Out at some place at Barnes. What was the name of it?"

"The White Hart?"

"That's it."

"Tell me," I said. "How did he seem? Cheerful?"

"Very. Why?"

"The last time I saw him he was thinking of giving up the struggle. He had had reverses."

I proceeded to the White Hart immediately after lunch. The fact that Ukridge was still at that hostelry and had regained his usual sunny outlook on life seemed to point to the fact that the clouds enveloping the future of Mr. Billson had cleared away, and that the latter's hat was still in the ring. That this was so was made clear to me directly I arrived. Inquiring for my old friend, I was directed to an upper room, from which, as I approached, there came a peculiar thudding noise. It was caused, as I perceived on opening the door, by Mr. Billson. Clad in flannel trousers and a sweater, he was earnestly pounding a large leather object suspended from a wooden platform. His manager, seated on a soapbox in a corner, regarded him the while with affectionate proprietorship.

"Hallo, old horse!" said Ukridge, rising as I entered. "Glad to see you."

The din of Mr. Billson's bag punching, from which my arrival had not caused him to desist, was such as to render conversation difficult. We moved to the quieter retreat of the bar downstairs, where I informed Ukridge of the undersecretary's invitation.

"I'll be there," said Ukridge. "There's one thing about good old Billson, you can trust him not to break training if you take your eye off him. And, of course, he realizes that this is a big thing. It'll be the making of him."

"Your aunt is considering engaging him, then?"

"My aunt? What on earth are you talking about? Collect yourself, laddie."

"When you left me you were going to try to get him the job of looking after your aunt's canary."

"Oh, I was feeling rather sore then. That's all over. I had an earnest talk with the poor simp, and he means business from now on. And so he ought to, dash it, with a magnificent opportunity like this."

"Like what?"

"We're on to a big thing now, laddie, the dickens of a big thing."

"I hope you've made sure the other man's a bachelor. Who is he?"

"Tod Bingham."

"Tod Bingham?" I groped in my memory. "You don't mean the middleweight champion?"

"That's the fellow."

"You don't expect me to believe that you've got a match on with a champion already?"

"It isn't exactly a match. It's like this. Tod Bingham is going round the East End halls offering two hundred quid to anyone who'll stay four rounds with him. Advertisement stuff. Good old Billson is going to unleash himself at the Shoreditch Empire next Saturday."

"Do you think he'll be able to stay four rounds?"

"Stay four rounds!" cried Ukridge. "Why, he could stay four rounds with a fellow armed with a Gatling gun and a couple of pickaxes. That money's as good as in our pockets, laddie. And once we're through with this job, there isn't a boxing place in England that won't jump at us. I don't mind telling you in confidence, old horse, that in a year from now I expect to be pulling in hundreds a week. Clean up a bit here first, you know, and then pop over to America and make an enormous fortune. Damme, I shan't know how to spend the money!"

"Why not buy some socks? I'm running a bit short of them."

"Now, laddie, laddie," said Ukridge, reprovingly, "need we strike a jarring note? Is this the moment to fling your beastly socks in an old friend's face? A broader-minded spirit is what I would like to see."

I was ten minutes late in arriving at the Regent Grill on the Wednesday of George Tupper's invitation, and the spectacle of George in person standing bare-headed at the Piccadilly entrance filled me with guilty remorse. George was the best fellow in the world, but the atmosphere of the Foreign Office had increased the tendency he had always had from boyhood to a sort of precise fussiness, and it upset him if his affairs did not run exactly on schedule. The thought that my unpunctuality should have marred this great evening sent me hurrying toward him full of apologies.

"Oh, there you are," said George Tupper. "I say, it's too bad——"

"I'm awfully sorry. My watch——"

"Ukridge!" cried George Tupper, and I perceived that it was not I who had caused his concern.

"Isn't he coming?" I asked, amazed. The idea of Ukridge evading a free meal was one of those that seem to make the solid foundations of the world rock.

"He's come. And he's brought a girl with him!"

"A *girl!*"

"In pink, with yellow hair," wailed George Tupper. "What am I to do?"

I pondered the point.

"It's a weird thing for even Ukridge to have done," I said, "but I suppose you'll have to give her dinner."

"But the place is full of people I know, and this girl's so—so spectacular."

I felt for him deeply, but I could see no way out of it.

"You don't think I could say I had been taken ill?"

"It would hurt Ukridge's feelings."

"I should enjoy hurting Ukridge's feelings, curse him!" said George Tupper, fervently.

"And it would be an awful slam for the girl, whoever she is."

George Tupper sighed. His was a chivalrous nature. He drew himself up as if bracing himself for a dreadful ordeal.

"Oh, well, I suppose there's nothing to do," he said. "Come along. I left them drinking cocktails in the lounge."

George had not erred in describing Ukridge's addition to the festivities as spectacular. Flamboyant would have been a suitable word. As she preceded us down the long dining room, her arm linked in George Tupper's—she seemed to have taken a liking to George—I had ample opportunity for studying her, from her patent-leather shoes to the mass of golden hair beneath her picture hat. She had a loud, clear voice, and she was telling George Tupper the rather intimate details of an internal complaint which had recently troubled an aunt of hers. If George had been the family physician, she could not have been franker; and I could see a dull glow spreading over his shapely ears.

Perhaps Ukridge saw it too, for he seemed to experience a slight twinge of conscience.

"I have an idea, laddie," he whispered, "that old Tuppy is a trifle peeved at my bringing Flossie along. If you get a chance, you might just murmur to him that it was military necessity."

"Who is she?" I asked.

"I told you about her. Flossie, the barmaid at the Crown in Kennington. Billson's *fiancée.*"

I looked at him in amazement.

"Do you mean to tell me that you're courting death by flirting with Battling Billson's girl?"

"My dear old man, nothing like that," said Ukridge, shocked. "The whole thing is, I've got a particular favor to ask of her—rather a rummy request—and it was no good springing it on her in cold blood. There had to be a certain amount of champagne in advance, and my funds won't run to champagne. I'm taking her on to the Alhambra after dinner. I'll look you up tonight and tell you all about it."

We then proceeded to dine. It was not one of the pleasantest meals of my experience. The future Mrs. Billson prattled agreeably throughout, and Ukridge assisted her in keeping the con-

versation alive; but the shattered demeanor of George Tupper would have taken the sparkle out of any banquet. From time to time he pulled himself together and endeavored to play the host, but for the most part he maintained a pale and brooding silence; and it was a relief when Ukridge and his companion rose to leave.

"Well! . . ." began George Tupper in a strangled voice, as they moved away down the aisle.

I lit a cigar and sat back dutifully to listen.

Ukridge arrived in my rooms at midnight, his eyes gleaming through their pince-nez with a strange light. His manner was exuberant.

"It's all right," he said.

"I'm glad you think so."

"Did you explain to Tuppy?"

"I didn't get a chance. He was talking too hard."

"About me?"

"Yes. He said everything I've always felt about you, only far, far better than I could ever have put it."

Ukridge's face clouded for a moment, but cheerfulness returned.

"Oh, well, it can't be helped. He'll simmer down in a day or two. It had to be done, laddie. Life and death matter. And it's all right. Read this."

I took the letter he handed me. It was written in a scrawly hand.

"What's this?"

"Read it, laddie. I think it will meet the case."

I read.

" '*Wilberforce.*' Who on earth's Wilberforce?"

"I told you that was Billson's name."

"Oh, yes."

I returned to the letter.

WILBERFORCE—

*I take pen in hand to tell you that I can never be yours. You will no doubt be surprised to hear that I love another and a better man, so that it can never be. He loves me, and he is a better man than you.*

*Hoping this finds you in the pink as it leaves me at present,*

Yours faithfully,
FLORENCE BURNS.

"I told her to keep it snappy," said Ukridge.

"Well, she's certainly done it," I replied, handing back the letter. "I'm sorry. From the little I saw of her, I thought her a nice girl—for Billson. Do you happen to know the other man's address? Because it would be a kindly act to send him a post card advising him to leave England for a year or two."

"The Shoreditch Empire will find him this week."

"What!"

"The other man is Tod Bingham."

"Tod Bingham!" The drama of the situation moved me. "Do you mean to say that Tod Bingham is in love with Battling Billson's girl?"

"No. He's never seen her!"

"What do you mean?"

Ukridge sat down creakingly on the sofa. He slapped my knee with sudden and uncomfortable violence.

"Laddie," said Ukridge, "I will tell you all. Yesterday afternoon I found old Billson reading a copy of the *Daily Sportsman*. He isn't much of a reader as a rule, so I was rather interested to know what had gripped him. And do you know what it was, old horse?"

"I do not."

"It was an article about Tod Bingham. One of those damned sentimental blurbs they print about pugilists nowadays, saying what a good chap he was in private life and how he always sent a telegram to his old mother after each fight and gave her half the purse. Damme, there ought to be a censorship of the press. These blighters don't mind *what* they print. I don't suppose Tod Bingham has *got* an old mother, and if he has I'll bet he doesn't give her a bob. There were tears in that chump Billson's eyes as he showed me the article. Salt tears, laddie! 'Must be a nice feller!' he said. Well, I ask you! I mean to say, it's a bit thick when the man you've been pouring out money for and watching over like a baby sister starts getting sorry for a champion three days before he's due to fight him. A champion, mark you! It was bad enough his getting mushy about that fellow at Wonderland, but when it came to being softhearted over Tod Bingham something had to be done. Well, you know me. Brain like a buzz saw. I saw the only way of counteracting this pernicious stuff was to get him so mad with Tod Bingham that he would forget all about his old mother, so I suddenly thought: Why not get Flossie to pretend that Bingham had cut him out with her? Well, it's not the sort of thing you can ask a girl to do without preparing the ground a bit, so I brought her along to Tuppy's dinner. It was a master stroke, laddie! There's nothing softens the delicately nurtured like a good dinner, and there's no denying that old Tuppy did us well. She agreed the moment I put the thing to her, and sat down and wrote that letter without a blink. I think she thinks it's

all a jolly practical joke. She's a lighthearted girl."

"Must be."

"It'll give poor old Billson a bit of a jar for the time being, I suppose, but it'll make him spread himself on Saturday night, and he'll be perfectly happy on Sunday morning when she tells him she didn't mean it and he realizes that he's got a hundred quid of Tod Bingham's in his trousers pocket."

"I thought you said it was two hundred quid that Bingham was offering."

"I get a hundred," said Ukridge, dreamily.

"The only flaw is, the letter doesn't give the other man's name. How is Billson to know it's Tod Bingham?"

"Why, damme, laddie, do use your intelligence. Billson isn't going to sit and yawn when he gets that letter. He'll buzz straight down to Kennington and ask Flossie."

"And then she will give the whole thing away."

"No, she won't. I slipped her a couple of quid to promise she wouldn't. And that reminds me, old man, it has left me a bit short, so if you could possibly manage——"

"Good night," I said.

"But, laddie——"

"And God bless you," I added, firmly.

The Shoreditch Empire is a roomy house, but it was crowded to the doors when I reached it on the Saturday night. In normal circumstances I suppose there would always have been a large audience on a Saturday, and this evening the lure of Tod Bingham's personal appearance had drawn more than capacity. In return for my shilling I was accorded the privilege of standing against the wall at the back, a position from which I could not see a great deal of the performance.

From the occasional flashes which I got of the stage between the heads of my neighbors, however, and from the generally restless and impatient attitude of the audience, I gathered that I was not missing much. The program of the Shoreditch Empire that week was essentially a one-man affair. The patrons had the air of suffering the preliminary acts as unavoidable obstacles that stood between them and the headliner. It was Tod Bingham whom they had come to see, and they were not cordial to the unfortunate serio-comics, tramp cyclists, jugglers, acrobats, and ballad singers who intruded themselves during the earlier part of the evening. The cheer that arose as the curtain fell on a dramatic sketch came from the heart, for the next number on the program was that of the star.

A stout man in evening dress with a red

handkerchief worn ambassadorially athwart his shirt front stepped out from the wings.

"Ladies and gentlemen!"

" 'Ush!" cried the audience.

"Ladies and gentlemen!"

A Voice: "Good ole Tod!" ("Cheese it!")

"Ladies and gentlemen," said the ambassador for the third time. He scanned the house apprehensively. "Deeply regret have unfortunate disappointment to announce. Tod Bingham unfortunately unable to appear before you tonight."

A howl like the howl of wolves balked of their prey or of an amphitheater full of Roman citizens on receipt of the news that the supply of lions had run out greeted these words. We stared at each other with a wild surmise. Could this thing be, or was it not too thick for human belief?

"Wot's the matter with 'im?" demanded the gallery, hoarsely.

"Yus, wot's the matter with 'im?" echoed we of the better element on the lower floor.

The ambassador sidled uneasily toward the prompt entrance. He seemed aware that he was not a popular favorite.

" 'E 'as 'ad an unfortunate accident," he declared, nervousness beginning to sweep away his aitches wholesale. "On 'is way 'ere to this 'all 'e was unfortunately run into by a truck, sustaining bruises and contusions which render 'im unfortunately unable to appear before you tonight. I beg to announce that 'is place will be taken by Professor Devine, who will render 'is marvelous imitations of various birds and familiar animals. Ladies and gentlemen," concluded the ambassador, stepping nimbly off the stage, "I thank you one and all."

The curtain rose and a dapper individual with a waxed mustache skipped on.

"Ladies and gentlemen, my first imitation will be of that well-known songster, the common thrush—better known to some of you per'aps as the throstle. And in connection with my performance I wish to state that I 'ave nothing whatsoever in my mouth. The effects which I produce—"

I withdrew, and two thirds of the audience started to do the same. From behind us, dying away as the doors closed, came the plaintive note of the common thrush feebly competing with that other and sterner bird which haunts those places of entertainment where audiences are critical and swift to take offense.

Out in the street a knot of Shoreditch's younger set were hanging on the lips of an excited orator in a battered hat and trousers which had been made for a larger man. Some stirring tale which he was telling held them spellbound. Words came raggedly through the noise of the traffic.

". . . like this. Then 'e 'its 'im another like that. Then they start—on the side of the jor—"

"Pass along, there," interrupted an official voice. "Come on there, pass along."

The crowd thinned and resolved itself into its elements. I found myself moving down the street in company with the wearer of the battered hat. Though we had not been formally introduced, he seemed to consider me a suitable recipient for his tale. He enrolled me at once as a nucleus for a fresh audience.

" 'E comes up, this bloke does, just as Tod is goin' in at the stage door—"

"Tod?" I queried.

"Tod Bingham. 'E comes up just as 'e's goin' in at the stage door, and 'e says, ' 'Ere!' and Tod says 'Yus?' and this bloke 'e says, 'Put 'em up!' and Tod says, 'Put wot up?' and this bloke says, 'Yer 'ands,' and Tod says, 'Wot, me?'—sort of surprised. An' the next minute they're fightin' all over the shop."

"But surely Tod Bingham was run over by a truck?"

The man in the battered hat surveyed me with the mingled scorn and resentment which the devout bestow on those of heretical views.

"Truck! 'E wasn't run over by no truck. Wot mikes yer fink 'e was run over by a truck? Wot 'ud 'e be doin' bein' run over by a truck? 'E 'ad it put across 'im by this red'eaded bloke, same as I'm tellin' yer."

A great light shone upon me.

"Redheaded?" I cried.

"Yus."

"A big man?"

"Yus."

"And he put it across Tod Bingham?"

"Put it across 'im proper. 'Ad to go 'ome in a keb, Tod did. Funny a bloke that could fight like that bloke could fight 'adn't the sense to go and do it on the stige and get some money for it. That's wot I think."

Across the street an arc lamp shed its cold rays. And into its glare there strode a man draped in a yellow mackintosh. The light gleamed on his pince-nez and lent a gruesome pallor to his set face. It was Ukridge retreating from Moscow.

"Others," I said, "are thinking the same."

And I hurried across the road to administer what feeble consolation I might. There are moments when a fellow needs a friend.

# INDEX

# ABOUT THE EDITOR

W. C. HEINZ was born in Mount Vernon, New York, in 1915, attended public schools there and was graduated from Middlebury College in 1937. From 1937 to 1950 he worked for the New York *Sun* as copy boy, reporter, rewrite man, feature writer, war correspondent and sports columnist. Since 1950 he has been a free lance, writing for, among other magazines, *Life, Look,* the *Saturday Evening Post, Collier's, Cosmopolitan, Esquire* and *True*. His work has been reprinted in more than two dozen anthologies, and he has five times won the E. P. Dutton Award for Best Magazine Sports Story of the year. In 1958 his first novel, *The Professional,* was published and was widely hailed as the best novel ever written about boxing. He lives with his wife and two daughters in Stamford, Connecticut.